Personnel and Human Resource Management in Canada

Personnel and Human Resource Management in Canada

Shimon L. Dolan
The University of Montréal

Randall S. Schuler
New York University

West Publishing Company
St. Paul ■ New York ■ Los Angeles ■ San Francisco

Copyediting   June Trusty

COPYRIGHT © 1987 By WEST PUBLISHING COMPANY
50 W. Kellogg Boulevard
P.O. Box 64526
St. Paul, MN 55164–1003

All rights reserved

Printed in the United States of America

Library of Congress Cataloging-in-Publication Data

Dolan, Shimon.
   Personnel and human resource management in Canada.

   Includes bibliographies and index.
   1. Personnel management—Canada.   I. Schuler,
Randall S.   II. Title.
HF5549.2.C3D65   1987   658.3'00971   87–2207
ISBN 0–314–32486–0

Dedicated to my wife Miri, and my children Keren and Tomer (S.L.D.)
To my brother Ed (R.S.S.)

Contents

Preface / xv

SECTION

I
Overview of Personnel and Human Resource Management in Canada / 1

1
Personnel and Human Resource Management / 2

PHRM in the News / 3
Personnel and Human Resource Management / 5
Functions and Activities of PHRM / 6
   Planning and Forecasting for Human Resource Needs / 6
   Obtaining Staff / 7
   Appraising and Compensating Employee Behaviour / 7
   Enhancing Human Potential / 8
   Establishing and Maintaining Effective Industrial Relations / 9
Systemic Relationships of PHRM Functions and Activities / 10
The Growing Importance of PHRM / 11
   Trends and Crises / 11
Strategic Purposes of PHRM / 14
   Productivity / 15
   Quality of Work Life / 15
   Legal Compliance / 15
Personnel and Human Resource Management in the Organization / 16
   A Brief Historical Overview / 16
   Personnel and Human Resource Management Roles / 16
   Extent and Scope of PHRM Activities / 18
Special Concerns in PHRM / 18
   Criteria for Evaluating PHRM / 20
   Strategic Involvement / 23
Organizing the PHRM Department / 23
   PHRM in the Organization / 25
   Centralization versus Decentralization / 25
   Who Is Responsible for PHRM? / 26
   PHRM Budgets / 27
Staffing the PHRM Department / 27
   Qualities of the PHRM Manager and Staff / 27
Careers in PHRM / 28
   How Much do PHRM Careers Pay? / 29
   Growing Professionalism in PHRM / 29
   Professional Certification/Accreditation / 30
The Plan of This Book / 31
   Purposes / 31

Themes / 32
For Whom Is This Book Written? / 32
Summary / 32
Discussion Questions / 33
Endnotes / 34

SECTION

II

Planning for Jobs and People / 37

2

Human Resource Planning / 38

PHRM in the News / 39
Human Resource Planning / 41
Purposes and the Importance of HRP / 41
Relationships with other PHRM Activities / 44
Four Phases of HRP / 45
Phase 1: Gathering, Analyzing, and Forecasting Supply and Demand Data / 46
Phase 2: Establishing Human Resource Objectives and Policies / 53
Phase 3: Human Resource Programming / 55
Phase 4: HRP Control and Evaluation / 58
HRP Roadblocks / 59
Important Changes in the 1990s Influencing HRP / 60
The Population and the Labour Force / 60
Trends and Changes in the Economy / 62
Changing Social Values / 64
Legislation, Regulation, and Government Activity / 65
Assessing HRP / 65
Summary / 66
Discussion Questions / 67
Case Study / 67
Endnotes / 68

3

Job Design and Job Analysis / 73

PHRM in the News / 74
Job Design and Job Analysis / 75
Purposes and Importance of Job Design and Job Analysis / 76
Relationships of Job Design and Job Analysis / 78
Legal Considerations in Job Design and Job Analysis / 80
Job Design / 80
Job Design Qualities / 81
Job Design Approaches / 85
Assessing Job-Design Appropriateness / 88
Job Analysis / 91
Collecting Job Analysis Information / 92
Job Descriptions / 92
Job Analysis Techniques / 94
Job-Focused Techniques / 96
Person-Focused Techniques / 101
Assessing Job-Analysis Methods / 106
Purposes of Job Analysis / 106
Practical Concerns / 107
Assessing Job Design and Job Analysis / 108
Summary / 110
Discussion Questions / 110
Case Study / 111
Endnotes / 113

SECTION

III

Staffing / 117

4

Recruitment and Employment Equity / 118

PHRM in the News / 119
Recruitment and Employment Equity / 121
Purposes and Importance of Recruitment / 121
Relationships of Recruitment with PHRM Activities / 122
Employment Equity Legal Considerations in Recruitment / 125
Sources and Methods for Obtaining Job Applicants / 128
Internal Sources / 128
Internal Methods / 129

External Sources / 131
External Methods / 136
Assessing Recruiting Methods / 137
Increasing the Pool of Potentially
  Qualified Applicants / 137
  Conveying Job and Organizational Information / 138
  Expanding Career and Job Opportunities / 139
  Alternative Work Arrangements / 141
Assessing Recruitment Activity / 145
Summary / 146
Discussion Questions / 147
Case Study / 147
Endnotes / 148

5
Selection, Placement, and Employment Equity / 152

PHRM in the News / 153
Selection, Placement, and
  Employment Equity / 154
  Purposes and Importance of Selection and Placement / 154
  Relationships of Selection and Placement with PHRM Activities / 155
Employment-Equity Legal
  Considerations / 157
  Legal and Normative Issues Affecting Selection and Placement / 158
Selection and Placement Information / 164
  The Organizational Context / 164
  The Job Context / 165
  The Job Qualities / 165
  The Job Applicant / 166
  Predictors and Criteria in Selection Decisions / 166
Obtaining Job Applicant Information / 167
  The Application Blank / 171
  The Selection and Placement Interview / 174
  Selection Tests / 178
  Types of Tests / 179
  Physical Ability Tests / 183
Summary / 187
Discussion Questions / 187

Case Study / 188
Endnotes / 189

6
Selection and Placement, Decisions and Employment Equity / 193

PHRM in the News / 194
Using Information in Selection and
  Placement Decisions and
  Employment Equity / 195
  Criteria: The Concept of Job Success / 195
  Problems in Measuring Job Success / 195
  The Single Predictor Approach / 196
  The Multiple Predictors Approach / 197
Selection and Placement Decisions and
  Employment Equity / 199
  Promotion and Transfer Decisions / 200
Assessing Selection and Placement
  Decisions and Employment
  Equity / 203
  Reliability / 204
  Validity / 205
  Utility Considerations: Base Rate vs. Predictor Rate / 211
  Selection Ratio / 212
  Utility and Cost: An Overview / 214
Socialization of New Employees / 215
  Purposes of Socialization / 216
  Methods of Socialization / 217
  Who Stays / 220
Summary / 221
Discussion Questions / 222
Case Study / 222
Endnotes / 224

SECTION
IV
Appraising / 227

7
Performance Appraisal I: Gathering the Data / 228

PHRM in the News / 229

Performance Appraisal / 231
- Purposes and Importance of Performance Appraisal / 232
- Relationships of Performance Appraisal / 233
- Legal Considerations in Performance Appraisal / 235
- Using Valid Performance Appraisal Instruments / 238

Performance Appraisal as a Set of Processes and Procedures / 239
- Criteria and Standards / 240
- Performance Appraisal Approaches / 241
- Assessing Performance Appraisal Techniques: Which Is Best? / 253
- Analysis of Future Performance / 254
- The Context of Appraisal Performance / 256
- Gathering Performance Appraisal Data / 258

Summary / 259
Discussion Questions / 260
Case Study / 260
Endnotes / 262

8
Performance Appraisal II: Utilizing the Data / 264

PHRM in the News / 265
Utilizing the Performance Appraisal Data / 266
- Inherent Conflicts in Performance Appraisal / 267
- Designing the Appraisal System / 269
- The Performance Appraisal Interview / 271

Improving Performance / 273
- Identifying Performance Gaps / 274
- Determining the Causes of Performance Gaps / 274

Strategies to Improve Performance / 275
- Positive Behavioural Strategies / 275
- Positive Organizational Strategies / 276
- Negative Behavioural Strategies / 278
- Employee Assistance Programs / 279
- Counselling / 280

Assessing Performance Appraisal Systems / 281
- Overall Performance Appraisal System Assessment / 282
- Specific Performance Appraisal System Assessment / 284

Summary / 284
Discussion Questions / 285
Case Study / 286
Endnotes / 286

SECTION
V
Compensating / 288

9
Total Compensation / 289

PHRM in the News / 290
Total Compensation / 292
- Purposes and Importance of Total Compensation / 292
- Relationships of Total Compensation / 294

Environmental Impact on Total Compensation / 296
- Legal Considerations in Total Compensation / 296
- Unions / 300
- The Market / 301

Basic Wage Issues / 301
- Job Evaluation / 301
- Common Discriminatory Aspects in Job-Evaluation Methods / 308
- Determining Job Classes / 310
- Establishing the Pay Structure / 310
- Individual Wage Determination / 313

Contemporary Issues in Wage and Salary Administration / 314
- Participation Policies / 314
- Pay Secrecy / 315
- Satisfaction with Pay / 315
- All-Salaried Workforce / 316

Assessing Total Compensation / 317
Summary / 318

Discussion Questions / 319
Case Study / 319
Endnotes / 320

10
Performance-Based Pay and Administration / 322
PHRM in the News / 323
Performance-Based Pay Systems / 325
   Purposes and Importance of Performance-Based Pay / 326
   Relationships of Performance-Based Pay / 327
   Legal Considerations in Performance-Based Pay / 328
Merit Pay Plans / 328
   Merit Pay Guidelines / 328
   Merit Versus Cost-of-Living Adjustments / 329
Incentive Pay Plans / 329
   Individual-Level Incentive Plans / 329
   Group-Level Incentive Plans / 334
   Organization-Level Incentive Plans / 336
Administrative Issues in Performance-Based Pay / 338
   Obstacles to Performance-Based Pay Plan Effectiveness / 338
   Auditing the Merit Pay System / 341
   Participation in Performance-Based Pay Plans / 342
Assessing Performance-Based Pay / 342
Summary / 344
Discussion Questions / 345
Case Study / 346
Endnotes / 347

11
Benefits Pay and Administration / 349
PHRM in the News / 350
Benefits Pay / 352
   Purposes and Importance of Benefits Pay / 353
   Relationships of Benefits Pay / 356
   Legal Considerations in Benefits Pay / 356
Private Protection Programs / 359
   Retirement Benefits / 359
   Early Retirement Benefits / 359
   Insurance Benefits / 360
   Supplemental Unemployment Benefits / 361
Pay for Time Not Worked / 361
   Off the Job / 361
   On the Job / 362
Employee Services and Perquisites / 362
   Golden Parachutes / 363
Administrative Issues in Benefits-Pay Compensation / 363
   Determining the Benefits Package / 363
   Providing Benefit Flexibility / 364
   Communicating the Benefits Package / 364
Assessing the Benefits of Indirect Compensation / 365
Summary / 366
Discussion Questions / 367
Case Study / 367
Endnotes / 368

SECTION VI
Enhancing Human Potential / 370

12
Training and Development / 371
PHRM in the News / 372
Training and Development / 374
   Purposes and Importance of Training and Development / 375
   Relationships of Training and Development / 375
   Legal and Policy Issues in Training and Development / 377
Determining Training Needs / 378
   Organizational Needs Analysis / 380
   Job Needs Analysis / 380

Contents

    Person Needs Analysis / 381
    Type of Training Needs / 381
Implementing Training Programs / 383
    Training Considerations / 383
    Training Programs / 387
    Selecting a Program / 392
    Problems and Pitfalls in Training / 393
Assessing Training Programs / 395
    Evaluation Designs / 396
Developing Employees' Potential / 399
    Facilitating Employee Development / 399
    Formal Programs of Employee Development / 400
Career Planning and Development / 402
    Individual-Centred Career Planning / 403
    Organization-Centred Career Planning / 404
Summary / 405
Discussion Questions / 406
Case Study / 406
Endnotes / 407

13
Quality of Work Life and Productivity / 410

PHRM in the News / 411
Productivity and the Quality of Work Life / 414
    Purposes and Importance of QWL and Productivity / 415
    Relationships of QWL and Productivity Programs / 416
    Policy Considerations in QWL and Productivity Programs / 417
Programs for QWL Improvements / 419
    Communicating with Employees: Organizational Surveys / 419
    Semi-autonomous Work Groups / 422
    Quality Circles / 425
    Organizational Restyling / 427
Programs for Productivity Improvements / 429
    Task Changes / 429
    Automation / 431

    Office Design / 432
    Productivity Improvements—The Total Management Approach / 433
Assessing QWL and Productivity Programs / 433
    QWL Programs / 433
    Productivity Programs / 433
Summary / 434
Discussion Questions / 434
Case Study / 435
Endnotes / 436

SECTION
VII
Maintaining Effective Industrial Relations / 439

14
Occupational Health and Safety / 440

PHRM in the News / 441
Occupational Health and Safety in Organizations / 443
    Purposes and Importance of Improving Health and Safety / 444
    Relationships of Occupational Health and Safety / 445
Legal Considerations of Occupational Health and Safety / 447
    The Canadian Jurisdictional Framework / 447
    Federal Health and Safety Legislation / 448
    Provincial Health and Safety Legislation / 449
    The Right to Know / 452
    The Right to Refuse Work / 452
    Joint Health and Safety Committees / 453
    Accident Reporting and Inquiries / 453
Work Hazards / 454
    Factors Affecting Occupational Accidents / 454
    Factors Affecting Occupational Diseases / 456
    Factors Affecting Low Quality of Work Life / 458

Sources of Organizational Stress / 458
Occupational Health and Safety Strategies for Improvement / 459
  Strategies for Health and Safety Improvement in the Physical Work Environment / 459
  Strategies for Health and Safety Improvement in the Socio-psychological Work Environment / 463
Assessing Occupational Health and Safety Activities / 464
  Physical Work Environment Strategies / 464
  Socio-psychological Work Environment Strategies / 464
Summary / 465
Discussion Questions / 465
Case Study / 466
Endnotes / 467

15
Employee Rights / 470
PHRM in the News / 471
Employee Rights / 473
  Purposes and Importance of Employee Rights / 474
  Relationships of Employee Rights / 475
Legal Considerations in Employee Rights / 476
  Employee Rights to Job Security / 476
  Employee Rights on the Job / 479
Strategies for Employee Rights / 482
  Employer Strategies for Employee Job Security Rights / 483
  Employer Strategies for Employee Rights on the Job / 485
Assessing Employee Rights Activities / 487
Summary / 488
Discussion Questions / 489
Case Study / 489
Endnotes / 490

16
Unionization / 492
PHRM in the News / 492

Unionization of Employees / 496
  Purposes and Importance of Unionization / 496
  Relationships of PHRM and Unionization / 497
Legal Considerations in the Unionization of Employees / 499
  The Early Days / 499
  Labour Relations Legislation Today / 500
The Attraction of Unionization / 504
  The Decision to Join a Union / 504
  The Decision Not to Join a Union / 506
The Development and State of Unionization / 507
  The Early Days / 507
  Today / 508
  Structure and Function of Unions in Canada / 510
The Organizing Campaign / 514
  The Campaign to Solicit Employee Support / 515
  Determination of the Bargaining Unit / 517
Assessing the Unionization of Employees / 517
Summary / 518
Discussion Questions / 519
Case Study / 519
Endnotes / 520

17
Collective Bargaining / 522
PHRM in the News / 523
Collective Bargaining / 526
The Collective Bargaining Process / 527
  Union-Management Relationships / 527
  Processes of Bargaining / 532
  Management Strategies / 535
  Union Strategies / 535
  Joint Union-Management Strategies / 536
Negotiating the Agreement / 537
  Negotiating Committees / 537
  The Negotiating Structure / 538
  Issues for Negotiation / 539
Conflict Resolution / 543
  Strikes and Lockouts / 543

Mediation / 545
Arbitration / 545
Contract Administration / 546
   Grievance Procedures / 547
   Grievance Issues / 549
   Management Procedures / 550
   Union Procedures / 550
Assessing the Collective Bargaining Process / 551
   Effectiveness of Negotiations / 551
   Effectiveness of Grievance Procedures / 551
Summary / 552
Discussion Questions / 553
Case Study / 553
Endnotes / 555

SECTION VIII
Contemporary Trends / 558

18
PHRM Agenda for the Future / 559
PHRM in the News / 560
Trends and Challenges in PHRM / 561
   Power of PHRM in the Organization / 563
   The Need for Professionalism in PHRM / 563
   PHRM and the Use of New Technology / 565
   Contemporary and Future Challenges / 568

International PHRM / 571
   PHRM in Japan / 572
   PHRM in West Germany / 575
Assessing PHRM in the 1990s / 578
   Qualitative Approaches / 579
   Quantitative Approaches / 582
Summary / 585
Discussion Questions / 585
Endnotes / 586

Appendixes / 588

A
List of Employment-Standards Legislation in Canada (updated as of January 1986) / 589

B
Selected Journals and Associations in Personnel and Human Resource Management / 593

Glossary / 597

Index / 614

Preface

Personnel and human resource management (PHRM) functions undoubtedly are more vital to companies today than ever before. Foreign competition, declines in productivity, the need to comply with vast and ever-changing laws and regulations, and the increasing demands for a more skilled and better educated work force are just a few of the many factors that have contributed to the importance of personnel and human resource management in modern organizations.

For many years, students at Canadian universities used U.S. textbooks in personnel and human resource management courses because few Canadian books were available on the subject. This practice generated much criticism from students and educators alike. Today, the increasing impact of federal and provincial legislation on the industrial relations scene, coupled with the uniqueness of the Canadian business environment, have made it clear that a textbook totally geared to Canada is sorely needed. This observation was reinforced by spirited discussions among academics and practitioners regarding the various shortcomings of PHRM education in Canada.

Personnel and Human Resource Management in Canada is designed to meet the growing needs of PHRM students, professionals, and academicians who want to keep up to date with the principles and contemporary challenges in the management of human resources in Canada. It is a vital resource for anyone working or intending to work in personnel in Canadian organizations, whether private or public, large or small, traditional or dynamic.

This book focuses on ways to manage human resource functions effectively. It presents the field's state of the art in research and practice by integrating theory and application, and by stressing the eclectic and interdisciplinary nature of personnel and human resource management. Analysis and discussion draw on a number of disciplines, including management, psychology, sociology, law, economics, ergonomics, medicine, and computer technology. Model PHRM practices are demonstrated with examples from Canadian firms.

To facilitate understanding of the complexities involved in managing human resources in Canada, each chapter contains several important features.

"PHRM in the News" opens each chapter and presents articles that highlight contemporary concerns in the management of human resources. This feature consists of recent examples taken from sources such as *The Financial Post*, *Financial Times*, and *Canadian Business*; monthly information service report bulletins such as *Human Resources Management in Canada*; and short articles from the business sections of *Maclean's*, the Toronto-based *Globe and Mail*, and Montréal's *The Gazette*.

A case study near the end of each chapter applies the material discussed in the chapter. The case studies depict various business situations in both the public and private sectors, in primary and high-tech industries, and in relatively small companies and very large firms.

Each chapter also contains a summary and discussion questions, which help the reader to focus on, and review, the essential points of each chapter. Two additional aids include an extensive set of up-to-date important references at the end of each chapter and, at the end of the book, a convenient subject index and a glossary containing key concepts discussed throughout the textbook.

In addition, the appendix to this book lists sources of PHRM information, a list of current employment laws in Canada, and a list of professional journals and PHRM associations in Canada.

We hope that the reader will find this book stimulating and thought-provoking, as well as informative and functional. In order to expand one's professional horizons beyond the coverage of this book, we encourage you to read our text *Canadian Readings in Personnel and Human Resource Management in Canada* (St. Paul: West Publishing Company, 1987), which contains complementary material to that included in this book.

Acknowledgements

In writing this book, we benefited from the advice, and assistance of many individuals and organizations. First, because this book represents an extensive revision of some texts written formerly by the second author, we wish to thank the publisher for allowing us to borrow and/or adapt relevant material. Second, we wish to acknowledge the following individuals, whose ideas have been directly or indirectly incorporated into this text: Dr. André Arsenault and Dr. Marie Reine van Ameringen of the University of Montréal; Professor Donald Pease of Boston University; Professor Steven Cronshaw of the University of Guelph; Professor Aharon Tziner of Tel Aviv University; Ms. Heidi Markowitz of Business Psychology Inc., Montréal; Romi Szawlowski of Pratt & Whitney Canada Inc.; and Robert Pelletier of M.S.P. Inc. in Montréal.

The following individuals also provided many good ideas and suggestions in their role as reviewers of different chapters of the book: Dr. Gordon Atherley, The Canadian Centre for Occupational Health & Safety; Professor Bernard Brody, The University of Montréal; Professor Thomas Janz, The

University of Calgary; Professor Rabindra Kanungo, McGill University; Professor Viateur Larouche, The University of Montréal; Professor Larry Moore, The University of British Columbia; Professor Roland Theriault, H.E.C., The University of Montréal; and Professor Gilles Trudeau, The University of Montréal.

We owe our sincere gratitude to the School of Management at Boston University for the technical support provided to the first author during his visit in 1985–86. In particular, we wish to mention the superb job done by Vincent Mahler, who word-processed the entire book, and Leslie Lomasson, head secretary in the Organizational Behaviour Department at Boston University, who typed and mailed the permission requests. We also thank Michelle Poirier and June Trusty for their help in editing the final draft of the book.

Finally we wish to express our deep appreciation to those at West Publishing without whom this book would never have been completed on schedule; namely, David Godden, who was our acquisition editor, and Roslyn Stendahl whose dedication, professionalism, and efforts guided this project throughout the production process.

Shimon L. Dolan
Montréal, Québec

Randall S. Schuler
New York, New York

January 1987

Personnel and Human Resource Management in Canada

SECTION

I

Overview of Personnel and Human Resource Management in Canada

CHAPTER 1
Personnel and Human Resource Management

CHAPTER 1

Personnel and Human Resource Management

PHRM in the News

Personnel and Human Resource Management

Functions and Activities of PHRM
Planning and Forecasting for Human Resource Needs
Obtaining Staff
Appraising and Compensating Employee Behaviour
Enhancing Human Potential
Establishing and Maintaining Effective Industrial Relations

Systemic Relationships of PHRM Functions and Activities

The Growing Importance of PHRM
Trends and Crises

Strategic Purposes of PHRM
Productivity
Quality of Work Life
Legal Compliance

Personnel and Human Resource Management in the Organization
A Brief Historical Overview
Personnel and Human Resource Management Roles
Extent and Scope of PHRM Activities

Special Concerns in PHRM
Criteria for Evaluating PHRM
Strategic Involvement

Organizing the PHRM Department
PHRM in the Organization
Centralization versus Decentralization
Who Is Responsible for PHRM?
PHRM Budgets

Staffing the PHRM Department
Qualities of the PHRM Manager and Staff

Careers in PHRM
How Much do PHRM Careers Pay?
Growing Professionalism in PHRM
Professional Certification/Accreditation

The Plan of This Book
Purposes
Themes
For Whom Is This Book Written?

Summary

Discussion Questions

Endnotes

PHRM in the News

People Count

Camco Inc., the country's largest appliance manufacturer, is a company that knows how to get the most out of its people. After eight years of operation, Camco decided to squash its pyramids and listen to its workers. "The trend here is toward greater participation and involvement in decision making," says Camco General Manager Bill James. "Our organization is flat—everyone talks to everyone. We're entrepreneurial and we formalize it, too. It feels like a young, dynamic company."

James has had his surprises. Employees have made recommendations that he thought would never work, but due to the commitment of the employees, the ideas did work far beyond anyone's expectations. Take the case of the glass microwave shelves. There were two groups of Camco employees installing shelves: different groups, different-sized shelves. Why not, suggested the employees, amalgamate the two groups into one and maybe produce a better-quality product as a result. Management accepted the proposition. The employees' brainwave went into effect in July 1984. James notes that the quality of work did improve and that the company will realize an estimated annual savings of $25 000.

"By being closer to our employees, our quality, productivity, profits and morale have leaped," says James. "Quality circles and productivity gains-sharing have had a remarkable impact. Productivity is 25% better than last year, employment has doubled to more than 400, and absenteeism has been reduced by 30%."

Source: Andrew Campbell, "Turning Workers into Risk Takers" *Canadian Business*, February 1985, p. 109. (Andrew Campbell is president of the Toronto-based consulting firm Campbell & Associates Inc.) Used with permission.

Productivity and Automation Matters

Industrial robots are hardly the glamorous creatures conjured up in science fiction stories and movies. Instead, they're hard workers able to carry out accurately and tirelessly the chores for which they have been programmed.

By the end of this year about 1290 will be on the job in Canadian plants and factories, where they'll be tackling such tasks as welding, assembling components, drilling, forging, grinding, packing, machine loading.

About 85% are in Ontario, home of the large automakers and the educational facilities that make up the major users. Indeed, Chrysler Canada Ltd. installed 125 robots in the Windsor, Ontario, plant it converted to mini-van production in 1983. This move increased hourly output by 20 units, without requiring any additional workers.

While robots boost productivity, they also eliminate jobs formerly assigned to human workers. This is of great concern to unions and those directly affected, who would like to see some government incentive for retraining displaced workers.

Most of the robots used in Canada are foreign-made, although Canadian input comes in the form of peripherals, software, and other products needed to get the entire robot system working.

A few Canadian companies have entered the high-tech and high-risk area of robot manufacturing, producing items such as the Canadarm, Spar Aerospace

Ltd.'s stellar performer, and the vision system from Diffracto Ltd. So far, only one Canadian firm—Clay-Mill Technical Systems Inc.—has designed and built its own industrial robot system.

Source: "Robots Find Niche on Factory Floor," *The Financial Post,* June 29, 1985, p. C1: (excerpt from a special report). Used with permission.

Discrimination Issues

TIMMINS—An Ontario Human Rights Commission Board of Inquiry has found that South Porcupine Hospital discriminated against an employee because of her marital status. Rosemary Mark was fired from her job as a part-time housekeeper at the hospital a few days after she was hired, because she worked in the same department as her husband. Under the Ontario Human Rights Code, employers may practice anti-nepotism policies at the hiring stage but cannot fire employees on the basis of marital status once they are hired. Mark was hired by a supervisor who was unaware of the hospital's unofficial policy of not employing married couples, particularly in the same department. The person normally in charge of hiring was away, and on his return he fired Mark. The Board ordered the hospital to pay Mark $1114 for lost wages, general damages and interest. The hospital must also notify her of any job vacancies for which she is qualified.

WINNIPEG—A Manitoba school bus driver, forced to retire when he reached age 65, must be reinstated and may continue to work as long as he performs his job satisfactorily and provides medical reports to his employer at regular intervals, a Manitoba Human Rights Board of Adjudication has ruled. After turning 65 earlier in the school year, William Delamare, a 31-year driver with a good record and in good health, was retired at the end of June 1983 by his employer, Inter-Mountain School Division. In light of medical evidence, adjudicator Aaron L. Berg ruled that "functional age assessment," not chronological age, "is in general the most reasonable and rational way to determine retirement ages for employees." The parties were given 30 days to negotiate a damage settlement.

TORONTO—The Supreme Court of Ontario has upheld an Ontario Human Rights Commission Board of Inquiry order against Commodore Business Machines Ltd. which found the company responsible for the conduct of one of its employees in a well-publicized sexual harassment case. Commodore was ordered to pay a total of $21 800 in damages plus lost wages and interest to six former employees who were found to have been sexually harassed by one of their foremen in 1978 and 1979.

Source: Human Resources Management in Canada, Report Bulletin No. 23, 1985, p. 4. Copyright © 1985 Prentice-Hall Canada Inc. Reprinted by permission of Prentice-Hall Canada Inc. All rights reserved.

These "PHRM in the News" excerpts underline several significant points:

1. Productivity is a dominant concern in organizations today. It is difficult to find a manager in any organization who is not concerned with productivity
2. People are key resources in achieving productivity improvements
3. Personnel and human resource management (PHRM) is critical to organizations because of the importance of productivity and the link between effective human resource utilization and productivity improvement
4. Failure to observe laws and regulations relevant to the utilization of human resources can result in substantial fines and penalties to the organization.

Effective PHRM is vital to organizations because it can improve organizational productivity and minimize fines and penalties. Furthermore, effective PHRM enables an organization to provide an enhanced quality of work life for its employees, because effective PHRM is based on respect and concern for and awareness of the rights and preferences of individuals. Despite the importance of PHRM to organizations, its ability to be effective is often challenged.[1]

In this book, the term **line manager** (or **supervisor**) refers to the person in charge of the employees who are working directly on the product that the organization produces. The terms **individual, person, worker**, or **workforce** are used as general references to employees. The term **employee** generally refers to the person who works for the line manager or the personnel manager; this person may also be called a non-managerial employee. Use of the term **subordinate** is avoided, except in Chapters 7 and 8, where the terms **subordinate** and **superior** are explained.

The terms **personnel manager** (or **executive**) or **personnel and human resource manager** refer to the person heading the PHRM department. In some organizations, the person holding this position is called the vice-president of personnel or the vice-president of employee relations.

Personnel and Human Resource Management

Effective personnel and human resource management is based on the recognition that the organization's workforce is vital to the accomplishment of the goals of the organization. PHRM utilizes several functions and activities to ensure that human resources are used effectively and fairly for the benefit of the individual, the organization, and society. Although the term "personnel" is still used in some organizations to refer to the department that deals with activities such as recruitment, selection, compensation, and training, the term "personnel and human resource management" is rapidly supplanting it. This is in recognition of the essential role that human resources play in an organization, the challenges involved in managing human resources effectively, and the growing body of knowledge and professionalism surrounding PHRM.[2] In return for this recognition, PHRM departments in organizations must meet these challenges *effectively* through numerous functions and activities.[3]

Functions and Activities of PHRM

Five PHRM functions and activities are described in this book, covering all of the functions and activities that PHRM departments in organizations actually perform:

- Planning and forecasting for human resource needs
- Obtaining staff
- Appraising and compensating employee behaviour
- Developing and enhancing human potential
- Establishing and maintaining effective industrial relations

Although the PHRM departments of many organizations may not currently be performing all of these functions, the trend is clearly moving in that direction. Therefore, it is useful to describe them all here.

Planning and Forecasting for Human Resource Needs

The two major activities of this function are

1. planning and forecasting the organization's short-term and long-term human resource requirements; and
2. analyzing the existing jobs to determine the skills, knowledge, and abilities that are needed, and designing jobs to accommodate the needs of both the individual and the organization.

These two activities are essential for effectively performing many other personnel and human resource management activities. For example, they help indicate (1) how many and what types of employees the organization needs today as well as tomorrow; (2) how the employees will be obtained (e.g., from outside recruiting or by internal transfers and promotions); and (3) the training programs required.

Although these two activities are so vital in the management of human resources, most organizations have only recently incorporated them into personnel departments. Today, in almost all of the North American 500-largest industrial companies, personnel managers are responsible for human resource planning; this was true for only a handful of companies 10 years ago. Some organizations are guided by simple notions of cost/benefit analysis in deciding to engage their personnel in manpower planning:

> At the organizational level, the need for effective manpower planning can be illustrated in terms of costs and benefits, that is, through costs associated with not forecasting and planning and through the benefits of engaging in systematic planning. The firm which is not planning to meet its manpower needs

is more likely to experience costs associated with being unable to meet market demands because of manpower shortages. Equally costly are losses and alienation of productive employees because of oversupply or through ineffective job placement and career progression.[4]

Other companies require their senior executives to submit five-year "executive resources" plans along with five-year business plans. If a division is planning to shift orientations (e.g., from marketing to production), the vice-president of PHRM at Tenneco, for example, must make certain that the vice-president of that division has a human resource plan to help implement the proposed shift.[5]

Obtaining Staff

Once the organization's human resource needs have been determined, they have to be filled. Staffing activities include:

- Recruiting job applicants
- Selecting from among the job applicants those most appropriate for the available jobs
- Orienting and placing the new job candidates

The organization must cast a wide net for potential employees in order to ensure a full and fair search for job candidates. Recruiting is an extremely important personnel function because the greater the number of applicants, the more selective an organization can be in its hiring.

To develop a pool of applicants, organizations use several sources of candidates, including consideration of current employees, advertising, employment services, executive recruiting services, college recruiting, referrals, and walk-ins.

After the candidates have been identified, standard procedures are used in selection process. These include obtaining completed application forms or résumés; interviewing the candidates; checking education, personal background, professional experience, and references; and various forms of testing. Regardless of the exact procedures used, these must comply with various government human rights regulations. Naturally, the goal of selection procedures is a match between a candidate's ability and the abilities required by the job.

Appraising and Compensating Employee Behaviour

After employees are on the job, it is necessary to determine how well they are doing and to reward them accordingly. If they are not doing well, the reason for this must be determined. This determination may indicate that the reward structure needs to be changed, that employee training is necessary, or that some type of motivation should be provided. To these ends, this function incorporates several activities associated with appraising and several associated with compensating.

Although performance appraisal can be painful for both supervisor and employee, it is a critically important activity, particularly because legal compliance dictates that employment decisions be made on the basis of performance. For example, promotional decisions should be based on an evaluation of employee performance.

Not all employees are "good" ones. Some may be continually absent, some may be alcoholics, or some may be late to work all the time. When employee rights, greater social responsibility, and the cost of replacing employees, are taken into account, however, organizations may find it preferable to assist employees to correct their undesired behaviour and to motivate them to perform as well as possible, rather than to terminate them.

Employees are generally rewarded on the basis of the value of the job, their personal contributions, and their performance. Although the provision of rewards based on level of performance can increase an employee's motivation to perform, many rewards are more generally given on the basis of the value of the job. However, rewards (namely, indirect benefits) provided just for being a member of the organization are rapidly increasing.

Which form of compensation is most fair? Which form is most effective for the organization? By what methods can jobs be evaluated fairly to determine their value? These concerns and others are part of the compensating activity, which includes:

- Administering direct compensation on the basis of job evaluation
- Providing performance-based pay
- Administering indirect compensation benefits to employees of the organization

It often is difficult to assess the types and levels of compensation that should be affected, but this process is very important. Appropriate compensation must be offered not only to attract good potential employees to the organization, and to motivate employees to perform well, but also to determine possible training and development needs. If generous compensation is offered and yet no appreciable level of employee improvement can be identified, perhaps further employee training is required.

Enhancing Human Potential

Two areas in which PHRM interest has grown in recent years are

1. determining, designing, and implementing employee training and development programs to increase employee ability, performance, and growth; and
2. improving the work environment, particularly in regard to the quality of work life and implementing productivity improvement programs.

Training and development activities include training employees, developing management, and helping employees to develop their careers. Enabling employees to pursue their own specific career goals provides them with a richer and more challenging career. For the organization, increased productivity is to be expected since the organization would be staffed by a more dedicated, high-performance workforce.

While the primary purpose of improving the physical and socio-psychological work environment is to improve conditions for both the employee and the organization, the primary purpose of training and development activities is to improve employee performance. In practice as well as in theory, however, there is some overlap. For example, as a result of programs designed to improve the work environment, employee performance may increase along with the employee's levels of satisfaction, responsibility, and self-control. One of the programs that is aimed at improving both the quality of work life and productivity is the quality circle effort. This is one of many programs now being used to increase productivity and one of several that is discussed in Chapter 13 of this textbook.

Establishing and Maintaining Effective Industrial Relations

An organization must take good care of its employees, compensate them properly, and provide conditions that make them want to stay. To maintain effective working relationships with its employees, an organization must

1. improve the work environment to maximize employee health and safety;
2. recognize and respect employee rights;
3. understand the reasons for unionization of employees, and the functions and structure of the union, in order to be able to effectively bargain and settle grievances with employees and the organizations representing them.

In addition to providing training and development programs, organizations also provide PHRM programs for health and safety improvements. In Canada, there are federal and provincial laws relating to occupational health and safety with which organizations must comply that often have a special influence in establishing and maintaining effective industrial relations, for example, by requiring unions and management to set up joint health and safety committees. Work-environment improvements not only ensure the physical safety and security of employees, but also enhance their socio-psychological well-being, and thus their productivity and quality of work life.

Increasingly, employees are gaining more rights. Consequently, employment decisions such as discharges, layoffs, and demotions must be made with care and backed up by evidence that such decisions are fair. It is important that all of the managers of an organization be aware of the employees' rights. The PHRM manager is in an excellent position to inform line managers of these rights.

When employees are unionized, their rights are protected by a union contract. PHRM personnel must become familiar with that contract and the issues that relate to how employees organize themselves in dealing with the organization and how the organization bargains and negotiates with its organized employees. This is necessary because, on the one hand, the formal union-management relationship can effectively define the extent to which other PHRM functions can be applied to the workforce. On the other hand, the union-management relationship can be instrumental in developing new PHRM programs, such as programs to improve productivity and quality of work life, or to improve compensation. This suggests that all of these PHRM functions and activities are interdependent.

Systemic Relationships of PHRM Functions and Activities

Rather than viewing PHRM as a set of five separate functions each with its own set of activities, it is more appropriate to view them as having systemic relationships with each other. That is, all five functions should be viewed as a unit, necessarily interrelated, serving the four major objectives of effective PHRM:

1. To attract qualified job applicants
2. To retain the desirable employees
3. To motivate the employees
4. To help employees to grow, develop, and realize their potential

These relationships are illustrated in Exhibit 1.1. Thus, to attract potentially qualified job applicants, it is not sufficient just to have an elaborate recruiting program. Attractive compensation and training programs also may be required. And so it is with any of the other PHRM functions and activities: doing one effectively requires taking the others into consideration. Because of the importance and prevalence of this systemic relationship of the PHRM functions and activities, a section in each chapter of this book is devoted to describing the relationships most relevant to the topic of that chapter.

PHRM functions and activities are important largely because they serve to attract, retain and motivate employees. Their recent and growing importance in organizations also is attributed to the recognition that PHRM can and does have an impact on the bottom-line goals of the organization. The term "bottom-line goals" refers to the organization's profitability and competitiveness or, in the case of non-profit and government organizations, to survival and the ability to do more with the same or fewer resources.[6] PHRM has this significant impact through three strategic purposes related to the bottom-line goals of the organization: **productivity, quality of work life**, and **legal compliance**. Thus, while the various PHRM functions and activities may serve the four major objectives, each also may serve these three strategic purposes and, consequently, be in line with the bottom-line goals of the organization. These relationships are illustrated in Exhibit 1.2.

The recent and growing importance of PHRM has been enhanced by trends and crises closely associated with its three strategic purposes. After a description of these trends and crises, the three strategic purposes are discussed in more detail.

The Growing Importance of PHRM

The current importance of PHRM is largely due to several trends and crises in society and to the recognition that PHRM can significantly influence the goals of organizations.

Trends and Crises

Four major trends and crises influencing the importance of PHRM are

1. The costs associated with effective human resource management
2. The productivity crisis

Systemic Relationships Among the Several PHRM Functions, Activities, and Objectives — Exhibit 1.1

Planning
- Human resource utilization
- Job design and analysis

Staffing
- Recruiting and respecting the law
- Selection and respecting the law

Appraising and Compensating
- Performance appraisals
- Compensation

Enhancing
- Training and development
- Improving quality of work life

Establishing and Maintaining
- Health and safety
- Employee rights
- Union-management relationships

PHRM Objectives
- Attract
- Retain
- Motivate
- Assist growth and development

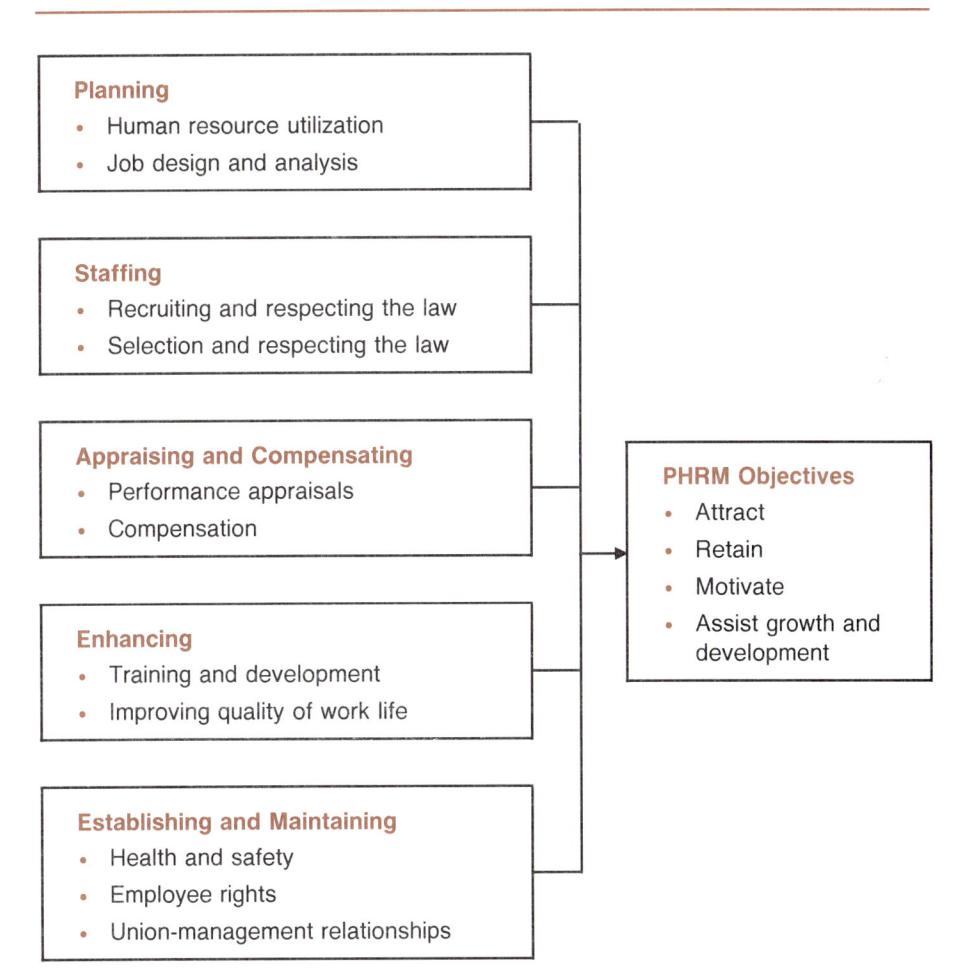

Exhibit 1.2   *Relationships Among PHRM Functions and Activities, Objectives, Strategic Purposes, and the Bottom-Line Goals (left to right)*

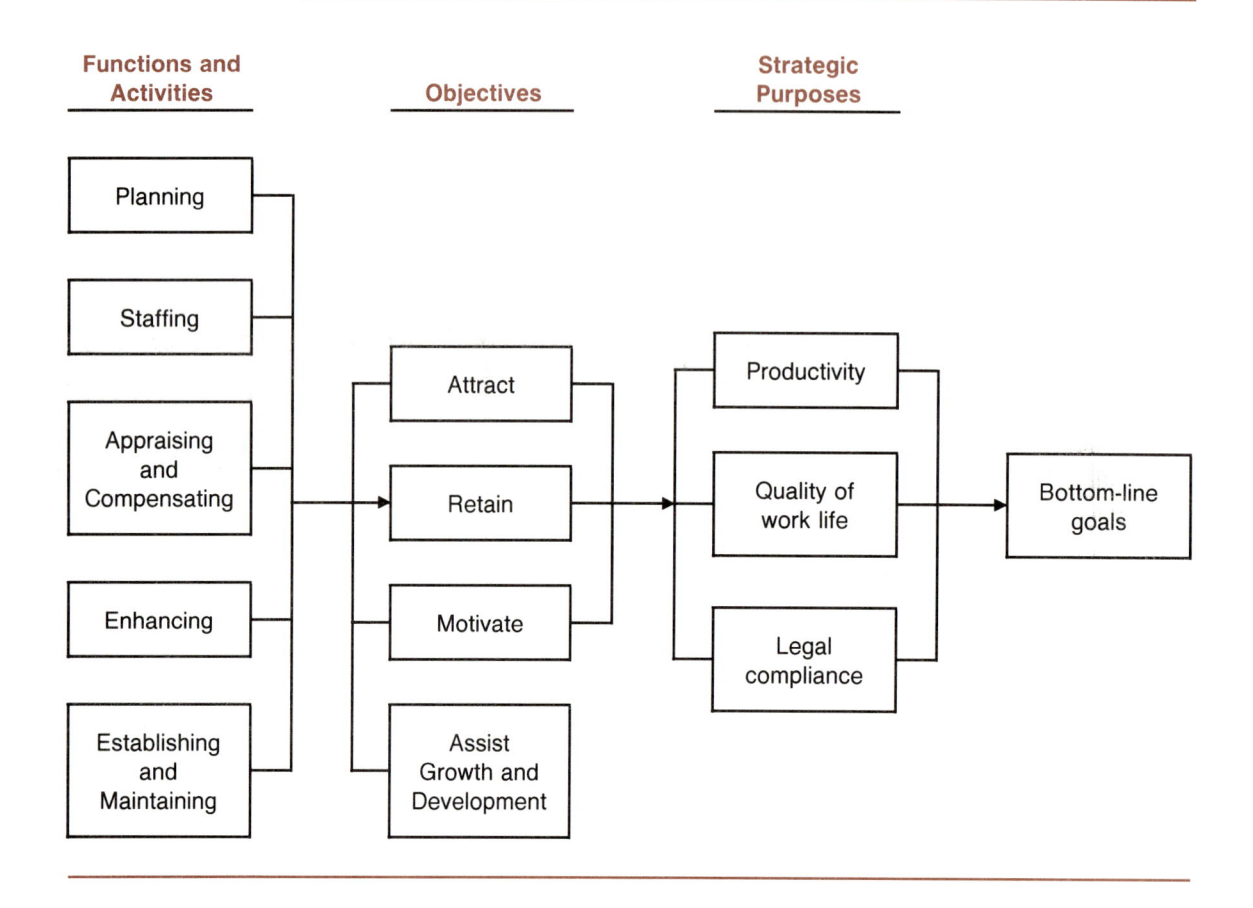

Functions and Activities:
- Planning
- Staffing
- Appraising and Compensating
- Enhancing
- Establishing and Maintaining

Objectives:
- Attract
- Retain
- Motivate
- Assist Growth and Development

Strategic Purposes:
- Productivity
- Quality of work life
- Legal compliance

→ Bottom-line goals

---

3. The increasing pace and complexity of social, cultural, legal, demographic, and educational changes
4. The symptoms of dysfunction in the workplace

Human Resource Management Costs. Today, corporations realize that it pays to be concerned with how they manage their human resources. They are aware, that their important assets are not just financial, but also human resources; it is crucial to have the right people to effectively operate an organization.[7]

PHRM activities designed to manage and develop human resources effectively result in significant reduction in accidents, absenteeism, and error rates, and a significant increase in morale and in the quality of the product or service, with productivity and profits being important by-products.[8]

The importance of PHRM has only recently been acknowledged by senior executives in organizations. For example, Laurent Thibault, executive vice-president of the Canadian Manufacturers' Association, admits that Canadian managers have been late in recognizing that human resources are critical to an organization. He states that, "They've considered the organization of the plant, the technology, and the equipment. But they didn't pay enough attention to whether the workplace was meeting the full needs of the employees."[9]

Productivity Crisis. Although Canada ranked third among the world's seven leading industrial nations in productivity gains during the late 1970s, the data gathered during the early 1980s and projections made by many economists suggest that a real productivity crisis will confront Canadian workers for the remainder of the 1980s and the early 1990s.

Canada had a productivity gain of 4.2% in 1978 compared with Japan's 8.3% or France's 4.9%. All of the other industrial nations reported smaller increments for that year: West Germany, 3.7%; Italy, 2.9%; the U.S., 2.5%; and the United Kingdom, 1.6%. The decline in Canadian productivity began in that year, according to a study conducted by Caron Belanger Woods Gordon, a Canada-wide accounting and management consulting firm. Rather than comparing the productivity with that of other nations, they analyzed the productivity trends and found a systematic decline in productivity gains. Projections for 1988 are even more gloomy, according to the study.[10] The Conference Board of Canada recently provided further evidence of this trend, as it forecast only a 3.7% increase in 1985 and a 2.4% increase in 1986, both down from the 1984 increase of 4.8%.[11]

Undoubtedly, many factors are contributing to this productivity crisis—changes in technology (see "PHRM in the News"), decreasing capital investment, limits on capacity utilization, and workflow interruptions. The importance of effective PHRM is central to productivity, so more effective utilization of human resources may be the best hope for stopping the slide in productivity.

Increasing Pace and Complexity of Change. Several cultural, educational, and social changes in Canada also have contributed to the growing importance of PHRM. For example, between 1970 and 1983, the participation rate of women in the labour force increased from 38% to 53%.[12] As a result, in 1983, women constituted 42% of the total labour force, up from 34% in 1970.[13] In the 1990s the participation of women in the workforce is expected to be even greater.

During the 1980s the number of workers in the 18-to-24 age group will decline, while the number in the 35-to-44 age group will increase. In Canada, the proportion of younger workers between the ages of 15 and 24 had already dropped from roughly 1 in 4 in 1976 to 1 in 5 in 1984. This trend will result in a shortage of young workers and a surplus of middle-aged workers with potentially frustrated career ambitions.

The current workforce is generally becoming better educated. In 1971 in Canada, 32% of the women and 38% of the men aged 15 and over had completed Grade 9 or less. In 1983, these percentages dropped to 20% and 21%, respectively.[14]

These high-quality human resources are potentially more productive, but also present a real challenge to organizations: "As society becomes better informed, it also tends to become more critical, less accepting of authority, and more cynical." [15]

Young workers appear to be particularly cynical about decisions made by supervisors and correspondingly more resistant to authority. Older workers, however, still tend to "reflect earlier values of society and are, therefore, more inclined to be organization people, to accept authority and to seek primarily the satisfaction of lower level needs at work." [16] Therefore, the effective management of human resources requires not only knowing how to manage and channel the skills of the young workers but also knowing how to manage a workforce with a mixed set of values. Other characteristics of the workforce are described in Chapter 2 of this textbook.

Symptoms of Dysfunction in the Workplace. Rapid social change has been accompanied by changes in the relationship between the worker and the job. Some of the terms used to describe what is happening in the workplace include *worker alienation, boredom*, and *job dissatisfaction*.[17] These symptoms are often associated with decreasing motivation and increasing counter-productive behaviour and worker demands in the workplace. Although these symptoms certainly can be found in most workplaces—factories or offices, public or private organizations—the extent to which these symptoms are reported to exist varies greatly.[18] Where they do exist, however, it appears that they can be eliminated through PHRM programs designed to involve employees more fully in decisions on the job.

A series of articles in *The Financial Post* reported the conclusions of a survey of top Canadian businesses that echoed the conclusions of Peters and Waterman's book, *In Search of Excellence*. They found that the best-run corporations in Canada are those that emphasize "people management," processes and structures through which managers deal with each other, their subordinates, their customers, and others in their environment.[19]

Such findings advanced the cause of improved PHRM in the organizations. PHRM officers have reported being pushed into the limelight of executive committee meetings and challenged to answer such questions as "What can we do to change the 'culture' of the firm?" and "How can we get our employees more involved?"

Another symptom being noticed in the workplace is the desire for a more explicit statement of the rights of employees. Among the rights that employees desire are the right to work, to know what one's job and its requirements are, to participate in decisions, to be appraised fairly and against objective performance criteria, to be accountable, and to be able to take risks and make mistakes.[20]

Strategic Purposes of PHRM

In the definition of PHRM, three major strategic purposes are identified. Although some organizations may value one purpose more than the others, all three are becoming tied more directly to the goals and purposes of the entire organization. The three strategic purposes are increased productivity, quality of work life, and legal compliance.

Productivity

Without a doubt, productivity is one of the most important goals of organizations.[21] Douglas Danforth, vice-chairman of Westinghouse Electric Corporation, indicates that the top management of his company considers productivity to be its highest priority.[22] Although individual PHRM managers and specialists can do little to influence the capital, material, and energy aspects that contribute to productivity, they can uniquely influence the utilization of the workforce, top management's human resource philosophy, and the personnel and human resource practices of the organization that also contribute to productivity. Thus, PHRM has a unique and timely opportunity to help improve productivity.[23] For instance, union-management co-operation can lead to improved productivity. The PHRM team of Canadair Ltd. and Lodge 712 of the International Association of Machinists and Aerospace Workers negotiated a unique productivity improvement plan that seems to be most successful.[24]

Quality of Work Life

The dissatisfying nature of industrial or clerical work is no longer disputed. Many of today's employees prefer a greater level of involvement in their jobs than was previously assumed. Many desire more self-control and a chance to make a greater contribution to the organization. Many employers seem to be equally convinced of the importance of improved quality of work life, particularly the importance of greater worker involvement in workplace decisions. Communicating with the employees and encouraging the employees to present their ideas is second only to increasing productivity as a major role that chief executive officers want to see their PHRM managers play. The Canadian Manufacturers' Association recognized the need for workforce participation when its president, Roy Phillips, stated that "To compete in the global village, the power of the people is necessary." [25]

Legal Compliance

Organizations must comply with many laws, guidelines, and court decisions in managing their employees. These laws and regulations affect almost all of the functions and activities utilized in PHRM. Therefore, PHRM representatives must constantly be involved in the process of complying with the current laws and regulations and court decisions. They also must be familiar with the actions of the various occupational health and safety commissions, and the federal and provincial Human Rights Commissions' guidelines (see "PHRM in the News"). If PHRM departments fail to keep abreast of what is happening and are unaware of the legal regulations with which organizations must comply, these organizations may find themselves paying out large sums of money for lawsuits and fines. Fortunately, PHRM departments and their managers can avoid these costs by constantly monitoring the legal environment for any changes, by complying with those changes, and by practising effective personnel and human resource management. Many examples of costly lawsuits that could have been avoided through the use of effective personnel practices are provided throughout this text. All of these examples, however, highlight just one of the many reasons that PHRM is so important, and why PHRM departments are gaining more recognition in organizations today.

Personnel and Human Resource Management in the Organization

A Brief Historical Overview

An authoritative history of the PHRM in Canada has yet to be written. However, many of the developments in this area reflect a combination of British and U.S. influences. Three major forces have helped to shape the evolution of the role of PHRM departments in Canadian business:

1. The slow change in general management philosophy, which has changed since the beginning of the century from the management of things to the management of people
2. The political pressures that eventually were translated into laws
3. The changes in the values of the larger society of which Canadian business is a part

Although PHRM can be very important to an organization, organizations have not always viewed the PHRM department that way. This was due, in part, to the limited role the PHRM department often played:

> To many businessmen, including many chief executives, the people who worked in "personnel" appeared to be a bunch of drones whose apparent missions in life were to create paperwork, recruit secretaries who couldn't type, and send around memos whose impertinence was exceeded only by their irrelevance.[26]

As a result of this perception, personnel directors seemed to be accomplishing nothing of any true importance. Today, for reasons already described, PHRM departments in many organizations are considered much more vital. Organizations are recognizing the prevalent crises and trends and the impact that PHRM can have on the bottom-line organizational goals. Consequently, the PHRM department is now becoming a key corporate division, and the executives who are now being put in charge of personnel departments are as interested in profits as any other executives.[27]

Personnel and Human Resource Management Roles

There are several roles that the PHRM department can play in an organization.[28] The more roles it plays, the more likely it is that it will be effective in (1) improving the organization's productivity, (2) enhancing the quality of work life in the organization, and (3) complying with all the necessary laws and regulations related to human resource utilization.

Policy Formulator. One role that the PHRM department can play is that of information provider, relaying to top management the information that relates to the concerns of the employees and the impact of the external environment.

PHRM staff can also advise in the process of policy formulation. The chief executive may still make policy statements, but these could be regarded as drafts of policy. Formal adoption of a final policy can take place after other executives, such as the personnel manager and line managers, have had a chance to provide their comments.

At Honeywell Limited there is an executive employee-relations committee, composed of five operating group vice-presidents and five staff vice-presidents. This committee is the senior policy board for employee-relations issues. This committee not only helps ensure extensive informational input into personnel policies but also increases the likelihood of their being accepted.

Provider and Delegator. In reality, PHRM programs succeed because line managers (at managerial and operational levels) make them succeed. The bread-and-butter job of the PHRM department, therefore, is to enable line managers to make things happen. In the more traditional personnel activities, such as selecting, interviewing, training, evaluating, compensating, rewarding, counselling, promoting, and firing, the PHRM department is basically providing a service to line managers. Since the line managers are ultimately responsible for their employees, many of them see these services as being useful. The PHRM department also can assist line managers by providing and interpreting information about fair employment practices equal-employment-opportunity legislation and health and safety standards.

The responsibilities of the PHRM department are to provide the services needed by the line managers on a day-to-day basis, to keep them informed of regulations and legislation regarding human resource management, and to provide an adequate supply of job candidates from which the line managers can choose. To fulfil these responsibilities, the PHRM department must be accessible. Otherwise the PHRM manager loses touch with the needs of the line managers.

Consider this typical statement made by a line manager: "If only the personnel people would visit us sometime, they might better understand what it is we do."[29] The PHRM staff should be as close to the people and the problems as possible. Because bringing the personnel staff close to the action is an organizing concern, this will be discussed in the section on departmental organizing later in this chapter.

Auditor. Although the PHRM department may delegate much of the implementation of personnel activities to line managers, it still is responsible for seeing that activities are implemented fairly and consistently. This is particularly true today because of fair-employment-practices legislation.

Various provincial and federal regulations are making increasingly sophisticated demands on organizations. Responses to these regulations can best be made by a central group supplied with accurate information, the needed expertise, and the blessing of top management.

Expertise also is needed for implementing many personnel activities, such as distributing employee benefits. And since having personnel experts on staff is costly, organizations hire as few as possible and centralize them. Their expertise then filters to other areas of the organization.

In organizations that have several locations and several divisions or units, there is often tension between the need to implement policy at the point of action (decentralization) and the need to implement it fairly across several divisions of an organization. There is also tension between the need for policy decentralization and the need to have the expertise necessary to comply with complex regulations and advise the best methods for carrying out personnel activities.

Innovator. An important and ever-expanding role for the PHRM department is that of providing up-to-date application of current techniques and developing and exploring innovative approaches to personnel problems and concerns.

> Naturally, the innovative role must be in tune with the times and the set of issues confronting a particular company. In periods of rising inflation and escalating wage and salary demands, the emphasis may be on compensation issues. In times of retrenchment and falling profits, creative work sharing and lay-off plans may be needed.[30]

Today, the personnel-related issues demanding innovative approaches and solutions revolve around how to improve productivity and the quality of work life while complying with the law in an environment of high uncertainty, high need for energy conservation, and intense international competition. How effective an organization is in addressing these issues depends upon how well it organizes and staffs its PHRM department. This situation is examined after a discussion of some trends for PHRM in the organization.

Extent and Scope of PHRM Activities

Another way to look at the current responsibilities of PHRM officers is to examine how they spend their time. A recent survey conducted by the American Society of Personnel Administration and the Bureau of National Affairs in the U.S. found that the PHRM unit's responsibility for different activities vary considerably. Exhibit 1.3 provides a good picture of how PHRM people spend their time.

Special Concerns in PHRM

Several special concerns exist in PHRM:

- *Openness* in PHRM activities, such as employee access to personnel files, employee participation in workplace decisions, and job posting[31]

- *Proactivity*, or the initiation of personnel and human resource management programs to improve productivity and the quality of work life without being ordered by the chief executive
- *A systems orientation*, that is, the diagnosis and assessment of trends and crises outside the organization as well as within it (but outside the PHRM department), and the impact of these on the organization and the effective utilization of its human resources
- *Evaluating PHRM effectiveness*
- *Strategic involvement* as well as operational and managerial involvement

Since the last two concerns are more encompassing, they will be discussed in detail.

Extent and Scope of PHRM Activities — Exhibit 1.3

Percent of Companies (Subject sample: 631)

Activity	Extent of PHRM Department's Responsibility — All	Some	None	No Such Activity at Company/Facility
Personnel records/reports/information systems	89	10	1	*
Legal compliance with employment regulations	86	12	1	1
Insurance benefits administration	85	10	5	*
Unemployment compensation administration	83	11	5	1
Wage/salary administration	79	18	3	*
Workers' compensation administration	77	14	9	*
Personnel research	75	6	1	18
Job evaluation	69	25	4	3
Pre-employment testing	66	9	3	22
Induction/orientation	62	34	3	1
Health/medical services	62	12	11	15
Promotion/transfer/separation processing	61	36	2	1
Retirement preparation programs	61	10	5	24
Vacation/leave processing	60	30	9	*
Recreation/social programs	58	29	8	5
Tuition aid/scholarships	58	19	12	11
Pension/profit-sharing plan administration	57	26	10	7
Employee assistance plan/counselling program	57	18	4	22
Recruiting/interviewing/hiring	56	42	2	*
Complaint/disciplinary procedures	54	43	2	1
Attitude surveys	48	9	5	38
Employee communications/publications	47	28	20	5
Human resource planning	46	40	4	10
Executive compensation administration	46	26	20	8
College recruiting	45	16	4	35

Continued on next page

Exhibit 1.3 Continued

Percent of Companies (Subject sample: 631)

Activity	Extent of PHRM Department's Responsibility — All	Some	None	No Such Activity at Company/Facility
Health and safety regulation compliance	44	37	17	3
Union/labour relations	44	15	3	39
Outplacement services	42	7	1	50
Supervisory training	40	44	12	4
Relocation services administration	40	19	7	34
Performance evaluation, non-management	39	44	14	4
Management development	36	44	11	9
Suggestion systems	32	17	10	41
Food services	32	6	28	34
Thrift/savings plan administration	31	13	8	47
Community relations/fund drives	30	35	28	7
Management appraisal/management by objectives	27	38	13	21
Career planning/development	26	41	5	28
Security measures/property protection	26	16	52	6
Organization development	24	43	13	20
Stock plan administration	21	11	9	59
Skill training, non-management	20	42	31	7
Productivity/motivation programs	17	49	13	21
Payroll processing	15	24	58	3
Public relations	14	30	48	8
Administrative services (mail, phone, messengers, etc.)	14	17	66	3
Library	10	5	37	48
Travel/transportation services administration	8	19	48	26
Maintenance/janitorial services	7	8	79	6

* Less than 0.45%

Source: "Personnel Activities Budgets and Staffs," American Society of Personnel Administration–Bureau of National Affairs Survey No. 47, June 21, 1984, p. 2. Reprinted by permission from *Bulletin to Management*, copyright 1984 by the Bureau of National Affairs, Inc., Washington D.C.

Criteria for Evaluating PHRM

PHRM often is not considered vital to an organization because it fails to demonstrate its effectiveness in line with the four objectives of PHRM and the three strategic purposes, as shown in Exhibits 1.1 and 1.2. Recognizing this, PHRM managers are starting to demonstrate their effectiveness just as other managers do, by *assessing* the costs and benefits of appropriate *criteria* and then comparing the costs of PHRM activities with the benefits resulting from those activities. In comparing the costs with the benefits, the PHRM manager demonstrates *effectiveness*. To be effective, PHRM must determine through assessment the relevant cost and benefit criteria.[32]

Benefit criteria for PHRM are those indicators against which comparisons can be made to demonstrate improvements or benefits to the organization. Three indicators are used as benefit criteria. These indicators and their specific components are:

Productivity
- Increased performance
- Reduced absenteeism
- Reduced turnover
- Reduced grievances

Quality of Work Life
- Increased job involvement
- Increased satisfaction
- Reduced stress
- Reduced accidents and illnesses

Legal Compliance
- Reduced or eliminated cost of fines
- Reduced or eliminated cost of lost contracts
- Enhanced community goodwill and general reputation

In general, productivity represents the efficiency with which an organization uses its workforce, capital, material, and energy resources to produce its product or service. Other things being equal, reducing the workforce but getting the same output improves productivity.[33] Similarly, if each employee's performance (quality or quantity) increases, total output increases and so does productivity. Reducing the absenteeism and turnover of good employees are other ways to increase productivity.[34]

Improving the quality of work life may result in increased performance and reduced absenteeism and turnover, but the quality of work life can also be measured in other ways.[35] For example, the more the individuals' preferences and interests are satisfied by the organization, the more likely it is that the employees will be more involved with their jobs; register higher satisfaction with their jobs, supervisors, and co-workers; suffer less from stress; and have fewer accidents and better health.

Finally, the goodwill of potential job applicants and the community can be diminished significantly if a company fails to comply with laws and regulations.

Cost criteria for PHRM are those indicators that are used to determine the costs or expense of the PHRM activities. Whereas the benefit criteria generally apply to all of the PHRM activities, the cost criteria are more specific to each activity. For example, cost criteria appropriate for the safety and health PHRM activity may be supervisory training; the addition of newer, safer equipment; the removal of hazards and waste materials; and job redesign. Cost criteria for recruitment may be advertising, training, and the payroll expense for the recruiters.

After determining the appropriate cost criteria (based on the specific PHRM activity of interest) and the appropriate benefit criteria (not all benefit criteria are equally relevant to each PHRM activity), these costs and benefits can be compared. This comparison is increasingly being made on the basis of dollars and cents for both the cost criteria and the benefit criteria. Whereas the value of the cost criteria is more specific to each PHRM activity, the value of the benefit criteria is more general. Consequently, the valuation of productivity, quality of work life, and legal compliance can be described here. A reference to cost criteria is presented separately in the assessment sections of each chapter.

Valuation of the benefit criteria in dollars and cents is most feasible for productivity and legal compliance. It is less feasible for quality of work life because of the difficulty in attaching a dollars-and-cents value to intangibles such as job involvement and satisfaction. Although it is not impossible to evaluate the quality of work life (the dollars-and-cents costs of accidents and illnesses can be determined readily), it may be more appropriate to relate quality of work life to the organization's ability to survive and adapt rather than to its profitability. These and related issues are discussed in the assessment sections of the following chapters, and will be summarized in Chapter 18.

Once the dollars-and-cents values of the benefit criteria and cost criteria are established, the PHRM department can demonstrate its effectiveness. A demonstration that the values of the cost criteria are no greater, or even less than, those in other organizations (similar or different) is one proof of effectiveness. The value of those comparisons can be enhanced by including relevant information on benefit criteria. Although it may be neither feasible to obtain nor valid to use dollars-and-cents valuation of the turnover of other organizations, it may be useful to compare *rates* of turnover or absenteeism. Thus, the PHRM department could demonstrate that the costs to the organization for managing its human resources are producing more benefits (using only a comparison of turnover rates) than in other organizations.

The PHRM department also can demonstrate its effectiveness by comparing the valuation of changes in benefit criteria levels with the valuation of the cost of specific PHRM activities. For example, if a new recruitment program is implemented and the absenteeism rate of the employees recruited with the new program declines 2%, the dollar costs of the program can be compared with the dollar gains obtained from reducing absenteeism.

Although this type of comparison can be useful in demonstrating the effectiveness of PHRM, it is not always possible to attribute certain changes, such as in absenteeism, to a particular program. For example, a downturn in the national economy at the time that the program was implemented may have been the *real* cause of the reduced absenteeism, rather than the recruitment program. To help prevent erroneous conclusions or false inferences from being drawn, the PHRM manager needs to be aware of varying types of research evaluation designs. These are presented in Chapter 12 on training and development. Other research and statistical issues useful to PHRM staff are presented throughout the following chapters. Also, a synthesis of PHRM assessment methods is detailed in Chapter 18.

Strategic Involvement

A relatively limited involvement in the affairs and goals of the total organization was consistent with the limited roles of auditor and provider that many PHRM departments used to play. It was not unusual for a PHRM manager to be concerned only with making staffing plans, providing specific job training programs, or running the annual performance appraisal program (the results of which were put in the personnel files and never really used). Consequently, the PHRM manager was concerned only with the short-term operational and managerial human resource needs. It would have been unusual for this PHRM manager to have been concerned with demonstrating the effectiveness of his or her department or even the effectiveness of the organization.

Now, because of the crises and trends described earlier, PHRM managers are becoming more involved in the total organization—where it is going, where it should be going—and are helping it to get there. As a consequence, they and their departments are playing all four roles (policy formulation, provider and delegator, auditor, and innovator) and utilizing the PHRM functions and activities on long- and medium-term bases as well as the traditional short-term basis. PHRM departments now engage in human resource management activities and functions at three levels—strategic, managerial, and operational. The requisite activities for each of these levels are shown in Exhibit 1.4.

PHRM departments are beginning to link PHRM activities to the needs of the organization. For example, PHRM departments are now recognizing that, as an organization's products go through different parts of their life cycle, different management skills are necessary. To be tied into the strategic needs of the organization, human resource planning must be attuned to the life cycles of the products of the organization.[36] With all of these considerations it is imperative that the PHRM department be adequately and appropriately organized and staffed.

Organizing the PHRM Department

For PHRM departments to be effective, they must not only be thoroughly involved in the organization but also well organized. The organization of PHRM includes the following needs:

- The need for the PHRM staff to be where the action is, and to identify with the organization as a whole
- The need for a fair and consistent application of personnel policies, regardless of how small or large or diversified the organization

Exhibit 1.4 Personnel and Human Resource Management Activities by Level

Level	Employee Selection/ Placement	Rewards (Pay and Benefits)	Appraisal	Development	Career Planning
Strategic (long-term)	Specify the characteristics of people needed to run business over long term Alter internal and external systems to reflect future	Determine how workforce will be rewarded over the long term, based on potential world conditions Link to long-term business strategy	Determine what should be valued in long term Develop means to appraise future dimensions Make early identification of potential	Plan developmental experiences for people running future business Set up systems with flexibility necessary to adjust to change	Develop long-term system to manage individual and organizational needs for both flexibility and stability Link to business strategy
Managerial (medium-term)	Make longitudinal validation of selection criteria Develop recruitment marketing plan Develop new markets	Set up five-year compensation plans for individuals Set up cafeteria benefits package	Set up validated systems that relate current conditions and future potential Set up assessment centres for development	Establish general management development program Provide for organizational development Foster self-development	Identify career paths Provide career development services Match individual with organization
Operational (short-term)	Make staffing plans Make recruitment plans Set up day-to-day monitoring systems	Administer wage and salary program Administer benefits packages	Set up annual or less frequent appraisal system Set up day-to-day control systems	Provide for specific job skill training Provide on-the-job training	Fit individuals to specific jobs Plan next career move

Source: M. A. Devanna, D. Fombrun, and N. Tichy, "Human Resource Management: A Strategic Perspective," *Organizational Dynamics*, Winter 1981.

- The need for the views of the PHRM department to be an integral part of personnel policy
- The need for the PHRM department to have sufficient power and authority to help ensure that personnel policies will be implemented without discrimination, but rather, legally and affirmatively
- The need for the PHRM department not just to react to personnel crises but to be active and innovative in dealing with human resource management

The PHRM department can be organized so that it effectively addresses only one or two of these needs. The way in which top management views personnel activities, and what it is willing to let the PHRM department do, will determine the actual organization.

PHRM in the Organization

The importance that an organization assigns to PHRM is reflected by the position of the department staff in the hierarchy. This in turn helps to determine the number of roles that the PHRM department plays and the levels at which these roles are played.

PHRM in the Hierarchy. For the effective fulfilment of the 4 personnel roles, top managers of the PHRM department should also be at the top of the organizational hierarchy. In fact, in more and more Canadian corporations, the top PHRM manager is placed in second position in the hierarchy, usually at the vice-presidential level and equivalent to other vice-presidents such as those of production, marketing, and finance.

Being at the top allows the PHRM manager to play a part in personnel policy formulation and to have the power necessary for its fair and consistent implementation. When PHRM has this much importance, it is likely to be performing the operational, managerial and strategic personnel activities that are necessary for PHRM.

Centralization versus Decentralization

The concept of centralization versus decentralization relates to the issue of the balance between getting PHRM personnel to where the action is and fairly and consistently applying personnel policies. It also is related to the balance between the benefits of having personnel generalists and of having personnel specialists. Under **centralization**, the essential decision making and policy formulation are done at one location (at headquarters); under **decentralization**, the essential decision making and policy formulation are done at several locations (in the divisions or departments of the organization).

With the recent increases in regulatory requirements for use of human resources and the increased expertise necessary to deal with complex personnel functions, organizations are moving away from personnel generalists toward PHRM specialists. At the same time, organizations, particularly larger ones, are moving personnel staff into the organization's divisions. As a result, there are trends to centralize some aspects of personnel and human resource management and to decentralize others.

For the personnel activities that require expertise, organizations generally hire specialists. But because of the expense, as few specialists as possible are hired. If an organization is large and has several plants or offices or divisions, the specialists are located in one place (at corporate headquarters) but serve all of the divisions. The PHRM activities requiring less specialized expertise are staffed by people at the divisional level, thereby increasing the autonomy of the divisions. Thus in a large, multi-division organization (which describes most of the largest industrial, retail, and financial organizations), there is generally a corporate personnel and human resource management department staffed largely with specialists, and several divisional personnel departments staffed largely with generalists. The PHRM department at headquarters then has two purposes:

- To develop and co-ordinate PHRM policy for the personnel staff at all locations, including headquarters
- To execute the PHRM functions and activities for all of the employees at headquarters

As the divisions grow, they begin to hire their own specialists and to administer their own PHRM department, similar to that found in most organizations without divisions. These specialists help to ensure a level of fairness and consistency in the administration of personnel activities in all of the divisions.

Who Is Responsible for PHRM?

Everyone should be responsible for PHRM, and as organizations demonstrate more openness and mutuality in their human resource management policies and practices, everyone will be.

The Managers. PHRM is the task of individuals who have specialized in, and are primarily responsible for, personnel management (personnel managers). It is also the task of individuals not specialized in, but often responsible for, the day-to-day implementation of personnel functions and activities (line supervisors and line managers). This is not meant to imply that the PHRM manager never implements personnel functions and activities or that the PHRM manager does not get involved in their development and administration. Indeed, line and personnel managers are interdependent in the effective management of human resources. But the effective management of human resources cannot occur without the support and direction of top management. Top management influences the number and execution of personnel functions and activities in an organization. This influence is best demonstrated by the roles that top management allows the PHRM manager and department to play in the organization.

The Employees. Increasingly, employees are taking a role in personnel and human resource management. For example, employees may be asked to appraise their own performance or the performance of their colleagues. Employees also may help to determine their own performance standards and goals. It is no longer uncommon for employees to write their own job descriptions. Perhaps most significantly, employees are taking a more active role in managing their own careers, assessing their own needs and values, and designing their own jobs. However, the PHRM department must help to guide this process.

PHRM Budgets

The money allocated by organizations to their PHRM departments continues to rise each year. For example, a U.S. survey points out that the per-employee personnel costs rose from $385 in 1980 to a median $433 in 1981 and rose again in 1982. Non-manufacturing business organizations tend to spend the most per employee ($503 in 1981) and non-business firms the least ($202 in 1982). Firms with up to 250 employees generally have the largest personnel budget as a percentage of the total company payroll (3.6%).[37] At present no comparable data exist for Canadian companies, but it is safe to estimate a similar trend.

Staffing the PHRM Department

Perhaps the most effective person who can head the PHRM department is an outstanding performer from the line organization. Since attracting a "superstar" means paying the person a higher salary than he or she has been receiving, the effect of the superstar accepting the position is to increase the PHRM department's credibility and prestige in the organization. However, even if the person is not a superstar, line experience gives the PHRM manager influence over the other line managers. To understand just how far some companies have gone in this area, consider IBM's policy of assigning line managers to work in the corporate personnel department for two or three years as part of their career development.

In addition, the well-trained personnel specialist often gains influence by becoming a personnel generalist through training and experience. The personnel specialist who wants to reach the top may benefit greatly by rotating through a line job in order to increase his or her ability to understand and deal with the entire organization.

Qualities of the PHRM Manager and Staff

How effectively an organization's human resources are managed depends largely the quality of the people in the PHRM department.

The PHRM Manager. What qualities should PHRM managers possess? To begin with, PHRM managers need to be effective. They must be able to identify problems, develop alternative solutions, and then select and implement the most effective one. In addition, they must develop and maintain an integrated and effective management information system for helping to identify problems and implement policy. They must be innovative and aggressive, and willing to take the risks that are incurred by serving as the conscience of the organization. Furthermore, they must be effective at selecting, building, and developing staff to carry out the five PHRM functions. Finally, they must be able to foster a co-operative climate throughout the organization.

PHRM Generalists. What qualities do the rest of the PHRM staff need, and from where do these people come? Line positions are one important source. A brief tour given by a line supervisor in a personnel position, usually as a personnel generalist, can convey to the PHRM department the knowledge, language, needs, and requirements of the line. As a result, the PHRM department can more effectively perform its service role. Another source of PHRM talent is non-managerial employees. In many organizations, PHRM positions are staffed with former hourly employees. Like line managers, these people bring with them information about the needs and attitudes of employees. In many cases they are particularly effective in their PHRM positions.

Personnel generalists should possess many of the same qualities as personnel specialists, but the level of expertise in a personnel specialty generally does not need to be at the same depth. The generalist, however, needs to have a moderate level of expertise in many PHRM activities and must be able to obtain more specialized knowledge when it is needed.

PHRM Specialists. Personnel staff specialists should have skills related to the speciality, an awareness of the relationship of that specialty to other PHRM activities, and a knowledge of the organization and where the personnel and human resource management department fits. Specialists who are new to an organization should also develop an appreciation for the political realities of the organization. Further, individuals in PHRM should guard against the development of "them" and "us" situations, remember that they are not in business to promote the latest fads—and be aware that companies are not in business to perpetuate PHRM departments. Universities are an important source of personnel specialists. Since specialists may work at almost any PHRM activity, qualified applicants can come from specialized programs in law, personnel psychology, labour and industrial relations, personnel management, counseling, organizational development, and medical and health sciences.

Careers in PHRM

PHRM as a field of employment is becoming very attractive. In it are many different types of jobs, many paying rather well. In addition, there is a high level of professionalism associated with the field.

How Much Do PHRM Careers Pay?

Now that you have a good idea what personnel and human resource management is, you may want to consider a career in PHRM. And, of course, it is important to know how much money the jobs pay. For example, in 1984–85, the mean salaries for several different types of PHRM jobs in Québec were as follows: [38]

Job Title	Mean Salary	Mean Bonus
Director of Industrial Relations (first level)	$53 125	$ 8 204
Director of Personnel	46 342	5 187
Director of Compensation	45 119	7 430
Director of Training and Development	43 195	2 847
Safety Specialist	37 075	2 807
Personnel Director (divisional level)	40 103	9 980

Salaries and bonuses are generally higher in larger organizations for individuals with more experience and more education. In addition, salaries are often higher in large metropolitan areas.

Although the opportunities in PHRM in Canada are attractive and expanding, opportunities are better for you if you enter the personnel field after gaining experience in a line position.

> In fact, it may be that these people with a few months or years of background and experience in line positions may be well ahead of those who do not have this perspective. In other words, while it may not be possible for graduating students to go directly into personnel administration, it also may not be wise for them to go directly into the field even if they have the opportunity.[39]

The background in a line position is helpful because it provides you with a better understanding of the organization. It also will give you more credibility with other line managers when you are in PHRM and are trying to work with them. Since there are many more line jobs than PHRM jobs, it will be easier to get a line job and demonstrate your skills and abilities there. It is possible then to transfer into the PHRM department.

Growing Professionalism in PHRM

PHRM is now a well-respected profession.[40] As with any profession, it follows a code of professional ethics and has an accreditation institute and certification procedures. The code of ethics that PHRM follows is shared by all professions:

- The practitioner must regard the obligation to implement public objectives and protect the public interest as more important than blind loyalty to an employer's preferences

- In daily practice, the professional must thoroughly understand the problems assigned and must undertake whatever study and research are required to ensure continuing competence and the best of professional attention and treatment
- The practitioner must maintain a high standard of personal honesty and integrity in every phase of daily practice
- The professional must give thoughtful consideration to the personal interests, welfare, and dignity of all employees who are affected by his or her prescriptions, recommendations, and actions
- Professionals must make sure that the organizations that represent them maintain a high regard and respect for the public interest and that they never overlook the importance of the personal interests and dignity of employees.[41]

Against the background of growing professionalism in PHRM, the Canadian specialists appear to be under-educated and under-trained. Although several formal programs are currently available for training PHRM specialists in many universities and colleges across Canada, only one in three practicing personnel managers has a university degree. Ten years ago, however, the proportion was only 1 in 5.[42]

Professional Certification/Accreditation

In 1976, the American Society for Personnel Administration (ASPA) helped establish an independent group called the ASPA Accreditation Institute (AAI). Its purposes are

- to provide colleges and universities with guidelines for curricular development;
- to help students select courses related to various career objectives;
- to help young practitioners keep up to date and maintain competence in their field;
- to help young practitioners establish career goals and development plans; and
- to help employers identify qualified practitioners.

The AAI has established two major categories of personnel practitioners, **generalists** and **specialists**. It accredits only active practitioners as generalists. Specialists include active practitioners, educators, and consultants, to name a few. One need not be a member of ASPA to be accredited, and about one in four of those accredited are not ASPA members. Specialists may be accredited (certified) in six functional areas:

1. Employment, placement, and personnel planning
2. Training and development
3. Compensation and benefits
4. Health, safety, and security

5. Employee and labour relations
6. Personnel research

For each of these areas there are "functional standards committees," consisting of experts who define the knowledge required for each function and develop bibliographies and examination questions. The accreditation exams are conducted and evaluated by The Psychological Corporation in the U.S.

Specialists are awarded two types of accreditation, *APS* (Accredited Personnel Specialist) and *APD* (Accredited Personnel Diplomate). The combination of education and experience must amount to six years for the APS and ten years for the APD. A Bachelor's degree is counted as four years, and a Master's degree counts as five years toward the total six-year (APS) and ten-year (APD) requirements.

Generalists also are awarded two types of accreditation, APM (Accredited Personnel Manager) and AEP (Accredited Executive in Personnel). The APM has a six-year requirement, and the AEP has a ten-year requirement.[43]

In addition to earning accreditation, practitioners can belong to a number of specialized associations, such as the American Compensation Association, the Training and Development Association, and others. There also are many research-oriented and practitioner-oriented journals and magazines of interest to the teacher as well as to the PHRM practitioner. The names and addresses for many of these journals and associations are found in Appendix B of this textbook.

Canada has been lagging behind in the move toward certification of personnel and human resource managers. While many people agree that a standardized education and minimum professional qualifications should be required from practitioners, accreditation is still voluntary and almost any individual can practice PHRM. Some provinces such as Quebec have restricted the use of the title "Industrial Relations Consultant" only to individuals who have successfully completed an Industrial Relations college degree program, or have practised for at least five years. Similar efforts at certification have been made in Ontario and Manitoba.

The Plan of this Book

This book is intended to serve the reader by fulfilling several specific purposes and maintaining several themes throughout each of the chapters.

Purposes

- To increase your expertise in the functions and activities of personnel and human resource management
- To assist you in being an effective manager of human resources

- To present the complexities, challenges, and trade-offs involved in being an effective manager of human resources
- To instill a concern and an excitement for effective personnel and human resource management
- To assist you in being a more effective line manager

Themes

There are three major themes in this book: applications and challenges, practical realities, and theory and research. Each of these is integral in illustrating the importance of PHRM and in demonstrating how PHRM can help organizations effectively utilize their human resources.

Applications and Practical Realities. Examples from organizations and PHRM managers are used to provide illustrations of the challenges and practical realities of the personnel activities being examined. Each chapter begins with several real-life, short scenarios and quotations, called "PHRM in the News." Cases are included at the ends of Chapters 2 through 17 to provide the reader with the opportunity to deal with the challenges and practical realities firsthand.

Theory and Research. Extensive use is made of current research and theory related to the effective use and management of human resources. You will receive not only a detailed description of all of the current PHRM functions and activities, but also an understanding of why PHRM functions and activities should work and how they actually do work. With this knowledge you can decide how to make the PHRM functions and activities work better. Assisting you in this is the section on assessment at the end of most chapters. This section contains suggestions on what data to gather in order to make assessments and, in turn, improvements on each activity.

For Whom Is This Book Written?

This book is written for those who will one day work in organizations or who already are working in an organization. Knowledge of effective PHRM functions and activities is vital for anyone working in organizations but particularly for managers and personnel staff (specialists or generalists). This is true whether your organization is private or public, large or small, slow-growing or fast-growing. Although the type and size of the organization may influence the size of the PHRM department, the functions and activities that are performed, and even the roles that are played, and effective management of human resources is always necessary.

Summary

This chapter has examined the growing importance of the functions and activities of personnel and human resource management, defined PHRM, and listed its purposes. Because of the increasing complexity of PHRM, nearly all organizations have established a department for it. However, not all of these departments perform all of the personnel functions and activities discussed in this chapter. A department's functions and activities, and the way it performs them, depend greatly on the roles that the department plays in the organization. There are four roles that a PHRM department can play. Organizations that are most concerned with effective personnel and human resource management allow their PHRM departments to play all four roles. When this is the case, it is likely that the PHRM departments have demonstrated their value to their organizations by showing how the PHRM functions and activities influence productivity, quality of work life, and legal compliance—all purposes associated with the organization's bottom-line criteria. In addition, it is likely that these PHRM departments are operating at all three levels in the organization: strategic, managerial, and operational. A PHRM department should demonstrate its effectiveness, perform all four roles and operate at all three levels in the organization. This can help the organization to attain its bottom-line goals.

The remaining chapters provide detailed information about each PHRM activity. Many references are provided to enable you to examine in more detail many of the topics discussed. These references are contained in the "Endnotes" of each chapter, along with points of clarification or explanation.

Discussion Questions

1. Why is PHRM growing in importance for organizations?
2. Summarize briefly the several functions and activities of PHRM.
3. Discuss what is meant by systemic relationships of PHRM functions and activities.
4. What is the usual bottom line goal of the organization, and how can PHRM have a significant impact on this?
5. What trends and crises are presently influencing PHRM activities in many organizations?
6. Identify and describe the four roles of PHRM departments and discuss why the more roles PHRM departments play, the more effective they are to the organization.
7. Why is assessing PHRM effectiveness important?
8. How can PHRM managers become proactive in demonstrating their effectiveness?
9. What are some key issues related to the organization of an effective PHRM department?
10. What is the difference between personnel generalists and personnel specialists?

Endnotes

1. J. Fitz-enz, "Measuring Human Resources Effectiveness," *Personnel Administrator*, July 1980, pp. 33–36. J. Ryan, "Meeting the Challenges of a Changing Business Environment," *Personnel Journal*, Oct. 1982, pp. 742–743. A. G. Franke, E. J. Harrick, and A. J. Klein, "The Role of Personnel in Improving Productivity," *Personnel Administrator*, March 1982, pp. 83–88.
2. Although the term "personnel" is still used in reference to PHRM departments in organizations, the trend is toward use of the term "PHRM." See S. J. Carroll and R. S. Schuler (eds.), *Human Resource Management in the 1980s* (Washington, DC: The Bureau of National Affairs, 1983), for a more complete description of this trend.
3. Effective PHRM implies that, whatever PHRM is being done, it is being done as well as possible to attain the maximum benefit possible for individuals, the organization, and society. However, just because a PHRM activity is being carried out does not mean that the human resources are being utilized effectively. Only when the activity is done effectively is there effective PHRM. In this book, each activity is described, including its strengths and shortcomings. Based on this, you should be able to play to the strengths of each activity in actual practice and reduce the shortcomings. Thus you will be able to practise *effective* PHRM.
4. L. F. Moore and L. Charach, *Manpower Planning for Canadians*. (Vancouver: Institute of Industrial Relations, University of British Columbia, 1979), p. 287.
5. "Personnel Widens Its Franchise," *Business Week*, Feb. 26, 1979, p. 116.
6. Or anything else important to the organizations, e.g., adaptability, growth, and survival. See K. S. Cameron and D. A. Whetten, *Organization Effectiveness: A Comparison of Multiple Models* (New York: Academic Press, 1983). J. L. Gibson, J. M. Ivancevich, and J. M. Donnelly, Jr., *Organizations*, 5th ed. (Plano, TX: Business Publications, Inc., 1985).
7. M. A. Devanna, D. Fombrun, and N. Tichy, "Human Resources Management: A Strategic Perspective," *Organizational Dynamics*, Winter 1981, pp. 51–67. For an excellent review of PHRM costs, see G. G. Flamholtz, *Human Resource Accounting*, 2nd ed. (San Francisco: Jossey-Bass Publishers, 1985).
8. T. Mills, "Human Resources: Why the New Concern? *Harvard Business Review*, March/April 1975, p. 133.
9. V. Emma, "CMA Turns to 'People Power'," *QWL Focus*, The News Journal of Ontario Quality of Working Life Centre, Ontario Ministry of Labour, 1983, vol. 3(2), pp. 12–13.
10. "Productivité: L'impératif en affaires pour les années 80," *Le Monde des Affaires*, 1984, no. 18, p. 13.
11. A. Gibson, "Quebec's Growth Expected to Slow to 3.2% This Year," *The Gazette*, July 25, 1985, p. B-5.
12. The participation rates are the number of individuals in the labour force expressed as a percentage of the total population aged 15 and over.
13. Statistics Canada, *Women in Canada: A Statistical Report*, Catalog 89–503E, March 1985.
14. Ibid.
15. F. E. Schuster, "Human Resource Management: Key to the Future," *Personnel Administrator*, Dec. 1978, p. 34.
16. Ibid., p. 35.
17. U.S. Department of Health, Education and Welfare, *Work in America*: Report of a special task force to the Secretary (Cambridge, MA: MIT Press, 1973). C. Kerr and J. M. Rosow (eds.), *Work in America, the Decade Ahead* (New York: D. Van Nostrand Company, 1979).
18. Ibid.: Kerr and Rosow.
19. *The Financial Post* (June 6, 13, 20, and 27, 1981). The study was conducted by the MacKinsey Canada Office, the management consulting firm for which Thomas J. Peters and Robert H. Waterman worked in the U.S. while writing *In Search of Excellence* (New York: Harper & Row Publishers, Inc., 1982).
20. For further discussion see A. Howard and J. A. Wilson, "Leadership in a Declining Work Ethic," *California Management Review*, Summer 1982, pp. 33–46, and L. Y. Jones, *Great Expectations: America and the Baby Boom Generation* (New York: Coward, McCann, and Geoghegan, 1980).
21. *Business Week*, Nov. 15, 1982, pp. 124–130. "Quality: The U.S. Drives to Catch Up," *Business Week*, Nov. 1, 1982, pp. 66–80. J. M. Rosow (ed.), *Productivity Prospects for Growth* (New York: D. Van Nostrand Company, 1981).
22. "More Jobs, and Better Productivity At Last," *Business Week*, June 1, 1981, p. 98.
23. E. K. Burton, "Productivity: A Plan for Personnel," *Personnel Administrator*, Sept. 1981, pp. 85–92; J. D. Hodgson, "An Impertinent Suggestion for Personnel," *Personnel Administrator*, Sept. 1981, pp. 85–92. H. C. White, "Personnel Administration and Organizational Productivity: An Employee View," *Personnel Administrator*, Aug. 1981, pp. 37–48.
24. D. A. Peach, "The Canadair-I.A.M. Productivity Improvement Plan," *Industrial Relations/Relations Industrielles*, 1982, vol. 37(1), pp. 177–197.
25. V. Emma, "CMA Turns to 'People Power'," *QWL Focus*, vol. 3(2), p. 12. For an excellent review of Ca-

nadian innovative approaches, see H. F. Kolodny, "Canadian Experience in Innovative Approaches to High Commitment Work Systems" in S. L. Dolan and R. S. Schuler (eds.), *Canadian Readings in Personnel and Human Resource Management* (St. Paul: West Publishing Co., 1987).

26. H. E. Meyer, "Personnel Directors Are Becoming the New Corporate Heroes," *Fortune*, February 1976, p. 84–89.
27. F. E. Schuster and F. K. Foulkes, "The Expanding Role of the Personnel Function," *Harvard Business Review*, March/April 1975. All rights reserved.
28. J. W. English, "The Road Ahead for the Human Resources Function," *Personnel*, March/April 1980, pp. 35–39. P. C. Gordon, " 'Magnetic' Management: The Real Role of Personnel," *Personnel Journal*, June 1980, pp. 485–487, 500. D. R. Hugar, AEP, "The Personnel Professional in the Small Organization," *Personnel Administrator*, April 1981, p. 41. T. W. Peters and Edward A. Mabry, "The Personnel Officer as Internal Consultant," *Personnel Administrator*, April 1981, pp. 29–32. H. C. White, APD, and Michael N. Wolfe, "The Role Desired for Personnel Administration," *Personnel Administrator*, June 1980, pp. 87–97.
29. F. K. Foulkes, "Organizing and Staffing the Personnel Function," *Harvard Business Review*, May–June, 1977.
30. Ibid., p. 147.
31. L. E. Albright, "Staffing Issues in the 1980s," in Carroll and Schuler (eds.), endnote 2.
32. J. Fitz-enz, "Quantifying the Human Resources Function," *Personnel*, March/April 1980, pp. 41–52. For an extensive discussion see D. R. Dalton, "Absenteeism and Turnover Measures of Personnel Effectiveness," in R. S. Schuler, J. M. McFillen, and D. R. Dalton (eds.), *Applied Readings in Personnel and Human Resource Management* (St. Paul: West Publishing Co., 1981), pp. 20–38. R. S. Schuler, "Occupational Health in Organizations: A Measure of Personnel Effectiveness," in Schuler, McFillen, and Dalton (eds.), pp. 39–53. P. M. Podsakoff, "Satisfaction and Performance Measures of Personnel Effectiveness," in Schuler, McFillen, and Dalton (eds.), pp. 3–19. D. R. Dalton, "Legal Compliance: A Measure of Personnel Effectiveness," in Schuler, McFillen, and Dalton (eds.), pp. 54–70. This topic is also discussed in terms of utility; for an excellent overview see F. L. Schmidt, J. E. Hunter, and K. Pearlman, "Assessing the Economic Impact of Personnel Program on Workforce Productivity," *Personnel Psychology*, Summer 1982, pp. 333–348. C. R. Day, Jr., "Solving the Mystery of Productivity Measurement," *Industry Week*, Jan. 26, 1981, pp. 61–66. F. J. Landy, J. L. Farr, and R. R. Jacobs, "Utility Concepts in Performance Measurements," *Organizational Behavior and Human Performance*, 1982, *30*, pp. 15–40. W. F. Cascio, *Costing Human Resources: The Financial Impact of Behavior in Organizations* (Reading, MA: Addison-Wesley, 1982). J. C. Pingpank, "Preventing and Defending EEO Charges," *Personnel Administrator*, Feb. 1983, pp. 35–40. L. J. Cronbach and G. C. Gleser, *Psychological Tests and Personnel Decisions* (Urbana, IL: University of Illinois Press, 1965). H. E. Brogden and E. K. Taylor, "The Dollar Criterion: Applying the Cost Accounting Concept to Criterion Construction," *Personnel Psychology*, 1950, *3*, pp. 133–154. H. C. Taylor and J. T. Russell, "The Relationship of Validity Coefficients to the Practical Effectiveness of Tests in Selection: Discussion and Tables," *Journal of Applied Psychology*, 1939, *23*, pp. 565–578. F. Krystofiak and J. Newman, "Evaluating Employment Outcomes: Availability Models and Measures," *Industrial Relations*, 1982, *21*, pp. 277–292. R. A. Katzell and R. A. Guzzo, "Psychological Approaches to Productivity Improvement," *American Psychologist*, April 1983, pp. 468–472. J. E. Hunter and F. L. Schmidt, "Quantifying the Effects of Psychological Interventions on Employee Job Performance and Work-Force Productivity," *American Psychologist*, April 1983, pp. 473–478. R. R. West and D. E. Logue, "The False Doctrine of Productivity," *The New York Times*, Jan. 9, 1983, p. F3. J. E. Ross, *Productivity, People and Profits* (Reston, VA: Reston Publishing Co., Inc., 1981). A. P. Brief and Associates, *Productivity Research in the Behavioral and Social Sciences* (New York: Praeger Publishers, 1984).
33. H. B. Henrici, "How Not to Measure Productivity," *The New York Times*, March 7, 1982, p. 2F.
34. For extensive discussion of these issues, see D. R. Dalton and W. D. Todor, "Turnover: A Lucrative Hard Dollar Phenomenon," *Academy of Management Review*, 7, 1982, pp. 212–218. T. E. Hall, "How to Estimate Employee Turnover Costs," *Personnel*, July/Aug. 1981, pp. 43–52. W. Mobley, *Turnover* (Reading, MA: Addison-Wesley, 1982). F. E. Kuzmits, "How Much is Absenteeism Costing Your Organization?" *Personnel Administrator*, June 1979, pp. 29–32. G. Johns, "Understanding and Managing Absence from Work," in Dolan and Schuler (eds.), see endnote 25.
35. "The New Industrial Relations," *Business Week*, May 11, 1981, pp. 85–93. P. H. Mirvis and E. E. Lawler III, "Measuring the Financial Impact of Employee Attitude," *Journal of Applied Psychology*, 62, 1977, pp. 1–8.
36. For an extensive discussion, see Devanna, Fombrun, and Tichy, endnote 7. See also S. M. Knomo, "Stage Three in Personnel Administration: Strategic Human Resources Management," *Personnel*, July/Aug. 1980, pp. 69–77. L. Dyer, "Human Resource Planning," in K. M. Rowland and G. R. Ferris (eds.),

Personnel Management (Boston: Allyn & Bacon, 1980), pp. 52–77. G. Mikovich, L. Dyer, and T. Mahoney, "The State of Practice and Research in Human Resource Planning," in Carroll and Schuler (eds.), endnote 2. N. M. Tichy, C. J. Fombrun, and M. A. Devanna, "Strategic Human Resource Management," *Sloan Management Review*, Winter 1982, pp. 47–61. L. J. Stybel, "Linking Strategic Planning and Management Manpower Planning," *California Management Review*, Fall 1982, pp. 48–56. Other qualities of organizations that influence PHRM are size, growth rate, and ownership. For a discussion of how, see D. J. Cosgrove and R. L. Dinerman, "Employee Relations in the Small, But Growing, Company," *Personnel Journal*, Aug. 1982, pp. 575–577. D. R. Hagar, "The Personnel Professional in the Small Organization," *Personnel Administrator*, April 1981, pp. 41–42. R. L. Mathis and G. Cameron, "Auditing Personnel Practices in Smaller-Sized Organizations: A Realistic Approach," *Personnel Administrator*, April 1981, pp. 45–49. B. R. Ellig, "Gearing Compensation to Market Cycles," *Management Review*, Nov./Dec. 1982, pp. 17–21. R. C. Gruver, "Personnel Management in the Small Organization," *Personnel Administrator*, March 1978, pp. 38–44. J. Klee, "Personnel Practices of the United Nations," *Public Personnel Management*, Jan./Feb. 1979, pp. 47–55. J. Kotter and V. Sathe, "Problems of Human Resource Management in Rapidly Growing Companies," *California Management Review*, Winter 1978, pp. 26–36. E. L. Loen, *Personnel Management Guides for Small Business* (Washington, DC: Small Business Administration, 1974). J. M. Rosow, "Human Dignity in the Public-Sector Workplace," *Public Personnel Management*, Jan./Feb. 1979, pp. 7–14. E. B. Roberts and A. R. Fusfeld, "Staffing the Innovative Technology-Based Organization," *Sloan Management Review*, Spring 1981, pp. 19–34.
37. S. Langer, "Budgets and Staffing: A Survey Part II," *Personal Journal*, June 1981, pp. 464–468. S. Langer, "The Personnel/Industrial Relations Report—An Overview of Current Staffing and Budgeting Ratios," *Personnel Journal*, Feb. 1980, pp. 95–98. M. G. Miner, "Personnel Budgets and Staffs, How Big Should They Be?" *Personnel Administrator*, July 1980, pp. 52–55.
38. *Les Affaires*, August 1985.
39. D. A. Greenwell, "Starting a Career in Personnel Administration," p. 16. Reprinted with permission from the September 1981 issue of the *Personnel Administrator*. Copyright 1981: The American Society for Personnel Administration, 30 Park Dr., Berea, OH 44017.
40. S. H. Applebaum, APD, "The Personnel Professional and Organization Development: Conflict and Synthesis," *Personnel Administrator*, July 1980, pp. 44–49. G. F. Brady, "Assessing the Personnel Manager's Power Base," *Personnel Administrator*, July 1980, pp. 57–61. F. R. Edney, "The Greening of the Profession," *Personnel Administrator*, July 1980, pp. 27–30, 42. "Playing on the Team," *Personnel Journal*, Aug. 1981, pp. 598–600. L. B. Prewitt, "The Emerging Field of Human Resources Management," *Personnel Administrator*, May 1982, pp. 81–87.
41. D. Yoder and H. Heneman, Jr., *PAIR Jobs, Qualifications, and Careers, ASPA Handbook of Personnel and Industrial Relations*, 1978, p. 18.
42. P. Kumar, "Personnel Management in Canada—A Manpower Profile," *The Canadian Personnel and Industrial Relations Journal*, Nov. 1979, 26, pp. 10–14. J. M. Cousineau "Labor Market Trends and Their Implications for PHRM Professionals in Canada," in Dolan and Schuler (eds.), endnote 25.
43. I. R. Weiss and A. D. Gowans Young, "Professional Certification Programs," *Personnel Administrator*, April 1981, pp. 63–68. Yoder and Heneman, endnote 41, pp. 29–30.

SECTION II
Planning for Jobs and People

CHAPTER 2
Human Resource Planning

CHAPTER 3
Job Design and Job Analysis

CHAPTER 2

Human Resource Planning

PHRM in the News

Human Resource Planning
Purposes and the Importance of HRP
Relationships with other PHRM Activities

Four Phases of HRP
Phase 1: Gathering, Analyzing, and Forecasting Supply and Demand Data
Phase 2: Establishing Human Resource Objectives and Policies
Phase 3: Human Resource Programming
Phase 4: HRP Control and Evaluation
HRP Roadblocks

Important Changes in the 1990s Influencing HRP
The Population and the Labour Force
Trends and Changes in the Economy
Changing Social Values
Legislation, Regulation, and Government Activity

Assessing HRP

Summary

Discussion Questions

Case Study

Endnotes

PHRM in the News

Human Resource Planning: Trends and Issues

How important is human resource planning today? The answer is almost a paradox: HRP is more important than ever, but not important enough. In a recent Hay survey of 927 human resources professionals, some 51% said that top management considers human resources planning to be "very important" or "fairly important"; just 16% thought that HRP was either "unimportant" or "neglected" in their organizations. However, when asked about the nature of their HRP programs, only 20% said that their programs were "formal"; another 45% indicated that programs were developed, but "informal"; a large 34% admitted that their programs were "rudimentary."

What is behind this apparently conflicting message? Is HRP one of those weatherlike corporate activities that everyone talks about but nobody can act on? Perhaps so—until recently. But now, demographic and business exigencies will push HRP to the forefront. Organizations who find the way to plan for their human resources needs will begin to enjoy a competitive advantage.

The current status of HRP

Today, we are well aware of the shift in the demographics of the work force. While the baby boom produced a glut of professional and managerial talent, the generation now entering behind them is dramatically smaller. Thus, at the middle and upper ends of the management and professional hierarchy, we have severe competition for responsibility and career growth.

By contrast, the entry level population which will occupy many of the rapidly increasing knowledge jobs is beginning to shrink dramatically. While the past five years has seen a concentration on streamlining and downsizing organizations, the next decade will see these activities occupying the same stage with efforts to attract, develop, and retain key professional and managerial employees.

Finally, to add to the complexity of the management task, some level of participative management is now the norm as employees insist on having a say in their work environments. (Over one-half of all participants in our HRP survey had introduced some form of participative management program in the last few years.) Organizationally, management expects Human Resources departments to contribute to profit, directly or indirectly. It's pay-for-performance all around! Job-related criteria for all types of personnel decisions are becoming mandatory, diminishing subjective appraisal and hiring decisions.

HRP: The future

Certainly productivity has always been a critical issue. Now, and in the future, doing more for less while being more competitive, may be the most pressing issue we face. New technologies are constantly being substituted for direct labour. Work redesign will maximize the utilization of scarce skills. Individuals will face greater accountability for achieving organizational goals.

Human resources planning professionals will examine the efficiency of staffing levels, the mix of positions, the development of talent, and job design, so that workers' talents are better matched to their tasks. They will work with whose who have been displaced— those whose jobs have become redundant.

As new technologies, such as state-of-the-art information systems, robots, and office automation are introduced, these planning professionals will be called on to answer questions such as: How can the work force assimilate these new technologies? What impact will these new technologies have on job design and on the organizational structure? Which skills will we need and which not?

What else? Management will become increasingly concerned with its ability to attract and retain skilled personnel. They may turn to the HRP function to find out how innovative incentive systems can help them in this area. Attention will also turn to the development of career paths that include both line and staff assignments. Such overlaps will help avoid duplicating the bloated staffs of the 70s which had little understanding of the day-to-day line issues.

Finally, there will be a strong need to study long-term public policy issues and assess their implications for HRP functions. Most certainly, human resources planning professionals will be concerned with the aging work force, permanent unemployment, and the economic impact of shifting from a manufacturing to a service economy.

As human resources planning becomes more measured and pragmatic in its approach, professionals will have to be more knowledgeable. When tribal survival was the key issue, it was not too difficult for the chief to decide who hunted and who gathered. Today, survival is still the issue. But the questions regarding it are myriad and complex. Human resources planning professionals will need to provide judicious and pragmatic answers.

Source: "The Planning Paradox: Human Resource Planning—Trends and Issues" (excerpts), *Management Memo*, No. 340, Hay Group, Inc., 1986. Used with permission.

New Jobs, New Skills, New Problems

In a growing number of modern offices across Canada, office workers pursue their tasks with a heightened sense of urgency. In the steno pools of major companies, secretaries tap feverishly at video display terminals. At telephone company switchboard offices in Ontario and Quebec, operators process an average of 700 long-distance calls a day at about 28 seconds per call. And at the headquarters of a major airline in Toronto, reservation agents race to deal with about 150 calls per shift at an average of 144 seconds each. In every case, a master computer silently records the employee's speed, accuracy, output, and the time spent away from work stations. "What has happened," said George Larter, president of Toronto Local 50 of the Communications and Electrical Workers of Canada, "is that a machine has become the supervisor."

The burgeoning use of computerized office equipment, which gives management the ability to monitor employees electronically, is part of a massive attempt by business to improve the way office workers process and record vast amounts of information. According to management consultants, the productivity of office workers has traditionally lagged behind that of industrial workers because there has been less capital investment in office equipment than in manufacturing technology.

The installation of computerized office machines has resulted in dramatic increases in productivity for many firms, including utilities, banks, retailers, and airlines.

In the process of installing computerized systems, some employers have also adopted the factory assembly-line approach to work. Each operation is subdivided into its specific elements, and every employee performs a single task. While routine operations computerized in that manner can be performed more quickly, the jobs have less variety and entail little responsibility or decision-making. Said a supervisor at a Toronto insurance company: "My section is like a sweatshop run on a piecework basis."

As a result, workers using office computers set up on an assembly-line basis often report that they suffer from more physical and stress-related ailments than they did before the introduction of computers. According to studies by academics and labor, the unexpected costs of computerization include higher staff turnover, increased absenteeism, and even outright acts of sabotage.

Source: Diana Swift, "The Electronic Supervisor" (excerpts), *MacLean's*, June 17, 1985, p. 32. Used with permission.

These two "PHRM in the News" articles highlight several important aspects of human resource planning. One aspect is that HRP is growing in importance as quickly as PHRM itself because of the vast number of changes occurring in society. Many of these changes are having and will continue to have a significant impact on the effective management of human resources. Consequently, PHRM must be aware of these changes and be responsible for translating or relaying these changes to the rest of the organization. In addition, HRP must develop PHRM programs to deal effectively with the changes. Such programs actually can assist an organization to survive and be profitable.[1]

Human Resource Planning

In general terms, **human resource planning** is the first step of any effective PHRM program. More specifically, HRP involves forecasting human resource needs for the organization, and planning the steps necessary to meet these needs. HRP is a process of developing and implementing plans and programs to ensure that the right number and types of individuals are available at the right time and place to fulfil organizational needs. As such, HRP is tied directly to strategic business planning.[2] And, because of the trend toward more strategic involvement by PHRM as discussed in Chapter 1, human resource planning is one of the fastest growing areas in PHRM, and one of the most important. HRP helps ensure that organizations fulfil their business plans[3] for the future in terms of financial objectives, output goals, product mix, technologies, and resource requirements. Once their business plans are determined, often with the assistance of the PHRM department, "The human resource planner assists in developing workable organizational structures and in determining the number and types of employees that will be required to meet financial and output goals."[4] After workable structures and the requirements for needed individuals are identified, the human resource planner develops personnel and human resource management programs to implement the structure and to obtain the individuals.

Purposes and the Importance of HRP

HRP is important to an organization because it serves many purposes. A major purpose is to identify future human resource demands and to develop programs to eliminate any discrepancies, in the best interests of the individual and of the organization. HRP also can reduce expenses associated with excessive turnover and absenteeism, low productivity, and an unproductive training program. More specifically, the purposes of HRP are to

- reduce personnel costs by helping management to anticipate shortages or surpluses of human resources, and to correct these imbalances before they become unmanageable and expensive;
- provide a better basis for planning employee development that makes optimum use of workers' attitudes;
- improve the overall business planning process;
- provide more opportunities for women and minority groups in future growth plans, and to identify the specific skills available;
- promote greater awareness of the importance of sound human resource management throughout all levels of the organization;
- provide a tool for evaluating the effect of alternative human resource planning actions and policies.[5]

All of these purposes are now more easily attained than ever before, thanks to computer technology. This technology allows vast numbers of job-related records to be maintained on each employee, in essence creating a human resource information system (this will be described in detail later). These records, which include information on employee job preferences, work experiences, and performance evaluations, provide a job history of each employee in an organization and a complete set of information on the jobs and positions held in the organization. This in turn can be used to facilitate the purposes of HRP in the interests of the individual as well as of the organization.[6]

A large number of environmental and organizational changes also are responsible for the growing importance of HRP and of PHRM. These changes are making it necessary for personnel and human resource management plans to be more future-oriented, comprehensive, and integrative. This perspective has a number of fundamental attributes: (1) it considers human resource costs to be an investment rather than an uncontrollable expense; (2) it is proactive rather than reactive or passive in its approach to developing human resource policies and resolving human resource problems; (3) it is characterized by a change in PHRM role perspective—the previous emphasis on the completion of personnel transactions is being replaced by a future-oriented approach in which the PHRM department acts as a controller of the organization's human resources; (4) it recognizes that there must be an explicit link between human resource planning and other organizational functions, such as strategic planning, economic and market forecasting, and investment and facilities planning; (5) it recognizes that such PHRM activities as recruitment, selection, labour relations, compensation and benefits, training, organizational planning, and career management must be visualized as dynamic, interconnecting activities rather than a series of separate and non-integrated functions; and, (6) it focuses on approaches that further both organizational and individual goals.[7]

One environmental change that is making HRP more important is recent legislation and voluntary province-wide pressure in support of affirmative action and other employment matters.[8] Equal employment opportunity and occupational safety and health legislation was established in many provinces in response to pressures and influences from the International Labor Office and U.S. case law.

Another important environmental change involves predictions about shortages in blue-collar occupations and entry level white-collar occupations by 1990, such as in tool and die making, bricklaying, and other skilled crafts. In addition, a shortage of jobs currently exists for shipbuilders, all categories of engineers including those in robotics, machinists, and mechanics.[9]

Along with shortages of jobs for certain types of occupations, there is a growing abundance of another category of job seekers—people in the 35- to 44-year-old age group. As discussed later in this chapter, the number of people entering this age group is increasing faster than the number of jobs available for them. Consequently, many of these people can probably anticipate relatively static income and rivalry with older workers for some period of time.

The new retirement options available to workers also are causing a shift in concern for staffing positions—but not in the direction expected. Workers now have options ranging from early retirement in their mid-50s to retirement in their 70s. However, more workers are staying on the job longer than anticipated. This fact, coupled with the protection given to employees under various human rights laws, has caused organizations to devote more time to managing these senior employees.

The increasing potential for managerial obsolescence is another critical change. Rapid changes in technology are making it difficult for professionals, engineers, and managers to remain up to date in their fields. Consequently, they must be provided with the opportunity for continued training. However, organizations are not sure how to do this, nor do they always recognize the potential for obsolescence. Nevertheless, "The unsolved problem of professional obsolescence posed by the production of knowledge is a threat to the growth potential of organizations and society as a whole." [10]

The general expansion and diversification of organizations also makes HRP more important. Trends toward multi-national operations are attended by difficulties in transferring workers, and in operating and staffing in foreign cultures.[11]

Another compelling reason for HRP is the investment an organization makes in its human resources.[12] Human assets, as opposed to some other assets, can increase in value—an employee who develops skills and abilities becomes a more valuable resource. Because an organization makes investments in its personnel either through direct training or job assignments, it is important that employees are used effectively throughout their careers. The dollar value of a trained, flexible, motivated, and productive workforce is difficult to determine, although attempts are being made to do so. At the Upjohn pharmaceutical company, a series of indexes has been developed to reflect the relationships between employee costs (treated as an investment) and organizational performance.[13] The indexes include:

- Pretax earning/Total employees
- After-tax earnings/Total employees
- Sales/Total employees
- Pretax earnings/Employee costs
- Employee costs/Value added
- Capital costs/Value added
- Pretax earnings/Value added
- Value added/Sales [14]

In addition, an increasing number of organization leaders are acknowledging that the quality of the workforce can be responsible for significant differences in short- and long-run performances. Many corporate executives are concluding that insufficient or unqualified manpower is at least as serious a production bottleneck as a scarcity of capital, and that manpower investments are as important a factor in company planning as the acquisition of plants, equipment, or materials.[15]

The final reason for the increased emphasis on human resource planning and programming is the growing resistance of employees to change and to relocation.[16] There is also a growing emphasis on self-evaluation and on valuing loyalty and dedication to the organization. All of these changes make it more difficult for an organization to assume that it can move its employees around arbitrarily, thus increasing the necessity of planning ahead.

All of these changes have increased the importance of PHRM. The implications for planning and program development will be described. First, however, is a discussion of techniques that are useful in determining human resource needs, and the relationships of HRP with other personnel activities.

Relationships with Other PHRM Activities

HRP is important because it influences almost all of the other PHRM activities. Although all of these relationships are important, perhaps two are most critical, as shown in Exhibit 2.1.

Staffing. HRP helps determine the human resource staffing needs of an organization. In conjunction with job analysis, it indicates how many and what types of people need to be recruited. Recruitment influences the pool of available job applicants, which in turn influences the needs for selection and placement. Thus, HRP can be viewed as a major input into an organization's staffing function. This relationship is highlighted again in the recruitment and selection chapters.

Career Management. HRP facilitates career management programs that aid an organization in retaining valued employees and keeping them from becoming obsolete.

Relationships of Human Resource Planning and Other Personnel Activities Exhibit 2.1

```
Human Resource Planning ─┬─ Organizational Needs: Staffing
                         │    • Recruitment
                         │    • Selection
                         │
                         └─ Individual Needs: Career Management
                              • Career management programs
                              • Career planning
```

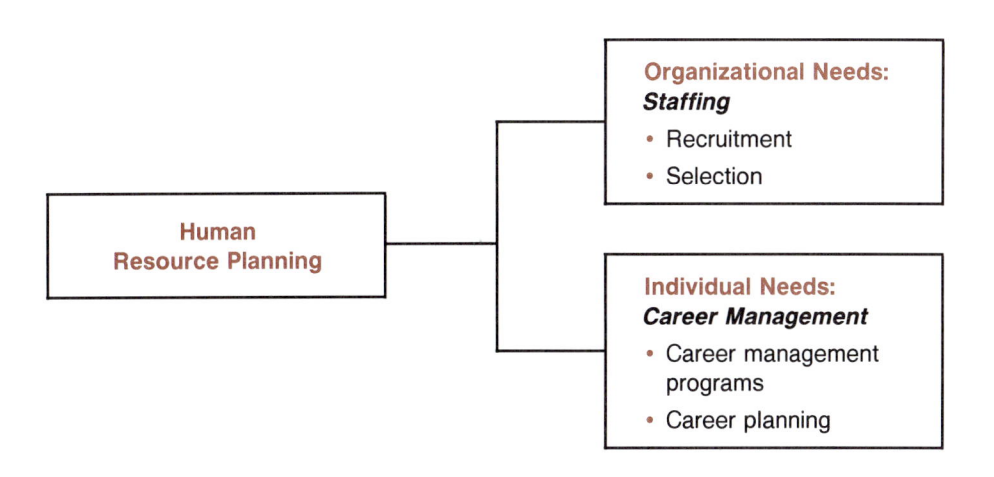

These programs play an important role in determining an organization's supply of human resources and, ultimately, its needs. For example, if these programs, along with career planning by employees, help reduce employee turnover and absenteeism, the organization can plan on a larger supply of qualified human resources and, therefore, a smaller need for additional people. Further discussion of these programs, along with the use of training and development, is contained in Chapter 12.

Four Phases of HRP

HRP is based on the determination of an organization's human resource needs—the identification of both the human resource supply and the human resource demand. Although these estimations are critical, until recently most organizations avoided making them or engaging in any of the four phases of HRP,[17] which are as follows:

1. Gathering, analyzing, and forecasting data in order to develop a human resource supply forecast (and create a human resource information system) and a human resource demand forecast (and add to the human resource information system)
2. Establishing human resource objectives and policies, and gaining approval and support for these from top management
3. Designing and implementing plans and action programs in such areas as recruitment, training, and promotion that will enable the organization to achieve its human resource objectives

4. Controlling and evaluating personnel plans and programs to facilitate progress toward human resource planning objectives [18]

Exhibit 2.2 shows the relationships among these phases as well as corporate goals and environmental components.

Phase 1: Gathering, Analyzing, and Forecasting Supply and Demand Data

The first phase of HRP involves developing data that can be used to determine corporate objectives, policies, and plans, as well as human resource objectives and policies. As shown in Exhibit 2.2, the human resource inventory and forecast are influenced in turn by these same factors. The interaction of these aspects of human resource planning helps determine the current human resource situation and future human resource needs.

As shown in Exhibit 2.3 (which further elaborates on the phases shown in Exhibit 2.2), there are five steps in Phase 1. Each is important for the success of human resource planning and programming. Step 1, consisting of an analysis of the human resource situation in an organization, has four aspects.

Analysis. Human resource analysis begins with an inventory of the current workforce in the organization and the current jobs in the organization. Analysis of both elements is necessary if the organization is to determine its capability to meet current and future human resource needs. Knowing the skills, abilities, interests, and preferences of the current workforce is only half of the inventory. The other half consists of knowing the characteristics of current jobs and how they are organized, and the skills required to perform them. An updated job analysis program facilitates this half of the inventory and the matching of employees with jobs.

Manual inventories have been used successfully for years in matching employees with jobs,[19] but the use of computers is making the compilation of these inventories much more efficient and is allowing for a more dynamic, integrative human resource program. Through computers, employees in separate divisions and different areas of the country are finding it easier to participate in the organization's network for matching jobs with employees.

A common computer-oriented information system used in the management of human resources is often referred to as a **human resource information system (HRIS)**:

> Any human resource information system is logically an inventory of the positions and skills extant in a given organization. However, HRIS is more than a simple aggregation mechanism for inventory control and accounting; it is the foundation for a set of management tools enabling managers to establish objectives for the use of their organization's human resources and to measure the extent to which those objectives have been achieved.[20]

A number of PHRM policy applications could be advanced by the proper set-up of HRIS in organizations: [21]

- Organizational demography, planning, and analysis—HRIS enhances the ability to track basic attributes such as age, sex, educational level, length

Human Resource Planning

The Human Resource Planning and Programming Process — Exhibit 2.2

```
                    ┌──────────────────┐
                    │  Environmental   │
                    │   components     │
                    │  top management  │
                    └────────┬─────────┘
                             ▼
                    ┌──────────────────┐
                    │  Organizational  │
                    │    objectives    │
                    │       and        │
                    │     policies     │
                    └──────────────────┘
```

Phase 1 — Human resource supply forecast ; Human resource demand forecast

Phase 2 — Human resource objectives and policies

Phase 3 — Current / Future ; Human resource programming ; Current / Future

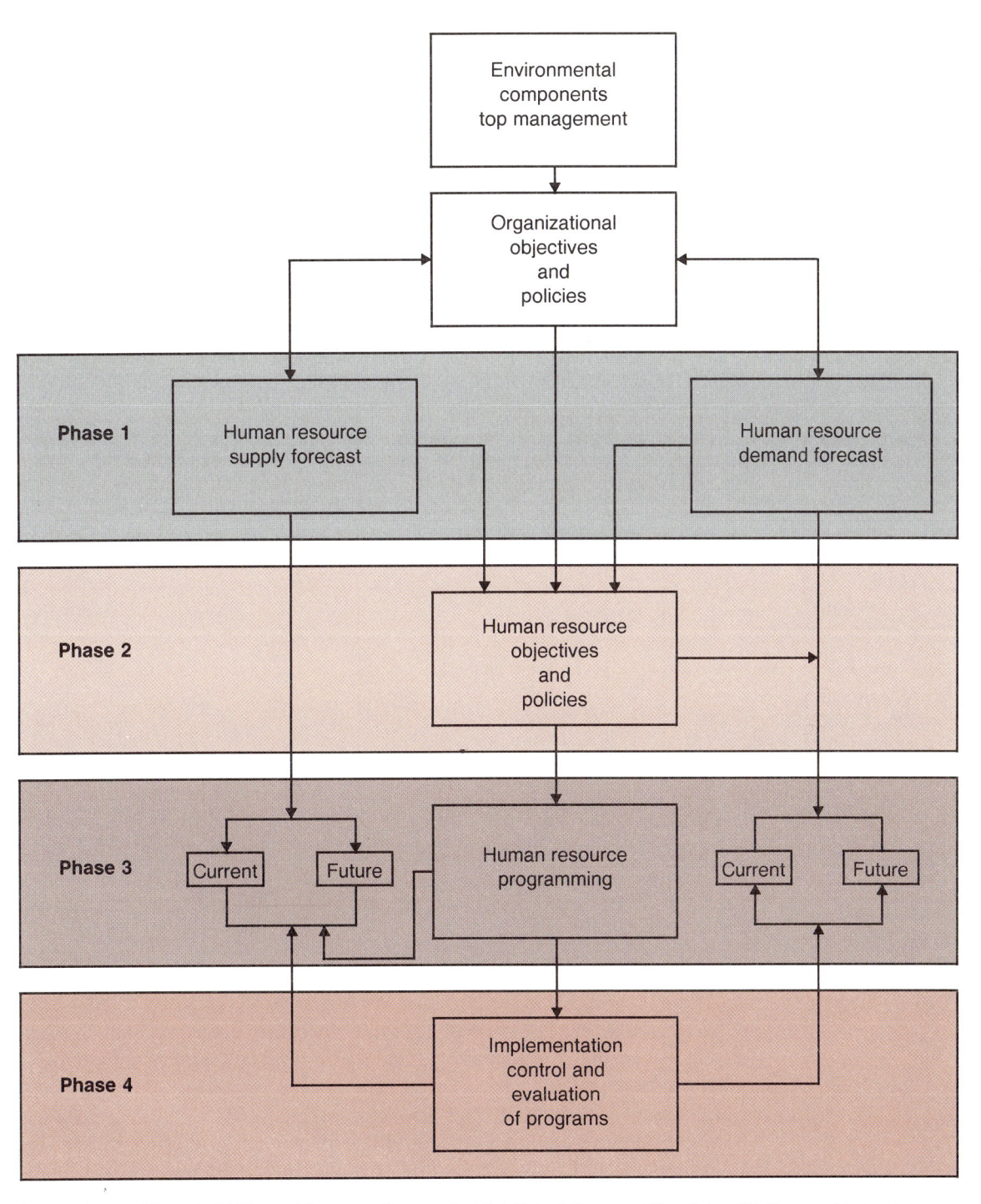

Phase 4 — Implementation control and evaluation of programs

Source: Adapted from G. W. Vetter, *Manpower Planning for High Talent Personnel* (Ann Arbor, MI: Bureau of Industrial Relations, Graduate School of Business Administration, University of Michigan, 1967), p. 29. Used with permission.

48   *Planning for Jobs and People*

Exhibit 2.3   Procedures and Steps for Human Resource Planning and Programming

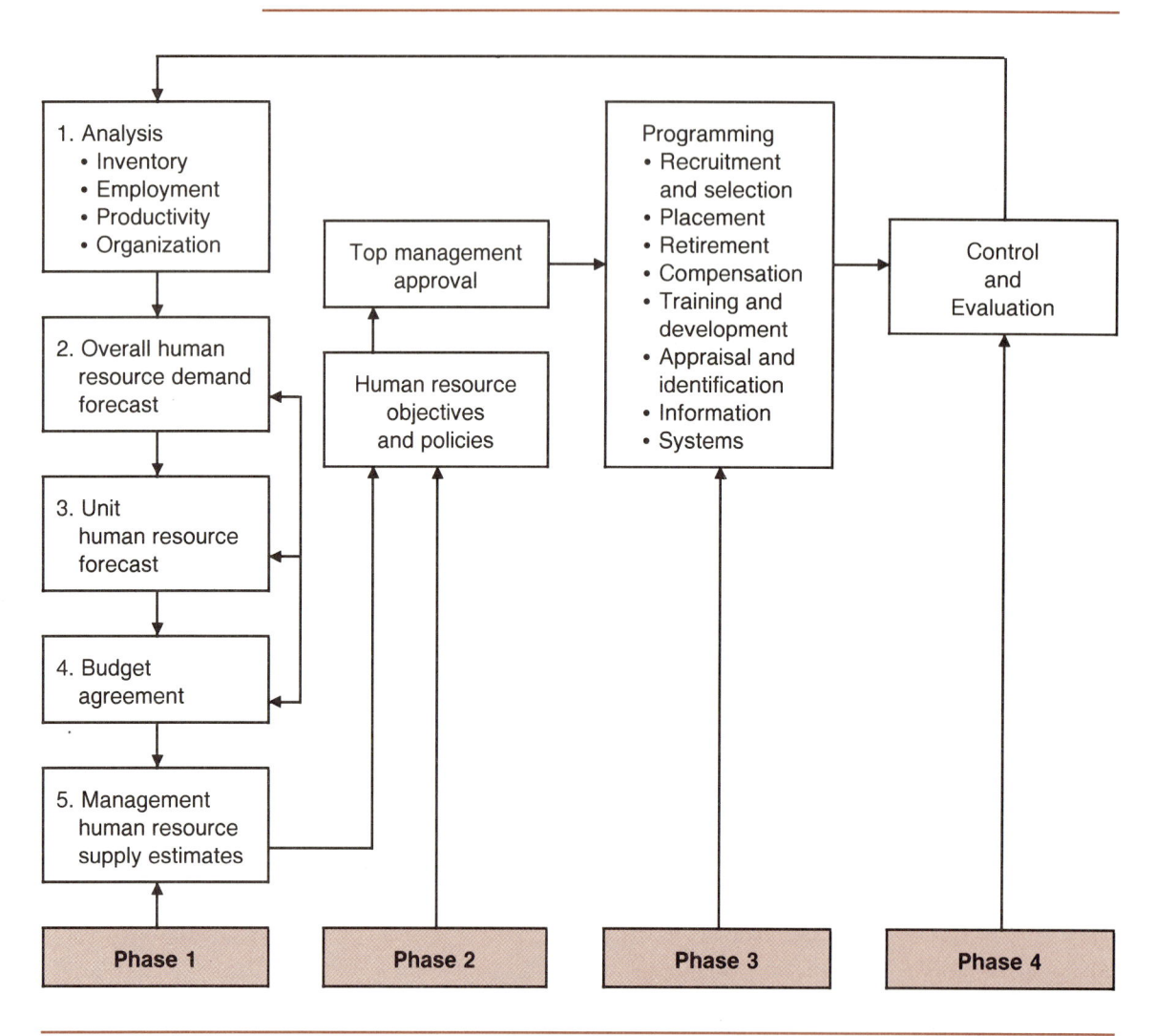

Phase 1
1. Analysis
   - Inventory
   - Employment
   - Productivity
   - Organization
2. Overall human resource demand forecast
3. Unit human resource forecast
4. Budget agreement
5. Management human resource supply estimates

Phase 2
- Human resource objectives and policies
- Top management approval

Phase 3
Programming
- Recruitment and selection
- Placement
- Retirement
- Compensation
- Training and development
- Appraisal and identification
- Information
- Systems

Phase 4
Control and Evaluation

Source: Adapted from G. W. Vetter, *Manpower Planning for High Talent Personnel* (Ann Arbor, MI: Bureau of Industrial Relations, Graduate School of Business Administration, University of Michigan, 1967), p. 34. Used with permission.

of service, race, etc., over time. This may facilitate decisions in such areas as succession planning, benefits/utilization analysis, and wage/productivity analysis.

- Employment equity planning and monitoring—HRIS could greatly enhance employment equity programming for women and other minorities; therefore it could help a company to conform to equity laws in Canada such as the proposed Bill C–62, which will require employers that come under the Canada Labour Code and federal contractors to develop employment equity plans.

- Scenario-building and forecasting—HRIS outputs can be used as a basis for forecasting the effects of alternative scenarios. This could aid in identifying future skills shortages or surpluses, career pathing, comparing past and projected recruitment, promotion and turnover patterns for high- and low-performing employees, etc.
- Productivity analysis and program evaluation—HRIS could be used to monitor the effects of training programs and other productivity improvement programs on various performance measures.[22]

A human resource analysis also examines the probable future composition of the society's workforce. Often this aspect is based on wage, occupational, and industrial groups. Historical data on workforce composition, along with current demographic and economic data, are used to make human resource projections. These projections are not specific to any single organization, but they often can provide an organization with useful information for its human resource plans, particularly for long-term needs. Examples of this type of data are presented later in this chapter.

The third aspect of human resource analysis involves the determination of labour productivity and its probable productivity in the future. Projected employee turnover and absenteeism, for example, influence the productivity of an organization's workforce at any one time and, thus, its future human resource needs. These projections might also suggest a need to analyze the reasons for turnover and absenteeism, and then form the basis for developing strategies to deal with them. It should be noted, however, that under certain circumstances, increased turnover is desirable. For example, if an organization suddenly finds itself with too many employees, increased turnover, particularly among poor performers, might be welcomed.[23]

The final aspect of the first step in HRP is the examination and projection of organizational structure. This helps determine the probable size of the top, middle, and lower levels of the organization, for both managers and non-managers. In addition, it provides information about changes in the organization's human resource needs and about specific activities or functional areas that can be expected to experience particularly severe growth or contraction.

The type of organization is a major factor in determining both structure and degree of change. As organizations become more technologically complex and face more complex and dynamic environments, more complex structures will evolve, with more departments and a greater variety of occupations. Therefore, the type of organization and its environment play an important role, not only in determining the organization's structure but also in providing information useful for forecasting its human resource needs.[24]

Human Resource Demand Forecast. An organization's demand for human resources can be determined by a variety of forecasting methods, both simple and complex. Forecasting results in approximations—not absolutes or certainties. The quality of the forecast depends on the accuracy of information and the predictability of events. The shorter the time horizon, the more predictable events are, and the more accurate the information.

Two classes of forecasting techniques are frequently used to project an organization's demand for human resources. These are **judgemental forecast** and **conventional statistical projections**.

The most common method of the judgemental forecast is the **Delphi technique**. At a Delphi meeting, a large number of experts take turns presenting forecast statements and assumptions. An intermediary passes each expert's forecast and assumptions to the others, who then make revisions in their own forecasts. This process continues until a viable composite forecast emerges. The composite may represent specific projections or a range of projections, depending on the positions of the experts.

The Delphi technique has been shown to produce better one-year forecasts than linear regression analysis.[25] Delphi techniques, however, do have some limitations. There may be difficulties, for example, in integrating the opinions of the experts. This technique appears to be particularly useful for generating insights into highly unstructured or undeveloped subject areas, such as human resource planning.[26]

A related method is the **nominal grouping technique**. Several people sit around a conference table and independently list their ideas on a sheet of paper.[27] After 10 to 20 minutes of this, they take turns expressing their ideas to the group. As these ideas are presented, they are recorded on larger sheets of paper so that everyone can see all of the ideas and refer to them in later parts of the session.

Although the two techniques are similar in process, the Delphi technique is more frequently used to generate predictions, and the nominal grouping technique is used more for identifying current organizational problems and potential solutions to them. Another judgemental forecast is called **managerial estimate**. Estimates of staffing needs are made by the top managers of the organization (top-down communication) or by lower level managers who make estimates and pass them up for further revisions (bottom-up communication) in order to form an overall demand forecast.[28]

Although all of these judgemental forecasts are less complex and rely on less data than those based on the statistical methods discussed next, these forecasts tend to dominate in practice.[29] The most common statistical procedures are simple linear regression and multiple linear regression analyses. In **simple linear regression analysis**, a projection of future demand is based on a past relationship between the organization's employment level and a variable related to employment, such as sales. If a relationship can be established between the level of sales and the level of employment, predictions of future sales can be used to make predictions of future employment. Although there may be a relationship between sales and employment, however, the relationship is often influenced by an organizational learning phenomenon. For example, the level of sales may double, but the level of employment necessary to meet this increase may be less than double. And if sales double again, the amount of employment necessary to meet this new doubling may be even less than that necessary to meet the first doubling of sales. An organizational learning curve usually can be determined by logarithmic calculations. Once the learning curve has been determined, more accurate projections of future employment levels can be established.

Multiple linear regression analysis is an extension of simple linear regression analysis. Instead of relating employment to one other variable related to employment, several variables are used. For example, instead of using only sales to predict employment demand, productivity data and equipment-use data also may be used. Because it incorporates several variables related to employment, multiple regression analysis may produce more accurate demand forecasts than linear regression analysis. It appears, however, that only relatively large organizations use multiple regression analysis.[30]

In addition to these two regression techniques, several other statistical techniques are used to forecast staffing needs. Such techniques include productivity ratios,[31] personnel ratios,[32] time series analysis,[33] and stochastic analysis.[34] Currently, little research exists regarding the use of these techniques for HRP.[35] These techniques and a brief description of each are presented in Exhibit 2.4.

Although most of the preceding techniques are used for forecasting the total organization's human resource demand, an additional technique is used by parts of the organization. The **unit demand forecasting** technique relies on labour estimates provided by the unit or functional area managers. This technique may produce forecasts of demands that, when added up for all unit managers, are discrepant with the total organization's forecasted demands. However, it encourages unit managers to be more aware of the skills, abilities, and desires of their employees. Such an awareness also may produce a higher-quality forecast. Of course, each unit may also use the same statistical techniques that are used for the total organization.

Since the use of unit demand forecasting often produces discrepant forecasts, reconciliation of the difference is necessary before planning can be undertaken. But the discrepancies often can provide a useful basis for questioning and examining the contributions of each unit in the organization as compared with what they demand.

Reconciling the Budget. This fourth aspect in the first phase of human resource planning and programming puts the whole activity into economic perspective. The human resource forecast must be expressed in terms of dollars, and this figure must be compatible with the organization's profit objectives and budget limitations.[36] Of course, the budget reconciliation process may also point up the importance of adjusting the budget to accommodate the human resource plan. This reconciliation stage also provides an opportunity to align the objectives and policies of the personnel department with that of the organization.

Forecasting Human Resource Supplies. Although forecasted supply can be derived from both internal and external sources of information, the internal source is generally most crucial and most available. As with forecasting

Exhibit 2.4 *Statistical Techniques Used to Project Staffing Demand Needs*

Name	Description
	Past levels of various workload indicators, such as sales, production levels, and value added are examined for statistical relationships with staffing levels. Where sufficiently strong relationships are found, a regression (or multiple regression) model is derived. Forecasted levels of the retained indicator(s) are entered into the resulting model and used to calculate the associated level of human resource requirements.
Productivity ratios	Historical data are used to examine past levels of a productivity index (P): $$P = \frac{\text{Workload}}{\text{Number of people}}$$ Where constant, or systematic, relationships are found, human resource requirements can be computed by dividing predicted workloads by P.
Personnel ratios	Past personnel data are examined to determine historical relationships among the employees in various jobs or job categories. Regression analysis or productivity ratios are then used to project either total or key group human resource requirements and personnel ratios are used to allocate total requirements to various job categories or to estimate requirements for non-key groups.
Time Series analysis	Past staffing levels (instead of workload indicators) are used to project future human resource requirements. Past staffing levels are examined to isolate seasonal and cyclical variations, long-term trends, and random movement. Long-term trends are then extrapolated or projected using a moving average, exponential smoothing, or regression technique.
Stochastic analysis	The likelihood of landing a series of contracts is combined with the personnel requirements of each contract to estimate expected staffing requirements. Potential applications in government contractors and construction industries.

Source: Adapted from L. Dyer, "Human Resource Planning," in K. Rowland and G. Ferris (eds.), *Personnel Management*. Copyright © 1982 by Allyn and Bacon, Inc. Used with permission.

demand, there are basically two techniques to help forecast internal labour supply—judgemental and statistical. Once made, the supply forecast can then be compared with the human resource demand forecast to help determine, among other things, action programming for identifying human resource talent and balancing supply and demand forecasts. However, most current forecasting of labour supply and demand is short-range and for the purposes of budgeting and controlling costs. Forecasts for more than a five-year period, when done, are used in planning corporate strategy, planning facilities, and identifying managerial replacements.[37]

Two judgemental techniques used by organizations to make supply forecasts are replacement planning and succession planning. **Replacement planning** uses replacement charts. These are developed to show the names of the current occupants of positions in the organization and the names of likely replacements. Replacement charts make it readily apparent where potential vacancies will occur, based on the present performance levels of the employees currently in the jobs. In the sample replacement chart shown in Exhibit 2.5, potential vacancies may occur in those jobs in which the incumbents are not outstanding performers. The incumbents are listed directly under the job titles. Those individuals likely to fill the potential vacancies are listed directly under the incumbents.

Note that the ages of individuals are omitted from the replacement chart so that age is not used in making the promotion decision; that would be in violation of human rights legislation. It also is important that the organization refrain from utilizing any age-related terms in describing its management philosophy and PHRM policies.

Succession planning is very similar to replacement planning except that succession planning tends to be longer term, more developmental, and more flexibile.[38] Other differences are shown in Exhibit 2.6. Although succession planning is widely practised, many employers using it tend to emphasize the characteristics of the managers and downplay the characteristics of the positions to which these managers eventually may be promoted.[39]

Until recently, statistical techniques were not widely used because of inadequate data bases, lack of software computer programs, shortage of trained professionals to use them, and the restrictive conditions under which the models are applicable.[40] They are now, however, gaining popularity. A sample of the more common statistical techniques is provided in Exhibit 2.7, briefly describing Markov analysis,[41] simulation (based on Markov analysis),[42] renewal analysis,[43] and goal programming.[44]

Phase 2: Establishing Human Resource Objectives and Policies

As was shown in Exhibit 2.2, Phase 2 in the HRP process is setting human resource objectives and policies. These objectives and policies are directly related to corporate objectives and policies.[45] The impact of the organization's objectives, policies, and plans on human resource planning is difficult to deny but, according to a recent survey, only about 25% of organizations achieve a substantial link between their general institutional planning and their manpower planning. An additional 45% reported only some link, while 20% had no link at all.[46]

One study found that 85% of the organizations surveyed were using a human resource information system, but that about one-third were operating at the departmental or divisional level rather than organization-wide. In addition, most HRISs were used for payroll processing, personnel listings, and placement, and less often for forecasting and human resource development planning.[47]

Planning for Jobs and People

Exhibit 2.5   Sample Employee Replacement Chart

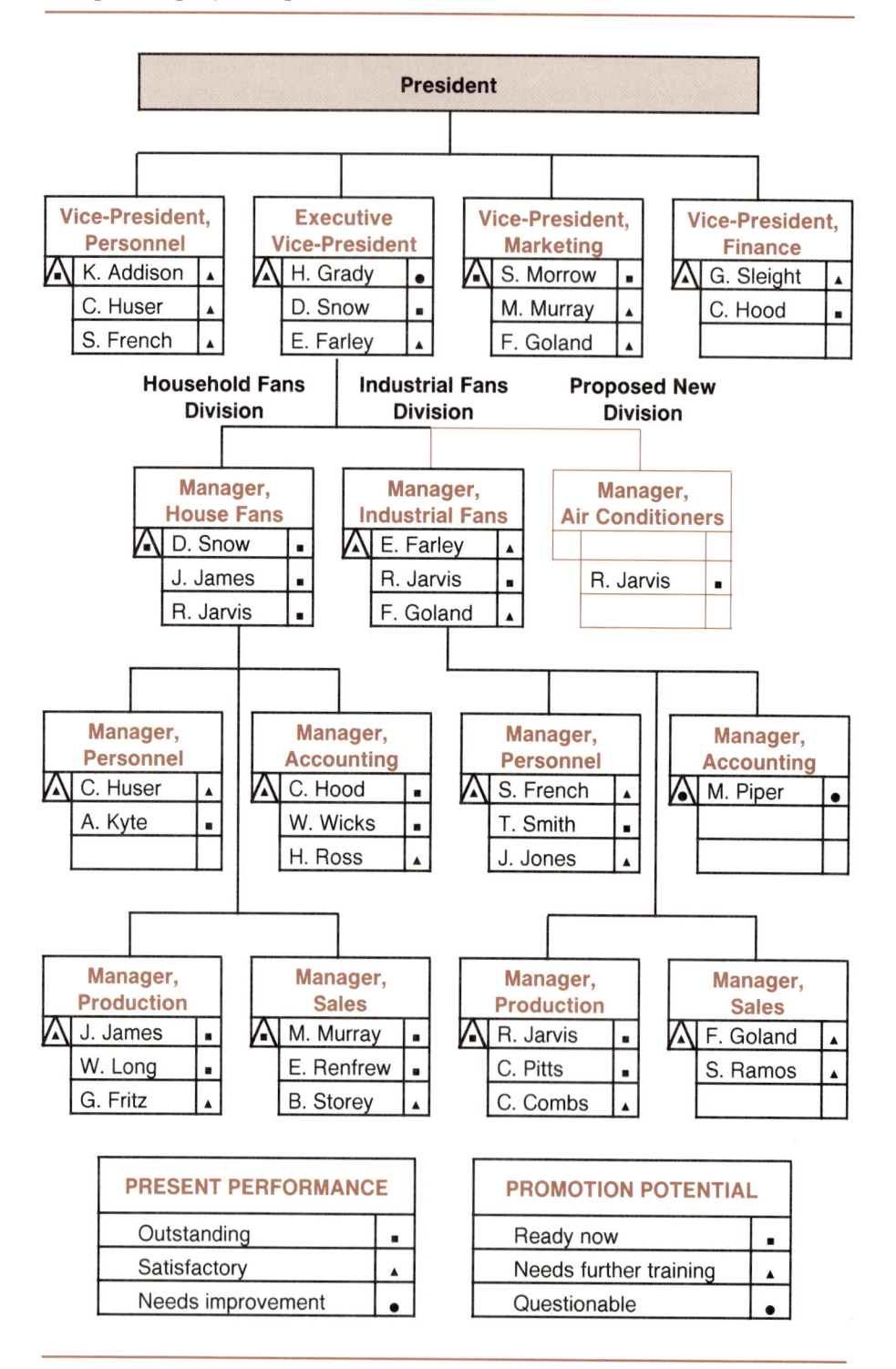

```
                                    President
        ┌──────────────────┬────────────────┬──────────────────┐
  Vice-President,     Executive      Vice-President,    Vice-President,
     Personnel      Vice-President      Marketing           Finance
  ▲ K. Addison ▲   ▲ H. Grady  ●   ▲ S. Morrow  ■    ▲ G. Sleight ▲
    C. Huser   ▲     D. Snow   ■     M. Murray  ▲      C. Hood    ■
    S. French  ▲     E. Farley ▲     F. Goland  ▲
```

Household Fans Division | Industrial Fans Division | Proposed New Division

```
     Manager,           Manager,              Manager,
   House Fans        Industrial Fans       Air Conditioners
  ▲ D. Snow   ■     ▲ E. Farley  ▲          R. Jarvis  ■
    J. James  ■       R. Jarvis  ■
    R. Jarvis ■       F. Goland  ▲
```

```
     Manager,         Manager,           Manager,          Manager,
     Personnel       Accounting          Personnel        Accounting
  ▲ C. Huser  ▲   ▲ C. Hood   ■      ▲ S. French ▲    ◐ M. Piper  ●
    A. Kyte   ■     W. Wicks  ■        T. Smith  ■
                    H. Ross   ▲        J. Jones  ▲
```

```
     Manager,         Manager,          Manager,          Manager,
    Production         Sales           Production          Sales
  ▲ J. James  ■    ▲ M. Murray ■     ▲ R. Jarvis ■    ▲ F. Goland ▲
    W. Long   ■      E. Renfrew ■      C. Pitts  ■      S. Ramos  ▲
    G. Fritz  ▲      B. Storey  ▲      C. Combs  ▲
```

PRESENT PERFORMANCE	
Outstanding	■
Satisfactory	▲
Needs improvement	●

PROMOTION POTENTIAL	
Ready now	■
Needs further training	▲
Questionable	●

Source: Adapted from *The Expanded Personnel Function, Studies in Personnel,* Policy 203 (New York: National Industrial Conference Board, 1966). Used with permission.

Exhibit 2.6: Contrasts Between Replacement and Succession Planning

Variable	Replacement Planning	Succession Planning
	0–12 months Best candidate available	12–36 months Candidate with best development potential
Commitment level	Designated preferred replacement candidate	Merely possibilities until vacancies occur
Focus of planning	Vertical lines of succession within units or functions	Development of a pool of talent: candidates with capability to take any of several assignments
Developmental action planning	Usually informal; merely a status report	Usually extensive: specific plans and goals set for each person
Flexibility	Limited by the structure of the plans, but in practice, decisions reflect a great deal of flexibility	Plans are conceived as flexible: intended to promote development and thinking about alternatives
Experience base applied	Each manager's best judgement based on personal observation and experience	Plans are the result of inputs and discussion from multiple managers
How candidates are evaluated	Observation of performance on the job over time; demonstrated competence: progress through the function	Multiple evaluations by different managers of the candidates on varied job assignments; testing and broadening early in careers

Source: James A. Walker, *Human Resources Planning* (New York: McGraw-Hill, 1980), p. 286. Reprinted with permission.

Though it may seem that HRP activity is too often divorced from the mainstream operations of the organization, the "PHRM in the News" items at the beginning of this chapter indicate the growing importance of HRP in determining an organization's goals, plans, and objectives. The relationship works both ways. Ideally, organizational policies, plans, and objectives influence the personnel inventory and forecasting analysis, and these in turn influence organizational policies, plans, and objectives by permitting the effective use of human resources in attaining the organization's goals.

Phase 3: Human Resource Programming

The third phase is an important extension of human resource planning. After the assessment of an organization's human resource needs, action programming must be developed to serve those needs. These action programs may be designed to increase the supply of the right employees in the

Planning for Jobs and People

Exhibit 2.7 *Statistical Techniques Used to Project Future Human Resource Supply Availability*

Name	Description
	Projects future flows to obtain availability estimates through a straightforward application of historical transition rates. Historical transition rates are derived from analyses of personnel data concerning losses, promotions, transfers, demotions, and perhaps recruitment.
Simulation (based on Markov Analysis)	Alternative (rather than historical) flows are examined for effects on future human resource availabilities. Alternative flows reflect the anticipated results of policy or program changes concerning voluntary and involuntary turnover, retirement, promotion, etc.
Renewal Analysis	Estimates future flows and availability by calculating: (1) vacancies as created by organizational growth, personnel losses, and internal geographical movements and (2) the results of decision rules governing the filling of vacancies. Alternative models may assess the effects of changes in growth estimates, turnover, promotions, or decision rules.
Goal Programming	Optimizes goals—in this case a desired staffing pattern—given a set of constraints concerning such things as the upper limits on flows, the percentage of new recruits permitted in each province, and total salary budgets.

Source: Adapted from L. Dyer, "Human Resource Planning," in K. Rowland and G. Ferris (eds.), *Personnel Management.* Copyright © 1982 by Allyn & Bacon, Inc. Used with permission.

organization (e.g., if the forecasts in Phase 1 showed that demand would exceed supply) or to decrease the number of current employees (e.g., if the forecasts showed that supply would exceed demand). Although many alternative programs could be proposed to address these needs, only two are presented here—one to increase and one to decrease the supply of employees.

Attraction: New Organizational Structures. As indicated earlier, "The human resource planner assists in developing workable organizational structures...." Workable structures are those that can serve the objectives of planning and programming to attract, retain, and motivate individuals.[48] It appears, however, that present organizational structures may not be as workable as they once were:

> Changes in our society, particularly in the values of the workforce, have seriously undermined the traditional relationship between organizations and their members. This has led to a crisis for organizations that may only be resolved by the evolution of new organizational forms.[49]

Some of the most apparent results of this crisis have been the decline in productivity, particularly quality of performance, and increases in absenteeism. Consequently, organizations have been losing their ability to utilize effectively the human resources available to them.

In general, present organizational structures can be characterized by supervisory control, minimal employee participation in workplace decisions, top-down communications, an emphasis on extrinsic rewards to attract, retain, and motivate employees (rewards such as pay, promotion, and status symbols), narrowly designed jobs with narrow job descriptions (see Chapter 3), and a primary concern for productivity and fitting people to jobs. This primary concern is translated into selecting people on the basis of their skills, knowledge, and abilities to meet the demands of the job. This concern is called **Match 1**.[50]

Sensing that these present organizational structure characteristics are no longer appropriate for attracting, retaining, and motivating individuals, some organizations such as Honeywell and Control Data are engaging in alternative structures.[51] These structures can be characterized by greater employee self-control, more employee participation in workplace decisions, bottom-up as well as top-down communications, recognition of employee rights, an emphasis on intrinsic rewards (such as senses of responsibility, meaningfulness, and achievement), and extrinsic rewards, more broadly designed jobs allowing for more worker discretion (see Chapter 3), and primary concerns for quality of working life (QWL), productivity, and fitting jobs to people. These primary concerns are translated into selecting individuals on the basis of their skills, knowledge, and abilities to meet the demands of the job (Match 1), and also on the basis of job and organizational characteristics to match the personality, interests, and preferences of the individuals.[52] This latter concern is referred to as **Match 2**. Match 1 is concerned with ensuring that employee skills, knowledge, and abilities match job demands, and Match 2 is concerned with ensuring that employee personality, interests, and preferences match job and organizational characteristics.

Although relatively few organizations are currently using alternative structures to improve their effectiveness, it appears that these alternatives offer human resource planners a way of providing workable structures to serve the employees. As described more extensively in Chapter 13, alternative structures, such as those described by Theory Z management, are proving effective in some organizations.[53] And as described in the remaining chapters, alternative structure concerns are being reflected in almost every PHRM function and activity. One reason that alternative structures are proving effective is the change in the social values of the workforce, as described later in this chapter.

Reduction: Dealing with Job Loss. Due to economic and technological conditions in the past few years, layoffs have become an increasing problem. Organizations therefore must become increasingly sensitive in dealing with their effects on employees, and either try to minimize these effects or eliminate the necessity for layoffs. Both of these efforts can be achieved through redundancy planning. **Redundancy planning** essentially is human resource planning associated with the process of laying off employees who are no longer needed—they are redundant. Involved in this planning may be outplacement counseling, buy-outs, job skill retraining opportunies, and job transfer opportunities.[54] Although redundancy planning has been limited to companies in only a few industries, it is suggested that this should be done in all industries.

Unions, of course, can also play a central role in redundancy planning. In one of Kruger's pulp and paper divisions in Montreal, union and management officials got together and established a redundancy plan that included such programs as attrition and early retirement. Other unions view redundancy planning as part of their participation in quality of working life projects. They view it as a necessary trade-off for increasing their voice in traditional management areas.[55] In Western Europe, trade unions are stepping up their efforts to win reductions in the number of hours worked per week, in an effort to stem the tide of swelling job displacement.[56]

Employees also play a role in employers' efforts at redundancy planning. Contrary to popular belief, many workers laid off as the result of a structural or technological change manage to find new jobs fairly quickly.[57] Therefore, possibly only a minority of redundant workers may need to be retrained and placed; the majority may need only counselling and placement. Also, *pre-retirement counselling* is used increasingly and may be particularly beneficial to redundancy planning.[58] This counselling can facilitate an employee's transition from work to non-work and can encourage employee retirement. Thus, human resource programming and planning may help an organization to reduce the bottlenecks discussed later, as well as to avoid or reduce the number of redundant workers by making sure that counselling programs are provided, and that potentially redundant employees are made aware of the counselling. It is important that both layoffs and counselling efforts not be used as methods of "getting rid of" older workers. It is particularly important that employees not perceive them as such.

Regardless of the human resource program implemented, however, it must be monitored and evaluated. This allows for controlling how well the program is being implemented and revising it as appropriate. Thus, control and evaluating are the necessary fourth phase in HRP.

Phase 4: HRP Control and Evaluation

Control and evaluation of human resource plans and programs are essential to the effective management of human resources. Efforts in this area are aimed at quantifying the value of human resources and recognizing human resources as an asset to the organization.

An HRIS facilitates program control and evaluation by allowing for more rapid and frequent collection of data to back up the forecast. This data collection is important not only as a means of control, but also as a method of evaluating plans and programs and making adjustments.

The collection of data should occur at the end of each year and at fixed intervals during the year. The evaluation should occur at the same time, in order to hasten revisions of existing forecasts and programs. It is likely that revisions will influence short-term, intermediate, and long-term forecasts.

Evaluation of human resource plans and programs is an important process not only for determining the effectiveness of HRP, but also for demonstrating the significance of both HRP and the PHRM department in the organization as a whole.

Possible criteria or standards for evaluating HRP include:

- Actual staffing levels against established staffing requirements
- Productivity levels against established goals
- Actual personnel flow rates against desired rates
- Programs implemented against action plans
- Program results against expected outcomes (e.g., improved applicant flows, reduced quit rates, improved replacement ratios)
- Labour and program costs against budgets
- Ratios of programs results (benefits) to program costs [59]

An important aspect related to evaluation, revisions, and adjustments is the issue of cause and effect. The model of PHRM presented in Chapter 1 is based on the principle of integrated, systemic activities. Therefore, if the recruiting program is not working well, it is not valid to conclude that the recruitment program needs revision. Perhaps the salaries offered to recruits are too low and not competitive with other organizations. It also is possible that, despite the best recruiting efforts, few acceptable applicants were available.

HRP Roadblocks

One of the key roadblocks to developing HRP has been the lack of top management support. This also has prevented PHRM departments from playing all of the major personnel roles discussed in Chapter 1. PHRM can help to overcome this roadblock with data and bottom-line (dollars-and-cents) facts that demonstrate the effectiveness of HRP and PHRM.

Another roadblock is the difficulty in integrating all of the personnel activities that are so necessary to make HRP work. A challenge for PHRM managers is to create a personnel system in which all the functions and activities discussed in Chapter 1 are integrated and co-ordinated in conjunction with the business plan of the organization. This will not only help remove a personnel planning roadblock, it also will enhance the effectiveness of all of the PHRM activities.

A third roadblock is the lack of involvement of line managers. Failure to involve line management in the design, development, and implementation of a human resource planning system is a common oversight for first-time planners. Personnel and human resource managers often are tempted to develop or adopt highly quantitative approaches to planning. These approaches often have little pragmatic value to line managers in dealing with problems such as reducing excessive turnover, identifying and training replacements for key positions, and forecasting staffing needs. Personnel planning, to be effective, must serve the line managers' needs.

Important Changes in the 1990s Influencing HRP

As the quotations at the beginning of this chapter illustrate, many changes are occurring that have a dramatic influence on organizations. In turn, these changes are affecting personnel management and increasing the importance of HRP. Because of the significance of these changes, it is important to discuss their impacts on human resources.[60]

The job of HRP encompasses the whole range of societal, demographic, economic, and government regulatory factors that influence changes in an organization's workforce. Just as PHRM is concerned with the "whole person," HRP must be increasingly aware of the total external environment that will shape the workforce and its concerns, as well as the particular environment that is influencing the current workforce.

The Population and the Labour Force

Several significant changes are taking place in the Canadian population and in the nature of the labour force. In addition, substantial changes are occurring in the nature of jobs and the dominance of certain industries.

Demographics. The counter clerk handing you your hamburger next time may not be the usual teenager. Rather, it may be some teenager's grandparent![61] The major reason is the shrinking supply of young workers. After more than two decades of growth, the nation's population between the ages of 16 and 24 has peaked. As shown in Exhibit 2.8, the 16-to-24 age group will continue to decline as a percentage of the total labour force and of the population. In the meantime, the 25-to-54 age group (particularly the 35-to-44 segment) will continue to rise. The 35-to-44 age group is expected to increase 32% between 1985 and 1995, from 3 565 000 to 4 705 000. These projections are made by Canada Employment and Immigration, which publishes both short- and long-term labour force projections. One document, *The Ford Occupational Imbalance Listing,* is a quarterly publication that estimates both labour market demands (by occupation) and supply characteristics. A longer-term projection is provided by the Canada Occupational Forecasting Program. Statistics Canada also publishes reports on a monthly, quarterly, and annual basis.

For example, Exhibit 2.8 shows the projected composition of the labour force by age for 1990 and 1995.[62] The implications are numerous. For instance, bottlenecks will occur in the promotion paths for the 35-to-44 age group for the next several years, because the number of middle-manager jobs for that group is expected to increase only moderately. The consequences of the bottlenecks may be increased militancy and dissatisfaction among the employees, and greater selection opportunities for employers. Employers, however, may have to accommodate these employees by making their present jobs more challenging and even by redefining "success" (in essence, changing the outcomes provided) by altering its current association with upward promotions.

Labour Force Age-Group Distribution

Exhibit 2.8

	Projected Numbers (Thousands)	
Age, Both Sexes	**1990**	**1995**
16 years and over	20 821	22 013
16 to 24	3 569	3 557
25 to 54	12 012	12 891
25 to 34	4 997	4 702
35 to 44	4 201	4 705
45 to 54	2 814	3 484
55 years and over	5 239	5 565
55 to 64	2 308	2 340
65 and over	2 931	3 225

Source: *Population Projections for Canada and the Provinces, 1976–2001*, Statistics Canada, catalogue no. 91–520. Reproduced with permission of the Minister of Supply and Services Canada.

The distribution of gender in these same categories could undergo several interesting changes. The total number of men in the labour force will continue to diminish, while the number of women will continue to increase. The number of women engaging in some form of paid work almost doubled between 1970 and 1983, and by the early 1980s, more than half of women aged 15 and over held jobs outside their homes. But while many more women have jobs, the circumstances of their working lives have not changed as radically—women are concentrated in relatively low-paying service and clerical occupations.[63] This trend toward increasing participation of women in the labour force is expected to continue over the next 10 years, and the percentage of women eligible to work will probably approximate the percentage of males. Women also are expected to occupy more professional and managerial positions where, until recently, their participation was very low.

Other population changes expected to occur in the 1990s include an increased life expectancy for men (from 69.5 years in 1978 to more than 70 years) and women (from 77.2 years in 1978 to 80 years), and more immigration. Extended projections indicate that the first decade of the twenty-first century will mark the "greying" of the workforce in North America, with a 42% increase in the 55-to-64 age category between 2000 and 2010.

All of these population and workforce trends are expected to present major challenges for HRP. Society may well wonder what these people are going to do: what jobs will be available for them and what will their job preferences be?

Job Preferences. Currently, the occupational makeup of the civilian labour force reflects much higher percentages of women than men in clerical positions, and higher percentages of men than women in managerial and administrative jobs and employed as craftworkers. One area, however, in which the number of female managers has grown considerably is personnel. From 1971 to 1981, the number of female directors of personnel multiplied 16 times. In 1981, close to 50% of all personnel officers were female.[64]

This increase, in part, resulted from reduction of gender stereotypes, changes in job titles, and legal mandates that encourage employers to hire females in previously male-dominated jobs, and vice versa.

Trends and Changes in the Economy

Most major companies devote substantial resources to economic forecasting, in addition to subscribing to the macroeconomic analyses of banks, insurance companies, private economists, and governmental agencies. Since economic conditions are certain to affect the future workforce and conditions of employment, they should be considered in HRP.

General Economic Conditions. One trend that will certainly affect human resource planning is the relative stagnation in the growth rate of productivity. Currently, the rate of inflation is at a moderate level and is not a major consideration in HRP. Yet, if inflation were to increase slightly, to 7%, for instance, the cost of most goods would double in less than 10 years. Similarly, wages and salaries would also double, to keep up with inflation. High inflation also would influence the cost of employer-paid fringe benefits, and further enhance the need for productivity gains and better workforce utilization. Consequently, faced with stagnation in productivity rates, the possible renewal of high inflation, and continued intense international competition, organizations are concerned with increasing productivity. This concern in turn is causing a significant economic shift toward increased automation, the use of robots, and advanced technologies. Exhibit 2.9 provides a summary of the major economic indicators, and Exhibit 2.10

Exhibit 2.9 Major Economic Indicators for Canada (March 1986)

	Latest Monthly Figures*	% Change from Year Ago
Average Weekly Earnings (November)	$425.15	3.5
Persons with Jobs (January)	11 200 000	4.8
Unemployed (January)	1 347 000	−9.2
Consumer Price Index** (January)	130.1	4.4
New House Price Index*** (December)	98.2	3.7
Department Store Sales (December)	$1 835 400 000	5.9
New Motor Vehicles Sales (November)	$1 696 400 000	26.2
Retail Sales (December)	$13 210 300 000	10.6

*Dollar figures are in current dollars and are not seasonally adjusted
**1981 = 100
***1976 = 100

Source: *Canadian Statistic Review*, Statistics Canada, catalogue no. 11–003E. Reproduced by permission of the Minister of Supply and Services Canada.

provides a summary of the Consumer Price Index. Updated versions of both should be consulted continually by PHRM departments.

Technologies, Automation, and Robots. The technologies in which Canada is advancing most rapidly and which have the most potential for enhancing productivity and workforce utilization are microelectronics, artificial intelligence, materials research, biotechnology, geology, and oil and energy exploration. A significant application of microelectronics will result in increased automation (and computerization) and the use of robots. Although using these products increases productivity dramatically, it also has a significant effect on the size of the needed workforce and the pride and self-esteem of employees.

Changes due to automation are occurring in white-collar as well as blue-collar occupations. For example, a recent survey of the impact of computers on human resource management in Canada revealed the following trends:

- The computerization of office, professional, and managerial tasks is changing dramatically. The survey projects that, at the current rate of change, by the 1990s the computer terminal or microcomputer will be a regular tool of the majority of all office, professional, and managerial employees.[65]
- Work quantity improvements usually took the form of slower growth in employment, rather than in work volume.[66]

It is feared that, although advances in robotics can help people by eliminating dull and dangerous jobs, their use may not only eliminate jobs, but also

---

Consumer Price Index: Percentage Change for January 1986   *Exhibit 2.10*

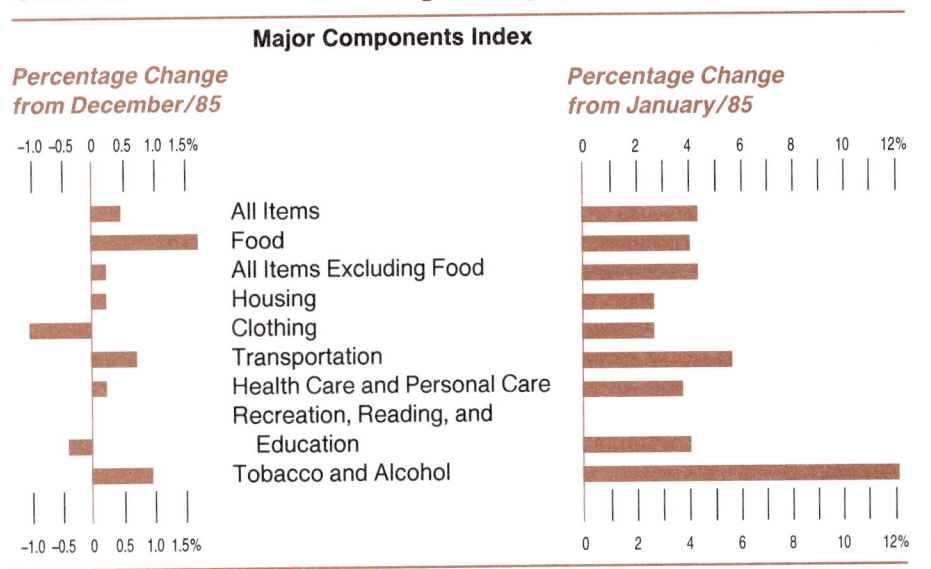

Major Components Index

Categories: All Items, Food, All Items Excluding Food, Housing, Clothing, Transportation, Health Care and Personal Care, Recreation, Reading, and Education, Tobacco and Alcohol

Percentage Change from December/85 (scale −1.0 to 1.5%)

Percentage Change from January/85 (scale 0 to 12%)

Source: *The Consumer Price Index,* Statistics Canada, catalogue no. 62–001. Reproduced by permission of the Minister of Supply and Services Canada.

take away the pride and self-respect of those displaced. Therefore, the human resource planning needs of the organization must be altered when robots are considered. Where use of robots is necessary, redundancy planning may be particularly useful.

Changing Social Values

Closely linked with changes in the population, the labour force, and the economy are changes in social values, interests, and preferences. The areas in which these changes are particularly important for HRP are values held by employees toward *work*, *mobility*, and *retirement*.

Values Toward Work. Stagnation in productivity is often related to the decline or disappearance of the value the workforce places on hard work. According to some, however:

> The work ethic has not disappeared. People today are willing to work hard at "good" jobs, providing they have the freedom to influence the nature of their jobs and to pursue their own lifestyles.[67]

People still value work, but the type of work that interests them has changed. They want jobs with challenge and they want jobs in which they are provided with the freedom to make some decisions. As suggested by survey results at General Electric and A.T.T., people do not necessarily seek or desire rapid promotions, particularly when this involves transferring to another geographical location. They do tend to seek influence and control—characteristics of the job and work situation integral to the quality of work life.[68] What the quality of work life represents, then, is personal control, self-respect, and power to influence what is going on.

By implication, HRP should involve the analysis of employees for their personalities, interests, and preferences as well as for skills, knowledge, and ability, and match these with the job and organizational characteristics. The result of this could be organizations with new, alternative structures that strive to fit organizational structure and individuals on both Match 1 and Match 2. Organizations may also have to fit structure with the environment. If this is the case and structure cannot be changed, the individuals may need to be selected for the existing type of structure.

Values Toward Mobility. The values that employees attach to work significantly affects their feelings about moving from job to job when it entails moving from one region of the country to another. Like the recently changing employee values toward work, the new values against mobility are having significant impact on PHRM, particularly in recruiting, training, promoting, and motivating managers and professionals. Large companies like Bell Canada, CN, and Air Canada are having a more difficult time getting their employees to move. This growing reluctance, however, may have some benefits for companies—in the past five years, the average cost to a company of moving a homeowning employee has tripled.

Values Toward Retirement. "Many fear golden years might become just brass." The North American predilection for early retirement appears to be waning, slowing a trend of the 1970s that would have put the average retirement age below 55 by the year 2000.[69] Many workers are bypassing provisions for early retirement (age 55 or 60) and even staying on the job past the traditional retirement age of 65. This is largely in response to inflation rates, concerns over the stability of the social insurance system, and federal and provincial legislation protecting the older employee.

One significant consequence of this change in value toward retirement is the bottleneck it creates in the promotional paths for younger employees, particularly minorities and women. Choice of later retirement adds to the problems for personnel managers caused by the changing demographics of the larger 35-to-44-year-old workforce group discussed earlier. PHRM managers will need to play the role of innovator very astutely to accommodate the older workforce, yet still retain and motivate the younger workforce.

Legislation, Regulation, and Government Activity

Perhaps at no time in history has governmental activity so greatly impinged on the human resource function in organizations. In some respects, the modern corporate personnel department has been shaped by the requirements of federal and provincial legislation. Study of the remainder of this book will make apparent the fact that all PHRM functions and activities are influenced and will continue to be influenced by legislation and regulation.

In summary, the changes in these four major areas—demographics, the economy, social values, and government regulation—probably will have significant impact on the management of human resources. Being able to anticipate these changes will aid a personnel and human resource manager in developing and implementing effective personnel planning programs. Once implemented, these programs need to be evaluated and revised continually.

Assessing HRP

Human resource planning can make or break an organization, particularly over the long term. Without effective human resource planning, an organization may find itself with a plant or an office without the people to run it productively. So, on a broad level, HRP activity can be assessed on the basis of whether or not the organization has the type of employees that it needs, at the right place, at the right time, and at the right salary.

At more specific levels, HRP activities can be assessed by how effectively the planning strategies attract new employees, deal with job loss, and adapt to the changing characteristics of the environment. Since an important part of HRP is forecasting, HRP can be assessed by how well its forecasts, whether of specific personnel needs or of specific environmental trends, compare with reality. Accuracy here can be crucial since it is unlikely that HRP can do well on a broad level if it fails to do well in forecasting. Several other criteria against which HRP can be assessed are those presented earlier in this chapter in the section entitled "Phase 4: HRP Control and Evaluation."

Summary

Nothing can be done about the performance of past management or the qualifications of today's management. But tomorrow's management can be as good as today's managers make it. This sums up the need for human resource planning and programming, at least for managerial employees. Of course, HRP also must be implemented for entry level and non-managerial employees, technical and professional employees. The changes occurring in our society are making HRP more critical and more complex. This is enhanced by the growing recognition of how closely HRP must be tied to an organization's overall business plan in order for the organization itself to be effective.

PHRM departments must actively strive to accomplish each of the four phases of HRP. The first phase is to determine the organization's current resources and what the future will be, in order to develop a forecast of human resource needs. In the second phase, the objectives and policies of the PHRM department must be compatible with the overall objectives of the organization. Action programs must be developed and implemented in the third phase. To help ensure the effectiveness of these programs, the fourth phase stipulates continual control and evaluation of the implementation and administration of each program. On the basis of the results of the evaluation, the programs can then be modified as necessary.

Roadblocks exist that increase the challenge of HRP, primarily the lack of top-management support. This support, however, can be gained by showing top management that the potential benefits of HRP include reduced personnel costs, better employee development, improved overall organizational planning, more opportunities for a better-balanced and more integrated workforce, and greater awareness of the importance of human resource management for the benefit of the individual and the organization.

Once top-management support for HRP has been gained, the PHRM department is prepared to move into the next important activity in planning for effect human resource utilization: job design and job analysis. HRP deals with the broader issues associated with human resource planning, while job design and job analysis deal with the more specific issues that are presented in the next chapter.

Discussion Questions

1. What type of questions would a personnel manager be most likely to ask when considering current challenges in HRP?
2. What is the essential goal of HRP?
3. Aside from identifying future organizational human resource needs and establishing programs for eliminating discrepancies while balancing individual and organizational interests, what are the other specific purposes of HRP?
4. Who is responsible for HRP, and what roles do these individuals play in determining the effectiveness of HRP?
5. Discuss the roadblocks to HRP and how each might be removed.
6. Provide a step-by-step overview of the four phases of HRP.
7. Identify and describe the most commonly used method of judgemental forecasting. What are its advantages and disadvantages?
8. Why are statistical methods of forecasting limited?
9. In what ways can an organization increase its ability to attract and retain better employees?
10. What are the two most salient results of evaluating human resource plans and programs?

CASE STUDY

Somebody's Got To Go

The Evermatic Company faces a dilemma soon to be faced by many other organizations. There has been pressure, and along with legislative moves, to discard compulsory retirement.

Evermatic is faced with a young workforce with no place to go. There are few opportunities for advancement within the company because more senior employees are maintaining their positions for much longer. Furthermore, the company, while successful, is not a rapidly expanding one. The immediate problem, of course, is that Evermatic is losing more and more of its capable people to other organizations that are expanding and therefore can provide more opportunities for promotion.

Evermatic is not alone in this dilemma. This is a potential problem of far-reaching importance to personnel departments and governments alike.

Case Questions

1. What are the implications, both positive and negative, of extending retirement age limits in industry?
2. What would you recommend to Evermatic?
3. Who has the "greater right," the young worker on the move or the older worker who wants to continue in his or her job?

Adapted from R. S. Schuler, S. A. Youngblood, and L. K. Trevino: *Instructor's Manual to Accompany—Effective Personnel Management* (2nd ed.), (St. Paul: West Publishing Co., 1986). Used with permission.

Endnotes

1. P. Donohue, "Human Resource Planning in a Recovering Economy," and C. Besler, "Canadian General Insurance: Coping with Success," in a feature report, *Planning for Productivity (Human Resource Management in Canada)*, October 1983, pp. 5140–5142 and 5129–5133, respectively. All rights reserved: Prentice-Hall Canada Inc., 1983.

2. G. Milkovich, L. Dyer, and T. Mahoney, "The State of Practice and Research in Human Resource Planning," in S. J. Carroll and R. S. Schuler (eds.), *Human Resource Management in the 1980s* (Washington, D.C.: The Bureau of National Affairs, Inc., 1983). E. H. Burack and N. J. Mathys, *Human Resource Planning: A Pragmatic Approach to Manpower Staffing and Development* (Lake Forest, IL: Brace-Park, 1979). E. C. Smith, "Strategic Business Planning and Human Resources: Part I, "*Personnel Journal*", August 1982, pp. 606–610; E. C. Smith, "Strategic Business Planning and Human Resources: Part II," *Personnel Journal*, Sept. 1982, pp. 680–682. L. J. Stybel, "Linking Strategic Planning and Management Manpower Planning," *California Management Review*, Fall 1982, pp. 48–56. L. Dyer, "Human Resource Planning," in K. M. Rowland and G. R. Ferris (eds.), *Personnel Management* (Boston: Allyn & Bacon Inc., 1982), pp. 52–77.

3. J. W. Walker, *Human Resource Planning* (New York: McGraw-Hill, 1980), uses the term "business plan." The term is used here to refer to those plans for the total organization (whether government, non-profit, or profit-oriented) that help drive the long- and short-range planning needs for human resource planning.

4. G. Milkovich and W. Glueck, *Personnel, Human Resource Management: A Diagnostic Approach*, 4th ed., Chapter 6 (Plano, TX: Business Publications, Inc., 1985).

5. E. W. Vetter, *Manpower Planning for High Talent Personnel* (Ann Arbor, MI: Bureau of Industrial Relations, Graduate School of Business, The University of Michigan, 1967). D. B. Gehrman, "Objective-Based Human Resource Planning," *Personnel Administrator*, Dec. 1982, pp. 71–75.

6. V. R. Ceriello, "The Human Resources Management System: Part I," *Personnel Journal*, Oct. 1982, pp. 764–767.

7. J. Laurie, "Gaining Acceptance for Your HRD Plan," *Personnel*, Dec. 1982, pp. 896–897. J. P. Muczyk, "Comprehensive Manpower Planning," *Managerial Planning*, Nov./Dec. 1981, pp. 36–41. E. H. Burack and T. J. McNichols, *Human Resources Planning, Technology, Policy Change* (Kent, OH: Comparative Administration Research Institute, 1973). C. F. Russ, Jr., "Manpower Planning Systems: Part I," *Personnel Journal*, Jan. 1982, pp. 40–45; C. F. Russ, Jr., "Manpower Planning Systems: Part II," *Personnel Journal*, Feb. 1982, pp. 119–123.

8. For an excellent history of the development of such programs as reaction to environmental changes, see L. J. White, "Equal Employment Opportunities: Challenges and Practice for Canadian Companies: Royal Bank Experience," in S. L. Dolan and R. S. Schuler (eds.) *Canadian Readings in Personnel and Human Resource Management* (St. Paul: West Publishing Co., 1987).

9. For general trends, see P. B. Fay, "Why Human Resource Planning Is Important" *Human Resources Management in Canada*, Prentice-Hall Canada Inc., 1983, pp. 20,011–21,014.

10. R. J. Szawlowski, "Training and Development in the High Technology Industry: Present and Future Trends," in Dolan and Schuler (eds.), see endnote 8.

11. C. G. Howard, "How Best to Integrate Expatriate Managers in the Domestic Organization," *Personnel Administrator*, July 1982, pp. 27–33. S. J. Carroll and R. S. Schuler, "Professional Human Resource Management," Carroll and Schuler (eds.), see endnote 2.

12. E. H. Burack and T. G. Gutteridge, "Institutional Manpower Planning: Rhetoric Verus Reality," *California Management Review*, Spring 1978, p. 17.

13. H. L. Dahl and K. S. Morgan, "Return on Investment in Human Resources," (Upjohn Company, unpublished manuscript, 1982) cited by Milkovich, Dyer, and Mahoney in Carroll and Schuler (eds.), see endnote 2. For a discussion of the human resource accounting concept, see J. B. Paperman and D. D. Martin, "Human Resource Accounting: A Managerial Tool?" *Personnel*, March/April 1977, pp. 41–50.

14. Milkovich, Dyer, and Mahoney, see endnote 2.

15. E. H. Burack and T. G. Gutteridge, "Institutional Manpower Planning: Rhetoric Versus Reality," © 1978 by the Regents of the University of California. Reprinted from *California Management Review*, vol. XX, no. 3, p. 14. By permission of the Regents.

16. "America's New Immobile Society," *Business Week*, July 27, 1982, pp. 58–62.

17. C. Mackay, "Human Resource Planning: A Four-Phased Approach," *Management Review*, May 1981, pp. 17–22.

18. For an extensive description of each of these phases, see J. J. Leach, "Merging the Two Faces of Personnel: A Challenge for the 1980's," *Personnel*, Jan./Feb. 1980, pp. 52–57. "Manpower Planning and Corporate Objectives: Two Points of View," *Management Review*, Aug. 1981, pp. 55–61. E. L. Miller and E. H.

Burack, "A Status Report on Human Resource Planning from the Perspective of Human Resource Planners," *Human Resource Planning*, 1981, pp. 33–40. S. M. Nkomo, "Stage Three in Personnel Administration: Strategic Human Resources Management," *Personnel*, July/Aug. 1980 pp. 69–77. G. S. Odiorne, "Developing a Human Resource Strategy," *Personnel Journal*, July 1981, pp. 534–536. J. A. Sheridan, "The Relatedness of Change: A Comprehensive Approach to Human Resource Planning for the Eighties," *Human Resource Planning*, 1979, pp. 123–133. N. C. Agrawal, "Human Resource Planning," in *Human Resources Management in Canada*, Prentice-Hall Canada Inc., 1983, pp. 20,011–20,046.

19. P. S. Greenlaw and W. D. Biggs, *Modern Personnel Management* (Philadelphia: Saunders, 1979), p. 83.

20. A. C. Hyde and J. M. Shafritz, "HRIS: Introduction to Tomorrow's System for Managing Human Resources," p. 70. Reprinted with permission from the March/April 1977 issue of *Public Personnel Management*, copyright 1977, International Personnel Management Association, 1850 K. Street, N.W. Washington, D.C. 20006. See also Ceriello, endnote 6; K. M. Rowland and S. L. Summers, "Human Resource Planning: A Second Look," *Personnel Administrator*, December 1981, pp. 73–80; A. J. Walker, "The Newest Job in Personnel: Human Resources Data Administrator," *Personnel Journal*, December 1982, pp. 924–927. J. C. Ullman and G. P. Huber, *The Local Jobs Bank Program* (Lexington, MA: D. C. Heath & Company, 1973); D. H. Brush and W. A. Owens, "Implementation and Evaluation of an Assessment Classification Model for Manpower Utilization," *Personnel Psychology*, 1979, 32, pp. 369–383.

21. The implications were extracted from E. B. Harvey and J. H. Blakely, "Maximizing Use of Human Resource Information Systems (HRIS), in S. L. Dolan, and R. S. Schuler (eds.), *Canadian Readings in Personnel and Human Resource Management* (St. Paul: West Publishing Co. 1987). For more information about HRIS, see S. Simon "The HRIS: What Capabilities Must It Have? *Personnel*, Sept./Oct. 1983, pp. 36–49. See also SKOPOS, *Personnel Data Base Systems for Micros* (Los Altos, CA: 1984), and *Executrack: A Microcomputer Succession Planning System* (Fairfield, IA: Corporate Education Resources, 1984).

22. Phillips R., "Equity in the Labour Market: The Potential of Affirmative Action," in R. S. Abella, *Equity in Employment*, research studies (Ottawa: Ministry of Supply and Services, 1984).

23. D. R. Dalton "Absenteeism and Turnover in Organizations," in R. S. Schuler, J. M. McFillen, and D. R. Dalton (eds.) *Applied Readings in Personnel and Human Resource Management* (St. Paul: West Publishing Co., 1980).

24. For a discussion of the structure-environment fit and the relationship of this fit with individual preferences and motivations, see J. R. Galbraith, *Organization Design* (Reading, MA: Addison-Wesley, 1977), and R. H. Miles, *Marco Organizational Behavior* (Santa Monica, CA: Goodyear Publishing Company, Inc., 1980).

25. M. J. Gannon, *Organizational Behavior* (Boston: Little, Brown, 1979) p. 97.

26. "Forecasters Turn to Group Guesswork," *Business Week*, March 14, 1970, p. 130.

27. For a more extensive discussion of group techniques, including the nominal group technique, see A. C. Delbecq, A. H. Van deVen, and D. H. Gustafson, *Group Technique for Program Planning* (Glenview, IL: Scott, Foresman, 1977). J. K. Murnigham, "Group Decision Making: What Strategy Should You Use?" *Management Review*, 1981, February, pp. 56–60. J. Lee, "An Alternative to the Nominal Group Technique Final Vote Procedure," *Appalachian Business Review* 1979, Winter, pp. 2–5. D. H. Gustafson, R. K. Sikula, A. Delbecq, and G. W. Walster, "A Comparative Study of Differences in Subjective Likelihood Estimates Made by Individuals, Interacting Groups, Delphi Groups, and Nominal Groups," *Organizational Behavior and Human Performance*, 1973, 9, pp. 280–291.

28. For a description of managerial estimates, see Walker, endnote 3.

29. H. Kahalas, H. L. Pazer, J. S. Hoagland, and A. Leavitt, "Human Resource Planning Activities in U.S. Firms," *Human Resource Planning*, 3, 1980, pp. 53–66.

30. G. Milkovich and T. Mahoney, "Human Resources Planning and PAIR Policy," in D. Yoder and H. Heneman (eds.), *PAIR Handbook*, vol. 4 (Berea, OH: American Society of Personnel Administration, 1976), G. Milkovich, L. Dyer, and T. Mahoney, "HRM Planning," in S. J. Carroll and R. S. Schuler (eds.), Human Resource Management in the 1980s (Washington, DC: Bureau of National Affairs, 1983), pp. 2.2–2.29. D. M. Atwater, E. S. Bress, R. J. Neihaus, and J. A. Sheridan, "An Application of Integrated Human Resource Planning Supply-Demand Model," *Human Resources Planning*, 5, 1982, pp. 1–15. E. P. Bloom, "Creating an Employee Information System," *Personnel Administrator*, Nov. 1982, pp. 67–75. B. W. Holz and J. M. Worth, "Improving Strengths Forecasts: Support of Army Manpower Management," *Interfaces, 10*, 1980, pp. 37–52.

31. S. Makridakis and S. C. Wheelwright (eds.), *Forecasting* (New York: North-Holland Publishing Co., 1979).

32. Makridakis and Wheelwright (eds.), see endnote 31. J. R. Hinrichs and R. F. Morrison, "Human Resource Planning in Support of Research and Development," *Human Resources Planning*, 3, 1980, pp. 201–210.

33. Burack and Mathys, see endnote 2, pp. 155–157.

34. N. K. Kwak, W. A. Garrett, Jr., and S. Barone, "A Stochastic Model of Demand Forecasting for Techni-

cal Manpower Training," *Management Science, 23,* 1977, pp. 1089–1098.
35. Milkovich, Dyer, and Mahoney, see endnote 2.
36. Vetter, see endnote 5, p. 35. P. S. Bender, W. D. Northup, and J. F. Shapiro, "Practical Modeling for Resource Management," *Harvard Business Review,* March/April 1981, pp. 163–175.
37. Burack and Gutteridge, see endnote 15, p. 20. R. B. Frantzreb, "Human Resource Planning: Forecasting Manpower Needs," *Personnel Journal,* Nov. 1981, pp. 850–857. N. Scarborough and T. W. Zimmerer, "Human Resources Forecasting: Why and Where to Begin," *Personnel Administrator,* May 1982, pp. 55–61.
38. Walker, see endnote 3. J. W. Walker and R. Armes, "Implementing Management Succession Planning in Diversified Companies," *Human Resource Planning, 2,* 1979, pp. 123–133.
39. Milkovich, Dyer, and Mahoney, see endnote 2. Dyer J. Carnazza, *Succession Replacement Planning: Programs and Practices* (New York: Center for Research in Career Development, Columbia Business School, 1982).
40. G. T. Milkovich and T. A. Mahoney, "Human Resources Planning Models: A Perspective," *Human Resources Planning Journal,* 1978, pp. 19–30.
41. See for example, S. H. Zanski and M. W. Maret, "A Markov Application to Manpower Supply Planning," *Journal of the Operational Research Society, 31,* 1980, pp. 1095–1102. J. F. Gillespie, W. G. Leininger, and H. Kahalas, "A Human Resource Planning and Validation Model," *Academy of Management Journal,* 1976, pp. 650–655.
42. G. T. Milkovich and F. Krystofiak, "Simulation and Affirmative Action Planning," *Human Resource Planning, 2,* 1979, pp. 71–80.
43. W. G. Piskor and R. C. Dudding, "A Computer Assisted Manpower Planning Model," in D. T. Bryant and R. J. Niehaus (eds.), *Manpower Planning and Organization Design* (New York: Plenum Press, 1978), pp. 145–154.
44. E. S. Bres, D. Burns, A. Charnes, and W. W. Cooper, "A Goal Programming Model for Planning Officer Successions," *Management Science, 26,* 1980, pp. 773–782.
45. D. B. Gehrman, "Objective-Based Human Resources Planning," *Personnel Journal,* December, 1981, pp. 942–946.
46. Burack and Gutteridge, endnote 15, p. 18.
47. Burack and Gutteridge cite a 1971 survey, *Corporate Manpower Planning,* conducted by Towers, Perrin, Foster, and Crosby.
48. Note that, in this section, the concern is for the structure-person fit, not the structure-environment fit. For a discussion of the latter, see Galbraith, and Miles, endnote 24. For a discussion of the structure-person fit, see L. Porter, E. E. Lawler III, and J. R. Hackman, *Behavior in Organizations* (New York: McGraw-Hill, 1975); D. Hellriegel, J. W. Slocum, Jr., and D. Woodman, *Organizational Behavior* (4th ed.), (St. Paul: West Publishing Co., 1986); L. F. Schoenfeldt, "Utilization of Manpower: Development and Evaluation of an Assessment-classification Model for Matching Individuals with Jobs," *Journal of Applied Psychology,* 1974, *59,* pp. 583–595.
49. Vetter, see endnote 5, p. 67. L. E. Davis, "Individuals and the Organization," *California Management Review,* Spring, 1980, p. 5.
50. For a discussion of the concerns and issues related to Match 1 and Match 2 (i.e., matching people on the basis of their abilities and reward preferences), see N. Schmidt and B. Schneider, "Current Issues in Personnel Selection," in K. M. Rowland and G. D. Ferris (eds.), *Research in Personnel and Human Resource Management* (Greenwich, CT: JAI Press, 1983). Note that although the term "individual skills, knowledge, and abilities" is used, this also can include other characteristics as well. For example, aptitudes can be included, since organizations do select on the basis of aptitudes, and since some aptitudes may be job-related, as discussed in Chapter 5.
51. L. McDonnell, "Honeywell Ponders Altering Corporate Style," *Minneapolis Tribune,* July 26, 1981.
52. Organizations are becoming aware of the importance of matching job rewards with an individual's personality, interests, and preferences, particularly the latter two. This is because of the growing recognition that an individual behaves in an organization on the basis of ability and motivation. In the past, organizations were concerned about ability. Now they also are becoming concerned about motivation, because employees do not always exhibit desirable behaviours, probably due in part to the fact that individuals' interests and preferences have changed. The influence of these changes on behaviour can be explained by expectancy- and reinforcement-theory concepts. Since these concepts are presented in Chapters 8 and 12, only brief mention is made here. Essentially, people behave in a manner that produces rewards, assuming that they believe they can do what is required to get the rewards. Consequently, if an organization wants its employees to come to work on time, it should reward them for doing so. If the employees believe they can get to work on time, they will try to do so, if the reward (or outcome) is worth it to them. Whether the reward is worth the effort depends on the employees' interests and preferences. Today, organizations are disturbed because some employees are not exhibiting desired behaviours. From a motivation perspective, this may be happening because the outcomes offered by organizations (e.g., pay, promotion, and status) are not as important to many employees as these once were.

Organizations concerned with the employees' changing interests and preferences now are offering different outcomes, such as organizational participation, job control, and job enrichment—all elements of alternative structures. Although this now appears to be working with some employees, organizations must think continually of alternative structures, offering different outcomes that will be seen as rewarding in light of the employees' changing interests and preferences. See also J. R. Gordon, "Using the People/Problem Management Dichotomy," *Personnel Administrator*, March 1983, pp. 51–57.

53. W. Ouchi, "Going from A to Z: Thirteen Steps to a Theory Z Organization," *Management Review*, May 1981, pp. 9–16. W. Ouchi, *Theory Z: How American Business Can Meet the Japanese Challenge* (Reading, MA: Addison-Wesley Publishing Company, 1981). For a Canadian example, see A. M. Jaeger, "The Applicability of Theory Z in Canada: Implications for The Human Resource Function," in Dolan and Schuler (eds.), see endnote 8.

54. P. F. Drucker, "Planning for Redundant Workers," *Personnel Administrator*, Jan. 1980, p. 32. "The Rise in Worker Buy-Outs," *The New York Times*, Feb. 23, 1983, pp. D1, D16.

55. For details, see the entire issue of *QWL Focus, The News Journal of Ontario Quality of Working Life Centre*, vol. 4(1), Spring 1984.

56. "The Unions Press to Cut the Work Week," *Business Week*, Aug. 31, 1981, pp. 60–61.

57. G. H. Cauble, "Alternatives to a Reduction in Force," *Personnel Journal*, June 1982, pp. 424–425. A. L. Otten. "Many Swedes 60 and Older Cut Working Hours Before Retirement Under Government Program," *The Wall Street Journal*, July 6, 1982, p. 46. J. S. Lublin, "More Managers Are Working Part-time: Some Like It, but Others Have No Choice," *The Wall Street Journal*, June 2, 1982, p. 50. N. R. Kleinfield, "A Human Resource at Allied Corp.," *The New York Times*, June 6, 1982, p. 4F. "Casting Executives as Consultants," *Business Week*, Aug. 30, 1982, pp. 46, 51. D. Henriksen, "Outplacement: Program Guidelines that Ensure Success," *Personnel Journal*, Aug. 1982, pp. 583–588.

58. "Helping Employees Through a Major Life Transition," *Behavioral Sciences Newsletter*, Feb. 26, 1981. W. Arnone. "Preretirement Planning: An Employee Benefit that Has Come of Age," *Personnel Journal*, Oct. 1982, pp. 760–762. B. Rosen, T. H. Jerdee, and R. O. Lunn, "Retirement Policies and Management Decisions," *Aging and Work*, Fall 1980, pp. 239–246. J. L. Wall and H. M. Shatshat, "Controversy Over the Issue of Mandatory Retirement," *Personnel Administrator*, Oct. 1981, pp. 25–30, 45. R. Jud, *The Retirement Decision* (New York: Amacom, 1981). M. Lyons, "The Older Employee as a Resource Issue for Personnel," *Personnel Journal*, March 1981, pp. 178–186. F. H. Cassell, "The Increasing Complexity of Retirement Decisions," *MSU Business Topics*, Winter 1978, pp. 15–24. P. Farish, "PAIR Potpourri," *Personnel Administrator*, December 1980, pp. 18–20. A. Finlayson, "The Lure of Early Retirement," *MacLean's*, February 1985, pp. 40–42.

59. Dyer in Rowland and Ferris (eds.), see endnote 2, p. 72.

60. G. S. Odiorne, "HRM Policy and Program Management—A New Look in the Eighties," in Carroll and Schuler (eds.), see endnote 2.

61. J. S. Lublin, "Effects of 'Baby Bust' Are Shrinking Ranks of Younger Workers," *The Wall Street Journal*, Sept. 10, 1981, pp. 1, 16.

62. Statistics Canada, *Population Projections for Canada and the Provinces 1976–2001*, Catalogue no. 91–520 (Ottawa: Department of Industry, Trade, and Commerce, 1979).

63. Statistics Canada, *Women in the Labour Force*, Catalogue no. 89–503E, March 1985.

64. Statistics Canada, census data, Catalogue no. 92–220.

65. D. Dimick, "Survey Report: The Influence of Computers on Human Resource Management in Canada," *Human Resources Management in Canada*, September 1984, Prentice-Hall Canada Inc., pp. 5,251–5,280.

66. Ibid., p. 5,252.

67. "Expectations that Can No Longer Be Met," *Business Week*, June 30, 1980, p. 84. J. Andrew, "In High School Today, Youths Are Absorbed with Material Goals," *The Wall Street Journal*, June 3, 1981, pp. 1, 22. A. Cherns, "Work and Values: Shifting Pattens in Industrial Society," *International Social Science Journal, 32*, 1980, pp. 427–441. R. M. Kanter, "Work in a New America," *Daedalus, Journal of the American Academy of Arts and Sciences, 107*, 1978, pp. 47–77. P. C. Grant, "Why Employee Motivation Has Declined in America," *Personnel Journal*, Dec. 1982, pp. 905–909. R. J. Erickson, "The Changing Workplace and Workforce," *Training and Development Journal*, Jan. 1980, pp. 62–65. P. Parrish, "PAIR Potpourri," *Personnel Administration*, July 1981, pp. 15–16. J. Holt, "Growing Up Engaged," *Psychology Today*, July 1980, pp. 14–16, 23–24. M. Sinetar, "Management in the New Age: An Exploration of Changing Work Value," *Personnel Journal*, Sept. 1980, pp. 749–755. W. H. Schmidt and B. Z. Posner, *Managerial Values and Expectations* (New York: AMACOM, 1982). R. L. Hannah, "The Work Ethics of Coal Miners," *Personnel Journal*, Oct. 1982, pp. 746–751. K. E. Debats, "The Continuing Personnel Challenge," *Personnel Journal*, May 1982, pp. 332–344. D. Yankelovich, "New Rules in American Life: Searching for Self-fulfillment in a World Turned Upside Down," *Psychology Today*, April

1980, pp. 35–91. R. Dubin, "Industrial Workers' Worlds: The 'Central Life Interests' of Industrial Workers," *Social Problems, 3*, 1956, pp. 131–142. R. Dubin, and J. E. Champoux, "Workers' Central Life Interest and Job Performance," *Social Problems, 3*, 1956, pp. 131–142. R. Dubin and J. E. Champoux, "Workers' Central Life Interests and Organizational Commitment of Blue-Collar and Clerical Workers," *Administrative Science Quarterly, 20*, 1975, pp. 411–421. J. W. Walker, "Training and Development," in S. J. Carroll and R. S. Schuler (eds.) *Human Resource Management in the 1980s* (Washington, DC: The Bureau of National Affairs, 1983). G. L. Staines and R. D. Quinn, *The 1977 Quality of Employment Survey* (Ann Arbor, MI: Survey Research Center, University of Michigan, 1977).

68. J. J. Mansell and T. Runkin, "Changing Organizations: The Quality of Working Life Process," *Ontario Quality of Life Centre,* occasional papers, series no. 4, September 1983.

69. J. Holt, "Retirement: A Time to Enjoy or Endure?" *The Personnel Administrator*, Nov. 1979, pp. 69–74. "Working for Life: The New Reality," *The Plain Dealer*, July 15, 1979, section 2, p. 2. J. M. Rosow and R. Zagar, "Work in America Institute's Recommendations Grapple with the Future of the Older Worker," *Personnel Administrator*, April 1980, pp. 77–79. S. R. McConnell, "Alternative Work Options for Older Workers: Part II—The Manager's View," *Aging at Work, 4,* 1981, pp. 81–87.

CHAPTER 3
Job Design and Job Analysis

PHRM in The News

Job Design and Job Analysis
Purposes and Importance of Job Design and Job Analysis
Relationships of Job Design and Job Analysis
Legal Considerations in Job Design and Job Analysis

Job Design
Job Design Qualities
Job Design Approaches
Assessing Job-Design Appropriateness

Job Analysis
Collecting Job Analysis Information
Job Descriptions

Job Analysis Techniques
Job-Focused Techniques
Person-Focused Techniques

Assessing Job-Analysis Methods
Purposes of Job Analysis
Practical Concerns

Assessing Job Design and Job Analysis

Summary

Discussion Questions

Case Study

Endnotes

PHRM in the News

The Electronic Supervisor

The new generation of office computers also makes it possible for employers to monitor what their employees are doing every minute they are on the job. Increasingly, labor and human rights advocates are criticizing that kind of precise and detailed surveillance as a gross invasion of privacy. Unions, including the 13,000-member Brotherhood of Railway and Airline Clerks, oppose matching monitoring as stressful and demoralizing. They charge that computers are too frequently used to discipline workers who are not keeping up with a predetermined pace.

Air Canada reservation clerks form one group that has consistently opposed computer monitoring. In 1970, the airline introduced a computerized booking system and in 1977 initiated electronic monitoring that timed the rate at which employees handled calls. According to the Canadian Air Line Employees' Association (CALEA), which represents the airline's 300 Toronto reservation clerks, the system has meant an average productivity improvement in the Toronto office of four percent per year.

Opponents of the system say that the reservation clerks feel threatened by computerized performance appraisals and believe they suffer from more stress-related illnesses than do other employees. Cheryl Kryzaniwsky, a reservation clerk and a CALEA member, said many of the Toronto employees are so wound up after work "that they cannot relax without a drink, a smoke, or a pill."

In its three-week strike against Air Canada, which ended March 19, 1984, CALEA failed to win its demand that the company cease monitoring the reservation clerks. Air Canada did, however, agree to review the problems that the union said were caused by the practice.

Employers can choose a less threatening approach when installing computerized systems. At Toronto-based Personal Insurance Co. of Canada, which computerized office work in 1979, executive vice-president Hans Johne was determined to avoid the practice of making clerks responsible for just one repetitive function, such as processing all automotive claims in one city. Instead, he made each clerk responsible for a complete range of services for a group of 2,000 policyholders. As well, clerks are never electronically audited. After six years under the new system, Johne reports that staff turnover is below the insurance industry average, while productivity is higher. Added Imperial Oil's Donlevy: "The technology itself is neutral. It is management's decision whether automation will enhance or degrade the quality of working life."

Still, if present trends continue, decisions on automation may be made not just by management, but by the courts. Aubrey Golden, a Toronto trial lawyer who recently computerized his 10-person office, but eliminated all the monitoring systems, said that he expects that computerized surveillance will soon be challenged under federal and provincial employment laws. If he is right, privacy in the workplace will become an even more crucial employment issue.

Source: Diana Swift, "The Electronic Supervisor," (excerpts), *MacLean's*, June 17, 1985, pp. 32–33. Used with permission.

Job Description and Discrimination

A miner who was refused employment because he needed eyeglasses will receive $8162.05 for lost wages plus the offer of another job, following a recent settlement approved by the Canadian Human Rights Commission. In March 1982, Rio Algom Ltd. refused Gaeton Jodouin a job as a timberman in its Elliot Lake mine because he failed to pass the required medical exam. Jodouin was told by the company doctor that the vision in his left eye was extremely poor, but correctable with eyeglasses. Jodouin visited an optometrist the same day, picked up his prescription lenses shortly after, and furnished the company doctor with the appropriate certificates. He was informed several days later that he did not get the job. Medical evidence provided during the investigation indicated that poor vision corrected by glasses would not affect the performance of a timberman in his job. In October 1983, the Commission appointed a conciliator to negotiate the settlement.

Source: Human Resources Management in Canada, Report Bulletin No. 24, 1985, p. 3. © 1986 Prentice-Hall Canada Inc. Reprinted by permission of Prentice-Hall Canada Inc. All rights reserved.

An analysis of any **worker-job interface** suggests that productivity and quality of work life problems are due in part to the way jobs are designed. Several authors have cautioned organizations against installing new technologies to increase productivity without consideration of the human element in the productivity equation.[1] The fear is that organizations will install these technologies the same way that they installed the old technologies, with the result of specialized and repetitive jobs for the workers. And although workers *then* performed those jobs, it appears that many workers *now* do not want to perform them, partly because the jobs are not interesting to them and they fail to provide workers with a sense of meaningfulness, responsibility, personal control, and challenge.

In addition to considering how workers may respond psychologically to their jobs—the extent to which they experience meaningfulness, responsibility, personal control, and challenge—consideration in job design should also be given to the potential physical compatibility between workers and jobs.

Once the jobs are designed, they must be filled by individuals who have the skills, knowledge, and abilities to perform them.[2] Knowing whether or not they have these attributes requires analysis of the jobs. Tests then can be developed that predict how well individuals are likely to perform the important aspects of specific jobs.

Job Design and Job Analysis

Many of the functions and activities of personnel and human resource management and the behaviour and attitudes of employees have their roots at the interface of employees and their jobs. As indicated in Exhibit 3.1, job analysis influences recruitment, selection, compensation, training and development, and performance appraisal. In turn, job analysis is a consequence of the way jobs are designed. The job design is influenced by several organizational qualities and union-management relationships.

Job design results in a set of purposes, task characteristics, and task duties in a given organizational setting, based on a set of unique organizational and personnel qualities. Job design is a creation-oriented task. **Job analysis** is the process of describing and recording several job aspects including the purposes, task characteristics, task duties, behaviour, and requisite skills and abilities in a given organizational setting.[3] Job analysis is a research-oriented task. Job analysis often results in two principal items: a **job description** and a **job specification**, as shown in Exhibit 3.1. These can be used in recruitment, selection, performance appraisal, compensation, and training.

This definition of job analysis suggests that job descriptions should contain more than a statement of the duties, conditions, and purposes of a job. They also should contain a description of the characteristics of the job, although generally this is no longer done. This definition also suggests that job specifications should contain more than an outline of the traditional set of skills, knowledge, and abilities necessary to perform the job duties successfully under the given condition. Job specifications should also contain a description of individual preferences, interests, and personality traits that might best be served by the job.

These two modifications of the traditional job description and job specification are in keeping with the concern for attaining two of the three major organizational human resource purposes of PHRM: high productivity and a high quality of work life. The other major purpose of PHRM—complying with legal regulations—is served in part simply by doing the job analysis. This chapter's section on job design explains how these modifications help to attain the two purposes and why such modifications are becoming necessary.

Purposes and Importance of Job Design and Job Analysis

Of the many purposes served by job design, the primary ones are to

- increase employee motivation;
- increase productivity and the quality of work life;
- serve as an alternative to promotion in career development;
- accommodate more women in traditionally male jobs; and
- make jobs available for older people, handicapped people, minorities, and native people.

It is becoming apparent that job design really does serve these purposes, which is making job design more important than ever before. Much of the work currently being done in organizations to improve productivity and the

Job Design and Job Analysis Relationship — Exhibit 3.1

Organizational qualities
- Technology
- Goals
- Design

Personnel qualities
- Union-management relations
- Philosophy
- Assumptions

Job-design qualities
- Characteristics
- Duties
- Purposes

Productivity | Job analysis | Quality of work life

Job specifications
- Skills
- Knowledge
- Ability

Job description
- Duties
- Characteristics
- Conditions
- Purposes
- Standards

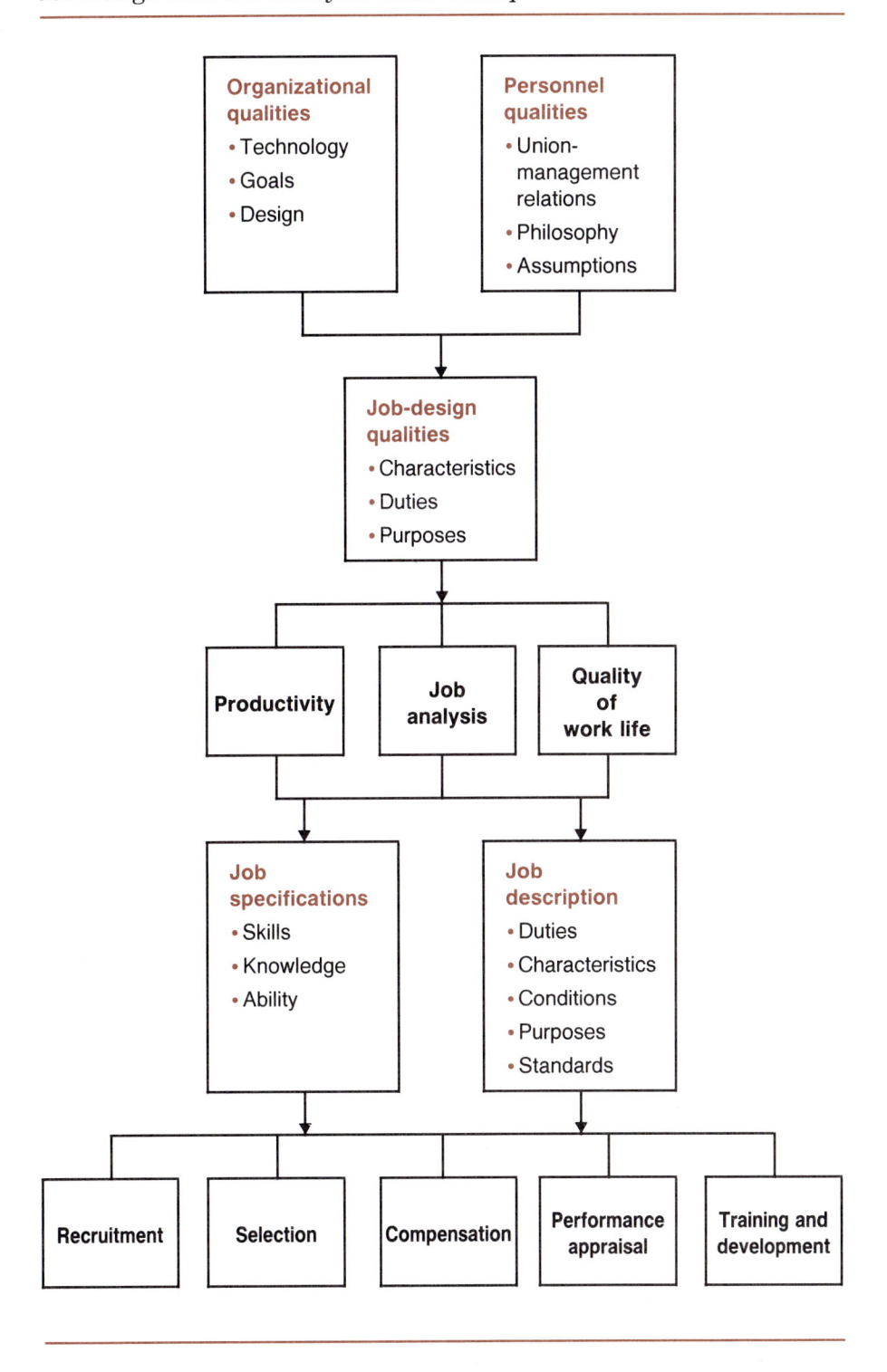

Recruitment | Selection | Compensation | Performance appraisal | Training and development

quality of work life is aimed at changing the workers' jobs, either by enriching individual jobs or by creating teams. This is being done in part because the results of assembly-line-type technology in offices and plants are worker boredom, alienation, high turnover, absenteeism, and lower productivity. Although many workers may still prefer assembly-line-type jobs, job-design knowledge is critical for effective PHRM. Because job design does relate to productivity and the quality of work life, it is discussed again in Chapter 13 in terms of job redesign to improve productivity and the quality of work life.[4]

As shown in Exhibit 3.1, job analysis is the basis of job descriptions and job specifications. While job analysis is necessary for making valid employment decisions such as selection, promotion, and performance appraisal determination, it also serves several other purposes including:

- Determining the relative worth of jobs, which is necessary to maintain external and internal pay equity
- Ensuring that companies do not discriminate and provide equal work opportunities, as legislated by various human rights Acts
- Aiding the supervisor and employee in defining the duties and responsibilities of each
- Providing a justification for the existence of the job and where it fits into the rest of the organization
- Determining the recruitment needs (when used together with the human resource planning needs discussed in Chapter 2) and providing the information necessary to make employment decisions
- Serving as the basis for establishing career development programs and paths for employees
- Serving as a means by which to convey to potential job applicants what will be expected of them, the general working conditions, and the types of individual preferences that the job may satisfy [5]

In addition to these many purposes, the importance of job analysis is enhanced by its extensive set of systemic relationships.

Relationships of Job Design and Job Analysis

Both job design and job analysis have extensive relationships with other PHRM activities, as well as with the goals and characteristics of the organization in general.

Organizational Goals and Technology. The design of jobs not only reflects the design and technology of the organization, but also its goals. Jobs are, in fact, very explicit statements by organizations of what they have determined to be the most appropriate means for accomplishing their goals. Furthermore, the stated goals and the subsequent standards of excellence that an organization establishes give clear cues to employees about what is important and where their efforts are required.

Since goals help to determine the products and environments of organizations, these goals also help to determine the criteria against which the behaviour of workers will be evaluated. The criteria and goals, in turn, also determine the kinds of individuals who will be attracted to the organization, evaluated highly, and promoted. Thus, organizational goals can help establish the reasons for jobs, the nature of the organization's expectations from the workers performing the jobs, and even the legitimacy of the job demands. Goals have several other consequences through their relationship with the structure of the organization, which is in turn related to the design of jobs.[6]

The type of technology being used by, and available for, an organization is also critical because it determines what types of job designs are possible and what types of jobs are appropriate for various organizational designs. For example, Canadian automobile manufacturers, with huge investments in plants and machinery to make cars on assembly lines, find it almost impossible to convert their car-making technology so that a group of workers could make one car in its entirety. The result is that most assembly jobs remain fairly segmented and repetitive. Furthermore, assembly-line technology determines the structure or design of the organization and, in turn, the most appropriate types of job designs.

Union-Management Relationships. Given that almost 40% of the Canadian workforce is unionized, union influence of employees is a major consideration. Without union support, organizations find it almost impossible to change the design of jobs. This is because job design can influence job classification—a critical concern for unions. In Chapters 13 and 17, the benefits that result when union and management work together in changing jobs to improve the quality of work life and productivity are discussed. These joint union-management efforts can become examples for non-union organizations, which might be well advised to seek union input when making job-design changes.

Recruitment and Selection. Without job analysis, in conjunction with HRP, the organization would be unable to specify what types of job applicants are needed, and when and where they are needed. This in turn could have negative consequences for organizational productivity and the validity of its selection procedures and decisions. Only with job-analysis information can an organization demonstrate specifically that its selection procedures are job-related.

Job design may become more important in recruitment and selection as the percentage of middle-age employees bulges in the 1990s. As described in Chapter 2, the number of middle-age employees is growing faster than the number of middle-manager jobs. Consequently, many employees will not receive expected promotions and will become frustrated. To deal with this frustration, organizations may need to redesign jobs to provide employees with challenge and growth despite the lack of promotion.

Appraising Performance and Training. To evaluate employee performance effectively, the appraisal method used must reflect the important aspects of the job (this relationship is discussed again in Chapter 7). Only by examining the skills required for a job, as defined in the job specifications, can the organization train and promote employees in conjunction with its human resource needs.

Compensation. Job analysis also plays a vital role in compensation activities. It is on the basis of job analysis that a job is evaluated. Since job evaluation determines the value of a job to the organization, it is often used to help determine how much an employee should be paid for doing that job. Job analysis also is important in ensuring that the level of pay for a job is fair in relation to other jobs, that employees in jobs of equal worth receive equal pay. It also can be used to provide insights into the comparable-worth considerations discussed in Chapter 9.

Legal Considerations in Job Design and Job Analysis

Today, the legal need for selection tests and performance appraisal that accurately predict job performance has made job analysis much more important. The various federal and provincial human rights legislations admonish the personnel specialist to do a thorough job analysis before selecting a personnel test or developing a measure of job performance.

Specific requirements will be discussed in more detail in the next three chapters, but one main requirement is that selection devices should be **content valid**. This means that test items should represent the actual on-the-job behaviour being measured. A case in point is the miner who was refused employment because he needed eyeglasses and therefore did not pass the physical examinations that were called for during the selection process (see "PHRM in the News"). Medical evidence in this case proved that poor vision corrected by glasses would not hinder his performance of this type of job.

Job Design

Because job design is concerned with job characteristics, duties, and purposes, the results of job design have a profound influence on employee productivity and the quality of work life. Unfortunately, this influence can be negative, for example when it results in employee boredom, absenteeism, and sabotage. On the other hand, this influence can be positive if it leads to feelings of greater achievement, responsibility, challenge, and meaningfulness. How would you design a job so that an employee would feel positive about it and motivated by it? An understanding of job-design qualities can make this task easier to perform. Chapter 13 also provides examples of how job-design qualities have been used to produce beneficial effects, such as increased employee satisfaction and job involvement, and lowered absenteeism and turnover.[7]

Job Design Qualities

As shown in Exhibit 3.1, there are three job design qualities—**characteristics, duties**, and **purposes**.

Characteristics. There are several critical job design characteristics.[8] These are

- **skill variety:** The degree to which a job requires a variety of different activities in carrying out the work, involving the use of a number of different skills and talents;
- **job significance:** The degree to which a job has substantial importance on the lives of other people, whether those people are in the immediate organization or in the world at large;
- **job identity:** The degree to which a job requires completion of a whole and identifiable piece of work—doing a job from beginning to end with a visible outcome;
- **autonomy:** The degree to which a job provides substantial freedom, independence, and discretion to the individual in scheduling the work and in determining the procedures to be used in carrying it out;
- **job feedback:** The degree to which carrying out the work activities required by the job provides the individual with direct and clear information about the effectiveness of his or her performance;
- **cognitive job elements:** These represent the elements or specific parts of a job, such as communicating, decision making, analyzing, information processing;
- **physical job elements:** These represent the specific parts of a job, such as lifting, lighting, colouring, sound, speed, and positioning;[9]
- **job overload:** There are two types of job overload. **Quantitative job overload** results when all duties cannot be performed in the allotted time. **Qualitative job overload** results when the employee is expected to perform duties that require more skills and abilities than the employee has;
- **role overload:** Performance in some jobs (for example, selling and managing) requires extensive interaction with other people. To the extent that there are too many other people with whom to interact, an employee experiences **quantitative role overload**. If these interactions require more skill and abilities than the employee has, **qualitative role overload** results; and
- **role underload:** As with role overload, performance in some jobs requires extensive interaction with others. A limited amount of this interaction is referred to as **quantitative role underload**. If this interaction requires a limited number of the employee's skills and abilities, then **qualitative role underload** exists.[10]

The importance of these characteristics is their association singly or in combination with several outcomes. For example, by themselves, the physical job elements help determine who can perform a job. Therefore, jobs can be more or less accessible to all job applicants, based on their physical job elements. In combination, several of these characteristics may influence employee motivation, performance, absenteeism, and turnover. For instance, the first five characteristics have been shown to be related to those employee outcomes through the impact of the characteristics on critical psychological states of employees, as shown in Exhibit 3.2.[11]

Duties. The specific activities and behaviours that comprise the job are called duties. Note that different employees may engage in different behaviour in carrying out a duty. For example, in reference to the job description of the animal keeper shown in Exhibit 3.3, one keeper could clean a cage from front to back, using a broom, and not leave a trace of debris, while another could clean a cage from back to front, using a mop, and leave slight traces of debris. The job description shown in Figure 3.3 illustrates other specific duties or activities that together form the essence of the animal keeper's job. As described later in this chapter, these duties are generally derived from the job analysis.

Purposes. The critical aspect of a job is the reason for its creation and its existence. Why does the job exist? How and why does it relate to the final product or goal of the organization? The design of a job whose purpose is to contribute only a small part of the total product of an organization will be very different from that of a job whose purpose is to contribute a large part to the total product. The former job may be designed into small, simple segments with minimal job identity and skill variety. The latter job may be designed into larger, more complex segments, with greater job identity and skill variety. As mentioned earlier, job design is also influenced by organizational goals, largely through their impact on the job-design approach selected.

Exhibit 3.2   *The Impact of the Core Job Characteristics on Employee Psychological States*

Core Job Characteristics	Critical Psychological States	Outcomes
Skill variety Job identity Job significance	Experienced meaningfulness of the work	Less absenteeism Less turnover
Autonomy	Experienced responsibility for outcomes of the work	High internal work motivation
Feedback from job	Knowledge of the actual results of the work activities	High quality of performance

Source: Adapted from J. R. Hackman and G. R. Oldham, *Work Redesign*, © 1980 (Reading, MA: Addison-Wesley, 1980), p. 77. Reprinted with permission.

| Position Description—Animal Keeper—WG=9 (Wage Grade) | Exhibit 3.3 |

Introduction

This position is located in the Office of Animal Management, The Zoological Park, and is directly supervised by the Curator of the assigned unit.

The function of the keeper is to perform the described duties, most of which require specialized skills that result in the proper care, feeding, exhibition, and propagation of a collection of wild and exotic animals, many of whom are rare and endangered. The keeper is also responsible for maintaining a presentable exhibit so that the animal may be shown to the public in an attractive setting. At this level, one is considered a journeyman in the craft of animal care.

All duties are performed in accordance with established policies and procedures of the Office of Animal Management. The incumbent is informed of any changes governing policies and procedures by the Animal Manager and/or Curator, who are available for consultation when new or unusual problems arise. Assignment areas will normally include any or all cages and enclosures in the assigned unit. The keeper receives technical supervision and daily work assignments from the Animal Manager of an assigned section of the unit.

Duties

1. Cleaning of animal enclosures, including hosing, sweeping, scrubbing, raking, and removal and disposal of manure, unconsumed food, and other refuse.
2. Maintenance of enclosure materials, such as trimming and watering of plants, and cleaning and maintenance of perches, nest boxes, feed containers, and decorative materials, and provision of nesting and bedding material.
3. Feeding and watering of all animals, including measurement and preparation of feed items and prepared diets, placement in feed pans or other containers, and timely distribution and placement in animal enclosures.

    Cleaning of service areas and of public areas adjacent to the animal enclosures.
5. Inspection of all animals at specific times to ensure security of animals in proper enclosures and to assure prompt reporting of illness or abnormal behaviour.

For these routine duties, the incumbent will adhere to standard operating procedures including lists of mandatory daily duties and the normal order and time in which they should be completed. Incumbent confers at all times with the Animal Manager of the assigned section when problem situations arise.

Prepares report on daily or periodic basis, as instructed, to be presented to the Animal Manager while working on an assigned line. May be asked to note and record relevant observations on animals and record these on the daily report. Examples, such as breeding encounters, nesting activity, courtship rituals, aggression between cage mates, feeding by offspring, would be considered relevant. The keeper may be expected to learn and be familiar with the terminology used in keeping the records, such as common names or scientific names of animals.

Maintains a close watch over the animals in the collection for symptoms of sickness, injury, or other unusual conditions and reports information to the Animal Manager and/or Curator or, in their absence, to the Veterinarian. When it is necessary, the keeper will capture, handle, crate, uncrate, transport, mark, force feed, or restrain any animal in the assigned area. This will involve aiding the Veterinarian in administering treatment to animals, or under instructions from the Animal Manager, independently giving prescribed medicines to an animal, administering first aid, and feeding and hand-rearing newborn or abnormal animals.

Continued on next page

Exhibit 3.3   Continued

The keeper will, in accordance with specifications, prepare the animal diets for all the animals in the assigned area when called upon to do so. The keeper will increase or decrease the diets as instructed by the Animal Manager and/or Curator and may recommend changes in feed and feeding sites from observations to the Animal Manager and/or Curator. All animals must be given water as required.

At this journeyman level, the keeper will use proper nest boxes, nest materials, and nest sites in attempting to get animals to breed and raise young. Uses proper techniques of young animal care, including correct methods of collecting and incubating eggs with special regard to preventing injury to the animals. The keeper may be asked to aid or participate in projects carried out by other NZP offices that involve the scientific study of the collection. The keeper may either under the supervision of the Curator, Animal Manager, or others, actively carry out an independent study project on the collection animals.

Incumbent assists Animal Manager in the development and construction of new exhibits. May be asked to collect exhibit materials such as logs, rocks, sand, dirt, and gravel. The keeper also monitors conditions of all exhibits in an assigned section, including plants and foliage, perches, logs, nesting boxes, and substrate materials. Maintains the exhibits in an assigned section in a clean and orderly condition.

The incumbent may be asked to train and instruct lower grade employees in any or all of the above duties assigned to the WG–9 animal keeper. Examples, such as animal husbandry techniques, understanding of the animals in an assigned section, and the zoological principles involved, as well as operating procedures.

Must be familiar with all safety, first aid, and emergency equipment and procedures in the unit. The keeper must be familiar with security procedures for all areas of the section, to prevent animal escapes, injury to visitors, and malicious damage to the animals.

Make recommendations to supervisors regarding establishment or modification of procedures that will make the unit more effective in reaching its objectives.

The keeper may be required to drive an automobile, scooter, or small truck, to do incidental driving such as transporting animals to other zoos, to depots of public transportation, or to the Conservation Centre.

May be required to work any assigned eight-hour shift during the 24–hours of operation and is subject to call at any time. Must be available for duty on weekends and holidays.

May be asked to pass the SI scuba diving certification test, so that aquatic vertebrate pools can be cleaned. On a routine basis, is required to mix and add chemicals to the filter systems for these pools.

Performs other related duties as assigned.

Physical Requirements and Conditions:

This position requires considerable walking, standing, heavy lifting up to 100 pounds, stooping, and other types of physical effort and dexterity in moving and distributing animals, animal feed, cage materials, equipment, and in opening and closing cage doors and gates. Although safety measures are taken, there is always a hazard of injury in working with exotic and unpredictable animals.

Incumbent will be required to work both indoors and outdoors during all types of weather, and may be required to work in areas that are hot, cold, dusty, odorous, or with high humidity, as well as in closed areas and cramped spaces.

Job-Design Approaches

Jobs can be designed in many different ways, four of which are discussed here. Other methods of designing jobs are essentially combinations of these four. Alternative job-design approaches differ primarily in regard to the three job design qualities. The four major job-design approaches to be discussed are **scientific** (traditional), **individual contemporary, team contemporary**, and **ergonomic**.

Scientific. Under the scientific approach, job analysts (typically, industrial engineers) took special pains to design jobs so that the tasks performed by employees did not exceed their abilities. In fact, the jobs designed by scientific management often resulted in work being partitioned into small, simple segments. These tasks lent themselves well to time and motion studies and to incentive pay systems, each for the purpose of obtaining high productivity. Scientifically designed jobs have been and still are important parts of many present organizational structures. The scientific approach to job design reflects the assumption that workers generally dislike work and are motivated only by economic rewards. Generally, the use of scientific design results in jobs with minimal levels of variety, significance, autonomy, feedback, and identity. Since the jobs are so small as a result of a high division of labour, they often have a qualitative underload and a narrow purpose. The only reward that employees received under scientific job design was monetary.

It soon became evident, however, that many workers did not like jobs designed according to the dictates of scientific management. In effect, the person-job relationship had been arranged so that achieving the goals of the organization (high productivity) often meant sacrificing important personal goals (the opportunity for interesting, personally challenging work).[12]

Organizations continued to treat the design of the job as inviolate, something not to be changed. Methods were developed to select people who would be satisfied with economic rewards and jobs with simple segments. It is not hard to understand why the success of this strategy was somewhat short-lived. As suggested in Chapter 2, some employees, although by no means all, appear to prefer jobs that involve some responsibility and autonomy, as well as good pay. Organizations have responded by designing jobs in other ways as part of creating alternative organizational structures.

Individual Contemporary. This approach and the team contemporary approach strive to achieve high productivity without incurring the human costs that are sometimes associated with the scientific approach. There are three individual contemporary job-design approaches: **job rotation, job enlargement**, and **job enrichment**.

Job rotation really does not change the nature of a specific job. However, it often does increase the number of duties that an employee performs, because the employee moves from one job to another after a specified period of time. The nature of each job's task characteristics may or may not be varied. It is reasonable, however, to assume that an *employee's* sense of identity and scope of purpose increases because he or she is performing several jobs.

Job enlargement differs from rotation by adding more duties to a specific job rather than by moving an employee around to experience the duties of several jobs. While the scientific approach seeks to reduce the number of duties, job enlargement seeks to increase this number. The characteristics of the duties, however, may be very similar.

Job enrichment differs from job enlargement by seeking to load a job vertically rather than horizontally. **Horizontal loading** means adding more duties with the same types of characteristics. **Vertical loading** means creating a job with duties with many different characteristics, for example, job identity, job significance, autonomy, feedback, and skill variety. The impact of this job enrichment design is illustrated in Exhibit 3.2 and discussed further in Chapter 13.

Team Contemporary. While the individual contemporary and scientific approaches design jobs for *individuals*, the team contemporary approach designs jobs for *teams of individuals*.[13] The final designs generally show a concern for the social needs of individuals as well as the constraints of the technology. In the team contemporary approach, teams of workers often rotate jobs and may follow the product they are working on from the beginning to the end of the production process. If the product is large, for example an automobile, teams may be designed around sections of the final car. Each group then completes only a section and passes its sub-product on to the next team. In the team contemporary design, each worker learns to handle several duties, many requiring different skills. Thus, the workers can satisfy their needs for achievement and task accomplishment and some needs for social interaction.

Two other techniques often associated with the team contemporary design are **group gain sharing** and **participation in decision making**. When faced with decisions, teams generally try to involve all members. If their decision and behaviour results in greater output, all team members share in the dollar benefits. Although individual employees also can be given increased participation, it is not generally considered to be part of individual job design as often as it is under a team contemporary approach.

Ergonomic. This approach is concerned with trying to design and shape jobs to fit the physical abilities and characteristics of individuals so that they can perform the jobs. The ergonomic approach is being used by organizations to redesign certain jobs to accommodate women and handicapped individuals. Often, this serves equal-employment-opportunity, affirmative-action objectives. It also is used in relation to retirement-alternative programs.[14]

Additionally, ergonomics can help organizations meet their legal obligations, as well as to better utilize their workforces. It has been shown that when jobs are designed along ergonomic principles, worker productivity is greater. In a U.S. study done by the National Institute of Occupational Safety and Health, two groups of employees working under an incentive-pay system were compared. The group working in ergonomically effective jobs were 25% more productive than the group working on the jobs designed without use of ergonomic principles. The Institute, along with several unions, also is actively involved in redesigning jobs, using ergonomic principles, to help reduce the incidence and severity of **carpal tunnel syndrome**. This syndrome is characterized by numbness, tingling, soreness, and weakness in the hands and wrists. It is caused or aggravated by jobs requiring repetitive hand motions. Redesigning jobs to eliminate these motions is being done successfully by companies such as Armco Inc. and the Hanes Corporation, using ergonomic principles.[15]

West Germany is engaged in considerable work in the area of ergonomics (see Chapter 18), and is considered to be the world leader in modifying assembly lines and increasing the workers' job cycle to minimize physical and mental strain and increase productivity.[16] Ergonomics, however, is not a panacea for an organization's legal employment obligations. In fact, not one of the four job-design approaches is a panacea for all of the purposes of job design. A summary assessment of the advantages and disadvantages of these four job approaches is shown in Exhibit 3.4. These are useful in assessing job-design appropriateness.

A Summary of Some of the Advantages and Disadvantages of the Four Job-Design Approaches

Exhibit 3.4

Approach	Advantages	Disadvantages
Scientific	Ensures predictability Provides clarity Fits abilities of many people Can be efficient and productive	May be boring May result in absenteeism, sabotage, and turnover
Individual Contemporary	Satisfies needs for responsibility, growth, and knowledge of results Provides growth opportunity Reduces boredom Increases quality and morale Lower turnover	Some people prefer routine and predictability May need to pay more since more skills needed Hard to enrich some jobs Not everyone wants to rotate
Team Contemporary	Provides social interaction Provides variety Facilitates social support Reduces absenteeism problem	People may not want interaction Requires training in interpersonal skills Group no better than weakest member
Ergonomic	Accommodates jobs to people Breaks down physical barriers Makes more jobs accessible to more people	May be costly to redesign some jobs Structural characteristics of the organization may make job change impossible

Assessing Job-Design Appropriateness

In Chapters 1 and 2, the concern that many people have for what they see as a decline in the productivity and the quality of work life in North American companies is discussed in detail. In trying to explain this phenomenon, many people point to the design of the jobs in organizations and their relationship with changing workforce values. They claim that most jobs are too simple and repetitive. Furthermore, many workers could do a lot more than they are now doing, and could be using more skills. Organizations, however, should resist the temptation to overcompensate for this by designing jobs with more complexity before analyzing the appropriateness of each job-design approach. Failure to analyze the characteristics of both the individuals and the organization may result in the selection of an inappropriate job design.[17] Consequently, these characteristics are reviewed here.

Personal Characteristics. Knowledge of an individual's characteristics is critical in determining an appropriate and feasible job design. If jobs are to be enriched successfully, employees must have the knowledge relevant to doing the new tasks. If the contemporary team approach is selected, employees will need interpersonal and problem-solving skills in order to work effectively as a group. Without these skills, the scientific approach may be more feasible and appropriate. Ergonomics may be the approach of choice if employees lack the physical strength or size to do a particular job. The way to determine whether the employees or job applicants have these skills, knowledge, and abilities is by testing (discussed further in Chapter 5).

Working on enriched jobs or in teams does not satisfy everyone, just as working on specialized, repetitive jobs is not boring and dull for everyone. Enriched jobs usually help satisfy individual personality, interest, and preference factors by providing more challenge, responsibility, and a sense of meaningfulness. Jobs designed using a group approach may satisfy some of the personality, interest, and preference needs, including the need for social interaction and support. Only those individuals with growth needs (e.g., knowledge of results, responsibility, and meaningfulness) are likely to exhibit the outcomes of job enrichment.[18] It may be useful then to match individuals with jobs on the basis of their skills, knowledge, and abilities, and personality, interests, and preferences.[19]

One way to measure individuals' personalities, interests, and preferences would be to administer the growth-need strength questionnaire shown in Exhibit 5.5 (Chapter 5). Another way is to administer the job-activity preference questionnaire, which measures individual preferences on 150 job elements, four of which are shown in Exhibit 3.5.[20] Other ways may include the personality measures and interest tests described in Chapter 5. Because of the limited research in this area, statements regarding the use of personality, interest, and preference factors and matching these factors with job rewards should be regarded as suggestions and areas requiring more systematic attention. To a lesser extent, the same is true for skill, knowledge, and ability factors, as suggested in Chapter 5.

Job Elements of the Work Preference Questionnaire

Exhibit 3.5

How *important* would you like each of the following job elements (job activities) to be in your work? Use the rating scale in giving your responses. Your total response score suggests how much you would prefer a job with these elements.

Rating Scale
0 No importance
1 Very minor
2 Low
3 Average
4 High
5 Extreme importance

I. Perceptual Interpretation

_____ 1. Using colour perception (telling the difference between things by colour)
_____ 2. Recognizing sound patterns (Morse code, heartbeats, etc.)
_____ 3. Recognizing sounds by loudness, pitch, or tone quality (tuning pianos, repairing sound systems, etc.)
_____ 4. Estimating speed of moving parts (rpm of a motor, speed of lathes, etc.)
_____ 5. Estimating speed of moving objects (vehicles, materials on conveyor belt, etc.)
_____ 6. Estimating speed of processes (chemical reactions, assembly operations, timing of food preparation, etc.)

☐ Total (your score on Dimension I)

II. Information Processing

_____ 7. Combining information (combining information, as to prepare weather report, to fly a plane, etc.)
_____ 8. Analyzing information (interpreting financial reports, determining why an engine will not run, diagnosing an illness, etc.)
_____ 9. Gathering, grouping, or classifying information (preparing reports, filing correspondence, etc.)
_____ 10. Coding or decoding (receiving Morse code, translating languages, shorthand, etc.)

☐ Total (your score on Dimension II)

III. Handling and Manipulating Activities

_____ 11. Arranging or positioning (placing objects, materials, etc., in a specific position or arrangement)
_____ 12. Physically handling objects, materials, etc.
_____ 13. Feeding/off-bearing (feeding materials into a machine or removing materials from a machine or piece of equipment)
_____ 14. Hand-arm manipulation (activities involving hand and arm movements, as in repairing automobiles, packaging products, etc.)

☐ Total (your score on Dimension III)

Continued on next page

Exhibit 3.5 Continued

IV. Communication of Decisions and Judgements

_____ 15. Advising (using legal, financial, scientific, clinical, spiritual, or other professional principles to counsel individuals)

_____ 16. Negotiating (dealing with others to reach an agreement or solution, i.e., labour bargaining, diplomatic relations, etc.)

_____ 17. Persuading (as in selling, political campaigning, etc.)

_____ 18. Teaching

_____ 19. Exchanging routine information (giving and receiving routine information as by ticket agent, taxi dispatcher, etc.)

_____ 20. Interviewing

_____ 21. Exchanging specialized information (as in a professional committee meeting, or when discussing a product design, etc.)

_____ 22. Public speaking

_____ 23. Writing (letters, reports, newspaper articles, etc.)

☐ Total (your score on Dimension IV)

Source: Reproduced with permission from *Workbook for Industrial Psychology*, E. J. McCormick, J. Tiffin, and J. R. Terbory, 1974. Job Elements of the Work Preference Questionnaire (WPQ) (formerly the Job Activity Preference Questionnaire [JAPQ]) is copyrighted by R. C. Mecham, A. F. Harris, E. J. McCormick, and P. R. Jeanneret, and is based in part on the *Position Analysis Questionnaire* (PAQ), which is copyrighted by the Purdue Research Foundation, Lafayette, IN.

Organizational Technological Systems, PHRM Practices, and Control Systems. The **technological system** of an organization refers to the machines, methods, and materials that are used to produce the organization's product.[21] The type of technology can strongly influence the job-design approach used. The assembly line is often used as an example of a technology that involves extremely repetitive and very simple jobs. Jobs that skilled workers and some managers perform generally are the opposite of assembly-line jobs. Both skilled workers and managers often can control the pace of their work and use a variety of skills.

Organizations sometimes can make the same product using very different types of technology. For example, in the manufacture of automobiles, General Motors, Ford, and Chrysler traditionally have chosen to use the assembly line. Volvo in Sweden, on the other hand, does not use an assembly line.[22] Volvo's switch in technologies had a major impact on the rest of the organization. Thus, in diagnosing the technological system, it is important to recognize (1) its impact on job design; (2) the variety of technologies that actually can be used in making a product; and (3) the organization's philosophy about its human resources.

PHRM practices in organizations generally are designed to provide fair and consistent treatment of workers. To ensure this, fixed job descriptions are written that often specify what a worker should do, as well as the methods the worker should use. These descriptions also specify the skills and abilities needed by workers. In turn, these descriptions and specifications are used in choosing selection tests and performance appraisal devices, in designing training programs, and in the important area of determining pay levels for jobs. These diverse areas all are affected when jobs are redesigned. Since these areas are usually under the control of different personnel specialists, they all have to be convinced of the need for the job-design change. Once they are convinced, their efforts must be co-ordinated. Without their support and co-ordination, any job-design effort is unlikely to be adopted or to succeed.

Control systems also can stand in the way of an organization adopting a new job design or a particular type of design. Control systems include such things as production and quality-control reports, scrap reports, attendance reports, and time sheets.[23] Because it is important to locate who is responsible for problems or errors, control systems often specify who is accountable, how things should be done, and from whom to get approval for doing something differently.

Although this helps reduce the complexity of each job and the responsibility of each worker, the effect is to set up impersonal boundaries. The boundaries then become critical in determining the way people behave and what they will do. Have you ever heard someone say, "I'm not responsible for that"?

To change control systems is just as difficult as changing personnel practices. Yet both of these need to be changed to facilitate job-design changes. Furthermore, particular types of job designs are unlikely to be adopted, given the philosophies of key decision makers. For example, if the top management or owners want to retain close control, or if they really do not think employees can act responsibly, it is likely that they will choose the scientific approach to job design rather than one of the contemporary approaches.

Summary. Although we are not prescribing which approach to job design an organization should select, many are considering one of the contemporary forms. Examples of some current programs are described in Chapter 13. Keep in mind that there are many other ways that PHRM can improve organizations: new spatial arrangement, new furniture, new compensation programs, and different selection and training programs, are several methods alternative to job-design changes. If the jobs are redesigned, they must also be re-analyzed. Although this process is costly, it is critical.

Job Analysis

As indicated earlier, job analysis serves many purposes in PHRM. Obviously, before any job can be analyzed, job analysis information must be obtained.

Collecting Job Analysis Information

Job analysis is the process of describing and recording many aspects of jobs. The aspects that can be described and recorded vary greatly (see Exhibit 3.6), often depending on the purposes to be served. Typically, information is collected by someone in the PHRM department in co-operation with a supervisor. Increasingly, it is becoming more common (and is less expensive) for the person currently doing the job to provide job information. Often a combination of the two is used. The method of information collection, the type of information collected, how it is used, and who has the final responsibility for compiling the results, often depends on whether the jobs and individuals are *exempt* or *non-exempt* (these terms are explained in Chapter 9).

Methods of Gathering. There are perhaps as many methods for gathering information as there are job aspects to describe. Some methods are (1) observation; (2) interviews with the job incumbent(s); (3) conferences with job analyst/experts; (4) observations by job analysts; (5) diaries kept by the job incumbent(s); (6) structured and unstructured questionnaires filled out by the incumbent(s) or observers such as the supervisor or job analyst; (7) critical incidents written by incumbent(s) or others who know the job; and (8) mechanical devices such as stop-watches, counters, and films.[24] The major outcome of the data-gathering phase of the job analysis is the job description.

Job Descriptions

Ideally, job descriptions should be detailed enough that the reader can understand (1) what is to be done (the domains, behaviour, duties, and the results); (2) what products are to be generated (the purposes of the job); (3) what work standards are applied (such as quality and quantity); (4) under what conditions the job will be performed; and (5) the task characteristics of the job.[25] Note that the task characteristics are included in order that individuals might select and be placed on jobs that match or suit their personality, interests, and preferences.

Typically, a single job description lists several aspects of a job along with the necessary skills, knowledge, and abilities. In total, a job description is likely to include:

- Job or payroll title
- Job number and job group to which the job belongs (as a result of job evaluation and for compensation purposes)
- Department and/or division where the job is located
- Name of the incumbent (optional) and name of the job analyst
- Primary function or summary of the job
- Description of the major duties and responsibilities of the job, sometimes with a percentage of time for each duty

Types of Information Obtained through Job Analysis

Exhibit 3.6

Work Activities Job-oriented activities (usually expressed in terms of what is accomplished; sometimes indicating how, why, and when a worker performs the activity)
- work activities/processes
- procedures used
- activity records (films, etc.)
- personal accountability/responsibility

Worker-oriented activities
- human behaviours performed in work (sensing, decision making, performing physical actions, communicating, etc.)
- elemental motions (such as those used in methods analysis)
- personal job demands (energy expenditure, etc.)

Machines, Tools, Equipment, and Word Aids Used

Job-Related Tangibles and Intangibles
- Materials processed
- Products made
- Knowledge dealt with or applied (such as law or chemistry)
- Services rendered (such as laundering or repairing)

Work Performance
- Work measurement (time taken)
- Work standards
- Error analysis
- Other aspects

Job Context
- Physical working conditions
- Work schedule
- Organizational context
- Social context
- Incentives (financial and non-financial)

Personal Requirements Job-related knowledge/skills (education, training, work experience, etc.) Personal attributes (aptitudes, physical characteristics, personality, interests, etc.)

Source: Adapted from E. J. McCormick, "Job and Task Analysis," in M. D. Dunnette (ed.), *Handbook of Industrial and Organizational Psychology,* pp. 652–653. Copyright © 1983 by John Wiley & Sons, Inc. Used with permission.

- Description of the skills, knowledge, and abilities required
- Relationship of the job to other jobs

Regardless of what is included in the job description, it is important that it be worded effectively. The *Handbook for Analyzing Jobs* suggests that, in job descriptions,

- a terse, direct style should be used;
- the present tense should be used throughout;

- each sentence should begin with an active verb;
- each sentence must reflect an objective, either specifically stated or implied in such manner as to be obvious to the reader. A single verb may sometimes reflect both objective and worker action;
- all words should impart necessary information; others should be omitted. Every precaution should be taken to use words that have only one possible connotation and that specifically describe the manner in which the work is accomplished;
- the description of tasks should reflect the assigned work performed and worker-trait ratings.[26]

An example of a typical job description containing many of these features is that of the animal keeper shown in Exhibit 3.3, although this job description does not provide information regarding performance standards, task characteristics, purposes of the job, or job conditions. Purposes, however, are implied in the introductory section. To date, job standards typically have not been specified in job descriptions. Increasingly, however, these are being included. Organizations sometimes include standards in the performance appraisal form to retain the flexibility. Information on task characteristics, such as the level of skills, variety, and identity, is also rarely included in job descriptions. Information regarding payroll, title, department, and the name of the analyst are normally included but are not shown here.

Exhibit 3.3 is a rather lengthy job description. A somewhat more typical example of a job description is shown in Exhibit 3.7.

Job Analysis Techniques

There are many procedures which can be used to determine what job information to collect, how to collect it, from whom to collect it, and how to organize and present it in job descriptions. Most of the procedures are structured: fixed forms and processes/systems are used to gather the job analysis data. When organizations use similar structured methods to analyze jobs, they can exchange compensation information and develop more valid methods of recruitment, selection, and performance appraisal.[27]

Structured techniques tend to divide into two types: those focusing on aspects of the job (job-focused) and those focusing on aspects of the individual (person-focused).[28] Some of the typical job-focused techniques include functional job analysis (FJA), the management position description questionnaire (MPDQ), the Hay plan, and methods analyses.[29] More behavioural-focused techniques include the position analysis questionnaire (PAQ), critical incidents, extended critical incidents, and the guidelines-oriented job analysis.

| Position Description (Exempt) | Exhibit 3.7 |

FUNCTIONAL TITLE: Corporate Loan Assistant	**DEPARTMENT:** Corporate Banking
	DIVISION:
FUNCTION CODE:	**LOCATION:** Head Office
INCUMBENT:	**DATE:** June 1986

NOTE: Statements included in this description are intended to reflect in general the duties and responsibilities of this classification are are not to be interpreted as being all inclusive.

RELATIONSHIPS:

Reports to: Corporate Account Officer A or AA: or Sr. Corporate Account Officer B or BB

Subordinate staff: None

Other internal contacts: Various levels of management within the Corporate Banking Department

External Contacts: Major Bank Customers

SUMMARY STATEMENT:

Assist in the administration of commercial accounts, to ensure maintenance of profitable bank relationships.

DOMAINS:

A. Credit Analysis (Weekly)
Under the direction of a supervising loan officer. Analyze a customer company's history, industry position, present condition, accounting procedures, and debt requirements. Review credit reports, summarizing analysis and recommending course of action for potential borrowers; review and summarize performance of existing borrowers. Prepare and follow-up on credit communications and reports and Loan Agreement Compliance sheets.

B. Operations (Weekly)
Help customers with banking problems and needs. Give out customer credit information to valid inquirers. Analyze account profitability and compliance with balance arrangements; distribute to customer. Direct Corporate Loan Note Department in receiving and disbursing funds and in booking loans. Correct internal errors.

C. Loan Documentation (Weekly)
Development required loan documentation. Help customer complete loan documents. Review loan documents immediately after a loan closing for completeness and accuracy.

D. Report/Information System (Weekly)
Prepare credit reports, describing and analyzing customer relationship and loan commitments; prepare for input into Information System. Monitor credit reports for accuracy.

E. Customer/Internal Relations (Weekly)
Build rapport with customers by becoming familiar with their products, facilities, and industry. Communicate with customers and other banks to obtain loan-related information and answer questions. Prepare reports on customer and prospect contacts and follow-up. Write memos on significant events affecting customers and prospects.

Continued on next page

Exhibit 3.7   Continued

F. Assistance to Officers (Monthly)
    Assist assigned officers by preparing credit support information, summarizing customer relationship, and accompanying on calls or making independent calls. Monitor accounts and review and maintain credit files. Co-ordinate paper flow to banks participating in loans. Respond to customer questions or requests in absence of assigned officer.

G. Assistance to Division (Monthly)
    Represent bank at industry activities. Follow industry/area developments. Help Division Manager plan division approach and prospect for new business. Interview loan assistant applicants. Provide divisional back-up in absence of assigned officer.

H. Knowledge and Skills (Any item with an asterisk will be taught on the job)
    Oral communication skills, including listening and questioning. Intermediate accounting skills. Writing skills. Researching/reading skills to understand legal financial documents. Organizational/analytical skills. Social skills to represent the bank and strengthen its image. Sales skills. Knowledge of bank credit policy and services.* Skill to use bank computer terminal.* Knowledge of bank-related legal terminology. Independent work skills. Work efficiently under pressure. Courtesy and tactfulness. Interfacing skills. Knowledge of basic business (corporate) finance. Skill to interpret economic/political events.

I. Physical Characteristics
    See to read fine print and numbers. Hear speaker 20 feet away. Speak to address a group of five. Mobility to tour customer facilities (may include climbing stairs). Use of hands and fingers to write, operate a calculator.

J. Other Characteristics
    Drivers licence. Willing to: work overtime and weekends occasionally, travel out of province every three months/locally weekly; attend activities after work hours; wear clean, neat business-like attire.

Typical Line of Promotion:
  From:
  To: Corporate Account Officer

_____   _____
Analyst   Incumbent   Date

                                          _____
                                          Superior   Date

Source: Used by permission of Biddle and Associates.

Job-Focused Techniques

The study of human work probably has not generally benefited from the systematic, scientific approaches that have been characteristic of other domains of inquiry, such as the study of physical phenomena, biological phenomena, or of the behaviour of humans through psychological and sociological research. However, the job-focused techniques described here have not been entirely unsystematic and lacking in the scientific approach.[30]

Functional Job Analysis (FJA). The United States Training and Employment Service of the U.S. Department of Labor developed functional job analysis to describe the nature of jobs in terms of people, data, and things, and to develop job summaries, job descriptions, and employee specifications. FJA was designed to improve job placement and counselling for workers registering for employment at state employment offices. This was part of an intensive research program directed toward producing the 1965 edition of the *Dictionary of Occupational Titles* (DOT). Today, many aspects of FJA are used by a number of private and public organizations.[31]

FJA is both a conceptual system for defining the dimensions of worker activity and a method of measuring levels of worker activity. The fundamental premises are that

- a fundamental distinction must be made between what gets done and what workers do to get things done. Bus drivers do not carry passengers; they drive vehicles and collect fares;
- jobs are concerned with data, people, and things;
- in relation to things, workers draw on physical resources; in relation to data, on mental resources; and in relation to people, on interpersonal resources;
- all jobs require the worker to relate to data, people, and things to some degree;
- although the behaviour of workers or the tasks they perform apparently can be described in an infinite number of ways, there are only a few definitive functions involved. Thus, in interacting with machines, workers feed, tend, operate, and set up; in the case of vehicles or related machines, they drive or control them. Although these functions vary in difficulty and content, each draws on a relatively narrow and specific range of worker characteristics and qualifications for effective performance;
- the functions appropriate to dealing with data, people, or things are hierarchical and ordinal, proceeding from the complex to the simple. Thus, to indicate that a particular function, e.g., compiling data, reflects the requirements of a job is to say that it also includes the requirements of lower functions, such as comparing, and that it excludes the requirements of higher functions, such as analyzing.[32]

The worker functions associated with data, people, and things are listed in Exhibit 3.8. The U.S. Training and Employment Service has used these worker functions as a basis for describing more than 30 000 job titles in the *Dictionary of Occupational Titles*.

In Canada, Employment and Immigration Canada has prepared a *Canadian Classification and Dictionary of Occupations*. It is an alphanumeric code that helps arrange jobs into occupational groups. This classification is based on, among other things, the kind of work performed, the materials or equipment used or produced, the standards to be met, the education or

| Exhibit 3.8 | Functions Associated with Data, People, and Things |

Data	People	Things
0 synthesizing	0 mentoring	0 setting up
1 co-ordinating	1 negotiating	1 precision working
2 analyzing	2 instructing	2 operating/controlling
3 compiling	3 supervising	3 driving/operating
4 computing	4 diverting	4 manipulating
5 copying	5 persuading	5 tending
6 comparing	6 speaking/signaling	6 feeding/offbearing
	7 serving	7 handling
	8 taking instructions/helping	

Source: Adapted from U.S. Department of Labor, Employment Service, Training and Development Administration, *Handbook for Analyzing Jobs* (Washington, D.C.: Government Printing Office, 1972), p. 73.

training required, the working conditions, and the relationship of the jobholder to co-workers.[33]

A PHRM manager who has to prepare job descriptions and job specifications can start with the Canadian Classification and Dictionary of Occupations to determine the general job analysis information and use the *Handbook for Analyzing Jobs* for more specific resource planning, recruitment, selection, placement, performance evaluation, training, and job design.

Management Position Description Questionnaire (MPDQ). Although the functional job analysis approach is complete, it requires considerable training to use well and is quite narrative in nature. The narrative portions tends to be less reliable than more quantitative techniques, such as the management position description questionnaire,[34] which is a method of job analysis that relies on the checklist method to analyze jobs. It contains 197 items related to the concerns and responsibilities of managers, their demands and restrictions, and miscellaneous characteristics. These 197 items have been condensed into 13 job factors including:

- Product, market, and financial planning
- Co-ordination of other organizational units and personnel
- Internal business control
- Products and services responsibility
- Public and customer relations
- Advanced consulting
- Autonomy of action
- Approval of financial commitments
- Staff service
- Supervision
- Complexity and stress

- Advanced financial responsibility
- Broad personnel responsibility

The MPDQ is designed for managerial positions, but responses to the items vary by managerial level within any organization and among different organizations. This questionnaire is appropriate for evaluating managerial jobs, determining the training needs of employees moving into managerial jobs, creating job families and placing new managerial jobs into the right job family, compensating managerial jobs, and developing selection procedures and performance appraisal forms.

The Hay Plan. Another method of analyzing managerial jobs is the Hay plan, which is used by a large number of organizations. Although less structured than the MPDQ and PAQ, it is systematically tied into a job evaluation and compensation system. Thus, use of the Hay plan allows an organization to maintain consistency not only in how it describes managerial jobs, but also in how it rewards them. The purposes of the Hay plan are management development, placement, and recruitment; job evaluation; measurement of the execution of a job against specific standards of accountability; and organization analysis.

The Hay plan begins with an interview between the job analyst and the job incumbent. The information that is gathered relates to four aspects of the incumbent's job: the objectives, dimensions, nature and scope of the position, and the accountability objectives. Information about the objectives allow the reader of the job description to know why the job exists in the organization. Information about dimensions conveys to the reader how much of the "show" the incumbent "runs" and the magnitude of the end results affected by his or her actions.

The real heart of the Hay job description is the information about the nature and scope of the position, which covers five crucial aspects:

1. How the position fits into the organization, including reference to significant organizational and outside relationships
2. The general composition of supporting staff. This includes a thumbnail sketch of each major function of any staff under the incumbent's position—size, type, and the reason for its existence
3. The general nature of the technical, managerial, and human relationship know-how required
4. The nature of the problem solving required: What are the key problems that must be solved by this job, and how variable are they?
5. The nature and source of control or of the freedom to solve problems and act, whether supervisory, procedural, vocational, or professional

Information related to the accountability objectives indicates the end-results required from the job, for which the incumbent is held accountable. There are four areas of accountability: organization (including staffing, developing, and maintaining the organization); strategic planning; tactical planning, executing, and directing the attainment of objectives; and review and control.

Because the Hay plan is based on information gathered in an interview (as opposed to the checklist method in the management position description questionnaire), the success of the plan depends on the skills of the interviewer. Interviewers can be trained to collect information useful for job descriptions, job evaluation, and compensation. The Hay plan results in one organization can be compared with those in other organizations to ensure external pay comparability. The Hay plan is discussed further in Chapter 9.

Methods Analysis. Conventional job analysis procedures and structured procedures generally focus on describing the job and its general duties, the conditions under which the duties are performed, and the levels of authority, accountability, and know-how required. Equally important, however, is a description of how to do the job as efficiently and effectively as possible. This is the purpose of methods analysis. Although methods analysis could be used for many jobs, it is more frequently applied to non-managerial jobs. In these jobs, individual activity units can often be identified more readily.

Methods analysis, or motion study, had its origins in industrial engineering. The following are some of the principles on which it is based:

- The movements of the two hands should be balanced, and the two hands should begin and end their motions simultaneously
- The hands should be doing productive work and should not be idle at the same time except during rest periods
- Motions of the hands should be made in opposite and symmetrical directions and at the same time
- The work should be arranged to permit it to be performed with an easy and natural rhythm
- Momentum and ballistic-type movements should be employed wherever possible to reduce muscular effort
- There should be a definite location for all tools and materials; these should be located in front of, and close to, the worker
- Bins or other devices should be used to deliver the materials close to the point of use
- The workspace should be designed to ensure adequate illumination, proper workplace height, and provision for alternated standing and sitting by the operator
- Wherever possible, jigs, fixtures, or other mechanical devices should be used to relieve the hands of unnecessary work
- Tools should be pre-positioned wherever possible in order to facilitate grasping them [35]

Proper application of these principles results in greater motion economy and working efficiency, according to the industrial engineers.

One form of methods analysis is **work measurement** or **time study**. In essence, work measurement determines standard times for all units of work activity in a given task or job. Combining these times gives a standard time of the entire job. These standard times can be used as a basis for wage-incentive plans (incentives generally are given for work performance that takes less than the standard time), cost determination, cost estimates for new products, and balancing production lines and work crews.[36]

Establishing standard times is challenging, since the time it takes to do a job can be influenced as much by the individual doing the job as by the nature of the job itself. Consequently, determining standard times often requires measurement of the actual effort the individual is exerting and the real effort required. This process often involves some guesswork.

Common methods of collecting time data and determining standard times include the stop-watch time studies, standard data, predetermined time systems, and work sampling for determining standard time.

Work Sampling. "Work sampling is the process of taking instantaneous samples of the work activities of individuals or groups of individuals."[37] Work sampling can be done in several ways: The job analyst can observe the incumbent at predetermined times; a camera can be set to take photographs at predetermined times; or, at a given signal, all incumbents can record their activity at that moment. The activities from these observations are timed and classified into predetermined categories. The result is a description of the activities by classification of a job and the percentage of time for each activity.

Person-Focused Techniques

Job-focused techniques describe jobs in terms of task or activity statements that culminate in a definition of the person-oriented content of the jobs. Person-focused or behaviour-focused techniques are behavioural statements resulting in the definition of the person-oriented content of jobs. Note that the two job descriptions, Exhibits 3.3 and 3.7, are both person-focused.

Position Analysis Questionnaire (PAQ). The PAQ is a structured questionnaire and contains 187 job elements. Seven additional items relating to amount of pay are included for research purposes only. The PAQ is organized into six divisions:

1. Information input: Where and how does the worker get the information used in performing the job? Examples are the use of written materials and near-visual differentiation
2. Mental processes: What reasoning, decision making, planning, and information-processing activities are involved in performing the job? Examples are the level of reasoning in problem-solving and coding/decoding
3. Work output: What physical activities does the worker perform, and what tools or devices are used? Examples are the use of keyboard devices and assembling/disassembling
4. Relationships with other people: What relationships with other people are required in performing the job? Examples are instructing, and contacts with the public or customers

5. Job context: In what physical or social contexts is the work performed? Examples are high temperatures and interpersonal conflict situations
6. Other job characteristics: What other activities, conditions, or characteristics are relevant to the job.[38]

In addition to describing the jobs on the basis of the six divisions and 187 elements, each element is also rated on one of six rating scales. The scales are (1) extent of use, (2) importance of the job, (3) amount of time, (4) possibility of occurrence, (5) applicability, and (6) other.

Using these six divisions and six rating scales, the nature of jobs is determined essentially in terms of communication/decision making/social responsibilities; performance of skilled activities; physical activity and related environmental conditions; operation of vehicles and equipment; and processing of information. Using these five dimensions, jobs can be compared and clustered. The job clusters then can be used for staffing decisions and the development of job descriptions and specification.[39]

The reliance of the position analysis questionnaire on person-oriented traits allows it to be applied to a variety of jobs and organizations without modification. This, of course, allows organizations to more easily compare their job analyses with those of other organizations.

Physical Abilities Analysis. A subject sub-set of abilities and job demands used to analyze jobs is physical proficiency. The physical abilities analysis uses nine abilities to analyze the physical requirements of tasks, including:

- Dynamic strength. This is defined as the ability to exert muscular force repeatedly or continuously over time
- Trunk strength. This is a derivative of the dynamic strength factor and is characterized by resistance of trunk muscles to fatigue during repeated use
- Static strength. This is the force that an individual exerts in lifting, pushing, pulling, or carrying external objects
- Explosive strength. This is characterized by the ability to expend a maximum of energy in one or a series of maximum thrusts
- Extent flexibility. This involves the ability to extend the trunk, arms, and/or legs through a range of motion in either the frontal, sagittal, or transverse planes
- Dynamic flexibility. This contrasts with extent flexibility in that the ability involves the capacity to make rapid, repeated flexing movements, in which the resilience of the muscles in recovering from distension is critical
- Gross body equilibrium. This is the ability to maintain balance in either an unstable position or when opposing forces are pulling
- Stamina. This is synonymous with cardiovascular endurance and enables the performance of prolonged bouts of aerobic work without experiencing fatigue or exhaustion.[40]

In analyzing jobs with physical abilities analysis, seven-point scales are used to determine the extent to which each job requires each of the seven abilities, from maximum performance to minimum performance.

With the presence of many voluntary affirmative-action programs, the need for organizations to know the precise physical requirements for jobs is increasing. Thus, the information from the physical abilities analysis can be very instrumental, along with job design, in matching workers to jobs. Other job analysis techniques that help organizations to comply with legal hiring requirements are the critical incident techniques, the extended critical incident technique, and the guidelines-oriented job analysis.

The Critical Incident Technique. One of the more frequently used job analysis techniques for developing behavioural criteria is the critical incident technique.[41] This technique requires that those who are knowledgeable about a job describe to a job analyst the critical job incidents—those incidents that they have observed over the past 6 to 12 months that represent effective and ineffective performance. The job analyst may prompt those describing the incidents by asking them to write down five key things at which an incumbent must be proficient, or to identify the most effective job incumbent and describe that person's behaviour.[42]

Those describing the incidents are also asked to describe what led up to the incident, what were the consequences of the behaviour, and whether the behaviour was under the control of the incumbent. After a number of critical incidents have been described and recorded, they are rated by their frequency of occurrence, importance, and the extent of ability required to perform them.

This information, often concerning a few hundred incidents for each job, is then clustered into job dimensions. These dimensions, which may often utilize only a sub-set of all of the critical incidents obtained, can then be used to describe the job.[43] They also can be used to develop performance appraisal forms, particularly behavioural-anchored rating scales (described in Chapter 7). The major disadvantages of this job analysis method are the time required to gather descriptions of the incidents, and the difficulty of identifying average performance; these methods often solicit the extremes of performance (e.g., ineffective or effective, or very bad or very good) and omit examples of average performance. This disadvantage, however, can be overcome by obtaining examples of all three levels of performance. This is what is done in the extended critical incident technique.

Extended Critical Incident Technique. Instead of beginning by having incumbents or others knowledgeable about the jobs list examples of effective and ineffective behaviour, this technique begins by having incumbents identify *job domains*.[44] These domains (described further in the discussion of guidelines-oriented job analysis) are essentially umbrellas under which many specific tasks can be included. For example, a job domain for a manager may be *training*. Specific tasks that can be placed under this domain include informally and formally teaching employees to learn new job skills, engaging in self-study on and off the job, and orienting new employees to the job and the organization.

The specific tasks that come under a given domain may vary from organization to organization. Consequently, after the job domains have been identified (often between 10 to 20 per job) and defined, the job analyst lists the tasks to be performed in each domain. The analyst lists these tasks after asking the incumbents to write examples or scenarios that reflect three different levels of performance for each domain. In describing these scenarios, the incumbents list the main event, the behaviour of the people in the scenario, and the consequences of that behaviour. Using scenarios collected from the incumbents, the analyst writes task statements. Each statement is essentially an example of one behaviour (or several in a domain that is described in the scenarios) indicating how frequently, the tasks are performed, the difficulty in doing so, and the importance of the task. An example of a scenario depicting excellent performance for a manager in one domain is shown in Exhibit 3.9.

With the information obtained thus far, job descriptions can be written. The extended critical incident technique can, however, be used to develop

---

Exhibit 3.9   *An Example of Excellent Performance for a Manager in One Job Domain*

Domain: Management and Supervision of Personnel Resources
Performance Level: Excellent

Once a year, Mary completes the performance evaluations for her six clerical staff members. These evaluations are used to make decisions about promotions and merit increases. They are also used to provide feedback to the workers. Recognizing the importance of these evaluations, Mary considers the behaviour of each staff member carefully and tries to identify both the strengths and weaknesses of their performance. Mary is careful not to rely on global impressions when completing her evaluations. Instead, she provides examples of the behaviours that indicate a worker's performance level. Mary then uses these evaluations to provide feedback to members of her staff. She recommends improvements when they are needed, and she acknowledges good performance as well. Thus, Mary's evaluations help to improve the effectiveness of her unit.

Why is this a useful scenario?

1. Because it describes

    Who: Mary, 6 staff members

    Main event: Performance evaluations done once a year

    Surrounding circumstances: Evaluations are used to make decisions about promotion, merit increases, and for feedback

    Behaviours: Identifies strengths and weaknesses, does not rely on global impressions, provides examples of behaviours that indicate performance levels, provides feedback, recommends needed improvements, acknowledges good performance.

    Consequences: Improves effectiveness of unit.

performance appraisal forms, to appraise performance, and identify training needs. This is done by having the incumbents (again, a different group to ensure validity) estimate the level of performance that each task statement represents, and place it in one of the domains identified initially by a previous group of incumbents.

If the incumbents are then asked to describe the abilities (physical and mental) necessary to perform the tasks in each domain, selection procedures can be developed. In this step, the incumbents are presented with a list of abilities with short definitions and asked to indicate the amount needed to perform satisfactorily the tasks in each domain. The identification of these abilities also can be used to write the job specifications or a job description.

Although the extended critical incident technique takes more time to develop than the critical incident technique method, it does gather a great deal more information from the incumbents, such as the needed abilities, performance levels, and the domains of the jobs. The extended critical incident technique also goes through several additional development steps. Both, however, are based on the identification of job behaviour and, as such, both are useful in performance appraisal and training. The same is true for the next job analysis method.

Guidelines-Oriented Job Analysis (GOJA). Another behaviour-focused job analysis technique is the GOJA. GOJA was developed in the U.S. as a response to the *Uniform Guidelines*, hence its name.[45] There are several steps in this type of analysis, each involving the job incumbents. Before any of these steps begin, the incumbents indicate their names, length of time on the job, experience, and the locations of the current job.

In the first step, incumbents list their job domains. Related duties in a job often fall into broad categories or groups. A category with related duties is called a domain. For example, a secretary may type letters, contracts, and memos. Since these duties are related, they are put into the same domain: typing. Jobs typically have several domains. In the job description shown in Exhibit 3.7, the job of corporate loan assistant has 10 domains.

After the domains are identified, the incumbents list the important or critical duties typically performed for successful job performance in each domain. Duties are observable work behaviour and something that incumbents are expected to perform. Often each domain contains several duties. Once the critical duties are identified, the incumbents indicate how frequently they are performed. Then each duty's degree of importance is determined. The several duties relevant to each of the ten domains for the corporate loan assistant are shown in Exhibit 3.7.

The next step is the incumbents' determination of the skills and knowledge required to perform each duty. Note that only those skills and knowledges that cannot be learned or acquired in eight hours or less are included. Rejecting an applicant who could have learned the necessary skills in less than eight hours is not a defensible practice. This is discussed further in the section on staffing.

The following step is the determination of the physical characteristics incumbents need to perform their job duties. Here the incumbents respond to five open-ended statements, each related to a physical characteristic.

The final step is a listing of other characteristics necessary to perform the job, such as any legally required licences or degrees. It also may indicate the necessity and frequency of overtime work and travel.

The results of the guidelines-oriented job analysis steps are a job description such as the one shown in Exhibit 3.7; an identified set of individual skills, knowledge, and abilities needed to perform the job; and a basis for developing job-related selection procedures and performance appraisal forms. The extended critical incident technique, the critical incident technique, and the guidelines-oriented job analysis, because they focus on behaviour, are useful for developing performance appraisal forms and identifying training needs. In addition, since skills (physical and mental) and knowledge are identified, selection procedures also can be developed, as described in Chapter 5. All three of these methods enhance employee understanding and validity of the job analysis, since job incumbents are involved in the process. This involvement, however, takes time.

Assessing Job-Analysis Methods

Confronted with several alternative job-analysis methods, the question is: Which is the best method to use? As with the selection of a job-design approach, the appropriateness of a specific job-analysis method depends on two major sets of considerations:[46] the purposes that job analysis serves, and practical concerns.[47]

Purposes of Job Analysis

A review of the earlier discussion indicates that the purposes served by job analysis include:

- Job descriptions, including specifications
- Job classification and evaluation for compensation
- Recruitment and selection information
- Performance appraisal development
- Identification of training and developmental needs
- Worker orientation
- Identification of human resource planning needs

An assessment of how well these purposes are served by each method is shown in Exhibit 3.10. In relation to job descriptions, the assessment of methods is determined by the extent to which it can be used to describe the job's range of duties, the worker requirements necessary to perform these duties, and the conditions under which they are performed. In relationship to the job classification and evaluation purpose, each method is assessed by how easily and how directly the job information collected can be used to establish job classes and families, and by how well internal equity distinctions are identified in using the method for job evaluation. In relation to performance appraisal, each method is assessed by how well it provides behavioural examples of performance and identifies the quality of those examples. Similarly, in training and development, each method is assessed in relation to how clearly behavioural examples of performance, and the skills and abilities required for that behaviour, are identified, thus allowing an evaluation of individuals against those requirements. Finally, the assessment of each method against human resource planning reflects how well the method facilitates a need analysis (see Chapter 12), an analysis that can be used to identify specific current and future human resource training needs, and what types of skills will be needed for future jobs.[48]

Practical Concerns

Several practical concerns are useful in assessing each job-analysis method, including:

- Versatility/suitability
- Standardization
- User acceptability
- User understandability
- Training required

Assessment of Several Job-Analysis Methods against Purposes of Job Analysis — Exhibit 3.10

Purposes	FJA	MPDQ	Hay Plan	PAQ	Critical Incident	Extended Critical Incident	GOJA
Job Descriptions	5	4	5	4	3	3	4
Job Classification and Evaluation	5	4	5	5	2	3	3
Recruitment and Selection	4	4	4	4	4	5	5
Performance Appraisal	3	3	4	3	4	5	5
Training and Development	4	3	3	3	4	5	5
Human Resource Planning	4	4	3	4	4	4	4

1: Serves this purpose inadequately
2: Serves this purpose somewhat inadequately
3: Serves this purpose adequately
4: Serves this purpose very adequately
5: Serves this purpose extremely adequately

- Readiness to use
- Time to completion
- Reliability and validity
- Purposes served
- Utility

In assessing each method against these concerns, the following definitions of each concern are used: **versatility/suitability** is the method's appropriateness for analyzing a variety of jobs. **Standardization** is the extent to which the method yields norms that allow comparisons with different sources of job-analysis data collection and at different times. **User acceptability** refers to the user's acceptance of the method, including its forms. **User understandability/involvement** refers to the extent to which those who are using the method, or are affected by its results, understand the method and are involved in the collection of the job-analysis information. **Training required** is the degree of training needed by those involved in using the method. **Readiness to use** is the extent to which the method is ready to be used for a job. **Time to completion** is the time required for the method to be implemented and the results of the method obtained. **Reliability and validity** refer to the consistency of the results obtained with the method, and the accuracy of those results in describing the duties, their importance, and the skills and abilities required to do the duties. **Purposes served** refers to the number of purposes listed above that are served by the method. To some extent, **utility** refers to the amount of overall benefit or value to be gained by the organization in using the method in relation to the costs incurred in its use. Using these several practical concerns, the assessment of each job-analysis method is presented in Exhibit 3.11.[49]

The assessment of the job-analysis methods presented in Exhibits 3.10 and 3.11 suggests that, overall, no method is clearly superior to others. Thus, in analyzing jobs as in designing jobs, several considerations must be weighed and any potential constraints identified. However, if the organization really wants to use job analysis as a critical base on which to develop and direct its PHRM activities, job-analysis techniques providing extensive person-focused information, such as the extended critical incident technique or the guidelines-oriented job analysis, may be most useful.

Assessing Job Design and Job Analysis

Both job design and job analysis are critical in PHRM. Assessment of job-design activities can be based on productivity measures such as employee performance, turnover, and absenteeism. If jobs are redesigned using the individual contemporary approach, turnover and absenteeism may be expected to decline. The monetary value of these benefits criteria can then be compared with the monetary costs incurred in redesigning the jobs. These costs may be substantial and may even exceed the value of the benefits.

Assessment of Several Job-Analysis Methods against Several Practical Concerns — Exhibit 3.11

Practical Concern	FJA	MPDQ	Hay Plan	PAQ	Critical Incident	Extended Critical Incident	GOJA
Versatility/Suitability	5	4	4	4	5	5	5
Standardization	5	5	5	5	3	3	3
User Acceptability	4	4	4	4	4	4	4
User Understandability/Involvement	4	4	5	4	5	5	5
Training Required	3	3	3	3	4	5	5
Readiness to Use	5	5	5	5	3	3	3
Time to Completion	4	4	4	4	3	3	3
Reliability and Validity	4	4	4	4	3	5	5
Purposes Served	4	3	3	4	3	4	4
Utility	4	4	4	4	3	4	4

1: Served to a very limited extent
2: Served to a limited extent
3: Served to an average extent
4: Served to an above average extent
5: Served to a great extent

Consequently, it is important to assess job-design projects in order to measure their effectiveness. This, however, may be more difficult to do in dollars-and-cents terms if the job redesign is assessed by the benefit criteria of satisfaction and involvement. Gains in these criteria may be substantial enough to justify the costs of the redesign, even if the other benefit criteria are relatively unaffected.

The assessment of job analysis can be done on the basis of how well it facilitates the organization's staffing needs, and whether it results in valid staffing procedures that comply with equal-employment legislation. Without job descriptions and worker specifications, potentially qualified job applicants cannot be identified and valid selection measures cannot be developed. Rather expensive recruiting efforts may result, along with noncompliance with equal-employment regulations. Effectiveness and validity can be used to assess job analysis but, more specifically, the number of qualified applicants to total applicants can be determined and the savings represented by avoidance of equal-employment violations can be calculated.

The financial benefit of these then can be compared with the cost of the job analysis method. The result may be a search for more appropriate and less expensive methods to analyze jobs.

Summary

The person-job interface is of vital importance to organizations today. This interface helps determine employee performance, satisfaction, and job involvement. Since the trend in these factors has been downward, in-depth study of the person-job interface is critical to both productivity and the quality of work life. Fortunately, job redesign efforts may be useful in both of these areas. The challenge to PHRM is to determine whether (and which) job design can improve productivity and the quality of work life, then implement the appropriate job-design program. Although many conditions must be considered in determining the appropriate job design, there are even more characteristics of jobs that can be changed or modified. These include skills variety, job significance, role overload and underload, and job overload and underload. With all of these characteristics subject to potential change, it becomes important to determine how individuals are likely to respond to them. This can be done by determining individuals' skills, knowledge, and abilities, along with their personality, interests, and preferences, which provide information on how well the individual will be *able* to do the job and how well the individual will *like* doing it.

Once jobs are designed, they must be analyzed and job descriptions and worker specifications must be written. Job analysis has a significant impact on the rest of the PHRM activities and on the organization's equal-employment considerations. The challenge, therefore, is finding the best or most appropriate way to analyze jobs. Because there are so many ways to analyze jobs, it becomes important to first identify what purposes are to be served. Different analysis methods might be useful in developing tests for selection and criteria for performance appraisal, and determining needs for training programs. A final selection then can be made with the consideration of several practical concerns.

Discussion Questions

1. How are job design and job analysis related?
2. What other areas of personnel management, besides job design, are related to job analysis?
3. List several strategic purposes of job design.
4. In what ways are job design and job analysis related to organizational goals and technology?
5. How are job design and job analysis affected by government legislation?
6. Who has the responsibility for job design and job analysis?

7. What is the difference between a job characterized by quantitative overload and one characterized by qualitative overload?
8. Identify and discuss the four job-design approaches.
9. Discuss and review the important considerations in selecting job-analysis methods.
10. In a nutshell, how might job-design and job-analysis activities be assessed in terms of their importance to organizations?

CASE STUDY

The Project Director

Dr. Betsy Morales has just been appointed project director of a research project on the effects of career counselling practices on female university students. The previous director had been fired after only six months on the job. The project is expected to be finished in two years, and funding sources expect quarterly progress reports. The project has been delayed for six months, half of the funds for the first year have been spent, and the staff, which was selected by the previous director, is experiencing severe conflicts and low morale. Dr. Morales's problem is to devise a plan to successfully complete the first-year's objectives with the existing staff, remaining funds, and limited time available.

History of the Case

Canada College was founded in 1912 as a private, independent, undergraduate, non-profit institution. The main campus of Canada College has grown steadily to its present population of more than 10 000 full-time students and 3600 part-time students. It continues to be a respected undergraduate institution, and is planning to offer graduate degrees in the near future.

As have so many other colleges, Canada College has begun to suffer the consequences of a reduced student-age population and cuts in financial aid to undergraduate students. In order to expand the potential student market, the Board of Trustees decided to initiate graduate programs. However, the college lacks the required research component at the graduate level. Once several research projects are underway, the president plans to develop an Institute for Social Research that he feels would give the College more visibility.

Dr. Stephen Flenglas, vice-president for external resources, was mandated to accomplish this task. He needed to get many research proposals going, and he reviewed many of the requests for proposals that had been offered by different federal and provincial agencies and foundations. Several of these proposals were of particular interest. He had expected the faculty to become interested in proposal writing, but he did not get the desired response. Although the faculty was informed of the new interest in research, it was not given any reason to become involved in the process with Dr. Flenglas. Many faculty members, particularly those without tenure, wanted to become the project director if they wrote winning proposals. Some wanted to know whether they would be relieved of teaching duties for a period of time while directing a project, and/or whether they would get a raise. Since the college had not established any clear guidelines on these issues, Dr. Flenglas was ambiguous in his replies.

Finally, Dr. Flenglas decided to hire a consultant to initiate the research thrust. The first research project awarded was a study on the effects of career counselling practices on female university students. It was a two-year project, with funds for the second year contingent on successful completion of the first-year's objectives. Dr. Flenglas was very happy with this award, since it would fit nicely into the plans for the Institute for Social Research. To direct this project, he thought a woman was appropriate. He decided to hire Elizabeth Boone, an experienced professional with an M.A. in education, who had been working as a counsellor in another college Upward-Bound program.

Exhibit 3.12 **Research Project Staff**

Dr. Betsy Morales, Director: Ph.D., Education, Simon Fraser University, 1975. Seven years executive director of the provincial Commission on the Status of Women and three years as member of the faculty of the School of Education at Canada College.

Zayra Lin, Researcher: M.A., Education, University of Toronto, 1982. Three years' experience as curriculum developer for a public school district, with particular expertise in the development of audio-visual educational materials.

Grace Peters, Researcher: M.A., Clinical Psychology, Memorial University of Newfoundland, 1980. Presently finishing doctorate dissertation in clinical psychology, York University. Seven years' experience as a clinical psychologist in a higher education environment, with particular expertise in research methodology.

Victoria Humphreys, Counselling Specialist: M.A., Educational Counselling, McGill University, 1965. Twenty years' experience as school counsellor at elementary and secondary levels.

Gloria Mosca, Secretary: Secretarial Sciences, Canada College, 1983. Five years of increasingly complex clerical duties at a junior college.

After six months as director of the research project, Elizabeth Boone had been fired. She was very bitter about her experience at Canada College, stating:

This project has left me angry and frustrated. I don't think I have ever been in such a situation. I am not an expert on women's issues, but it is something that interests me and that I wanted to learn more about. I have an M.A. in Education, and three years of experience as an Upward-Bound counselor. With a good staff, I wouldn't have had any problem with this project. But I didn't have any luck at all with the staff. I admit that this was in part because I didn't have any experience in hiring, but also I was under strong pressure to hire certain persons.

Aside from my friend Zayra, who was very helpful, I was stuck with an arrogant doctorate student recommended by Dr. Flenglas. She carried around her books on research methods and statistics almost as a banner of how much she knew. And then there was Victoria, whom I hired because of all her counselling experience. It turned out that she was always showing off about her experience, almost as if my younger age was a problem. Her husband was chronically ill and she was absent a lot. I would not be surprised if she quits. Even the secretary was a problem. I mean, she was efficient, but I think the position of secretary is very personal and confidential, and I would have liked to have chosen my own. Yet, the college has this policy of giving priority to current clerical personnel when new positions open, and I had no input in deciding who would be my secretary.

With such a weak staff, I found myself doing all the work alone, and trying to get advice from people outside the college. I'm sure that while I sought advice, they were gossiping behind my back. I should add that I have a very difficult family life, with four children from my first marriage, and three from my husband's first marriage living at home. Yet I gave this project so much energy. I was very excited at the subject of this project, and also the prospect of more money and status. I did all the work that was done for this project alone. Yet, instead of firing the staff, I got fired.

Following this event, the president called upon Dr. Morales to be the project director. In a private meeting with Dr. Morales, he acknowledged that morale among the team was very low, the project was behind schedule, and the remaining funds were limited. In order to help Dr. Morales carry out her new duties effectively, he prepared a short project staff background information list as shown in Exhibit 3.12.

Case Questions

1. What mistakes can you infer were committed by Elizabeth Boone, the first project director?

2. How are job-design issues related to this case?
3. Demonstrate the systematic relations among job analysis, reward systems, performance appraisal, and staff development.
4. If you were assigned the job of Dr. Morales, the new project leader, how would you proceed to overcome the problems?

Endnotes

1. For example, see J. R. Hackman and G. R. Oldham, *Work Redesign* (Reading, MA: Addison Wesley, 1980).
2. In the U.S., the essence of Title VII of the Civil Rights Act of 1964, the Equal Opportunity in Employment Act of 1972, and various court decisions, is that employment decisions be made on the basis of whether or not the individual will be able to perform the job. In order to determine this, job analyses should be conducted by organizations to help them determine what skills, knowledge, and abilities are needed by individuals to perform the job. Once this is known, selection procedures can be developed. Chapters 4 through 6 of this book expand on the job-relatedness of selection procedures.
3. More traditional definitions of job analyses are found in C. P. Sparks, "Job Analysis," in K. M. Rowland and G. R. Ferris (eds.), *Personnel Management* (Boston: Allyn and Bacon, 1982), pp. 78–100. E. J. McCormick, "Job and Task Analysis," in M. D. Dunnette (ed.), *Handbook of Industrial and Organizational Psychology* (New York: John Wiley & Sons, 1983), pp. 651–696. E. J. McCormick, *Job Analysis: Methods and Applications* (New York: AMACOM, a division of American Management Association, 1979). J. Ghorpade and T. J. Atchison, "The Concept of Job Analysis: A Review and Some Suggestions," *Public Personnel Management*, 1980, 9, pp. 134–144. In these sources, job analysis is the process of determining, either by structured or unstructured methods, the characteristics of work, often according to a set of prescribed dimensions, for the purpose of producing a job description.
4. For more information on the purposes and importance of job design, see J. Richard Hackman, and G. R. Oldham, *Work Redesign* (Reading, MA: Addison-Wesley Publishing Company, 1980). R. W. Griffin, *Task Design* (Scott, Foresman and Company, 1982). T. Rendero, "Job Analysis Practices," *Personnel*, Jan.–Feb. 1981, pp. 4–12.
5. For more discussion on the purposes of job analysis, see E. Prien, "Multi-Domain Job Analysis," paper presented in a workshop at the National I-O and OB Graduate Student Convention, April 23–25, 1982, University of Maryland. R. A. Ash and E. L. Levine, "A Framework for Evaluating Job Analysis Methods," *Personnel*, Nov.–Dec. 1980, pp. 53–59. P. van Rijn, *Job Analysis for Selection: An Overview* (U.S. Office of Personnel Management, Examination Services Branch, Office of Personnel Management, Aug. 1979). McCormick in Dunnette, see endnote 3, p. 683. Sparks, see endnote 3, pp. 81–88.
6. Aldag and Brief, endnote 4. Hackman and Oldham, endnote 4. Griffin, endnote 4. J. W. Slocum, Jr., and H. P. Sims, Jr., "A Typology for Integrating Technology, Organization and Job Design," *Human Relations, 33*, 1980, pp. 193–212. J. R. Hackman, "The Design of Work in the 1980s," *Organizational Dynamics*, Summer 1978, pp. 3–17. J. L. Pierce, "Job Design in Perspective," *Personnel Administrator*, Dec. 1980, pp. 67–74. J. R. Hackman, "Work Design," in J. R. Hackman and J. L. Suttle, *Improving Life and Work* (Santa Monica, CA: Goodyear Publishing Company, 1977).
7. Many ideas in this section reflect the ideas found in Aldag and Brief, see endnote 4; Hackman and Oldham, endnote 4; Griffin, endnote 4; and B. Schneider, A. Reichers, and T. M. Mitchell, "A Note on Some Relationships between the Aptitude Requirements and Reward Attributes of Tasks," *Academy of Management Journal*, 1982, 25, pp. 567–574. B. Schneider, *Staffing Organizations* (Santa Monica, CA: Goodyear, 1976). E. J. McCormick and J. Tiffin, *Industrial Psychology*, 6th ed. (Englewood Cliffs, NJ: Prentice-Hall Inc. 1974). L. H. Lofquist and R. V. Davis, *Adjustment to Work* (New York: Appleton-Century-Crofts, 1969).
8. This list is meant to be suggestive and not all-inclusive of job characteristics. Furthermore, not all of the characteristics used here are objective. Rather, they are based on an individual's subjective perceptions of the job; thus, they cannot be used directly in job-design efforts, but must be used based on the subjective perceptions of jobs. See Hackman and Oldham (endnote 4) for a discussion of these issues, particularly as they enter into job-redesign programs.
9. More cognitive and physical elements can be found in McCormick in Dunnette (see endnote 3) in his description of the position analysis questionnaire.
10. All of these job characteristics could be summated to form a single construct called **task complexity**.

Measuring such a construct could be done using separate measures for each characteristic or one overall measure. Either method may produce similar results when examining the relationships among the job characteristics and outcomes, such as employee motivation and morale. See D. R. Frew, "Diagnosing and Dealing with Task Complexity," *Personnel Administrator*, Nov. 1981, pp. 87–96.

11. Hackman and Oldham, endnote 4. J. R. Hackman, "Work Design," in J. R. Hackman and J. L. Suttle (eds.), *Improving Life at Work* (Santa Monica, CA: Goodyear Publishing Company, 1977).

12. J. R. Hackman, "Work Design," in J. R. Hackman and J. L. Suttle (eds.), *Improving Life at Work*, p. 101. Copyright © 1977. Reprinted by permission of Goodyear Publishing Company, Inc., Santa Monica, CA.

13. Hackman and Oldham, endnote 4. P. G. Gyllenhammar, "How Volvo Adapts Work to People," *Harvard Business Review*, July–Aug. 1977, pp. 102–113. "Stonewalling Plant Democracy," *Business Week*, March 28, 1977, pp. 78–82. M. S. Fisher, "Work Teams: A Case Study," *Personnel Journal*, Jan. 1981, pp. 42–45. "Moving Beyond Assembly Lines," *Business Week*, July 27, 1981, pp. 87, 90. A. F. Alber and M. Blumberg, "Team vs. Individual Approaches to Job Enrichment Programs," *Personnel*, Jan.–Feb., 1981, pp. 63–75.

14. Ergonomics is based in part upon knowledge of biomechanics. For a description of this, see M. A. Campion and E. J. Phelan, "Biomechanics and the Design of Industrial Jobs," *Personnel Journal*, Dec. 1981, pp. 949–952; Y. M. Shkop and E. M. Shkop, "Job Modification as an Alternative to Retirement," *Personnel Journal*, July 1982, pp. 513–516.

15. J. S. Lublin, "Unions and Firms Focus on Hand Disorders that Can Be Caused by Repetitive Tasks," *The Wall Street Journal*, Jan. 14, 1983, pp. 25, 37.

16. W. B. Werther, Jr., K. Davis, H. F. Schwind, H. Das, and F. C. Miner, Jr., *Canadian Personnel Management and Human Resources*, 2nd ed. (Toronto: McGraw-Hill Ryerson Ltd., 1985, p. 96). German Engineers Work on Humanization, *QWL Focus*, Quality of Working Life Centre vol. 3(2), 1983, pp. 23–25.

17. According to G. R. Oldham, this point cannot be stressed enough, since the success or failure of job enrichment experiments depends on so many other aspects of the organization.

18. The impact of growth-need strength is not great all of the time, nor does it serve as a moderator for all outcomes. See Hackman and Oldham (endnote 4) for a review of the research and issues.

19. This discussion can be extended to an analysis of the question, "Should people be selected to fit jobs or should jobs be made to fit people?" For views on this question, see J. R. Hackman, G. R. Oldham, R. Janson, and K. Purdy, "A New Strategy for Job Enrichment," *California Management Review*, Summer 1975, pp. 57–71; and J. R. Hackman, J. L. Pearce, and J. C. Wolfe, "Effects of Changes in Job Characteristics on Work Attitudes and Behaviors," *Organizational Behavior and Human Performance*, 1978, 21, pp. 289–304. For a discussion on why the use of the word "preference" is generally used here instead of the word "need," and why interests and preferences are a reasonable substitute for need, see G. Salancik and J. Pfeffer, "An Examination of Need-Satisfaction Models of Job Attitudes," *Administrative Science Quarterly*, 1977, 22, pp. 427–456.

20. The job-activity preference questionnaire was developed by R. C. Mecham, A. F. Harris, E. J. McCormick, and P. R. Jeanneret, and is reported and described in McCormick and Tiffin, see endnote 7.

21. T. Burns and G. M. Stalker, *Management of Innovation* (London: Tavistock, 1961). J. Woodward, Management and Technology (London: H. M. Stationary Office, 1958). R. D. Daft, Organization and Theory Design (St. Paul: West Publishing Co., 2nd ed. 1986).

22. B. Goranzon et al., *Job Design and Automation in Sweden* (Stockholm: The Swedish Center for Working Life, 1984).

23. For an excellent discussion of control systems, see E. E. Lawler III and J. R. Rhode, *Information and Control in Organizations* (Pacific Palisades, CA: Goodyear Publishing Company, 1976).

24. See McCormick in Dunnette (endnote 3) for an extensive description of these methods.

25. Note that only information related to selecting people on the basis of their abilities to do the job is legally required. Information on employee interests and preferences is suggested here in order to make better selection decisions and to enhance the employee's quality of work life experience.

26. McCormick, 1979, endnote 3, p. 64. M. A. Jones, "Job Descriptions Made Easy," *Personnel Journal*, May 1984, pp. 31–34.

27. "Job Analysis," *Employee Relations Law Journal*, 1981, pp. 586–587.

28. G. P. Latham and K. N. Wexley, *Increasing Productivity through Performance Appraisal* (Reading, MA: Addison-Wesley, 1981).

29. Other forms include the occupation analysis inventory, job elements method, task inventory paired with CODAP, work elements inventory, and the time span of discretion. For a description of these, see Sparks, endnote 3, pp. 88–91; E. J. McCormick, *Job Analysis: Methods and Applications* (New York: AMACOM, 1979); E. Jacques, *Time-Span Handbook* (London: Heineman Educational Books Ltd., 1964); E. Jacques, *Measurements of Responsibility* (New York: Wiley, 1972); and J. W. Cunningham, R. R. Boese, R. W. Webb, and J. J. Pass, "Systematically Derived Work Dimensions: Factor Analysis Inventory," *Journal of Applied Psychology*, 68, 1983, pp. 232–252. In addition to the use of these forms, job

analysis also can be conducted by direct observation, without any checklist.
30. McCormick, 1979, endnote 3, p. 67.
31. McCormick, endnote 3, p. 111.
32. S. A. Fine, "Functional Job Analysis: An Approach to a Technology for Manpower Planning," *Personnel Journal*, Nov. 1974, pp. 813–818. See also Department of Labor, *Dictionary of Occupational Titles*, vol. 2, 3rd ed. (Washington, DC: Government Printing Office, 1965); Department of Labor, Manpower Administration, *Handbook for Analyzing Jobs* (Washington, DC: Government Printing Office, 1972); Department of Labor, *Task Analysis Inventories: A Method of Collecting Job Information* (Washington, DC: Government Printing Office, 1973); and J. Markowitz, "Four Methods of Job Analysis," *Training and Development Journal*, Sept. 1981, pp. 112–121.
33. Canada Employment and Immigration, *Canadian Classification and Dictionary of Occupations*, 1971, vol. 5, pp. 1–2. Originally published in 1971, the CCDO was revised in 1985.
34. W. W. Tornow and P. R. Pinto, "The Development of a Managerial Job Taxonomy: A System for Describing, Classifying, and Evaluating Executive Positions," *Journal of Applied Psychology in Personnel Management*, 2nd ed. (Reston, VA: Reston Publishing Company, 1982), p. 61.
35. H. T. Amrine, J. Ritchey, and D. S. Hulley, *Manufacturing Organization and Management*, 3rd ed. (Englewood Cliffs, NJ: Prentice-Hall, 1975), p. 130. Reprinted by permission of Prentice-Hall Inc.
36. McCormick, 1979, endnote 3, pp. 77, 79.
37. McCormick, 1979, endnote 3, p. 83.
38. E. J. McCormick and J. Tiffin, *Industrial Psychology*, 6th ed. (Englewood Cliffs, NJ: Prentice-Hall Inc. 1974), p. 53. Reprinted by permission of Prentice-Hall Inc. The position analysis questionnaire is copyrighted by the Purdue Research Foundation and, along with related materials, is available through the University Book Store, 360 West State Street, West Lafayette, IN 47906. Further information is available through the PAQ Data Processing Division at that address. For a description of the validation of a short form of the questionnaire, see S. M. Colarelli, S. A. Stumpf, and S. J. Wall, "Cross-Validation of a Short Form of the Position Descriptive Questionnaire," *Educational and Psychological Measurement*, 1982, *42*, pp. 1279–1283. The position analysic questionnaire has been adapted for professional and managerial jobs: see J. C. Mitchell and E. J. McCormick, "Development of the PMPQ: A Structural Job Analysis Questionnaire for the Study of Professional and Managerial Positions" (Purdue Research Foundation, Purdue University, PMPQ Report #1, 1979).
39. Sparks, endnote 3, p. 87.
40. Sparks, endnote 3, p. 92. These physical proficiencies are taken from the extensive work of E. A. Fleishmann in *Structure and Measurement of Physical Fitness* (Englewood Cliffs, NJ: Prentice-Hall, 1964); "Toward a Taxonomy of Human Performance," *American Psychologist*, 1975, *30*, pp. 1017–1032; and "Evaluating Physical Abilities Required by Jobs," *Personnel Administrator*, 1979, *42*, pp. 82–92.
41. J. C. Flanagan, "The Critical Incident Technique," *Psychology Bulletin*, 1954, *51*, pp. 327–358.
42. Latham and Wexley, endnote 28, pp. 49–51.
43. These incidents can be used to form the basis for behavioural-anchored rating scales (see Chapter 7). If they are, many incidents are generally deleted. See Latham and Wexley, endnote 28, p. 54. Note that the job description developed may not contain examples of average performance, just very good and very bad.
44. Extended critical incident technique was developed and is described by S. Zedeck, S. J. Jackson, and A. Adelman, in a *Selection Procedures Reference Manual* (Berkeley, CA: University of California, 1980).
45. Guidelines-oriented job analysis is a specific technique developed by a consulting firm, as is the Hay plan. The guidelines-oriented technique is from Biddle and Associates, and is described here with their permission. Although this technique was developed in response to the *Uniform Guidelines* in the U.S., this does not imply that it is the only technique that complies with the *Guidelines*. In fact, according to the *Guidelines* (Sec. 14A), "Any method of job analysis may be used if it provides the information required for the specific validation strategy used" (i.e., content, construct, or empirical). See also G. A. Kesselman and F. E. Lopez, "The Impact of Job Analysis on Employment Test Validity for Minority and Non-Minority Accounting Personnel," *Personnel Psychology*, Spring 1979, pp. 91–108; and L. S. Kleiman and R. H. Faley, "Assessing Content Validity: Standards Set by the Court," *Personnel Psychology*, Fall 1978, pp. 701–713.
46. Much of the discussion of assessing job analysis methods is based on the extremely thorough work reported by R. A. Ash and E. L. Levine in "Evaluation of Seven Job Analyses," unpublished manuscript, University of South Florida, July 17, 1981. See also E. L. Levine, R. A. Ash, and N. Bennett, "Exploratory Comparative Study of Four Job Analysis Methods," *Journal of Applied Psychology*, 1980, *65*, pp. 524–535; R. A. Ash and E. L. Levine, "A Framework for Evaluating Job Analysis Methods," *Personnel*, Nov.–Dec. 1980, pp. 53–59; Sparks, endnote 3; Latham and Wexley, endnote 28.
47. The assessment of job analysis methods here is meant to be suggestive, not exhaustive and definitive. The reader is urged to review the references in endnote 46.
48. In addition, part of the assessment of each method for compensation includes how well equal-pay provi-

sions would be served. The assessment of each method for recruitment and selection incorporate how well the method serves the equal-opportunity validity requirement, i.e., content, construct, and empirical validity showing for selection methods used. In respect to performance appraisal, the assessment incorporates how well the method serves in developing job-related appraisal forms.

49. Note that the assessments of the several job-analysis methods presented in Exhibits 3.10 and 3.11 represent extrapolation from several sources including job analysts (the Ash and Levine study), academic researchers (Cascio; Sparks; Latham and Wexley) and by an evaluation of the written documents describing each method. For a more extensive discussion of this topic see L. Fogli, "Job Analysis and Organizational Effectiveness" (Berkeley, CA: Graduate School of Business, dissertation for Ph.D. in Business Administration, 1978).

SECTION III
Staffing

CHAPTER 4
Recruitment and Employment Equity

CHAPTER 5
Selection, Placement, and Employment Equity

CHAPTER 6
Selection and Placement, Decisions and Employment Equity

CHAPTER 4

Recruitment and Employment Equity

PHRM in the News

Recruitment and Employment Equity
Purposes and Importance of Recruitment
Relationships of Recruitment with PHRM Activities
Employment Equity Legal Considerations in Recruitment

Sources and Methods for Obtaining Job Applicants
Internal Sources
Internal Methods
External Sources
External Methods

Assessing Recruiting Methods

Increasing the Pool of Potentially Qualified Applicants
Conveying Job and Organizational Information
Expanding Career and Job Opportunities
Alternative Work Arrangements

Assessing Recruitment Activity

Summary

Discussion Questions

Case Study

Endnotes

PHRM in the News

CEO Emphasizes Recruitment Strategy as Key to Success

"If you're a nine-to-five person, you'll never get anywhere." That is the belief of Antoine Turmel, the retired president and chief executive officer of Québec food merchandiser Provigo Inc., and one of this year's additions to the Canadian Business Hall of Fame.

Last year, the group, which includes Provigo supermarkets, Provigo affiliate stores such as IGA and Axep, Provi-Soir, Pinto and Red Rooster convenience stores, Provigo-owned drug stores and Sports Experts franchises, rang up $4.7 billion in sales in North America.

The 67-year-old Turmel's disdain for punching clocks transformed sales of $190,000 and a small Eastern Townships holding company 40 years ago into Canada's number-two food distributor.

He did it by what he calls "hard work" and a "common-sense analysis" of the relationship between customers, food retailers, and wholesalers.

Provigo Inc. was created in 1969 when Turmel merged Denault's $47-million annual sales with two equally large Québec wholesalers based in Montréal and Chicoutimi.

Between 1970–85, the new company's sales doubled every five years. That spectacular growth was the result of Provigo's daring takeover of a grocery and drug wholesaler twice its size, Ontario-based M. Loeb Ltd., in 1977. Its warehouse operations in Ontario, western Canada, and California, as well as its affiliated stores, provided the beachhead for Provigo's nationwide expansion.

"One of the reasons for Provigo's success was I was clairvoyant enough to realize it's better to recruit people with a good academic background and teach them the grocery business than to build the other way around," Turmel says.

He initiated Provigo's management-trainee program, schooling that has spring-boarded several former Provigo executives into Québec politics recently. Former Provigo vice-president Paul Gobeil is now in charge of cutting $1 billion in government spending as the president of Québec's Treasury Board.

Source: J. Henderson, "Food for Thought for Making it Big," *The Financial Post* (special report), May 17, 1986. Used with permission.

Manitoba Hydro Project to Hire Northerners First

WINNIPEG (CP)—A policy to hire natives and northerners first may disappoint some of the thousands of job seekers who have inquired about work at a giant hydroelectric station in northern Manitoba.

The Limestone generating station is expected to employ 400 this year, 1,160 next year, and 1,800 in 1987–88. So far, about 7,000 job inquiries from across the country have flooded provincial government information offices.

Elaine Hunter, an official with the information office in Winnipeg, said that, given the government's preference for hiring northern residents, she cannot offer an opinion on the likelihood of employment.

"It depends on the uptake of jobs by northerners," she said. "I wish I could tell people their chances, but I just don't know."

The Manitoba Energy Authority has registered about 3,000 northern Manitobans for training programs on the multi-billion-dollar project, expected to start by the end of summer.

The cost of the training is expected to reach $25 million over five years.

"The training will be for everything from laborers to engineers," Energy Authority spokesman Peter Ferris said.

Mr. Ferris said that, under the preferential hiring clause brought in by the Manitoba New Democratic Party government, someone must have lived in the north for at least five years to qualify. The project also has some preference for northerners of native ancestry, he said.

The cost of completing Limestone is expected to be anywhere from $2.5 billion to $3 billion over eight years. The 1,200 megawatt station was given the go-ahead for an early start after a $3.2 billion export sale to Northern States Power Ltd. of Minneapolis.

So far, few job seekers have come to the isolated site on the Nelson River in the northeastern corner of Manitoba.

"With all the hiring to be done out of Thompson and Winnipeg, we don't really expect to see too many," said Gary Hanna, administrator for the local government district of the community of Gilliam, Man.

With only a 40-room hotel in the community of 1,100, Mr. Hanna said, people looking for work at the nearby dam site could encounter difficulty in finding a place to live.

Mr. Hanna said he is to meet provincial and federal officials soon to discuss a policy for dealing with destitute job seekers who drift into town.

Source: The Globe and Mail, July 8, 1985, p. 4. Reprinted with permission from The Canadian Press.

Affirmative Action

PINAWA, MAN.—Atomic Energy of Canada, Ltd. has agreed to set up a full-fledged affirmative action program at its Whiteshell nuclear research establishment in Pinawa, Manitoba, under the terms of a settlement approved by the Canadian Human Rights Commission. The settlement was worked out between the Crown corporation, the Commission, and an employees' group which filed a complaint of sex discrimination in 1982. The group charged that the research establishment's policies and practices restricted employment opportunities for women. At that time, women occupied only 14% of technical positions, and were not represented at all in any of the three levels of management. Under the terms of the settlement, Whiteshell must examine its employment practices, policies, and procedures on hiring women, and make other employees aware of the program. Management training and career development is to be provided with a view to increasing the number of women in management, in scientific/engineering and in other nontraditional job categories. The settlement also includes a schedule for monitoring the program's effectiveness.

Source: Human Resources Management in Canada, Report Bulletin No. 33, November 1985, p. 4. Reprinted with permission of Prentice-Hall Canada Inc. All rights reserved.

These "PHRM in the News" features illustrate the importance of recruitment for organizations and several of the purposes that it can serve.

Recruitment is important because the success of an organization's hiring program depends on it. Recruiting a large pool of potentially qualified applicants aids an organization in selecting applicants who will perform well. Recruitment also is important because it facilitates an organization's fulfilment of its equal-employment-opportunity commitments. Requiring organizations to develop new ways to recruit facilitates these commitments.

This chapter discusses the purposes of recruitment, the relationship of the recruitment activity to other personnel activities and functions, internal and external sources of job applicants, and legal issues related to recruitment, and it provides an assessment of the recruitment activity.

Recruitment and Employment Equity

Recruitment generally is defined as searching for and obtaining potential job candidates in sufficient numbers and of high enough quality that the organization can select the most appropriate people to fill its job needs.[1] In addition to filling job needs, the recruitment activity should be concerned with filling the needs of job candidates.[2] Consequently, recruitment should not only attract individuals to the organization but also increase the chance of retaining the individuals once they are hired. Of course, the recruitment activity must be done in compliance with an extensive set of rules and legal regulations. Thus, **recruitment** is specifically the set of activities and processes used to obtain legally a sufficient number of the right people at the right place and time so that the people and the organization can select each other in their own best short-term and long-term interests. This definition reflects the relationship between recruitment and several other personnel activities.

Purposes and Importance of Recruitment

The general purpose of recruitment is to provide a pool of potentially qualified job candidates. More specifically, the purposes of recruitment are to

- determine the present and future recruitment needs of the organization in conjunction with the human resource planning and programming activity and the job analysis activity;
- increase the pool of job applicants with minimum cost;
- help increase the success rate of the selection process by reducing the number of obviously under-qualified or over-qualified job applicants;
- help reduce the probability that job applicants, once recruited and selected, will leave the organization after only a short period of time;
- meet the organization's responsibility for affirmative action programs and other legal and social obligations regarding the composition of its workforce;
- start identifying and preparing potential job applicants who will be appropriate candidates;

- increase organizational and individual effectiveness in the short and long terms;
- evaluate the effectiveness of various techniques and locations of recruiting for all types of job applicants.[3]

Several important activities are part of recruitment. They include determining the organization's short- and long-range needs by job title and level in the organization; staying informed of job market conditions; developing effective recruiting materials; developing a systematic and integrated program of recruitment in conjunction with other personnel activities and with the co-operation of the line managers; obtaining a pool of qualified job applicants; recording the number and quality of job applicants produced by the various sources and methods of recruiting; and following up on applicants (those hired and not hired) in order to evaluate the effectiveness of the recruiting effort. In addition, all of these must be done within a legal context that may affect an organization's recruitment and selection policies and procedures. An example of how the legal-political context can influence an organization's recruitment and selection, is illustrated by the "PHRM in the News" articles at the beginning of this chapter.

Conducting all of these activities effectively enables the organization to avoid costly legal battles and settlements and to select only those applicants who are indeed qualified. Because the recruiting activity is as much concerned with getting job applicants to stay once they have been selected as it is with getting an initial pool of potentially qualified job applicants, it should also lead to a higher quality of working life. In essence, effective recruiting helps an organization attain the three general purposes of PHRM, as discussed in Chapter 1.

Relationships of Recruitment with PHRM Activities

Recognizing the relationships that recruitment has with other personnel activities is necessary for the effective management of human resources. Recruitment is closely related to human resource planning, job analysis, and training (see Exhibit 4.1), the three main activities that can be used to identify appropriate job candidates. An organization's human resource information system can then help to tie all of these activities together.

Human Resource Planning. Recruiting programs are developed around three components of planning: strategic business planning, job/role planning, and human resource planning.[4] Strategic business planning determines the organization's goals, future products and services, growth rate, location, legal environment, and structure. Job/role planning, which follows strategic business planning, specifies what needs to be done at all levels in order to meet the strategic business plans. Human resource planning determines what types of jobs the organization needs to fill, and thus, the skills, knowledge, and abilities needed by job applicants.

Components of the Recruitment Activity   *Exhibit 4.1*

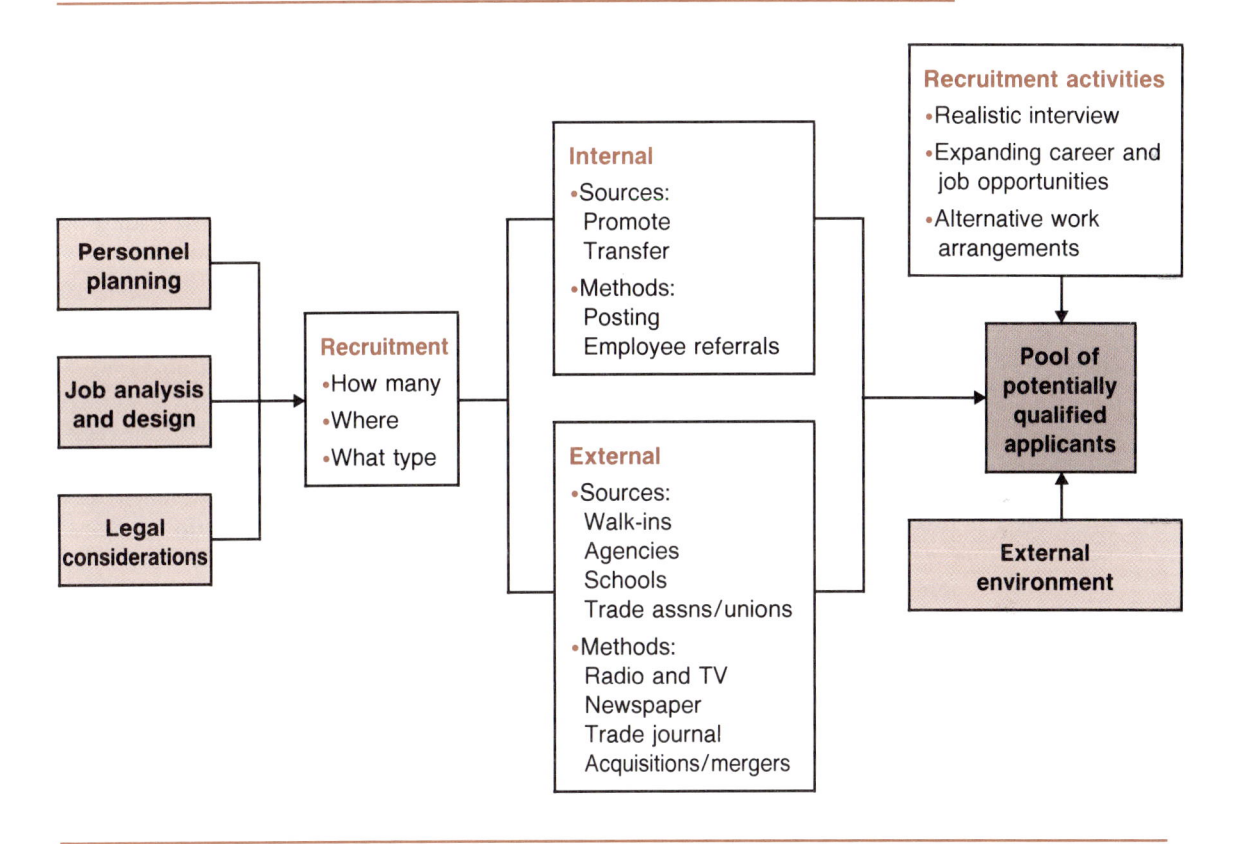

```
Personnel
planning ──┐
           │
Job analysis├──► Recruitment ──► Internal                          ──► Recruitment activities
and design │    • How many      • Sources:                              • Realistic interview
           │    • Where           Promote                                • Expanding career and
Legal      │    • What type       Transfer                                 job opportunities
considerations                  • Methods:                               • Alternative work
                                  Posting                                  arrangements
                                  Employee referrals                              │
                                                                                  ▼
                                External                          ──► Pool of
                                • Sources:                             potentially
                                  Walk-ins                             qualified
                                  Agencies                             applicants
                                  Schools                                  ▲
                                  Trade assns/unions                       │
                                • Methods:                             External
                                  Radio and TV                         environment
                                  Newspaper
                                  Trade journal
                                  Acquisitions/mergers
```

As part of the human resource planning, programs are established in close co-ordination with recruiting to indicate where and how the individuals with the needed skills, knowledge, and abilities will be found. Results of past recruiting efforts can be used to determine where particular types of individuals may be located again.[5] Caution must be used here, however, because use of past sources may result in the organization's inability to fulfil its legal considerations, such as its affirmative action programs for minorities, women, and the handicapped.

The recruitment process, to be done effectively, requires a great deal of information. This information also must be centralized so that all of the personnel activities related to recruitment can be co-ordinated. A human resource information system, as indicated in Chapter 3, can be useful for recruitment, since it can rapidly simulate organizational changes and conditions and thereby determine future personnel needs.

Job Design and Job Analysis. Although personnel and human resource planning identifies the organization's jobs needs, it is the job analysis activity that is essential for identifying the necessary skills, knowledge, and abilities, and the appropriate individual preferences, interests, and personality traits for each job type in each organizational setting.

> It is very difficult, if not impossible, to do effective recruiting unless the job qualifications are defined, preferably upon initiation of the employment requisition. No internal or external recruiting should begin until there is a clear and concise statement of the education, skills, and experience requirements and the salary range for the job. In larger organizations, this information is readily available in job descriptions and salary structures. Yet numerous hours and dollars are spent in recruiting, particularly recruiting advertising, where the applicant is required to play a "guessing game" about the job qualifications required.[6]

Recruitment based on job analysis helps to ensure that the people who are hired have the ability to do the job. However, recruitment must also match the personalities, interests, and preferences of the applicants with the characteristics of the job and organization if it is to serve the long-term interests of the organization and the individual. These job characteristics (considered rewards if preferred by the applicant) can include monetary compensation, favourable hours of work, training program availability, safe working conditions, and career opportunities in the organization. The design of the job also can be an important characteristic (or reward), as discussed in Chapter 3. Since all of these components are important personnel activities, they are further discussed in later chapters. However, it is important to note here that these characteristics (job and organizational) are capable of satisfying the preferences, interests, and personality traits of many different potential employees and can result in satisfied employees who are less likely to quit their jobs.

Training and Development. If recruiting activities produce a large pool of qualified job applicants, the need for employee training may be minimal. But if recruiting activities produce a large but unqualified pool of job applicants, the organization will be faced with heavy training costs. Some organizations have no other choice but to recruit people who are not yet ready to perform on the job. This usually results from shortage of skills within the labour market. Recruiting decisions often include a trade-off: should the organization expand its labour market and import skilled workers from other markets (regions or countries), or should the organization settle for less qualified candidates and assume a massive investment in training? This dilemma is somewhat typical of the aeronautic industry in Canada during rapid growth periods.[7]

Organizations also can accommodate handicapped job applicants by developing specialized training programs, thus making it easier to recruit and retain disabled individuals. For example, Sears, Roebuck & Company has been conducting an affirmative action program for the disabled since 1947; Control Data Corporation provides suddenly disabled employees with computer training to help them get back on the job; and IBM has a program to train and place severely handicapped people in entry-level computer jobs.

The results of these companies' training efforts is to make employment easier for handicapped employees and to encourage the same employees to stay on the job.[8] Thus, these training efforts help the companies to meet their equal-opportunity-employment goals.

The External Environment. Often, the type of employee an organization needs depends on the external environment. For example, the current shortage of skilled workers is presenting organizations with a real challenge to recruit skilled workers in sufficient numbers.[9] In times of national economic recession, some executives may worry whether they can find a job, but chief financial officers and others who can cut costs still get calls from recruiters. One way in which these cost cutters often can effect savings is by helping the personnel department to revise its medical and life insurance plans in order to achieve benefit cost control.[10]

Employment Equity Legal Considerations in Recruitment

Legal considerations, obligations, and requirements play a critical role in the recruitment activities of most companies in Canada. Although much of the legislation facing PHRM is directed at employment decisions such as hiring, firing, health and safety, and compensation, it essentially begins with the organization's search for job applicants, whether the search is made inside the organization or outside. Some of these legal aspects are discussed here. Other equal-employment-opportunity legislation applicable to staffing are discussed in the next two chapters. The equal-employment-opportunity legal considerations discussed here are relevant to an organization's recruitment activity because they essentially help identify who will be selected and, therefore, who should be recruited. Thus, the legal considerations discussed here are mainly those resulting from affirmative action programs.

Affirmative Action Programs and Recruiting. The Canadian Human Rights Act gives the Canadian Human Rights Commission great latitude in pursuing its enforcement. One way for the Commission to comply with the intent of the Act is by improving equal employment opportunities for special groups (see the "PHRM in the News" section) through **affirmative-action programs**.

Section 15(1) of the Act specifies special programs as a legitimate mechanism for improving the opportunities of a specific group through the elimination, reduction, or prevention of discrimination.

> It is not a discriminatory practice for a person to adopt or carry out a special program, plan, or arrangement designed to prevent disadvantages that are likely to be suffered by, or to eliminate or reduce disadvantages that are suffered by, any group of individuals, when those disadvantages would be or are based on or related to race, national or ethnic origin, colour, religion, age,

sex, marital status, or physical handicap of members of that group, by improving opportunities respecting goods, services, facilities, accommodation, or employment in relation to that group.

Such programs are developed by employers to remedy past discrimination or to prevent discrimination in the future. This usually implies organizational self-evaluation with regard to hiring, promotion, and compensation practices. If discrepancies are found, it would benefit the personnel department to check the criteria used for different personnel decisions, adjust them if necessary, and make sure that they are consistently applied.

In August 1984, a federal human rights tribunal issued its first decision with regard to *mandatory* affirmative-action programs.[11] The tribunal ordered Canadian National Rail to hire women for one in four non-traditional or blue-collar jobs in its St. Lawrence region, until they hold 13% of such jobs. CN Rail also was required to implement a series of other measures, varying from abandoning certain mechanical aptitude tests to modifying the way it publicizes available jobs. The decision arose from a complaint laid against CN Rail in 1979 by Montréal lobby group (Action Travail de Femmes). The goal of 13% would roughly correspond to the proportion of women in blue-collar jobs in industry generally.

Other Considerations. Gender labeling of jobs and stereotyping can result in the exclusion of women from certain jobs. This was illustrated by a study of the Canadian Broadcasting Corporation. Among other findings, the study reported that (1) most jobs in the CBC were segregated, and (2) when a woman did summon enough courage to apply for one of these "men only" jobs, she was actively discouraged by the male interviewers.[12]

In order to avoid such problems, many Canadian companies have set up voluntary affirmative-action programs. One of these, with a special emphasis on avoidance of gender discrimination, is in effect at the Royal Bank of Canada:[13]

Policy and Responsibility

The Royal Bank accepts applications and fills positions without regard to gender, ensuring that the male and female composition within the bank reflects the qualified candidates available in the workforce population. The bank has a promotion-from-within policy, and promotions also reflect the attempt to have a representation of men and women in the internal workforce.

The policy of equal employment opportunity is emphasized through both internal and external communication channels.

1. *Internally*, this is accomplished through
   (a) the personnel administration manual, which is available in all units and accessible to employees at any time;
   (b) the annual report to staff, which provides an annual statement and update;
   (c) a videotape presentation that discusses the nature of opportunity, power, and numbers in the context of equal opportunity;
   (d) the bank bulletin, which keeps employees up to date about important equal employment opportunity changes;

(e) internal communication publications such as "Interest" magazine and "Cheque Marks." Women are also portrayed in staff publications and video communications. The Public Affairs Department has developed editorial guidelines to ensure that language and editorial treatment is unbiased;

(f) orientation packages for new employees, which contain information regarding bank policy on equal employment opportunity;

(g) regular discussions held with individual personnel departments and more formal presentations included at personnel courses and conferences. Senior management and the EEO Co-ordinator address groups in all branches about equal-employment-opportunity issues

2. *Externally*, this is communicated in the following ways:

(a) The bank's equal-employment-opportunity policy and program is often published in outside newspapers and magazine articles

(b) The bank takes an active role in talking with and counselling other companies about affirmative action

(c) Women as well as men are portrayed in publications and advertising, including those relating to employment practice

(d) Written and verbal notification of EEO policy is made available to all recruiting sources

(e) The bank's equal opportunity policy is included in recruitment brochures

The EEO Co-ordinator works to ensure bank-wide commitment to the EEO objectives, and works with individuals and departments in managing equal employment opportunity issues. The Co-ordinator provides a central source of information in this area, reviews the program's effectiveness, makes recommendations to senior management, and is expected to

- compile quarterly monitoring information and provide analysis of the data to senior management for review with field units;
- review problems and concerns bank-wide, recommend changes, and implement corrective action;
- handle and deal with complaints concerning discrimination;
- ensure a continued awareness on the part of all bank staff members on issues related to equal employment opportunity;
- represent the bank's position outside the organization;
- gather information from outside the organization on equal employment and affirmative action matters; and
- monitor the activities of personnel, human resource development, and compensation to ensure that activities are in compliance with the bank's objectives.

Analysis

The EEO Co-ordinator maintains a listing by gender for job levels, divisions, and streams. The listing is produced and analyzed on a quarterly basis, is reviewed with the heads of departments, and appropriate recommendations are provided.

Utilization is monitored by comparing the estimated available female workforce with the bank's actual female workforce. To determine the availability of non-officer positions and entrance level positions, the bank examines the external workforce on the basis of the following factors:

1. The size of the female workforce
2. General availability of women with requisite skills in the area that the bank can reasonably recruit
3. Availability of women seeking employment

Sources and Methods for Obtaining Job Applicants

Now that we are aware of the legal considerations of recruitment, it is possible to examine sources of potentially qualified job applicants, and the methods used to recruit them. After looking at the internal sources and methods, the external sources and methods are examined.

Internal Sources

Internal sources include present employees, friends of employees, former employees, and former applicants. Promotions, demotions, and transfers can also provide applicants for departments of divisions within the organization.[14]

Promotions. The case for promotion from within rests on several sound arguments. One is that internal employees usually are better qualified. "Even jobs that do not seem unique require familiarity with the people, procedures, policies, and special characteristics of the organization in which they are performed."[15] Another is that employees are likely to feel more secure and to identify their long-term interests with the organization that considers them first when job openings occur. Availability of promotions within an organization can also motivate employees to perform better, and internal promotion can be much less expensive to the organization in terms of both time and money. To lure applicants from outside of the organization can be an expensive process. The cost to the company of relocating the new recruit and his or her family may range from $10 000 to $50 000. Further, the new recruit often must be brought in at a higher salary than those currently in similar positions in the organization. The result, particularly if the new recruit fails to contribute as expected, is dissatisfaction among the current employees. In addition, the incentive value of promotions diminishes.[16]

Disadvantages of a *promotion-from-within policy* may include an inability to find the best qualified person, and in-fighting, inbreeding, and a lack of varied perspectives and interests. If an organization has a policy of promotion from within, it must identify, select, and pressure candidates to accept the promotions. When done during times of rapid organizational growth, almost any employee may be promoted, regardless of qualifications, because the organization faces a managerial shortage. Rapid growth may temporarily obscure managerial deficiencies, but when the growth rate abates, the company will be faced with a surplus of managers whose poor performance becomes obvious.[17]

Based on these advantages and disadvantages, most organizations use a combination of internal promotion and external recruiting. Many organizations tend to obtain particular types of employees from particular sources. For example, many organizations are more likely to hire highly trained professionals and high-level managers from the outside than to promote from within.[18]

Transfers. Another way to recruit internally is by transferring current employees without promotion. Transfers often provide employees with the more broad-based view of the organization that better qualifies them for future promotions. For this reason, outside job applicants also might be more attracted to a company that provides transfers,

However, recent trends suggest that transfers or promotions that involve relocation may not be as attractive as they once were, except in companies that provide some sort of relocation counselling. Approximately 60% of the largest 500 Canadian companies now use this type of service when they relocate their employees.[19]

One of the major issues in promoting or transferring candidates from within is the question of whether seniority or performance/merit should be used as the criteria. Unions seem to prefer promotion and transfer based on seniority, and organizations prefer promotion or transfer based on ability.

Occasionally the criterion for promotions is personal judgement. This is particularly true for middle- and upper-level managerial positions. It is difficult to defend this criterion under legal guidelines. Therefore many organizations use test results from managerial assessment centres as one alternative to personal judgements and impressions. Since assessment centres are used more frequently as a selection device than as a recruiting device, they are discussed more extensively in Chapter 6.

Once the criteria or criterion is established, the candidates need to be identified. This is done through several internal methods of recruitment.

Internal Methods

As Exhibit 4.2 indicates, there are many methods for internally advertising job vacancies. Candidates also can be identified by word of mouth, company personnel records, promotion lists, and lists generated by the skills inventory in an organization's human resources information system. Since the job posting (notice on the bulletin board) method is a frequently used method, it is discussed here, along with informal contacts, particularly employee referral programs.[20]

Exhibit 4.2   *Methods for Advertising Job Openings Internally*

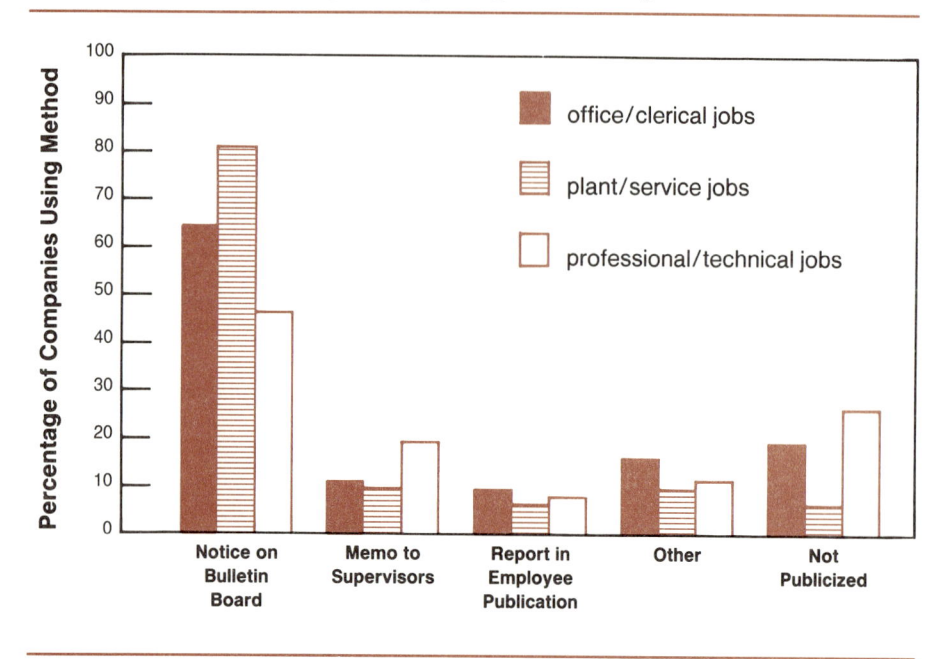

Source: Adapted from "Employee Promotion and Transfer Policies," Personnel Policy Forum Survey No. 120, January 1978, p. 2. Reprinted by permission of *Personnel Policy Forum,* copyright 1978 by the Bureau of National Affairs, Inc. Washington, D.C.

Job Posting. In essence, job posting is extending an open invitation to all employees, through prominent display of notices, to apply for a job vacancy.[21] This serves five purposes:

1. To provide opportunity for employee growth and development
2. To provide equal opportunity for advancement to all employees
3. To create a greater openness in the organization by making opportunities known to all employees
4. To increase staff awareness regarding salary grades, job descriptions, general promotion and transfer procedures, and what comprises effective-to-outstanding job performance
5. To communicate organization goals and objectives while allowing each individual the opportunity to self-select the best possible fit for himself or herself in the organization job structure [22]

Although job postings are usually found on bulletin boards, they also can be found in company newsletters and publications, circulated in employee lounges, and announced at staff meetings. Generally, all openings for management positions are posted. Sometimes specific salary information is posted, but job grade and pay range are more typical. Job posting improves morale because it is a fair way of providing opportunities; it provides employees with the opportunity for job variety; it facilitates the matching of jobs to employee skills and needs; and it provides a good way to fill positions at a low cost. There are, however, several disadvantages to job posting that counteract these benefits:

- It can lengthen the process of filling vacancies.
- Conflicts are sometimes created if it appears that a qualified internal candidate has been passed over in favour of an outsider.
- Conversely, the system may lose credibility if it appears that the successful candidate within the department has been identified in advance and the manager is merely going through the motions in considering outsiders.
- The morale of the unsuccessful candidates may suffer if feedback is not timely or carefully handled.
- Choices can be more difficult for the selecting manager if two or three approximately equally qualified candidates are encountered.
- Information about the posted jobs, such as salary or position grade, may trigger objections from employees who perceive inequities with their position evaluations or salaries.
- Supervisory-subordinate relationships may be jeopardized by subordinates who frequently apply for jobs in other departments.

Employee Referral Programs. These are essentially word-of-mouth advertisements that usually involve rewarding employees for referring skilled employment applicants to organization.[23] This method has proven to be a low cost-per-hire way of recruiting applicants, even though in many cases the applicants come from outside of the organization. This method is particularly useful for finding the type of managerial and skilled applicants who are in very short supply. For successful referrals, employees may receive a financial bonus (in some companies, it may exceed $500), particularly if they refer someone with a skill that is in high demand, such as robotics engineers.

One major concern with the employee referral program is that it is potentially discriminating: individuals often are inclined to refer those who are of the same race or sex. There are potential legal problems inherent in this type of situation. In addition, cliques and nepotism could develop, with negative effects on work habits.

External Sources

Recruiting internally does not always produce enough qualified job applicants. This is particularly true for organizations that are growing rapidly or that have a large demand for high-talent professional, skilled, and managerial employees. Therefore, organizations often need to recruit from external sources. Recruiting from the outside has a number of advantages, including bringing in people with new ideas. It is often cheaper and easier to hire an already trained professional or skilled employee, particularly when the organization has an immediate demand for scarce labour skills and talents. External sources also can supply temporary employees, who provide the organization with much more flexibility than permanent employees.

Surveys show that organizations use multiple sources for all occupational groups, but some sources are used more than others to recruit professional and managerial candidates.[24]

Information about the supply of certain types of labour is published monthly by Employment and Immigration Canada, local Canada Employment Centres, provincial departments of labour, and industry association newsletters. There are more than 800 Canada Employment Centres located across Canada, with more than 23 000 employees to assist employers in meeting their recruitment needs.

Information regarding labour force characteristics on a national, provincial, or even city-by-city basis is contained in the monthly *Labour Force Survey*, published by Statistics Canada. Another related service of Statistics Canada is the Help-Wanted-Index. It is published four times a year and provides an analysis of the help-wanted advertisements that are placed in 18 major newspapers across Canada. The survey attempts to indicate the number of jobs available in various categories.

Job Search Techniques. As illustrated in Exhibit 4.3, the single most frequent method of job search for all unemployed persons in Canada, regardless of occupation, education, and gender in 1977, and for females and males individually in 1982, was the informal method of contacting prospective employers directly.[25] Exhibit 4.3 also shows, in descending order of importance, the use of Canada Employment Centres, ads in the newspapers, and checking with friends and relatives.

Walk-ins. In the walk-in method, individuals become applicants by walking into an organization's employment office. This method, like employee referrals, is relatively informal and inexpensive and is almost as effective as employee referrals in resulting in employees who are likely to stay.[26] Unlike referrals, however, non-referred applicants may know less about the specific jobs available and usually come without the implicit recommendation of a current employee. This may be a disadvantage in comparison to referrals since current employees usually recommend only applicants who are likely to be satisfactory.[27]

Although walk-ins may be a relatively inexpensive source of applicants, the walk-in method is not used extensively by managerial, professional, and sales applicants. It tends to be a passive source of applicants, and thus may not provide the specific types of applicants needed nor be of any help in fulfilling affirmative action and equal employment considerations. These drawbacks may be reduced by attracting walk-ins through open-house events, the type of activity that is more likely to attract all types of applicants from the nearby community. However, sufficient numbers of some applicants often can be attained only by using other sources.[28]

Employment Agencies. Employment agencies are the second most popular source of employment for Canadians (see Exhibit 4.3). The public employ-

Job Search Techniques by Unemployed Individuals by Occupation and Sex for 1977 and 1982 Exhibit 4.3

	1977							April 1982		
Search Technique	Mgmt. and Prof.	Clerical, Sales, Service	Blue-Collar Workers	Univ. Degree	Post-Sec. Cert.	High School	None or Elemen.	Male	Female	Both
Contacted Employers Directly	73.5	74.4	60.7	70.9	68.9	69.3	64.5	75.0	68.9	72.5
Canada Employment Centre	58.8	51.3	61.1	51.6	58.6	60.2	61.8	51.0	46.0	49.0
Checked with Private Employment Agency	11.8	5.1	5.0	12.9	6.9	4.9	3.3	NA	NA	NA
Checked with Union	2.9	2.6	3.7	3.2	5.2	3.2	6.6	NA	NA	NA
Checked with Friends/Relatives	14.7	12.8	12.1	16.1	12.1	12.8	11.2	NA	NA	NA
Placed or Answered Ads	29.4	17.9	12.2	25.8	17.2	15.4	7.2	NA	NA	NA
Looked at Ads	44.1	41.0	32.7	48.4	43.1	42.1	28.3	41.9	48.5	44.5
Used Other Methods	2.9	2.6	0.9	3.2	1.7	0.2	0.7	38.2	32.4	35.8

Source: Adapted from A. Hasan and S. Gera "Aspects of Job Search in Canada," Discussion Paper No. 156 (Ottawa: Economic Council of Canada, 1980); and Statistics Canada, *Labour Force Surveys.*

ment agencies in Canada are the **Canada Employment Centres**. As indicated earlier, these federal employment agencies exist in every province. Their work is co-ordinated by Employment and Immigration Canada, which operates a nationwide, computerized job bank to which all provincial employment offices are connected. When an employer has a job opening, the personnel department notifies all of the Canada Employment Centres about the job and its requirements and the job is posted on the Centres job boards.

Prospective employees are interviewed by a Centre counsellor. If the counsellor's assessment of the applicant is positive, a referral is made to the prospective employer.

The effectiveness of the Centres' placement activities was recently studied, and the results are mixed. Although Canada Employment Centres comprise the second most important source for recruiting, the labour market is exposed to only one in three job seekers, and actually places only one in five.[29] Almost half of the vacancies filled are in clerical, sales, and service occupations, and very few placements are made in primary, managerial, and professional occupations.[30]

Private employment agencies tend to serve two groups of job applicants: unskilled workers and professional and managerial workers. The agencies that deal with unskilled workers often provide job applicants that employers would have a difficult time finding otherwise. Many of the employers looking for unskilled workers do not have the resources to do their own recruiting or have only temporary or seasonal demands for unskilled labour.

Private agencies play a major role in recruiting professional and managerial applicants. These agencies supply services for job applicants of all ages; many, however, have had some work experience beyond college. During the past 10 years, the executive recruiting industry has grown phenomenally.

The fees charged by these agencies range up to 33% of the first year's total salary and bonus package of the available job. The search firm receives this money whether or not they are successful in finding someone who is eventually selected for the job. Even if the firm is successful in finding someone who is hired, the cost may be much greater than the fees charged by the employment agency. This is because, in the pre-screening process, the employment agency may have rejected a candidate who would have done well or misidentified a candidate who will not do well. These two errors, discussed in Chapter 6 as false negative and false positive, respectively, pose additional costs for the organization.[31] To keep costs minimal, the organization should monitor closely the employment agency's activities.[32]

These agencies sometimes pre-screen job applicants who currently are working for other organizations. Consequently, in addition to the expense, this method of dealing with a potential candidate is apt to be very secretive.

Approximately 30 firms (some are branches of multi-national management consulting firms) offer executive search services in Canada. In 1980, they were estimated to have combined billings in excess of $25 million.[33]

Temporary Help Agencies. The use of temporary help agencies, which provide applicants for part-time positions, is growing as skilled and semi-skilled individuals find it preferable to work less than a 40-hour week, or simply to work on their own schedule. Temporary employees also have a chance to work in a variety of organizations and therefore have the opportunity to satisfy preferences for workplace variety.

Organizations are using temporary help agencies more than ever because workers with certain skills can be obtained only through them. This is particularly true for small companies that are not very visible or cannot spend the time to recruit for themselves. Also, organizations often need people only for a short time. Thus, organizations benefit from being able to get these people without an extensive search, while retaining the ability to reduce their workforce without costly layoffs and potential unemployment compensation payments. Although temporary employees may require higher rates of pay than the organization's permanent staff, they generally forego indirect compensation in the form of various benefits, which are discussed in Chapter 11.

Ted Turner, vice-president of the Canadian Association of Temporary Services, was quoted as saying that the growth rate of the temporary employment industry for 1984 was 20 times that of the regular workforce.[34]

Professional/Trade Associations and Labour Organizations. In some industries, such as the construction industry, skilled workers are recruited through the local labour organization. Since contractors often hire seasonal workers, a union hiring hall is a convenient channel for finding many candidates.

Trade and professional associations also are important sources for recruiting. They often have newsletters and hold meetings, which can be used to post employment opportunities. Meetings also can provide employers and potential job applicants with an opportunity to meet. Some communities and schools have picked up on this idea and now bring together large numbers of employers and job seekers at "job fairs." Of course, these fairs provide limited interview time and thus serve only as an initial step in the recruitment process, but they are an efficient source for both employers and job hunters.

Technical and Educational Institutions. High schools, vocational and technical schools, and colleges and universities are important sources of recruits for most organizations, although their importance varies depending on the type of applicant sought. For example, if an organization is recruiting for managerial, technical, or professional applicants, colleges and universities are the most important source. When an organization is seeking plant/service and clerical employees, high schools or vocational schools would be more effective sources.

Recruiting at colleges and universities is often an expensive process, even if the recruiting visit eventually produces new employees. Studies conducted in the U.S. showed that approximately 30% of the applicants hired from college leave the organization within the first five years of initial employment. This rate of turnover is even higher for graduate business management students.[35]

Some people attribute this high rate of turnover to the lack of job challenge provided by organizations. Organizations claim, however, that people just out of college have unrealistic expectations. Partly because of the expense, organizations are questioning the necessity of hiring college graduates for some of their jobs. Many universities, on the other hand, suggest that on-campus recruitment is the most popular method for students looking for their first jobs, and they provide placement and counselling centres that facilitate the job search for their graduates.[36]

External Methods

Radio and Television. Many organizations looking for applicants of all types engage in extensive advertising on radio and television. Companies are reluctant to use these media because they fear that

- it is too expensive;
- it will make the company look desperate; and
- it will damage the firm's conservative image.

Yet, organizations that are desperate to reach certain types of job applicants, such as skilled workers, use these media. In reality, however, there is nothing desperate about using radio or television. Rather it is the *content* and *delivery* that may imply some level of desperation. Recognizing this, organizations are increasing their recruitment expenditures for carefully designed radio and television advertisements, with very favourable results.

Newspapers and Trade Journals. Social and national newspaper advertising traditionally has been the most common method of external recruiting,[37] because a large number of potential applicants can be reached at a relatively low cost-per-hire. Newspaper ads are used to recruit for all types of positions, from the most unskilled to the most highly skilled and top managerial positions. The ads range from the simple, matter-of-fact type to highly creative eye-catching productions.[38] The average 1985 advertising cost for high-level jobs was in excess of $3500 per professional person recruited.[39]

Trade journals enable organizations to aim at a much more specific group of potential applicants than the newspapers. Ads in trade journals often are more elaborate, and the paper stock quality is better than newsprint. Unfortunately, long lead times are required and thus the ads can become outdated.

Preparing ads to be placed in newspapers and trade journals or on radio and television requires considerable skill. Many organizations hire advertising firms to do this rather than spend the time and money to do it themselves. Selecting an advertising agency must be done with as much care and search as is used in selecting a private recruiting agency.

Acquisitions and Mergers. Employees are obtained as a by-product of acquisitions and mergers. Although a merger or acquisition will provide some new employees with valuable skills, the overall result will be a large pool of employees, some of whom may no longer be necessary in the new organization. However, this situation may enable an organization to develop a new strategic business plan, such as a new product line, because the qualified personnel are right at hand.

Because mergers and acquisitions often present the need to displace excess employees, and a number of employees will have to be integrated into a new organization rather quickly, the PHRM department should be involved with the relevant factors of acquisitions and mergers.

Assessing Recruiting Methods

Based on a survey of personnel executives conducted by the U.S. Bureau of National Affairs, the most effective recruiting methods varied across occupations.[40] For example, private employment agencies were most effective for sales, professional, technical, and management positions, whereas walk-ins were most effective for office/clerical and plant/service positions.

While the results of the survey are informative, they represent only the perceptions that personnel executives have regarding what is effective. If a cost/benefit analysis were done on each method, the results could be quite different. Such an analysis would require that the costs involved in using a method of recruiting be measured and then compared with the benefits derived. The travel, hotel, and salary costs incurred by a recruiter visiting a college campus for example, would be easy to determine. The benefits from the college recruiting, however, can be very difficult to measure in dollar amounts. Is the length of time a person stays on the job a benefit from recruiting? If it is, can this benefit be translated into dollars and cents? Presently, it appears difficult to determine the monetary benefits of recruiting methods.[41] It might be more feasible, for example, to record the length of time that hired applicants acquired by each recruiting method stay on the job, and then compare the results. These results can then be compared with the costs of each method.

Another way that the utility of each method can be determined is by comparing the number of potentially qualified applicants hired by each method for each occupational group. The methods resulting in the hiring of the most qualified applicants in each occupational group could be considered to be the most effective, even if not the least expensive.

Increasing the Pool of Potentially Qualified Applicants

Although organizations may use both external and internal sources of recruitment, they may not always obtain a sufficient number of qualified applicants, or be able to retain those employees of most value to the organization. This is particularly true in highly competitive markets and for highly skilled individuals.[42] The organization can, however, enhance recruitment through the enticements it offers, such as relocation assistance, career development programs, or child-care services. As an added benefit, many things that companies are doing to increase applicant pools also increase the probability that once hired, the person will stay.

Before looking at what the organization can do to attract potentially qualified applicants, it is useful to look first at the applicants. If organizations want to attract candidates, they need to know how candidates are attracted and by what.[43] To find out *how* candidates are attracted, one must know where they get their information regarding job availability. As discussed in the previous section on assessing recruiting methods, different types of candidates learn about job availability through different sources, so the method used should change to suit the type of candidate sought, based on proven effectiveness.[44]

Knowing *what* attracts candidates involves knowing what makes an organization attractive to prospective employees,[45] for instance, the nature of the job and what it can offer to the individual. The nature of the job is defined by its duties, purposes, characteristics, and performance standards, as discussed in Chapter 3. What the organization provides can include traditional direct and indirect compensation, or several newer forms of indirect compensation that motivate better employee performance. Although an organization may become attractive by offering high initial levels of traditional direct and indirect compensation, this may be too costly for an organization and may not be attractive to all individuals. New forms of indirect compensation as a means of increasing the pool of potentially qualified applicants are discussed later in this chapter. The traditional forms of direct and indirect compensation are discussed more extensively in Chapters 9, 10, and 11.

After learning about an available job through one of the several sources shown in Exhibit 4.3, the individual needs to know more about the nature of the job and the organization's compensation programs. For some individuals, other employees may be the source of this information, while for others it is the organization itself. Because advertisements, pamphlets, and recruiting agencies are generally unable to convey all of this information, the organization often needs to rely on the recruitment interviews with external candidates for the conveyance of knowledge about the job and its compensation. For internal candidates, job information may be more critical, so a job-matching program may be more appropriate. After discussing these two means of conveying job and organizational information—recruitment interview and job matching—several new forms of indirect compensation are discussed in this chapter. They are organized under two categories: expanding career and job opportunities, and alternative work arrangements.

Conveying Job and Organizational Information

The traditional approach to recruiting is concerned with matching the abilities of the job applicant with the skills required by the job (Match 1 only). The more recent approach to recruiting adds the matching the personality, interests, and preferences of the job applicant with the job and organizational characteristics (Match 1 and Match 2). Effective PHRM strives to achieve both Match 1 and Match 2 as a means for recruiting job applicants who not only can do the job, but who will stay. The job interview and job matching programs can be instrumental in providing accurate information and, therefore, making it likely that recruits will get what they expect and stay.

Job Interview. A vital aspect of the recruitment process is the **job interview**. A good interview provides the applicant with a realistic preview of the job, and can result in stimulating an applicant's interest in joining an organization. A bad interview can result in applicants rejecting the possibility of working for the organization.

All other things being equal, the chance of a person accepting a job offer increases when interviewers show personal interest in, and concern for, the applicant. In addition, it has been found that college students feel most positive toward the recruitment interview when they can use at least half of the interview time to ask questions of the interviewer, and when they are not embarrassed or put on the spot by the interviewer.

The content of the recruitment interview is also important. Organizations often assume that it is in their best interest to tell a job applicant only the positive aspects of the organization. However, studies by the life insurance industry have reported that providing realistic (positive and negative) information actually increases the number of recruits. In addition, those who receive realistic job information are more likely to remain with the organization.[46]

Assuming that the job applicants pass an initial screening, they should be given the opportunity to interview a potential supervisor and even potential co-workers. The interview with the potential supervisor is crucial, because this is the person who often makes the final decision.

Job Matching. **Job matching** is a systematic effort to identify the people's skills, knowledge, and aptitudes, and their personality, interests, and preferences, to facilitate matching them to job openings. Increasing pressure on organizations to maintain effective recruitment, selection, and placement of new and current employees may make an automated job-matching system worthwhile. For example, Citibank's job-matching system for non-professional employees evolved from an automated system designed to monitor job requisition and internal placement processes. The system is currently used to identify suitable positions for staff members who wish to transfer or who are seeking another job due to technological displacement or reorganization, and to ensure that suitable internal candidates have not been overlooked before external recruiting begins. Thus, the system appears not only to help recruit people and ensure that they stay, but also to provide a firm basis for job-related recruitment and selection procedures.

There are two major components of a job-matching system: **job profiles** and **candidate profiles**. The job profiles are elaborate job descriptions and specifications. The candidate profiles contain information regarding the candidate's experience or skills related to specific jobs. These jobs are the same ones described in the job profiles. It also lists the candidates' job preferences and interests. With these profiles, the organization can identify many more potentially qualified job applicants for specific jobs than previously.

Expanding Career and Job Opportunities

Organizations can enhance the attractiveness of the organization and increase its applicant pool by providing career opportunities, by breaking down job stereotyping, by aiding in job relocation, and by providing child-care assistance.

Career Opportunities. The decision to provide career opportunities involves several choices for the organization. First, should the organization have an active policy of promotion from within? Second, should the organization be committed to a training and development program to provide sufficient candidates for internal promotion? If the answers to these questions are "yes," then the organization must identify career ladders consistent with organizational and job requirements, and with employee skills and preferences.

An organization may identify several career paths for different groups or types of employees. This concept is based on the premise that an organization cannot afford to recruit applicants for lower-level jobs when they already possess those skills necessary for higher-level jobs. This actually occurs, however, with many people recruited from college. Although they essentially are over-qualified for their first jobs, the organization hires them for more difficult future jobs. This approach is partially to blame for the higher turnover rate of new college graduates. It also is a cause for concern regarding legal compliance. Employers may claim that a college degree is necessary for the second or third job, thus possibly leading to discriminatory barriers to recruitment and promotion.

One way to reduce the possibility of discrimination is for an organization to establish career ladders and career paths.[47] When organizations have career ladders and paths with clearly specified requirements, anchored in sound job analyses, the organization can present a better legal defence for its recruitment policy. Organizations with clearly defined career ladders also may have an easier time attracting and recruiting qualified job applicants, and a better chance of keeping employees. Career paths are also discussed in Chapter 12.

An attractive way to begin recruitment is to offer temporary career opportunities to individuals, particularly those who are less apt to be familiar with organizational life. Two of the most popular temporary opportunities are summer internships for college students and internships for middle-aged women looking for new careers.

Reducing Job Stereotyping. In Chapter 2, job stereotyping based on gender or other discriminatory factors is discussed in detail. To reduce this stereotyping organizations should "de-sex" job titles, avoid using the "old-boy network" for recruitment, and never consider that only males are suitable for some positions. Although these changes will help increase the pools of applicants for many more jobs, particularly the top jobs, the increases are likely to be gradual, based on the progress experienced in the 1970s.[48] Organizations should be aware that job stereotyping still appears to pervade the recruitment and selection procedures involving older employees.[49]

Relocation Assistance. Organizations are finding that employees are more reluctant to relocate, and that it is more necessary to provide relocation assistance.[50] With high interest and inflation rates, the costs of relocation have soared for both the individual and the organization. Providing low-interest mortgages to employees who have to sell their houses in one town and buy houses in the new town (often with mortgages at much higher interest rates) is one increasingly common form of relocation assistance.

Child-care Assistance. Many Canadian employers are providing some kind of child-care services for their employees. The provision of such benefits may cause reductions in turnover, tardiness, and absenteeism, and improvements in recruiting success, morale, productivity, public relations, and product quality.[51] There is a wide spectrum of child-care services that organizations can undertake to meet the needs of working parents, including:

- *Supporting existing facilities:* Employers can help to lower program costs for participants and, at the same time, improve the quality of child-care services by contributing funds or products or by donating some types of assistance.
- *Setting up information and referral systems:* To help eliminate some of the worries of being a working parent, the personnel department can keep a current list of child-care centres, including fee schedules and eligibility requirements.
- *Subsidizing employees' child-care costs:* Providing vouchers and "sub-letting" child-care centre slots are the two most common ways of underwriting child-care expenses. In the former, the employer issues a voucher for use at any participating centre, which then bills the company for the amount of the voucher. Under the latter arrangement, management reserves a number of slots in a centre and then passes along to employees the savings associated with the group rate.
- *Establishing a child-care centre:* Where community services are deficient, management can set up its own child-care program for workers or even join with other area employers to form a community centre.[52]

Although providing these types of programs is expensive, it probably is less costly than the less effective recruitment, increased absenteeism, and turnover that result from not having these programs. However, to help keep costs in line and to provide the most appropriate assistance, the personnel department should conduct a careful analysis of the organization's needs for this type of service and a careful review of what is available in the community. In Canada, the provision of day-care services to working parents is much more prevalent in the health and service industries than in the industrial sector. The results of a number of studies indicate that, although such assistance by an employer aids in the attraction and retention of some employees, the reduction of absence and tardiness is not apparent.[53] In 1985 there were an estimated 91 work-site day-care centres across Canada, and many employers provided this service for different reasons.[54]

Alternative Work Arrangements

This may be the decade in which Canadians free themselves from the tyranny of the time clock. Already, a significant number of Canadians have done so by working under one of several types of alternative, flexible work arrangements. The growing number of single-parent families, the high costs of commuting, the preference for larger blocks of personal time, and the desire of older workers to reduce their hours will all reinforce the trend toward flexible scheduling. Far from contributing to, or representing a decline in, the work ethic, alternative work arrangements strengthen it by reducing the stresses caused by the conflict between job demands, family needs, educational needs, and the desire for leisure. Thus, organizations can only enhance their recruiting attractiveness by offering alternative as well as standard work schedule arrangements.[55]

Standard Work Schedules. These include the standard day, evening, and night work sessions and 40-h-per-week schedules. (In the 1860s, the average work week was 72 h; 12 h per day, six days per week. It was 58 h in 1900 and is approximately 40 h per week today.) Standard work schedules also include overtime work, part-time work, and shift work over a 40-h week.

Someone who does shift work might work from 08:00 to 16:00 one week, 16:00 to 24:00 the next, and 24:00 to 08:00 the next. Since the end of World War I, shift work systems have become more prevalent in industrialized countries. Currently, about 20% of all industrial workers in Europe, the United States, and Canada are on shift-work schedules.[56] The percentage of employees on part-time schedules also has increased steadily.

All of these standard work schedules have advantages and disadvantages, as shown in Exhibit 4.4, but traditionally they provide little choice to employees. Initially, employees may have some choice in the schedules they choose but, after that, the working days of the week (generally five) and the hours of the working day (generally eight) are fixed. Because employee preferences and interests may change, what may once have been an appropriate work schedule might become inappropriate. If alternative arrangements are not provided, the employee may leave the organization. Furthermore, the organization may have a difficult time attracting a group of employees who are satisfied with the same schedule. Thus, provisions for non-standard work schedules become more necessary.[57] Employees often are given a choice between a non-standard schedule and a standard schedule, as well as a choice of hours, days, and total number of hours of work per week.

Flextime Schedules. This is the most popular non-standard work schedule with organizations because it decreases absenteeism, increases employee morale, induces better labour-management relations, and encourages a high level of employee participation in decision making, self-control, and discretion.[58]

Simply stated, **flextime** is a work schedule that gives employees daily choice in the timing of work and non-work activities. Flex-time involves three components. **Band width** refers to the maximum length of the work day. This band (often ranging between 10 and 16 h) is divided into core time and flexible time. **Core time** is when the employee *has* to work; **flexible time** allows the employee freedom to choose when to complete the required number of work hours that day.

Advantages and Disadvantages of Standard Work Schedules

Exhibit 4.4

Type of Schedule	Advantages	Disadvantages
Regular	Allows for standardization, predictability, and ease of adminstration: consistent application for all employees	Does not fit needs of all employees; not always consistent with preferences of customers
Shift	More effective use of plant and equipment: allows continuous operation and weekend work	Can be stressful, particularly if rotating shifts; lower satisfaction and performance
Overtime	Permits more efficient utilization of existing workforce; cheaper than alternatives: allows flexibility	Job performance may decline; may not be satisfying and may contribute to employee fatigue
Part-time	Allows scheduling flexibility to the organization, enabling it to staff at peak and unusual times; cheaper than full-time employees	Applicable to only a limited number of jobs; increased costs of training; no promotion opportunities

Source: "Part-time and Temporary Employees," ASPA–BNA Survey 25. *Bulletin to Management,* December 5, 1974, p. 5. Reprinted by permission from *Bulletin to Management,* copyright 1974 by The Bureau of National Affairs, Inc., Washington, D.C.

Among the advantages of flextime is its ability to increase employee productivity, although it does not necessarily do so. It also allows organizations to accommodate employee preferences, some of which may be legally protected, such as accommodation of time off for religious leave. The disadvantages are that it forces the supervisor to do more planning, sometimes makes communications between employees (particularly with different schedules) difficult, and requires more record-keeping of employees' hours. Furthermore, most flextime schedules still require employees to work five days per week.

Compressed Work Weeks. Provisions for employees who want to work fewer than five days per week have led to **compressed work weeks**. By extending the work day beyond the standard eight hours, employees generally need to work only three or four days per week to complete a standard 40-hour work week. Compressed work weeks are becoming particularly popular for certain occupations, such as nursing.

Although the compressed work week gives employees larger blocks of free time (three- or four-day weekends), it is easier for some employees to work five days for eight hours each day. The company, however, can make better use of its equipment and can decrease turnover and absenteeism by instituting compressed work weeks. Scheduling and legal problems also accompany compressed work week arrangements, but legal exceptions can be made, and scheduling can become a joint process between supervisor and employee.

In Metro Toronto, a survey shows that approximately 35% of firms are using one or more of the above systems. The same survey revealed that in those firms the use of alternative methods had the following impact: [59]

- Tardiness was virtually eliminated
- Short-term absenteeism was reduced by more than 50%
- Morale was improved
- Hours of business could be expanded without overtime costs to the organization
- Potential employees found the arrangement attractive

Permanent Part-Time Work and Job Sharing. Sometimes productive employees cannot maintain a full-time commitment to the organization. Traditionally, part-time work has meant filling positions that only lasted for a short time, such as those in retail stores during holiday periods. Now some organizations have designated **permanent part-time positions**. A permanent part-time work schedule may be a shortened daily schedule (perhaps from 13:00 to 17:00) or an odd-hour shift (perhaps from 17:00 to 21:00). Organizations can also use permanent part-time schedules to fill in the remainder of a day composed of two 10-h shifts (representing a compressed work week).

Job sharing is a particular type of part-time work. In job sharing, two people divide the responsibility for a regular full-time job. Both may work half the job, or one could work more hours than the other.

Part-time workers generally receive little or no indirect compensation, but workers on permanent part-time and job-sharing schedules often do. The benefits to these workers are not equal to those of full-time workers but are prorated according to the amount of time they work.

Both permanent part-time and job sharing provide the organization and employees with opportunities that might not otherwise be available. They provide organizations with the flexibility to meet actual staffing demands, and do so with employees who are at least as productive, if not more so, than regular full-time employees. Employees benefit from being able to enjoy permanent work with less than a full-time commitment to the organization.

Statistics Canada estimated that less than 1% of Canadian workers shared jobs as of 1983.[60] Nevertheless, the subject of permanent part-time employment is becoming a hot issue between union and management in Canada. While management views part-time work as a way to control labour costs more efficiently, for unions the issue is a double-edged sword: while they want to improve the conditions of part-timers through extended benefits and pension coverage, they must balance that against their concern that part-timers are cutting into the future growth of full-time jobs. In 1985, 5000 flight attendants and support crews of CP Air engaged in a labour dispute over this matter.[61] While Statistics Canada estimated that 16% of all employees worked on part-time schedules (less than 30 h per week according to the official definition), this practice is used often by large department stores. For example, at Simpsons Limited, permanent part-time employees represent 60% of the labour force. Similar figures apply to Woodward Stores and Eaton's. In the banking industry, only 147 000 employees (about 5%) are permanent part-time workers.[62] Growth in this direction is projected for the years to come.[63]

Assessing Recruitment Activity

The recruitment activity is supposed to meet the criteria of attracting the right people at the right time, within legal limits, so that both people and organizations can select each other based on their respective short-run and long-run interests. Assessment of recruitment should be based on how well it meets those criteria and on the basis of the more specific criteria shown in Exhibit 4.5. The criteria in Exhibit 4.5 are grouped by the stage of the recruitment process to which they are most applicable.

Recruitment is not concerned only with attracting people, but rather, with attracting those whose preferences and interests probably will be matched by the organization and who have the skills, knowledge, and aptitudes to perform adequately. It is only by matching these two sets of personal factors with the organization's needs that the recruitment activity will result in productive employees who will remain with the organization. Thus, as shown in Exhibit 4.5, job performance and turnover are benefit criteria for recruitment whose value could be assessed.

Another benefit criterion by which recruiting can be assessed is legal compliance. Job applicants must be recruited fairly and without discrimi-

Some Criteria for Assessing Recruitment — *Exhibit 4.5*

Stage of Entry	Type of Criteria
Pre-entry **Entry**	Ability of the organization to recruit newcomers Initial expectations of newcomers Choice of organization by the individual (needs being matched with climate)
Post-entry	Initial job attitudes, such as • satisfaction with one's job • commitment to the organization • descriptive statements about the job (to be compared with the expectations held as an outsider) • thoughts about quitting Job performance Job survival and voluntary turnover rates

Source: From J. P. Wanous, *Organizational Entry.* © 1980, Addison-Wesley Publishing Company, Inc., Reading, MA, p. 62, Table 3.3. Reprinted with permission.

nation. During the entry and post-entry stages, they also must receive fair opportunities to be matched to appropriate jobs and to perform to their maximum abilities. Thus, the value of the costs saved (benefits gained) from not paying fines should be assessed for both recruitment and selection.

In addition to assessing each benefit criterion of recruitment, each method or source of recruitment can be evaluated. For example, for each method, such as radio advertising or employee referrals, the cost per applicant and cost per hire can be determined. One can determine the value of the benefit criteria for each method, such as the average length of time that the employee stays with the organization and the average level of performance of each employee. All of these costs and benefits of each method can then be compared. On the basis of this comparison, some methods may be used more, some dropped, and some modified to reduce the costs. Similarly, recruiting sources can be assessed.

Summary

Recruiting is a major activity in an organization's human resource planning and management program. After human resource needs have been established and job requirements have been identified through job analysis, a program of recruitment can be established to produce a pool of job applicants. These applicants can be obtained from internal or external sources.

For recruiting to be effective, it must not only consider the needs of the organization, but also those of society and the individual. Society's needs are most explicitly defined by various federal and provincial regulations in the name of equal employment opportunity. The needs of individuals figure prominently in two aspects: attracting candidates and retaining desirable employees.

Once legal considerations are established, the organization must recruit a sufficient number of potentially qualified applicants so that the individuals selected are adequately matched to the job. This matching will help to ensure that the individuals will perform effectively and not leave the organization. Organizations can attract and retain employees by numerous methods and through various sources. Although some methods and sources are more effective than others, the ones chosen often are determined by the type of applicant sought.

If the traditional sources and methods fail to produce a sufficient number of potentially qualified applicants, organizations should consider making available programs and services to attract applicants, such as alternate work-schedule arrangements, child-care facilities, and by expanding career opportunities. Recognition of employee rights, as discussed in Chapter 15, and improvements in the quality of work life, as discussed in Chapter 13, are other considerations that can make an organization more attractive to potential employees.

Discussion Questions

1. What contemporary challenges do organizations face in recruiting job applicants?
2. What are the purposes of recruitment and how do those purposes affect other organizational activities?
3. How are strategic business planning, job role planning, and human resource planning systems systematically related to recruitment efforts?
4. Discuss why the cost of training and development of employees is so closely tied to recruitment programs.
5. In what way are legal considerations related to recruitment?
6. What is meant by the concept of under-utilization?
7. What are the best methods for recruiting potentially qualified applicants? Give examples to substantiate your answers.
8. What interview characteristics are often related to increasing an applicant's desire to work for an organization and increasing the applicant's likelihood of staying once hired?

CASE STUDY

The Promise

Stan Fryer, project leader at General Instruments, knew that today would be one of those proverbial Mondays that managers so often fear. Stan's boss and group manager, Marguerite Albrecht, had left town on business the previous Friday and would not return until the following week. General Instruments, a defence contractor, employs nearly 500 engineers, and designs and manufactures a number of electronic navigation systems. Recruiting qualified engineers has been difficult for the company because of the competitive market in Metropolitan Toronto and the fairly substantial cost-of-living increase for anyone relocating to the area.

Stan's immediate problem this morning concerned a new engineer recruit, June Harrison, a single 23-year-old systems engineer who was hired three weeks previously after graduation from the University of Calgary. Much to Stan's surprise, June had submitted her letter of resignation, stating personal reasons as the cause for her departure. In addition to the letter of resignation, Stan also had a memo from June's supervisor, Lou Snider, describing the events leading up to June's resignation.

It seemed, as well as Stan could reconstruct the events, that June was expecting overtime pay on this week's paycheque because of the extra hours she had put in over the previous three weeks. Lou, however, had neglected to file the proper payroll paperwork so that June could receive her overtime pay in the current pay period. This did not surprise Stan, given Lou's prior history of not getting the job done in other supervisory positions at General Instruments. Apparently, Stan's boss had reprimanded Lou for filing so much overtime for his section. So Lou decided to spread out some of the overtime charges over several pay periods.

What Lou hadn't realized was that June had finally secured an apartment in downtown Toronto (she had been renting a room in a nearby hotel) and had committed herself to make a three-month payment and deposit from the amount she expected to receive for both her regular overtime work. When June realized what was going to happen, she called Marguerite to set up a meeting to discuss how she could cover her housing expense. June remembered that when she was being recruited, Marguerite had told her to contact her if she ever needed anything or had any problems settling into her new job. Marguerite was in a bit of a rush to get to a staff meeting, so she agreed to see June early the following day. When June reported to Marguerite's office the next morning, she was understandably upset when the secretary told her that Marguerite had left town on a business trip. She returned to her office and drafted her resignation letter.

As Stan contemplated how to resolve his problem, he recalled the speech that Marguerite had given him two years previously when Stan joined General Instruments. Marguerite made clear her distaste for young engineers who had a tendency to live beyond their means and to count on bonuses and overtime as if they were regular assured components of their paycheques. Despite this, Stan decided that the company must try to arrange for a loan covering June's housing expenses and, more importantly, to persuade her to reconsider her hasty decision.

No sooner had Stan decided on a course of action than June appeared in his doorway. She had done some thinking over the weekend after talking with another General Instruments project engineer, a temporary employee hired for the duration of a single project. It seemed that temporary employees earned about 20% more than comparable permanent employees at General Instruments, although they received considerably fewer benefits, such as retirement and health insurance. June made a proposal to Stan: She would retract her resignation letter if the company would permit her, in effect, to quit and be rehired as a temporary project engineer. Otherwise, she planned to leave General Instruments and accept an offer she had received from an engineering firm in her home city of Calgary.

As Stan listened, he wondered how Marguerite would handle this situation. In his own mind, June's proposal sounded more like blackmail.

Case Questions:

1. What, in your estimation, created this problem?
2. What recruitment practices might improve General Instruments' ability to attract new engineers?
3. Could June's problem have been prevented? How?
4. If you were Stan, what would you do?

Source: Adapted with permission from R. S. Schuler and S. A. Youngblood, *Effective Personnel Management*, 2nd ed. (St. Paul: West Publishing Co., 1986), pp. 145–146.

Endnotes

1. C. J. Coleman, *Personnel: An Open System Approach* (Cambridge, MA: Winthrop, 1979). P. G. Greenlaw and W. D. Briggs, *Modern Personnel Management* (Philadelphia: Saunders, 1979).
2. B. Schneider, *Staffing Organizations* (Santa Monica, CA: Goodyear, 1976).
3. R. H. Hawk, *The Recruitment Function* (New York: AMACOM, a division of American Management Associations, 1967).
4. E. H. Schein, "Increasing Organizational Effectiveness through Better Human Resource Planning and Development," *Sloan Management Review*, Fall 1977, pp. 1–20.
5. R. Stoops, "Are You Ready for the Coming Recruitment Boom?" *Personnel Journal*, July 1982, pp. 490, 492. R. Stoops, "Recruitment Strategy," *Personnel Journal*, February 1982, p. 102.
6. H. A. Acuff, "Improving the Employment Function," *Personnel Journal*, June 1982, p. 407. Reprinted with the permission of *Personnel Journal*, Costa Mesa, CA. All rights reserved.
7. Information based on the authors' discussions during 1985 with R. Szawlowski, Manager, Manpower Planning and Development, Pratt & Whitney Canada Inc. See also R. Szawlowski, "Training and Development in the High Technology Industry: Present and Future Trends," in S. L. Dolan and R. S. Schuler (eds.) *Canadian Readings in Personnel and Human Resource Management* (St. Paul: West Publishing Co. 1987).
8. Bureau of National Affairs, *Bulletin to Management*, Sept. 24, 1981, p. 3.
9. L. C. Thurow, "Wanted: More Skilled Workers," *New York Times*, Sunday, May 3, 1981. *Basic Skills in the*

U.S. Work Force (New York: Center for Public Resources, 1983).
10. H. Kelin, "Financial Officers Often in Demand as Companies Seek Cost-Cutters," *The Wall Street Journal*, Nov. 22, 1982, p. 33. "When the Slump Helps Service Firms Prosper," *Business Week*, May 10, 1982, p. 42.
11. M. Gibb-Clark, "CN ordered to recruit more women in landmark human-rights decision," *The Globe and Mail*, August 23, 1984, pp. 1–2.
12. H. C. Jain, "Human Rights: Issues in Employment," *Human Resources Management in Canada*, 1983, p. 50,012.
13. Based on L. J. White, "Equal Employment Opportunities, Challenges, and Practice for Canadian Companies: Royal Bank Experience," in S. L. Dolan and R. S. Schuler (eds.), *Canadian Readings in Personnel and Human Resource Management* (St. Paul: West Publishing Company, 1987); and "Equal Employment Opportunities at the Royal Bank" (interview with M. G. Bucknell), *APHRQ*, vol. 6, No. 8–9, 1983, p. 15.
14. Only promotion and transfers are considered as internal methods of recruitment. Recruiting by demotions is done infrequently. Demotions are discussed in Chapters 8, 15.
15. L. R. Sayles and G. Strauss, *Managing Human Resources* (Englewood Cliffs, NJ: Prentice-Hall, 1977), p. 147.
16. A. Patton, "When Executives Bail Out to Move Up," *Business Week*, Sept. 13, 1982, pp. 13, 15, 17, 19. For a review of the costs of relocations, see H. Z. Levine, "Relocation Practices," *Personnel*, Jan.–Feb. 1982, pp. 4–10. See also the entire issue of *Personnel Administrator* (April 1984).
17. H. Klein, "Fast Promotions Haunts Some in a Recession," *The Wall Street Journal*, March 19, 1982, p. 29.
18. J. P. Campbell, M. D. Dunnette, E. E. Lawler III, and K. E. Weick, Jr., *Managerial Behavior, Performance and Effectiveness* (New York: McGraw-Hill, 1970).
19. M. Axmith and B. Moses, "Career Planning and Relocation Counselling: An Emerging Personnel Function," Dolan and Schuler, endnote 13.
20. Based on S. L. Mangum, "Recruitment and Job Search: The Recruitment Tactics of Employers," *Personnel Administrator*, June 1982, pp. 96–104; and *Personnel Practices Forum*, 1979, Bureau of National Affairs.
21. J. R. Garcia, "Job Posting for Professional Staff," *Personnel Journal*, Oct. 1981, pp. 796–798.
22. T. Rendero, "Consensus," *Personnel*, Sept.–Oct. 1980 (New York: AMACOM, a division of the American Management Associations, 1981), p. 5.
23. R. Stoops, "Employee Referral Programs: Part I," *Personnel Journal*, Feb. 1981, p. 98; Part II, pp. 172–173.

24. H. C. Jain, "Employment Tests and Discrimination in the Hiring of Minority Groups," in H. C. Jain, *Contemporary Issues in Canadian Personnel Administration* (Scarborough, Ontario: Prentice-Hall, 1974).
25. Sources for the data comes from A. Hasan and S. Gera, "Aspects of Job Search in Canada," Discussion Paper No. 156 (Ottawa: Economic Council of Canada, 1980); and Statistics Canada, *Labour Force Surveys*.
26. P. J. Decker and E. T. Cornelius, "A Note on Recruiting Sources and Job Survival Rates," *Journal of Applied Psychology*, 1974, 64, pp. 463–64. D. P. Schwab, "Recruiting and Organizational Participation," in K. M. Rowland and G. R. Ferris (eds.), *Personnel Management* (Boston: Allyn and Bacon, Inc., 1982), pp. 103–128.
27. Mangum, endnote 20, p. 99.
28. R. Kenney, "Open House Complements Recruitment Strategies," *Personnel Administrator*, March 1982, pp. 27–32.
29. Sunder Mangum, "The Placement Activity of the Canadian Employment Agency," *Industrial Relations* (Canada), vol. 38(1), 1983, pp. 72–94.
30. Ibid.
31. For a discussion of the false negatives and positives see S. Rubenfild and M. Crino, "Are Employment Agencies Jeopardizing Your Selection Process?" *Personnel*, Sept.–Oct. 1981, pp. 70–78. See also W. J. Bjerregaard and M. E. Gold, "Employment Agencies and Executive Recruiters: A Practical Approach," *Personnel Administrator*, May 1981, pp. 127–131, 135. W. J. Bjerregaard and M. E. Gold, "Executive Utilization of Search Consultants," *Personnel Administrator*, Dec. 1980, pp. 35–39, R. J. Cronin, "Executive Recruiters: Are They Necessary?" *Personnel Administrator*, Feb. 1980, pp. 31–34. B. Horovitz, "Where Headhunters Hunt," *Industry Week*, Feb. 9, 1981, pp. 43–47. C. E. Kur and P. G. Some, "An Untapped Source of Consulting Help," *Personnel Administrator*, Dec. 1980, pp. 29–33.
32. D. Diamond, "For Rent: Nomadic Engineer (Expensive)," *The New York Times*, Sept. 27, 1981, Section F, p. 6.
33. As quoted in H. C. Jain, "Staffing: Recruitment and Selection," in *Human Resource Management in Canada* (Scarborough, Ontario: Prentice-Hall, Canada Inc., 1983), p. 25,022.
34. P. Donohue, "Light and Dark on the Hiring Scene," *Human Resource Management in Canada* (Scarborough, Ontario: Prentice-Hall Canada Inc., 1984), "Current Matter," February 1984, pp. 5, 168). D. L. Chicci and C. L. Krapp, "College Recruitment from Start to Finish," *Personnel Journal*, August 1980, pp. 653–657. T. Rendero, "Consensus," *Personnel*, May–June 1980, pp. 4–10. P. Zollman, "There's Jobs in Abundance for Americans with Skills," *Columbus Dispatch*, May 20, 1979, pp. 1, 8.

35. A. E. Marshal, "Recruiting Alumni on College Campuses," *Personnel Journal*, April 1982, pp. 264–266.
36. *The Globe & Mail*, October 1, 1982, p. R4.
37. R. Stoops, "Advertising in Trade Journals," *Personnel Journal*, Sept. 1981, p. 678. R. Stoops, "A Marketing Approach to Recruitment," *Personnel Journal*, Aug. 1981, p. 608. An extension of advertising in newspapers and journals is direct mail advertising. For a description see R. Stoops, "More on Direct Mailing Advertising," *Personnel Journal*, March 1982.
38. Bureau of National Affairs, *Personnel Policies Forum*, 1979.
39. Data for 1985 was supplied by Gestion MDS Inc., a management consulting firm in Montreal; for the beginning of 1982, similar figures were reported by *The Globe & Mail*, Jan. 12, 1982, p. B2, which reported the advertisement costs as being $2700 per person.
40. Relatively little work has been done on the assessment of recruitment method effectiveness. See Schwab, endnote 26, pp. 111–113 for a review of what has been done.
41. K. S. Teel, "Estimating Employee Replacement Costs," *Personnel Journal*, December 1983, pp. 956–960.
42. For a review, see Schwab, endnote 26. See also J. Ullman, "Interfirm Differences in the Cost of Search for Clerical Workers," *Journal of Business*, 1968, 41, pp. 153–165. G. J. Stigler, "Information in the Labor Market," *Journal of Political Economy*, 1962, pp. 94–105. A. Rees, "Information Networks in Labor Markets," *American Economic Review*, 1966, pp. 559–566.
43. Limited information is available on the general effectiveness of recruiting methods, so each organization should do its own analysis.
44. J. H. Greenhaus and O. C. Brenner, "How Do Job Candidates Size Up Prospective Employers?" *Personnel Administrator*, March 1982, pp. 21–25. "Summer Internships Receive High Marks from College Students," *The Wall Street Journal*, Aug. 27, 1981, pp. 1, 20. "Firms Providing Business Internships Lure Middle-Aged Women Looking for Careers," *The Wall Street Journal*, Sept. 2, 1981, p. 23. R. L. Lattimer, "Developing Career Awareness among Minority Youths: A Case Example," *Personnel Journal*, Jan. 1981, p. 17. R. S. Greenberger, "An Oversupply of College Graduates Forces Some into Lower-Level Jobs," *The Wall Street Journal*, Feb. 25, 1982, p. 27.
45. For a discussion of the realistic job review or preview see J. P. Wanous, *Organizational Entry* (Reading, MA: Addison-Wesley, 1980). J. H. Greenhaus, C. Seidel, and M. Marinis, "The Impact of Expectations and Values on Job Attitudes," *Organizational Behavior and Human Performance*, 1983. M. D. Hakel, "Employment Interviewing," in K. M. Rowland, and G. R. Ferris (eds.), *Personnel Management* (Boston: Allyn and Bacon Inc., 1982), pp. 153–154. R. R. Reilly, B. Brown, M. R. Blood, and C. Z. Malatesta, "The Effects of Realistic Previews: A Study and Discussion of the Literature," *Personnel Psychology*, 1981, 34, pp. 823–834. R. D. Arvey and J. G. Campion, "The Employment Interview: A Summary and Review of the Recent Literature," *Personnel Psychology*, 1982, 35, pp. 281–322.
46. P. Sheibar, "A Simple Selection System Called Job Match," *Personnel Journal*, Jan. 1979, pp. 26–29, 53. See also L. Albright, "Staffing Policies and Procedures," in S. J. Carroll and R. S. Schuler, *Human Resource Management in the 1980s* (Washington, DC: The Bureau of National Affairs, 1983).
47. H. L. Wellbank, D. T. Hall, M. A. Morgan, and W. C. Hamner, "Planning Job Progression for Effective Career Development and Human Resources Management," *Personnel*, March–April 1978, pp. 54–64.
48. B. Rosen and T. H. Jerdee, "Too Old or Not Too Old," *Harvard Business Review*, Nov.–Dec. 1977, pp. 97–106.
49. M. Magnus and J. Dodd, "Relocation: Changing Attitudes and Company Policies," *Personnel Journal*, July 1981, pp. 538–548. G. F. Milbrandt, "Relocation Strategies: Part I," *Personnel Journal*, July 1981, pp. 551–554. See also *Personnel Administrator*, Dec. 1982.
50. A. Brooks, "Job Help for Wives," *The New York Times*, Aug. 30, 1981, Section F, p. 8.
51. "Child Care: Larger Number, Positive Effects," *Bulletin to Management* (Washington, DC: BNA), Nov. 25, 1982, p. 7.
52. S. A. Coltrin and B. Barendse, "Is Your Organization a Good Candidate for Flextime?" *Personnel Journal*, Sept. 1981, pp. 712–715. L. F. Copperman, F. D. Keast, and D. G. Montgomery, "Old Workers and Part-Time Work Schedules," *Personnel Administrator*, Oct. 1981, pp. 35–38. T. E. Currey, Jr., and D. N. Haerer, "The Positive Impact of Flextime on Employee Relations," *Personnel Administrator*, Feb. 1981, pp. 62–66. P. Farish, "PAIR Potpourri," *Personnel Administrator*, June 1981, p. 10. D. J. Petersen, "Flextime in the United States: The Lessons of Experience," *Personnel*, Jan.–Feb. 1980, pp. 21–31. D. Stetson, "Work Innovation Improving Morale," *The New York Times*, Sept. 20, 1981, p. 53. "Why Flextime Is Spreading," *Business Week*, Feb. 23, 1981, pp. 455–460.
53. Dolan, S. L., "Working Mothers' Absenteeism: Does Workplace Day-Care Make a Difference?" in D. Vredenbourgh and R. S. Schuler, (eds.), *Effective Management Research and Applications* (Proceedings of the Eastern Academy of Management, Pittsburgh, 1983), pp. 48–51.
54. R. Wright, "Work-Site Day Care in Canada," Feature report in *Human Resource Management in Can-*

ada, (Scarborough: Prentice-Hall Canada, 1985), pp. 5,421–5,431.
55. T. A. Mahoney, "The Rearranged Workweek: Evaluations of Different Work Schedules," *California Management Review*, Summer 1978, pp. 31–39. A. R. Cohen and H. Gadon, *Alternative Work Schedules: Integrating Individual and Organizational Needs* (Reading, MA: Addison-Wesley, 1978). M. Maurice, *Shift Work* (Geneva, Switzerland: Internal Labor Office, 1975). D. L. Tasto and M. J. Collegan, *Shift Work Practices in the United States* (Washington, DC: National Institute for Occupational Safety and Health, 1977).
56. R. T. Golemiewski, and R. J. Hills, "Drug Company Workers Like New Schedules," *Monthly Labor Review, 100*, 1977, pp. 65–69. R. T. Golemiewski, R. Hills, and M. S. Kagna, "A Longitudinal Study of Flextime Effects: Some Consequences of an OD Structural Intervention," *Journal of Applied Behavioral Sciences, 4*, 1974, pp. 503–532.
57. S. D. Nollen, "Does Flextime Improve Productivity?" *Harvard Business Review, 57*, 1979, pp. 16–18, 76, 80.
58. R. H. Crowder, Jr., "The Four-Day, Ten-Hour Workweek," *Personnel Journal*, Jan. 1982, pp. 26–28. "A Full-Time Job—Weekends Only," *Business Week*, Oct. 15, 1979, pp. 151–152. A. R. Cohen and M. Gadon, R. B. Dunham, and D. L. Hawk, "The Four-Day/Forty-Hour Week: Who Wants It?" *Academy of Management Journal, 20*, 1977, pp. 644–655. M. D. Fottler, "Employee Acceptance of the Four-Day Workweek," *Academy of Management Journal, 20*, 1977, pp. 656–668. J. S. Kim and A. F. Campagna, "Effects of Flextime on Productivity: A Field Experiment in a Public Sector Setting," Paper presented at the National Academy of Management, Detroit, MI, 1980. V. Schein, E. Maurer, and J. Novak, "Impact of Flexible Working Hours on Productivity," *Journal of Applied Psychology, 62*, 1977, pp. 463–465. R. B. Dunham and J. L. Pierce, "The Design and Evaluation of Alternative Work Schedules," *Personnel Administrator*, April 1983, pp. 67–75.
59. The Toronto Transit Commission, *The Variable Work Hours Book*, 1981.
60. *The Gazette*, Montréal, Monday, July 8, 1985.
61. *Financial Post*, August 3, 1985.
62. Ibid.
63. J. Wallace, "The Changing World of Part-time Work: Implications for Human Resource Managers," Feature article in *Human Resources Management in Canada*, May 1986, pp. 15,519–15,524; and "Highlight from a Survey of Part-time Employment in Federally Regulated Industries," *Human Resources Management in Canada*, May 1986, pp. 15,531–15,535.

CHAPTER 5

Selection, Placement, and Employment Equity

PHRM in the News

Selection, Placement, and Employment Equity
Purposes and Importance of Selection and Placement
Relationships of Selection and Placement with PHRM Activities

Employment-Equity Legal Considerations
Legal and Normative Issues Affecting Selection and Placement

Selection and Placement Information
The Organizational Context
The Job Context
The Job Qualities
The Job Applicant
Predictors and Criteria in Selection Decisions

Obtaining Job Applicant Information
The Application Blank
The Selection and Placement Interview
Selection Tests
Types of Tests
Physical Ability Tests

Summary

Discussion Questions

Case Study

Endnotes

PHRM in the News

Hiring Age Restriction Not Bona Fide Occupational Requirement

OTTAWA—Air Canada's practice of refusing to hire pilots over the age of 27 is not a bona fide occupational requirement (BFOR), the Federal Court of Appeal has ruled. The case is the first concerning age of entry into employment to reach the Canadian courts, according to the Canadian Human Rights Commission. The ruling upholds an earlier decision of a Commission review tribunal. It is significant because it helps define what constitutes a BFOR under Section 14 of the Canadian Human Rights Act. According to Commission general counsel Russell Juriansz, it prevents employers from making a blanket refusal to hire a class or group of people unless they can prove they cannot deal with those applicants on an individual basis.

Section 14 of the Act allows for exceptions from the general rule of nondiscrimination in employment and services. The Commission is in the process of developing policies and guidelines for complaints dealing with Section 14.

Source: Human Resources Management in Canada, Report Bulletin No. 29, p. 4, Article 29.8, July 1985. © 1985, Prentice-Hall Canada Inc. Reprinted with permission.

Another Case of Age Discrimination in Hiring

SMITHS FALLS—A 40-year-old applicant for a position as police constable who never made it beyond the initial screening stage was a victim of age discrimination, an Ontario Human Rights tribunal has ruled. John Underwood filed a complaint of age discrimination against the Smiths Falls Board of Police Commissioners with the Ontario Human Rights Commission after he learned that a fellow applicant for an advertised opening for a police constable had earned an interview. Underwood, who had worked in corrections, had military experience and was a member of the Ontario Provincial Police Auxiliary, felt he was better qualified. During the investigation, which was obstructed to some extent by the police force, it was revealed that hiring criteria were, to say the least, arbitrary. Moreover, two other 40-year-old applicants with comparable and possibly even better qualifications were also rejected at the initial screening level. The age of one was circled on his application form.

In determining that age was a factor in the screening process, the tribunal pointed out that the resulting injury was made all the more serious "by the discrimination having been practiced by a public body whose judgements are bound to be more publicized and far more likely to be assumed by the public to be sound, than would those of a private organization." Underwood, who would have had to take a pay-cut had he been hired, was awarded $3,000 in damages for mental anguish. The police board was also ordered to submit to a review of its application forms and recruitment policies and procedures.

Source: Human Resources Management in Canada, Report Bulletin No. 33, pp. 3–4, March 1986. © 1986, Prentice-Hall Canada Inc. Reprinted with permission.

Staffing

These "PHRM in the News" articles highlight the increased impact of federal and provincial human rights legislation on staffing decisions made by organizations. In one case, the focus is on the Canadian Human Rights Act and the Canadian Human Rights Commission, the agency created by the amended Act in 1983. These news articles also indicate how costly selection decisions can be when made counter to employment equity laws.

Personnel and human resource managers also face other concerns in making these decisions, including (1) how to collect information on job applicants; (2) how to make selection and placement decisions; (3) how to validate tests used in making selection decisions; and (4) how to make the entire set of selection and placement procedures more useful. These concerns, along with the extensive legal considerations, raise several contemporary challenges in making selection, placement, and equal-employment-opportunity decisions.

Selection, Placement, and Employment Equity

Selection is the process of gathering information for the purposes of evaluating and deciding who should be hired, under legal guidelines, for the short- and long-term interests of the individual and the organization.[1] **Placement** is concerned with ensuring that job demands and job and organizational characteristics match individual skills, knowledge, and abilities,[2] as well as preferences, interests, and personality.[3] Concern here for both matches is consistent with our emphasis on serving the individuals as well as the organization. Thus, discussion of selection and placement is consistent with, and builds on, this emphasis prescribed in recruitment, job analysis, and job design. Selection and placement are treated as a unit because they share many common qualities. For example, both use information about the characteristics and qualities of the organization, the job, and the individual. They also share many of the same purposes and goals.

Purposes and Importance of Selection and Placement

Selection and placement procedures provide the backbone of organizations—their human resources. Through effective selection and placement, organizations can obtain and retain the human resources most likely to serve their needs, and probably also improve their organizational productivity. Since there are likely to be productivity differences between employees, selecting only those employees likely to perform well may result in substantial productivity gains. For example, in a study of budget analysts, the dollar value of the productivity of the superior performers (top 15%) was $23 000 per year greater than that of low performers (bottom 15%). In another study, of computer programmers, the dollar value difference was $20 000 per year.[4]

Effective selection and placement are critical to any organization, and involves the fulfilment of several purposes, including to

- fairly, legally, and in a non-discriminatory manner evaluate and hire potentially qualified job applicants;
- help fulfil hiring goals and quotas specified in affirmative action programs;
- evaluate, hire, and place job applicants in the best interests of the organization and of the individual;
- engage in selection and placement activities that are useful for initial hiring as well as future selection and placement of the individual (for example, in promotions or transfers); and
- make selection and placement decisions with consideration for the uniqueness of the individual, the job, the organization, and the environment, even to the extent of adapting the job or organization to the individual.[5]

In order to serve these purposes effectively, selection and placement activities must be integrated with several other PHRM activities, because of the extensive set of systemic relationships that exists between them.

Relationships of Selection and Placement with PHRM Activities

The success of an organization's selection and placement procedures depends on their relationships with several other personnel and human resource activities. As Exhibit 5.1 illustrates, selection and placement decisions begin with a pool of potentially qualified job applicants, an analysis of the qualities of the jobs that are open, and a description of the organizational context. As discussed in the three previous chapters, these are directly related to recruitment, job analysis, and human resource planning activities.

Job Design and Job Analysis. Selection and placement decisions should be made to benefit the individual and the organization. In order to do this, the qualities of the available jobs must be identified clearly. When the essential job dimensions and worker qualifications are known, selection devices can be developed. Selection devices developed on the basis of a job analysis are more likely to be job-related—and therefore more effective and more likely to satisfy legal considerations because content validity can be more easily demonstrated.[6]

However, selection devices based on job analysis tend to focus on the worker's skills, knowledge, and ability to do the job (Match 1). It is also necessary to use information about job and organizational characteristics so that job applicants can be placed in jobs that match their preferences, interests, and personality (Match 2). As noted in Chapters 3 and 4, serving these two matches helps to ensure that the short-run and long-run interests of both the individual and the organization are served.[7]

Recruitment. The success of selection and placement activities depends on the effectiveness of the recruiting activity. If recruiting does not provide a large pool of potentially qualified job applicants, it is difficult for the orga-

Staffing

Exhibit 5.1 **Components of Selection and Placement Activity**

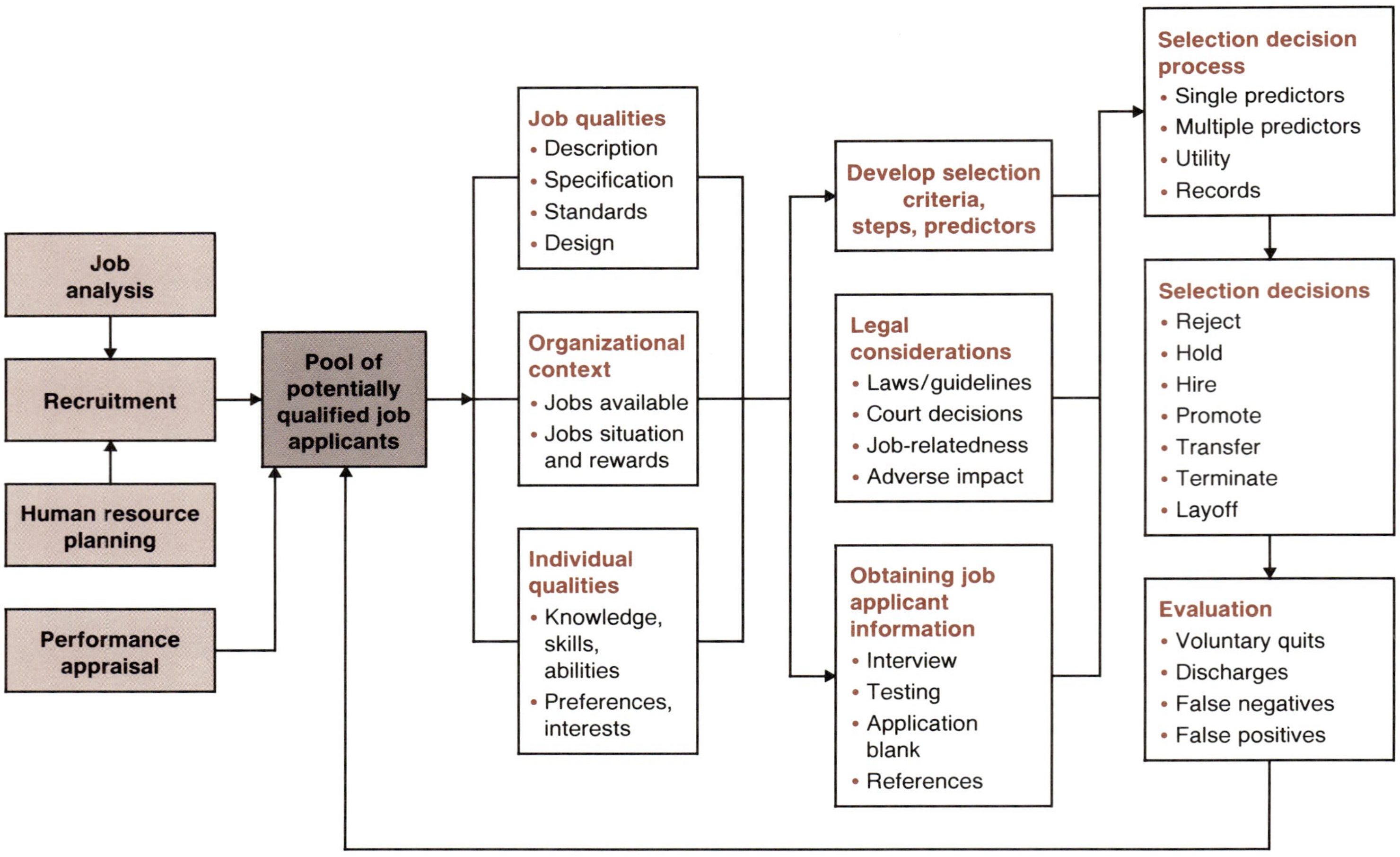

nization to select and place individuals who will perform well and not quit. If the pool is too small, the potential effectiveness of the selection and placement activities is lessened because the selection ratio tends to become large (see Chapter 6).

Human Resource Planning. Human resource planning can facilitate the organization's selection decisions by projecting when and how many such decisions will need to be made. If staffing needs for new jobs are identified, the PHRM department may need to anticipate new selection procedures and job-relatedness studies. Human resource planning also can facilitate selection decisions by ensuring that the maximum number of potential job applicants, particularly those within the organization, is identified, particularly for promotion decisions. This can be done with the use of an extensive, up-to-date human resource information system, described in Chapter 2. This information system can be used to store extensive banks of data on employees and jobs that can be readily matched when job openings are identified.

Performance Appraisal. Performance appraisals are a source of feedback that indicate whether the selection devices do indeed predict performance. If the criteria used in performance appraisal are not job-related (e.g., the appraisals are not built on job analysis) or the criteria are not communicated, it is difficult for the organization to develop and use selection devices to meaningfully predict employee performance (see Chapters 3 and 7). In other words, the selection and placement devices cannot be validated, are unable to serve their purposes, and cannot be shown to be job-related empirically.

Because the relationships of selection and placement to other PHRM activities are critical, it is important that these relationships be taken into consideration in the design of selection and placement activities. In addition, an extensive set of equal-employment-opportunity considerations also should be incorporated into selection and placement functions.

Employment-Equity Legal Considerations

The legal requirements to be met are becoming so numerous and complex that employment-equity legislation is becoming a first consideration in making employment decisions. Knowing the impact that legislation has on the selection and placement decision process is a second consideration. Both of these considerations are the responsibility of the PHRM manager. A growing number of employers have been voluntarily devising employment-equity and affirmative action policies in order to comply with the various federal and provincial human rights statutes. Prominent among some of these organizations are Bell Canada, Canadian National, the Canadian Broadcasting Corporation, the Royal Bank of Canada, the federal government, and several provincial governments.[8]

As of April 1986, however, Bill C–62 was passed, requiring all employers to file reports with the Minister of Employment and Immigration Canada in relation to employment equity. Details of such reports are specified in the Bill.

Legal and Normative Issues Affecting Selection and Placement

Determining exactly what an organization's equal-employment obligations are is made complex by an extensive web of federal, provincial, and local legislation, guidelines, quasi-judicial bodies (such as panel of arbitrators), and the Canadian Human Rights Commission rulings. Some of the most important developments affecting employment, with a special emphasis on staffing considerations, are outlined below.[9]

Historical Developments of Public Policy on Equity in Employment. Government commitment in Canada to equal rights in employment has grown steadily since World War II. For many decades following Confederation, Canadian jurisprudence provided little assistance in establishing the legal right to equitable treatment in the workplace.

There can be little doubt that the remarkable achievements of the *Universal Declaration of Human Rights*, proclaimed by the United Nations General Assembly on December 10, 1948, was a key catalyst. This was followed by the International Labour Organization's adoption of the policy of equal remuneration for male and female workers for work of equal value. What followed in Canada was a decade of fair practices legislation in the area of employment, beginning with Ontario's Fair Employment Practices Act (1951) and including two federal acts, the Canada Fair Employment Practices Act (1953) and the Female Employees Equal Pay Act (1956).

In 1958, the International Labour Organization provided another important foundation for government action when it adopted the Discrimination (Employment and Occupation) Convention (No. 111). This Convention required each ratifying country to promote equality of opportunity and treatment in employment, with the aim of eliminating discrimination. Canada ratified the Convention in 1964.

The ratification of the Convention corresponded with the emergence of new legislative initiatives in many provincial jurisdictions. Spurred in part by the work of the International Labour Organization and in part by the conservative interpretation applied by the courts, new human rights legislation was passed in all provinces. Perhaps most importantly, the administration of the new Acts was eventually placed in the hands of provincial human rights commissions, where a more proactive and developmental approach could be expected.

A commitment to equal rights by all jurisdictions is increasing at the federal level. The 1970 Royal Commission on the Status of Women, numerous studies on the economic position of native people, the Special House of Commons Committee on the Disabled and the Handicapped, the Special Committee on Participation of Visible Minorities in Canadian Society, the ratification of the International Covenants on Human Rights, the Federal Action Plan for Women, the Canadian Human Rights Act, and the Charter of Rights and Freedoms, have all derived from a deep-rooted concern with making the ideal of equality a social and economic reality.

The Canadian Human Rights Act, 1976–77, established the Canadian Human Rights Commission to enforce anti-discrimination laws and to promote observance of human rights and equality. The government has also instituted an affirmative action program in the private sector in order to test the effectiveness of voluntary programs in removing employment discrimination and correcting the effects of past discrimination. Besides prohibiting intentional discrimination on a wide variety of grounds (including six physical handicaps), the Human Rights Act explicitly accepts the systemic definition of discrimination that formed the basis of U.S. affirmative action and anti-discrimination programs. Under this definition, the Human Rights Commission examines the impact of an employment decision or transaction rather than the employer's intent, to determine whether it is discriminatory.

The Canadian Human Rights Act also explicitly permits the implementation of special programs that will prevent or reduce disadvantages to certain designated groups or remedy the effects of past discrimination against those groups. The Act also gives the Commission the ability to order the implementation of affirmative action programs where discrimination had been found. Canada further confirmed its commitment to the principle of affirmative action in passing the Constitution Act of 1982. As of April 17, 1985, under Section 15(2) of the Charter of Rights and Freedoms, the legality of special programs or affirmative action cannot be questioned. The courts are now entitled, pursuant to Section 24, to order ameliorative measures for disadvantaged groups.[10]

In 1983 the Abella Commission on Equality in Employment was appointed. This appointment stemmed from the U.S. experience, as well as from mounting public pressure for government action to define more specifically the appropriate remedies in cases of discrimination. Judge Rosalie Abella was appointed to enquire into the most efficient, effective, and equitable means of promoting employment opportunities for, and eliminating systemic discrimination against, four designated groups: women, disabled people, native people (aboriginal), and visible minorities. The inclusion of visible minorities in the Commission's mandate was significant in that, prior to that date, visible or racial minorities had not been designated as a target group for employment programs on a national basis. In its final report, the Commission recommended that organizations set mandatory equity programs.

In the United States there is abundant evidence that women have increased their participation rates and their representation in senior management jobs much more rapidly than they have in Canada, and minority representation in the workforce has increased dramatically as a result of affirmative action. There also is evidence that employers have come to support affirmative action, believing that it enhances their human resource systems and business practices.[11]

In Canada, however, only a few resource industries have implemented any kind of mandatory program. In these cases, there is dramatic proof of their effectiveness in increasing the numbers of designated group members employed.[12] The Commission found, by contrast, that the success of voluntary affirmative action programs, which have been promoted by both federal and provincial governments, has been either limited or impossible to measure.

In making the decision to recommend legislation, the Commission claimed to be ensuring the right to freedom from discrimination rather than merely hoping for it. It is argued that the laws reflect commitment and clearly define the limits of acceptable behaviour. The authors write, "A government genuinely committed to equality in the workplace will use law to accomplish it and thereby give the concept credibility and integrity."

While the Abella Commission limited its recommendations to federally regulated companies, recommendations were made that would ensure that the 89% of Canadian workers who work in non-federally regulated companies would benefit. It is urged that provincial and territorial governments pass equity legislation, with requirements being as consistent as possible with federal legislation. In the absence of universal legislation, the federal government was urged to encourage employment equity in the private sector through the use of contract compliance. We have, of course seen how contract compliance was used to ensure equality for designated groups in the United States. The granting of contracts to enhance equality in employment would be completely consistent with Treasury Board policy, which states that contracts will be let in such a manner as to relate to national policies and objectives.[13]

On July 1, 1983, the Canadian Human Rights Act was amended. It now bars discrimination in federal jurisdiction on 10 grounds: race, national or ethnic origin, skin colour, religion, age, gender, marital status, family status, disability, and conviction of an offence for which a pardon has been granted. Some of the other changes relating to employment include the following:

- All individuals covered by a collective agreement are protected against discrimination by the union, whether or not they are members of the union
- The Canadian Human Rights Commission can deal with allegations that an employer, employee organization, or organization of employers has a policy that limits the job opportunities of certain groups, even if no individual victim comes forward. This is intended to make it easier for the Commission to deal with systemic discrimination practices and policies that raise barriers against the employment of specific groups such as women and native people
- Employers are made responsible for discrimination by their employees, officers, or agents, in the course of their work, unless all of the following conditions are met: (a) the employer did not consent to the discrimination, (b) the employer exercised "all due diligence" to prevent the discrimination, and (c) the employer acted subsequently to mitigate or avoid the effects of the discrimination.

Discrimination Defined: Indirect or Systemic Discrimination. **Methods of** assessing qualifications for employment have evolved over time to suit the needs of a particular type of worker in a particular type of labour market. The Canadian Human Rights Act (as well as numerous boards of inquiry in several provinces) has borrowed the legal definition of discrimination from U.S. case law.[14] Systemic discrimination refers to any employment system or practice that, while equitable in intent and in application, has a differential and negative impact on women or minorities. In the U.S. the concept of systemic discrimination was articulated by the Supreme Court in Griggs v. Duke Power Co. (1971). In this case the court indicated that intent does not matter; it is the consequences of an employer's actions that determine whether it may have discriminated under Title VII of the Civil Rights Act. Systemic discrimination is pervasive in Canadian employment systems. Often it can be detected only by a statistical examination of the results of an employment practice, designed to measure the ratio of successful women and minorities to successful major group members.

The Legal Status of the Systemic Discrimination Concept. The approach adopted in the Griggs Case, which was a watershed for U.S. jurisprudence, also became the prevailing view in Canada. A similar if somewhat slower process has taken place in Canada. Proving intent has been an important concept in Anglo-Canadian law. In Dritnell v. Michael Brent Personnel Place (1968) and MacBean v. Village of Plaster Rock (1975), boards of inquiry in two provinces found that intention or motive must be evident to prove discrimination. A 1975 case seemed to severely limit the chances for a systemic interpretation when in Ryan v. Chief of Police, Town of North Sydney, the Board of Inquiry rejected the idea that a height and weight requirement constituted employment discrimination against women because of very heavy adverse impact.[15]

This was followed by what must be considered Canada's "Griggs" case, Singh v. Security and Investigation Services Ltd. (1976). In this case, Singh, for religious reasons, insisted on the right to wear a turban rather than the traditional hat of the company's uniform. Again, this case involved a crucial change in approach—discrimination was defined by the Board of Inquiry in terms of its effect on the protected group rather than the intent or motivation of the alleged violation.

Although the board took a clear position, it also recognized that business necessity was an acceptable defence, stating:

> First one decides whether the employee's request is important and valid, i.e., not trivial or arbitrary. Second, one determines the extent of the inconvenience that would be caused to the employer if the request were granted. Finally the inconvenience to the employer and the importance of the request from the standpoint of the employee must be balanced.

Subsequently, the Singh case was supported by a number of similar decisions. In Colfer v. Ottawa Board of Commissioners of Police (1979), an Ontario board of inquiry found height (1.75 m/5'9") and weight (72.5 kg/160 lbs.) requirements to be discriminatory, and in Foster v. B. C. Forest Products Ltd., a British Columbia Board found that a height/weight requirement had an adverse impact and was not a good indicator of strength or of the ability to do a job. Similar reasoning was used in Grole v. Sechelt Building Supplies Ltd. (1979).

Despite these decisions, a number of issues could have limited severely the impact of a systemic approach. First, the "business necessity" defence can present a substantial obstacle. Difficulties arise if the complainant is forced not only to prove a negative proposition but also to assume the responsibility, including costs, for presenting evidence on technical matters. Courts have generally held, however, that once the basic elements of the case have been proven—prima facie evidence of discrimination—the onus shifts to the respondent to establish business necessity. Such reasoning was found in Foster and Colfer as well as in Bone v. CFL and Robertson v. Metropolitan Investigation Security Canada Ltd. (1979).

A second problem can arise in reference to the acceptability of vague and subjective definitions of "business necessity." The Colfer decision, however, made it clear that evidence in support of business necessity must demonstrate an acceptable level of rigour. In an important decision in 1982, the Supreme Court of Canada ruled unanimously against a mandatory retirement age of 60 for firefighters in the borough of Etobicoke. The defence of a bona fide occupational requirement was rejected as insufficient because it was impressionistic and relied on general assertions. Evidence to support the borough's claim must, the court ruled, cover the detailed nature of the duties to be performed, the conditions existing in the workplace, and the effect of these conditions, particularly on people near retirement age.

In line with the Act's clear reference to practices that discriminate "indirectly," many boards of inquiry established under the Canada Human Rights Act have found systemic discrimination to be prohibited. Settlements and decisions relating to religious accommodation and weight and height requirements, for example, have helped define what constitutes systemic discrimination in federal jurisdiction.

A setback of this view on the federal level occurred in 1983, when a federal Court of Appeal ruled (2–1) that Sections 7 and 10 of the Canadian Human Rights Act are not sufficiently comprehensive to include indirect or systemic discrimination (CNR v. K. S. Bhinder). The courts concluded that some missing words, found in the U.S. 1964 Civil Rights Act, were necessary if the existing Canadian Act was to be interpreted to include systemic discrimination. This decision raised a serious challenge to the legal status of systemic discrimination. Some provinces, such as in Ontario, amended their own human rights Acts to clarify the situation.

Analysis of Systemic Discrimination. Systemic discrimination is not necessarily the result of conscious attempts to exclude certain groups. For this reason it involves an analysis of results and empirical validity rather than an examination of motivation and intent. Employers intent on identifying and removing systemic discrimination therefore must ascertain where target group workers are under-represented, given their availability according to requisite skills. If certain restrictive or exclusionary practices are indicated by an analysis of the the composition of the workforce, they can be analyzed more intensively.

The goal of this analysis would be to determine whether or not employment practices having an adverse impact are necessary for the safe and efficient operation of the enterprise. This determination requires two steps.

First, it is imperative to determine whether there is an alternative system or practice that will meet the employer's objective with little or no differential race or gender impact. If a suitable alternative does exist, the exclusionary practice cannot be justified as necessary. Second, if no alternative exists, it is necessary to analyze the validity of the practice, to determine whether a practice accomplishes its predictive or evaluative function.

Three methods of determining validity are commonly used, all of which are discussed in detail in Chapter 6.

1. The **criterion-related approach** involves measuring the predictive capability of a standard or practice. For example, does the possession of a Grade 12 diploma predict job success? To determine requirement, one must make a comparison between those who do and those who do not have a Grade 12 diploma, using objective measures of job success.
2. The **construct validity approach** requires a careful analysis of the identified characteristics required—the constructs—and the tasks required for successful job performance. This is necessary to determine whether the constructs themselves, such as an aptitude test, are likely to predict job performance. Can a reasonable causal link be demonstrated? While popular with industrial psychologists, the construct validity approach is less acceptable for justifying adverse impact unless backed up by criterion-related validity.
3. The **content approach** measures the degree to which the items on a test or in a selection practice are representative and appropriate for those tasks actually performed. If the test content approximates the tasks (for example, a program-drafting test for systems analysts), validity can be shown.

The systemic approach, with its emphasis on impact and business necessity rather than on intent, provides an objective measure for determining whether discrimination exists. It downplays the question of individual blame and concentrates on rationalizing employment systems based on valid business need. Solutions are oriented toward achievement of realistic goals rather than toward attitudinal change.

Despite the emphasis on systemic discrimination, intentional discrimination, whether individual or broadly based, must not be ignored. Both forms of discrimination adversely affect certain groups, therefore, both must be understood so that PHRM managers can develop effective remedies that are capable of eliminating or reducing discrimination.

In general, discrimination can be established by looking at the composition and treatment of an organization's current workforce or by looking at the number of individuals from various groups who are selected after applying to the organization. In other words, discrimination based on relevant labour market comparisons addresses discrimination vis-à-vis the current workforce. Discrimination based on employment standards that exclude protected group applicants, women, and minorities at a higher rate than other groups is discrimination vis-à-vis selection of individuals. Generally discrimination vis-à-vis selection is referred to as "adverse impact."

Essentially, the various bases listed above can be classified either as a basis for prima facie discrimination (referring to the current labour force) or a basis for prima facie adverse impact (referring to staffing decisions). These distinctions between discrimination and adverse impact are made primarily to highlight the difference between illegal employment practices that can be determined on the bases of what an organization looks like (a static snapshot of the workforce composition) or what an organization does (how it processes job applicants and makes decisions on current employees). These distinctions are not necessarily made by everyone involved in equal-employment-opportunity programs, but they do capture the essence of it: understanding, locating, and removing illegal employment practices and their resultant adverse or unfair effects.

With these distinctions in mind, note that another basis for evidence of prima facie discrimination is really a prima facie case of adverse impact. It is often referred to as the "bottom-line criterion." If, for example, a company hires 50% of all white male applicants who apply in a particular job category, then it must hire at least 40% (80% × 50%) of all natives who apply and 40% of all women and other protected groups. Originally this bottom-line criterion was aimed at identifying adverse impact for an entire set of selection procedures rather than for any single part of the procedures. Another basis that can be used to establish a case of prima facie discrimination is referred to as *systemic discrimination*. In essence, this means that there is evidence of systemic discrimination against employers who employ available minorities and women at substantially lower rates than do other employers in the same labour market who employ persons with the same general level of skills.

Bona Fide Occupational Qualifications and Seniority Systems. All jurisdictions have a bona fide occupational qualification exemption in respect to gender discrimination in employment. An example of a court ruling regarding bona fide occupational requirement is provided in the first "PHRM in the News" article. The burden of proof, however, rests with the employer in all provincial jurisdictions except for New Brunswick.[16]

Seniority systems in unionized companies, if specified in the collective agreement, may discriminate against women, if for example, males acquire more seniority than females. In such cases, males will obtain more rights such as preferred jobs, preferred schedules, and a lower possibility of layoff through the application of the rule last-in-first-out.

Selection and Placement Information

Job applicants also should obtain information about the organization with which they are going through selection and placement procedures. As discussed in Chapter 4, it is advisable for organizations to convey realistic information about the job and organization to the applicant.[17]

The Organizational Context

Information about the organizational context necessary for effective selection and placement identifies the jobs available, job situations, and legal constraints. Job openings usually are identified through the organization's human resource planning and programming or through direct requisitions from supervisors. Because many organizations do not effectively plan human resource needs, supervisor requisitions often are the major source of information about job openings. However, in view of some forecasts of managerial and professional shortages by the early 1990s, more organizations are beginning to program systematically for their human resource needs. Managerial succession programs are evidence of this systematic effort. Without effective human resource planning, job availability is often not determined until job vacancies exist. Consequently, recruitment, selection, and placement may be undertaken without full understanding of the jobs that are open or performed so quickly that a thorough recruitment and selection process is not possible.

Job performance can be determined only in part by the individual. Such organizational characteristics as compensation policies, group pressures, philosophy of management, and quality of supervision also determine an individual's level of performance. In fact, there are many job situations in which employee performance actually is determined by the pace of the machines more than by any qualities of the employee. Because these aspects of the organization and job situation are so important, they must be accounted for in selection and placement procedures. These organizational characteristics should also be conveyed to job applicants in order for them to determine if the characteristics match their interests and preferences. For example, two jobs may require the same technical skills, but if one is isolated and the other is part of a larger group, the selection process should take into account the personalities and preferences of applicants regarding in which type of situation they prefer to work. The job situation not only influences employee performance but also determines job rewards.

The Job Context

In order to choose a job realistically, job applicants must know the conditions under which the job is performed.[18] Physical conditions, time pressures under which the work is performed, the hours of work, and where the work is performed should all be made clear to the applicant.

The Job Qualities

Information about job requirements and specifications is obtained from the job analysis. This information is needed to match individual skills, knowledge, and aptitudes with job demands. In addition to job-analysis information, job-design information should also be provided so that the qualities or characteristics of the job are known. This is critical in helping job applicants to determine if their preferences and interests would be satisfied by the job characteristics. As discussed in Chapter 3, the job-design characteristics and information about individuals' preferences, interests, and personalities also can be used in redesigning jobs and in placing applicants in more appropriate jobs. To further aid the applicants in choosing jobs and in performing well once hired, standards of performance and other job-related expectations (e.g., rate of absenteeism tolerated) should be obtained from the job analysis and conveyed to the applicants.

The Job Applicant

Information about the organizational context, job context, and job qualities constitute only about half of the information needed to match individual skills, knowledge, and abilities to job demands and interests and preferences to job and organizational characteristics. The remaining half comes from the job applicant. Information about an individual's skills, knowledge, and abilities, and personality, interests, and preferences in conjunction with that about the organization and job, is the basis for predicting how successfully a job applicant will perform the job criteria. Therefore, these pieces of information are often called *predictors*. More specifically, when they are used to make selection decisions, they are called *tests*.

However, while the word "test" usually is defined to include all methods by which information to make selection decisions is gathered, in this chapter the word refers exclusively to the written tests. In the next chapter, "test" is used to refer to all forms of information gathering, as discussed in this chapter.

Gathering predictor information from job applicants is very critical in selection and placement. When used in conjunction with criteria information, it is the essence of making selection and placement decisions.

Predictors and Criteria in Selection Decisions

Selection decisions in organizations are generally made on the basis of job applicants' predictor scores. These scores are used because they predict how well the applicants, if hired, will perform according to the job performance criteria. Typically, selection decisions are made using scores from several predictors that are administered to the job applicants sequentially or in steps. Consequently, selection decisions are also made in steps.

Predictors for Selection and Placement Decisions. What the organization wants is a predictor or set of predictors that will enable it to anticipate how a job applicant will perform according to the criteria established for the job.[19]

The more commonly used predictors are interviews, application blanks, and written tests. Since selection and placement decisions are made on the basis of the information obtained by these predictors, each is discussed in more detail after the discussion of criteria for, and steps in, selection and placement decisions.

Criteria for Selection and Placement Decisions. It is important that the criteria selected are critical to the job that the organization wants to fill, that they are job-related. For example, in the animal keeper's job (Chapter 3), it is more critical to ensure that cages be cleaned every day and animals be fed properly than to ensure that the animal keeper dresses nicely and smiles. According to the job description of the animal keeper, other criteria or standards also are important to the job. Establishing the exact criteria and their relative importance is crucial to developing valid predictors and having a valid performance appraisal system.

The exact criteria also are important because they help to determine the type of information that should be obtained from the job applicants and, to some extent, the method used to gather that information. For example, if a low rate of absenteeism is an appropriate criterion, a check of references on employment history or a preference test may be used. If quantity of performance is identified as a criterion, a written test measuring an applicant's skills, knowledge, and aptitude may be used.[20]

The base for determining the appropriate, relevant, and important criteria is the job analysis, as described in Chapter 3. Compare the relationship between the job dimensions of the corporate loan assistant in Exhibit 3.7 and the knowledge and skills identified as being necessary to perform the duties of the assistant's job in Exhibit 5.2. The skills, knowledge, and abilities were identified by the job incumbents who also identified the job dimensions, as discussed in Chapter 3 (see the discussion of guidelines-oriented job analysis). Since those job dimensions were identified as being the essence of the job, they essentially are the job criteria. These criteria are behaviours rather than outcomes such as quantity of output or rate of absenteeism, the distinctions between which are clarified in Chapter 6. To make a selection decision then, one must determine whether the skills, knowledge, and abilities identified as necessary to perform specified behaviours (job-dimensions criteria) are present. The methods by which each skill or behaviour is to be measured are indicated in the matrix in Exhibit 5.2. These measures become the predictors of the applicant's future performance in each job dimension.

After the important criteria are identified, predictors must be chosen that will indicate how well an applicant is likely to perform on the basis of the criteria. This process is neither easy nor inexpensive. If done correctly, however, it results in selection and placement decisions that are effective and meet legal requirements.

Steps in Selection and Placement Decisions. Selection and placement decisions are very important to the organization,[21] so PHRM managers often use several predictors to make them. The information is generally gathered in steps, a typical example of which is shown in Exhibit 5.3.

Obtaining Job Applicant Information

The major information-gathering procedures for selection and placement decisions are interviews, written tests, and background information and references supplied by the applicant.

It is important to note that gathering and using information about the individual, particularly to predict performance, generally represents con-

168 Staffing

Exhibit 5.2 Selection Plan Matrix

FOR: ____CORPORATE LOAN ASSISTANT____   DATE: _____

Practices, Procedures, and Tests Used in Selection

1	2		3	4	5	6	7	8	9	10	11	12	13
Coding		**Short Title**	**R=Rank**		**SAF**					**DAI**	**BI/REF**		**PAF**
A	**B**												
		Knowledges/Skills											
MQ		1. Communication	R		X					X	X		X
MQ		2. Math			X					X	X		X
MQ		3. Writing			X					X	X		X
MQ		4. Reading			X					X	X		X
MQ		5. Researching			X					X	X		X
MQ		6. Organizing	R		X					X	X		X
MQ		7. Listening	R		X					X	X		X
MQ		8. Social skills			X					X	X		X
MT	B	9. Sales	R		X					X	X		X
MQ		10. Interpret	R		X					X	X		X
WT		11. Bank policy											X
MT	C	12. Bank services	R		X					X	X		X
WT		13. Computer											X
WT		14. Credit report											X

MQ=Minimum qualification. **MT**=May be trained or acquired on the job (desirable). Preference may be given to those who possess this knowledge/skill. When used on a physical characteristic, **MT** means a reasonable accommodation can be made. **WT**=Will be trained or acquired on the job. Not evaluated in the selection process. **WT**=Will be trained or acquired on the job because it can be learned in a brief orientation, i.e., 8 h. or less. Not evaluated in the selection process. **MQ/MT**=Lower level is minimum qualification; higher level may be trained or acquired on the job (desirable). **MQ/WT**=Lower level is minimum qualification; higher level will be trained or acquired on the job. **WT** part is not measured in the selection process. **MT/WT**=Lower level may be trained or acquired on the job; higher level will be trained or acquired on the job. **WT** part is not measured in the selection process. **R**=Rank. Applicants may be ranked by their level of work skills. This is differentiating among those who possess more and who will probably perform the duties better. Not all the differentiating knowledges, skills, physical characteristics, and "other characteristics" are ranked.
SAF=Supplemental application form. **WKT**=Written knowledge test. **ST**=Skills test. **PCD**=Physical capability demonstration. **SOI**=Structured oral interview. **DAI**=Departmental appointment interview. **BI/REF/**=Background investigation/Reference check. **ME**=Medical examination. **PAF**=Performance appraisal form.

Source: Biddle & Associates, Inc. Used with permission.

Steps in Selection   *Exhibit 5.3*

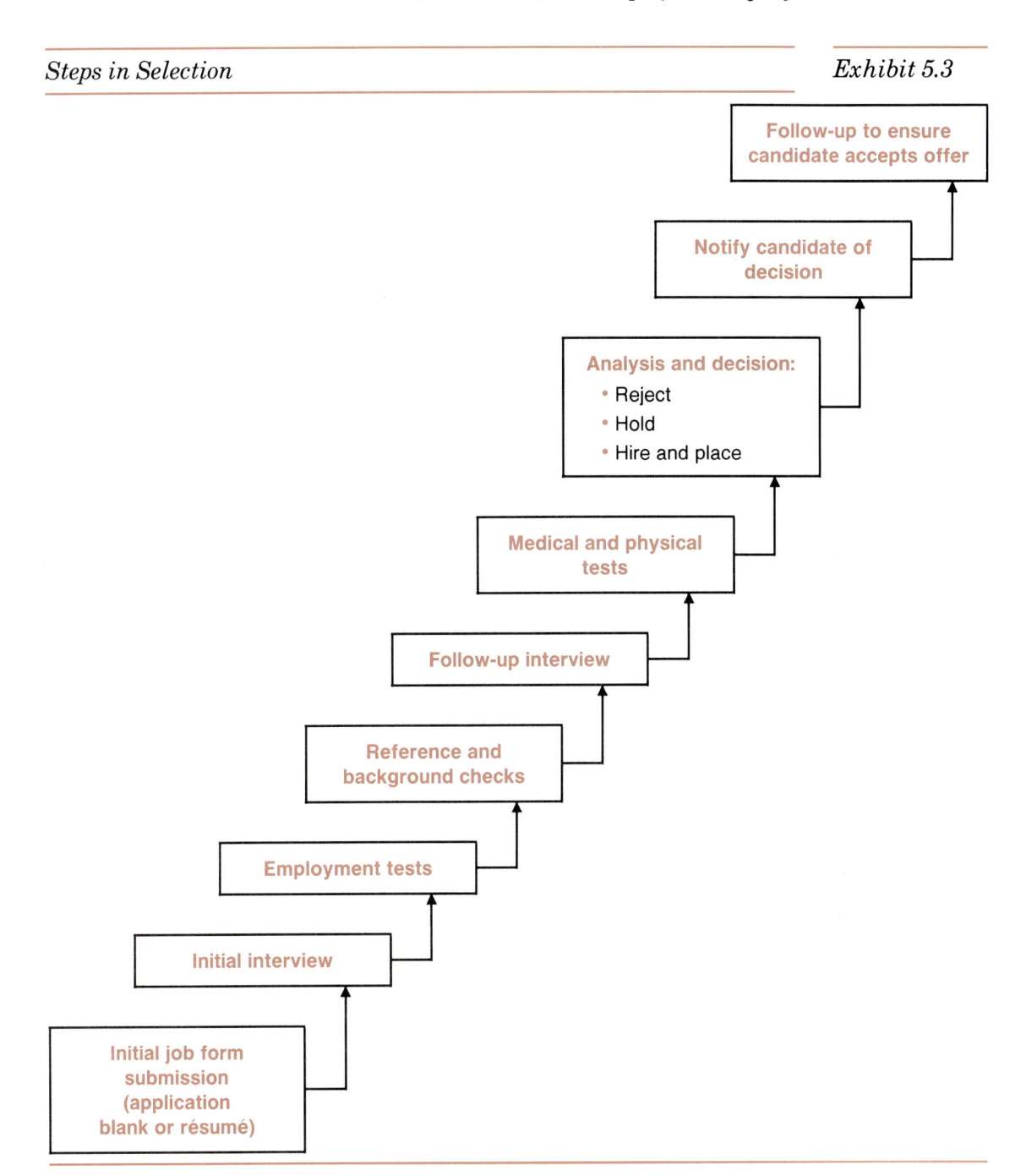

Steps (bottom to top):

1. Initial job form submission (application blank or résumé)
2. Initial interview
3. Employment tests
4. Reference and background checks
5. Follow-up interview
6. Medical and physical tests
7. Analysis and decision:
   - Reject
   - Hold
   - Hire and place
8. Notify candidate of decision
9. Follow-up to ensure candidate accepts offer

cern only for the match between an individual's skills, knowledge, and abilities and the job demands (Match 1). This match appears most subject to legal considerations and traditionally has been of major interest to organizations because it is directed primarily at predicting how well the individual is likely to perform on the job. However, information concerning the individual's preferences, interests, and personality (Match 2) should be gathered because it may, when used in combination with information about job rewards, enhance employee satisfaction and reduce absenteeism and voluntary turnover. It also may enhance employee performance, particularly the quality of it, due to the elevated job involvement resulting from a match between employee interests and preferences and job rewards.[22]

Regardless of the type of information gathered, its relationship with important criteria must be demonstrated, not merely assumed. The degree of difficulty in demonstrating this connection may vary with the type of information gathered, for two reasons (1) lack of precision or reliability in the method by which the information is gathered or in the predictor that is being measured (e.g., there are more than 100 different intelligence tests); (2) a weakness in the relationship between the predictor that is being measured and the important criteria. Generally it is easier to demonstrate job-relatedness for predictors based on information about skills, knowledge, and aptitude than for predictors based on information about interests and preferences.[23] This demonstration is highlighted in the discussion of empirical, content, and construct validity in the next chapter.

All of this information can be gathered, but its job-relatedness must be demonstrated. The same is true of information that does not neatly fall into either of the personal characteristics categories. This "other" category includes intelligence, general knowledge (not job-relevant knowledge), leadership, judgement, dexterity, spatial ability, commonsense, and number of years of education and experience. The level of difficulty in demonstrating the job-relatedness of this type of information may be approximately equivalent to that for interests and preferences information.

Although demonstrating job-relatedness may be easiest with skills, knowledge, and aptitudes information, skills that can be learned in fewer than eight hours, or that are going to be taught on the job, should not be used to make selection decisions. Furthermore, if job applicants need only a specified minimum level of a knowledge, skill, or ability, the only information that should be obtained is whether the applicants meet the minimum levels. If having more of one skill or ability is likely to result in better performance, then information about that particular skill or ability should be obtained so that applicants can be ranked. When making decisions that relate to firing, demotion, layoff (where a bona fide seniority system does not exist), or discipline, it is more appropriate to measure the employees' task or job performances rather than their skills, knowledge, or abilities.

If physical abilities are being measured, job accommodation must be considered (see the discussion of ergonomics in Chapter 3). If reasonable accommodation cannot be made to a handicap that interferes with performing the essential duties of the job, the applicant can be rejected.

In addition to gathering information on skills, knowledge, and aptitude, personality, interests, and preferences, and whatever falls into the "other category," employers can gather information about other characteristics, terms, and conditions of employment. "Other characteristics" usually are items that are required as minimum qualifications for a job: licences required by law, willingness to travel, willingness to work split-shifts or weekends, willingness to work under adverse conditions such as confined facilities and high noise levels, willingness to comply with uniform requirements or employer grooming codes that are related to the business, or possession of tools necessary for the job and not provided by the employer. Very rarely will "other characteristics" be used to rank applicants—applicants either possess them or they do not—and level or amount of possession will make no difference in how well the candidate will perform the job. Applicants can be disqualified from consideration if they are unwilling to comply with a required "other characteristic."

Evaluation of a candidate's type of education or experience is a useful way of ensuring that the candidate for hire, transfer, training, or promotion does have the necessary background required for the job. Evaluation of the content of the education or experience, however, should be done as it relates to the job-required skills, knowledge, and abilities. It is important not to fall into the trap of evaluating the number of years of education or experience a candidate has had as proof that he or she possesses specific knowledge and skills.[24]

Armed with an understanding of the types of information that should be gathered, it is important to discuss the ways in which job applicant information is most frequently obtained. When making selection decisions, employers should consider the fact that some information should not be gathered, primarily because it is discriminatory. This type of information is identified in the following discussion.

The Application Blank

The first step in the process of selection, as shown in Exhibit 5.3, is the application blank. For many professional and managerial jobs, applications may be replaced by résumés. Unfortunately these résumés, as with references indicated on application blanks, are increasingly less likely to reflect reality and should be used only in collaboration with other information.[25] The **application blank** is a form that requests information about the job applicant's background and present conditions, including current address and telephone number. Although application blanks formerly requested a great deal of information (sometimes even a photograph), legal constraints have reduced the content substantially.

Information that generally should not be requested in an application blank or during an interview because of the difficulty in demonstrating job-relatedness or because it is discriminatory includes:

- The name of a member of the clergy as a reference
- Questions about whether one has children and who will care for them
- Height and weight, unless absolutely job-related
- Marital status
- Education level or degree (except for professionals where licences are required)

- Conviction record, unless strongly related to the job
- Nature of military discharge
- Citizenship
- Credit history
- Relatives and friends working for the employer
- Questions about age, colour, sex, religion, national origin, race

On grounds of discrimination, almost all federal and provincial human rights Acts prohibit the questioning of individuals regarding age (except for the Northwest Territories and the Yukon), colour, religion, ethnic or national origin, marital status, sex, and race. Some provincial legislatures prohibit questions to do with language (Québec), mental handicap (Ontario and Saskatchewan); pardoned offence (federal government and Ontario); physical handicap (all provinces except for B.C., the Northwest Territories, and the Yukon); and sexual orientation (Saskatchewan).

These prohibitions do not preclude application blanks as a source of job-related information. In order to use this information in the most effective job-related way, organizations sometimes weight the information, giving some information on the form more importance as a predictor of performance than other information. In essence this procedure results in what is called a **weighted application blank**, which can be extremely effective in predicting such things as turnover. Weighted application blanks often are developed through the use of multiple regression or multiple stepwise regression analysis. Based on the results of the analysis, the relative importance (thus, the weight) of the information on the application blank can be determined and used in selection decisions.[26]

As an addition to the application blank or even as a substitute, employers may administer a *biographical information blank*, which generally requests more information from the applicant than does an application blank. For example, in addition to requesting information about name, present address, references, skills, and type of education, the biographical information blank may request the applicant to indicate preference for such things as working split-shifts, being transferred, working on weekends, or working alone. Exactly which items are asked should be a reflection of the nature of the job. If the job does require split-shift working, this form should include questions regarding preference for split-shifts, since the answers may be a good predictor of turnover. Other information often gathered on a biographical information blank is an applicant's work history and pre-work history. For example, an applicant may be asked to indicate whether he or she worked while in high school or had a car in high school. This information, along with other biographical background information, is gathered on the assumption that past behaviours and experiences may be important predictors of future behaviours and experiences, particularly job performance. Using these data for selection assumes behavioural consistency—that past behaviour is the best indicator of future behaviour, which is not always a valid assumption.

Research on Application Blanks/Biographical Data. Research shows that if the application blank/biographical data is carefully constructed, it could be a very useful tool for predicting job success. The literature is filled with studies of how well these methods predict turnover of white and black workers, respectively.[27] While the predictive validity is extremely impressive, it is also notable that the application blank method was considered to be fair to members of both of these racial groups.

Other issues relevant to this type of predictor have to do with the honesty of the people responding to the questions. The limited information that we have on these issues suggests that most people do not lie. However, people seem to be more honest when they think their answers will be verified. Therefore, it is important to avoid questions that cannot be verified. For example, an application for a secretarial job at the Calgary Symphony Orchestra should not include the question: Do you like classical music? Questions like this lead quite naturally to responses that are perceived by the candidate to be desired by the organization.

A second issue is the stability of the application over time. Most studies show validity decay. Changes in applicant pools, job-market conditions, and in the jobs themselves cause the validity of the information to fluctuate. Therefore a periodic check and revision of items is desirable.

In sum, research shows that, relative to other selection procedures, questionnaires for biographical data are among the most valid. One researcher notes, "If they gave an Academy Award for the most consistently valid predictors used to forecast job performance, biographical information (as a general class) would be the winner."[28] However, surveys indicate that although most organizations use application blanks, fewer than a third of the larger employers bother to validate them, thereby potentially running the risk of being guilty of discrimination.[29] A final point is that, due to the very large sample sizes needed to validate both methods, they are not practical for many Canadian organizations.

Reference Checks/Letters of Recommendation. Another way of gathering information is by reference verification. Although listed as the fourth step in selection (Exhibit 5.3), it may be done earlier. While reference verification is widely practised, its use has raised some legal concerns because it could lead to discriminatory practices.

Referrals also can come under fire. An example is the case of a settlement accepted by the Canadian Human Rights Commission against an employment agency in Halifax, which had failed to refer a fully-trained woman to a job vacancy for an orderly because the employer has specified it wanted a man.[30]

On the other hand, it is felt that employers should be free to discriminate among job applicants, particularly when seeking performance-related information about them. However, this can lead to infringement of an individual's privacy. This potential conflict promises to remain a central issue in personnel management for the next several years.

Research on Reference Checks and Recommendations. Research has demonstrated that the references listed by the candidate may not be as valid as those obtained from a former employer, peers, and subordinates. In addition, some of the most reliable information can be obtained during face-to-face interviews, by observing whether the non-verbal responses coincide with what is being said.[31] Most studies indicate that few employers consider written references alone to be a reliable source of data. Only references from former immediate supervisors who have recently observed the applicant in a work situation seem to be accurate predictors of the applicant's success in a new job.

The Selection and Placement Interview

Although aptitude, achievement, personality, interests, and preferences are more reliably assessed by written tests or carefully developed situational tests, the interview remains a very popular method of obtaining information.[32] However, while it appears to be a good procedure for gathering factual background information, it is not a particularly good procedure for making assessments, because it is too subjective.[33] Nevertheless, employers continue to use the interview for both data gathering and decision making, despite the pressure by agencies such as the various federal and provincial commissions on human rights to use more objective methods of gathering information, i.e., methods or procedures that are more precise and reliable.[34] Such agencies are concerned about interviews because the results can be unreliable (e.g., two people interviewing the same applicant can come up with different findings and conclusions), and because they can be used to obtain discriminatory information.

A case in point is Segrave v. Zellers (1975), in which the complainant alleged that he was refused employment because of his gender and marital status. The applicant was interviewed by Zellers' female personnel officer who told him that there were only women in the position for which he was applying. Also, in the preliminary interview he was rejected for further processing on grounds of his "undesirable marital status." The Ontario board of inquiry found that Zellers had discriminated against Segrave on both gender and marital status grounds and ordered the company to remedy its hiring practices.

Because interviews are used so frequently, they will be discussed here in detail to show how they can be used to provide information that is more reliable, job-related, and non-discriminatory.

As shown in Exhibit 5.3, the interview process is important at two points—at the beginning and at the end of the selection procedure. The way in which the interview is conducted depends on the type of job being filled. In the case of middle- and upper-level managerial and executive jobs, individuals often submit résumés by mail or through an employment agency. An initial interview appointment is made over the phone if the organization is interested in the applicant. For lower-level management and non-management jobs, an individual may see a job advertised in the newspaper or posted on the organization's bulletin board and request an application blank for completion and submission. The initial interview may follow.

Frequently, several individuals interview the applicant, particularly applicants for middle- or upper-level managerial or executive positions. Often these interviewers ask for in-depth information about motivation, attitudes, and experience. These interviews are for the purpose of making assessments, not just for gathering information. Even the initial interview has an assessment aspect, because a reject/pass decision could be made at that stage. Therefore, both interview stages are crucial.

Types of Interviews. Interviews can be categorized according to the techniques and format used. One common interview is the depth interview. The interviewer has only a general outline of topics to be covered, and often pursues them in an unstructured or non-patterned way. The interviewees may be allowed to expand on any question. Because the quality of an unstructured interview depends on the skill of the interviewer, which is difficult to guarantee, organizations often use a patterned or structured interview. This interview, in order to ensure consistency, actually resembles an oral questionnaire (to be discussed in Chapter 13). But because it is structured, validation studies indicate that the patterned interview can be quite useful in predicting job success.

As indicated above, several individuals may interview an applicant. This is called a panel interview, and because of its cost, is usually reserved for managerial job applicants. Another type of interview that may be used for certain types of managerial job applicants is called the stress interview. The types of jobs (managerial or non-managerial) for which applicants would be subjected to a stress interview are those in which it is important to remain calm and composed under pressure. In the stress interview, the applicant may be intentionally annoyed, embarrassed, or frustrated by the interviewer to see how the applicant reacts. Although this may be a particularly good format for certain types of jobs such as those found in law enforcement and the military, it appears to be less job-related for most organizational jobs.

Regardless of the interview format and technique used, there are several problems that can adversely affect interviews. An awareness of them can help reduce their likelihood of occurrence. The PHRM department can play a key role by making sure that the people doing the interviewing are aware of the problems, are trained in how to avoid them, and are reinforced for conducting interviews correctly.[35]

Common Interview Problems. There are several problems that interviewers often encounter,[36] relating to the interview as a procedure for gathering information as well as for assessing that information:[37]

- Interviewers sometimes do not seek applicant information on all of the important dimensions needed for successful job performance or for success in meeting other criteria. Often the interviewers do not have a complete description of the job being filled, an accurate appraisal of its critical requirements, or the conditions under which the job is performed. Nevertheless, for performance and legal reasons, it is important that all the information obtained be job-related.
- When there are several interviewers, they sometimes overlap in their coverage of some job-related questions and miss others entirely. In fact, it

may happen that an applicant has not had four interviews but one interview four times.

- Interviewers may make "snap" judgements early in the interview, blocking out further potentially useful information. Research has found that most interviewers make a decision within the first four to five minutes of an interview. In the remainder of the interview they search for cues and clues to substantiate the impressions they formed in the initial phase of the interview.[38]
- Interviewers permit one trait or job-related attribute to influence their evaluation of the remaining qualities of an applicant. This process, called the **halo effect**, occurs when an interviewer judges an applicant's entire potential for job performance on the basis of one characteristic, such as how well the applicant dresses or talks. The halo effect may lead to poor and/or discriminatory choices by the interviewer; it may also affect the choices made by the job applicant. To the applicant, the interviewer is a symbol of the company, although he or she represents a sample size of only one. Nevertheless, the applicant often places more importance on his or her estimate of the representative of the company than on judgements based on the company literature.[39]
- Interviewers sometimes have not organized the various selection elements into a system. Exhibit 5.3 depicts an order in the selection activities, but often these activities are not done in as orderly a fashion. Key references may not be checked before the intensive interviews, resulting in interviews with unqualified applicants. Occasionally, applicants are treated differently, some given certain tests and others not. This may be a result of lack of clarity on who was to do what. Regardless, the result is unfair and ineffective selection practices.
- Information from interviews with an applicant is not integrated and presented in a systematic manner.
- If several interviewers share information on an applicant, they may do so in a very haphazard manner. They may not identify job-related information or seek to examine any conflicting information. This casual approach to decision making may save time and confrontation—but only in the short run. In the long run, everyone in the organization will pay for poor hiring decisions.
- Managers' judgements often are affected by pressure to fill the position, resulting in a lowering of standards. Managers also may hire an applicant because of low salary demands. Personnel managers can reduce this possibility by not revealing applicant salary demands to the line managers responsible for hiring. The best philosophy is to select the best person for the job first and then to be concerned with the salary.
- Managers' judgements regarding an applicant are often affected by the available applicants.

Two concepts—**contrast effect** and **order effect**—are important here. First, a good person looks better in contrast with a group of average or below-average people (contrast effect). An average person looks below-average or poor in contrast with a group of good or excellent people. Second, there are two important order effects—first impression and last impression. At times a first impression (**primacy effect**) is important and lasting; the first person may become the standard used to evaluate the quality of all of the other people. But an interviewer, particularly at the end of a long day of interviewing, may be more likely to remember the last person better than many of the other people (**recency effect**). Average applicants should be aware of this and take advantage of these effects. For example, they should try to get an interview in the middle of an interviewer's schedule and be interviewed around the time that less qualified applicants are being interviewed.

Overcoming Potential Interview Problems. There are several ways to overcome the above problems. The methods suggested below are essentially ways to increase the validity and reliability of the interview, to increase its job-relatedness, the scope of qualifications measured, and the consistency and objectivity of the information gathered.

- *Gather only job-related information:* That is, use only information from job-related questions as predictors of future performance. This requires that a job analysis be done on the jobs to be filled and, if possible, validation of the predictors being used. Increasing job-relatedness can be facilitated by structuring the interview and using multiple interviewers. This procedure increases the validity by increasing the reliability of the interview results. (These issues are examined in more detail in Chapter 6.)
- *Use past behaviour to predict future behaviour:* Essentially, concentrate on getting information about the applicant's past job behaviour. This background information can be obtained conveniently in the initial interview. It is most useful to obtain specific examples of performance-related experiences and the events surrounding those examples.
- *Co-ordinate the initial interview and succeeding interviews with each other and with other information-gathering procedures:* Job-related information should be combined in an objective, systematic manner. The co-ordination and systematic combination of information can aid in reducing the risk of quick decisions, bias, and the use of stereotypes in selection. Also assisting in this reduction is the final step.
- Involve several managers in interviewing and in the final decision. Although the final decision may be made by only one person, several should be involved in gathering the information and assessing its merits.

Non-verbal Cues in Interviews. Another important aspect of the interview is the non-verbal component—information communicated without words. Things such as body movements, gestures, firmness of handshake, eye contact, and physical appearance are all non-verbal cues. Interviewers often put more importance on the non-verbal cues than on the verbal.

> It has been estimated that, at most, only 30 to 35% of the meaning conveyed in a message is verbal; the remainder is non-verbal. Similarly, in terms of

attitudes or feelings, one estimate is that merely 7% of what is communicated is verbal, while non-verbal factors account for the remaining 93%.[40]

Therefore, it is important to be aware of non-verbal cues. "In fact, one of the reasons that non-verbal cues are so powerful is that in most cases interviewers are not aware of them as possible causal agents of impression formation."[41]

What to Ask. Interviewers may ask anything that, when combined with other information about the job applicant, can be a useful predictor of how well the applicant will perform once hired. Useful questions include:

- Has the applicant performed in a similar capacity before?
- How does the applicant feel about present job qualities and organizational context?
- If the applicant is changing jobs, why is a change being made?
- What are the applicant's career objectives?
- Does the applicant like working closely with people?
- Does the applicant feel that any particular environmental conditions are necessary for best performance?[42]

Questions not to ask or information not to gather in an interview are the same as that discussed for the application blank.

Selection Tests

Testing is another important procedure for gathering, transmitting, and assessing information about an applicant's aptitudes, experiences, and motivations. The most common types of written tests measure aptitude, achievement, and interests and preferences.

The validity and reliability of written tests are of utmost importance for both the organization and the job applicant. Validity and reliability help to ensure that an applicant will perform at a certain level, and will help to provide the job applicant with a sense of fairness and legality in the selection procedure. While a test that leads to rejection of people on any of the grounds specified by the federal and provincial human rights Acts is prohibited, test validity as it relates to discrimination has not yet received as much attention in Canada as in the U.S. No component of staffing has generated more controversy and criticism since the early 1960s in the U.S., than the use of written tests.[43] Controversy and criticism centre around questions of test fairness, cultural bias, validity, and test item characteristics such as vagueness and irrelevancy.

Many of the tests used in Canada were developed in the U.S., and validated with different groups of workers. An examination of the catalogue of psychological tests offered by the Institute of Psychological Research in Québec, for example, reveals that less than 5% of all of the tests offered were properly validated in Canada and/or on a Québec-relevant basis.[44] If this estimate is correct, a serious potential problem relating to discrimination exists.

While it is essential for each organization to use its own staff to validate the tests it uses, there is no need for it to develop its own tests. This could become too costly. The PHRM manager can select from more than 1000 tests that are commercially available. Most of these are distributed by a few management consulting firms that are ready to adapt and/or further develop the tests to accommodate the organizational needs.

Although many tests typically used for employment decisions are valid predictors of job criteria for many jobs in a variety of organizations, they should not be used exclusively. The best approach is to use a test, or a battery of tests, in conjunction with other selection procedures (bio-data, interviews, simulations, etc.). This concept of multiple predictors will be discussed further in Chapter 6.

In Canada, it is estimated that 20% to 25% of all employers use tests to obtain information on job candidates.[45] The following examples represent just some of the tests that can be used to measure individuals' skills, knowledge, and aptitudes, and interests and preferences. In addition, if these tests are given but are not used in making selection decisions, the equal-employment-opportunity legal considerations do not apply. For example, personality, interests, and preference tests may be given to help place new employees in the appropriate job context after the hiring decision is made. However, even though the legal considerations are not as applicable in these placement decisions, the decisions still should be made consistent with the legal considerations.

Types of Tests

Tests can be classified on the basis of information sought regarding the applicant's personal characteristics and habits. These include aptitude tests, achievement or proficiency tests, and preference, interest, and personality tests.

Aptitude Tests. **Aptitude tests** measure the potential of individuals to perform. Measures of general aptitude, often referred to as general intelligence tests, include the Wechsler Adult Intelligence Scale and the Stanford-Binet test. These tests are used primarily to predict academic success in a traditional setting. Thus several multi-dimensional aptitude tests were developed for organizations, including Differential Aptitude Tests, the Flanagan Aptitude Classification Test, the General Aptitude Test Battery, and the Employee Aptitude Survey. Because they are standardized, these tests are not specific to any particular job. Yet they are reliable and general enough to be used in many job situations, particularly for indicating the contribution that more specific tests can make.[46]

Another group of aptitude tests, called **psychomotor tests**, evaluate a combination of mental and physical aptitudes. Two of the more widely used psychomotor tests are the MacQuarrie Test for Mechanical Ability and the O'Connor Finger and Tweezer Dexterity Tests. The MacQuarrie test measures skills in tracing, tapping, dotting, copying, locating, arranging blocks, and pursuing. This test seems to be a valid predictor for success as an aviation mechanic or stenographer. The O'Connor test is a valid predictor for power sewing-machine operators, dental students, and other occupations requiring manipulative skills.[47]

A final group of aptitude tests relates to personal and interpersonal competence. A **personal competence test**, the Career Maturity Inventory, measures whether individuals know how to make appropriate and timely decisions for themselves, and whether they really put forth the effort to do so. It includes five competence tests related to problems, planning, occupational information, self-knowledge, and goal selection. The better the score on these five competency tests, the more likely an individual is to make career decisions resulting in higher satisfaction and performance.[48]

Interpersonal competence tests have been designed to measure social intelligence. These include aspects of intelligence related to information, non-verbal, which is involved in human interactions where awareness of attention, perceptions, thoughts, desires, feelings, moods, emotions, intentions, and actions of other persons and of the individual is important.[49]

Achievement Tests. **Achievement tests** predict an individual's performance on the basis of what he or she knows. Validation is required of any test used by an organization, but validating achievement tests is a rather straightforward process. The achievement tests almost become samples of the job to be performed. However, hiring on the basis of achievement tests may exclude applicants who have not had equal access to the opportunities to acquire the skills. It also should be noted that some achievement tests are less job-related than others.

Paper-and-pencil achievement tests tend to be less job-related because they measure the applicant's knowledge of facts and principles, not the actual use of them. For example, you could take a paper-and-pencil test measuring your knowledge of tennis and pass with flying colours, and yet play the game very poorly. Although this is a serious drawback to these tests, they continue to be used in many areas because of their widespread acceptance. For example, admission to the legal profession is through the bar exam, and the medical profession is entered through medical boards. Paper-and-pencil tests are used in these cases because they are assumed to be related to performance in the actual job. Of course, job-relatedness can be a necessary legal defence for the use of paper-and-pencil tests, as well as of all other tests.

The **recognition test** is often used in advertising and modelling to select applicants. The applicants bring to the job interview portfolios of samples of the work that they have done. However, portfolios contain no clues to the conditions or circumstances under which they were done. Some organizations may insist on seeing written samples from school work for jobs where written expression may be important. Recognition tests are really examples of past behaviour.

Simulation tests are used to see how applicants perform now. Only the task itself—not the situation in which the task is performed—is recreated. Even so, simulation can be extremely useful as a training and practice device. Simulations are particularly good preparation for events that happen only once, like the first moon landing.

Some achievement tests overcome the artificiality of simulations by using the actual task in the actual working conditions. These are called **work sample tests**. Work sample tests frequently are given to applicants for secretarial jobs. Applicants may be asked to type a letter in the office where they would be working. There is still some artificiality in work sample tests, however, because the selection process itself tends to promote some anxiety and tension. Nevertheless, work samples are used rather extensively because of their applicability and validity.[50]

Anxiety and tension may not be artificial for certain jobs, such as a managerial job under time pressure. Therefore, a work sample test referred to as the **in-basket exercise** has been created to test for that type of job. Its objective is to create a realistic situation that will elicit typical on-the-job behaviours. Situations and problems encountered on the job are written on individual sheets of paper and set in the in-basket. The problems or situations described to the applicant involve different groups of people—peers, subordinates, and those outside the organization. The applicant is asked to arrange the papers by priority, and occasionally may need to write an action response. The applicant usually is given a set time limit to take the test but is often interrupted by phone calls meant to create more tension and pressure.

Other work sample tests used in managerial selection are the **leaderless group discussion** and **business games**.[51] In the former, a group of individuals are asked to sit around and discuss a topic for a given period of time. IBM uses this method, in which each individual makes a five-minute presentation of a candidate for promotion (generally a fictitious person) and then defends this candidate in a group discussion.

Business games are living cases. That is, individuals must make decisions and live with them as they would in the in-basket exercise. Because in-basket exercises, leaderless discussion groups, and business games all tend to be useful in managerial selection, they often are all used in assessment centres.

In an **assessment centre**, job applicants or current employees are evaluated as to how well they might perform in a managerial or higher-level position. More than 20 000 North American companies use this method, and its use grows each year because of its validity in predicting the job applicants who will turn out to be successful and those who will turn out to be unsuccessful.[52]

In Canada, some of the organizations that regularly use assessment centres include the Federal Public Service Commission, the Montreal-based Steinbergs Supermarket chain, Ontario-Hydro, and Northern Electric.

An assessment centre usually is attended by from six to a dozen people who have been chosen by the organization to undergo assessment. The centre is usually run by the organization for one to three days, and normally off the organization's premises. The performance of attendees usually is evaluated by organization managers who are trained assessors. An excellent example of the use of an assessment centre is General Motors' Manufacturing Supervisors Assessment Program. The purpose of the assessment program and the exercises and tests is to help determine potential promotability of applicants to first-line supervisory positions.

The General Motors assessment centre program measures eight areas of qualification, identified through job analyses and other research as being essential to good performance in manufacturing supervision. These are

1. organizing and planning;
2. analyzing;
3. decision making;
4. controlling;
5. oral communications;
6. interpersonal relations;
7. influencing; and
8. flexibility.

The program also provides an overall evaluation of each candidate's qualifications.

> The program content includes a wide range of evaluation techniques, such as group problems, interviews, in-baskets, tests, videotape exercises, and questionnaires. These are designed to simulate the situations and problems that manufacturing supervisors regularly encounter on their jobs. As candidates go through these exercises, their performance is observed by a specially trained team of observers/evaluators (assessors) drawn from the local management group. The assessors then, meet after the candidates have finished the program, to discuss the candidates and prepare evaluations, based on the combined judgments of all the assessors, of the candidates in the areas of performance listed above.[53]

The composite performance of the exercises and tests is often used to determine an assessment centre attendee's future promotability and the organization's human resource planning requirements and training needs, as well as to make current selection and placement decisions. The composite performance evaluation is generally shared with the attendee, who in turn can use this information for his or her own personal career planning purposes.

Personality, Interest, and Preference Tests. Designed to measure an individual's preferences and interests, personality, interest, and preference tests focus on the individual's traits or characteristics, and sometimes are referred to as **personality inventories**. Inventories are distinguished from tests because there are no right or wrong answers to the former. Several common multi-dimensional tests of personality are the Edwards Personal Preference Schedule, the California Psychological Inventory, the Gordon Personal Profile, the Thurstone Temperament Survey, the Guilford-Zimmerman Temperament Survey, and the Minnesota Multiphasic Personality Inventory.

These personality inventories are useful for predicting the performance of employees such as sales-clerks and clerical workers.[54] At present, however, the utility of personality tests for selection for most jobs appears limited. They may be useful, however, for placement and career counselling after a selection decision has been made. This is true also for personality measures such as those measuring tolerance for ambiguity and locus of control. These measures may be useful in selection decisions, particularly if the open job is set in a context of change and uncertainty. If this is the case, selecting individuals with a high tolerance for ambiguity may prove effective.

Placement and career decisions also can be facilitated by **interest tests**. Two major interest tests are the Strong Vocational Interest Blank and the Kuder Preference Records. Both are essentially inventories of interests. Although generally not predictive of performance on the job, they can predict which occupation will be more in tune with an individual's interests. Many people take the Kuder Preference Records in high school to find out what jobs or occupations might match their interests. Records are grouped into 10 vocational categories—outdoor, musical, computational, scientific, persuasive, artistic, literary, musical, social service, and clerical. Specific jobs can be identified within each of the 10 groupings. Both of these interest tests should be used with caution. It is unlikely that either could predict performance on a job, nor are they always valid for predicting the specific type of job that one should choose within a vocational or occupational grouping.

Preference tests are useful in matching employee preferences with job and organizational characteristics. One scale that may be used to infer an individual's preferences for a specific job design is the preference test from the Job Diagnostic Survey, a sample of which appears in Exhibit 5.4.

Physical Ability Tests

In Chapter 3, nine physical abilities are listed, including such things as dynamic strength, trunk strength, and static strength. Although in Chapter 3 they serve as items in analyzing the physical requirements of tasks, they can also be used as a basis in the selection of job applicants. Used in conjunction with the physical abilities analysis presented in Chapter 3, job-related **physical ability tests** can be developed and utilized in selection.

Ensuring that physical ability tests are job-related is important. Through the process of attempting to demonstrate job-relatedness of physical ability tests such as those for dynamic strength, potentially non-job-related tests (previously assumed to be job-related) may be identified and either modified or replaced.[55] This process may also suggest job modifications that can provide more equal employment opportunity, particularly for women and handicapped individuals (reasonable accommodation here is a necessity in any case), and at the same time maintain the integrity of the job.

A misuse of the physical ability test is illustrated in the following example. The case involved the firing of an experienced waitress on the first day on the job because she had a limp. The British Columbia Council of Human Rights awarded the waitress $2000 as compensation for the humiliation and mental anguish she suffered, and found the operator of the restaurant guilty of discrimination on the basis of physical handicap. The waitress in this case had more than 11 years of experience. She used a built-up shoe and walked with a limp as a result of polio, which she contracted as

Exhibit 5.4 *Sample Preference Test from the Job Diagnostic Survey*

Listed below are a number of characteristics that could be present on any job. People differ about how much they would like to have each one present in their own jobs. We are interested in learning *how much you personally would like* to have each one present in your job.

Using the scale below, please indicate the *degree* to which you would like to have each characteristic present in your job.

Would mildly like having this			Would strongly like having this			Would very strongly like having this
1	2	3	4	5	6	7

____ 1. High respect and fair treatment from my supervisor
____ 2. Stimulating and challenging work
____ 3. Chances to exercise independent thought and action in my job
____ 4. Great job security
____ 5. Very friendly co-workers
____ 6. Opportunities to learn new things from my work
____ 7. High salary and good fringe benefits
____ 8. Opportunities to be creative and imaginative in my work
____ 9. Quick promotions
____ 10. Opportunities for personal growth and development in my job
____ 11. A sense of worthwhile accomplishment in my work

Source: J. R. Hackman and G. R. Oldham, *Task Design*, © 1980 (Reading, MA: Addison-Wesley, 1980), p. 136. Reprinted with permission.

a child. This handicap, however, did not prevent her from providing good service.[56]

Medical Examinations. A medical examination is often one of the final steps in the selection process. While many employers give standard medical examinations to all job applicants, special examinations may be given to only a sub-set of applicants. For example, production job applicants may be given X-rays of their backs while office job applicants may not.

The advantages of conducting medical examinations of employees could be numerous, including:

- It might entitle the employer to accrue lower life insurance rates for company-wide plans
- It might avoid heavy fines by ensuring compliance with provincial or local health regulations, particularly in food and similar industries and in hospitals where the risk of communicable diseases is high

- It could predict some proneness to disease such as lower back pain when ergonomic and technological conditions are inadequate

Medical examinations, however, should be used only to screen out applicants when the results of the exam indicate that job performance would be affected adversely.

Medical examinations can be used in conjunction with physical ability tests to help ensure that proper job accommodation is made and to provide a record for the employer in order to prevent employees from collecting on Workers' Compensation claims for pre-existing injuries.[57]

A more recent use of medical examinations is to screen applicants on the basis of their genetic makeup. **Genetic screening**, as it is called, is based on the premise that some individuals may be more sensitive than others to workplace elements such as chemicals.[58] The screening is done on the basis of an analysis of an applicant's blood or urine sample. With approximately 55 000 chemicals in use in industry presently and 800 being added annually, the benefits of genetic testing to the millions of Canadian workers exposed to those chemicals daily are apparent. Both employees and job applicants should be told about their genetic susceptibility so that they can decide whether they want to work in this type of environment. However, some legal as well as ethical questions must be asked: Should companies be permitted to select employees according to their inherited probability of contracting occupational illness? Who should bear the cost of adapting workplaces for the employees most susceptible?

Presently there are no laws that deal with genetic testing in the workplace. As will be discussed in Chapter 14, the various Canadian occupational health and safety organizations have to date shown little or no interest in investigating genetic screening. A recent report concludes that genetic screening is still a relatively new issue, but one that will most likely develop during the reminder of the 1980s and in the 1990s.[59]

However, genetic screening may prove to be more appropriately used as information for placement rather than selection. If all applicants are shown to have equal sensitivity to a workplace chemical, genetic screening information may be used to facilitate workplace modification.

Lie Detector Tests. Increasing numbers of organizations routinely ask job applicants to submit to a **polygraph test** as part of the selection procedure. This is particularly true in situations where the applicant is being considered for a fiduciary position or has access to pharmaceuticals or any small consumer items that have resale value. A 1978 survey in the U.S. showed that approximately 20% of the country's largest organizations used lie detector tests to check on applicants' background and honesty. Currently, it is estimated that between 7 and 10% of job applicants are not who they say they are![60] although information about the use of polygraph tests in Canada is sketchy, one author estimates that this practice is also widely used in Canadian companies.[61]

Although there is no federal law forcing job applicants or employees to take a polygraph test in order to be hired or promoted, many companies may ask them to sign a release indicating that they are taking the test voluntarily. Generally, the job applicant or employee should be prepared to answer questions honestly, particularly as these questions pertain to what is on the application blank. Refusal to answer questions about religion, sexual activity, politics, and other non-job issues is appropriate. However, the test-taker may want to bring this to the potential employer's attention after the test. Typically, organizations hire polygraph examiners and place them in an office away from the company with which the applicant is seeking employment.

Recently the use of polygraph testing has been challenged on both psychometric and ethical grounds. On psychometric grounds, people question both the validity and reliability of the readings. The polygraph does not measure lies, but rather variations in a person's breathing, blood pressure, and pulse. With this information, a trained operator interprets the responses. Given that the average length of training for an operator is usually six to eight weeks, opponents of polygraph-use question the proficiency of these operators. Low inter-operator reliability in interpreting results may be the greatest drawback to using this instrument as a selection device.[62] A second problem is related to its constitutionality and the invasion of privacy of those tested.[63] As a result of those concerns, twelve U.S. states recently passed laws banning the use of polygraph tests for employment purposes.[64] Nineteen states have laws about licensing requirements for operators.[65]

In Canada, a Royal Commission inquiring into Metropolitan Toronto police practices concluded that some of the deficiencies of the polygraph were that it is crude and many of the operators are unskilled in its use as a scientific instrument. Justice Monard who headed the Commission was amazed to hear the naïve and dogmatic pronouncements made by the polygraph operators and called for legislative control in this field. As of today, there are no legislative efforts in this regard.

Because of the costs and complications involved in using polygraph tests, companies are beginning to use paper-and-pencil honesty tests to predict individuals who are likely to lie or steal.

Honesty Tests. The theory behind the **honesty test** is that attitudes are accurate predictors of behaviour: a thief believes everybody steals, thinks he is normal, and will accept dishonest behaviour. A thief will probably enjoy stories of successful crimes and might answer "yes" to the question: Have you ever been so entertained by the cleverness of a crook that you hoped he would get away with it?[66] Other sample questions in a typical honesty test may include the following:[67]

- Would you tell your boss if you knew that another employee was stealing from the company?
- Is it all right to borrow company equipment to use at home if the property is always returned?
- Have you ever wished you were physically more attractive?

Honesty tests are legal, they are less costly than the polygraph, easier to score, and almost anybody can administer them. Given that the honesty test is a spin-off of the polygraph, however, they suffer the same criticism, particularly with regard to their validity and reliability. Very little research has been conducted on the validity and reliability of these paper-and-pencil tests and the little information that is known is anecdotal in nature. For example, one retail chain indicated that employee theft was cut by 28% after the Reid Report (a popular honesty test) was put into use.[68]

Summary

The various categories in which applicant information is gathered are skills, knowledge, and aptitude; personality, interests, and preferences; and what was termed as "other." In general, employment tests for achievement and physical ability, interviews, and weighted application blanks can be demonstrated without extreme difficulty to be related to job criteria, particularly performance, for measuring skills, knowledge, and aptitudes. While employment tests for aptitude may be demonstrated to be associated with job criteria, the association is indirect and thus it may be more difficult to establish job-relatedness. The employment tests for personality, interests, and preferences, biographical information blanks, and interviews present some difficulty in demonstration of their association with job criteria, their association with some specific job criteria, e.g., rate of absenteeism, may not. Nevertheless, their appropriateness may be better established by demonstrating their association with quality of work life criteria such as job involvement, satisfaction, and even stress. As a result, personality, interest, and preference measures presently should be considered as information more for placement than selection decisions until more evidence is gathered.

For the gathering of information in the "other" category, both employment aptitude tests and interviews are used, affording a versatility that employers seem to appreciate.

Information on other characteristics such as work preferences, special licences, physical condition of the applicant, and current residence information also are necessary. The most popular ways of obtaining this information appear to be medical examinations, application blanks, reference checks, honesty tests, and lie detector tests.

This chapter examined the nature and purpose of selection and placement procedures and how these relate to other personnel activities. It also examined in detail the legal considerations, such as human rights laws, bona fide occupational requirements, business necessity, job-relatedness, and adverse impact, in making selection and placement decisions.

Discussion Questions

1. What issues can be raised when an organization hires women or a minority person to increase the number of minority employees hired?

2. How are selection and placement activities related?
3. What are the advantages of having personnel departments co-ordinate selection and placement activities?
4. Identify and summarize the major legal guidelines affecting selection and placement activities.
5. List several grounds on which groups or classes of individuals could demonstrate a prima facie case of discrimination against an employer.
6. Where does selection and placement information come from, and what is it used for?
7. While the interview is still the primary method used in selection and placement, what problems arise from its use?
8. What is the bottom line in gathering and assessing information from the job applicant, with respect to future selection and placement in the organization?

CASE STUDY

The New Test

While attending an executive development seminar, Peter Gray, vice-president of Human Resources for Squish, a medium-sized pharmaceutical company employing about 500 people, learned of a new test for selecting salespeople. The reports of successful application of the test by the test manufacturer were so positive that Gray decided to give serious consideration to its use at Squish.

"This test looks like it will be the best solution to our salespersonnel turnover problem," he told John White, Squish president. "I'm trying to hire 10 new salespeople right now. Anything that would facilitate better selection and less turnover would be welcomed," replied White. Gray decided to order a sample test from the New York company that published it. He felt that Squish could not afford to develop its own tailor-made test, and that it would be appropriate for the situation to use the U.S. test.

He received a supply from the publisher and administered the test to 18 applicants. Test results were the prime consideration in making the final selection of the eight people to whom he ultimately offered the positions. Applicants Marie Toulouse and Jim White-Cloud asked Gray why they had not been hired, and he explained that their test scores were "substantially below the U.S. norms." Several months later, Squish received a complaint from the local Commission of Human Rights alleging that the company's selection test was improper because it tended to screen out French-Canadian and native people.

Case Questions

1. From a testing point of view, what seems to be the problem here?
2. Could Squish have avoided the discrimination charge? How?
3. What steps should a small or medium-sized company take to develop and implement a testing program to select salespeople?
4. What alternative methods could have been used to select salespeople?
5. What should this company have done to ensure that the test it bought was a valid selection device for its purposes?

Endnotes

1. N. Schmitt and B. Schneider, "Current Issues in Personnel Selection," in K. M. Rowland and G. D. Ferris (eds.), *Research in Personnel and Human Resource Management* (Greenwich, CT: JAI Press, 1983), for a more inclusive definition of selection and placement. See also L. E. Albright, "Staffing Issues," in S. J. Carroll and R. S. Schuler (eds.), *Human Resource Management in the 1980s* (Washington, DC: Bureau of National Affairs, 1983).
2. This traditional concern with selection and placement is consistent with the legal environment: the equal-employment-opportunity laws are directed toward ensuring that all individuals are selected on the basis of job-related predictors. Ensuring that employee preferences are matched with job and organizational characteristics is not a legal concern.
3. B. Schneider, *Staffing Organizations* (Pacific Palisades, CA: Goodyear Publishing Company, Inc., 1976). B. Schneider, A. E. Reichers, and T. M. Mitchell, "A Note on Some Relationship Between the Aptitude Requirements and Reward Attribute of Tasks," *Academy of Management Journal*, 1982, 25, pp. 567–574, where the case is made for being concerned with both matches. Note that whereas selection deals with matching individuals and jobs by picking only a few of many individuals, placement deals with taking all individuals and matching them with jobs, generally after the selection is made. Note also that much of the work on quality of work life is concerned with the worker preference-job characteristic match. This is discussed in further detail in Chapter 13.
4. F. L. Schmidt and J. E. Hunter, "Research Findings in Personnel Selection: Myths Meet Realities in the 1980s," *Public Personnel Administration: Policies and Procedures for Personnel* (New York: Prentice-Hall, 1981), for a description of these results and calculation of dollar costs and benefits. See also F. L. Schmidt, J. E. Hunter, and K. Pearlman, "Assessing the Economic Impact of Personnel Programs on Productivity," *Personnel Psychology*, Summer 1982, pp. 238–348.
5. S. T. Rickard, "Effective Staff Selection," *Personnel Journal*, June 1981, pp. 475–478.
6. Refer to Chapter 3 for a brief discussion of validity, and to Chapter 6 for a more extensive discussion.
7. F. A. Malinowski, "Job Selection Using Task Analysis," *Personnel Journal*, April 1981, pp. 288–291.
8. H. C. Jain, "Human Rights: Issues in Employment", *Human Resources Management in Canada*, Prentice-Hall Canada, 1983, pp. 51,001–50,140.
9. Part of this review is based on a text published by the Public Affairs Division of the Canada Employment and Immigration Commission. D. Rhys Phillips: *Equity in the Labour Market: The Potential of Affirmative Action*, 1983. Reproduced with permission of the Minister of Supply and Services Canada.
10. For more details, see P. Scott "Equality in Employment: A Royal Commission Report," *Current Readings in Race Relations*, vol. 2, no. 4, Winter 1984/85 (Toronto: Urban Alliance on Race Relations).
11. R. Gilbert Scheaffer, "Nondiscrimination in Employment and Beyond," *The Conference Board*, 1980.
12. J. Slovick & Associates, "Native Employment Programs of Amok Ltd., Syncrude Canada, Eldorado Nuclear Ltd.," Canada Employment & Immigration Commission, 1980.
13. N. Kinsella, "A Renewed Federal Contracts Program: An Instrument for Progressive Affirmative Action," Canada Employment & Immigration Commission, 1979, p. 3.
14. H. Jain, endnote 8, p. 50,023.
15. D Rhys Phillips, endnote 9, p. 65.
16. H. Jain, endnote 8, p. 50,029.
17. J. B. Miner and M. G. Miner, *Personnel and Industrial Relations*, 3rd ed. (New York: MacMillan, 1977), pp. 88–123.
18. R. R. Reilly, B. Brown, M. R. Blood, and C. Z. Malatesta, "The Effects of Realistic Previews: A Study and Discussion of the Literature," *Personnel Psychology*, 1981, 34, pp. 823–834 for a discussion of the relevant issues. See also J. H. Greenhaus, C. Seidel, and M. Marinis, "The Impact of Expectations and Values on Job Attitudes," *Organizational Behavior and Human Performance*, 1983.
19. A more extensive discussion of predictors and criteria and their relationship is presented in Chapter 6 of this book.
20. For an excellent discussion about criteria for selection and placement decisions see Schmitt and Schneider endnote 1. Important concepts about criteria are contamination, deficiency, sensitivity, discriminability, relevance, and practicality.
21. F. L. Schmidt and J. E. Hunter, "Research Findings in Personnel Selection: Myths Meet Realities in the 1980s," *Public Personnel Administration: Policies and Procedures for Personnel* (Englewood Cliffs, NJ: Prentice-Hall, 1980). B. Schneider, *Staffing Organizations* (Santa Monica, CA: Goodyear, 1976).
22. Schmitt and Schneider endnote 1. In their concern for Match 2 these authors also use preferences, personality, and interests, a practice followed by many organizations in making selection decisions, particularly when seeking managerial candidates. When used, these measures enable employers to predict

how well an individual will fit in, stay on the job, interact with others (essential for managers), and perform (most of which is interacting). Schmitt and Schneider suggest using personality, interests, and preferences to predict satisfaction and absenteeism also. This is consistent with the usage here.

23. These statements and suggestions are based on "Educational Requirements," *FEP Guidelines*, no. 186(1); "Experience Required," *FEP Guidelines*, no. 206(9), 1982; "Nepotism," *FEP Guidelines*, no. 190(5), 1981; "Arrest Records," *FEP Guidelines*, no. 190(5), 1981; "The Importance of Record Keeping," *Personnel Guidelines for Managers and Supervisors*, Biddle & Associates, Inc., 1982.

24. *Personnel Guidelines for Managers and Supervisors*, Biddle & Associates, Inc., 1982.

25. K. Johnson, "Rise of the Resume Sleuth," *The New York Times*, Jan. 9, 1983, p. 12. F. R. Richlefs, "Resume Flood Posing Problems in Job Market," *The Wall Street Journal*, Feb. 24, 1981, p. 21. J. Andrew, "Resume Liars Are Abundant, Experts Assert," *The Wall Street Journal*, April 24, 1981, p. 35.

26. D. G. Lawrence, B. L. Salsburg, J. G. Dawson, and Z. D. Fasmen, "Design and Use of Weighted Application Blanks," *Personnel Administrator*, March 1982, pp. 47–53, 101.

27. W. F. Cascio, "Turnover, biographical data, and fair employment practice," *Journal of Applied Psychology*, 1976, *61*, pp. 576–580.

28. P. M. Muchinsky, *Psychology Applied to Work*, (Homewood, IL: The Dorsey Press, 1983), p. 124.

29. G. T. Milkovich and W. F. Glueck, *Personnel: Human Resource Management (A Diagnostic Approach)*, 4th ed., (Plano, TX: Business Publications, Inc., 1985), p. 301. For a detailed discussion of bio-data, see also W. A. Owens "Background Data," in M. D. Dunnette (ed.) *Handbook of Industrial and Organizational Psychology*, (NY: John Wiley & Sons, 1983), pp. 609–649.

30. H. Jain, endnote 8, p. 50,028.

31. R. Deland, "Recruitment: Reference Checking Methods," *Personnel Journal*, June 1983, p. 460.

32. This is the case, even though it may be more difficult to get reliable information from an interview than from other means, such as paper and pencil tests. See J. C. Sharf, "Personnel Testing and the Law," in K. M. Rowland and G. R. Ferris (eds.), *Personnel Management* (Boston: Allyn & Bacon, 1982), p. 172.

33. For an excellent discussion of interviewing see M. D. Hakel, "Employment Interviewing," in K. M. Rowland and G. R. Ferris (eds.), *Personnel Management* (Boston: Allyn and Bacon, 1982), pp. 129–155. *Interview Guide for Supervisors* (Washington, DC: College and University Personnel Association, 1981). S. G. Ginsburg, "Preparing for Executive Position Interviews: Questions the Interviewer Might Ask—or Be Asked," *Personnel*, July–Aug. 1980, pp. 31–36. "Editor to Reader," *Personnel Journal*, Feb. 1981, pp. 82–87. R. D. Arvey and J. E. Campion, "The Employment Interview: A Summary and Review of Recent Literature," *Personnel Psychology*, 1982, *35*, pp. 281–322. "Reader to Editor," *Personnel Journal*, Aug. 1980, p. 618. J. D. Latterell, "Planning for the Selection Interview," *Personnel Journal*, July 1979, pp. 466–467. T. J. Neff, "How to Interview Candidates for Top Management Positions," *Business Horizons*, Oct. 1980, pp. 47–52. E. D. Pursell, Michael A. Campion, and Sarah R. Gaylord, "Structured Interviewing: Avoiding Selection Problems," *Personnel Journal*, Nov. 1980, pp. 907–912. W. T. Wolz, "How to Interview Supervisory Candidates for the Ranks," *Personnel*, Sept.–Oct. 1980, pp. 31–39. N. Schmitt, "Social and Situational Determinants of Interview Decisions: Implications for the Employment Interview," *Personnel Psychology*, 1976, *29*, pp. 79–101.

34. This is true despite its low reliability and its fallibility. This is confirmed in L. Ulrich and D. Trumbo, "The Selection Interview Since 1949," *Psychological Bulletin*, 1965, *63*, pp. 100–116. M. D. Hakel, "Employment Interviewing," in K. M. Rowland and G. R. Ferris (eds.), *Personnel Management* (Boston: Allyn & Bacon, 1982), p. 131. See also M. D. Dunnette and W. C. Borman, "Personal Selection and Classification Systems," *Annual Review of Psychology*, 1979, *30*, pp. 477–525.

35. Evidence that training helps is reported in A. P. Goldstein and M. Sorcher, *Changing Supervisory Behavior* (New York: Pergamon, 1974). Hakel, endnote 34, p. 154.

36. W. C. Byham, "Common Selection Problems Can Be Overcome," *Personnel Administrator*, August 1978, pp. 42–47.

37. Since 1976 much research on interviewing has gone from the validity type to the judgemental processes taking place in the interview, particularly by the interviewer. However, little research has been done on the validity of interviews with information gained from judgemental research. Schmitt and Schneider, endnote 1. Hakel, endnote 34.

38. E. C. Mayfield, S. H. Brown, B. W. Hamstra, "Selection Interview in the Life Insurance Industry: An Update of Research and Practice," *Personnel Psychology*, 1980, *33*, pp. 725–740.

39. C. W. Downs, "What Does the Selection Interview Accomplish?" *Personnel Administrator*, 1968, *31*, p. 100.

40. J. D. Hatfield and R. D. Gatewood, "Nonverbal Cues in the Selection Interview," *Personnel Administrator*, Jan. 1978, p. 35. Reprinted with permission. Copyright © 1978.

41. Ibid., p. 37.

42. Albright in Carroll and Schuler, endnote 1. Note that part of the criticism of testing is the issue of privacy invasion versus the issue of liberty. Consequently, it is recommended that organizations in-

form job applicants of the procedures used in gathering information, particularly from paper-and-pencil tests. The Life Insurance Marketing and Research Association also recommends that organizations using tests inform those taking tests of the following:
- That the test is only one step in the hiring process
- What the test measures and that it does so with validity and reliability
- Why it is being used
- What passing or failing means to them and about them

Life Insurance Marketing and Research Association, *Recruitment, Selection, Training and Supervision in Life Insurance* (Hartford, CT: Life Insurance Marketing and Research Association, 1966). See also "The Interview," *FEP Guidelines*, no. 202(5), 1982.

43. See Albright, endnote 1, and Schmidt and Hunter, endnote 4, on the use of tests. See also M. L. Tenopyr, "The Realities of Employment Testing," *American Psychologist*, 1981, 36, pp. 1120–1127, which suggests that even if tests were dropped, the impact on women and minorities could be minimal. For an excellent review and overview of testing see A. K. Wigdor and W. R. Garner (eds.), *Ability Testing: Uses, Consequences, and Controversies, Part I and Part II* (Washington, DC: National Academy Press, 1982). For an evaluation of the current state of testing see M. D. Dunnette and W. C. Borman, "Personnel Selection and Classification Systems," *Annual Review of Psychology*, 1979, 30, pp. 477–525.

44. Data supplied is an estimate suggested by Gestion MDS, a management consulting firm operating in Montreal.

45. M. Tefft, "Why More Firms Rely on Psychological Tests," *Financial Post*, Dec. 12, 1981. M. Dewey, "Employers Take Hard Look at the Validity and Value of Psychological Screening," *The Globe & Mail*, Feb. 7, 1981, p. 81.

46. Schneider, endnote 3.

47. J. B. Miner and M. G. Miner, *Personnel and Industrial Relations*, 3rd ed. (New York: MacMillan, 1977). See also R. R. Reilly, S. Zedeck, and M. L. Tenopyr, "Validity and Fairness of Physical Ability Tests for Predicting Performance in Craft Jobs," *Journal of Applied Psychology*, 1979, 64, pp. 262–274. J. D. Arnold, J. M. Rauschenberger, W. G. Soubel, and R. M. Guion, "Validation and Utility of a Strength Test for Selecting Steelworkers," *Journal of Applied Psychology*, 1982, 67, pp. 588–604.

48. D. Goleman, "The New Competency Tests: Matching the Right Jobs," *Psychology Today*, Jan. 1981, pp. 35–46.

49. J. P. Guilford, *The Nature of Human Intelligence* (New York: McGraw-Hill, 1967), p. 77.

50. See L. B. Plumke, "A Short Guide to the Development of Work Sample and Performance Tests, Second Edition," pamphlet from the U.S. Office of Personnel Management, Washington, DC, Feb. 1980, for an extensive review and guide of these tests. Note also the interchangeability of the words "work sample" and "performance tests." See also R. M. Guion, *Personnel Testing* (New York: McGraw-Hill, 1965). J. J. Asher and J. A. Sciarrino, "Realistic Work Sample Tests: A Review," *Personnel Psychology*, 1974, 27, pp. 549–553.

51. M. M. Petty, "A Multivariate Analysis of the Effects of Experience and Training Upon Performance in a Leaderless Group Discussion," *Personnel Psychology*, 1974, 27, pp. 271–282. See B. M. Bass and G. V. Barnett, *People, Work and Organizations* (2nd ed.) (Boston: Allyn & Bacon, 1981), for business games.

52. S. L. Cohen, "Pre-Packaged vs. Tailor-Made: The Assessment Center Debate," *Personnel Journal*, Dec. 1980, pp. 989–995. L. A. Digman, "How Well-Managed Organizations Develop Their Executives," *Organizational Dynamics*, Autumn 1978, pp. 65–66. L. C. Nichols and J. Hudson, "Dual-Role Assessment Center: Selection and Development," *Personnel Journal*, May 1981, pp. 350–386. T. C. Parker, "Assessment Centers: A Statistical Study," *Personnel Administrator*, Feb. 1980, pp. 65–67. J. C. Quick, W. A. Fisher, L. L. Schkade, and G. W. Ayers, "Developing Administrative Personnel Through the Assessment Center Technique," *Personnel Administrator*, Feb. 1980, pp. 44–46, 62. J. D. Ross, "A Current Review Of Public Sector Assessment Centers: Cause for Concern," *Public Personnel Management*, Jan.–Feb. 1979, pp. 41–46.

53. Used by courtesy of General Motors Corporation. For more excellent discussion on assessment centers see Albright, endnote 1; Sharf, endnote 32, pp. 156–183; V. R. Boehm, "Assessment Centers and Management Development," in K. M. Rowland and G. R. Ferris (eds.), *Personnel Management* (Boston: Allyn & Bacon, 1982), pp. 327–362. F. D. Frank and J. R. Preston, "The Validity of the Assessment Center Approach and Related Issues," *Personnel Administrator*, June 1982, pp. 87–94. R. B. Finkle, "Managerial Assessment Centers," in M. D. Dunnette (ed.), *Handbook of Industrial and Organizational Psychology* (Chicago: Rand McNally, 1976). S. D. Norton, "The Empirical and Content Validity of Assessment Centers vs. Traditional Methods for Predicting Managerial Excess," *Academy of Management Review*, 1977, 2, pp. 353–361. R. J. Klimoski, and W. J. Strictland, "Assessment Centers: Valid or Merely Prescient," *Personnel Psychology*, 1977, 30, pp. 353–361. G. F. Dreher and P. R. Suckett, "Some Problems with Applying Content Validity Evidence to Assessment Center Procedures," *Academy of Management Review*, 1981, 6, pp. 461–566. P. R. Sackett and G. F. Dreher, "Some Misconceptions About Content-Oriented Validation: A Rejoinder to Norton," *Academy*

of Management Review, 1981, *6*, pp. 567–568. W. F. Cascio and V. Silbey, "Utility of the Assessment Center as a Selection Device," *Journal of Applied Psychology*, 1979, *64*, pp. 107–118.
54. E. E. Ghiselli, *The Validity of Occupational Aptitude Tests* (New York: Wiley, 1966).
55. See K. Stabiner, "The Storm Over Women Firefighters," *The New York Times Magazine*, Sept. 26, 1982, for descriptions of such attempted demonstrations.
56. *Human Resources Management in Canada*, Prentice-Hall Canada Inc., Report Bulletin No. 31, p. 4.
57. T. H. Murray, "Genetic Testing at Work," *Personnel Administrator*, Sept. 1985, pp. 91–102.
58. See the full text of the *MacNeil/Lehrer Report* (New York: WNET-TV and the PBS Television Network), July 20, 1982, for a discussion of the issues surrounding genetic screening.
59. S. L. Dolan and B. Bannister, "Emerging Issues in Employment Testing," paper presented at the *4th International Congress of Work Psychology in the French Language*, Montreal, May 5–7, 1986.
60. "Personal Business," *Business Week*, July 27, 1981, pp. 85–86. The extent of polygraph usage is demonstrated by fact that, in the U.S., 50% of all retail firms and 20% of all corporations and many banks use polygraph tests: *U.S.A. Today*, Feb. 1981, p. 16.
61. H. Jain, endnote 8, p. 25,043.
62. D. T. Lykken, "The Case Against the Polygraph in Employment Screening," *Personnel Administrator*, Sept. 1985, pp. 59–65.
63. Kahn et al., "The Intimidation of Job Tests," *AFL-CIO Federationist*, January 1979.
64. R. L. Mathis and J. M. Jackson, *Personnel-Human Resource Management*, 4th ed. (St. Paul: West Publishing Co., 1985), p. 249.
65. J. A. Belt, "The Polygraph: A Questionable Personnel Tool," *Personnel Administrator*, August 1983, pp. 65–69.
66. P. R. Sackett, "Honesty Testing for Personnel Selection," *Personnel Administrator*, Sept. 1985, pp. 67–76.
67. "Saint vs. Sinner? Score Yourself Honestly," *Omaha World Herald*, Oct. 18, 1981, p. 7A.
68. Example cited in Mathis and Jackson, endnote 64, p. 250.

CHAPTER 6

Selection and Placement Decisions and Employment Equity

PHRM in the News

Using Information in Selection and Placement Decisions and Employment Equity
Criteria: The Concept of Job Success
Problems in Measuring Job Success
The Single Predictor Approach
The Multiple Predictors Approach

Selection and Placement Decisions and Employment Equity
Promotion and Transfer Decisions

Assessing Selection and Placement Decisions and Employment Equity
Reliability
Validity
Utility Considerations: Base Rate vs. Predictor Rate
Selection Ratio
Utility and Cost: An Overview

Socialization of New Employees
Purposes of Socialization
Methods of Socialization
Who Stays

Summary

Discussion Questions

Case Study

Endnotes

PHRM in the News

CBC Will Reinstate and Pay Back-wages for Work Dismissal

ST. JOHN'S—The Canadian Broadcasting Corporation must reinstate and pay back wages to a broadcast reporter who was fired after her husband became a director of Petro Canada, following the order of an independent Canadian Human Rights Commission tribunal. Rosann Cashin's contract with the CBC was not renewed after her husband Richard was appointed to the high-profile position in July 1981. The tribunal found that Cashin had been discriminated against on the basis of her marital status, but it dismissed her complaint of sexual discrimination. The CBC argued that Cashin's dismissal was justified because she no longer fit the bona fide occupational requirement that broadcasters be perceived to be objective. The Commission originally upheld that argument when it dismissed the complaint in June 1982; however, the dismissal was set aside by the Federal Court of Appeal in April 1985. The matter was referred back to the Commission and the independent tribunal was subsequently appointed. In addition to lost wages of an amount still to be determined, Cashin was awarded $2500 for hurt feelings.

Source: Human Resources Management in Canada, © 1986 Prentice-Hall Canada, Inc. Report Bulletin No. 35, p. 4, article 35.7 (January 1986). All rights reserved. Used with permission.

Hotel Seeks Out Special Employees

While parking a guest's car at our Yorkville [Toronto] hotel, the valet noticed the engine overheating. He discovered a radiator hose was broken. On his lunch hour, he bought a new hose and immediately installed it.

Late on a cold February night, a guest arrived at our hotel in Ottawa. On the way to her room, she complained of a sore throat to the bellman. Five minutes later, he returned with a humidifier, a thermos of hot tea, and a cold remedy. All unasked for.

Such impressions are no accident. We encourage our employees to develop this kind of attitude—what might be called a "managerial perspective." We let them know we value their creativity and sense of personal responsibility for making sure the guest's experience is special.

Selecting the right people to begin with—managers or employees—is critical. When we opened the Four Seasons in Philadelphia, for example, we received 20,000 applications and hired 350 people. Most job applicants are seen by at least four managers, and every person hired is interviewed by the general manager.

The selection system for managers is even more stringent. We use clinical psychologists to help us in assessing and enhancing the skills of our general managers.

Source: J. W. Young (senior executive with Four Seasons Hotels Ltd.), "Hotel Seeks Out Special Employees," *The Financial Post,* June 7, 1985, p. 19. Used with permission.

These "PHRM in the News" articles point out several factors that are important to organizations in making selection and placement decisions.

The first and most important is that job-related qualifications are the foundation on which fair employment practices are built. What organizations must do in making selection and placement decisions is to gather and use only valid information (i.e., information about an applicant that accurately predicts how well the applicant is likely to do on the job if selected). Because "valid" means "job-related" in this context, selection decisions based on valid predictors are in the best interests of the organization's productivity and legal concerns. Although using them may not be difficult, developing them often is. Many alternative ways to demonstrate validity exist, each with its own unique characteristics.[1]

Chapter 5 highlighted the legal and normative issues surrounding staffing activities; this chapter completes our discussion of selection and placement by addressing how this information is used to make valid employment decisions.

Using Information in Selection and Placement Decisions and Employment Equity

The methods for collecting selection and placement information—interviews, tests, and applications blanks—are outlined in Chapter 5. Using one method alone in making the decision is called the **Single predictor approach**; using several methods in combination is called **the multiple predictor approach**.

Criteria: The Concept of Job Success

Much careful consideration must be given to what is meant by "success" on a job. What does it mean being a good manager? A good worker? Instruments are available to measure success, but not everyone in the field is in agreement as which are best. The term "criteria" to the PHRM specialist means the evaluation norms that are used to measure such things as the performance, aptitudes, or skills of an individual.[2] In the psychological literature two types of criteria are mentioned: the **ultimate criterion** and the **actual criterion**. The ultimate criterion is a theoretical construct, an abstract idea that can never actually be measured. It represents a complete set of ideal factors that constitute a successful person. The actual criterion is the measurable, referring to real factors that are used to determine or measure success. For example, some organizations use the periodic results of a performance appraisal, or the number of days the individual was absent.

Problems in Measuring Job Success

The relationships between the ultimate and the actual criteria can be expressed in terms of two problems: deficiency and contamination. Exhibit 6.1 shows the degree of overlap between the ultimate and actual criteria. The circle represents the conceptual content of each type of criterion. The true and valid elements of job success are represented by the shaded area (the criterion relevance).

Criterion Deficiency. **Criterion deficiency** is the degree to which the actual criteria fail to overlap the ultimate criteria, for instance, the evaluation fails to include an important job dimension in the measurement of overall success on the job although there is always some degree of deficiency in the actual criteria, it can be reduced by careful job analysis.

Criterion Contamination. **Criterion contamination** refers to the actual criteria which, in fact, are unrelated to the ultimate criteria, for instance, rating the quality of the coffee prepared by one of the workers. Contamination consists normally of two parts. One part, called **bias**, is the extent to which the actual criteria systematically measures something other than what the job is supposed ultimately to entail. The second part, called **error**, is the extent to which the actual criteria are not related to anything at all.

Consequently, in order to relate any selection instrument (predictor) to any measure of job success, the first task is to carefully examine the multiple dimensions of the job, and attempt to reduce both deficiency and contamination. This is usually done through effective use of job analysis, as explained in Chapter 3.

The Single Predictor Approach

When PHRM managers use only one piece of information or one method for selecting an applicant, they are taking the **single predictor approach**.

Exhibit 6.1 Criterion Deficiency, Relevance, and Contamination

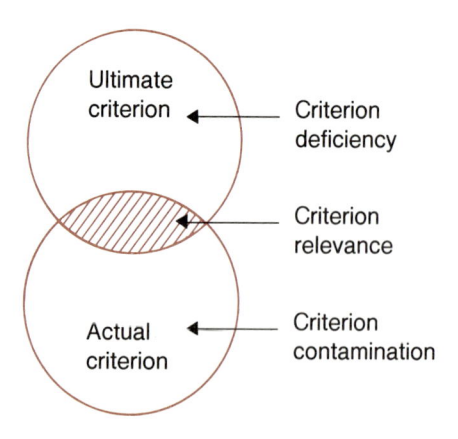

Single predictors are used by many organizations to select employees, particularly when these predictors can readily be validated. This occurs most frequently when a single predictor captures the essence (or the major dimension) of the job, thereby making it easy to validate:

> A few hiring tests are easy enough to validate, especially those in which the candidate actually performs a task he/she will have to perform on the job. It makes obvious good sense, for example, to require a candidate for a secretarial job to pass a typing test, and generally the equal-opportunity establishment accepts such tests.[3]

But for the vast majority of jobs, a single predictor cannot be used, nor can a single dimension, such as typing, be used to demonstrate the essence of the job. Many jobs can be fully described only with several job dimensions (duties), as illustrated in the job descriptions shown in Chapter 3. For such jobs, several predictors, such as written tests and application blanks, are used in making the selection and placement decisions.

The Multiple Predictors Approach

When several sources of information are combined, as was illustrated in Exhibit 5.3, selection and placement decisions are made with a **multiple predictors approach**. There are several ways to combine information from different sources. The type of job typically influences what information is gathered and how it is combined. Generally the information is combined by using one of the following: (1) a non-compensatory approach, (2) a compensatory approach, or (3) a combination of these two approaches.[4]

Non-compensatory Approach to Multiple Predictors. Two major models are used in making selection decisions based on a non-compensatory approach. One is the multiple cut-off model and the other is the multiple hurdle model. Both models are based on the idea that the job to be performed has several dimensions and thus several predictors are appropriate in making the selection decision.

In the **multiple cut-off approach**, an applicant must exceed fixed levels of proficiency on *all* of the predictors in order to be accepted. A failing or low score on one predictor cannot be compensated for by a higher than necessary score on another predictor. For example, an applicant for an air traffic controller's job cannot compensate for failure on a visual recognition test. That is the reason that this is called the **non-compensatory approach**.

The **multiple hurdle approach** is similar to the multiple cut-off approach except that decisions are made sequentially. In the multiple cut-off approach, selection is made only from the applicants who score at or above the required minimal levels of proficiency on each of the measures being used as predictors. In contrast, when a multiple hurdle approach is used, applicants must first pass one hurdle (a test) before they go on to the next hurdle. For example, they may need to first pass a paper-and-pencil test before an interview can be arranged.

In the multiple hurdle approach an applicant may not need to attain or exceed a minimum score on each predictor in order to be selected. Sometimes low scores on a predictor result in a provisional acceptance of the applicant, which enables the organization to assess how the applicant performs on the job. If the applicant performs well on those dimensions on which he or she had low scores, the applicant, now an employee, may be granted full acceptance. Although this multiple hurdle approach helps ensure higher success rate for the final acceptance decisions, it necessitates hiring applicants who otherwise would not have been hired if the multiple cut-off approach had been used, and who might not make it beyond provisional acceptance. Thus, there is some cost involved in using multiple hurdles, although it may result in more applicants who eventually are accepted.[5]

Common Pitfalls in the Multiple Hurdle Approach. Given that in the multiple hurdle model, a decision regarding the next hurdle is contingent on passing successfully the past hurdle, the question arises: How do you arrange the various hurdles? Many organizations sequence the different hurdles based on comfort and convenience considerations, although convenience does not necessarily reflect the validity of the hurdle. Ideally, therefore, the hurdles should be sequenced in terms of their relative validity—the more important should be first, and the least important should be placed last. Imagine for example, a hospital that wishes to hire a cook. Following the successful passing of several hurdles that included application blanks, interviews, and even simulation, the medical examination, which is the last hurdle, reveals that the candidate has tuberculosis, and cannot work in the kitchen because of this communicable disease. In cases like this, the proper approach would be to deduct from the criterion (see previous section) the most important requirements for the job, and schedule the hurdles in this order. Consequently, the medical examination (a bona fide occupational requirement) will be put first. It is highly recommended that an employer using a multiple hurdle approach consider the order and sequence of the various hurdles not as a function of convenience, but rather as a function of validity.

Compensatory Approach to Multiple Predictors. Both of the above models assume that doing well on one predictor cannot compensate for doing poorly on another one. In situations where this assumption is not applicable, the multiple regression approach is used. This is a **compensatory** approach, which assumes that good performance on one predictor can compensate for poor performance on another predictor. A low score on ability, for example, can be compensated for by a high score on motivation. Based on this assumption, a statistical analysis of multiple regression can then be used to combine predictors to predict job criteria.

Combined Approach to Multiple Predictors. Many organizations use the combined approach, often starting at the recruitment stage. The combined approach may use aspects of both the non-compensatory and compensatory approaches. Generally, the multiple cutoff approach, or part of it, is used first: "You have to get through the door before we'll interview you." Once in the interview setting, the compensatory approach applies. For example, an organization may establish one minimum requirement—an undergraduate degree in accounting or a high grade-point average. If this condition is met, other characteristics are negotiable. Thus, when organizations decide to use multiple predictors they need to assess the characteristics of the jobs to determine the appropriate number of predictors and the extent to which predictor scores can compensate for each other.

Until there is a legal challenge, the employer does not have to demonstrate validity or defend the predictors used. However, it might prove to be most cost-effective for an organization to use only valid predictors, and to make sure that each one meet the bottom-line criterion discussed in the previous chapter. In addition to demonstrating the job relatedness of the selection procedures used, employers also should be able to show that non-job-related procedures and information did not enter into the decision-making process.

Selection and Placement Decisions and Employment Equity

Selection and placement decisions are attempts to place the right person in the right job. The right person may be found inside or outside the organization. Whether a person is "right" depends on the match between the person's skill, knowledge, and aptitude and job skill demands, and between the person's personality, interests, and preferences and job and organizational characteristics. An organization may want job applicants to fill newly created jobs, or jobs that have become vacant as a result of retirement, transfer, or voluntary quitting. Vacancies also may be created by demotions and discharges. Demotions and discharges are discussed further in Chapters 8 and 15.

The decision may be made to hire a new job applicant or to transfer or promote one from within the organization. The decision also may be to not hire a particular applicant or set of applicants, but rather to do more recruiting, or even to put on hold some applicants who are qualified but for whom no jobs currently are open. Although generally not defined as such, demotion and termination are essentially final selection or placement decisions. These decisions should be thought of as such since they are subject to the same legal considerations as hiring, transfer, and promotion decisions, which is why these are included in Exhibit 5.1.

Selection decisions also can be made to bring in candidates from the outside to fill higher level jobs in the organization. This may lower morale, particularly for those internal candidates who feel passed over. Therefore, many organizations prefer to promote from within. And as the 34 to 44-

year-old age group increases in the 1990s, transfers will become the alternative to promotions, at least in providing challenge and variety for valued employees.

Promotion and Transfer Decisions

Most organizations have policies of promoting from within. A U.S. survey reports that 76% of all of the organizations surveyed have a policy of filling their job openings with current employees.[6] Some job vacancies, however, are filled by outside sources, particularly highly skilled jobs or when the organization has been caught by surprise and has no individual ready internally to take the job. To help prevent surprises, organizations like Xerox, IBM, Canadian Pacific, and the Ontario Ministry of Transportation and Communications have managerial succession programs. In these programs, which are part of the organization's human resource planning and forecasting, current top managers identify employees who may one day be able to take over their jobs or other executive jobs in the organizations. Exhibit 6.2 is an example of a typical human resource forecasting form, used by the Ontario Ministry of Transportation and Communications. Potential candidates identified by the managers are assessed by top management, which also identifies back-up incumbents. All of the factors, specified on the form (Exhibit 6.2) result in an equation for supply and demand for certain job levels. If a shortage is recognized, strategies for development and/or inside recruitment are devised.

Types of Promotion and Transfer. Promotions can occur within a department, a division, or an entire organization. They also can occur between two non-managerial positions (for example, from Typist I to Typist II), between managerial positions, and between non-managerial and managerial positions.

Although promotions generally refer to vertical moves in the organization, promotions may occur when an employee moves to another job at the same level but with more pay or status. A transfer generally refers to a move at the same level and at the same pay.

Making Promotion and Transfer Decisions. Immediate supervisors play a major role in deciding whom to promote or transfer.

> In many cases, the immediate supervisor must search for qualified candidates and make a choice when a vacancy arises. This process may be carried out in close consultation with one or more higher level supervisors who ultimately have to approve the choice. On the other hand, the immediate supervisor may have almost total control over the decisions.[7]

Immediate supervisors may have most control when a new job is being created, and may be able to determine exactly who will be promoted by writing a job description that fits only that specific individual. This is not necessarily a fair practice, but it is a common one. It is important to remember, however, that promotion decisions are just another selection decision and as such must be done without discrimination.

Succession Planning/Human Resource Forecasting Form Exhibit 6.2

Job Level	Current Strength	Losses	Back-up	Future Demand	Imbalance		
					Surplus	Shortage	Promotionally Blocked

Source:
Human resource inventory

Sources:
Current job incumbents
Retirement
Transfers out of function
Resignations

Sources:
High-potential people
Mobility and career development preferences, from managers and employees.

Source:
Strategic and operational business plans.

Action Plans:
Development
Recruitment
Reassignment

Source: Adapted from L. J. Reypert, "Succession Planning in the Ministry of Transportation and Communication, Province of Ontario," *Human Resource Planning*, 1981, vol. 4, no. 3. Reprinted by permission of the publisher. Copyright 1981 by the Human Resource Planning Society.

Identifying Candidates for Promotion and Transfer. Candidates may be identified by word of mouth, inspection of the organization's personnel records, (this is easy if the organization has a computerized human resource information system), promotion lists based on performance or managerial ratings, and formal programs for identifying potential candidates for promotion, such as assessment centres. The human resource information system is also valuable here because it can store information on employee preferences and interests,[8] which help to ensure that candidate identification can be made with consideration for both Match 1 and Match 2. Appropriate matching also helps to reduce the number of employees turning down promotions or leaving a job to which they were only recently promoted or transferred.

Comparing Candidates. Methods for identifying candidates also can be used to evaluate and compare them. Although many companies administer a battery of tests to assess mental ability, personality, and interests, one study concluded that tests aften are ignored as a decision-making device for internal promotions.

Instead, job experience, performance history, and assessment centre results often are used to evaluate internal candidates. Interviews also are used, although mainly for external candidates. Recently, research has pointed out the critical role that a powerful sponsor (mentor) can play in helping a bright subordinate to climb up in the hierarchy. In some organizations, seniority plays a role in comparing candidates.

One strategy used by managers who favour a particular candidate is the **confirmation approach**. To make the selection process appear legitimate, a manager may select several candidates, in addition to the favourite, for others to evaluate. The manager, however, deliberately selects other candidates who are far less qualified than the favourite. Although there is a choice, it is more apparent than real.

Making the Final Choice. Making a decision is difficult if different types of information are available for competing job applicants. Even if this is the case, however, all of the candidates can be screened quickly, and only those with an obvious potential to do well need to be retained as candidates. Those remaining then can be evaluated. Although this may not result in selection of the best candidate, the one who is chosen should at least perform adequately.

Why Not the Best? All too often, the best people are not the ones who are promoted or transferred.[9] There are several reasons for this apparent anomaly.

First, staff people often are not considered for line jobs. Many organizations promote only line managers to upper management. Exceptions to this tradition are occurring, however. IBM has a company policy of promoting managers in and out of line and staff jobs.

Second, decentralized departments and divisions operate like independent organizations. When vacancies occur, a department or division tends to select only from its own employees and not from the total organization. Decentralization also can result in a separate performance appraisal system for each division; even if divisions did obtain candidates from other divisions, they could be hard to evaluate.

A third reason that the most qualified person may be overlooked is related to discrimination:

> Probably one of the more overlooked banks of promotable talent is the huge reservoir of women in the workforce. Except in service industries such as banks, insurance companies, and advertising firms, women have been largely ignored in management promotions.[10]

Ignoring women, older employees, and minorities, besides being illegal, means selecting managers from a small percentage of employees. The following case illustrates the kind of problems in which this practice could result.

Regarding older employees, in 1985 the Federal Court of Appeal ruled that an Air Canada practice of refusing to hire pilots over the age of 27 is not a bona fide occupational requirement, which helped to define what constitutes a requirement of this type under Section 14 of the Canadian Human Rights Act. This case ruling also will probably apply to questions regarding promotions.

In 1985, the Supreme Court of Canada ruled that fixing a compulsory retirement age is discriminatory. In this case, the Supreme Court struck down a mandatory retirement policy forcing school teachers to retire when they turned 65. The judges stated that, despite the collective bargaining agreement and the Manitoba Public Schools Act, the policy contravened the province's human rights Act (Craton v. Manitoba Public Schools).

This decision will have widespread impact on forced retirements in all of the provinces whose human rights Acts prohibit age discrimination in employment (see Chapter 5). Section 15 of the federal Charter of Rights also prohibits age discrimination without setting upper age limits, but it has not yet been tested in court. However, an Ontario case has been launched by the Ontario Confederation of University Faculty Associations that will test the primacy of the Charter over the Ontario Human Rights Act.

Fourth, the best person may not be promoted because subjective, personal criteria are used in selection rather than objective criteria. Subjective criteria include how well they are liked by the manager, how they dress, and how popular they are.

Finally, many competent managers are refusing promotion if it means moving to another location. Increasingly, members of dual-career families are refusing promotions involving a geographic change because the change may require a career sacrifice on the part of the spouse.

Assessing Selection and Placement Decisions and Employment Equity

The quality and effectiveness of selection and placement decisions can be judged by the number of good employees acquired as a result of these decisions. The hiring of good performers naturally leads to an increase in overall organizational productivity. When an organization makes selection and placement decisions based on activities that benefit organizational productivity, it is making decisions using predictors that are valid and serve its legal considerations. Using predictors that do not result in selection and placement decisions that benefit productivity is counterproductive and generally not consistent with legal considerations.

Obtaining and using predictors that are valid is only part of making effective selection and placement decisions. The other parts include predictor reliability, base rate versus selection rate, the selection ratio, and the overall utility (costs and benefits) of the decisions. Consequently, it is useful to examine these several parts in assessing the nature of the tradeoffs made during the selection and placement decisions.

Reliability

Reliability means the consistency or stability of a predictor. A predictor should yield the same estimate during repeated usage under identical conditions. In organizational studies, two types of reliabilities are commonly identified: test-retest reliability, and internal consistency reliability.

Test-retest reliability. The simplest way to assess a predictor's reliability is to measure something at two points in time and compare the scores. For example, an IQ test can be administered to a group of applicants three months before the hiring decision and again a month before it. The two sets of scores then are correlated, and the coefficient that results is called the coefficient of stability, because it reflects the stability of the test over time. The higher the coefficient of stability, the more reliable is the measure. As a rule of thumb, stability coefficients of approximately +.70 are professionally acceptable.[11]

Internal Consistency Reliability. This refers to the extent to which the predictor has an homogeneous content. It concerns the degree to which the different items of a predictor (a test, for example) are measuring the same thing. Because psychological tests are used extensively in selection decisions (see Chapter 5), an examination of the different ways to assess the test internal consistency is presented here.

One common method is called **split-half reliability**. During the scoring of the test, the items/questions are divided or split in half. For each person, two scores are computed and these scores are then correlated. If the test is internally consistent, the correlation coefficient that results is usually high.

A closely related technique for assessing internal consistency reliability is to compute a coefficient called **Gronbach Alpha** or **Kuder-Richardson 20**. Conceptually, each item of a test is thought to be a mini-test in itself and is correlated with the response to every other item. This generates a matrix of inter-item correlations that are averaged to obtain a composite measure of the item similarity or homogeneity of the test. Both reliability coefficients are very popular in PHRM research.[12]

Because any type of reliability can influence validity, the U.S. *Uniform Guidelines* require that estimates of reliability be reported for all selection procedures, if available. Furthermore, these estimates should be made for relevant race, gender, and ethnic subgroups. In Canada, the various human right Acts have not addressed reliability issues.

Validity

Validity refers to how accurate the predictor is as a forecaster. Validity is distinguished from reliability in the sense that it refers to the accuracy and precision, rather than to consistency. Also, reliability is inherent in a test or a predictor, while validity depends on the use of the test. Validity concerns the appropriateness of using a given predictor for drawing inferences about the criteria (Exhibit 6.1). For example, a given test may be valid for predicting an employee's direct performance, but invalid for predicting attendance.

Several types of validity are discussed in psychological research. Five types of validity are particularly relevant to selection and placement decisions:

1. Empirical or criterion-related
2. Content
3. Construct
4. Face
5. Differential

Although all of these types of validity are important, the strategies used to collect the information to demonstrate them are significantly different. Employers should be familiar with all of them, so that they can demonstrate the validity of their predictors in defence against adverse impact charges.

Empirical or Criterion-Related Validity. This type of validity refers, as its name suggests, to how much a predictor relates to a measure of job success. There are two types of empirical validation strategies—concurrent and predictive—as shown in Exhibit 6.3.

Concurrent validity involves determination of the relationship between a predictor and a job-criterion score for all employees involved in the study at the same time. For example, to determine the concurrent validity of the correlation between years of experience and job performance, PHRM staff would collect from each person in the study information about years of experience and performance scores. All persons in the study would have to have been working in similar jobs, generally in the same job family or classification. Then a correlation would be computed. In concurrent validity, there is no time interval between collecting the predictor and the criterion data: the two variables are assessed concurrently. This validation strategy is simpler, quicker, and less expensive to use than the predictive criterion-related validity. It is, however, less accurate, because results obtained by already-working employees may not be completely accurate when applied to a group of applicants who have not yet worked for the firm.[13]

Exhibit 6.3   Criterion-related Validation Strategies

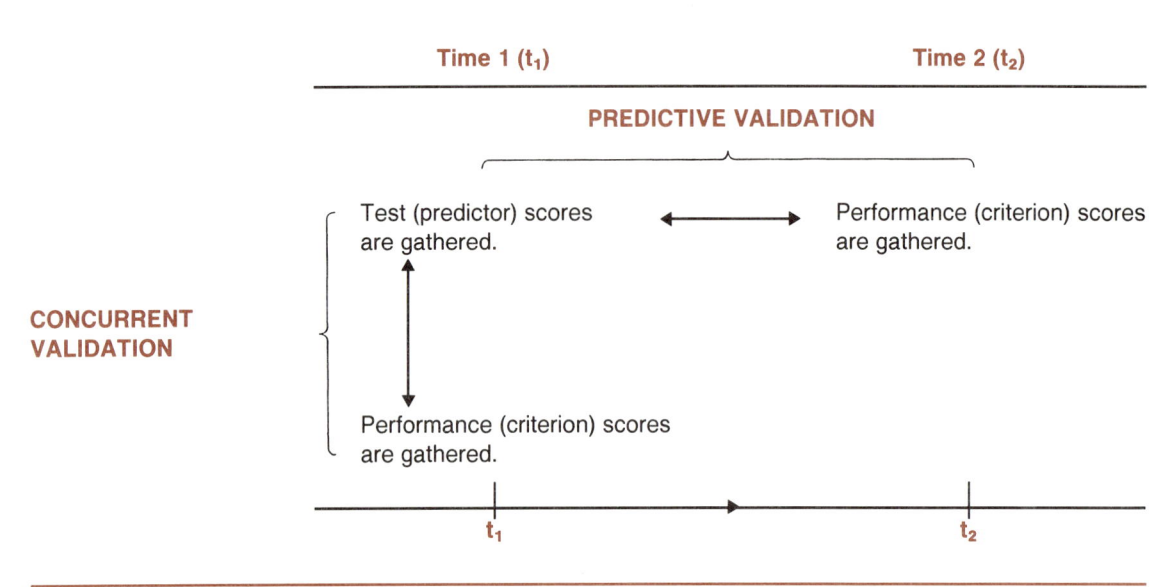

```
                    Time 1 (t₁)                              Time 2 (t₂)
                  ─────────────────────────────────────────────────────
                                  PREDICTIVE VALIDATION
                              ⌒─────────────────────────⌒
                    Test (predictor) scores    ←――→   Performance (criterion) scores
                    are gathered.                     are gathered.
                         ↑
CONCURRENT               │
VALIDATION               ↓
                    Performance (criterion) scores
                    are gathered.
                  ─────┼───────────────────────────────────┼──────────
                       t₁                                  t₂
```

Source: R. S. Schuler and S. A. Youngblood, *Effective Personnel Management,* 2nd ed. (St. Paul: West Publishing Co., 1986), p. 205. Used with permission.

Predictive validity determination is similar to that of concurrent validity, except that the predictor is measured some time before the criterion is measured, as shown in Exhibit 6.3. Thus, the predictive validity of a predictor could be determined by measuring an existing group of new employees with it and waiting to gather their criterion measure later on by hiring a group of job applicants, regardless of their initial score on the predictor, and measuring them on their criterion later. If only those who initially score higher on the predictor also score higher on the criterion, the validity of the measure is empirically demonstrated. Because this procedure is somewhat expensive, most organizations tend to employ the concurrent validation strategy.

In both concurrent and predictive validity, predictor scores are correlated with criterion data. The resulting correlation is referred to as **validity coefficient**. The correlation is important because it describes the statistical likelihood that a predictor will predict the actual job success. A job applicant who passes a welding test, for example, should be able to perform successfully as a welder, if the test is valid.

It is important to note that there is a range of validity. The degree of validity for a particular test is indicated by the magnitude of the correlation coefficient, which ranges from -1 or $+1$ (most valid) to 0 (least valid). In fact, -1 and $+1$ show perfect validity (perfectly correlated), and 0 shows the absence of validity (perfectly uncorrelated). Perfect validity comes in two forms: **perfectly positive validity** $(+1)$ means the two variables move in the same direction; and **perfectly negative validity** (-1) means they move in the opposite direction.

The correlation coefficient discussed here measures the extent or degree of linear relationship between two sets of values, for example, scores on a test (predictor) and performance scores. Illustrations of several linear relationships with validities of +1, −1, and 0 can be represented by plotting actual data of test-criterion relationship on **scattergrams**, as shown in Exhibit 6.4.

But what do these values of validity mean in the real world? Perfect validity means that future performance on the job is perfectly predictable from a job applicant's score on selection tests. If the test lacked validity, it would be impossible to predict on the basis of test scores whether one job applicant would be a better performer than the other. Generally, most tests used by organizations have less than perfect validity: these tests are not perfect predictors of performance. However, as long as a test has some validity it is useful to the organization because it can indicate which applicants are most likely to be the best performers.

Validity is the heart of many PHRM decisions. The more valid (job-related) the test, the more efficient selection and placement decisions can be. An important aspect of empirical validity is the relevance or appropriateness of the criterion being correlated with the predictor.[14] The criteria should, of course, be relevant and important to the jobs in question. The job in question, could also resemble other jobs for which the predictors are correlated.[15]

On many occasions employers are not able to present empirical data for empirical validity determination.[16] Consequently, other methods of validation are necessary. The most common are content and construct validity.

Content Validity. **Content validity** differs from empirical validity in that it estimates or judges the relevance of a predictor as an indicator of performance without collecting actual performance information. The administration of a typing test as a selection device for hiring typists is a

Relationships Between Test Scores and Performance Scores — Exhibit 6.4

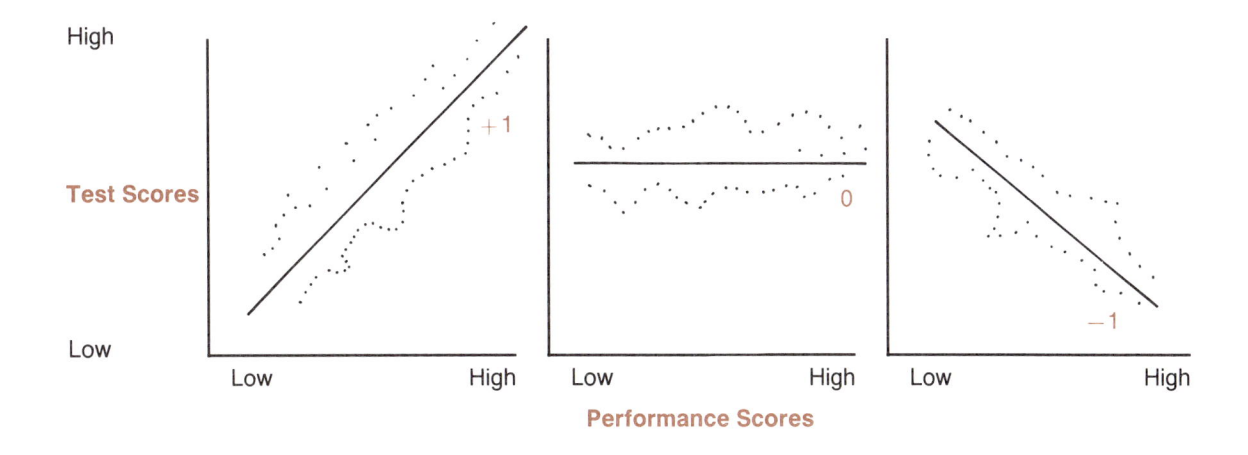

classic example of a predictor judged to have content validity.[17] Content validity refers to predictors that measure skills, knowledge, or abilities related to those required of the actual job. Therefore, to demonstrate content validity, it is necessary to know the duties of the actual job and the individual skills, knowledge, and aptitudes needed to perform those duties. As discussed in Chapter 3, information about job tasks and responsibilities can be obtained by using several standardized forms, and then it can be used to develop job descriptions. These descriptions can be used in turn to make judgements about the individual skills, knowledge, and aptitudes necessary to perform the tasks. Unlike criterion-related validity, no statistical correlation is involved in assessing content validity. Rather, experts in the field provide the assessment of relevance. A similar type of validity based on experts' judgment is called face validity.

Face validity is concerned with the appearance of the test items. Do they appear to be relevant for such a test? While estimates of content validity are normally given by the test developers, estimates of face validity are given by test takers. Consequently, one may logically conclude that, given that test developers are more professional, content validity is far more useful than face validity. However, in order for the experts to develop an appropriate test, they must be familiar with the domain of job behaviour, which must be specified by the organization. Clearly then, job analysis is a critical element in the validation process. Job analysis should be regarded as the starting point and the thread that ties together a basic selection and validation study (see Exhibit 6.5, which is an extension of Exhibits 3.7 and 5.2). It is also a critical activity in determining construct validity.

Construct Validity. Instead of showing a direct relationship between test results or other selection information (e.g., education or experience levels) and job criteria, selection methods seek to measure, often by tests, the degree to which an applicant possesses abilities and aptitudes (psychological traits) that are deemed necessary for job criteria. These underlying psychological traits are called constructs and include, among many others, intelligence, leadership ability, verbal ability, interpersonal sensitivity, and analytical ability—essentially, the characteristics of the "other" category of applicant information. Constructs deemed necessary for doing well on the job are inferred from job behaviours and activities indicated in the job analysis.

Construct validity requires demonstrating that a relationship exists between a selection procedure or test (a measure of the construct) and the psychological trait (construct) that it seeks to measure. For example, does a case analysis test reliably measure to what degree the person possesses analytical ability? In order to demonstrate construct validity, one would need data showing that high scorers on the test actually are able to analyze more difficult material and are better thinkers than low scorers on the test, and that analytical ability is related to the duties shown in the job description.

Content, construct, and empirical validities are illustrated in Exhibit 6.6, which uses some of the information contained in the job description of the animal keeper in Exhibit 3.3.

Steps in the Process of Validation   *Exhibit 6.5*

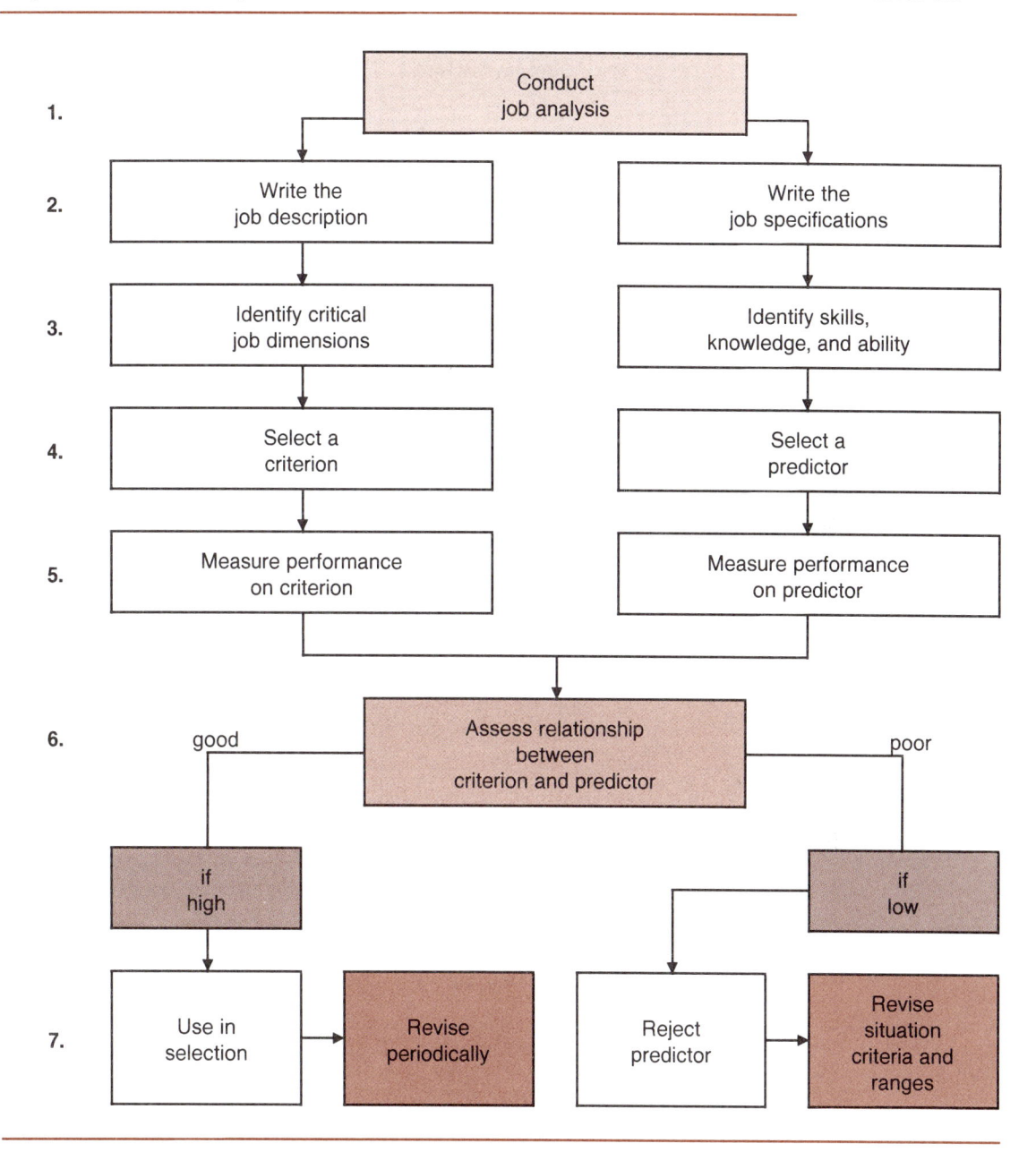

1. Conduct job analysis
2. Write the job description / Write the job specifications
3. Identify critical job dimensions / Identify skills, knowledge, and ability
4. Select a criterion / Select a predictor
5. Measure performance on criterion / Measure performance on predictor
6. Assess relationship between criterion and predictor
   - good → if high
   - poor → if low
7. If high: Use in selection → Revise periodically
   If low: Reject predictor → Revise situation criteria and ranges

Differential Validity. So far, validity, particularly empirical validity, has been discussed as the extent to which a predictor or set of predictors actually predicts.[18] If an individual scores well on a valid predictor, that person is likely to do well in the future. But there may be situations in which the predictor is valid for some people and not valid, or less valid, for others. For

Exhibit 6.6 Illustration of Three Types of Validation Processes

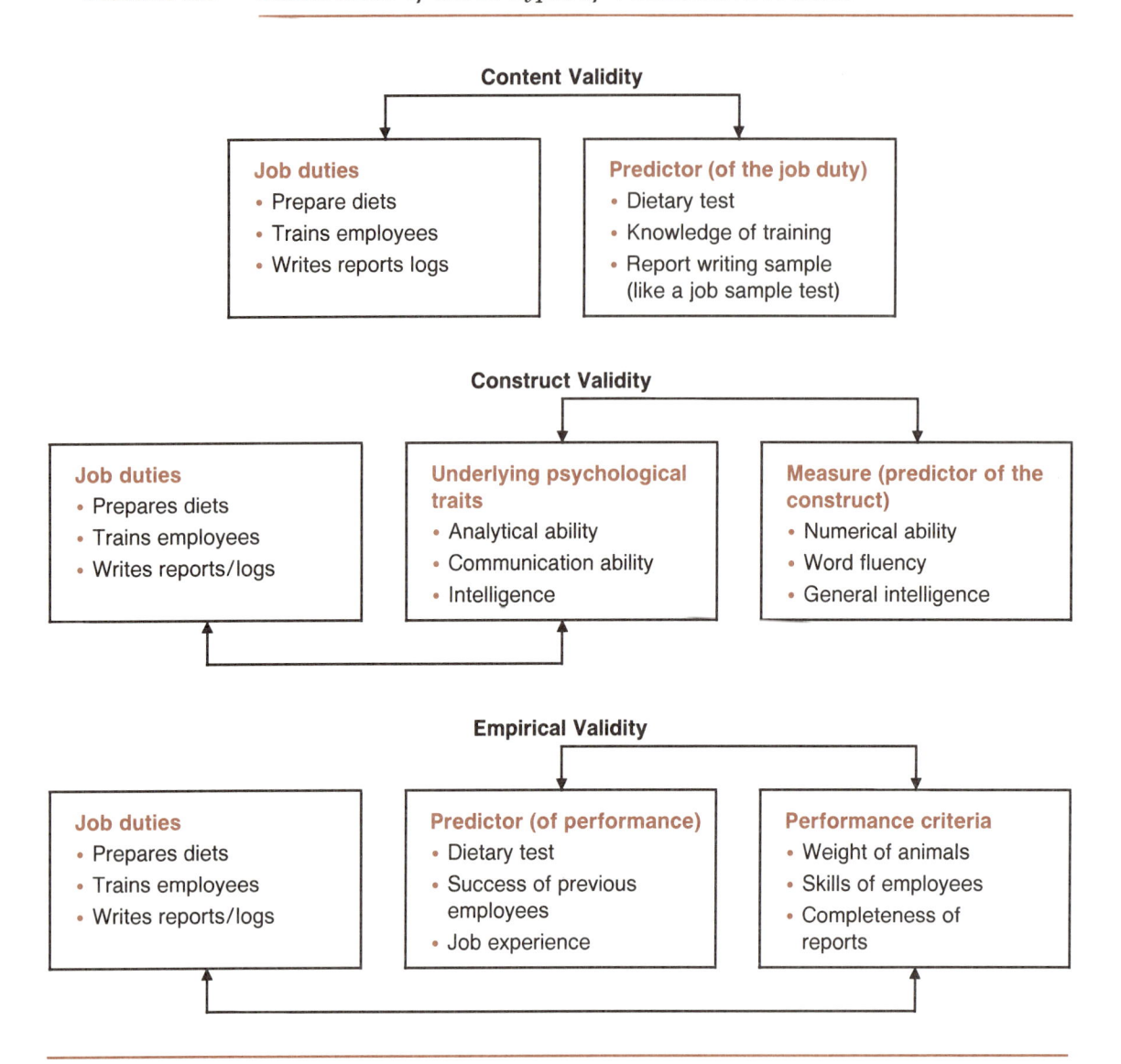

Content Validity

Job duties	Predictor (of the job duty)
• Prepare diets • Trains employees • Writes reports logs	• Dietary test • Knowledge of training • Report writing sample (like a job sample test)

Construct Validity

Job duties	Underlying psychological traits	Measure (predictor of the construct)
• Prepares diets • Trains employees • Writes reports/logs	• Analytical ability • Communication ability • Intelligence	• Numerical ability • Word fluency • General intelligence

Empirical Validity

Job duties	Predictor (of performance)	Performance criteria
• Prepares diets • Trains employees • Writes reports/logs	• Dietary test • Success of previous employees • Job experience	• Weight of animals • Skills of employees • Completeness of reports

Source: R. S. Schuler and S. A. Youngblood, *Effective Personnel Management*, 2nd ed. (St. Paul: West Publishing Co., 1986), p. 209. Used with permission.

example, a person with high verbal ability may perform well on a job regardless of the individual's score on a manual dexterity test. But for a person with low ability, high scores on the manual dexterity test may be necessary for the individual to perform well. Thus, the manual dexterity test is a valid predictor of performance for only the person with low ability, and not for the person with high ability. Therefore, the manual dexterity test is a valid predictor of performance only for the person with low ability and can be described as having differential validity.

Since any test may have differential validity, it is important for a personnel department to conduct several validity studies for any test being used. Differential validity studies must be done for minorities in relationship to the majority group. The argument here is that a test valid for one group (e.g., whites) may not be valid for another group (e.g., native people). Similarly, separate validity studies must be conducted for the same or similar jobs when they are carried out in different conditions or in different organizations.[19] The practical necessity, however, for doing either separate validity studies for separate groups of employees, or the same for similar jobs under different conditions, is questioned by the concept of validity generalization.

Validity Generalization. The essence of validity generalization is that a test or predictor predicts in the same manner for all individuals in the same or similar jobs in the same or similar organizations.[20] That is, if two similar jobs exist in two parts of an organization or in two different organizations, a given selection test should be equally valid for both jobs. This assumes, however, that some degree of similarity in jobs and conditions can first be identified.[21] Similarity of jobs and conditions are judged by results of job analyses. If validity generalization can be substantiated successfully, an organization can save a great deal of time and money by developing valid, job-related predictors. In sum, if the validity of a predictor for a job has been established, it may be utilized as a predictor in another, perhaps newly created, similar job.

Utility Considerations: Base Rate vs. Predictor Rate

As long as the predictor used for selection decisions has less than a perfect validity (r = 1.00), all personnel selection will entail some errors. The objective, of course is to minimize these errors as much as possible. While using predictors, PHRM managers operate on the premises that

1. some job applicants will perform better than others;
2. the better performers can be identified; and
3. using predictors will result in a greater success rate than not using them at all. In other words, they assume that the **predictor rate** (the number of true decisions relative to the total number of decisions) will significantly exceed the **base rate** (the proportion of applicants who would succeed on the job in any event if they are selected randomly).

The concepts of **false negatives, false positives, true positives,** and **true negatives** are useful in assessing these utility considerations. In selecting employees, an organization wants to make as many true decisions as possible (both positive and negative), and to minimize the number of false decisions. Using a test with a predictor rate higher than the base rate does this. For example, if the base rate is .5 (half of the applicants who are hired randomly turn out to be good performers) and the predictor rate is .8 (80% of the selection decisions are effective), many more true decisions will be made using the predictor. This can be illustrated using two scattergrams, each plotting 100 applicants hired, one showing a .5 base rate and the other a .8 predictor rate. **Cut-off score** is used to categorize the employees as being good performers or poor performers, and those who would be hired or rejected if the predictor was used. The two scattergrams are shown in Exhibit 6.7.

In scattergram A there is essentially no relationship between test score and total performance. Note that, of 100 subjects, an equal number of applicants turned out to be true positive, false positive, true negative, and false negative. The number of correct decisions is 50, so the predictor rate does not exceed the base rate of .5.

In scattergram B, however, the number of individuals in the four categories is not equal. In fact, false positive and false negative are each 10, and true positive and true negative are each 40, so 80 correct decisions were made in this case, as opposed to only 50 in the previous case. This illustrates that using tests with predictor rates exceeding base rates tends to improve the utility of the selection process. Final evaluation of the real utility of the selection process, however, must incorporate a number of additional variables, which will be discussed next.

Selection Ratio

A further important concept in evaluating selection and placement procedures is the **selection ratio**, which is defined as the proportion of individuals actually hired in relation to the number who applied. For example, only 10 individuals out of 200 applicants might be hired. This would represent a selection ratio of $10/200$ or 5%.

Generally speaking, a selection system has greater value when the selection ratio is small—when there are many more applicants than jobs. The fewer applicants, the lower the chance that this pool contains the best possible applicant. With few applicants, more care must be taken in matching them to the jobs available. If an organization must hire anyone who applies because there are so few applicants, the validity of the selection and placement devices becomes irrelevant. This is particularly true when there is only one type of job available.

In these situations, the chance is low that all of the people hired will perform well. Consequently, the organization may need to establish extensive training programs, which may be costly. The organization could try to attract more job applicants by raising wages, but that might cause many of the current employees to become unhappy if they detect pay inequities. Therefore, it pays an organization to attract as many potentially qualified applicants initially as possible and thereby reduce its selection ratio. Without choice, the utility of selection devices is minimal; with choice, utility may be high and there is a greater probability that the applicants chosen will do well and be satisfied.

Selection and Placement Decisions and Employment Equity 213

Effects of Predictor and Base Rate for Tests with Two Levels of Validity

Exhibit 6.7

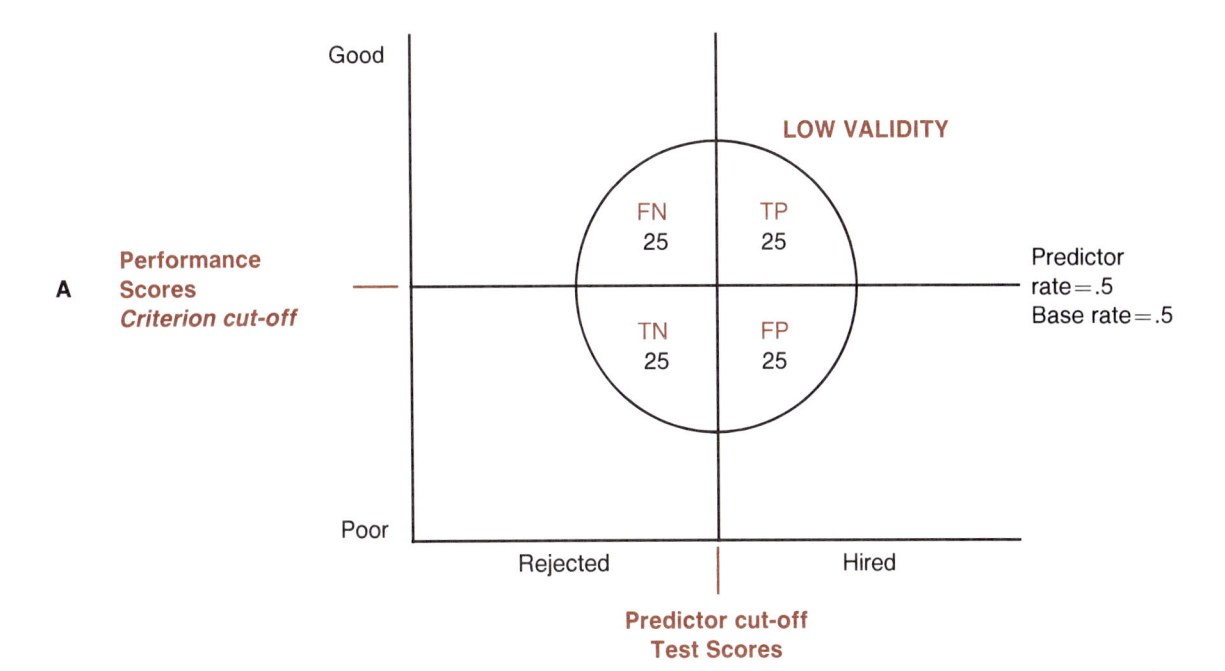

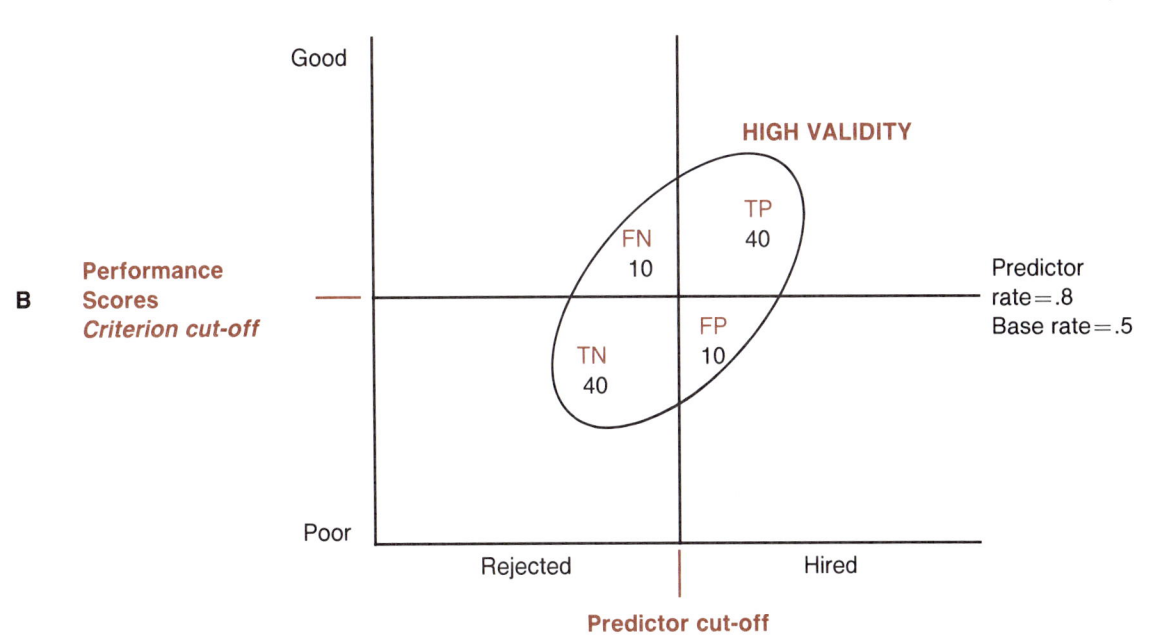

A

Performance Scores
Criterion cut-off

Good / Poor

LOW VALIDITY

	Rejected	Hired
Above criterion	FN 25	TP 25
Below criterion	TN 25	FP 25

Predictor rate = .5
Base rate = .5

Predictor cut-off
Test Scores

B

Performance Scores
Criterion cut-off

Good / Poor

HIGH VALIDITY

	Rejected	Hired
Above criterion	FN 10	TP 40
Below criterion	TN 40	FP 10

Predictor rate = .8
Base rate = .5

Predictor cut-off
Test Scores

Subject sample = 100

Key:
TP = true positive **FP** = false positive **TN** = true negative **FN** = false negative

Utility and Cost: An Overview

The value of the selection decision can be attributed to four critical variables:

1. *Criterion Validity and Reliability:* As job analyses are conducted more carefully, and validity and reliability of the measure of job success is defined to include relevant behaviours that are consistent, the utility of the selection procedure will increase.
2. *Predictor Validity and Reliability:* As the magnitude of validity (regardless of its type) and reliability increases, so does the utility of the selection procedures.
3. *Base Rate:* As the differential between the base rate and predictor rate increases (assuming that the predictor rate is higher than the base rate), the utility of the selection procedures increases.[22]
4. *Selection Ratio:* As the selection ratio becomes smaller, the cost of testing increases and the utility of the selection procedures decreases. The reason is that, although every candidate must be tested, only a few will be selected.

The utility of these four criteria may be changed significantly by the cost involved, particularly the costs of potentially alternative selection procedures. For example, it might be more useful for an organization to use a particular selection test with a validity of .4 rather than another with a validity of .5 if the costs of developing and using the latter are double those of the former. The relative gains must be compared against these relative costs. The test with the higher validity may result in gains several times larger than those from the test with lower validity.

Therefore, organizations should use specific selection and placement procedures that result in the highest gain in relation to costs. Generally, those procedures producing potentially greater gains tend to be both more job-related and more costly. Consequently, it is important to consider both the benefits derived from effective selection decisions versus the costs of the more effective procedures. The costs to consider include both actual and potential costs, as detailed below:

1. *Actual costs* (costs actually incurred in hiring applicants):
   (a) Recruiting and assessment costs—Salaries of staff, advertising expenses, travel expenses, and personnel evaluation test costs.
   (b) Induction and orientation costs—Administrative costs of adding the employee to the payroll, salary of the new employee, and salaries of those responsible for orienting him or her to the new job.
   (c) Training costs—Salaries of training and development staff, salary of the new employee during training, and costs of any special materials, instruments, or facilities for training.
2. *Potential costs* (costs that might be incurred if a wrong selection decision is made):
   (a) Costs associated with hiring a person who subsequently fails—Record keeping; termination costs; costs of undesirable job behaviour,

such as materials or equipment damaged; loss of customers or clients; loss of good will; and costs incurred in replacing a failed employee.

(b) Costs associated with rejecting a person who would have been successful on the job—Competitive disadvantage if he or she is hired by another firm (for example, loss of a top sports celebrity to a competing team), and the cost of recruiting and assessing an additional applicant to replace the rejectee.[23]

In addition to comparing the costs and benefits of alternative selection and placement procedures, organizations should also compare the costs and benefits of techniques other than selection and placement to identify increases in job performance and employee retention. In part, the costs and benefits of alternatives versus those of selection and placement are influenced by other basic criteria.

In evaluating alternatives to selection and placement, it is important to consider the impact that these alternatives will have on PHRM activities. For example, if an organization is considering dropping its selection and placement procedures, the state of its training and development activity should be considered. If an organization is considering changing the design of its jobs, the interests and preferences and the skills, knowledge, and aptitudes of its current employees should be considered (discussed in further detail in Chapters 3 and 13). These considerations, in addition to the cost-benefit determinations, are important in a total utility assessment because they represent a **feasibility assessment**. Some alternatives may be more cost-effective to use than selection and procedures, but they may not be feasible. For example, it may not be feasible to increase the complexity of jobs because top management will not remove the assembly-line technology.

In addition to selection and placement procedures, organizations need to predict the extent to which the hired candidates will stay with the organization. Retaining good people is critical for all organizations. In some instances, organizations are unable to retain good employees because their selection system did not incorporate such issues as over-qualifications for a job. For example, a candidate with a Ph.D. in English literature, who happens to possess good typing skills, is not likely to remain in a low-level secretarial position. If the organization does not provide career opportunities beyond the entry position, such a candidate will seek other employment. Hiring either over-qualified candidates or under-qualified candidates could result in a false negative situation. What PHRM managers should consider is the fit between candidate skills, knowledge, and aptitudes and the job requirements.

Another factor relating to retention has to do with the quality of the orientation and socialization process.

Socialization of New Employees

It is unlikely that recruitment and selection processes will produce new employees who know the values, norms, and behaviour patterns of the organization. Therefore, the organization must socialize new employees. Socialization can be difficult, particularly when organizational values differ from a new employee's values. If the organization is not successful in socializing new employees, they eventually leave the organization.

Socialization has been defined as (1) the process by which people acquire the knowledge, skills, and dispositions that make them more or less able members of their organizations; (2) the processes of situational adjustment and commitment; (3) a continuing interaction between individuals and those who seek to influence them; and (4) the development of new attitudes, values, and competencies leading to a new self-image and the new behaviours that are needed to meet new role demands.[24] Socialization continues throughout the relationship between the organization and the employee. **Socialization**, then, is the process by which employees learn the norms, values, attitudes, and behaviours appropriate for their roles in the organization.

An important aspect of this definition is that socialization is concerned with the roles played rather than with the jobs occupied by employees. Although employees need specific skills to perform their jobs and are trained to perform them, they also need an awareness of the basic goals of the organization, the means to attain those goals, their responsibilities, and the acceptable behaviour patterns for the roles they are expected to play. Employees acquire this information by being socialized, formally and informally, through continuing contacts and experiences with others.

Purposes of Socialization

Ensuring Predictability. Socialization is important because it increases the predictability of employee behaviour—predictability that employees will act in the interests of the organization, be loyal, be productive, and remain with the organization. When an organization asks how it can find people that it can depend on, it usually means people who will help perpetuate the organization, improve it, and always consider the organization first when making decisions.

Many organizations use, intentionally or unintentionally, their recruitment and selection activities to find such people. Organizations usually recruit from familiar sources that have in the past supplied good applicants, or recruit individuals who are already socialized. For example, business organizations tend to recruit and hire students from schools that have specialized business courses rather than those from schools where the emphasis is on the social sciences. But recruitment and selection from an old familiar source may not always be feasible or legal. Recruitment from new sources will provide new employees with unpredictable norms, values, and behaviours, often necessitating extensive socialization efforts.

Substituting for Rules to Guide Behaviour. Socialization tends to be extremely useful as a substitute for rules and regulations or direct supervision when employees are working in remote locations. In this respect, it is useful particularly for sensitive jobs involving company secrets and research activities, and in jobs that are continuously changing, where appropriate rules and regulations cannot be kept up to date.

Increasing Performance and Satisfaction. Socialization conveys others' expectations regarding the new employees. If socialization activities can minimize employees' uncertainty and conflict, the employees are most likely to be satisfied with their roles. It must be noted that increased satisfaction results only if the employees accept socialization; if they do not, they are less likely to be satisfied. In another sense, effective socialization may help employees to learn the desired behaviours, values, norms, and policies of the organization more quickly.

Reducing Anxiety. Effective socialization activities should reduce the anxiety of new employees. At Texas Instruments, it was discovered through interviews that new employees suffered a great deal of anxiety. The interviews revealed that

- their first days on the job were anxious and disturbing ones;
- "new employee initiation" practices by peers intensified anxiety;
- anxiety interfered with the training process;
- turnover of newly hired employees was caused primarily by anxiety;
- new operators were reluctant to discuss problems with their supervisors; and
- supervisors had been unsuccessful in translating motivation theory into practice.[25]

Anxiety was reduced after the initial socialization activity (often referred to as "orientation") was extended to include more information about the new job situation and supervisors. In addition, questionnaire analysis indicated that supervisors felt that they lacked the skills to socialize new employees, and tended to provide very little feedback to new employees about their performance.

As a consequence, Texas Instruments initiated a three-day supervisory training program to establish procedures for bringing new employees on board. In addition, a one-day workshop for supervisors and their new employees was designed to increase communication and resolve any discrepancies. The results of these training programs were a 50% reduction in tardiness and absenteeism, an 80% reduction in waste, a 50% reduction in training time, and a 66% cut in training costs.[26]

Methods of Socialization

Major methods of achieving employee socialization include the following:

- Realistic job previews
- Orientation programs
- Job assignments

Realistic Job Previews. One method of preventing the inaccurate expectations of employees regarding their roles in the organization is the realistic job preview, a process by which job applicants are presented with a balanced view of the positive and negative features of work in a particular organization.

This strategy is critical for retaining qualified applicants. While the traditional approach by many companies was to "sell" the job by presenting an optimistic picture, the realistic job preview presents both positive and negative features of the job. Most studies indicate that not only does a realistic picture not adversely affect the number of candidates willing to accept the job, but also that a significantly longer retention is reported for these candidates.[27]

Orientation Programs. Orientation programs frequently are used to brief new employees on benefit programs and options, to advise them of rules and regulations, and to provide them with a folder or handbook of the policies and practices of the organization.

Orientation programs also usually contain information about employment equity practices, safety regulations, work times, coffee breaks, the structure and history of the organization, and sometimes the products or services of the organization. Typically, however, the orientation program does not inform employees about the real politics or strategy of the organization. The fact that the organization may soon be going out of business, might merge with another company, or even be planning for an extensive layoff, is not information that would be provided in the program.[28] Nevertheless, orientation programs are useful for factual information, and a handbook can be used to tell employees where to get additional information.

Orientation programs are usually co-ordinated by the PHRM department. Some organizations ask line managers or representatives from other departments or sections to be present and to explain their vision of the work. There is, in fact, a trend toward increased involvement of line managers in orientation sessions. A sample from an employee departmental orientation is presented in Exhibit 6.8.

Orientation programs usually are conducted within a week of an employee's initial employment date. Organizations that put off orientation programs run the risk of letting the new employees gain critical information about the company from current employees. This may not be accurate and thus not in the best interests of the organization and the new employees.

Orientation programs are effective if they transmit appropriate and timely information to new employees regarding values, norms, attitudes, and behaviours. Some experts refer to this process as a "psychological contract." The contract contains an implicit set of expectations that the company and employee have of each other.[29] A successful psychological contract may lead to an increase in employee motivation and commitment to the organization.

Orientation programs represent only one portion of the socialization process. Many of those programs last for only a few hours, and organizations

Sample Items to be Included in Departmental Orientation

Exhibit 6.8

Department functions
Goals and current priorities
Organization and structure
Operational activities
Relationships of functions to other departments
Relationships of jobs within the department

Job duties and responsibilities
Detailed explanation of job based on current job description and expected results
Explanation of why the job is important, how the specific job relates to others in the department and company
Discussion of common problems and how to avoid and overcome them
Performance standards and basis of performance evaluation
Number of daily work hours and times
Overtime needs and requirements
Extra duty assignments (e.g., changing duties to cover for an absent worker)
Required records and reports
Check-out on equipment to be used
Explanation of where and how to get tools, have equipment maintained and repaired
Types of assistance available: when and how to ask for help
Relations with federal and provincial inspectors

Policies, procedures, rules, and regulations
Rules unique to the job and/or department
Handling emergencies
Safety precautions and accident prevention
Reporting of hazards and accidents
Security, theft problems and costs
Cleanliness standards and sanitation (e.g., cleanup)
Relations with outside people (e.g., drivers)
Eating, smoking, and chewing gum, etc., in department area
Removal of things from department
Damage control (e.g., smoking restrictions)
Time clock and time sheets
Breaks and rest periods
Lunch time and duration
Making and receiving personal telephone calls
Requisitioning supplies and equipment
Monitoring and evaluating of employee performance
Job bidding and requesting reassignment
Going to cars during work hours

Tour of department
Rest rooms and showers
Fire alarm box and fire extinguisher stations
Time clocks
Lockers
Approved entrances and exits
Water fountains and eye-wash systems
Supervisors' quarters
Supply room and maintenance department
Sanitation and security offices
Smoking areas
Locations of services to employees related to department
First aid kit

Introduction to department employees

Source: W. D. St. John, "The complete employee orientation program," *Personnel Journal*, May 1980, p. 377. Reprinted with the permission of *Personnel Journal*, Costa Mesa, CA. All rights reserved.

rarely conduct a follow-up program. Therefore, other formal methods are also used. In fact, the socialization process in some companies such as IBM, Procter & Gamble (in the U.S.), and VIA Rail (in Canada) envisions interacting with potential candidates prior to long-term engagement. At VIA Rail, a permanent team of trainers are assigned to orient the newcomer to the different operations. This information-orientation session lasts five full weeks.[30]

Job Assignments. The important socializing aspects of job assignments are the characteristics of the initial job, the nature of early experiences on the job, and the first supervisor. The initial job often determines the new employee's future success. The more challenge and responsibility the job offers, the more likely it is that an employee will be successful with the organization.[31] A challenging but not overwhelming job assignment implies that the organization values the employee and believes that he or she can do well. Sometimes organizations give new employees simple jobs or rotate them through departments to give them a feeling for different jobs. However, employees may interpret these practices to mean that the organization does not yet trust their abilities or loyalties.

An employees' experiences in new jobs and with new supervisors help to prepare them for the acquisition of the appropriate values, norms, attitudes, and behaviours. Supervisors of new employees can serve as role models and set expectations. The positive influence that a supervisor's expectations can have on the new employee is referred to as the **Pygmalion effect**. If the supervisor believes that the new employee will do well, the employee is more apt to live up to these expectations.[32]

The key to individual success in the first job assignment is the way the organization (via the direct supervisor) deals with success and failure. Employees will develop positive feelings toward the organization if they are not punished for initial failure; are given clear feedback on their achievements and shortcomings; are provided with an explanation of why they are succeeding or failing; and if they find out that they can count on their supervisors to provide instrumental guidelines in case of failure. It is therefore important to alert line managers to the impact of their initial behaviour on the ultimate success of their new employees.

Who Stays

Selection and placement decisions can be assessed by measuring employees' satisfaction with work, the extent to which they feel their skills and abilities are being used, their needs are being satisfied, and their level of involvement with the job and the organization is sufficient. Since employee skills, satisfaction, and involvement can change, PHRM managers must continually monitor them. Regular, periodic organizational surveys are one method of doing this.

The organization's interests are often closely related to the individual's. If the best person is selected and placed in a job, the organization will gain from having a productive employee who is satisfied, who attends work regularly, and who stays with the organization. Thus, selection and placement decisions can be measured from the organization's viewpoint by employee satisfaction and performance, and by low absenteeism and turnover rates.

Summary

The last two chapters are based on the assumption that an essential goal of selection and placement is to place the right person in the right job in order to serve the short- and long-term interests of both the organization and the individual. This means that organizations should make selection and placement decisions based on information about an individual's motivation and the rewards of the job and organization, as well as on an individual's abilities and the demands of the job. Only by considering both matches can the major purposes of selection and placement be attained.

Selection and placement decisions, therefore, require a great deal of information. There are many ways by which organizations can gather information for selection and placement decisions. It can be done through interviews, application blanks, references, and numerous paper-and-pencil and job sample tests. The methods used to gather selection information should depend on the type of information needed and the validity of the methods. Determining the type of job information to be sought is a function of the difficulty in demonstrating its job-relatedness. This, in turn may be a function of both the type of information sought and the method used.

In the process of gathering information, however, the organization must be aware of several legal considerations. Failure to do so may result not only in lawsuits, but also in decisions to hire less than the best qualified job applicant. Legal considerations are also important when the organization actually combines the information gathered to make the final selection and placement decision. The best way for organizations to ensure that they are making selection decisions with respect to employment-equity considerations, is for their PHRM managers to stay abreast of pertinent legal developments and to implement fair and affirmative human resource policies and practices.

Organizations obtain qualified employees by using valid selection instruments. Within this parameter, organizations can continue to improve their selection and placement decisions by identifying and utilizing more job-related predictors. This should be done within a cost-benefit framework to ensure that if two predictors are equally job-related, the less costly one should be used.

Another way to help enhance the effectiveness of an organization's selection and placement decisions is to engage in effective socialization of employees, since this can help reduce turnover or other negative possible behaviours. Most new employees do not know about the values, norms, attitudes, and behaviours that an organization expects of its members. Socialization attempts to provide the individual with this information. Organizations use many methods in their efforts to socialize new employees, including the initial job assignment, the manner of recruitment and selection, and the formal orientation program.

After selection and socialization, organizations must monitor the performance of new employees. This is critical for the overall success of the organization and for each of the other PHRM activities.

Discussion Questions

1. Why are the best candidates for promotion often overlooked?
2. What approaches are available to managers for gathering information to make selection and placement decisions?
3. What explanations are there for predictor tests that accurately predict performance for some employees while the same tests do not predict performance for other employees?
4. What does the term "criteria" mean? What are some problems associated with measuring a criterion?
5. What does the term "validity" mean, and why is it important in selection and placement decisions?
6. How does the issue of base rate versus predictor rate affect selection and placement decisions?
7. The value of selection and placement varies as a result of what basic criteria?
8. Define several types of validity that organizations can use in assessing selection and placement decisions.
9. What is the difference between compensatory and non-compensatory approaches using multiple predictors in selection and placement decision making?
10. What are the major legal issues in selection and placement of employees?
11. Why is reliability important for validation?
12. How can organizations identify candidates for promotion and transfer?
13. Why is the socialization of employees important to the organization?

CASE STUDY

Free Throws or Foul Shots?

Jack Rush stared across the airport grounds toward Montréal as the airliner lifted off the runway for a non-stop flight to Vancouver. It was January and Jack Rush, assistant athletic director at the University of British Columbia, was returning home from the National University Athletic Association annual meeting, a meeting that had produced, in Jack's opinion, a major change in the conduct of major collegiate athletics for the upcoming years.

For Jack, the annual meeting made history by passing, for the first time, minimum academic standards for freshman eligibility to compete in collegiate athletics at large institutions. In a controversial vote, members of the association had voted by a two-to-one margin to approve the regulation that entering freshmen must have a combined score of at least 700 on the Scholastic Aptitude Test and must acquire a minimum grade-point average of 2.0 in 11 academic high-school courses. Freshmen with an overall 2.0 high-school average but who did not meet either of these minimum requirements might receive a grant-in-aid but would have to forfeit a year of eligibility and would not be permitted to play or practice with the team. The regulation would go into effect on August 1, 1990.

Jack was worried about the impact of this new regulation on athletic recruiting, particularly for basketball, and weighed several alternatives on the long trip home. By the time the plane touched down, he had devised a project for his graduate assistant, Michelle Desroches.

Michelle, a former collegiate basketball star, was in her second year of the MBA program at the university, and was hoping to land a job in sports administration after graduation. She had been assigned a graduate assistantship under Jack and had assisted Jack on a variety of projects during the past year. Michelle enjoyed her position because it enabled her to use some of her business training. For example, she recently had concluded a six-month project that produced a set of job descriptions for each position in the athletic de-

Data for 28 Athletes — Exhibit 6.9

Scholastic Aptitude Test Combined Score	Freshman Grade-point Average	Race	Sex
200	1.25	W	M
300	1.00	NW	M
400	1.37	NW	M
400	1.75	W	M
400	2.75	NW	F
500	1.25	W	F
500	1.75	W	F
500	2.50	NW	F
550	2.13	NW	F
600	1.75	NW	F
600	2.75	NW	M
600	3.00	NW	F
700	2.13	W	M
700	2.25	NW	F
700	2.63	W	M
750	1.87	W	F
750	2.13	NW	M
750	2.75	NW	F
850	2.75	W	M
900	2.25	NW	M
900	2.50	W	F
1000	2.25	W	F
1000	2.37	W	M
1100	3.00	W	M
1200	1.87	NW	M
1200	2.75	W	F
1300	3.25	W	F
1450	1.25	NW	M

M = male; F = female
W = white; NW = Non-white

partment, which, among other things, would be helpful for training new staff members. As she entered Jack's office for their weekly meeting, she wondered if Jack would give her another challenging project.

Michelle was not disappointed. Jack explained the outcome of the annual athletic association meeting and expressed his concern about the impact of the new policy on the recruitment and future success of the major sports programs at their university, particularly basketball. After some discussion, he suggested that perhaps some information on the academic performance of freshman athletes in both the men's and women's basketball programs over the past few years could be gathered and analyzed in relation to the corresponding Scholastic Aptitude Test scores of these freshman recruits. Michelle arranged to meet with Jack one week later, after she had assembled the basic information from the registrar's office.

Before the week was out, though, the local newspaper contacted Jack for his reaction to the new ruling. He declined comment except to say that his staff had taken the matter under consideration. When the news story ran in the Friday afternoon edition, special emphasis was placed on the potential impact of the ruling, given the University of British Columbia's past successful recruitment of athletes from all over the province, particularly those of Asian origin.

By the time Michelle and Jack met again the following week, reaction to the staffing implications of the new ruling had really begun to heat up. The athletic director scheduled a staff meeting for three days later, and Jack hoped that Michelle's background research would be helpful.

Michelle showed him the data she had assembled (see Exhibit 6.9) regarding the freshman athletes recruited by the university in both the men's and women's basketball programs who subsequently completed at least their first year at the school. As Jack studied the information, he wondered if, somehow, it could be prepared for presentation at the athletic staff briefing meeting.

Michelle remembered a validation exercise she had done for her elective course in personnel management. She asked Jack to give her an evening to work up the information contained in the table and to let her make the presentation to the staff during their meeting. Statistics were never Jack's strong suit; moreover, Michelle was bright and capable, and so, somewhat reluctantly, he agreed to Michelle's request.

Endnotes

1. For a discussion of issues of validity of selection instruments, see R. D. Arvey, *Fairness in Selecting Employees* (Reading, MA: Addison-Wesley, 1979).
2. M. L. Blum and J. C. Naylor, *Industrial Psychology* (New York: Harper & Row, 1968), p. 174.
3. L. Smith, "Equal Opportunity Rules Are Getting Tougher," *Fortune*, June 1978, p. 154.
4. Most typically, the several predictors of success would be determined using a multiple regression model that combines and weighs the relative importance of the predictors. For greater detail on multiple regression in selection decisions see W. G. Cascio, *Applied Psychology in Personnel Management*, 2nd ed. (Reston, VA: Reston Publishing Inc., 1982), p. 210.
5. For a discussion of the multiple hurdle approach see L. J. Cronbach and G. C. Gleser, *Psychological Tests in Personnel Decisions*, 2nd ed. (Urbana, IL: University of Illinois Press, 1965). For multiple cut-offs, see L. S. Buck, *Guide to the Setting of Appropriate Cutting Scores for Written Tests: A Summary of the Concerns and Procedures* (Washington, DC: U.S. Office of Personnel Management, 1977). For a discussion of the multiple regression approach see J. Cohen, "Multiple Regression as a General Data Analytic System," *Psychological Bulletin*, 1968, 70, pp. 426–443; A. K. Korman, "Personnel Selection: The Basic Models," in A. K. Korman, *Industrial and Organizational Psychology* (Englewood Cliffs, NJ: Prentice-Hall Inc., 1971).
6. H. J. Sweeney and K. S. Teel, "A New Look at Promotion from Within," *Personnel Journal*, Aug. 1979, p. 532.
7. M. London, "What Every Personnel Director Should Know about Management Promotion Decisions," *Personnel Journal*, Oct. 1978, p. 551.
8. A. J. Walker, "Management Selection Systems that Meet the Challenge of the '80s," *Personnel Journal*, Oct. 1981, pp. 775–780. E. J. McGarrell, Jr., "An Orientation System that Builds Productivity," *Personnel Administrator*, Oct. 1984, pp. 75–85.
9. D. D. McConkey, "Why the Best Managers Don't Get

Promoted," *The Business Quarterly*, Summer 1979, pp. 39–43, published by the School of Business, University of Western Ontario, London, Ontario.
10. Ibid., p. 40. See also W. List, "Women, a Force to be Reckoned with in the Canadian Economy," *The Globe and Mail*, July 15, 1985, p. B7.
11. P. M. Muchinsky, *Psychology Applied to Work* (Homewood, IL: The Dorsey Press, 1983), p. 97.
12. For example, see N. H. Nie, C. H. Hull, J. G. Jenkins, K. Steinbrenner, and D. H. Brent, *Statistical Package for the Social Sciences*, (NY: McGraw-Hill, 1985).
13. For further discussion of the two strategies, see A. Anastasi, *Psychological Testing*, 4th ed. (New York: MacMillian, 1976). S. L. Dolan and D. Roy, "La sélection des cadres," Monograph no. 11, Chapter 5 École de relations industrielles, University of Montréal 1980).
14. Other issues here that influence results of empirical validity studies relate to characteristics of the criterion or the predictor. For an excellent discussion of these see N. Schmitt and B. Schneider, "Current Issues in Personnel Selection," in K. N. Rowand and G. R. Ferris (eds.), *Research in Personnel and Human Resource Management* (Greenwich, CT: JAI Press, 1983).
15. Demonstrating job-relatedness of predictors through evidence of other similar jobs is the essence of validity generalization.
16. Or employers may lack a sufficient number of jobs on which to demonstrate traditional empirical validity. An alternative method is a type of empirical validity referred to as **synthetic validity**. In synthetic validity, a systematic analysis of all jobs is made, from which job dimensions common to several jobs in the total set can be identified. Empirical validity then can be established for separate tests for each of the job dimensions. The validities of the separate tests all relevant to the dimensions in a single job can then be combined to present evidence of quasi-empirical validity. See also J. J. Balma, "The Concept of Synthetic Validity," *Personnel Psychology*, 1959, *12*, pp. 395–396; Cascio, endnote 4, p. 215; M. L. Blum and J. C. Naylor, *Industrial Psychology: Its Theoretical and Social Foundations* (rev. ed.) (New York: Harper & Row, 1968).
17. R. S. Barrett, "Is the Test Content-Valid: Or, Who Killed Cock Robin?" *Employee Relations Law Journal*, vol. 6, no. 4 (1981), pp. 584–600. R. S. Barrett, "Is the Test Content-Valid: Or, Does it Really Measure a Construct," *Employee Relations Law Journal*, vol. 6, no. 3 (1981), pp. 459–475. S. Wollack, "Content Validity: Its Legal and Psychometric Basis," *Public Personnel Management*, Nov.–Dec., 1976, pp. 397–408. E. P. Prien, "The Function of Job Analysis in Content Validation," *Personnel Psychology*, 30, 1977, pp. 167–174. L. S. Kleiman and R. H. Faley, "Assessing Content Validity: Standards Set by the Court," *Personnel Psychology*, 31, 1978, pp. 701–713.

18. Differential validity is actually a sub-set of empirical validity in this case because it implies that empirical validities are determined for two or more groups rather than for one larger group. Differential validity is an important concept because it is in part the essence of test fairness, i.e., the notion that the way a test predicts for one group of individuals will be the way it predicts for another group. If a test has differential validity, it predicts differently for two or more groups. For detailed discussion of differential validity and test fairness, see Cascio, endnote 4, pp. 163–176.
19. This is really only feasible, however, when an employer has a large enough number of jobs and individuals to enable statistical studies to be used.
20. For an extensive review of validity generalization see Cascio, endnote 4; F. L. Schmidt, J. E. Hunter, and J. R. Caplan, "Validity Generalization Results for Two Job Groups in the Petroleum Industry," *Journal of Applied Psychology*, 66, 1981, pp. 261–273.
21. The emphasis on similar jobs and similar conditions is important because, if the same jobs are in two different places (even if in the same organization), the conditions in one place may prevent employees from varying their performance, so predictions for performance would be different for applicants in that group than in another where performance could and does vary.
22. R. D. Arvey, *Fairness in Selecting Employees*, (Reading, MA: Addison-Wesley, 1979), pp. 35–37. Copyright © 1979 by Addison-Wesley. Reprinted with permission. Arvey provides an excellent in-depth discussion of these issues.
23. M. D. Dunnette, *Personnel Selection and Placement* (Monterey, CA: Brooks/Cole, 1966), pp. 174–175. Copyright © 1966 by Wadsworth, Inc. Reprinted by permission of the publisher. Also see Cascio, endnote 4, pp. 220–226, for a discussion of the evaluation of utilities of different selection and placement procedures. W. F. Cascio and V. Silbey, "Utility of the Assessment Center as a Selection Device," *Journal of Applied Psychology*, 1979, 64, pp. 107–118.
24. J. P. Wanous, *Organizational Entry* (Reading, MA: Addison-Wesley, 1980), pp. 167–197. See also D. T. Hall and J. G. Goodale, *Human Resource Management: Strategy, Design and Implementation* (Glensview, IL: Scott, Foresman & Company, 1986), Chapter 10.
25. E. R. Gomersall and M. S. Myers, "Breakthrough in On-the-Job Training," *Harvard Business Review*, July–August, 1966, p. 64.
26. Ibid. See also T. W. Johnson and G. Graen, "Organizational Assimilation and Role Rejection," *Organizational Behavior and Human Performance*, 8 (1973), pp. 72–87; M. Lubliner "Employee Orientation," *Personnel Journal*, April 1978, pp. 207–208.
27. Wanous, endnote 24.

28. D. F. Jones, "Developing a New Employee Orientation Program," *Personnel Journal*, March 1984, pp. 86–87. H. E. Gerson and L. P. Britt "Hiring—The Dangers of Promising Too Much," *Personnel Administrator*, March 1984, pp. 5–7, 112.
29. Hall and Goodale, endnote 24, p. 285.
30. "Chez VIA Rail," *Formation et Emploi*, May–June 1985, pp. 14–16.
31. D. Berlew and D. T. Hall, "The Socialization of Managers: Effects of Expectations on Performances," *Administrative Sciences Quarterly*, Sept. 1966, pp. 207–223.
32. J. S. Livingston, "Pygmalion in Management," *Harvard Business Review*, July–August 1969, pp. 81–89.

SECTION IV
Appraising

CHAPTER 7
Performance Appraisal I: Gathering the Data

CHAPTER 8
Performance Appraisal II: Utilizing the Data

CHAPTER 7

Performance Appraisal I: Gathering the Data

PHRM in the News

Performance Appraisal
Purposes and Importance of Performance Appraisal
Relationships of Performance Appraisal
Legal Considerations in Performance Appraisal
Using Valid Performance Appraisal Instruments

Performance Appraisal as a Set of Processes and Procedures
Criteria and Standards
Performance Appraisal Approaches

Assessing Performance Appraisal Techniques: Which Is Best?
Analysis of Future Performance
The Context of Appraisal Performance
Gathering Performance Appraisal Data

Summary

Discussion Questions

Case Study

Endnotes

PHRM in the News

Seven Assumptions that Block Performance Improvement

Peak productivity levels, reached and maintained by improved human resources (HR) performances, should be the ultimate goal of all HR managers.

Most managers have access to an extensive array of tools, techniques, and processes designed to assist them in areas such as planning, budgeting, decision-making, and quality control. However, few managers have a systematic approach to handling one of the major management responsibilities—maximizing the productivity of human resources.

Our work with dozens of organizations in Canada, the United States, and abroad suggests that managers lack this systematic approach largely because they make a number of assumptions that blind them to significant opportunities for performance improvement.

Consider each of the following seven commonly made assumptions and the degree to which each acts as an obstacle within your organization. At the conclusion, you are invited to test your group's performance management IQ

1. The most significant productivity improvements result from actions directed at the people in the job
2. Training, reorganization, goal-setting, and positive reinforcement are effective productivity improvement interventions
3. People understand what's expected of them on the job
4. The organization reward system supports productive, high-quality performance
5. The annual performance appraisal provides the feedback that employees need to improve or sustain performance
6. There is no need to be concerned with those parts of the organization that are meeting or exceeding their goals
7. The key ingredient in performance improvement is that elusive and intangible variable, motivation

Most managers hold at least some of these seven assumptions. As a result, they tend to either avoid human performance concerns or react to them with "solutions" that do not improve the situation.

When they were provided with a process for diagnosing the performance system by examining not only the people, but also the environmental factors within their control, when they were furnished with a set of tools for implementing improvements that addressed the needs they had identified, then they were able to systematically and effectively confront the performance issues that have such a significant impact on productivity. They were on their way to attaining peak performance.

Testing Your Organization's Performance Management IQ

The seven assumptions cited here inhibit human productivity. However, there is no reason for managers in your organization to allow them to continue to do so. The first step is to test the extent to which your organization makes some of the common mistakes in performance management. Test your organization's performance management IQ by considering the following questions:

- Do managers in your organization address human performance problems as systematically as they address technical problems?
- Do managers diagnose performance problems before implementing a solution?
- Do managers take actions to improve performance in non-problem areas as well as in problem areas?
- Do managers examine factors in the environment as well as the employees when troubleshooting a performance problem?
- Is your performance appraisal system based on performance outputs, i.e., on specific results expected and corresponding measurements?
- Do employees in your organization have output-focused job descriptions and standards of performance that describe the quality and quantity of work expected?
- When employees do a good job, do they receive positive consequences that outweigh any negative consequences?
- Do employees receive specific, timely, understandable, balanced (positive and negative), and constructively delivered feedback on performance?
- Do the workflow, resources, job procedures, and equipment contribute to efficient, effective performance?
- Is training based on identified skill or knowledge needs?
- Are supervisors and managers provided with a set of skills to manage human performance?

Each question that you answered "no" or "I don't know" represents an opportunity to improve human performance in your organization.

Source: Excerpts from N. B. Wright, "Seven Assumptions that Block Performance Improvement," *Business Quarterly,* Summer 1984, pp. 10–12. Used with permission of the author.

MBO and More: The Alcan Experience

In addition to job descriptions and the organalysis process, Alcan's integrated communications system has three other parts: a modified management-by-objectives (MBO) process, zero-based budgeting and, most critical of all, a short- and long-term planning process.

From my discussions with other senior managers who question the value of MBO and our own efforts to develop an effective MBO program, I suspect that there are two calamitous pitfalls in the implementation of MBO.

The first is an over-emphasis on technicalities. In the early stages of developing an MBO program, it is easy to become mesmerized by the complex technicalities of measurement. How do you set objectives so that an individual's performance in achieving them can be fairly measured? How do you differentiate between the providential factors and those over which an individual has some degree of influence? And how do you account for an individual's performance in achieving an objective when his ability to do so is partially dependent on others?

Our experience also has convinced us that it is critical to limit the number of objectives. In *In Search of Excellence,* Thomas J. Peters and Robert H. Waterman, Jr., contend that the number of objectives should be only three or four. Our experience suggests an MBO system, if properly designed, can cope with up to 10.

Also, from the top down, a rigorous effort should be made to assure that there is a satisfactory balance between long- and short-term objectives. At Alcan, we compensate for the ramifications of including longer-term objectives in an individual's annual performance evaluation by limiting their attainment of objectives to 50% of a person's annual rating. The other half depends on how the person has carried out his or her principal accountabilities or performed overall.

Source: R. A. Gentles, "Alcan Integration of Management Techniques Raises Their Effectiveness," *Management Review*, April 1984, p. 31. Reprinted by permission of the publisher, from AMA Forum, © AMA Membership Publications Division, American Management Association, New York. All rights reserved.

These "PHRM in the News" articles illustrate different aspects of performance appraisal as a critical tool in the management of human resources. The first article talks about seven common assumptions made by PHRM managers that inhibit proper use of performance appraisal systems in organizations and eventually block performance improvements. The second article points out some common pitfalls as well as potential advantages of the application of an MBO program in an organization.

Given that performance appraisals are vital to organizations, widely used, and represent an amalgamation of data, two chapters are devoted to this topic. This chapter discusses the various aspects related to the gathering of the appraisal information. It also describes the purpose of performance appraisal and its relationships with other HRM functions. Chapter 8 discusses use of the appraisal information, particularly that obtained from the performance appraisal interview. Moreover, it identifies deficiencies in performance and describes strategies to eliminate them. It also examines the elements in diagnosing and assessing how effectively an organization is conducting performance appraisal.

Performance Appraisal

Although employees may learn about how well they are performing through informal means, such as co-workers telling them what a great job they are doing or their superiors giving them an occasional pat on the back, **performance appraisal** is discussed here as a formal structure.[1] It can be defined as a system of measuring, evaluating, and influencing an employee's job-related attributes, behaviours and outcomes, and level of absenteeism, to discover at what level the employee is presently performing on the job. This leads to a determination of how productive the employee is, and whether he or she can perform as effectively or more effectively in the future so that the employee, the organization, and society all benefit.[2]

The term "performance appraisal system" encompasses all of the following:

- The form(s) or method(s) used to gather the appraisal data
- The job analysis conducted to identify the proper job elements (criteria) against which to establish standards to be used in examining the appraisal data

- An assessment of the validity and the reliability of the methods used
- The characteristics of the rater and ratee that may influence the outcome(s) of the interview process
- The process involved in utilizing the appraisal information for development and evaluation
- An assessment of how well the performance appraisal system is utilized in relation to stated objective

In this chapter, the terms **supervisor** and **manager** are generally discarded, because both the appraiser and the appraisee may be managers or supervisors. Thus, the term **superior** or **rater** is used to denote the person doing the appraising, and the term **subordinate** or **ratee** is used to refer to the employee whose performance is appraised. The terms superior and subordinate are used in this chapter only for clarity; they do not imply that the person doing the appraising (the rater) is "better" than the appraisee (the ratee) or that the subordinate is "inferior" to the superior.

Purposes and Importance of Performance Appraisal

Productivity improvement concerns all organizations, particularly when the rate of productivity increases is relatively small. Although the productivity of most organizations is a function of technological, capital, *and* human resources, many organizations have not sought to increase productivity through improving the performance of their human resources.[3] The relationship of employees to productivity can be measured and evaluated. Such measurable outcomes such as the quality and quantity of performance, and absenteeism are all critical influences on productivity. Employee **job performance** describes how well an employee performs his or her job while **absenteeism** refers to whether the employee is in attendance to perform his or her job. Although both may be important job criteria, they are often discussed separately.

In this chapter, emphasis is placed on job performance since performance appraisal forms are generally developed to measure it. Occasionally absenteeism is included on the form, although job performance is generally measured by an employee's job-related **attributes** (e.g., extent of co-operativeness or initiative), **behaviour** (e.g., feeding the animals), or **outcomes** (e.g., quantity of output). The conditions under which each of these criteria are appropriate are discussed later.

The fact that job performance and absenteeism can have a significant impact on productivity has not been entirely lost on organizations, however. While the dollar value of increased job performance can be substantial, the financial benefit from reduced absenteeism alone is enormous. The cost of absenteeism to the Canadian economy in 1982 was estimated at somewhere between $3 billion and $8 billion.[4] Further, it is estimated that at Bank of Montreal branches across Canada, 54 000 hours per week are lost due to absenteeism, which is translated to a direct cost of $18 million per year in salaries alone.[5]

Performance appraisal also has a strategic importance because an effectively designed performance appraisal form serves as a **contract** between the organization and the employee. This contract acts as a control and evaluation system that enables performance appraisal to better serve a multitude of purposes:

- *Management development*: The performance appraisal provides a framework for future employee development by identifying and preparing individuals for increased responsibilities
- *Performance measurement*: It establishes the relative value of an individual's contribution to the company and helps evaluate individual accomplishments
- *Performance improvement*: It encourages continued successful performance and helps individuals to identify and correct their weaknesses, resulting in greater effectiveness and productivity
- *Compensation*: It helps determine appropriate pay for performance and equitable salary and bonus incentives based on merit or results
- *Identification of potential*: It identifies candidates for promotion
- *Feedback*: It outlines what is expected from employees against actual performance levels
- *Human resource planning*: It audits management talent to evaluate the present supply of human resources for replacement planning
- *Legal compliance*: It helps to establish the validity of employment decisions made on the basis of performance-based information (also helps to defend management actions such as demotions, transfers, or terminations)
- *Communication*: It provides a format for dialogue between superior and subordinate and improves the understanding of personal goals and careers
- *Clarification of supervisory understanding of the job*: It forces superiors to be aware of what their subordinates are doing.

Performance appraisal can also serve as a tool for research.[6] The preceding purposes often are condensed into two general categories: *evaluative* and *developmental*. The evaluative purposes include decisions on pay, promotion, demotion, layoff, and termination. The developmental purposes include research, feedback, management and career development, human resource planning, performance improvement, communications, and improving supervisory job knowledge. These two categories will be used in the discussion of the purposes served by different performance appraisal methods.

Relationships of Performance Appraisal

Performance appraisal has critical relationships with job analysis, selection and placement, compensation, and training.

Job Analysis. The foundation of the performance appraisal is the job analysis. If a formal job analysis has not been conducted to establish the validity of the performance appraisal form, and thus the job-relatedness of an evaluation criteria, the company may be accused of discrimination.

In fact, such a case has been submitted recently to arbitration in the province of Québec. In this case, a group of television producers at Radio-Québec were denied tenure, after having worked for the company for an average of five years. The decision was made by the administration in Radio-Québec, based on a performance appraisal form that had never been validated (i.e., no formal job descriptions were conducted for the job of a producer).[7]

Selection and Placement. Performance appraisal information is vital for making a number of selection and placement decisions. First, it helps increase the likelihood that those applicants selected from a large pool will perform better on the job than those who are not selected. Second, because empirical validation of a selection test requires the calculation of a correlation between test scores and performance scores, performance appraisal results are necessary. Without them, performance scores cannot be established.

Because of their evaluative purpose, it is particularly important that the appraisal form(s) be based on job analysis. This helps produce job-related performance appraisal forms that can increase the likelihood of selecting good performers, and meeting the various human rights requirements. In addition, if promotions in the organization are based strictly on performance (rather than seniority), promotion decisions are more defensible when performance appraisal systems are used.

Compensation. One of the purposes of performance appraisal is to motivate employees. Performance appraisal can be used in this regard by serving as a basis upon which to distribute compensation. A valid appraisal of employee performance is necessary in order for an organization to provide contingent rewards (that is, those based on performance).[8] Performance appraisal information can be used in determination of pay levels as well as pay increments (discussed in Chapters 9 and 10).

Training. Because employee performance is in part determined by employee ability as well as by motivation, training can improve performance. In order to provide the appropriate training, however, it is necessary to be aware of the employee's current level of performance and any aspects of performance that are unsatisfactory. It also is necessary to know if the undesirable performance is caused by a lack of ability or motivation, or by the situation. In order to gain this knowledge, performance appraisal is necessary. Performance appraisal, used in conjunction with job analysis, is therefore necessary for implementing effective pre-employment training programs.

These relationships of performance appraisal to other PHRM activities are shown in Exhibit 7.1. Also shown in this exhibit are the rather extensive legal considerations relevant to appraising employee performance.

Processes and Procedures of Appraising Employee Performance *Exhibit 7.1*

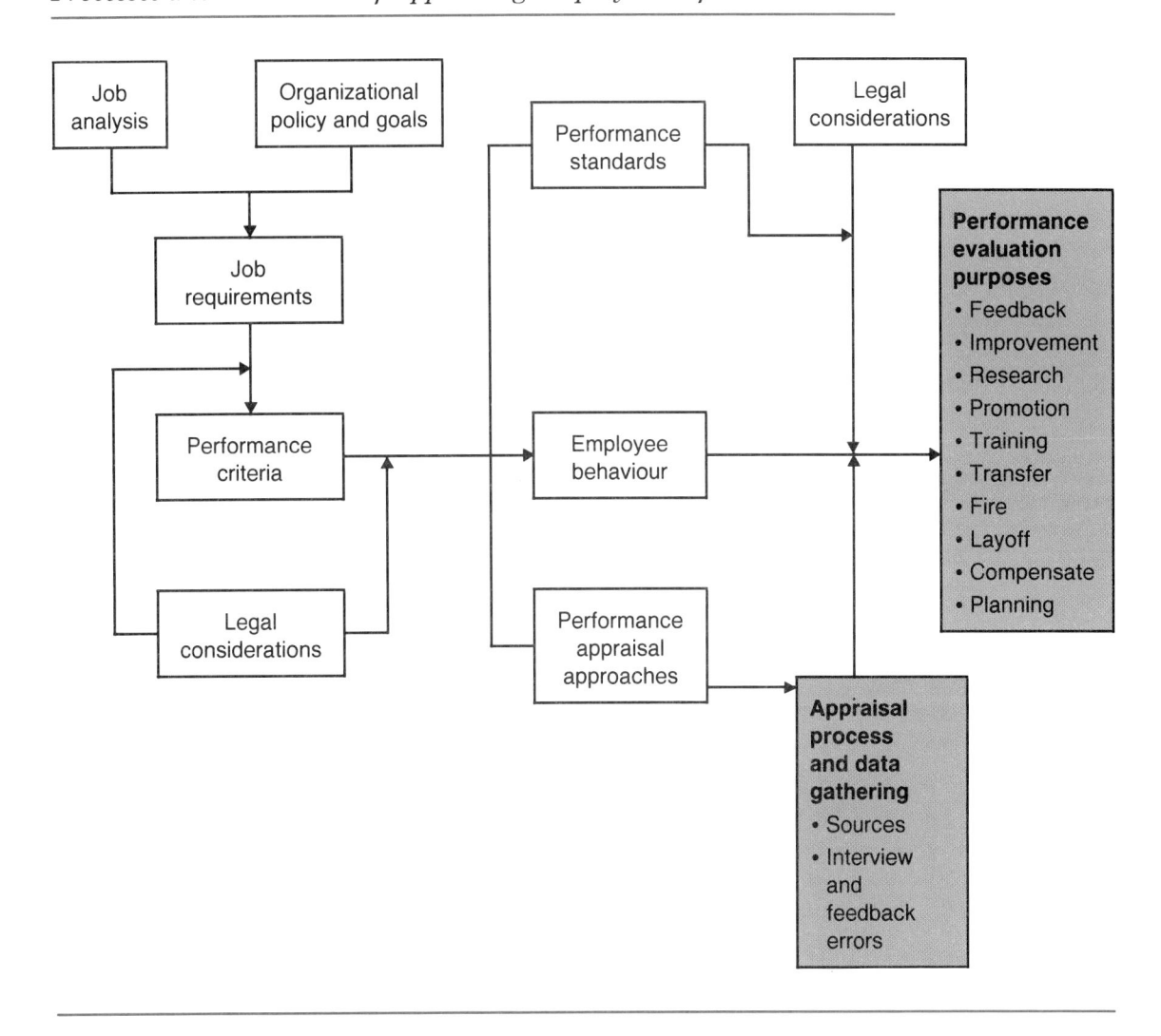

```
┌──────────┐  ┌──────────────┐                      ┌──────────────┐
│   Job    │  │ Organizational│     ┌────────────┐  │    Legal     │
│ analysis │  │ policy and goals│   │ Performance│  │considerations│
└────┬─────┘  └──────┬───────┘     │  standards │  └──────┬───────┘
     │               │              └─────┬──────┘         │
     │               ▼                    │                │
     │        ┌──────────────┐            │         ┌──────────────────┐
     │        │     Job      │            │         │  Performance     │
     │        │ requirements │            │         │  evaluation      │
     │        └──────┬───────┘            │         │  purposes        │
     │               │                    │         │  • Feedback      │
     │               ▼                    │         │  • Improvement   │
     │        ┌──────────────┐    ┌──────────────┐  │  • Research      │
     └───────▶│ Performance  │───▶│  Employee    │─▶│  • Promotion     │
              │  criteria    │    │  behaviour   │  │  • Training      │
              └──────┬───────┘    └──────────────┘  │  • Transfer      │
                     ▲                              │  • Fire          │
                     │                              │  • Layoff        │
              ┌──────┴───────┐     ┌──────────────┐ │  • Compensate    │
              │    Legal     │     │ Performance  │ │  • Planning      │
              │considerations│     │  appraisal   │ └──────────────────┘
              └──────────────┘     │  approaches  │
                                   └──────┬───────┘
                                          │         ┌──────────────────┐
                                          └────────▶│ Appraisal        │
                                                    │ process          │
                                                    │ and data         │
                                                    │ gathering        │
                                                    │ • Sources        │
                                                    │ • Interview      │
                                                    │   and            │
                                                    │   feedback       │
                                                    │   errors         │
                                                    └──────────────────┘
```

Legal Considerations in Performance Appraisal

Many observers of the Canadian labour scene agree that legal requirements have a major effect on the development of performance appraisal systems. The federal Charter of Rights and Freedoms and the various federal and provincial human rights laws require that selection procedures be valid, meaning that all staffing decisions should be based strictly on job-related criteria. Much of the legal context was described in detail in Chapters 4 and 5. Unlike the U.S. experience, the appropriateness of the job criteria via performance appraisal systems has not been directly and legally contested yet. Most of the legal tests (as described in Chapters 4 and 5) apply to staffing practices. However, in a number of court cases and arbitration hearings involving layoffs, dismissals, and even promotions, indirect references to PA have been made.[9] One can conclude from the early cases that, whenever arbitrary management decisions are contested, courts and boards of inquiry tend to rule in favour of the employee.

Establishing Valid Performance Criteria: Cases. In the case of Sorel v. Tomerson Saunders Ltd. (1985), Justice Gibbs of the British Columbia Supreme Court ruled that the company could not dismiss an employee with so much seniority (37 years of uninterrupted service) "... without warning, without notice, and without cause." Sorel was awarded $254 556 in compensation for lost benefits. In the case of B. L. Means et al. v. Ontario Hydro (1984), seven black employees alleged discrimination in layoffs by Ontario Hydro. The layoffs were made on the basis of an informal ranking system. Management used vague criteria for assessing the rank of workers and failed to keep written records of the ranking to support the layoffs. The Board of Inquiry ruled in favour of four of the complainants, and concluded that because Ontario Hydro failed to use "objective" criteria, the possibility of racial discrimination existed.

Another example of an employer's failure to justify its actions was a case involving a fire security company that hired a man of East Indian ancestry to be its assistant controller Almeida v. Chubb Fire Security Division (1984). The assistant controller worked for the company for six years. During this time, four new Caucasian controllers were hired despite the company's usual policy of promoting from within. Shortly after the fourth appointment, the company dismissed the assistant controller, who then filed a complaint with the Ontario Human Rights Commission. The dismissed assistant controller alleged that both the failure to promote him and his dismissal were "motivated by a discriminatory bias."

The assistant controller presented evidence that, during his early months with the company, his performance was highly regarded by management. About seven months after the assistant controller was hired, the controller left the company. The assistant controller "assumed and discharged many of the controller's responsibilities during the interim period before the appointment of a new controller." His salary was raised in appreciation of his efforts but he was not promoted to the position of controller. During the term of the new controller, the assistant controller raised his qualifications by obtaining the degree of Registered Industrial Accountant. Over the space of several years, four controllers were hired in succession, and during each interim period, the assistant controller "ably discharged" the duties normally handled by the controller. When the assistant controller did not receive the appointment for the fourth time his work deteriorated and he "no longer fully co-operated with the incumbent of the controller's position." Approximately eight months later, the assistant controller was dismissed for his *inadequate work performance.*

At the hearing, the Board of Inquiry referred with approval to an American decision that stated that a person complaining of racial discrimination must first establish that

- he belongs to a racial minority;
- he applied and was qualified for a job opening;
- he was rejected; and
- after his rejection, the position remained open and the employer continued to seek applicants with the complainant's qualifications.

According to the Board, once the person lodging the complaint has established these facts then the employer, in its defence, must offer reasonable explanation for its actions.

In this case, the employer was able to justify itself for not promoting the assistant controller the first time because the assistant controller did not then have his degree as a Registered Industrial Accountant. The employer was also able to justify not promoting the assistant controller when the vacancy occurred for the fourth time. The evidence disclosed that the assistant controller's resentment at being passed over on previous occasions had influenced his attitude and his work had deteriorated. The employer also was able to justify the dismissal of the controller on this ground.

However, the Board did not accept the employer's reasons for not promoting the assistant controller on the other occasions when the controller's post became vacant. The employer claimed that the assistant controller lacked "people skills," and was unable to get along with management. However, the employer did not present evidence to support these claims. Moreover, there was evidence that the company never seriously considered the assistant controller for promotion. For example, the assistant controller's superiors had not been questioned about his work performance.

The Board of Inquiry found the company guilty of discrimination and ordered it to pay damages to the assistant controller. The amount of the damages was based on what the assistant controller's salary would have been if he had been promoted the second time that the controller's position became vacant up to the time that the final appointment of a controller was made.[10]

When criteria of performance are clear, organizations can make hiring, firing, or promotional decisions, for example, without violating the laws. A Board of Inquiry in Ontario dismissed a racial discrimination complaint directed against the Metropolitan Toronto Police Board of Commissioners. A police constable of East Indian racial origin and a "Sikh by religion" complained that he had been refused reclassification and was ultimately dismissed for race-related reasons. At the hearing, the constable's superiors claimed that the reasons for the refusal to reclassify and the dismissal were based on the facts that the constable was unable to get along with his fellow officers and had broken police rules. The evidence indicated that the reasons for the constable's inability to get along with his fellow officers were not based on their disliking him on racial grounds.

Fellow officers testified that they objected to working with the dismissed constable because he was overbearing, he drove dangerously, he had a "hostile" manner of dealing with the public, he demonstrated cruelty toward animals, and "would not take direction and advice easily from more experienced officers." Moreover, evidence was presented that on one occasion he wore improper attire in court and on another occasion failed to remain in court, in contravention of the rules. The "culmination incident" was the officer's failure to report an accident in which he was involved, and his attempts to deny being involved when confronted. The Board of Inquiry, in dismissing the constable's complaint, said that the constable's "problem was not racial. If he had shown reliability and competence in his performance as an officer, he would have been accepted by his fellow officers and would not have had problems in getting along with them. His problem was a personal one rather than a racial one." [11]

Considering all of the above cases, it appears that the most efficient way to determine whether the appraisal criteria are job-related is to begin with a careful job analysis. As described in Chapter 3, this can help to ensure that the criteria accurately portray job performance (i.e., are not deficient and are not contaminated; see Chapter 6).

Once the appropriate job criteria are established, standards marking the level of employee performance that is either desirable or acceptable can be set. In order to ensure that the essence of performance on a job is captured, several criteria may be required. These criteria can be established in various ways. For example, methods analysis (described in Chapter 3) can establish the number of units of output considered acceptable in job performance. For jobs where units of output may not be relevant, standards may be derived through managerial dictate or definition, historical records, comparison with other jobs, comparison with similar jobs in other companies, and by profitability (relevant for managers of profit centres).

Using Valid Performance Appraisal Instruments

Once the criteria are established, forms (instruments) must be used to gather information about the criteria (critical job components). For example, if **quantity of output** is a critical job criterion, having a supervisor comment only on how personable the employee is may lead to an inappropriate appraisal. If this appraisal is used for an employment decision, a prima facie case of adverse impact or discrimination may result. Appraisal forms on which the rater indicates by a checkmark his or her evaluation of an employee on things such as leadership, attitude toward people, and loyalty (attributes) are often referred to as **subjective forms**. They are in contrast to appraisals in which the evaluation is done against specifically defined behaviour, level of output, level of specific goal attainment, or number of days absent (behaviour and outcomes). These appraisals are often called **objective forms**. These different forms will be discussed in more detail in Chapter 8.

Communicating Performance Criteria and Standards. Once performance criteria and standards have been identified, employees should be told what these are. Can you imagine being in a class and not knowing how your grade will be determined? Many employees, unfortunately, indicate that they *do not know* on what basis they are being evaluated. A summary of the broad legal guidelines for appraisal systems (emerging from the cases reported earlier, as well as from the various chartes of human rights) is shown in Exhibit 7.2.

Performance Appraisal as a Set of Processes and Procedures

Exhibit 7.2 shows many processes and procedures that are essential for both achieving the purpose of evaluation and serving the many legal considerations. It is important to discuss these processes and procedures, starting with the establishment of criteria and standards.

Prescriptions for Legally Defensible Appraisal Systems — *Exhibit 7.2*

- Procedures for personnel decisions must not differ as a function of the race, gender, colour, national origin, marital status, creed, or age of those affected by such decisions.
- Objective-type, non-rated, and uncontaminated data should be used whenever it is available.
- A formal system of review or appeal should be available for appraisal disagreements.
- More than one independent evaluator of performance should be used.
- A formal, standardized system for the personnel decision should be used.
- Evaluators should have ample opportunity to observe ratee performance (if ratings must be made).
- Ratings on traits such as dependability, drive, aptitude, or attitude should be avoided.
- Performance appraisal data should be empirically validated.
- Specific performance standards should be communicated to employees.
- Raters should be provided with written instructions on how to complete the performance evaluation forms.
- Employees should be evaluated on specific work dimensions rather than a single overall or global measure.
- Behavioural documentation should be required for extreme ratings (e.g., critical incidents).
- Rater should be trained in conducting the performance appraisal.
- The content of the appraisal form should be based on a job analysis.
- Employees should be provided with an opportunity to review their appraisals.
- Personnel decision makers should be trained on laws regarding discrimination.

Source: Modified from H. J. Bernardin and W. F. Cascio, "Performance Appraisal and the Law," in R. S. Schuler, S. A. Youngblood, and V. L. Huber (eds.), *Readings in Personnel and Human Resource Management*, 3rd ed. (St. Paul: West Publishing Co., 1987).

Criteria and Standards

To serve the organization's purposes and meet legal requirements, a performance appraisal system must accurately appraise employee performance. If the appraisal system is to uncover employees' potential for greater responsibilities and promotions, it must also provide accurate data about such potential. In addition, the system must yield consistent data (be reliable) about what it is supposed to measure (be valid).

A reliable performance appraisal system produces the same appraisal of a subordinate regardless of *who* is doing the appraising at any given point in time. Over time, a reliable performance appraisal system should produce the same results from the same rater if the actual performance of the subordinate has not changed. A performance appraisal system may be unreliable due to numerous errors in rating as described in a later section in this chapter on superior-subordinate relationships.

A valid performance appraisal system must specify **performance criteria** that are job-related and important, and can be determined easily through job analysis. Employees' contributions to the organization can be evaluated based on the degree to which they perform those activities and attain those results specified in the job analysis. For example, if selling 100 units per month is the only important result of an employee's job, then the appraisal system should measure only the number of units sold. In this case, there is only one performance criterion.

Generally, job analysis identifies several performance criteria that reflect employees' contributions. For example, selling 100 units per month may be accompanied by such criteria as "effects of remarks to customers," "consistency in attendance," and even "effects on co-workers." If all of these performance criteria are determined to be important by the job analysis, they all should be measured by the performance appraisal.

If the form used to appraise employee performance does not address the job behaviour, and results identified in the job analysis, the form is said to be **deficient**. If the form includes appraisal of anything either unimportant or irrelevant to the job, it is **contaminated**. Many performance appraisal forms actually used in organizations measure some attributes and behaviour of employees unrelated to the employee's job. These forms are contaminated and in many cases also deficient.[12]

Standards must be identified to evaluate how well employees are performing. By using standards, performance criteria take on a range of values. For example, selling 100 units per month may be defined as excellent performance, and selling 80 units may be defined as average. Organizations often use historical records of employees' performance records to determine what is possible and to establish what constitutes average or excellent performance. Standards also can be established by the time and motion studies and work sampling described in Chapter 3. These methods often are used for blue-collar non-managerial jobs, but many organizations employ other methods to evaluate how well their managers perform. One of these methods is **management by objectives**, to be discussed later in this chapter. Increasingly, managers also are being evaluated against standards of profitability, revenues, and costs.

Performance Appraisal Approaches

There are four major approaches to performance appraisal: **comparative standards, absolute standards** (quantitative and qualitative), **management by objectives** or goals, and **direct or objective indexes**.

Comparative Standards. There are several *comparative methods* of evaluation, all comparing one subordinate to the others. The first is the **straight ranking**, in which a superior lists the subordinates in order from best to worst, usually on the basis of overall performance. The second method is the **alternative ranking**, which takes place in several steps. The first step is to put the best subordinate at the head of the list and the worst subordinate at the bottom. The superior then selects the best and worst from the remaining subordinates. The middle position on the list is the last to be filled by this method. Ranking approaches could be used quite efficiently not only by a single supervisor but also by the subordinates themselves. They could be particularly useful in generating performance data for a group of individuals who perform similar tasks as a team. Exhibit 7.3 shows a type of form used by many university professors to allow students to assess each other's contributions to a team project.[13]

The **paired comparison method** is more time-consuming but may provide better information. Each subordinate is compared to every other subordinate, two at a time, on a single standard or criterion or, alternatively, on the overall performance. The subordinate with the second-greatest number of favourable comparisons is ranked second, and so on.

All of the comparative methods discussed so far give each person a unique rank. This suggests that no two subordinates' performances are too close to differentiate—a point that some have disputed. The **forced distribution method** was designed to overcome this complaint and to incorporate several factors or dimensions (rather than a single factor) into the ranking process. The term "forced distribution" is used because the superior must assign only a certain proportion of subordinates to each of several categories in respect to each factor.

A common forced distribution scale may be divided into five categories. A fixed percentage of all subordinates in the group must fall within each of these categories. One problem with this method is, of course, that the performance of a group may be too similar to divide among the fixed percentages. In fact, all four comparative methods assume that there are good and bad performers in all groups. You may know from experience, however, of situations where all of the people in a group actually perform identically. Forced distribution methods are ineffective in these situations. Many universities' letter-grading systems are based on forced distribution. Exhibit 7.4 shows a typical example of the forced distribution method.

Exhibit 7.3 Peer Evaluation Form

Purpose:
This form provides you with an opportunity to assess the performance of your group members. Remember that these evaluations are a factor in your participation grade. Please feel free to comment in detail on the back of this form.

Procedure:
Write each group member's name, including your own, in the spaces provided. Rank each individual in each category. Use a ranking of 1 to 6, where 1=the best, 2=second best, and 6=the worst.

Name of Group Member	Group Responsibility A. Does his/her share of the work B. Is prepared for meetings		Group Interaction C. Contributes to discussions D. Is receptive to constructive criticism		Overall Evaluation E.
	A.	B.	C.	D.	E.
1.					
2.					
3.					
4.					
5.					
6.					

PLEASE MAKE ADDITIONAL COMMENTS ON THE BACK OF THIS FORM.

SIGNATURE: _____

Problems Identified with Comparative Approaches. Regardless of the specific comparative approach, all are based on the assumption that performance is best captured or measured by one criterion: overall performance. Since this single criterion is a global measure and is not anchored in any objective index, such as units sold, the result can be influenced by rater subjectivity. The rankings may lack behavioural specificity and may be subject to legal challenge. Further, in the rank order method for example, it is not specified how good the "best" is or how bad the "worst" is; the *level* of performance is unclear. This may result in arbitrary ranking. In addition, a major limitation of the paired comparison method is that the

Forced Distribution Method of Performance Appraisal Using Five Performance Categories with a Sample of 100 Students

Exhibit 7.4

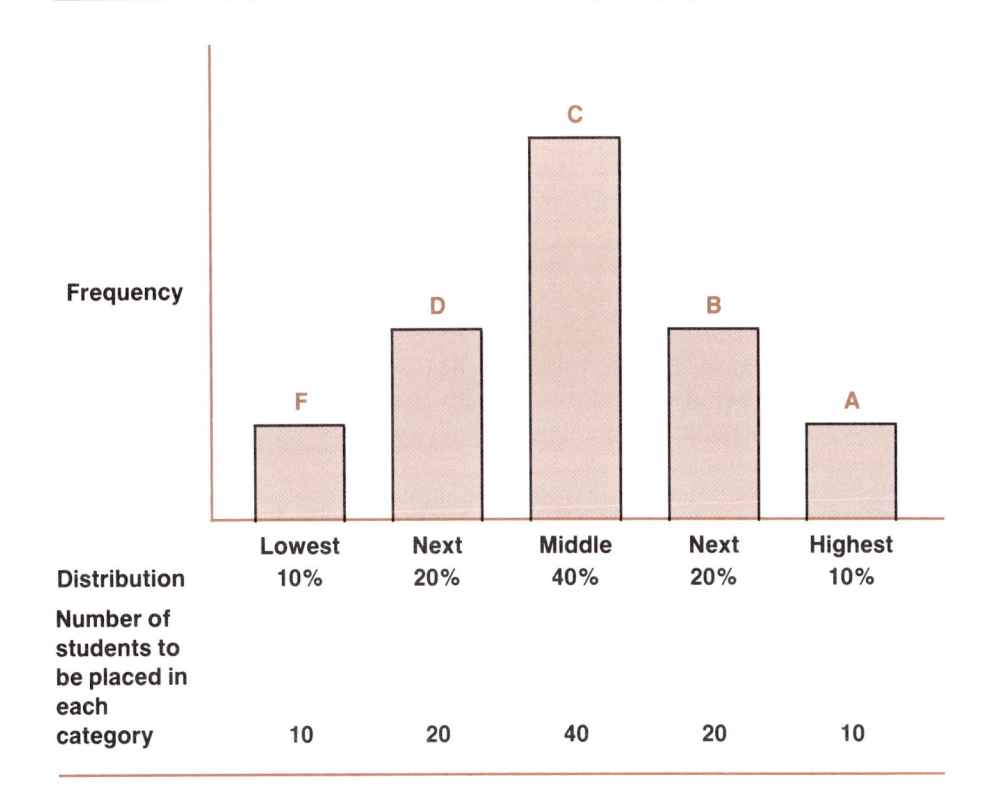

Distribution	Lowest 10%	Next 20%	Middle 40%	Next 20%	Highest 10%
Number of students to be placed in each category	10	20	40	20	10

number of comparisons becomes too great to perform with large numbers of employees.

Concerning the forced distribution, in Exhibit 7.4 the normal distribution was assumed (and forced). Therefore, it is impossible for all students (employees) to be rated "excellent." Proponents of this method, however, claim that it encourages healthy competition among employees who know that their level of performance ultimately will be judged against that of their peers. Opponents of this approach claim that forced distribution may lead to individualism and non-cooperation. Moreover, some raters claim that the procedure creates artificial distributions among employees.[14]

Absolute Standards. In the comparative approach to performance evaluation, the superior is forced to evaluate each subordinate in relationship to the other subordinates, often based on a single overall dimension. In contrast, the absolute standard approach allows superiors to evaluate each subordinate's performance independently and often on several dimensions of performance.

One of the simplest absolute standards forms is the **narrative essay**. Using this form, the rater can describe the ratee's strengths and weaknesses and suggest methods for improving the employee's performance. Since these essays are unstructured, they often vary in length and detail. Consequently, comparisons of ratees within a department or across departments are difficult. Furthermore, the essay form provides only qualitative data. However, qualitative appraisals are enriched by the inclusion of critical incidents, behavioural checklists, and forced-choice forms. Finally because some supervisors have better written communication skills than others, variation in quality may result.[15] This method should not be used with supervisors who do not have these skills, or do not have the time required to write an essay (often the case with first-line supervisors).

Using the **critical incidents** technique, the superior observes and records things that subordinates do that are particularly effective or ineffective in accomplishing their jobs.[16] These incidents generally provide descriptions of the ratee's behaviour and the situations in which that behaviour occurred. For example, a negative critical incident for a life insurance salesperson might be "lied to the client when insurance was sold." A positive one might be "responded to a client complaint in a prompt and cordial manner."

When the superior then provides feedback to the subordinate, it is based on specific behaviour rather than personal characteristics or traits such as dependability, forcefulness, or loyalty. This feature of the critical incident technique can increase the chances that the subordinate will improve, since he or she learns more specifically what is expected.

Proponents of the critical incident technique focus on its simplicity and behavioural focus. Another advantage is that it also eliminates the "recency effect," hence performance incidents are recorded throughout the year. Thus, the supervisor may not be subject to "recent behaviour" biases. In addition, many claim that it would be more logical to spend a fraction of the time to record the critical incidents than to "use more sophisticated and time-consuming methods (which suffer from many errors and biases) just to arrive at the conclusion that most of your employees performed at average capacity."[17] Critical incidents can point out the "best" and "worst" performers, absence of information (incidents) can be attributed to a mediocre performance.[18]

Drawbacks of the critical incident technique include the superior's necessity to keep records (little black books) on each subordinate, its non-quantitative nature, the fact that the incidents are not differentiated in terms of their importance to job performance, and the difficulties in comparing subordinates when the incidents recorded for each one are quite different. To overcome some of these drawbacks, (1) supervisors need to be trained in using the method, and (2) predetermined, job-related critical incidents could be established as part of the criteria.

The **weighted checklist** can be developed by using the critical incident technique. After a number of critical incidents are gathered from several superiors or expert raters knowledgeable of the job, the incidents can be used to construct checklists of weighted incidents. The rater merely has to check the incidents that each subordinate performs. The form may be designed to include frequency response categories (e.g., "always," "very often," and "infrequently"). With this form the rater checks the frequency category for each incident for each subordinate. This method saves the rater time and can yield a summary score. Nevertheless, the rater does not know the relative importance of each incident, thus making it difficult for him or her to give feedback.

To reduce the potential for leniency rating error (rating everybody high, as will be discussed below) and to establish a form that allowed for a more objective comparison of ratees, the **forced-choice form** was developed. The forced-choice method differs from the weighted checklist because it forces superiors to evaluate each subordinate by choosing which of two items in a pair better describes the subordinate. The two items in a pair are matched to be equal in *desirability* but of differential relevance to job performance or discriminability. The degrees of desirability and discriminability are established by individuals familiar with the jobs. A sample form is shown in Exhibit 7.5. Through use of this format, leniency error is minimized and validity and reliability may be enhanced. Although the forced-choice scale can be very useful, the raters are essentially unaware of how their ratings of their subordinates are interpreted. This not only makes feedback difficult, but also it reduces the trust that the rater has in the organization. These scales also are expensive to develop, and the cost-benefit analysis of its use is not readily apparent.

In addition to these qualitative techniques are several quantitative techniques. Quantitative techniques differ from the qualitative techniques by generally requiring the rater to assign a specific numerical value to a personal attribute (trait) or behaviour shown by the ratee, rather than simply to indicate whether or not a ratee has exhibited the attribute or behaviour. There are three quantitative techniques: the conventional or graphic rating scale, the behaviourally anchored rating scale, and the behavioural observation scale.

The **conventional rating** is the most widely used form of performance evaluation (see Exhibit 7.6).[19] Conventional forms vary in the number of dimensions of performance that they measure. The term *performance* is used advisedly here because many conventional forms use personality characteristics or traits rather than actual behaviours as indicators of per-

---

Forced Choice Pairs with Equal Desirability and Differential Discriminability for the Animal Keeper   Exhibit 7.5

Prepares Proper Diets	Likes The Animals	Cleans Cages Thoroughly	Makes Friends with Others Quickly
Desirability Index		**Desirability Index**	
4.20	4.37	4.83	4.68
Discrimination Index		**Discrimination Index**	
4.56	1.25	4.10	1.72

formance. Frequently used traits are *aggressiveness, independence, maturity,* and *sense of responsibility*. Many conventional forms also use indicators of output such as quantity and quality of performance. Conventional forms vary in the number of traits and indicators of output that they incorporate. They also vary in the range of choices (one of which is to be checkmarked) for each dimension and the extent to which each dimension is described.

Exhibit 7.6   Conventional Form for Employee Performance Appraisal

DATE COMPLETED

NAME	DATE OF BIRTH	DATE OF EMPLOYMENT	OFFICE LOCATION BRANCH DEPARTMENTAL	DEPARTMENT
PRESENT JOB TITLE	**CONVERSION CODE**	**YEARS IN PRESENT POSITION**	**SIN**	**EDUCATION**

Quality of Work General excellence of output with consideration to accuracy—thoroughness—dependability—without close supervision.	☐ Exceptionally high quality. Consistently accurate, precise, quick to detect errors in own and others' work.	☐ Work sometimes superior but usually accurate. Negligible amount needs to be redone. Work regularly meets standards.	☐ A careful worker. A small amount of work needs to be redone. Corrections made in reasonable time. Usually meets normal standards.	☐ Work frequently below acceptable quality. Inclined to be careless. Moderate amount of work needs to be redone. Excessive time to correct.	☐ Work often almost worthless. Seldom meets normal standards. Excessive amount needs to be redone.
Quantity of Work Consider the amount of useful work over the period of time since the last appraisal. Compare the output of work to the standard you have set for the job.	☐ Output consistently exceeds standard. Unusually fast worker. Exceptional amount of output.	☐ Maintains a high rate of production. Frequently exceeds standard. More than normal effort.	☐ Output is regular. Meets standard consistently. Works at steady average speed.	☐ Frequently turns out less than normal amount of work. A low producer.	☐ A consistent low producer. Excessively slow worker. Unacceptable output.
Co-operation Consider the employee's attitude toward the work, the employee's fellow workers, and supervisors. Does the employee appreciate the need to understand and help solve problems of others?	☐ Always congenial and co-operative. Enthusiastic and cheerfully helpful in emergencies. Well-liked by associates.	☐ Co-operates well. Understands and complies with all rules. Usually demonstrates a good attitude. Liked by associates.	☐ Usually courteous and co-operative. Follows orders but at times needs reminding. Gets along well with associates.	☐ Does only what is specifically requested. Sometimes complains about following instructions. Reluctant to help others.	☐ Unfriendly and unco-operative. Refuses to help others.
Knowledge of the Job The degree to which the employee has learned and understands the various procedures of the job and their objectives.	☐ Exceptional understanding of all phases. Demonstrates unusual desire to acquire information.	☐ Thorough knowledge in most phases. Has interest in and potential toward personal growth.	☐ Adequate knowledge for normal performance. Will not voluntarily seek development.	☐ Insufficient knowledge of job. Resists criticism and instruction.	☐ No comprehension of the requirements of job.

Continued on next page

Continued   *Exhibit 7.6*

Dependability — The reliability of the employee in performing assigned tasks accurately and within the allotted time.	☐ Exceptional. Can be left on own and will establish priorities to meet deadlines.	☐ Very reliable. Minimal supervision required to complete assignments.	☐ Dependable in most assignments. Normal supervision required. A profitable worker.	☐ Needs frequent follow-up. Excessive prodding necessary.	☐ Chronic procrastinator. Control required is out of proportion.
Attendance and Punctuality — Consider the employee's record, reliability and ability to conduct the job within the unit's work rules.	☐ Unusual compliance and understanding of work discipline. Routine usually exceeds normal.	☐ Excellent. Complete conformity with rules but cheerfully volunteers time during peak loads.	☐ Normally dependable. Rarely needs reminding of accepted rules.	☐ Needs close supervision in this area. Inclined to backslide without strict discipline.	☐ Unreliable. Resists normal rules. Frequently wants special privileges.
Knowledge of Company Policy and Objectives— Acceptance, understanding, and promotion of company policies and objectives in the area of the employee's job responsibilities.	☐ Thorough appreciation and implementation of all policies. Extraordinary ability to project objectively.	☐ Reflects knowledge of almost all policies related to this position.	☐ Acceptable but fairly superficial understanding of job objectives.	☐ Limited insight into job or company goals. Mentally restricted.	☐ Not enough information or understanding to permit minimum efficiency.
Initiative and Judgement — The ability and interest to suggest and develop new ideas and methods; the degree to which these suggestions and normal decisions and actions are sound.	☐ Ingenious self-starter. Superior ability to think intelligently.	☐ Very resourceful. Clear thinker—usually makes thoughtful decisions.	☐ Fairly progressive, with normal sense. Often needs to be motivated.	☐ Rarely makes suggestions. Decisions need to be checked before implementation.	☐ Needs detailed instructions and close supervision. Tendency to assume and misinterpret.
Supervisory or Technical Potential — Consider the employee's ability to teach and increase skills of others, to motivate and lead, to organize and assign work and to communicate ideas and instructions.	☐ An accomplished leader who earns their respect and can inspire others to perform. An articulate and artful communicator, planner and organizer.	☐ Has the ability to teach and will lead by example rather than technique. Speaks and writes well and can organize and plan with help.	☐ Fairly well-informed on job-related subjects but has some difficulty communicating with others. Nothing distinctive about spoken or written word.	☐ Little ability to interpret or implement. Seems uninterested in teaching or helping others. Careless speech and writing habits.	☐ Unable to be objective or reason logically. Inarticulate and stilted in expression.

Conventional forms are used extensively because they are relatively easy to develop, permit quantitative results that allow comparisons across ratees and departments, and include several dimensions or criteria of performance. But because the rater has complete control in the use of the forms, they are subject to several types of error including leniency, strictness, central tendency, and halo (to be discussed later in this chapter). Often, separate traits or factors are grouped together and the rater is given only one box to checkmark. Another drawback is that the descriptive words often used in such scales may have different meaning to different raters. Terms such as "motivation," "co-operation," and "social skills" are subject to many interpretations, particularly when used in conjunction with words such as "outstanding," "average," or "very poor."

In addition to their potential for error, conventional forms are criticized because they cannot be used for developmental as well as evaluative purposes. They fail to tell a subordinate how to improve and they are not useful for the subordinate's career development needs. Consequently, when actually used, organizations often modify the conventional form and add space for short essays so that the appraisal results can be used for developmental as well as evaluative purposes.

However, even when essays are added, the results are still subject to the errors of the conventional forms and the essay forms described earlier. Thus, even the modified form is not the most appropriate for giving feedback and improving subordinates' performance.

The **behaviourally anchored rating scale (BARS)** was developed to provide results that subordinates could use to improve performance. They were also designed so that superiors would be more comfortable giving feedback in behavioural terms. The first step in the development of a BARS is to collect incidents that describe competent, average, and incompetent behaviour for each job category, like the critical incidents method of job analysis. These incidents are then categorized into broad overall categories or dimensions of performance (e.g., administrative ability and interpersonal skills). Each dimension serves as one criterion in evaluating subordinates. Another group of individuals lists the critical incidents pertinent to each category. Exhibit 7.7 illustrates an example of one such criterion, *organizational skills*, and the critical incidents listed as pertinent to it.[20] Also shown in this exhibit is the next step, the assignment of a numerical value (weight) to each incident in relation to its contribution to the criterion.

Armed with a set of criteria with behaviourally anchored and weighted choices, the superiors rate their subordinates with a form that is relatively unambiguous in meaning, is understandable, justifiable, and relatively easy to use.[21] Yet it also has its shortcomings. Since most BARS forms use a limited number of performance criteria many of the critical incidents generated in the job analysis stage may not be used. Thus, the raters may not find appropriate categories to describe the behaviour of their subordinates. Similarly, even if the relevant incidents are observed, they may not be worded in exactly the same way on the dimension. Thus, the rater may not be able to match the observed behaviour with the dimension and anchors. A procedure that overcomes these and other limitations of the BARS but retains its advantages is called the **behavioural observation scale (BOS)**.[22]

The BOS and the BARS are essentially the same except in the development of the scales or dimensions, the scale format, and scoring procedures. They are even similar in this area to the extent that expert raters or judges rate the incidents from the job analysis in terms of the degree to which

A Behaviourally Anchored Rating Scale for Instructors or Industrial Trainers

Exhibit 7.7

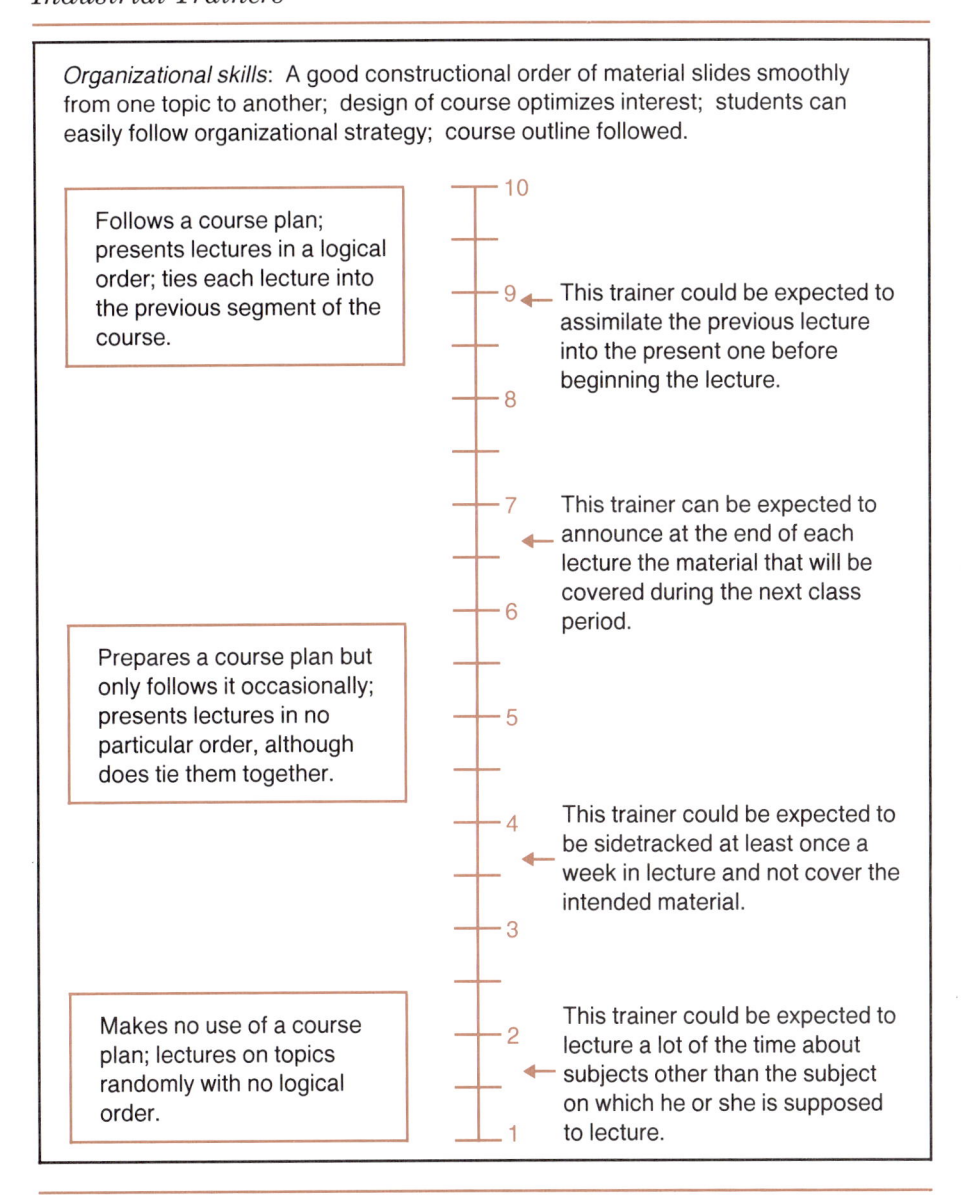

Organizational skills: A good constructional order of material slides smoothly from one topic to another; design of course optimizes interest; students can easily follow organizational strategy; course outline followed.

Scale	Anchor (left)	Anchor (right)
10	Follows a course plan; presents lectures in a logical order; ties each lecture into the previous segment of the course.	
9		This trainer could be expected to assimilate the previous lecture into the present one before beginning the lecture.
8		
7		This trainer can be expected to announce at the end of each lecture the material that will be covered during the next class period.
6		
5	Prepares a course plan but only follows it occasionally; presents lectures in no particular order, although does tie them together.	
4		This trainer could be expected to be sidetracked at least once a week in lecture and not cover the intended material.
3		
2	Makes no use of a course plan; lectures on topics randomly with no logical order.	This trainer could be expected to lecture a lot of the time about subjects other than the subject on which he or she is supposed to lecture.
1		

Source: Adapted from H. J. Bernardin and R. W. Beatty, *Performance Appraisal: Assessing Human Behavior at Work* (Boston: Kent Publishing Co., 1984), p. 84. © 1984 by Wadsworth, Inc. Reprinted by permission of Kent Publishing Company, a division of Wadsworth, Inc.

each incident represents effective job behaviour. BOS and BARS are different, however, in their scale development (i.e., in the use of statistical analysis to select items for building each dimension of performance). For BOS, statistical analysis is used to identify those behaviours or critical incidents

Appraising

that most clearly differentiate effective from ineffective performers. For BARS, expert raters perform this function. The major ways in which BOS differs from BARS are the rating scale format and summated scoring procedure used for each dimension as shown in Exhibit 7.8, which is based on the critical incidents from the job description of the animal keeper (Exhibit 3.3).

The advantages of BOS are several, including (1) it (like BARS) is based on a systematic job analysis; (2) its items and behavioural anchors are clearly stated; (3) it, in contrast to many other methods, allows participation of employees in the development of the dimension (through the identification of critical incidents in the job analysis) that facilitates understanding and acceptance; and (4) it is useful for performance feedback

---

Exhibit 7.8 *Sample BOS Items for the Animal Keeper Illustrating Both Effective and Ineffective Performance*

Effective Performance

1. The animal keeper keeps the cages clean without having to be told.

Almost Never				Almost Always
1	2	3	4	5

2. The animal keeper prepares the right diets for each of the animals.

Almost Never				Almost Always
1	2	3	4	5

3. The animal keeper instructs others who are in lower salary grades, when they ask for assistance.

Almost Never				Almost Always
1	2	3	4	5

Ineffective Performance

1. The animal keeper insults zoo patrons.

Almost Always				Almost Never
1	2	3	4	5

2. The animal keeper fails to lock the cages after they are cleaned.

Almost Always				Almost Never
1	2	3	4	5

3. The animal keeper forgets to provide water for the animals.

Almost Always				Almost Never
1	2	3	4	5

On an actual form the items would neither be grouped nor identified as effective and ineffective performance.

and improvement since specific goals can be tied to numerical scores (ratings) on the relevant behavioural anchor (critical incident) for the relevant performance criterion or dimension.

The limitations of BOS are connected with some of its advantages, particularly the time and cost for its development as compared with forms such as for the conventional rating. Remember that a BOS is developed and used for each job category. The costs of this may be greater than all of the benefits. Furthermore, several dimensions that essentially are behaviours may miss the real essence of many jobs. This is particularly true of managerial and highly routinized jobs, where the essence of the job may be the actual outputs produced, regardless of the behaviour used to obtain them. When these conditions exist, some argue that a better method is one that is goal-oriented or that appraises performance against output objectives.

Objectives-Based Approaches. The two most common types of output performance-measuring systems for managerial employees are **management by objectives** (MBO) and **responsibility centres**. MBO is probably the most popular method used to evaluate managers.[23] Its popularity appears to result from its congruence with people's values and philosophies (for example, the belief that "it is important to reward people for what they accomplish"). MBO is also popular because it can attain greater individual-organizational goal congruence and reduce the likelihood that managers will be working on things unrelated to the objectives and purposes of the organization (goal displacement). The essence of how MBO works can be described in four steps. The first step is to establish the goals that each subordinate is to attain. In many organizations, superiors and subordinates work together to establish the goals. The goals can refer to desired outcomes to be achieved, means (activities) for achieving the outcomes, or both.

The second step involves the setting of a time-frame within which the subordinate must meet the objective. As subordinates perform, they can budget their time by knowing what there is to do, what has been done, and what remains to be done.

The third step is a comparison of the actual level of goal attainment against the agreed-on goals. The evaluator explores reasons why the goals were not met or were exceeded. This step helps determine possible training needs. It also alerts the superior to conditions in the organization that may affect a subordinate's performance but over which the subordinate has no control.

The final step is to decide on new goals and possible new strategies for achieving goals not previously attained. Subordinates who successfully reach the established goals may be allowed to participate even more in the goal-setting process the next time.[24]

Although the use of goals in evaluating managers is effective in motivating their performance, it is not always possible to capture all of the important dimensions of a job in terms of outputs. How the job is done (job behaviour), may be as critical as the outcomes. For example, it may be detrimental to an organization if a manager meets his or her goal by unethical or illegal means. And even if output measure can capture the essence of the job, there is still the concern about establishing goals that are of equal difficulty for all managers and that are sufficiently difficult to be challenging.

Because MBO is used as more than a performance appraisal method (it is also a motivational instrument when employees are involved in the goal-setting sessions), it is mandatory to make sure that the objective(s) agreed on are a function of the employees' skills, knowledge, and abilities. Otherwise, the implementation of MBO might be counter-productive and demoralizing. The following example illustrates this concern.

In a recent case, a large fast-food franchise organization had decided to implement an MBO for its unit managers. A group of unit managers negotiated collectively a fixed increase in sales as compared to the previous year's sales in the same unit (for a similar period). Although the unit managers agreed to the fixed objective (and to the financial bonus that was used as an incentive for attaining this objective), the results after the end of the first year generated ample dissatisfaction and low motivation for many of the managers.

These managers complained that the single criterion (increased sales) was not within their direct control. Factors such as type of neighbourhood, price of meat, and the marketing and advertising generated by the head office, all contributed to the attainment (or non-attainment) of the objective, more than their own effort. This led to random attainment of the objectives: some managers exerted much effort but did not attain the objective, and vice versa. A management consultant who was brought in to resolve the problem suggested replacing the sales criterion with other criteria that are more intimately linked to an individual's skills, knowledge, and abilities (management of personnel; neatness of the unit, etc.).

This example suggests that although MBO sounds plausible theoretically, there may be many operational problems in implementing such a program. To help avoid some of the problems encountered in establishing goals in the MBO approach, some organizations have implemented responsibility centres. These centres appear to be most relevant in appraising the performance of managers.

Under the responsibility centre approach, profit, cost, or revenue centres are established (and become criteria), and the performance of the managers of those centres is evaluated in relation to one or a combination of those criteria. To develop these centres, an organization essentially creates many independent sub-organizations. To the extent that real independence cannot be created, the responsibility centre approach becomes a less appropriate form on which to evaluate managerial performance. The centre concept gives each manager a great deal of freedom to succeed or fail.

An approach similar to MBO is the **work standards approach**, which uses more direct measures of performance and is usually applied to non-managerial employees. Instead of asking subordinates to negotiate their own performance standards or goals as in MBO, organizations determine these through past experience (e.g., what has been done on this job before), time-study data, and work sampling. To produce time-study data, information is collected pertaining to how long it takes a worker to do a certain task under particular circumstances (for example, how long it takes a secretary to type a business letter in an office setting with only normal interruptions from the telephone and visitors). If unique job circumstances are ignored, more habitual data can be used to establish standards and goals. Although the standard data approach is more efficient than time-study because each job does not have to be examined, if job circumstances are important, the standard data may produce inapplicable results. Time-study and standard data are useful on jobs that are relatively repetitive and noncomplex. With jobs that are less repetitive and more complex, the work sampling technique is more appropriate. Using this technique, it is determined how workers allocate their time among various job activities.

The disadvantages of the work standards approach is that it requires time, money, and co-operation to develop. Often co-operation of the job incumbents is necessary, and the problems inherent in this are presented in Chapter 3. Without co-operation, however, the data are neither reliable nor valid. What workers do—a necessary ingredient in work sampling—may reflect what tasks they like and dislike instead of what they should do or the importance of the task. As with MBO, the essence of job performance may not be captured entirely by set standards and goals. In addition, although set standards may provide clear direction to the employees and the goals may be motivating, these may also induce undesirable competition among employees to attain their standards and goals. This method will be motivating only if the competition does not lead to undesirable consequences and if the employees do not want to participate in the standard- and goal-setting process.

Direct Index Approach. This approach differs from the first three primarily in how performance is measured. The first three approaches, except the objective-based approach, depend on a superior's evaluation of a subordinate's performance. There is a certain amount of subjectivity in these cases. However, the **direct index** approach measures subordinate performance by objective, impersonal criteria such as productivity, absenteeism, and turnover. For example, a manager's performance may be evaluated by the turnover or absenteeism rate of that manager's employees. For non-managers, measures of productivity may be more appropriate. Measures of productivity can be broken into measures of quality or quantity. Quality measures include scrap rates, customer complaints, and number of defective units or parts produced. Quantity measures include units of output per hour, new customer orders, and sales volume.

Assessing Performance Appraisal Techniques: Which Is Best?

Although performance appraisal involves a set of many processes and procedures, the system often revolves around the technique itself. Consequently, attention should be focused on assessing the available appraisal techniques so that organizations can choose the best one for their purposes.[25]

Criteria for Assessment. To determine which appraisal technique is best, one must ask the question "Best for what?" That is, what purpose is the technique supposed to accomplish, or what performance is it supposed to measure? The purposes of performance appraisal are generally evaluation and development, but an effective appraisal technique should also be free from error, reliable, valid, and cost effective, and allow comparisons across subordinates and departments in an organization.

Which Technique is Best? Research information on this question is limited, but does reinforce the necessity of first identifying the purposes the organization wants to serve with performance appraisal. Each technique can then be assessed in relation to the following criteria:

- *Developmental:* Motivating subordinates to do well, providing feedback, and aiding in human resource planning and career development
- *Evaluational:* Promotion, discharge, layoff, pay, and transfer decisions and, therefore, the ability to make comparisons across subordinates and departments
- *Economic:* Cost of development, implementation, and use
- *Freedom from error:* Halo, leniency, and central tendency and the extent of reliability and validity
- *Interpersonal:* The extent to which superiors can gather useful and valid appraisal data that facilitates the appraisal interview

An assessment of the appraisal techniques in relationship to each of these criteria is shown in Exhibit 7.9.

Analysis of Future Performance

The approaches discussed so far appraise *past* and *current* performance. Occasionally it is useful to appraise how employees would perform on a *future* job (generally one to which they might be promoted). The **assessment centre** method, which is used to determine the managerial potential of employees, evaluates individuals as they take part in large number of activities conducted in a relatively isolated environment. In a typical assessment centre, an employee may spend two or three days going through a series of activities, including management games, leaderless group discussions, peer evaluations, and in-basket exercises. An example of the criteria by which organizations evaluate future job performance is shown in the General Motor company's assessment centre discussed in Chapter 5.

Advantages of the assessment centre include its validity and its ability to give more employees a chance to have their potential as future managers tested and recognized. Occasionally, employees find themselves placed in jobs or parts of the organization that are less visible to top management. If, in addition, they have a supervisor who fails to make fair evaluations of present performance, they may find themselves "buried" in the organization. An assessment centre program, which most employees can attend by volunteering, helps reduce the likelihood that employees with management potential will get passed over.

Evaluation of Performance Appraisal Techniques

Exhibit 7.9

Criteria for Evaluation	Relative Approach		Absolute Approach				Objectives-based Approach				Direct Indexes	
	Straight Ranking	Forced Distribution	Critical Incidents	Weighted Checklist	Forced Choice	Conventional	BARS	BOS	MBO	Work Standards	Output	Absenteeism
Developmental[a]	1	1	2	2	1	1	2	2	3	2	1	1
Evaluational[b]	3	2	1	1	2	2	2	2	3	3	3	3
Economic[c]	3	3	2	1	1	3	1	1	1	1	3	3
Freedom from Error[d]	3	3	1	2	2	1	2	2	2	2	2	2
Interpersonal[e]	1	2	2	2	1	1	3	3	2	2	2	2

1 = low level; 2 = medium level; 3 = high level.

a. Extent to which subordinates are motivated to improve performance and can develop their careers.
b. Extent to which the form enables the company to make decisions, such as for promotions, salary increase, or layoffs.
c. Extent to which the costs, time, and ease in development and use of form are minimized.
d. Extent to which errors in evaluation such as halo, leniency, low validity, and reliability are minimized.
e. Extent to which form facilitates supervision.

Source: Adapted with permission from R. S. Schuler and S. A. Youngblood, *Personnel Management,* 2nd ed. (St. Paul: West Publishing Co., 1986), p. 250.

On the other hand, some potential limitation of the assessment centre method include its cost, its focus on competition rather than co-operation, and its creation of "crown princes and princesses."[26] The creation of a special class of employees is less likely, however, under a program where they can either be nominated by their supervisors or volunteer on their own initiative. The nature of the activities in the centre, including the degree of co-operation or competition established, can be regulated to match the needs of the organization and its environment. The relatively high cost of the assessment approach (as much as $6000 per employee) suggests that the organization, to justify its use of the centre, must clearly identify the benefits gained from a better and bigger pool of potential managers.

Once performance potential has been identified, organizations can establish management inventory systems to facilitate the human resource planning activity (see Chapter 2). Using the same information, organizations can also establish career planning and training programs to eliminate any gaps between current qualifications possessed and needed skills (see Chapter 12).

Appraising

The Context of Performance Appraisal

Regardless of the form or technique used to gather performance appraisal data, the validity and reliability of the data and even the feasibility of gathering the data may be influenced by the superior-subordinate relationship, the nature of the job, and organization conditions.[27]

Superior-Subordinate Relationships. Important aspects of the superior-subordinate relationship are personal characteristics of the superior, characteristics of the superior in relation to those of the subordinate, the superior's knowledge of the subordinate and the job, and the subordinate's knowledge of the job. For ease of discussion, these can be grouped into problems with the superior and problems with the subordinate.

Basically, four problems may arise with the superior. The first is that superiors may not know what employees are doing or may not understand their work well enough to appraise it fairly. This particular problem occurs more frequently when a manager has a large span of control—a large number of responsibilities and a large number of employees working in different areas. This problem also occurs when the tasks of the employees are varied and technically complex or changing.

The second problem is that even when superiors understand and know how much work subordinates do, they may not *have* performance standards for evaluating that work. Because of the resulting variability in standards and ratings, subordinates may receive unfair (invalid) evaluations. This unfairness may be particularly obvious when comparing the evaluations of subordinates working for different superiors.

The third problem is that superiors may *use* inappropriate standards: they may allow personal values, needs, or biases to replace organizational values and standards. The last major problem related to the superior, although important in itself, also is important because it often leads to some of the errors listed above, particularly the halo and leniency errors: superiors do not like, and where possible resist, making ratings, particularly ones that need to be defended or justified in writing. This resistance also may stem from the inherent conflicts between organizational and individual goals in performance appraisals discussed in the next chapter. The result is often inadequate or inaccurate evaluations. Superiors may consider performance appraisals too time-consuming. For example, they may perceive that appraisals take time away from their "real job," or fail to see how performance appraisals reveal meaningful knowledge about the behaviour of people in organizations.

The general result is any one of several errors in evaluation ("previously defined" or "to be defined here"). The most common errors occur when superiors rate an employee or group of subordinates on several dimensions of performance. Frequently, a superior will evaluate a subordinate similarly on all dimensions of performance just on the basis of the evaluation of one dimension—the one perceived as perhaps the most important. This effect is the **halo error**. When superiors tend to give all of their subordinates favourable ratings, they are said to be committing an **error of leniency**. An

error of strictness is just the opposite. An **error of central tendency** represents a tendency to evaluate all subordinates as average. A **recency-of-events error** is a tendency to evaluate total performance on the last or most recent part of the subordinate's performance. This error can have serious consequences for a subordinate who performs well for six months or a year but then makes a serious or costly error in the last week or two before evaluations are made.

These errors can occur intentionally or unintentionally. Some superiors, for example, may intentionally evaluate their best performers as slightly less than excellent to prevent them from being promoted out of the superior's group. On the other hand, some superiors may unintentionally evaluate certain subordinates less favourably than others merely because they "don't look like good performers." A female subordinate, for instance, may be perceived by a male superior as having such traditional female qualities as dependence, passiveness, and kindness. He perceives the qualities of independence, initiative, and impersonalism as being necessary for a good performance, so he will evaluate this subordinate less favourably. A supervisor may also incorrectly evaluate a subordinate simply on the basis of personal liking or disliking of the subordinate. Halo and leniency errors often result when superiors do not want to take time to consider each performance criterion separately for each subordinate. The leniency error is often committed by superiors because it is difficult for them to give negative feedback, particularly when sufficient justification is lacking.

Even the most valid and reliable appraisal forms cannot be effective when superiors commit these all-too-common errors. But many of these errors can be minimized if

- each performance dimension addresses a single job activity rather than a group of activities;
- the rater can observe the behaviour of the ratee on a regular basis while the job is being accomplished;
- terms like "average" are not used on a rating scale, since different raters have various reactions to such terms;
- the rater does not have to evaluate large groups of employees;
- raters are trained to avoid such errors as leniency, strictness, halo, central tendency, and recency of events; and
- the dimensions being evaluated are meaningful, clearly stated, and important.[28]

Superior-oriented problems in performance appraisal are problematic indeed. However, subordinates also present problems. First, they may not know what is expected of them. People may not be performing simply just because they do not know what is expected of them. This is not because they do not have the ability, it is because they just do not know how to apply it. This is true regardless of the level of difficulty of the job.

The second problem is that subordinates may not be able to do what is expected. Of course, this may be corrected by training or job matching. However, it is not always easy to spot performance inabilities. The PHRM manager can play an important role in these cases, working with superiors to spot reasons for performance deficiencies. Using the performance appraisal to identify and remove performance deficiencies is discussed in the next chapter.

The Nature of the Job. To a considerable extent, the potential value of any performance appraisal system is dependent on the nature of the subordinate's job. The quality or quantity of performance in many jobs may be beyond the subordinate's control. This is particularly true for very routine jobs and where the pace of the jobs is controlled by machines. Also, when jobs are highly interdependent, it is difficult to separate the individual's performance from that of the group.

Organizational Conditions. Organizational conditions over which subordinates may have little control but which are likely to influence their performance (more often negatively than positively) include tools, equipment and availability of supplies, as well as heat, light, and noise levels.[29] If only the subordinates' outcomes, not their behaviour, are appraised, and if organizational conditions are adversely affecting performance, performance evaluations are likely to be unfair. As a result, subordinates are likely to either quit the job or lower their commitment. A condition that may influence performance as much as the use of the performance appraisal is whether the subordinates are unionized. If employees are unionized, performance appraisals may not even be used. Unions have traditionally favoured the use of seniority to determine wage increases, promotions, transfers, and demotions.

Gathering Performance Appraisal Data

Performance appraisal data can be gathered by many sources. The sources include a ratee's supervisor, subordinates (if the ratee is a manager or supervisor), peers, and the ratee himself or herself.

Appraisal by Superiors. The superior is the immediate boss of the subordinate being evaluated. It is assumed that the superior is the one who knows best the job of the subordinate and the performance of the subordinate. But there are drawbacks to appraisal by the superior:

- Since the superior may have reward and punishment power, the subordinate may feel threatened
- Evaluation is often a one-way process that makes the subordinate feel defensive. Thus, little coaching takes place; justification of action prevails
- The superior may not have the necessary interpersonal skills to give good feedback
- The superior may have an ethical bias against "playing God"
- The superior, by giving punishments, may alienate the subordinate

Because of the potential liabilities, organizations may invite other people to share in the appraisal process, even giving the subordinate greater input.

Allowing other people to participate in the performance appraisal creates a greater "openness" in the performance appraisal system, thus helping to enhance the quality of the superior-subordinate relationship.

Self-Appraisal. The use of self-appraisal, particularly through subordinate participation in setting goals, was made popular as an important component of MBO. Subordinates who participate in the evaluation process may become more involved and committed to the goals. It appears that subordinate participation may also help clarify employees' roles and reduce role conflict.[30]

Self-appraisals are often effective tools for programs focusing on self-development, personal growth, and goal commitment. On the other hand, self-appraisals are subject to systematic biases and distortions when used for evaluative purposes.[31] These biases and distortions may be important topics of discussion in the performance appraisal session between superior and subordinate.

Peer Appraisal. Peer appraisals appear to be useful predictors of subordinate performance.[32] They are particularly useful when superiors lack access to some aspects of subordinates' performance. However the validity of peer appraisals is reduced somewhat if the organizational reward system is based on performance and is highly competitive, and if there is a low level of trust among subordinates.[33]

Appraisal by Subordinates. Perhaps many of you, particularly as students, have had the chance to evaluate an instructor. How useful do you think this evaluation process is? A significant advantage of appraisal by students is that many instructors are unaware of how they are being perceived by their students. They may not realize that students fail to understand some of their instructions. It is the same in a work setting—subordinates' appraisals can make superiors more aware of their impact on their subordinates.

Sometimes, however, subordinates may evaluate their superiors solely on the basis of personality or serving the needs of subordinates rather than those of the organization. Of course, subordinates may inflate the evaluation of their superiors, particularly if they feel threatened by them and have no anonymity.[34]

Summary

Appraising employee performance is a critical PHRM activity. This chapter examined performance appraisal as a set of processes and procedures consisting of developing reliable and valid standards, criteria, and performance appraisal techniques. To ensure the effectiveness of performance appraisal, PHRM managers must be concerned with implementation and monitoring of all of these aspects of the performance appraisal system with an awareness of legal considerations.

The effectiveness of performance appraisal depends on several components of appraisal, not just one (such as the appraisal technique). Recognition of the importance and role of the subject in the performance appraisal system has helped focus attention on such components of appraisal as the superior-subordinate relationship, job qualities, and organizational conditions. Also of particular importance is the manner in which the raters process appraisal information and make evaluation decisions. This is examined in more detail in the next chapter.

Despite the best-laid plans for an effective performance appraisal system, PHRM professionals often are frustrated by the failure of line managers to consistently apply and use the system. A number of obstacles can contribute to rater resistance to a performance appraisal system: raters may not have the opportunity to observe subordinates' performances, raters may not have performance standards, raters as human judges are prone to errors, or raters may view performance appraisal as a conflict-producing activity and therefore avoid it. The next chapter describes the proper use of performance appraisal systems.

Discussion Questions

1. In what ways can a performance appraisal system help an organization?
2. What is involved in a performance appraisal system?
3. What are the purposes of performance appraisal?
4. Discuss the points that the boards of inquiry have implicated as important in a legally viable performance appraisal system.
5. How can performance appraisal forms be developed so that supervisory errors in performance appraisal can be minimized?
6. What criteria are important in answering the question: "Which is the best performance appraisal form?"
7. What relationships exist among performance appraisal and other PHRM activities?
8. Who is responsible for the efficacy of the performance appraisal system?
9. What is the primary difference between the behavioural observations scale and the behaviourally anchored rating scale?
10. What are some typical errors in performance appraisal?

CASE STUDY

Alleged Discrimination in Performance Appraisal

Micheline, Marielle, Louise, and Nicole were surprised to receive an internal memo from the director of personnel services inviting them to be present at a formal performance appraisal session to be conducted that afternoon. They had worked as temporary producers for Telé-Montréal,

Inc. for an average of five years, and could not recall such sessions having been held in the past. In fact, none of the other producers at the station were involved. The individual performance interviews were conducted by the director of personnel, the production supervisor, and the director of professional services.

To their surprise, they discovered that, based on the results of a recent performance appraisal, a decision had been reached to demote each of them to the position of assistant producer. Each of the four employees was given a brief summary of the reasons for this decision, and then was asked to sign a statement indicating that she had been told of the results of the superior's evaluation. All four left their interviews feeling shocked, angry, and helpless.

The next morning, the four decided to get together to learn more about the decision and the performance evaluation system used by Telé-Montréal, Inc. They learned the following from Johana Watson, the personnel director, regarding the new performance appraisal system:

Telé-Montréal had decided to reorganize their operation and to implement a new performance appraisal system for all of their professional employees. With the help of the National Management Consulting Firm, Inc., they developed a "bias-free" performance appraisal policy that included the following elements:

- Each producer was to be assessed on the basis of four criteria: creativity; versatility; management of technical, material, and budgetary resources; and management of human resources
- Evaluation was to be conducted on an annual basis
- Evaluation was to be carried out by a committee of three supervisors, which will be guided by the following rating scale in assessing each dimension:

  –Performance that surpasses the job demands   5 points
  –Performance that satisfactorily meets the job demands   3 points
  –Performance that exhibits average satisfaction of the job demands   2 points
  –Performance that is inferior to the job demands   1 point

- A differential weighting was to be applied for the criteria: creativity; management of human resources; and management of technical, material, and budgetary resources were to have factors multiplied by four, and versatility was to be multiplied by two.
- The total score compiled for each employee was then interpreted as follows:

Meaning	Score
Non-satisfactory performance	30 or less
Minimal performance	30 – 40
Satisfactory performance	40 – 50
Excellent performance	50 +

Finally, according to Watson, "Given that this performance appraisal procedure has been tested and used by many Canadian organizations to their complete satisfaction, it is probably a very valid procedure." And further, "This sophisticated nu-

---

Breakdown of Producers' Performance Appraisals Telé-Montréal, Inc.   *Exhibit 7.10*

Producer's Name	Creativity	Versatility	Management of Mat., Tech., Budget	Human Resources	Total
Louise	4 × 3 = 12	2 × 3 = 6	4 × 2 = 8	4 × 2 = 8	34
Nicole	4 × 2 = 8	2 × 2 = 4	4 × 2 = 8	4 × 3 = 12	32
Micheline	4 × 1 = 4	2 × 3 = 6	4 × 2 = 8	4 × 2 = 8	26
Marielle	4 × 2 = 8	2 × 4 = 8	4 × 1 = 4	4 × 1 = 4	24
John	4 × 3 = 12	2 × 3 = 6	4 × 3 = 12	4 × 4 = 16	46
André	4 × 4 = 16	2 × 3 = 6	4 × 3 = 12	4 × 3 = 12	46
Marcel	4 × 3 = 12	2 × 4 = 8	4 × 4 = 16	4 × 4 = 16	52
David	4 × 2 = 8	2 × 3 = 6	4 × 4 = 16	4 × 4 = 16	46

merical and highly accurate system leads Télé-Montréal, Inc. to believe that in no way can they 'perform poorly' in utilizing this new performance appraisal system."

On learning of the new system, the four producers demanded to see the detailed breakdown of their assessment, along with those of other producers. Johana Watson agreed and produced the data (Exhibit 7.10). When asked why the producers were not given a detailed job description, Watson answered, "Don't tell me that after working as assistant producers for two years and then as producers, you don't know what your job is?"

This answer did not satisfy the four and they filed a formal complaint alleging discrimination (possibly sexual discrimination) with the Human Rights Commission of Québec.

Case Questions

Put yourself in the position of the Human Rights Commission investigator. Based on the limited information available, decide whether there is any justification to the complainants' charges. In making your decision, consider the following questions: (1) Are issues of reliability involved in this case? If so, what sources of errors must you consider? (2) Are issues of validity involved in this case? If so, what sources of errors must you consider? (3) Is the measuring instrument itself an issue here? (4) Are problems of administration an issue here?

Another way to analyze the case is by assigning to yourself the role of a lawyer for the complainants: How would you build the case? What would you emphasize?

Endnotes

1. For more information, see S. J. Carroll, Jr., and C. E. Schneier, *Performance Appraisal and Review (PAR) Systems* (Glenview, IL: Scott-Foresman, 1982). G. Latham and K. Wexley, *Increasing Productivity through Performance Appraisal* (Reading, MA: Addison-Wesley, 1981). Both of these sources present excellent detail on performance appraisal as a system and as a single form or technique.
2. For slight variations of this definition, including the fact that it is a dynamic, multi-dimensional construct, see Latham and Wexley, ibid., p. 4; Carroll and Schneier, ibid., pp. 2–3; M. J. Kavanagh, "Evaluation Performance," in K. M. Rowland and G. R. Ferris (eds.), *Personnel Management* (Boston: Allyn and Bacon, 1982), pp. 187–225; and E. Eichel and M. E. Bender, *Performance Appraisal: A Study of Current Techniques* (New York: AMACOM, 1984).
3. Latham and Wexley, endnote 1, p. 2.
4. A. Mikalachkiki and J. Gandz, *Managing Absenteeism* (London, Ontario: University of Western Ontario, School of Business Administration, 1982).
5. "Absenteeism Costs Bank $18 Million a Year: Survey," *First Bank News*, February 1983, p. 2.
6. For other descriptions of these purposes, see L. L. Cummings and D. P. Schwab, *Performance in Organizations: Determinants and Appraisal* (Glenview, IL: Scott, Foresman & Company, 1973); M. Beer, "Performance Appraisal: Dilemmas and Possibilities," *Organizational Dynamics*, Winter 1981, pp. 24–36. Carroll and Schneier, endnote 1. See also the entire issue of *Personnel Administration* of March 1984.
7. Based on one of the authors' "expert witness" reports, submitted to the Association of Producers in Radio-Québec, July 1985.
8. For a description of the impact of contingent rewards based on performance behaviour, see G. P. Latham, L. L. Cummings, and T. R. Mitchell, "Behavior Strategies to Improve Productivity," *Organizational Dynamics*, Winter 1981, pp. 4–23; W. Nord, "Improving Attendance through Rewards," *Personnel Administration, 34*, 1971, pp. 41–47; E. Pedalino and V. Gamboa, "Behavior Modification and Absenteeism: Intervention in One Industrial Setting," *Journal of Applied Psychology, 59*, 1974, pp. 694–698; C. E. Schneier, "Behavior Modification in Management: A Review and a Critique," *Academy of Management Journal, 17*, 1974, pp. 528–548; P. J. Stonich, "The Performance Measurement and Reward System: Critical to Strategic Management," *Organizational Dynamics*, Winter 1984, pp. 45–47; R. Kanungo, "Reward Management: A New Look," in S. L. Dolan and R. S. Schuler (eds.), *Canadian Readings in Personnel and Human Resource Management* (St. Paul: West Publishing Co., 1987).
9. H. F. Schwind, "Performance Appraisal: The State of the Art," in S. L. Dolan and R. S. Schuler (eds.), *Canadian Readings in Personnel and Human Resource Management* (St. Paul: West Publishing Co., 1987).
10. Excerpts taken from *The Employment Law Report*, June 1985, vol. 6, no. 6, pp. 45–46. Used with permission of the publisher, Concord Publishing, Toronto.
11. Ibid., pp. 45–46.
12. For extensive discussion of these issues, see H. J.

Bernardin and R. W. Beatty: *Performance Appraisal: Assessing Human Behavior at Work* (Boston: Kent Publishing Co., 1984). A call for overcoming the criterion bias in Canadian organizations is also made in S. F. Cronshaw, "Future Directions for Personnel Psychology in Canada," *Canadian Psychology* (Special industrial/organizational issue), 1986.

13. This form has been used successfully in many of the authors' courses where a team project was required. The participation score for team performance was part of the overall student evaluation.
14. P. M. Muchinsky, *Psychology Applied to Work* (Homewood, IL: The Dorsey Press, 1983), p. 257.
15. S. Pinsker, "The Written About and Those Who Write," *Business*, April–June 1983, p. 54.
16. J. C. Flanagan, "The Critical Incident Technique," *Psychological Bulletin*, 1954, *51*, pp. 327–358.
17. Normal distribution assures that, within one standards deviation from the mean.
18. This method is used successfully by one of the authors of this book to assess student performance. Not only does it facilitate the rater's work (assuming normal distribution among the students), but the ratees were found to be most satisfied with this method in comparison to alternative assessments of their work.
19. F. J. Landy and D. A. Trumbo, *Psychology of Work Behavior*, rev. ed. (Homewood, IL: Dorsey, 1980). W. F. Cascio, *Applied Psychology in Personnel Management*, 2nd ed. (Reston, VA: Reston Publishing Company, Inc., 1982). R. L. Mathis and J. H. Jackson, *Personnel, Human Resource Management*, 4th ed. (St. Paul: West Publishing Co., 1985), p. 345.
20. Modified from an exhibit in Bernardin and Beatty, endnote 12, p. 84.
21. Bernardin and Beatty, endnote 12, pp. 82–88.
22. G. Latham and K. Wexley, "Behavioral Observation Scales for Performance Appraisal Purposes," *Personnel Psychology*, 1977, *30*, pp. 255–268.
23. As reported in Carroll and Schneier, endnote 1, p. 39, 60% of the organizations use MBO to evaluate managers.
24. L. Olivas, "Adding a Different Dimension to Goal Setting Processes," *Personnel Administrator*, October 1981.
25. B. McAfee and B. Green, "Selecting a Performance Appraisal Method," *Personnel Administrator*, June 1977, pp. 61–64. "Appraising the Performance Appraisal," *Business Week*, May 19, 1980, pp. 153–154. E. Yager, "A Critique of Performance Appraisal Systems," *Personnel Journal*, February 1981, pp. 129–133.
26. Carroll and Schneier, endnote 1, p. 205. W. F. Cascio and V. Silbey, "Utility of the Assessment Center as a Selection Device," *Journal of Applied Psychology*, 1979, *64*, pp. 107–118.
27. R. E. Lefton, V. R. Buzzotta, M. Scerberg, and B. L. Karaker, *Effective Motivation through Performance Appraisal* (New York: Wiley, 1977). L. L. Cummings and D. P. Schwab, "Designing Appraisal Systems for Information Yield," *California Management Review*, Summer 1978. Bureau of National Affairs, "Employee Performance, Evaluation, and Control," *Personnel Policies Forum*, no. 108, Feb. 1975. R. I. Lazar and W. S. Wikstrom, *Appraising Managerial Performance: Current Practice and Future Directions* (New York: Conference Board, Inc., 1977). A. H. Locher and K. S. Teel, "Performance Appraisal: A Survey of Current Practices," *Personnel Journal*, May 1977, pp. 245–247. *Personnel Practices in Factory and Office Manufacturing*, Studies in Personnel Policy 194 (New York: National Industrial Conference Boards, 1964). Bernardin and Beatty, endnote 12.
28. J. L. Gibson, J. J. Ivancevich, and J. M. Donnelly, *Organizations: Behavior, Structure, Processes*, 5th ed. (Dallas, TX: Business Publications, 1985), p. 614.
29. L. H. Peters and E. J. O'Connor, "Situational Constraints and Work Outcomes: The Influence of Frequently Overlooked Construct," *Academy of Management Review, 5*, 1980, pp. 391–397.
30. R. S. Schuler, "A Role and Expectancy Perception Model of Participation in Decision Making," *Academy of Management Journal*, June 1980, p. 338.
31. Cummings and Schwab, endnote 6, p. 106.
32. J. S. Kane and E. E. Lawler III, "Methods of Peer Assessment," *Psychological Bulletin, 3*, 1978, pp. 555–586.
33. Cummings and Schwab, endnote 6, p. 105.
34. B. McAfee and B. Green, "Selecting a Performance Appraisal Method," *Personnel Administrator*, June 1977, pp. 61–64. M. E. Schick, "The Refined Performance Evaluation Monitoring System: Best of Both Worlds," *Personnel Journal*, Jan. 1980, pp. 47–50. "Appraising the Performance Appraisal," *Business Week*, May 19, 1980, pp. 153–154. P. C. Grant, "How to Manage Employee Job Performance," *Personnel Administrator*, Aug. 1981, pp. 59–65. W. J. Birch, "Performance Appraisal: One Company's Experience," *Personnel Journal*, June 1981, pp. 456–460. E. Yager, "A Critique of Performance Appraisal Systems," *Personnel Journal*, Feb. 1981, pp. 129–133.

CHAPTER 8

Performance Appraisal II: Utilizing the Data

PHRM in the News

Utilizing the Performance Appraisal Data
Inherent Conflicts in Performance Appraisal
Designing the Appraisal System
The Performance Appraisal Interview

Improving Performance
Identifying Performance Gaps
Determining the Causes of Performance Gaps

Strategies to Improve Performance
Positive Behavioural Strategies
Positive Organizational Strategies
Negative Behavioural Strategies
Employee Assistance Programs
Counselling

Assessing Performance Appraisal Systems
Overall Performance Appraisal System Assessment
Specific Performance Appraisal System Assessment

Summary

Discussion Questions

Case Study

Endnotes

PHRM in the News

Performance is a Key to Career Development

My focus will be on the conditions which should exist for a career program to work well—in other words, the "right" environment.

We think about the "right" environment for career planning and development in terms of several areas. They include succession planning, performance management, employee communication, training and development, rewards, and benefits.

Career planning requires an effective succession-planning process, which, in turn, must be carried out under the umbrella of corporate philosophies and directions.

Each year, we sit down with regional management teams and discuss the status of each of our management and specialist people. The input from these sessions is used in our management succession-planning process, which then gets reviewed and reshaped by executive management.

The aim is to integrate corporate succession needs and individual career goals.

At the individual level, performance in the current job is an important factor in determining career direction. Our performance-management process includes objective setting and review, as well as assessment of performance and career potential.

The personal-development plan involves discussion between manager and employee on strengths, development areas, action plans, career preferences, and potential.

Source: Excerpt from a presentation by J. Reid, Manager, Human Resources Planning and Development, Canada Trust, at a Best Companies Conference. Appeared in *The Financial Post* (Special Report), June 7, 1986, p. 20. Used with permission.

The Art of Firing

The majority of employers stumble into a termination with little knowledge of the potential consequences and even less sensitivity to the human dynamics involved. Management commonly procrastinates before reaching the decision to dismiss. Eventually a manager terminates an employee in anger, without assessing the long-term implications of such action. What the corporation may regard as a humane approach often amounts to false kindness, with adverse consequences for both the company and the individual.

For many employers, the greatest difficulty they encounter on termination is the actual communication of the fact of dismissal. Firing a top-level executive is never painless: it can have a disruptive effect on corporate morale and exacts a heavy psychological toll on those directly involved. Modern-day executives find the ordeal of firing a colleague a stressful experience to be avoided whenever possible. No one wishes to be placed in a position where he must be unkind. The action taken must be rationalized by those engaged in it, and explained to those other employees who may feel they may be next.

Tension is inherent in the termination process and inevitably takes its toll. In the short run, it will mean that the terminating executive will be unable to carry on his normal corporate tasks because of the time taken up by problems created by the dismissal. In the long run, he may be called upon to justify his actions in a courtroom under cross-examination.

The cost of ill-considered terminations has been increasing annually. The court awards have reached 24 months' salary and benefits for termination without cause and without adequate notice. Settlements run even higher for senior executives of substantial service and status. In addition to payments of salary and benefits, courts have awarded damages for mental distress and, in certain circumstances, damages for loss of reputation. Awards may also include punitive damages, where an employer fires an employee in a brutal manner.

With some careful planning, it is possible to contain an otherwise unpleasant situation by making it absolutely clear, concise, and humane. Preparation is essential; otherwise the meeting will degenerate into accusations and finger pointing, and both parties may make the situation much worse than necessary.

Once it has been decided that the employee must be terminated and the terms and conditions of severance have been reviewed with the company's lawyer, it then becomes important to decide what must be communicated to the employee, how this information will be communicated, and by whom. The timing of the meeting is crucial, and the environment in which the meeting takes place is also important. The person responsible for the termination must carefully prepare a checklist of the matters that he will cover in the interview and stick to it.

Source: Excerpts from Brian A. Grosman, "The Art of Firing," *Fire Power* (Markham, Ont.: Penguin Books Canada Ltd., 1985). Copyright © Brian A. Grosman 1984. Reprinted by permission of Penguin Books Canada Limited.

These "PHRM in the News" articles illustrate two important points in utilizing performance appraisal information. First, it can be very useful for a company to utilize performance appraisal data as part of a career development program for its employees. Second, when organizations attempt to develop strategies to improve performance on the basis of performance appraisal information, they may encounter difficulties in establishing a policy that is fair. For example, it can be very difficult for a supervisor to tell a subordinate about poor performance, even though this is a necessity.

This chapter discusses issues and potential solutions associated with providing subordinates feedback via the performance appraisal interview. Also, issues associated with improving performance, including a paradigm for diagnosing causes of performance gaps, are presented. Finally, an overall assessment of the performance appraisal system is presented.

Utilizing the Performance Appraisal Data

Performance appraisal data are used for a variety of purposes, including (a) for *evaluation* (salary, promotion, demotion, transfer, and layoff decisions), and (b) for *development* (counselling, coaching, improving, and career planning decisions). The major way in which organizations utilize performance appraisal is through the interview between the superior and subordinate. Although the performance appraisal interview is used to gather additional performance data, its major use as discussed here is to feed back performance appraisal data to the subordinate. On the basis of this feedback, the intended purposes of performance appraisal are served. The success of the process depends on how the appraisal system is designed and how the interview is conducted.

An understanding of the inherent conflicts in performance appraisal is pertinent to the discussion of the design of the system and the conduct of the interview, so these conflicts will be discussed first. Then methods of improving performance deficiencies are examined.

Inherent Conflicts in Performance Appraisal

The purposes of performance appraisal can be either evaluative or developmental. Although the performance appraisal system should serve both sets of purposes for organizations, doing so often creates conflicts.[1]

Goal-oriented Conflicts. From organizational and individual goals three sets of conflicts can be singled out. One is between the organization's evaluative and developmental goals. When pursuing the evaluative goal, superiors have to make judgements affecting their subordinates' careers and immediate rewards. Communicating negative judgements can lead to the creation of an adversarial, low-trust relationship between superior and subordinate. This in turn inhibits the superior's ability to perform the problem-solving, helper role that is essential in serving the developmental goal.

A second set of conflicts arises from the various goals of the individual being evaluated. On the one hand, individuals want valid feedback that gives them information about how to improve and where they stand in the organization. On the other hand, they want to verify their self-image and obtain valued rewards. In essence, the goals of individuals imply a need for evaluator openness (giving valid feedback for improvement) and also protectiveness (allowing the individual to maintain a positive self-image and obtain rewards).

The third set of conflicts arises between the goals of the individual and the goals of the organization. One conflict is between the organization's evaluation goal and the individual's goal of obtaining rewards. Another conflict is between the organization's developmental goal and the individual's goal of maintaining self-image. The nature of these conflicts is shown in Exhibit 8.1.

Consequences of Inherent Conflicts. Among the several consequences of the inherent conflicts described above are ambivalence, avoidance, defensiveness, and resistance. Ambivalence is a consequence for both the superiors and the subordinates. Superiors are ambivalent because they must act as judge and jury in telling subordinates where they stand, both because the organization demands it and the subordinates want it. Yet, they are uncertain about their judgements and how the subordinates will react to

Exhibit 8.1 **Conflicts in Performance Appraisal**

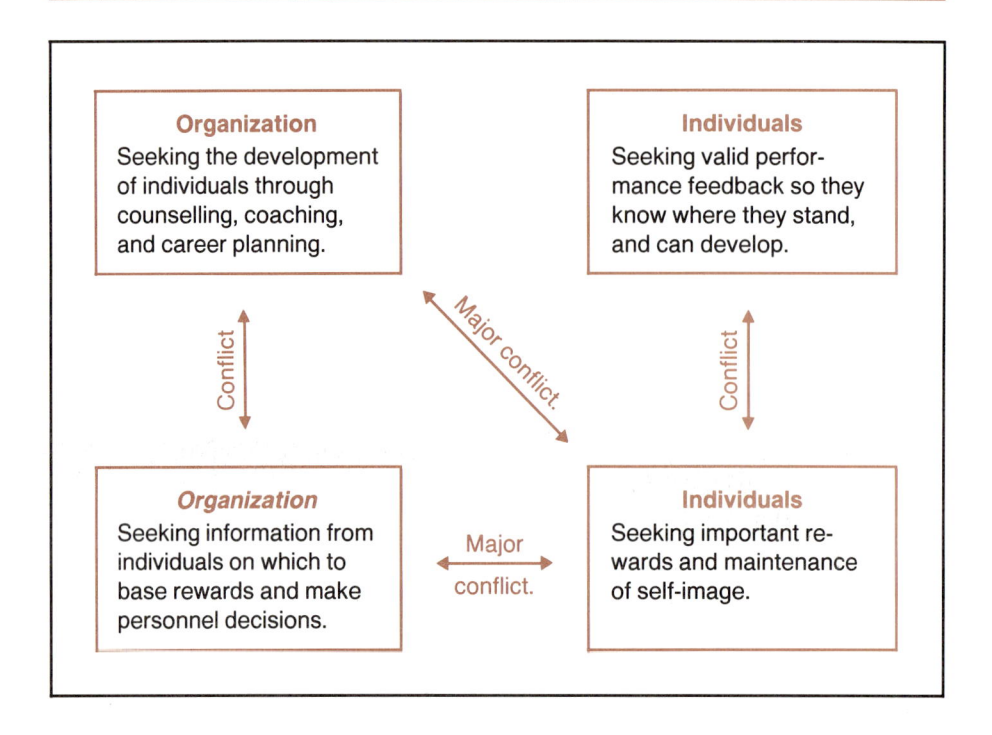

Organization Seeking the development of individuals through counselling, coaching, and career planning.	**Individuals** Seeking valid performance feedback so they know where they stand, and can develop.
Organization Seeking information from individuals on which to base rewards and make personnel decisions.	**Individuals** Seeking important rewards and maintenance of self-image.

Vertical arrows between the upper and lower boxes on each side are labelled *Conflict*. A diagonal arrow from upper-right to lower-left is labelled *Major conflict*. A horizontal arrow between the two lower boxes is labelled *Major conflict*.

Source: M. Beer, "Performance Appraisal: Dilemmas and Possibilities," *Organization Dynamics,* Winter 1981 (New York: AMACOM, a division of American Management Association), p. 27. Reprinted by permission of the author.

receiving negative feedback. This feeling is intensified when superiors are not trained in giving feedback.

Subordinates are equally ambivalent because they want honest feedback, yet they want to maintain their self-image (that is, they really want only positive feedback) and to receive rewards. Additionally, if they are open with their superiors in identifying undeveloped potential, they risk the chance that the superiors may use this to evaluate them unfavourably.

A consequence of this joint ambivalence is avoidance. Subordinates, to avoid negative feedback, may avoid seeking appraisal data in general and may attempt to play down the importance of performance appraisal data. The superiors meanwhile avoid giving appraisals, convinced that the subordinates really would rather not know. This process is sometimes called the "vanishing performance appraisal." [2]

If organizations both demand that superiors engage in the performance appraisal process, and that they give negative feedback (to support current and future decisions regarding layoffs, terminations, and demotions), the superiors may resort to the "sandwich approach." Here the superiors squeeze the negative feedback between two pieces of positive feedback. When this is done, subordinates may report never having received negative feedback, even though superiors will report giving it.

Subordinates and superiors also become defensive during performance appraisals. The subordinate becomes defensive in responding to negative feedback that threatens his or her self-image and chance for gaining rewards. This is corroborated by the results of a study at General Electric, where it was found that

- criticism has a negative effect on achievement of goals;
- praise has little effect one way or the other;
- the average subordinate reacts defensively to criticism during the appraisal interview;
- defensiveness resulting from critical appraisal produces inferior performance;
- the disruptive effect of repeated criticism on subsequent performance is greater among those already low in self-esteem;
- the average General Electric employee's self-estimate of performance before appraisal placed him at the 77th percentile; and
- only 2 out of 92 participants in the study estimated their performance to be below average.[3]

Accordingly, subordinates attempt to blame others for their performance, challenge the appraisal form, and demand that their superiors justify their appraisals. Initially at least, subordinates are not inclined to apologize for their behaviour and seek ways to improve; in fact, they resist efforts by the superiors to engage in problem solving. Consequently, the superiors spend most of their time trying to defend their appraisals and resisting the efforts of the subordinates to have their appraisals altered. The appraisal process is uncomfortable for both participants, particularly when poor performance and negative feedback are involved. But even if good performance is involved, the superiors still have to make evaluation decisions, in order to reinforce further those who excel and to have a relative comparison to other levels of performance. Because appraisals are uncomfortable, yet necessary, it is important to seek ways to make the process better. The appraisal system and the appraisal interview can both be designed to minimize many of the problems just discussed.

Designing the Appraisal System

Several features can be incorporated into the design of the appraisal process to reduce the problems caused by conflict inherent to performance appraisal.

Separate Evaluation and Development. Because many subordinates react defensively to evaluations that are negative, they initially do not want to consider ways to improve. Consequently, attempts by the superiors to engage in developmental activities such as problem solving are likely to be futile. For problem-solving to be effective, the subordinates must be open to suggestion and the superiors must play the role of helper, not judge or prosecutor. Thus, if organizations want to serve both the evaluation and development purposes effectively, there should be two appraisal interviews. One interview can focus on evaluation and the other, at a different time of the year, on development.[4]

Use Appropriate Performance Data. During the appraisal, the superiors should always utilize performance data that focus on specific behaviours or goals. Data that focus on personal attributes or characteristics are likely to prompt more defensiveness because they are more subjective and because they address the subordinate's self-image.

As shown in the previous chapter, superiors can facilitate specific performance feedback through their selection and use of the appropriate appraisal forms. Specifically, if superiors want to use performance data on behaviours, a critical incident technique or a BOS method would be effective, while performance data on goals would be more effectively displayed using an MBO or work standards approach. Using these appraisal forms allows the supervisors to monitor *what* subordinates are doing as well as *how* they are doing.

Separate Current and Potential Performance Appraisal. Current performance of subordinates may have little to do with their performance potential. Yet superiors may unconsciously incorporate evaluations of performance potential into evaluations of current performance unless there exists a specific and separate form for appraisal of potential. One consequence of this confusion might be an appraisal of current performance that represents an averaging of current and potential performance appraisal. This can result in unfair appraisals, particularly for subordinates who may not be interested in being promoted yet perform adequately in their present jobs. Thus, separate appraisal forms for current and potential performance could help to eliminate the averaging effect and the unfairness that may result for some subordinates.

Upward Appraisals. To encourage openness in the performance appraisal and to improve superior-subordinate relationships, subordinates could be allowed to engage in appraisal of their superiors. Upward appraisal can help put into better balance, if not equalize, the power of the superior vis-à-vis the subordinate. Such a balance is useful in reducing the hierarchical character of the superior-subordinate relationship that contributes much to defensiveness and avoidance in the performance appraisal.

Organizations and superiors facilitate the upward appraisal process by providing forms for subordinates to use and by engaging in other human resource policies and procedures indicative of openness. They allow employees to participate in deciding their own pay increases (Chapter 9), or in analyzing their own jobs (Chapter 3).

Self-Appraisal. Furthering this openness and power-equalization approach in performance appraisal is a policy of self-appraisal. Self-appraisal is likely to provide more information for the superior and result in a more realistic appraisal of the subordinate's performance and a greater acceptance of the final appraisal by subordinates.

The Performance Appraisal Interview

To further enhance the effectiveness of the performance appraisal, several considerations should be made regarding the actual performance appraisal interview.

Types of Interviews. There are essentially four major types of interviews: (1) tell and sell; (2) tell and listen; (3) problem-solving; and (4) mixed.[5] The **tell and sell**, or directive, interview is used to let subordinates know how well they are doing and to sell them on the merits of setting specific goals for improvement, if needed. This type of interview is efficient and is effective in improving performance, particularly for subordinates with little desire for participation. This type of interview may be most appropriate in providing evaluation.

The **tell and listen** interview provides the subordinates with chances to participate and establish a dialogue with their superiors. The purpose of the tell and listen interview is to communicate the supervisors' perceptions of the subordinates' strengths and weaknesses, and to let the subordinates respond to those perceptions. The superiors summarize and paraphrase the responses of their subordinates but generally do not establish goals for performance improvement. Consequently, the subordinates may feel better but their performance may not change.

In the **problem-solving**, or participative problem-solving, interview, an active and open dialogue is established between the superior and the subordinate. Not only are perceptions shared, but solutions to problems or differences are sought, presented, and discussed. Goals for improvement are established mutually by the superior and subordinate. This type of interview is generally more difficult for most superiors to conduct, so training in problem solving is usually necessary and beneficial.[6]

Conducting a **mixed interview** also requires training, because it is a combination of the tell and sell and the problem-solving interviews. Skills are needed to do the tell and sell and the problem-solving interviews, and to make the transition from one to the other. As explained above, it is desirable to use the tell and sell interview for evaluation and the problem-solving interview for development, but separate interviews for each purpose may not be feasible. Consequently, a single interview must accomplish both purposes. This single interview may begin with the subordinate listening to the superior provide an appraisal of performance, followed by a participative discussion of what and how performance improvements can be made (problem solving), and conclude with agreed-upon goals for improvement.

Interview Effectiveness. A mixed interview can be an effective format by which to structure an interview, but overall interview effectiveness is dependent on more than simply following the format. The necessary characteristics for an effective interview include:

- Scheduling so that subordinate as well as superior are aware of and agree on an appropriate time for the interview
- Agreeing on the content of the interview; foremost should be whether the interview is for evaluation or development, or both
- Agreeing on the process—how differences are to be resolved, how problems are going to be solved, and the topical flow of the interview
- Selecting and using a neutral location in which the interview can be held, including neither the superior's nor the subordinate's work locations.[7]

The appraisal interview would be more effective if it also had the following characteristics:

- High levels of subordinate participation. This increases the subordinate's acceptance of the superior's appraisal and enhances satisfaction
- Superior's support of and trust in the subordinate, which helps to increase the openness of the interview and the subordinate's acceptance of the appraisal and the superior
- Open, two-way discussion of performance problems and joint problem solving, which can lead to improvement in the subordinate's performance
- A setting of specific and challenging goals to be achieved by the subordinate serves to increase the chances for improved performance
- Provision for effective feedback rather than criticism. This can enhance the quality of the subordinate-superior relationship and the subordinate's performance.

Since superiors have the opportunity to provide feedback on an informal, daily basis as well as in the formal performance appraisal interview, it is useful to examine the process of effective feedback.

Effective Feedback. Whether negative or positive, feedback is not always easy to give. Fortunately, several parameters of effective feedback have been determined.

1. Effective feedback is *specific rather than general*. Telling someone that he or she is too domineering is probably not as useful as saying, "Just now you were not listening to what I said, but I felt I either had to agree with your arguments or face attack from you."
2. Effective feedback is focused on *behaviour rather than on the personal* characteristics. It is important to refer to what a person does rather than to what type of person the employee seems to be. Thus, a superior might say that a person talked more than anyone else at a meeting rather than saying that he or she is a loudmouth. The former allows for the possibility of change; the latter implies a fixed personality trait.
3. Effective feedback also *takes into account the needs of the receiver* of the feedback. Feedback can be destructive when it serves only the evalua-

tor's needs and fails to consider the needs of the person on the receiving end. Feedback should be given to help, not to hurt.
4. Effective feedback is *directed toward behaviour that the receiver can control*. Frustration increases when people are reminded of shortcomings over which they have no control or a physical characteristic they can not change.
5. Feedback is most effective when it is *solicited rather than imposed*. Receivers should actively seek feedback by asking the evaluator questions.
6. Effective feedback involves *sharing information rather than giving advice*, leaving receivers free to decide for themselves about the changes to make in accordance with their own needs.
7. Effective feedback is *well-timed*. In general, immediate feedback is most useful, provided it is directed constructively at recent behaviours.
8. Effective feedback *concerns limited information*. Although an evaluator may have much information, he or she should provide only as much as the receiver can use. Overloading a person with feedback reduces the possibility that it will be used effectively. An evaluator who gives more than can be used is more often than not satisfying some need of his or her own rather than helping the other person.
9. Effective feedback *concerns what is said or done and how—not why*. Telling people your interpretation of their motivations or intentions tends to alienate them and contributes to a climate of resentment, suspicion, and distrust; it does not contribute to learning or development. If appropriate for the situation, the evaluator can express uncertainty regarding the receiver's motives or intent, and ask for an explanation. It is not constructive to assume knowledge of why a person says or does something.
10. Effective feedback is *checked to ensure clear communication*. One way of doing this is to have the receiver paraphrase the feedback, to see if it corresponds to what the evaluator had in mind. No matter what the intent, feedback often is threatening and thus subject to considerable distortion or misinterpretation.

Effective systems, interviews, and feedback will all increase the likelihood of an effective performance appraisal system. This will not eliminate performance problems but, in the best case, an effective performance appraisal system will aid organizations in identifying performance problems and in developing strategies to solve them.

Improving Performance

Improving performance is a process of identifying performance deficiencies or or gaps, understanding their causes, and then developing strategies to remove those deficiencies.

Identifying Performance Gaps

As discussed in the previous chapter, employee job performance is appraised in terms of attributes, behaviours (including absenteeism), and outcomes or goals. Just as these serve to identify performance, they also serve to identify performance gaps. If, for example, an employee had a performance goal of reducing the scrap rate by 10%, but only reduced it by 5%, there is a performance gap. Thus, the discrepancy between actual performance and set goals can be used to spot performance gaps. This method is valid as long as the goals are measurable and are not contradictory.

Another method of identifying performance gaps is by **comparing subordinates, units, or departments with one another**. Organizations with several divisions often measure the overall performance of each division by comparing it with all other divisions. The divisions that are ranked on the bottom are identified as having performance gaps. However, whether ranking individuals or units, identifying performance gaps by comparisons does not provide an effective diagnosis of the *cause* of the performance gaps.

The other method by which gaps can be identified is by **comparisons over time**. For example, a manager who sold 1000 record albums last month but only 800 albums this month appears to have a performance gap, but the clause is not apparent readily. The month in which 1000 albums were sold may have been at the peak of the buying season. The month in which only 800 albums were sold, the employee may have had to attend an important conference vital to longer-run record sales, accounting for the fewer sales.

Determining the Causes of Performance Gaps

Before examining the processes used by managers in determining the causes of performance gaps and deficiencies, it is useful to discuss determinants of employee performance. Exhibit 8.2 illustrates that an employee's behaviour that directly influences performance is complex because it is affected by diverse variables, experiences, and events. The factors that determine behaviour fall into three major categories: (1) individual variables (i.e., abilities and skills, background variables, and demographic variables), (2) psychological variables (i.e., perception, attitudes, personality, learning, and motivation), and (3) organizational variables (i.e., resources available, leadership, reward system, structure, and the job design).

The determinants of behaviour identified in Exhibit 8.2 can lead supervisors to ask specific questions regarding the causes of performance deficiencies:

1. Does the employee have the skills and abilities to perform the job?
2. Does the employee have the adequate resources to perform the job?
3. Is the employee aware of the performance problem?
4. When and/or under what circumstances did the performance problem surface?
5. What is the reaction of the employee's co-workers to the performance problem?

Variables That Influence Behaviour and Performance   *Exhibit 8.2*

Individual variables

Abilities and skills
Mental
Physical

Background
Family
Social class
Experiences

Demographic
Age
Race
Sex

Individual behaviour (e.g., what a person does)

Performance (e.g., desired results)

Organizational variables
Resources
Leadership
Rewards
Structure
Job Design

Psychological variables
Perception
Attitudes
Personality
Learning
Motivation

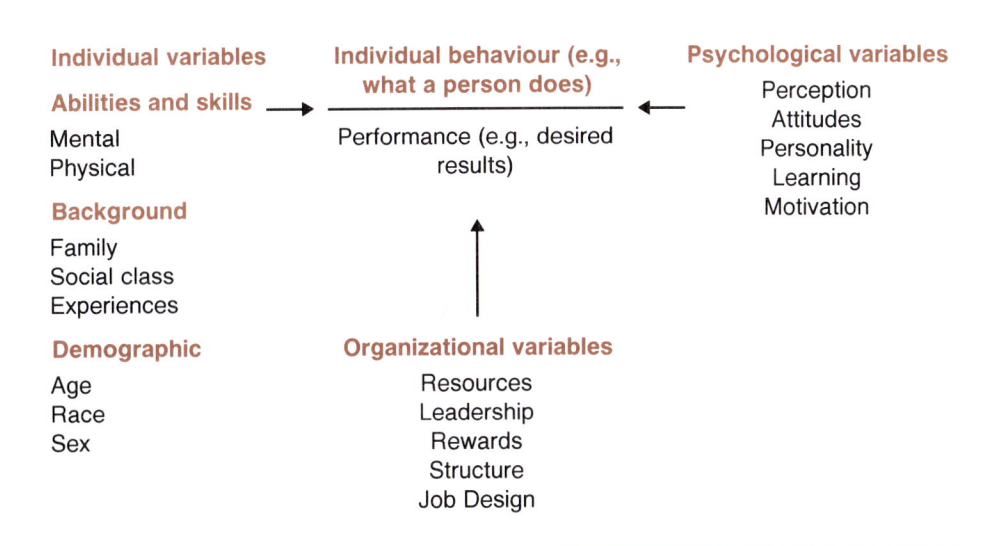

Source: J. L. Gibson, J. M. Ivancevich, and J. M. Donnelly, Jr., *Organizations,* 5th ed., (Plano, TX: BPI, Inc., 1985), p. 56. © 1985 by Business Publications, Inc. Used with permission.

6. What can the manager *do* to help alleviate the performance problem?
7. Does the employee have the right attitudes/motivation to perform on the job?

A more systematic approach by which to analyze performance deficiencies is shown in Exhibit 8.3. Using this approach, the manager can utilize a standard checklist in the process of determining the likely causes for a performance deficiency. The next step is to develop remedial strategies to improve performance.

Strategies to Improve Performance

Strategies to improve performance can be categorized into two groups: those that are implemented to *reduce or control* actual deficiencies, and those that are implemented to *prevent* deficiencies from occurring. Although many strategies are implemented on both bases, they are discussed in only one category.

Positive Behavioural Strategies

If subordinates exhibit job behavioural deficiencies, a positive behavioural strategy may be effective. The positive approach to improvement involves efforts to encourage desirable job behaviours by establishing behavioural criteria and setting up reward systems that are contingent upon desired behaviours.[8] Implementing this strategy requires development of accurate behavioural measures of performance. This can be done by using the critical incident technique to identify critical behaviours of effective and ineffective performance, as described in Chapter 3. If the organization already uses a behaviour-based performance appraisal form, such as BARS or BOS, these can be used instead of the critical incident technique. Use of behavioural criteria should help to eliminate many rating errors, thus improving the validity of the appraisals.

Once these behavioural criteria are established, the subordinates should be made aware of them. Goals then can be established for each behavioural dimension and rewards specified for goal attainment. To obtain maximum benefit from the goal-setting process, the goals should be relatively challenging, specific, clear, and acceptable to the subordinates.

Positive Organizational Strategies

A positive organizational control strategy used specifically to reduce absenteeism is called **earned time**. Earned time is a new approach to the way

---

Exhibit 8.3   *Diagnosing Performance Deficiencies*

Check which of the following factors affecting an individual's performance or behaviour apply to the situation that you are analyzing.

1. **Skills, knowledge, and aptitudes of the individual**   YES   NO
   A. Does the individual have the skills to do as expected?   ____   ____
   B. Has the individual performed previously as expected?   ____   ____

2. **Personality, interests, and preferences of the individual**
   A. Does the individual have the personality or interest to perform as expected?   ____   ____
   B. Does the individual clearly perceive what's actually involved in performing as expected?   ____   ____

3. **Opportunity for the individual**
   A. Does the individual have a chance to grow and use valued skills and abilities?   ____   ____
   B. Does the organization offer career paths to the individual?   ____   ____

4. **Goals for the individual**
   A. Are there goals established?   ____   ____
   B. Are the goals very specific?   ____   ____
   C. Are the goals clear?   ____   ____
   D. Are the goals difficult?   ____   ____

5. **Uncertainty for the individual**
   A. Is the individual certain about what rewards are available?   ____   ____
   B. Is the individual certain about what to do?   ____   ____
   C. Is the individual certain about what others expect?   ____   ____
   D. Is the individual certain about job responsibilities and levels of authority?   ____   ____

paid absence is accumulated and used. Under earned time, employees have more of a choice in the way they use their paid off-time. Thus the responsibility for the use of earned time is their own. Accumulating earned time depends on the preferences of each employee. Rather than dividing benefits into specific numbers of days for vacation and personal leave, sick leave, or short-term disability, earned time lumps these days into one package. These days can be used for any purpose the employee chooses, or the employee can elect to receive a cash payment for them at the time of voluntary termination. Earned time is available for use as soon as it is earned on the job. In effect, earned time is "no-fault absence."[9]

The essence of the program is that the number of earned time days for which an employee may receive time off or a cash payment is less than the previous total of sick, vacation, jury duty, and all other benefit days combined. For example, the previous total combined may be divided by 2, 3, or 4 to get the earned time. And earned time is available for use without the employee having to meet a plethora of special requirements. The program's prime advantages are (1) reduction in unplanned absences; (2) reduction in employee-supervisory conflict over legitimacy of absences and individual responsibility; and (3) flexibility for use of time to suit individual priorities.

Continued   *Exhibit 8.3*

6. **Feedback to the individual**
   A. Does the employee get information about what is right and wrong (quality or quantity) with performance?
   B. Does the information received tell the employee how to improve performance?
   C. Does the employee get information frequently?
   D. Is there a delay between the time the employee performs and receiving information on that performance?
   E. Can the information easily be interpreted by the employee?

7. **Consequences to the individual**
   A. Is it punishing to do as expected (immediate)?
   B. Is it punishing to do as expected (long-term)?
   C. Do more positive consequences result from taking alternative action (immediate)?
   D. Do more positive consequences result from taking alternative action (long-term)?
   E. Are there no apparent consequences of performing as desired?
   F. Are there no positive consequences of performing as desired?

8. **Power for the individual**
   A. Can the individual mobilize resources to get the job done?
   B. Can the individual influence others to get them to do what is needed?
   C. Is the individual highly visible to others higher up in the organization?

Source: R. S. Schuler and S. A. Youngblood, *Effective Personnel Management*, 2nd ed. (St. Paul: West Publishing Co., 1986), p. 273. Used with permission.

Appraising

Negative Behavioural Strategies

Unlike positive behavioural strategies that seek to encourage desirable behaviour patterns through systems of reward, negative strategies seek to discourage unwanted behaviour by punishing it.[10] A negative strategy is commonly utilized in many organizations because of its ability to achieve relatively immediate results. Its negative effects can be reduced by incorporating several "*hot stove principles*" including to

- provide ample and clear warning. Many organizations have clearly defined steps of disciplinary action. For example, the first offence might elicit an oral warning; the second offence a written warning; the third offence, a disciplinary layoff; the fourth offence, discharge;
- administer the discipline as quickly as possible. If a long time elapses between the ineffective behaviour and the negative consequence, the employee may not connect one with the other;
- administer the same discipline for the same behaviour for everyone, every time. Discipline must be administered fairly and consistently; and
- administer the discipline impersonally. Discipline should be based on a specific behaviour, not a specific person.[11]

While disciplinary strategies are the most common and most favoured absence-control techniques among personnel managers, they do have several negative side-effects. Such strategies are stressful for supervisory staff to handle,[12] and extensive use of discipline leads to an increase in expensive, time-consuming grievances.

Because the immediate supervisor or manager plays the major role in administering discipline, to increase its effectiveness the PHRM department and the organization should

- allow managers and supervisors to help select their own employees;
- educate managers and supervisors about the organization's disciplinary policies and train them to administer the policies; and
- set up standards that are equitable to employees and that can easily and consistently be implemented by managers and supervisors.

By taking these steps an organization not only reduces the likely negative effects generally associated with discipline, but also it helps to ensure that employee rights are respected (this is discussed further in Chapter 15). This is further ensured by the establishment of fair work rules, and of work policies that are consistently applied and enforced.

No organization can operate safely and efficiently without work rules and policies. Generally, employers make the rules and policies, supervisors enforce them, and employees follow them. However, employers must ensure that such rules and policies are reasonably related to appropriate management goals, are fair and not discriminatory, and are communicated clearly to employees.

It pays an organization to be consistent in the enforcement of its rules and policies. It also pays an organization to provide other strategies to reduce undesirable behaviours that influence job performance and absenteeism.

Employee Assistance Programs

Employee assistance programs (EAPs) are designed specifically to assist employees with chronic personal problems that might hinder their job performance and attendance. Such programs often are used with employees who are alcoholics, have drug dependency problems, suffer from stress-related illnesses, or have severe domestic problems. Since these problems may be caused in part by the job, many Canadian employers are taking the lead in establishing employee assistance programs.

In Canada, employee assistance programs seem to be of even greater need than in other countries, given the alarming statistics on the consumption and impact of alcohol on Canadians. It has been estimated that 3.5% to 7% of the active workforce, amounting to between 350 000 and 700 000 of Canada's 10 000 000 employed individuals, experience *severe* alcohol-related problems. These contribute to lower productivity, absenteeism, lowered worker morale, and accidents at work, and have been estimated to cost Canadian industry about $21 million dollars per day.[13] The Gallup International Research Institute provided even more alarming figures, by finding Canadians to be among the "world leaders" in alcohol consumption. The survey indicated that 77% of the adult Canadian population consume alcohol, 26% of whom consume a great quantity, and 17% a moderate amount.[14] The impact of alcohol intake is estimated to exacerbate child abuse, marital disruption, social aggression, and violent crimes.[15]

A variety of employee assistance programs have been developed by Canadian organizations to directly assist the employee in dealing with personal problems. Some of the approaches developed include:

- In-house programs in which the company provides its own staff of professionals
- Public service agency programs (e.g., Addiction Research Foundation, Canadian Mental Health Association, Family Service Association)
- Consortium programs, in which several companies join together to provide the necessary professional assistance
- Employee Recovery Programs developed by the Canadian Labour Congress. These programs train union members as facilitators in linking the troubled employee with the appropriate community resource
- Programs developed through the services of management consultants.[16]

Each approach has its own merits, and each is effective in different situations and at different companies.

However, many of the employees who need such assistance programs fail to utilize them unless they are confronted with the alternative of being fired. The success rate of those who do attend such programs, however, is high, and the results often are substantial gains in employee job performance and reductions in absenteeism. Success has been reported by many

Appraising

Canadian organizations such as the Royal Bank of Canada (Access Program), and the federal government. Of particular interest are the results reported for Project HELP, an employee assistance program of the Canadian Mental Health Association. In the case of Warner-Lambert Canada Ltd., it has been estimated that the company has saved about $200 000 as a result of its employee assistance program. This company also reported that 80% of the savings were due to a reduction in absenteeism,[17] with the other 20% divided between group insurance savings and reduced time loss due to accidents.[18] In another example, Eldorado Resources Ltd. (1334 employees) was able to cut its absenteeism rate nearly in half, and increased its employee assistance program user rate to 17% from an initial 2.6%.[19]

Finally, a national committee of the Canadian Mental Health Association has researched and developed ideas and potential plans for a mental health in the workplace program, with an agenda for the 1980s. The report indicates that, although stress is normal in the workplace and in everyday living, stress may be heightened by changes in working conditions, advancements in technology, and accelerated changes in society in general. The report also suggests that 15 to 30% of the workforce is believed to be seriously handicapped by emotional problems at any time, and that such problems cost employers money in a variety of areas, both direct and indirect costs. The report points out that the workplace is the ideal medium to reach the highest concentration of people and provide them with mental health education programs and programs for early intervention in emotional problems. It is the latter that an employee assistance program addresses.[20]

Counselling

To change the habits of chronically absent employees, some companies have devised a counselling program that stresses problem-solving and goal-setting techniques. This approach focuses on the estimated 5 to 10% of the workforce that has a history of absenteeism. Before beginning the actual counselling with individual employees, supervisors take the following steps:

- Identify the consistently worst offenders. Make a list of all employees who have a record of repeated absences, regardless of the presumed legitimacy or the underlying reasons for missing work
- Centralize the absenteeism data. Records and information should be accumulated, analyzed, and maintained in one central location
- Collect long-term data. Absenteeism records on individuals should be kept for a sufficiently long period to show that a clear pattern exists

Once the decision is made to meet with an employee, supervisors should do the following:

- Examine the attendance record with the employee
- Be sure that the employee is aware of the severity of the problem, as well as the organization's attendance standards

- Prepare a brief, accurate memo at the session's end outlining the problem, noting the reasons given by the employee, and specifying whether or not the employee responded with a desire to improve.

If the first session has not produced a significant change, a second counselling session should be scheduled. Participants in this session should include the employee, the employee's supervisor, a union representative (if applicable), and higher management officials. An upper-level manager should be present to ensure that due process protection (Chapter 15) is provided for the employee. Results of the second counselling session should be documented.

If the employee shows no improvement after the second session, another session can be held, which also should include a high-level manager. At this stage it should be made clear that the responsibility for meeting the expected standard of attendance, and thereby continuing employment, rests on the employee. The employee should be allowed to take a day off with pay in order to decide whether he or she wishes to resign or to commit to a long-term program of positive improvement. If there is no sign of improvement after this step, it may be necessary to discharge the employee.

Whether employee counselling is an appropriate remedy depends on an analysis of the behavioural determinants, as shown in Exhibit 8.3. This is also true for the other strategies. For example, if the undesirable performance is caused by a lack of positive consequences for desirable behaviours, supervisor praise, organizational recognition, or monetary compensation attached to these behaviours may produce better results than counselling. If employees are not performing well due to a lack of information about their progress, increased feedback or the establishment of goals may be appropriate.

The effectiveness of programs designed to improve performance can be assessed by determining the costs of the program, the cost of the current performance gap, and the extent to which it can be reduced by the program (its benefits). In general, this method also is useful for assessing the entire performance appraisal system.

Assessing Performance Appraisal Systems

The purposes of performance appraisal are both evaluative and developmental. That is, appraisal information is used as input for making evaluation decisions on such functions as

- salary increases or decreases;
- demotions;
- layoffs;
- promotions/transfers; and
- terminations.

Appraisal information also is used as input for developmental purposes including

- spotting training needs;
- motivating employees to improve;
- providing feedback;
- counselling of employees; and
- spotting performance deficiencies.

Although all organizations may not desire to use performance appraisal to serve both of these purposes, all should be concerned with the legal requirements that must be met. When performance appraisal is used to serve evaluation and development purposes and to meet the legal requirements, it is affecting the three organizational human resource goals: productivity, quality of work life, and legal compliance. Assuming that organizations want to serve these three purposes, how can they assess how well their performance appraisal systems are doing?

Overall Performance Appraisal System Assessment

Before assessing specific aspects of an organization's performance appraisal system, it may be useful to perform an overall assessment. An overall assessment suggests quickly how well the system is operating and may provide an added stimulus for a more specific assessment.[21]

Personnel and human resource managers could ask members of the organizations, both managers and non-managers, about specific aspects of the performance appraisal system, but this would be very time-consuming. An alternative is for the members of the organization, both supervisors and subordinates, to respond to a questionnaire such as the one shown in Exhibit 8.4. As indicated in the scoring of the questionnaire, there are the sub-categories (A + B + C) that sum to form an overall assessment score of the system. The three sub-categories correspond to the major purposes of appraisal, with categories A and B assessing the developmental purpose and category C assessing the evaluation purpose. The assessment of the evaluation purpose includes administrative features of appraisal, that is, whether performance appraisal records are maintained and how accessible they are. These features also facilitate the developmental purpose of performance appraisal.

By using this overall performance appraisal assessment questionnaire, the organization can determine how effective, in general, its system is. Scores of nine or ten in each sub-category suggest that the system serves its purpose well, while scores of four to eight suggest average service, and scores of two or three suggest it does not serve its purpose well. Totalling the scores of the three sub-categories results in an overall assessment of how well the purposes of appraisal are being met. Scores of 26 to 30 suggest quite well, scores of 21 to 25, good, 11 to 20, average, and less than 11, quite poorly. Because of the breakdown of the form, scores that indicate there is room for improvement (e.g., average scores or less) also highlight specific areas that should be assessed in depth.

Organizational Performance Appraisal Questionnaire Evaluation

Exhibit 8.4

Instructions

Respond to the following six statements by indicating the extent to which you agree (or disagree) that the statements accurately describe performance appraisal in your organization. Some statements refer to your experiences in appraising your subordinates' performance, others refer to your experiences in being appraised yourself. Try to reflect as accurately as you can the current conditions in your organization, based on your experiences.

SA = Strongly Agree	**A** = Agree	**?** = Neither Agree nor Disagree	**D** = Disagree
		SD = Strongly Disagree	

1. I have found my boss's appraisals to be very helpful in guiding my own career development progress.   SA A ? D SD
2. The appraisal system we have here is of no use to me in my efforts toward developing my subordinates to the fullest extent of their capabilities.   SA A ? D SD
3. Our performance appraisal system generally leaves me even more uncertain about where I stand after my appraisal than before.   SA A ? D SD
4. The appraisal system we use is very useful in helping me to clearly communicate to my subordinates exactly where they stand.   SA A ? D SD
5. When higher levels of management are making major decisions about management positions and promotions, they have access to and make use of performance appraisal records.   SA A ? D SD
6. In making pay, promotion, transfer, and other administrative personnel decisions, I am not able to obtain past performance appraisal records that could help me to make good decisions.   SA A ? D SD

Scoring

Use the following grid to determine point scores for each item by transferring your responses onto the grid. Place the number in the box at the bottom of each column, then add pairs of columns as indicated.

		Statement Number					
		1	2	3	4	5	6
Response	SA	5	1	1	5	5	1
	A	4	2	2	4	4	2
	?	3	3	3	3	3	3
	D	2	4	4	2	2	4
	SD	1	5	5	1	1	5

□ + □ → A   □ + □ → B   □ + □ → C

A + B + C = □

Source: Copyright © 1981 by M. Sashkin. All rights reserved. Used by special permission. See also M. Sashkin, *Assessing Performance Appraisal* (San Diego: University Associates, 1981).

Specific Performance Appraisal System Assessment

The specific assessment of an organization's performance appraisal system requires the examination of several aspects of the entire system. Answers to the following questions can provide an assessment of the specific components:

- What purposes does the organization want its performance appraisal system to serve?
- Do the appraisal forms effectively elicit the information needed to serve these purposes? Are these forms compatible with the jobs for which they are being used, that is, are they job-related? Are the forms based on behaviours or outcomes that might be included in a critical incident?
- Are the appraisal forms designed to minimize errors and ensure consistency?
- Are the processes of the appraisal effective? For example, are the appraisal interviews done effectively? Are goals established? Are they developed jointly? Do superiors and subordinates accept the appraisal process?
- Are superiors relatively free from task interference in doing performance appraisal?
- Are the appraisals being implemented correctly? What procedures have been set up to ensure that the appraisals are being done correctly? What supporting materials are available to aid superiors in appraising their subordinates?
- Do methods exist for reviewing and evaluating the effectiveness of the total system? Are there goals and objectives for the system? Are there systematic procedures for gathering data to measure how well the goals and objectives are being met?

By addressing these questions and taking corrective action where necessary, an organization's performance appraisal system is more likely to serve its purposes and the broader organizational human resource goals of productivity, quality of work life, and legal compliance. An organization just beginning to design an appraisal system should incorporate the information produced by answering these questions into the initial design and implementation of its system.

Summary

Appraising performance is a critical PHRM activity because its results can be used for several evaluational and developmental decisions and actions. In this chapter, two critical components of utilizing the performance appraisal data were discussed: feeding back the data to the subordinate via the performance appraisal interview, and spotting performance deficiencies and developing strategies for improvement.

It was suggested that in providing effective feedback to subordinates, superiors should use the appropriate and specific performance data, that the purposes of evaluation and development should be served separately, that current and potential performance appraisal discussions should be separated, and that there should be upward appraisals. The effectiveness of the performance appraisal interview session in providing feedback also can be enhanced if the performance appraisals are conducted in a legally defensible way. To do this, the organization and the PHRM department must conduct evaluations of all employees, using only objective judgements whenever possible and letting subordinates review their performance appraisals and records.

Programs for identifying and correcting performance deficiencies were identified. Such programs begin with a determination of the causes of the performance deficiencies. When these deficiencies are traced to employee motivation rather than ability, several programs designed either to control or prevent these behaviours can be developed and implemented.

The assessment of the entire performance appraisal system and specific components of it can increase its effectiveness. Such assessments are necessary to help determine how well the evaluational and developmental purposes are being attained, and if the legal considerations are being observed. On the basis of such assessments, revisions in current appraisal methods can be made and more effective strategies for improving performance can be developed and implemented. Once done, an organization has a much better basis on which to make other PHRM decisions, particularly those associated with compensation and training and development, topics that are addressed in the later chapters.

Discussion Questions

1. What is involved in the utilization of performance appraisal?
2. What kinds of conflict emerge when assessing performance?
3. What considerations are there in designing an effective performance appraisal system?
4. Identify and discuss several different types of interviews used in performance appraisal.
5. What characteristics of the interview are likely to enhance and facilitate the effectiveness of performance appraisal?
6. What characteristics of feedback and goals inhibit acceptable levels of individual performance?
7. To what causes are performance deficiencies associated, and what are the respective strategies used to correct those performance deficits?
8. What information is critical in determining how to improve employee performance?
9. What are the critical issues in determining the utility of a specific performance appraisal system?

CASE STUDY

The Pain of Performance Appraisal

Joe Swersky sat at his desk looking over the performance appraisal form he had just completed on Bill Cox, one of his insurance underwriters. Bill was on his way to Joe's office for their annual review session. Joe dreaded these appraisal meetings, even when he did not have to confront the employees with negative feedback.

Two years earlier, Essex Insurance Company, which had experienced very rapid growth, had decided to implement a formal appraisal system. All supervisors had been presented with the new appraisal form, which included five different subcategories in addition to an overall rating. Supervisors were asked to rate employees on each dimension, using a scale from 1 (unacceptable) to 5 (exceptional). They also were advised to maintain a file on each employee into which they could drop notes on specific incidents of good or poor performance during the year to use as "documentation" when completing the appraisal form. They were told they could give an overall rating of 1 or 5 only if they had substantial documentation to back it up.

Joe had never given one of these ratings because he was not diligent about recording specific incidents for each employee. He believed it was just too time-consuming to write up all of the documentation necessary to justify such a rating. There were several employees in his department who deserved a 5 rating in Joe's opinion, but so far no one had complained about not receiving one.

Bill was one of Joe's "exceptional" workers. Joe had three or four specific examples of exceptional performance in Bill's file, but looking over the form could not clearly identify the category in which they belonged. "Oh, well," Joe said to himself, "I'll just give him 3 and 4 ratings. I don't have to justify those, and Bill has never complained before."

One of the categories was "Analyzing Work Materials." Joe had never understood what that meant or whether it was relevant to the job of insurance underwriter. He had checked 3 (satisfactory) for Bill, as he did on all of the evaluations he did. He understood the meaning of the other categories—Quality of Work, Quantity of Work, Improving Work Methods, and Relationships with Co-workers—although he was confused as to what a 3 or a 4 indicated about each category.

Bill knocked on Joe's door and came in. Joe looked up and smiled. "Hi, Bill. Sit down. Let's get through this thing so we can get back to work, OK?"

Case Questions

1. What problems do you see with the appraisal system Joe is using?
2. What are Bill's likely reactions to being told by Joe that he scored only 3 and 4 ratings even though he is one of Joe's exceptional workers?
3. What suggestions do you have for improving the performance appraisal system?
4. What suggestions do you have for improving Joe?

Endnotes

1. For an extensive discussion of individual and organizational goals and their inherent conflicts see L. W. Porter, E. E. Lawler III, and J. R. Hackman, *Behavior in Organizations* (New York: McGraw-Hill, 1975), S. L. Dolan and A. Arsenault, "Stress, Santé et Rendement au Travail," Monograph No. 5., School of Industrial Relations, University of Montreal, 1980; and S. L. Dolan and D. Balkin, "A Contingency Model of Occupational Stress," *International Journal of Management*, September 1987.

2. For a discussion of the vanishing performance appraisal and other career issues, see D. T. Hall, *Careers in Organizations* (Glenview, IL: Scott, Foresman & Company, 1976).

3. H. H. Meyer, E. Kay, and J. R. P. French, Jr., "Split Roles in Performance Appraisal," *Harvard Business Review*, Jan.–Feb. 1965, p. 125.

4. R. S. Schuler, "Taking the Pain Out of the Performance Appraisal Interview," *Supervisory Management*, Aug. 1981, pp. 8–13. "Training Managers to

Rate Their Employers," *Business Week*, March 17, 1980, pp. 178–179. K. N. Wexley, "Performance Appraisal and Feedback," in S. Kerr (ed.), *Organizational Behavior* (Columbus, OH: Grid, 1979), pp. 241–262. C. Cammon, D. A. Nadler, and P. H. Mirvis, *The Ongoing Feedback System: A Tool for Improving Organizational Management* (Ann Arbor, MI: Survey Research Center, University of Michigan, 1975). K. S. Teel, "Performance Appraisals: Current Trends, Persistent Progress," *Personnel Journal*, April 1980, pp. 296–301, 316. R. R. Catalenello and John A. Hooper, "Managerial Appraisal," *Personnel Administrator*, Sept. 1981, pp. 75–81.

5. For further information, see N. R. F. Maier, *The Appraisal Interview* (New York: Wiley, 1958). G. P. Latham and K. N. Wexley, *Increasing Productivity Through Performance Appraisal* (Reading, MA: Addison-Wesley, 1981), pp. 152–54. S. J. Carroll and C. E. Schneier, *Performance Appraisal and Review Systems* (Glenview, IL: Scott, Foresman & Company, 1982), pp. 160–189.

6. Latham and Wexley, endnote 5, pp. 154–155.

7. M. Beer, "Performance Appraisal: Dilemmas and Possibilities," *Organizational Dynamics*, Winter 1981, 26, pp. 34–35.

8. L. S. Mosher, "Preventing Poor Past Practices from Becoming Future Policies," *Personnel Administrator*, March 1978, pp. 19–20. W. R. Flynn and W. F. Stratton, "Managing Problem Employees," *Human Resource Management*, Summer 1981, p. 31. D. A. Nadler and E. E. Lawler III, "Motivation—A Diagnostic Approach," in J. R. Hackman, E. E. Lawler III, and L. W. Porter (eds.), *Perspectives on Behavior in Organizations* (New York: McGraw-Hill Book Co., 1977). M. C. Meyer, "Demotivation—Its Cause and Cure," *Personnel Journal*, May 1978, pp. 260–266.

9. R. J. Bula, "Absenteeism Control," *Personnel Journal*, June 1984, pp. 57–60. G. Johns, "Understanding and Managing Absence from Work," in S. L. Dolan and R. S. Schuler, *Canadian Readings in Personnel and Human Resource Management* (St. Paul: West Publishing Co., 1987).

10. J. E. Belohlav and Paul O. Papp, "Making Employee Discipline Work," *Personnel Administrator*, March 1978, pp. 22–24. H. Behrend, "Absence Problems—Are Attendance Bonus Schemes the Answer?" *Management Decisions*, vol. 18, no. 4, 1979, pp. 212–216. F. E. Kuzmits, "No Fault: A New Strategy for Absenteeism Control," *Personnel Journal*, May 1981, pp. 387–390. J. M. McDonald, "What is Your Absenteeism I.Q.?" *Personnel*, May–June 1980, pp. 33–37.

11. For an excellent discussion of the application of discipline in organizations, see R. D. Arvey and J. M. Ivancevich, "Punishment in Organizations: A Review, Propositions and Research Suggestions," *Academy of Management Review*, 1980, 5, pp. 123–132. W. C. Hamner and D. W. Organ, *Organizational Behavior: An Applied Psychological Approach* (Dallas, TX: Business Publications, Inc., 1978) pp. 73–88. R. J. Hart, "Crime and Punishment in the Army," *Journal of Personality and Social Psychology*, 36, 1978, pp. 1456–1471. J. P. Muczyk, E. B. Schwartz, and E. P. Smith, *First and Second Level Supervision* (Indianapolis: Bobbs-Merrill, 1980). H. P. Sims, Jr., "Further Thought on Punishment in Organizations," *Academy of Management Review*, 5, 1980, pp. 133–138. R. J. House and M. L. Baetz, "Leadership: Some Empirical Generalizations and New Research Directions," in B. Staw (ed.), *Research in Organizational Behavior*, vol. 2 (Greenwich, CT: JAI Press, 1980). G. R. Oldham, "The Motivational Strategies Used by Supervisors: Relationships to Effectiveness Indicators," *Organizational Behavior and Human Performance*, 15, 1976, pp. 66–86. Additional considerations in dealing with performance problems are presented in Chapter 15 on employee rights, particularly the use of termination as a way of correcting performance gaps.

12. G. Johns, "Did You Go to Work Today?" *Montréal Business Report*, 4th quarter, 1980, pp. 52–56; G. Johns, "Understanding and Managing Absence from Work," in Dolan and Schuler (eds.), endnote 9, 1987.

13. "Special Report on Alcohol Statistics," Minister of National Health and Welfare and the Minister of Supply and Services Canada, 1981, p. 22.

14. Source: La Presse, August 2, 1985, p. A4.

15. "Special Report on Alcohol Statistics," Minister of National Health and Welfare and the Minister of Supply and Services Canada, 1981, p. 22.

16. D. Wheeler, "Employee Assistance Programs" in *Human Resources Management in Canada* (Prentice-Hall Canada Inc., 1983), pp. 5093–5097.

17. Ibid., pp. 5094–5095.

18. "Project HELP," Canadian Mental Health Association, Metropolitan Toronto Branch, Toronto, 1983.

19. B. Conway, "Employee Assistance at Eldorado," in *Human Resources Management in Canada* (Prentice-Hall Canada Inc., August 1983), pp. 5085–5091.

20. Canadian Mental Health Association, "Mental Health and the Workplace—An Agenda for the 1980's," Canadian Mental Health Association, National Office, Toronto, 1983. For more information about stress, absenteeism, and performance, see A. Arsenault and S. L. Dolan, "The Role of Personality, Occupation and Organization in Understanding the Relationship between Job Stress, Performance and Absenteeism," *Journal of Occupational Psychology*, 1983, vol. 50, pp. 227–240.

21. M. Sashkin, "Appraising Appraisal: Ten Lessons from Research for Practice," *Organizational Dynamics*, Winter 1981, pp. 37–50.

SECTION V
Compensating

CHAPTER 9
Total Compensation

CHAPTER 10
Performance-based Pay and Administration

CHAPTER 11
Benefits Pay and Administration

CHAPTER

9

Total Compensation

PHRM in the News

Total Compensation
Purposes and Importance of Total Compensation
Relationships of Total Compensation

Environmental Impact on Total Compensation
Legal Considerations in Total Compensation
Unions
The Market

Basic Wage Issues
Job Evaluation
Common Discriminatory Aspects in Job-Evaluation Methods
Determining Job Classes
Establishing the Pay Structure
Individual Wage Determination

Contemporary Issues in Wage and Salary Administration
Participation Policies
Pay Secrecy
Satisfaction with Pay
All-Salaried Workforce

Assessing Total Compensation

Summary

Discussion Questions

Case Study

Endnotes

PHRM in the News

Productivity Outpaces Hourly Wages

Productivity, a major concern of economists and international investors, rose more than did hourly compensation levels in Canada, Japan, and West Germany in 1984, according to a report released by the United States Department of Labor last week.

As a result, unit labor costs fell in these three countries while they remained virtually unchanged in the United States. Unit costs rose by about 2% in Denmark and about 4% to 5% in France, Italy, Norway, Sweden, and the United Kingdom.

This reflected a relatively small increase of less than 4% in hourly compensation levels for Canada, the U.S., Japan, and Sweden, 6% to 9% in Denmark, France, Norway, and the U.K., 10% in Italy, and 12% in Sweden. In fact, Canada had the smallest increase of all countries measured, and that increase was well below that of the previous year. In all countries except Sweden, hourly compensation rose less than the average trend since 1973.

However, when measured in U.S. dollars rather than national currencies, unit labor costs fell significantly in all countries except Japan. The U.S. dollar remained unchanged relative to the Japanese yen, but appreciated by about 5% against the Canadian dollar and by 7% to about 13% against the European currencies.

Source: "Productivity Outpaces Hourly Wages," *Financial Times of Canada*, June 17, 1985, p. 18. Reprinted with permission of Financial Times of Canada.

Business Must Lobby to Stop Equal-pay Laws

WINNIPEG (CP)—The business community has to prevent pay equity legislation from going ahead or soon it may have to pay women as much as men for doing comparable jobs, a U.S. lawyer said yesterday.

"Unless the business community is willing to actively participate in the comparable-worth debate, we might be looking at this epitaph in the not-so-distant future: 'Gee, it was such a far-out idea, I never thought it would get this far'," Washington lawyer John Tysse said.

Mr. Tysse made the comments before 160 members of the Winnipeg Chamber of Commerce, two weeks after the Manitoba New Democratic Party Government introduced legislation that requires women to be paid as much as men doing comparable jobs.

Manitoba is the first province to bring forward such legislation.

Mr. Tysse, a former director of labor law for the U.S. Chamber of Commerce, said it has been proven that in areas of the United States where the business community has not voiced opposition, similar legislation has gone forward.

Mr. Tysse also said that pay equity will hurt those it is intended to help—those in female-dominated, lower-paying jobs.

Putting comparable-worth legislation into effect would reduce the incentive of women to be integrated into the workplace, Mr. Tysse said.

"Ask yourself how comparable worth would help a secretary whose job is eliminated because her employer cannot afford to absorb pay increases without productivity increases," he said.

Source: "Business Must Lobby to Stop Equal-Pay Laws," *The Globe and Mail*, July 1985, p. 4. Reprinted with permission of The Canadian Press.

Minimum Wage Law No Help to Unskilled

VANCOUVER—Terry Segarty, British Columbia's Minister of Labour, has a problem, and is resolved to do something about it in the fall.

British Columbia has the lowest minimum wage rate in the country—$3.65 per hour—and tremendous pressure has been placed on him to raise it at least to $4 per hour, the average level obtaining in the other nine provinces.

At first blush, this would seem like a good idea, even one that is long overdue. If, as its name implies, the minimum wage law can boost wages up to whatever level is prescribed, that is to say set a floor under incomes for the poor, then why not?

But a moment's reflection will show that this is a mirage. For example, if prohibiting compensation below some arbitrarily determined level can really enhance salaries, why stop at the paltry, mean, and niggardly $4 level? Why not go for, say, $40 per hour, or even better yet, really reach for the stars and demand that no employee be paid less than $400 per hour?

The answer is obvious. To mandate that a skilled craftsman with a productivity level of $25 be paid $400 is to invite disaster. Any employer who complied would rack up $375 per hour in red ink. Even at the more modest $40 per hour, any such firm would still lose $15 per hour—and thus be forced into eventual bankruptcy.

No, the reason wages are as high as they are has nothing whatever to do with legal compulsion. It is because productivity is relatively great in this country and because salaries tend to be equal to productivity levels, that we enjoy our relative prosperity.

True, a minimum wage level of $4 would not threaten the livelihood of the person who can produce $25-worth of goods and services per hour, but it certainly can put at risk the jobs of people with lesser skills. For example, the employment of a person who can only create goods valued by the market at $3.25 per hour, would be obliterated by a minimum wage level of $4 per hour.

How can we test the economic principle that high minimum wage levels lead to relatively increased unemployment rates for unskilled workers? One way is to calculate the unemployment rates of youthful Canadians as a percentage of those of the more highly productive adult employees, and compare them with the minimum wage levels in each of the provinces. (For our table, we choose workers between 20 and 24 as our control because this is the youngest group subject to the "adult" minimum wage law.)

The results are painfully obvious. Manitoba, with the highest minimum wage level ($4.30) has an unemployment rate for its young workers that is 1.9 times as high as that for the rest of the population. Saskatchewan, with the next greatest level ($4.25) weighs in with the second biggest relative unemployment rate for youth—1.6 times as high as the rest of the population. And at the bottom of the pack in terms of the disenfranchisement of their young people, come British Columbia and Alberta with two of the country's lowest minimum wage levels.

Are you listening, Mr. Segarty?

Source: W. Block, "Minimum Wage Law No Help to Unskilled," *The Financial Post*, August 17, 1985, p. 9. Used with permission of *The Financial Post* and the author. (Mr. Block is senior economist of the Frazer Institute).

These "PHRM in the News" articles highlight several significant and timely issues about total compensation in Canadian companies. The first point is the important relation of salary and wage cost to productivity, and the competitiveness of Canadian companies in this respect with companies in other nations. Canadian wage costs are among the highest in the world today. Equally important are the legal considerations affecting total compensation, particularly regarding pay for different jobs. Federal equal-value laws have been in force for several years and similar laws have been enacted in Québec and in Manitoba, and now other provinces are considering the passage of these laws in their constituencies. Some suggest that a comparable-worth law might be counter-productive to the employees it is supposed to help. The second "PHRM in the News" item summarizes this view.

The third article raises another important point about total compensation: what are the effects of minimum wage laws on unskilled labour? The evidence suggests that although the legislative policies are well intentioned, they may reduce opportunities for employment.

This chapter discusses a number of issues critical to the concept of total compensation. More specifically, the chapter addresses itself to the following topics:

1. How wage and salary levels for jobs are determined
2. The different methods used to establish job worth and conduct job evaluation
3. Some of the most pertinent issues in salary administration, including market surveys, equity issues, and pay secrecy
4. The legal considerations related to total compensation

Total Compensation

Total compensation is the activity by which organizations evaluate the contributions of employees in order to distribute direct and indirect monetary and non-monetary rewards within legal regulations and the organization's ability to pay.[1]

As Exhibit 9.1 indicates, there are two categories of **direct compensation** (rewards)—the *basic wage* and *performance-based pay*—and three categories of **indirect compensation** (rewards)—*protection programs, pay for time not worked*, and *employee services and perquisites*.[2] The basic wage is discussed in this chapter and performance-based pay is discussed in the next chapter. Indirect compensation is covered in Chapter 11.

Purposes and Importance of Total Compensation

Total compensation is important because it serves to

- *attract potential job applicants:* The total compensation program can help

Components of Total Compensation   Exhibit 9.1

```
                         Total compensation
                         /               \
        Intrinsic rewards              Extrinsic rewards
          (job factors)                   (monetary)
                                         /           \
                           Indirect compensation    Direct compensation
                          /        |        \         /          \
                Protection    Pay for time   Employee services   Basic wage   Performance-
                 programs     not worked     and perquisites                   based pay
```

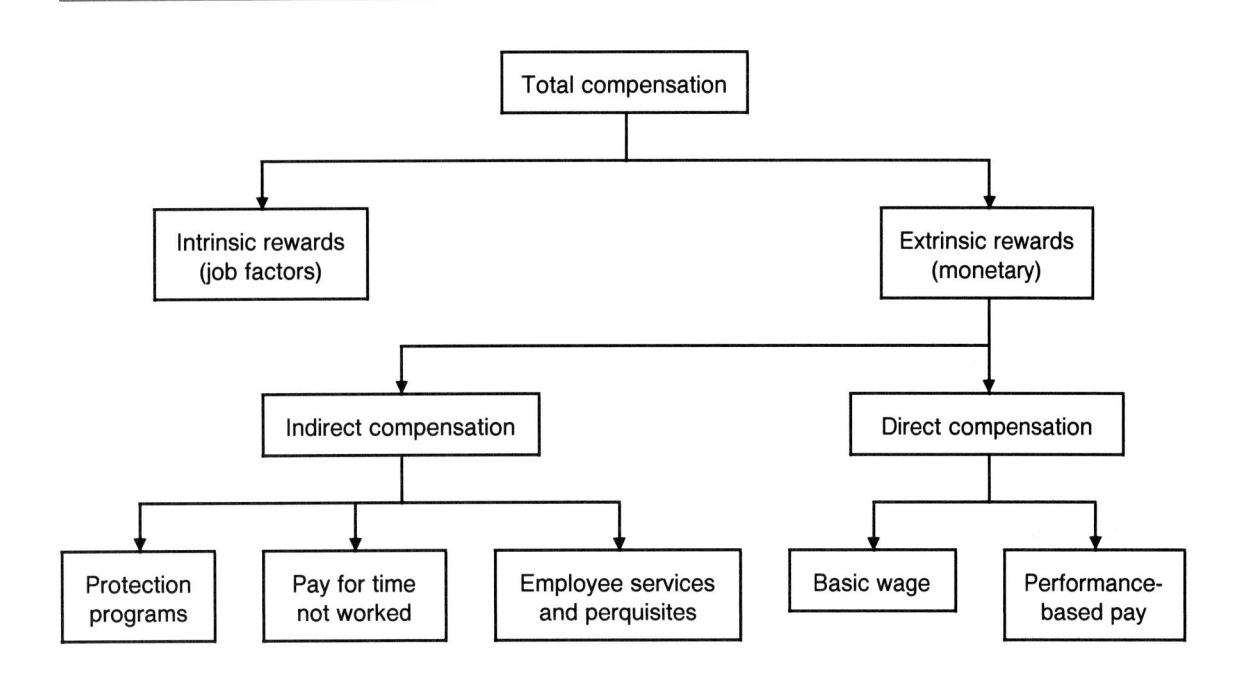

Source: Adapted from J. F. Sullivan, "Indirect Compensation: The Years Ahead," © 1972 by the Regents of the University of California. From *California Management Review*, vol. XV, no. 2, p. 65, table 1, by permission of the Regents.

to assure that pay is sufficient to attract the right people at the right time for the right jobs;

- *retain good employees:* Unless the total compensation program is perceived as internally equitable and externally competitive, good employees are likely to leave;
- *motivate employees:* Total compensation can help to produce a motivated workforce by tying rewards to performance, that is, by providing incentives for productivity;
- *administer pay within legal regulations:* Because several legal regulations are relevant to total compensation, organizations must be aware of them and avoid violating them in their pay programs; and
- *facilitate organizational strategic objectives and control labour costs:* To create a rewarding and supportive climate and to attract the best applicants, an organization can design an attractive total compensation package. As a result, organizational objectives such as rapid growth, survival, or innovation can more readily be achieved.[3] Total compensation policy also can aid the organization in estimating and controlling its labour costs.

Although serving these purposes is important, effective and attractive total compensation is costly. Approximately 50% of an organization's costs are those of compensation. Furthermore, an ever-growing percentage of these compensation costs is being spent on indirect rather than direct compensation.[4] In addition, failure to abide by the legal regulations can be very costly for an organization.

The ability that compensation has to attract, retain, and motivate individuals is related to the importance people place on money. Because compensation, in both direct and indirect forms, has the potential to satisfy the many various needs of different individuals, it can take on varying degrees of importance.

However, employees often are willing to join an organization and to perform in it for reasons other than just the money. Some of the non-monetary rewards an organization can provide are job status and prestige, job security, safety, job responsibility, and variety. As shown in Exhibit 9.2, these are all status symbols, social rewards, or task-self rewards. Although these rewards can be critical, all three chapters on compensation primarily discuss monetary rewards, direct and indirect, that usually are regarded as the major part of compensation in most organizations.

Relationships of Total Compensation

Total compensation, being one of the most important PHRM activities to individuals as well as organizations, has an extensive set of relationships with other PHRM activities. It relies extensively on certain PHRM activities (e.g., job analysis and performance appraisal for input in determining total compensation), and it influences other PHRM activities, such as recruitment, selection, union-management relations, and human resource planning.

Recruitment and Selection. Employees differ in the value they attribute to pay. If PHRM departments can determine how important pay is to individuals, they can recruit people to fill specific jobs with specific pay policy options. It appears that in order to attract and retain even the best applicants, maximum pay levels (i.e., the most competitive) need not be offered. Individuals make job-choice decisions on the basis of several factors, including the location of the organization, its reputation as a place to work, what friends think of the company, as well as the nature of the job and the pay level offered. Consequently, rather than taking the job that pays the most, individuals often take the job that satisfies as many of these factors as possible.[5]

Union-Management Relations. Wage levels and individual wage determinations can be influenced greatly by the existence of a union. A union's influence includes not only wage gains but also wage concessions. A union also can play an important role in the job evaluation process and may determine the type of pay plan an organization will have. Extensive discussion of this is provided in Chapter 17.

Organizational Rewards

Exhibit 9.2

Monetary Rewards, Including Fringe Benefits		Status Symbols	Social Rewards	From the Task—Self Rewards
Pay	Theatre and sports tickets	Office size and location	Friendly greetings	Interesting work
Pay raise	Recreation facilities		Informal recognition	Sense of achievement
Stock options	Reserved company parking	Office with window	Praise	Job of more importance
Profit sharing			Smile	
Bonus plans	Work breaks		Evaluative feedback	Job variety
Christmas bonus	Sabbatical leaves	Carpeting		Job-performance feedback
Provision and use of company facilities	Club memberships and privileges	Drapes	Compliments	Self-recognition
		Paintings	Non-verbal signals	
Deferred compensation, including other tax shelters	Discount purchase privileges	Watches	Pat on the back	Self-praise
		Rings	Invitations to coffee/lunch	Opportunities to schedule own work
	Personal loans at favourable rates	Formal awards/ recognition	After-hours social gatherings	
Pay and time-off for attending work-related training programs and seminars	Free legal advice			Working hours
	Free personal financial planning advice	Wall plaque		Participation in new organizational ventures
Medical plan, including free physical examinations	Free home protection—theft insurance			Choice of geographical location
	Burglar alarms and personal protection			Autonomy in job
Company auto	Moving expenses			
Pension contributions	Home purchase assistance			
Product discount plans				
Vacation trips				

Source: P. M. Podsakoff, C. N. Greene, and J. M. McFillen, "Obstacles to the Effective Use of Reward Systems," in R. S. Schuler and S. A. Youngblood (eds.), *Readings in Personnel and Human Resource Management,* 2nd ed. (St. Paul: West Publishing Co., 1984).

Human Resource Planning. Compensation also can be integral to the organization's strategic planning. A manufacturer of a line of technology-based products developed a strategic vision of itself as a leader in new technologies. Since accomplishing this could have disrupted the current business (located in Ontario), the company decided to acquire small entrepreneurial companies in British Columbia. The parent company quickly realized that these smaller companies required different management styles and a different pay system. Therefore, managers' base salary in these small companies was set significantly lower than those in the parent company, but the potential size of their annual bonus is four times greater![6]

Job Analysis. Compensation also is integrally related to job analysis. The job evaluation process that determines the relative worth of jobs is based in large measure on how the job is described in the formal job description. Job evaluation and job analysis influence the basic compensation structure for the organization, including the job classes and individual and job wage rates.

Performance Appraisal. The relationship between compensation and performance appraisal is perhaps the most important for individuals, particularly in organizations where salaries are performance-based. Without the ability to measure performance in a reliable and valid way, linking such an important reward as pay to the results may lead to diminished motivation and lowered performance (conditions appropriate for performance-based pay are discussed in Chapter 10). Where promotions are available as one type of reward for performance, the performance evaluation system can have added significance.

A summary of these relationships, along with a list of administrative issues discussed in Chapters 10 and 11, is shown in Exhibit 9.3. Also shown in Exhibit 9.3 are several aspects of the environment that influence an organization's total compensation process and hence its ability to attract, retain, and motivate employees for productivity and quality of work life improvements. Since the environment is so critical, it is discussed in detail here and will be discussed further in the next two chapters.

Environmental Impact on Total Compensation

The major aspects of the environment that are critical influences on total compensation are legal considerations, unions, and the market. Each has its own unique impact.

Legal Considerations in Total Compensation

As with many of the PHRM activities, there are several provincial and federal laws as well as human rights commission decisions that affect total compensation. Some of the most important laws are summarized in Exhibit 9.4. Other laws that affect not only compensation but general minimum standards of employment by province are listed in Appendix A at the end of this book. A synoptic summary of Exhibit 9.4 reveals that all provinces and the federal government have provisions for minimum wage, minimum pay for overtime, and compensation for non-work (vacation pay). Furthermore, with the exception of Alberta, British Columbia, New Brunswick, and Prince Edward Island, all other provinces have provisions for equal-pay legislation. Some of the most important of these laws are presented here.

The Canada Labour Code (Part III, amended 1985). This is the most comprehensive law, regulating several aspects of compensation and affecting all employees under federal jurisdiction. This law regulates the minimum wage, overtime pay, minimum age, and documentation of hours worked. All provinces have similar legislation.

Exhibit 9.3　　The Aspects and Processes of Compensating Employees

Job evaluation
- Ranking
- Classification
- Point
- Factor comparison
- Hay
- Skill based

Basic structure
- Job classes
- Individual and job wage rates

Performance appraisal

Human resource planning

Environment impact
- Law
- Unions
- Market

Job analysis

Administrative issues
- Secrecy
- Participation
- Satisfaction
- Lump sum
- All-salaried

Total compensation
- Direct pay
- Performance based pay
- Indirect pay

Attract
- Pay level
- Direct
- Indirect

Retain
- Equity
- Consistency

Motivate
- Pay for performance

Control labour costs

Productivity

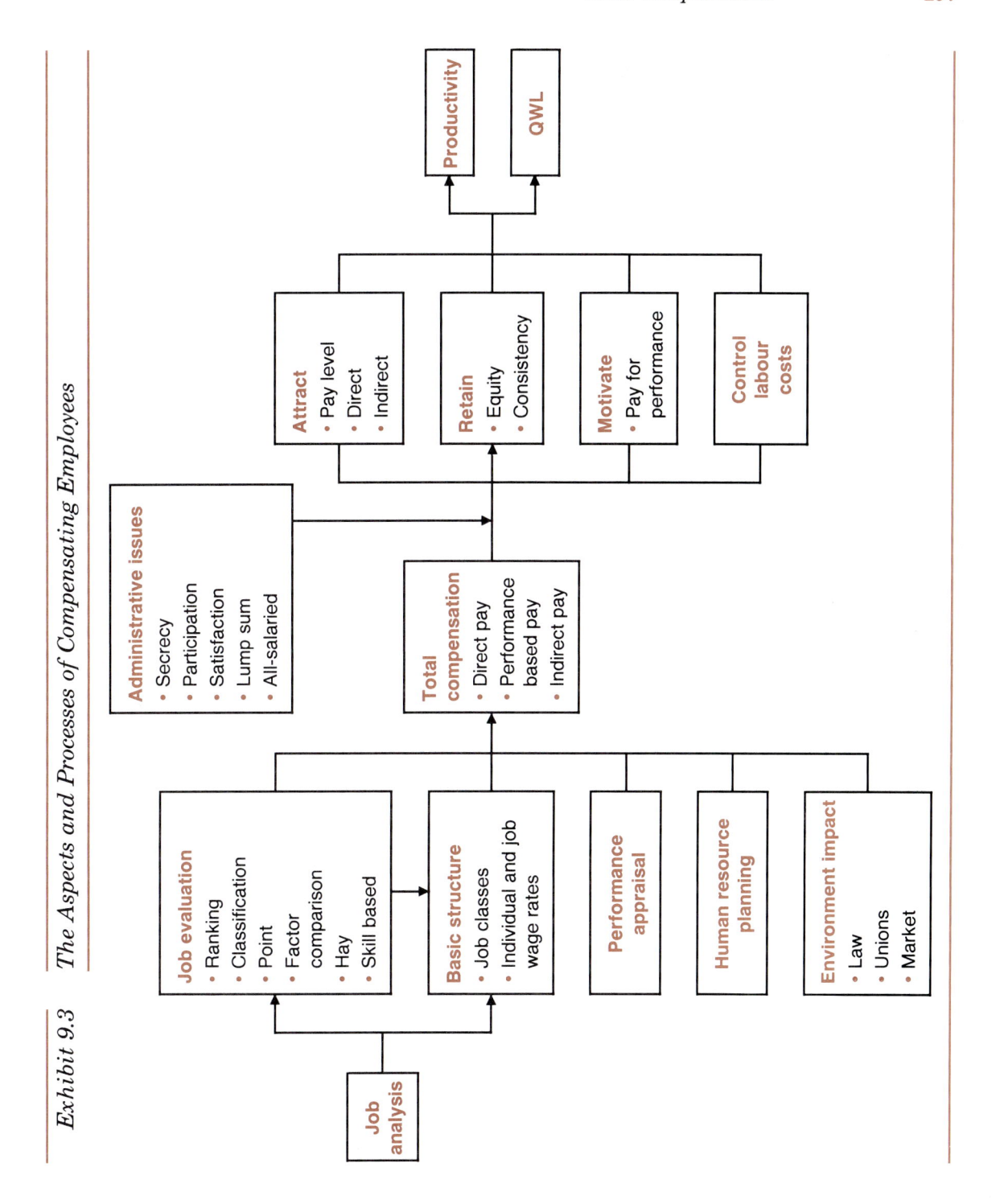

QWL

Exhibit 9.4   *Minimum Employment Standards for Total Compensation: Major Legislation by Province for 1985*

Province	Minimum Wage (per hr)	Overtime (per hr)	Vacation Pay (% of annual wage)	Equal-Pay Legislation
Alberta	$3.80	1 1/2	4%	none
British Columbia	3.65	1 1/2 (1st 3 hr) 2 (over 3 hr)	2%	none
Manitoba	3.85	1 1/2	no information	yes
New Brunswick	3.80	no information	4%	none
Newfoundland	4.00	min. $6.00	4%	yes
Nova Scotia	4.00	1 1/2	4%	yes
Ontario	4.00	no information	4%	legislation in progress
Prince Edward I.	4.00	min. $6.00	4%	none
Québec	4.00	1 1/2	4% up to 10 a	yes
Saskatchewan	4.50	1 1/2	4%	yes
Federal Employees	3.50	1 1/2	4% up to 6 a;	yes
	3.50	1 1/2	6% over 6 a	yes

Source: Data compiled from "Employment Standards (September 1985–January 1986)," *Human Resources Management in Canada*, Prentice-Hall Canada Inc.

The Code states that overtime must be paid at a rate of at least 1½ times normal pay for any hour that exceeds 40 h per week. It also sets a minimum wage. In 1985, employees under the age of 17 were entitled to a minimum wage of $3.25 per hour, and all other federal employees were entitled to a minimum of $3.50 per hour. Trainees and apprentices employed by the federal government are exempt from this provision.

Several provincial laws also influence wages paid to employees and the hours they can work. All provinces have minimum-wage laws covering employees not covered by federal minimum-wage laws, although the amounts vary. The minimum wage varied in 1985 from $3.65 per hour in British Columbia to $4.50 per hour in Saskachewan. The minimum wage might have a significant effect on organization expenses, as well as on the level of unemployment in the province (see "PHRM in the News"). The 1985 laws covering minimum vacation pay also differed from province to province. The required mimimums were the lowest in British Columbia (2% of annual pay); most of the other provinces enforced a minimum of 4%.

The Canada Labour Code, along with the Canada Labour Standards Regulations (SOR/72–7) contains provisions for hours of work. Employees may not work more than 48 h per week except in cases of an emergency. The Code also requires that employers keep detailed records on hours worked, pay rates, amount of overtime, deductions and additions to pay, and various miscellaneous information related to compensation. The relevant compensation records must be kept for at least 36 months after the work has been performed and should be available for inspection.

Certain categories of employees are exempt from the Code, or from certain provisions of it. For instance, managerial and professional employees are not covered by the hours-of-work provisions; in fact, they are called *exempt employees*, meaning that they do not need to be paid overtime for work beyond 40 h per week.

Employee exemption depends on responsibilities, duties, and salary. Generally, executives, administrative, and professional employees are exempt not only from the overtime requirements of the Code, but also from the minimum-wage provision. Employees paid by the hour or the day usually are non-exempt, while individuals who are paid a salary (monthly or bi-weekly) are exempt. This practice, however, is changing rapidly and it is difficult to generalize whether salaried or piecework employees are exempt or not.

Because these compensation laws vary from province to province, and are constantly changing, PHRM managers are well advised to keep up to date with changes. Most of these laws are enforced by the provincial Ministry of Labour, and up-dated information can be obtained by contacting its office.

The Canada Labour Code and the Financial Administration Act (Bill C–34) were amended as of March 1, 1985. Substantial changes were made to existing provisions of the Code regarding maternity leave, child-care leave, reinstatement, bereavement leave, sick leave, and sexual harassment provisions were added. Other changes related to compensation included the holiday pay entitlements, penalties for employers who do not comply with provisions of the law (with fines of up to $100 000), and minimum-wage exemptions for trainees.

Equity Laws.   Several federal and provincial equity laws passed since the 1960s influence the individual wage determination. For example, the discriminatory practice of establishing or maintaining differences in wages between male and female employees employed in the same establishment and performing work of equal value (as defined in the Canadian Human Rights Act and the Equal Wages Guidelines) is prohibited by the Canada Labour Code. Inspectors appointed by the Minister of Labour can file complaints with the Canadian Human Rights Commission when they have reason to believe the prohibition is not being observed. Similar statutes have been enacted by most provinces. These Acts require that companies found guilty of pay discrimination must make up past discrepancies as well as equalize the pay at the time discrimination is discovered. Nevertheless, as will be discussed later, the comparable pay concept is very difficult to demonstrate.

Although the various pay-equity acts are meant to ensure that employees with similar seniority, performance, and background who are doing the same work are paid the same, regardless of gender, age, national origin, religion, etc. (as specified in the various human rights Acts), evidence exists that suggests that employees are still being paid differentially primarily because of gender. On a national scale, although the proportion of women in the labour force has increased dramatically, their earnings in Canada are about 64% of those of men. The percentage varies by occupation, and almost universally was lower in the 25 to 34 age group.[7]

There are several possible reasons for the wage discrepancies, one of which is outright sexual discrimination. Another is that women may work in jobs that are valued less (based on job evaluation results) than jobs occupied by men. This reasoning has given rise to the issues of *comparable worth*, and the demand for equal pay for jobs of comparable value. Given that most pay equity Acts provide legal coverage only when men and women are performing the same job, it is very difficult to enforce comparable worth unless there are differences in performance, seniority, or other conditions. However, the evidence suggests that many employers make an attempt to comply with the provisions of the laws. The gap in wages for men and women, although it exists, has narrowed since the early 1980s. For example, data on wage discrimination, published by Statistics Canada for 1981, shows that the average employment income for women was slightly more than one-half that for men.[8]

Comparable-Worth Issues. Comparable worth is likely to be a significant compensation issue in the 1990s. As suggested before, the heart of the comparable-worth theory is the contention that while the "true worth" of jobs may be similar, some jobs (often held by women) are paid at a lower rate than others (often held by men). The resulting differences in pay that are disproportionate to the differences in the true worth of jobs, therefore, amount to wage discrimination. According to comparable-worth advocates, legal protection should be provided in these cases.

As shown in Exhibit 9.4, pay-equity legislation was instituted in a number of provinces, as well as in the federal government. Given that this legislation is recent (except for Québec and Manitoba), the legal test so far has been very limited. In one case, the Ste. Anne de Bellevue Veterans Hospital near Montréal had to increase a woman's salary by $10 000 and pay $14 262 in back wages for past discrimination.[9] In another case, a job evaluation in a Saskachewan hospital failed to support differential pay for male and female dominated jobs (Beatrice Harwatiuk v. Pasqua Hospital).[10]

Unions

Unions and associations have had a major impact on wage structures, wage levels, and individual wage determinations, even in companies that are not organized. Union actions influence every phase of compensation from early stages of job analysis and job evaluation to the final determination of specific wage rates and the selection of the criteria used to set those roles. Although unions generally do not conduct job evaluation programs, in many instances they do help design, negotiate, or modify company programs. Even if union interests are not completely served in the job-evaluation process, they can be served at the bargaining table. In fact, serving the interests of members at the bargaining table puts job evaluation into perspective for the union as well as the management.

Since 1980, the trend toward higher pay and benefit demands by unions has slowed dramatically. This has been due in large part to the serious financial difficulties of organizations and their need to survive. In fact, conditions have become so severe in several industries that workers have actually voted to take pay cuts in order to prevent layoffs, as a consequence of take-back negotiations between the union and management. Concessionary bargaining is presented in Chapter 17.

The Market

Both union and management base final wage rates and levels are far more than the results of job evaluation and wage surveys, although both often rely on wage surveys. The surveys illustrate wage rates for comparable work in other sections of the industry, and wages paid in the locality or the relevant labour market. It is necessary for organizations to be aware that paying what the market will bear—for instance paying women and minorities less because they will accept it just to get a job—is no excuse for wage discrimination.

In addition to the market wage levels, other criteria for wage determinations are labour market conditions (the number of people out of work and looking for work), past history of the organization's wage structure, fringe benefits, indexes of productivity, company profit figures or turnover data, and the Consumer Price Index, which helps to determine cost-of-living increases.

In the determination of wage rates, the market impact is used both directly and indirectly. Directly, the market provides comparisons against which organizations can establish pay rates for certain jobs. The rates of these jobs in turn are used as benchmarks, to establish pay rates for all other jobs. When used indirectly, organizations first perform a job evaluation on their existing jobs, then establish pay grades and classes, and then study the market to see what other organizations are paying. Whether used directly or indirectly, however, the market rates generally are not the ones used by an organization. The final rates usually represent a composite of market rate information and answers to pay-policy questions such as "Does the organization want to be a pay leader?" and "For what does the organization want to pay: job content, seniority, performance, or cost of living?" These usually are the central issues in basic wage determination in most organizations.

Basic Wage Issues

There are four basic wage issues that represent most activities in many compensation departments: (1) determination of the value of jobs—job evaluation; (2) determination of job classes; (3) establishment of pay structure; and (4) individual wage determinations.

Job Evaluation

Job evaluation is important when organizations are concerned about establishing *internal equity* among the different jobs in the organization. The amount paid for a job could be decided on the basis of a manager's impression of what the job should pay or is worth, but to help to ensure internal equity, more formal methods are often used. Job evaluation is the comparison of jobs by the use of formal and systematic procedures to determine their relative worth within the organization.[11] After jobs are formally evaluated, they are grouped into classes or grades. Within each class, jobs are then arranged in order of importance, and ranges of pay are established with the aid of wage surveys.

Although organizations generally compensate individuals on the basis of their job performance and personal contributions, organizations implicitly recognize job-related contributions by assigning pay in accordance with the difficulty and importance of jobs. Most organizations use some type of formal job evaluation or informal comparison of job content to determine the relative worth of job-related contributions. It is usually only in the formal job-evaluation process, however, that job-related contributions are explicitly specified.

There are four essential steps in the job-evaluation process. The first step is a thorough job analysis (see Chapter 3), which provides information about the job duties and responsibilities and about employee requirements for successful performance of the job.

The second step is deciding what the organization is paying for—that is, determining which factors will be used to evaluate jobs (although not all methods of job evaluation explicitly use factors). The factors are like yardsticks used to measure the relative importance of jobs. Since these factors help determine what jobs are paid (*jobs* and not people at this point), they are called **compensable factors**. The factors used by organizations vary widely, but they all presumably reflect job-related contributions. Accountability, know-how, problem-solving ability, and physical demands are examples of these factors. The factors chosen should

- represent all of the major aspects of job content for which the company is willing to pay (compensable factors), typically skill, effort, responsibility, and working conditions;
- avoid excessive overlap or duplication;
- be definable and measurable;
- be easily understood by employees and administrators;
- not be excessively costly to install or administrate; and
- be selected with legal considerations in mind.

Since jobs in organizations vary so greatly in terms of their job content, more than one job evaluation often is conducted. Occasionally, the number of job evaluations reflects the number of distinct groups of employees found in the company.

After compensable factors are determined, their relative importance must be defined. The relative importance is reflected by differential points or degrees (weights) assigned to each of the compensable factors. The weights assigned to the factors usually are determined by the employer's judgement of the relative importance of the factors to the organization. An illustration of differential weighting is provided in Exhibit 9.5.

Sample of Point Rating Method

Exhibit 9.5

Compensable Factor	1st Degree	2nd Degree	3rd Degree	4th Degree	5th Degree
Basic knowledge	15	30	45	60	—
Practical experience	20	40	60	80	—
Complexity and judgement	15	30	45	60	—
Initiative	5	10	20	40	—
Probable errors	5	10	20	40	—
Contacts with others	5	10	20	40	—
Confidential data	5	10	15	20	25
Attention to functional detail	5	10	15	20	—
Job conditions	5	10	15	—	—
For Supervisory Positions Only					
Character of supervision	5	10	20	—	—
Scope of supervision	5	10	20	—	—

The third step, though, is to design a system for evaluating jobs in the organization according to the compensable factors chosen in the second step. There are many basic methods of job evaluation that organizations can adapt to their own needs. Several job evaluation methods to choose from are discussed below.

Since the fourth step in the process of job evaluation is to decide who will conduct the job evaluation and use the evaluation methods, it is important to examine the operation of job evaluation methods in detail. There are two common non-quantitative methods of job evaluation: **ranking** and **job classification**. The **point-rating method, Hay plan**, and **factor-comparison method** are more quantifiable.[12] Newer methods of job evaluation are called **skill-based evaluation**.

Since job evaluation is the crux of many of the discussions of equal pay and job comparability, as you read the discussion on job evaluation, bear in mind the issue of true worth and the difficulty in really determining it through evaluation.

Ranking Method. Job-analysis information can be used to construct a hierarchy or ladder of jobs, which reflects their relative difficulty or value to the organization. This is the core of the **ranking method**. Although any number of compensable factors could be used to evaluate jobs, the job analyst often considers the whole job on the basis of just one factor, such as difficulty or value.

This method is convenient when there are only a few jobs to evaluate and when one person is familiar with them all. As the number of jobs increases and the likelihood that one individual will be familiar with all of them declines, detailed job-analysis information becomes more important and ranking is often done by committee. When a large number of jobs are to be ranked, key or benchmark jobs are used for comparison.

One of the difficulties in the ranking method is that it is effective only when all jobs are different from each other. Often it is difficult to make fine distinctions between similar jobs, and thus disagreements arise. Because of these difficulties, ranking is generally adopted only by small organizations.

Job-Classification Method. The **job-classification method** is similar to the ranking method, except that classes or grades are established and the jobs are then placed into the classes. Jobs are usually evaluated on the basis of the whole job, often using one factor such as difficulty or an intuitive summary of factors. Again, job analysis information is useful in the classification, and benchmark jobs are frequently established for each class. Within each class or grade, there is no further ranking of the jobs. Exhibit 9.6 illustrates class definitions, with examples of typical jobs in each class.

Although many organizations use job classification, the largest user of this method has been the Canadian Public Service Commission, which is gradually replacing this approach with more sophisticated methods. It also is commonly used for managerial and engineering/scientific jobs in the private sector.[13]

One advantage of this method is that it can be applied to a large number and wide variety of jobs. As the number and variety of jobs in an organization increases, however, the classification of jobs tends to become more

---

Exhibit 9.6 *Illustration: Class Definitions and Benchmarks*

Class II

Ability to perform unskilled routine jobs that are almost entirely manual, requiring the use of simple tools or equipment.

Jobs usually do not require a knowledge of company methods or the exercise of judgement and decision.

Versatility may be the prime characteristic and assignments will coincide with ability to assume tasks dependent on training and skill. Work performed under direct or limited supervision.

Benchmarks

Casual plant and field labour	Guard
Car and truck loaders	Janitor
Apprentice factory mechanic	Apprentice machine operator

Class III

Ability to perform tasks of a semi-skilled nature, either manual or non-manual. Mechanically must have ability to operate or to examine machines for defects, dismantle, reassemble, and adjust for efficient operation without direct or constant supervision.

May have ability to perform work of non-mechanical status, but work that requires the making of some general decisions as to quality, quantity, operations, and the exercising of independent judgement.

Benchmarks

Stockroom clerk	General truck operator
Semi-skilled mechanic	Research technician
Semi-skilled machine operator	

subjective. This is particularly true when an organization has a large number of plant or office locations, in which case jobs with the same title may differ in content. Because it is difficult to evaluate each job separately in such cases, the job title becomes a more important guide to job classification than job content.

A major disadvantage of the job classification method is that the basis of the job evaluations is either one factor or an intuitive summary of many factors. The problem with using one factor, such as difficulty (skill), is that it may not apply to all jobs. Some jobs may require a great deal of skill, but others may require a great deal of responsibility. This does not mean that jobs requiring much responsibility should be placed in a lower classification than jobs requiring much skill. Perhaps both factors could be considered together. Jobs should be evaluated and classified on the basis of all factors valued by the organization. However, "This balancing of the compensable

---

Continued *Exhibit 9.6*

Class IV

Ability to perform work of a skilled or specialized nature. Mechanically must have the ability to set up, repair, overhaul, and maintain machinery and mechanical equipment without being subject to further check. Must have ability to read blueprints, material specifications, and the use of basic shop mathematics, or comparable experience with the company layout to offset these requirements.

Work may be specialized or of a non-mechanical nature, requiring the ability to plan and perform work where only general operations methods are available and requires the making of decisions involving the use of considerable ingenuity, initiative, and judgement. Work under limited supervision.

Benchmarks

Skilled machinist	Packaging supervisor
Skilled electrician	Shipping supervisor
Skilled mechanic	

Class V

Ability to perform work of the highest level in a trade or craft. This skill may be recognized with a licence or other certification after formal apprenticeship training, or after a considerable period of formal on-the-job training by demonstrated competence to perform equivalent level of skill.

Other employees to be considered for classification into grade V must regularly supervise others in the technical and other aspects of the work, perform other supervisory functions, and may, in addition, perform work of a non-supervisory nature.

Benchmarks

Master electrician	Factory supervisor
Master (chief) mechanic	Maintenance planner
Power plant–chief engineer	

Source: G. T. Milkovich and W. F. Glueck, *Personnel, Human Resource Management: A Diagnostic Approach*, 4th ed., pp. 524–525. © Business Publications, Inc., 1985. Used with permission.

factors to determine the relative equality of jobs often causes misunderstandings with the employees and the labor leaders."[14] To deal with this disadvantage, many organizations use more quantifiable methods of evaluation.

Point-Rating Method. The most widely used method of job evaluation is the **point-rating method**, which consists of assigning point values to previously determined compensable factors and adding them to arrive at a total. There are several advantages of the point-rating method:

1. The point-rating plan is widely used throughout industry, permitting comparisons on a similar basis with other firms
2. The point-rating plan is relatively simple to understand. It is the simplest of quantitative methods of job evaluation
3. The point values for each job are easily converted to job and wage classes with a minimum of confusion and distortion
4. A well-conceived point-rating plan has considerable stability. It is applicable to a wide range of jobs over an extended period of time. The greatest assets here are consistency, uniformity, and widespread applicability
5. The point-rating method is a definitive approach requiring several separate and distinct judgement decisions

The limitations of the point-rating method are few. They include relatively high cost and difficulty to administer, and the method could generate lobbying for reclassification and an inequity in transfer from point to monetary value. But a particularly critical limitation is the assumption that all jobs can be described with the same factors. Many organizations avoid this problem by developing separate point-rating methods for different groups of employees. Exhibit 9.5 lists 11 compensable factors used by one organization to evaluate the jobs in supervisory, non-supervisory, and clerical categories. Exhibit 9.5 also describes what is associated, by degree and points, with each one of the factors, and sets out the specifications for the degrees or levels within that factor. Some factors are more important than others, as shown by the different point values. For example, the second degree of practical experience is worth four times as much as the second degree of job conditions. Each job is evaluated only on its compensable factors. The PHRM department determines which degree of a factor is appropriate for the job, and then the points assigned to each degree of each factor are totalled. Levels of compensation are determined on the basis of the point totals.

The point-factor method, as with other job-evaluation plans, incorporates the potential subjectivity of the job analyst. It therefore has the potential for wage discrimination. *Bias* or *subjectivity* can enter (1) in the selection of the compensable factors; (2) in the relative weights (degrees) assigned to factors; and (3) in the assignment of degrees to the jobs being evaluated. At stake here are equal pay and job comparability. In order to make sure that its point-factor evaluation system is free from potential bias and is implemented as objectively as possible, an organization may solicit the input of the job incumbent, the supervisor, and job-evaluation experts, as well as its PHRM department.

Hay Plan. A method with only three general factors is shown in Exhibit 9.7. This method, generally known as the **Hay plan**, is a widely used method for evaluating managerial and executive positions. The three factors—know-how, problem solving, and accountability—are used because they are assumed to be the most important aspects of managerial and executive positions. For all practical purposes there are eight factors: three sub-factors in know-how, two in problem solving, and three in accountability. In deriving the final point profile for any job, however, only the three major factors are assigned point values.

Hay Plan Compensable Factors — *Exhibit 9.7*

Mental Activity (problem solving)	**Know-How**	**Accountability**
The amount of original, self-starting thought required by the job for analysis, evaluation, creation, reasoning, and arriving at conclusions	The sum total of all knowledge and skills, however acquired, needed for satisfactory job performance (evaluates the job, not the person)	The measured effect of the job on company goals
Mental activity has two dimensions:	Know-how has three dimensions:	Accountability has three dimensions:
• The degree of freedom with which the thinking process is used to achieve job objectives without the guidance of standards, precedents, or direction from others	• The amount of practical, specialized, or technical knowledge required	• Freedom to act, or relative presence of personal or procedural control and guidance; determined by answering the question, "How much freedom has the job holder to act independently?"; for example, a plant manager has more freedom than a supervisor under his or her control
• The type of mental activity involved; the complexity, abstractness, or originality of thought required	• Breadth of management, or the ability to make many activities and functions work well together; the job of company president, for example, has greater breadth than that of a department supervisor	• Dollar magnitude, a measure of the sales, budget, dollar value of purchases, value added, or any other significant annual dollar figure related to the job
Mental activity is expressed as a percentage of know-how for the obvious reason that people think with what they know. The percentage judged to be correct for a job is applied to the know-how point value; the result is the point value given to mental activity.	• Requirement for skill in motivating people	• Impact of the job on dollar magnitude, a determination of whether the job has a primary effect on end results or has instead a sharing, contributory, or remote effect
	Using a chart, a number can be assigned to the level of know-how needed in a job. This number—or point value—indicates the relative importance of know-how in the job being evaluated.	Accountability is given a point value independent of the other two factors.

The total evaluation of any job is arrived at by adding the points (not shown here) for know-how, mental activity, and accountability.

Factor-Comparison Method. The point-rating method, regardless of the number of factors and degrees of each factor, derives a point total for each job. Several very different types of jobs can have the same total points. After the total points are determined, jobs are priced—often according to groups or classes, much as they would be using the job-classification method. The **factor-comparison method** avoids this step between point totalling and pricing by assigning dollar values to factors and comparing the amounts directly to the pay for benchmark jobs. In short, factor comparison is similar to point rating in that both use compensable factors. However, the point method uses degrees and points for each factor to measure jobs, whereas the factor-comparison method uses benchmark jobs and money values on factors.

The wage rates for the benchmark jobs are determined by the market. Although this is a quick method by which to set wage rates, it has the potential to perpetuate the traditional pay differentials between jobs because it is against these jobs that the wage rates for other jobs are determined. Moreover, the process of determining the rates of other jobs is actually in the hands of the wage and salary analyst who might be subjective, furthering the potential for wage discrimination. This method therefore has come under attack from the job comparability advocates, who claim it allows or causes pay discrimination.[15] Only about 10% of employers that do formal job evaluation use the factor-comparison method.[16] The complexity of the above explanation indicates why this is the case.

Skill-Based Evaluation. Whereas the first five job evaluation plans "pay for the job," **skill-based evaluation** is based on the idea of "paying for the person." This type of evaluation is concerned with the skills of the employees and therefore, incorporates training programs to facilitate skill acquisition by employees.[17]

The idea of paying for the person, or at least the person/job combination rather than for just the job, is not new. Many professional organizations have been doing this for a long time, such as universities, law offices, and research and development labs. What is new, however, is paying for the person in blue-collar jobs. One of the more visible examples of skill-based evaluation for blue-collar jobs is carried out by the Steinbergs Frozen Food Division in Montréal or Shell Sarnia in Ontario. Their plans are based on the starting rate given to all new employees. After coming on board, employees are advanced one pay grade for each job they learn. People can be trained for jobs in any order and at any price. Members of each employee's team ensure that the jobs are taught correctly, and they determine when the employee has mastered a job. Employees reach the top pay grade in the plant after learning all jobs.

Common Discriminatory Aspects in Job-Evaluation Methods

Ranking Methods. Jobs usually performed by women are often perceived to have low social status and may, therefore, be under-compensated.

Classification Methods. Job families, such as clerical and secretarial, which consist almost completely of women, are often allotted low wage rates. Generally, in the classification system, no mechanisms exist for comparison with other job families, so that the wage range for classes of under-valued incumbents remain lower than the range set for other classifications. This discriminatory aspect of evaluation is validated and becomes systemic when compensation rates are based on labour-market pay data. The under-valued remain under-valued.[18]

Point-Factor Method. Wage scales normally are adjusted to reflect both labour market rates and the subjective assessment of raters as to the relative importance of the job. For example, the total point score can be adjusted to fit the pay data, so that while some jobs might be allowed a certain dollar amount per point, jobs with a tendency to be under-valued, as are many women's jobs, could be assigned less than that regardless of the necessary skill, effort, and responsibility factors for the job.[19]

Factor-Comparison Method. A high degree of subjectivity is present in the selection of benchmark jobs, and in the definition of worth and the determination of the degree or involvement of each compensable factor. As with other systems, worth is in part determined by external pay rates, rather than in terms of contribution to the organization.[20]

Reducing Bias Discrimination. A number of discriminatory aspects are common to all systems of job evaluation, except skill-based systems. Many factors, for example, are based on men's jobs, and are weighed accordingly. Moreover, since most of those involved with devising pay structures for "women's jobs" have little understanding of, or direct experience with, the work, many of these jobs are under-valued. Consequently, the following guidelines could be used in order to reduce biases in job evaluation systems:

1. Ensure that those associated with the analysis and evaluation of jobs are aware of and understand the issues concerning women's jobs and the possible discriminatory aspects of systems
2. Ensure that the actual job content is analyzed and evaluated, and not the person doing the job
3. Conduct comprehensive and structured job analyses to screen factors, job families, and benchmarks in terms of discriminatory aspects
4. Ensure that factors associated with work usually done by women, such as manual dexterity, accuracy, continuous routine, and concentration, are weighted on a comparable basis with factors associated with jobs usually done by men
5. Discuss all aspects of work usually done by women with incumbents to determine previously unrecognized or under-valued factors, such as physical and mental effort and skill, responsibility, and varied working conditions
6. Ensure that where more than one evaluation system is established for different types of jobs, discriminatory aspects are not present

7. Maintain records of job analyses, the definition and weighting of factors, the scores for each job, and the reasons for rating decisions
8. Inform all involved employees of job-evaluation procedures [21]

A new system of job evaluation that is supposed to be bias free has been recently introduced to Canadian organizations. The system is called JEBOR (Job Evaluation by Operations Research) and it is based on computer software. Companies such as Gulf Canada, Olympia, and York and Epton Industries, Inc. have been experimenting with the system. Unlike other systems, JEBOR's evaluations are made only by employees—superiors, peers, or subordinates—with direct knowledge of the jobs being rated. Using a computer's user-friendly language, JEBOR could be tailored to the company's own values and if equity philosophies are included in these values, the system accounts for them during the compilation of the ranking data.

Determining Job Classes

Once the job evaluations have been conducted, and before salaries are determined, job classes are created. Job classes are based on the results of the job evaluation. Determining **job classes** means grouping together all jobs that are similar in value; for example, all clerical jobs or all managerial jobs. The jobs within the same class may be quite different, but they should be roughly comparable in value to the organization. All jobs in each class are assigned one salary or range of salaries.

One reason for grouping jobs into classes is efficiency of salary administration. Also, it can be hard to justify the small differences in pay that might exist between jobs if job classes are not created. Finally, small errors that occur in evaluation of the jobs can be eliminated in the classification process. On the other hand, employees can find fault with the classification results if their jobs are grouped with jobs they feel are less important. Additionally, the jobs that are grouped together may be dissimilar when there are too few classes of jobs. Using only a few classes is most appropriate when many of the jobs in the organization are of similar value.

Establishing the Pay Structure

Once jobs are evaluated and job classes are determined, wage rates or ranges need to be established. Although job classes are determined for the purpose of establishing wage rates, job classes often are based on wage rates that already exist. This practice may seem somewhat reversed, but it is common in organizations. Most organizations have firmly established pay schedules, and therefore need to determine job classes only when many new jobs are introduced or if the organization has never really had a sound job-analysis program. A newly established organization is likely to be small, and therefore would price its jobs based on surveys of what other organizations are paying.

Wage and Salary Surveys. Wage surveys can be used to develop compensation levels, wage structures, and even payment plans (the amount and kind of direct and indirect compensation). Whereas job evaluation helps to ensure internal equity, wage surveys provide information to help ensure external equity. Both types of equity are important if an organization is to be successful in attracting, retaining, and motivating employees. In addition, survey results also can indicate compensation philosophies of competing organizations. For example, a large electronics company may have a policy of paying 15% above the market rate (the average of all rates for essentially the same job in an area); a large service organization may choose to pay the market rate; a large bank may decide to pay 5% less than the market rate.

Most organizations use wage surveys extensively. Separate surveys are published for different occupational groupings, so many larger organizations subscribe to several surveys. For example, there are surveys for clerical workers, professional workers, managers, and executives. Separate surveys are conducted not only because there are such wide differences in skill levels, but also because labour markets are so different. An organization surveying clerical workers may need to survey only companies within a 16-km radius, whereas a survey of managerial salaries may cover the entire country.

An example of the results of a survey for management compensation in Canada for 1985 is provided in Exhibit 9.8. In this survey, if all positions had been considered at their market value, both in terms of job and actual compensation paid to the incumbent, the discrepancies would be close to zero and the mean ratio participants/market values would all be at 1.00. The organizations can have liberal or restrictive policies, but the overall average should result in showing a central group value of 1.00. Discrepancies from this ideal central value can be attributed primarily to biases from the participants in evaluating jobs and in compensating their incumbents. Compensation surveys reflect, of course, regional and provincial differences. During the early 1980s, for example, a salary survey for executives in Canada indicated a rapid increase in salary in western Canada (Alberta and British Columbia) as compared with other regions. This tendency, however, was reversed by the mid-1980s. In 1984 many organizations reported no salary increases, and in addition, half of the organizations surveyed, particularly from western Canada, reported pay reductions.[22]

Once the survey data are collected, the organization must decide how to use them. The organization could use only the average wage and salary levels from all of the companies in the survey to determine its own levels, or could weight the wage and salary levels of companies by the number of employees. Another option would be to use the wage and salary ranges from all of the companies to determine its own wage and salary ranges. After selecting the wage and salary information it wants, the organization develops a grade structure with pay rates for job categories.

Grade Structure. A typical example of a grade structure is shown in Exhibit 9.9. This grade structure is based on job evaluation points associated with a point-factor evaluation. The boxes shown are associated with a range of job-evaluation points (the job class) and the range of pay grades.[23] In essence, these **pay grades** are the job classes. Consequently, there may be

Exhibit 9.8 *Management Comparative Compensation for Canada (1985)*

Position	Salary Policy	Current Salary	Total Cash Compensation
Direction of Operations	1.001	1.032	1.047
Production	.957	.973	.997
Production Support	.967	.948	.972
Finance	1.064	1.052	1.125
Financial Control	1.000	.980	1.005
Treasury	1.055	1.026	1.017
Internal Audit	.974	.975	.895
Corporate Planning	.988	1.013	1.084
Systems and Data Processing	.969	.971	1.003
Legal and Secretarial	.988	.990	1.119
Public Relations	.975	.974	1.096
Procurement and Purchasing	1.001	.996	1.069
Human Resources	1.010	.982	1.033
Personnel	.965	.942	1.075
Labour Relations	1.026	.987	.975
Medical, Health, and Safety	.976	.958	—
Engineering	.949	.943	.950
Research and Development	1.020	.989	1.036
Marketing	1.039	.999	1.017
Sales	.987	.982	.979
Advertising	1.026	.969	1.004
Actuarial	1.066	1.059	.944
Underwriting	.946	.939	.927
Policyholder Service	.937	.933	.798
Branch and Agency Management	.910	.991	1.032
Lending	.943	.990	.880
Investment	1.032	1.014	1.056
Mortgage Loans	1.056	1.085	—
Real Estate	.959	.963	.869

Source: "Management Comparative Compensation for 1985: A Study of the National, Regional and Functional Situation in Canada," *Multi-Services Professionals*, (Montréal: M.S.P. Inc., 1985), p. 8. Used with permission.

several different jobs within one box, but they are very similar in job-evaluation points.

As illustrated, the boxes generally ascend from left to right. They may also vary in shape. This reflects increased job worth and the associated higher pay levels (shown on the vertical axis) for more valued jobs. The pay levels are established using market information, to help ensure external equity.

The wage rate for each job then is determined by locating or determining its grade and moving over to a point on the vertical axis, as done for Job A in grade II in Exhibit 9.9. Note that there are minimum and maximum pay limits to the jobs in each grade. Staying within those limits (the range) is essential to maintaining internal equity, assuming that the job evaluation system is valid.[24]

Establishing a Grade Structure Based on Job Evaluation

Exhibit 9.9

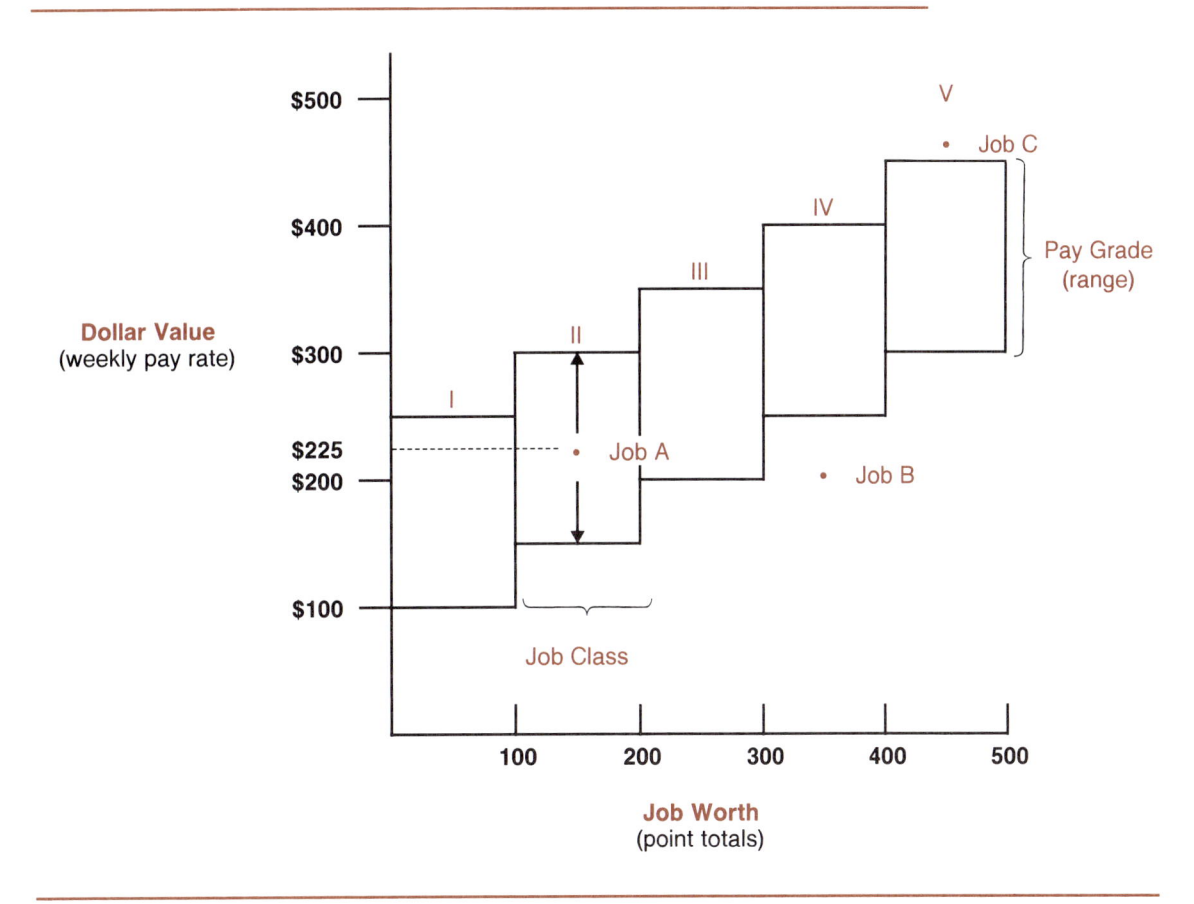

[Chart: Dollar Value (weekly pay rate) on vertical axis vs. Job Worth (point totals) on horizontal axis, showing five stepped pay grades I–V. Job A plotted at ~$225 in grade II (range $150–$300, midpoint $225); Job B plotted in grade IV; Job C plotted in grade V. "Job Class" bracket spans 100–200 on horizontal axis. "Pay Grade (range)" bracket indicates grade V range.]

Source: Adapted with permission from R. S. Schuler and S. A. Youngblood, *Effective Resource Management* (St. Paul: West Publishing Co., 1986), p. 312.

For an employee to obtain a significant salary increase requires that he or she must move or be promoted into a job in the next higher grade. However, an employee also can receive a pay raise within a given grade. Generally, each job has a rate range. As illustrated, Job A has a range from $150 per week to $300 per week. The mid-point of this range is $225. Initially, an employee may start at the bottom of the range and go up. Many companies, however, attempt to keep the bulk of their employees paid at the mid-point range (average salary).

Individual Wage Determination

Once the wage structure has been determined, the question is: How much do we pay each individual? For example, consider Maya and John, both of whom work on the same job. If the rate range were $1500 to $2000 per month, Maya might be paid $2000 and John $1750. What might account for the pay differential? Although performance contribution would be an appropriate explanation, personal factors such as seniority, gender, age, size of family, experience, and appearance also have been found to influence individual wages. Age and seniority, in fact, are frequently perceived to be rather important factors.[25] In certain cases, variables such as an employee's potential, negotiating skills, and leverages also play a role in determining compensation levels.[26]

In actuality, individual wage determinations often are based on both personal factors and performance. Thus, age and seniority as well as performance may influence Maya's and John's pay. However, many managers would argue that pay differences based on performance are more equitable than those based on such personal factors as seniority, while unions regard seniority as a sacred cow. They believe that seniority should be the critical factor in determining pay rate for a number of reasons: (1) rewarding seniority means recognizing experience: assuming a maturity curve for many jobs, the argument is that the senior people in the organization contribute the most; (2) it may be seen as recognition for past performance; and (3) it is a recognition of employees' loyalty to the organization. Many Japanese companies, for example, reward seniority more than performance for similar reasons.

Contemporary Issues in Wage and Salary Administration

There are several contemporary issues in wage and salary administration, four of which have particular importance: (1) to what extent employees should be able to participate in choosing their forms of pay and in setting their own wages; (2) the advantages and disadvantages of pay secrecy; (3) employee requirements for pay satisfaction; and (4) whether all employees should be salaried. More administration issues are addressed in the next two chapters.

Participation Policies

For many employees, total compensation generally represents a mixture of direct salary and indirect benefits. These indirect benefits may represent as much as 40% of total compensation, but employees generally have no choice as to which indirect benefits they receive. Management defends this policy on the grounds that it is capable of selecting the proper benefits and because of the cost advantage in buying the same benefits for all employees. Yet the proliferation of varied indirect pay arrangements has created a smoked-glass effect, through which the attitudes and desires of the recipient can be seen only darkly, if at all. Employees often receive costly benefits they neither want nor need and, in many cases, do not even know about. And even in cases where employees are aware of all of the particular forms of compensation that they are receiving, they tend to under-value the benefits.

What are the alternatives? The popular form of participation for executive-level employees is the **cafeteria approach** (also called "flexible compensation") in which individuals select from a variety of compensation "entrees" those items that they want. The cafeteria approach tends to be favoured by a majority of executives, even if the administrative costs are deducted from their annual pay. This approach is discussed further in Chapter 11.

A newer method of employee participation allows employees to set their own wage rates. One way of doing this is by letting the employees decide who should get a raise by voting on the matter. Under this system, the employee's name, hourly wage, and photograph are posted for six consecutive working days in a common area. The employees then vote with a majority ruling. Although top-level managers cannot vote, they can veto a raise. This has not happened yet; experience with the system demonstrates that employees can responsibly set their own wages given they trust management and have a sufficient understanding of the "cost of doing business."[27]

Pay Secrecy

Ask anyone who works for a living how much money he or she makes, and you are likely to encounter a range of responses from evasion to outright hostility. Such responses, however, should not be surprising. According to organizational etiquette, it is considered gauche to ask others their salaries. In a study at E. I. du Pont de Nemours, all employees were asked if the company should disclose more payroll information so that everyone would know everyone else's pay. Only 18% voted for an open pay system.

Nevertheless, some companies practise open salary administration because they feel it is the right thing to do. For example, the Polaroid Corporation has established a pay-level structure for its exempt salaried employees and, in keeping with its policy of openness, involves those employees in making salary decisions. Employees are also involved in the job-evaluation process to get a broad understanding of the process by which job value is established.[28]

Satisfaction with Pay

If organizations want to minimize absenteeism and turnover through compensation, they must make sure that employees are satisfied with their pay. And since motivation to perform is not always a function of satisfaction with pay, it is necessary to know the specific facets of pay satisfaction. With this knowledge, organizations can develop pay practices that are more likely to result in satisfaction with pay. Perhaps the three major determinants of satisfaction with pay are pay equity, pay level, and pay administration practices.

Pay Equity. **Pay equity** refers to what people feel they deserve to be paid in relation to what others deserve to be paid. The tendency is for people to determine what they and others deserve to be paid by comparing what they give to the organization with what they get out of the organization. By comparing themselves with others, people may decide whether or not they are being paid fairly. If they regard this comparison as fair or equitable, they are more likely to be satisfied. If they see this comparison as unfair they are likely to be dissatisfied, and reduce their work efforts.[29]

A current issue in pay equity deals with top executive compensation: Are they paid too much? In the U.S. and Canada, it is estimated that, on the average, top executives earn 12 to 18 times as much as the lowest-paid employees.[30] As a point of interest, Japan's top-level managers earn only six times as much and, for further contrast, in Rumania, the gap is closer to that of the U.S. and Canada (1:18). But, in the Soviet Union, the gap is 1:40, which many people suggest generates a high level of dissatisfaction not only among workers but also the general public.

Pay Level. **Pay level** is an important determinant of the perceived amount of pay. People use this perception and compare it to what they feel they should receive. The result of the comparison is satisfaction with pay if the "should" level of pay equals the actual level of pay. Pay dissatisfaction results if the actual level is less than the "should."

Pay Administration Practices. If the employer is to attract new employees and keep them satisfied with their pay, the wages and salaries offered should approximate the wages and salaries paid to other employees in comparable organizations (i.e., external equity must exist). Also, the pricing of jobs can enhance pay satisfaction when it is perceived to adhere to a philosophy of equal pay for jobs of comparable worth. The worth of jobs must be evaluated according to the factors considered most important by the employees and the organization, so that internal equity exists.[31]

Furthermore, pay-for-performance systems must be accompanied by a method for accurately measuring the performance of employees and must be open enough so that these employees can see clearly the performance-pay relationship. This is discussed further in the next chapter.

Compensation rates and pay structures should be continually reviewed and updated and revised as necessary. Over time, the content of a job may change, thus distorting the relationship between its actual worth and its evaluated worth.

Finally, employees must perceive that the organization is looking out for their interests as well as its own. An atmosphere of *trust* and *consistency* must exist. Without this, pay satisfaction probably will be low, and pay administration will become a target for complaints regardless of the real issues.

All-Salaried Workforce

Although there is some evidence that all employees prefer to be on salary rather than to be paid on an hourly basis, most organizations distinguish between their employees by method of pay. That is, salary status is usually reserved (along with a parking space) for management, and the non-management employees, except clerical workers, are paid on an hourly basis.

Some organizations nevertheless have put all of their employees on salary. IBM has had an all-salaried workforce since the 1930s. The all-salary concept shows a general respect for the entire workforce, which is treated as mature and responsible. The policy therefore establishes an atmosphere of trust and respect.

Although there is little hard evidence to support the effectiveness of the all-salaried concept, it appears to be a practical way to increase productivity and the quality of work life, two factors involved in the assessment of total compensation.[32]

Assessing Total Compensation

In assessing how effectively an organization administers its compensation program, the following major purposes of total compensation must be considered:

1. Attract potentially qualified employees
2. Motivate employees
3. Retain qualified employees
4. Administer pay within legal constraints
5. Facilitate organizational strategic objectives and control labour costs

In order to attain these purposes, employees generally need to be satisfied with their pay. This means that the organization's pay levels should be extremely competitive, that employees should perceive internal pay equity, and that the compensation program should be properly administered. It also means that compensation practices must adhere to the various provincial and federal wage and hour laws, including comparable worth considerations. Consequently, an organization's total compensation can be assessed by comparing its pay levels with other organizations, by analyzing the validity of its job evaluation method, by measuring employee perceptions of pay equity and performance-pay linkages, and by determining individual pay levels within jobs and across jobs.

Attracting, motivating, and retaining employees are worthy purposes of total compensation and can facilitate organizational objectives. Attaining them at a lower rather than higher cost also can facilitate an organization's strategic objectives. This can be done by replacing non-deductible pay expenditures (expensive perquisites such as cars and club memberships) with deductible pay expenditures, such as contributions to employee stock-ownership plans. This replacement, of course, must be done with consideration for the differential impact of alternative pay expenditures on attracting, motivating, and retaining employees. These differentials can increase the effectiveness of the total compensation dollar.

Since total compensation is composed of base pay and performance-based and indirect pay, the assessment here is incomplete. The next two chapters will provide a more comprehensive assessment.

Summary

This chapter examined many of the important aspects of one of the most significant PHRM activities in an organization. Perhaps no single issue evokes as much emotion as learning that one's level of pay is less than another's, or finding out that another person got a bigger raise even though he or she did less to earn it. There are, in addition, many other pay-related issues of concern to PHRM managers in organizations. One in particular is the concept of comparable worth and its impact on organizations. Comparable worth is the "true value" of a job, and should be used in determining compensation rates. Currently, compensation rates of many jobs actually reflect the fact that men occupy certain jobs and women occupy others.

Although determining true value of a job is an important concept, it is difficult to measure or determine precisely. The use of sound job-evaluation procedures can assist an organization in determining the true value of jobs. Sound procedures, involve (1) using a single set of factors (i.e., just one evaluation system or plan) rather than one for the clerical staff, one for the blue-collar workers, and yet another for the supervisory group; (2) selecting factors that reflect the working environment and the organization's objectives; (3) developing factors and relative weights free of bias; (4) eliminating as much as possible the subjective measurement error in evaluating position; (5) eliminating bias in the evaluation committee that reviews job evaluation results on jobs; and (6) sustaining an updated system to ensure that factors or evaluations do not become outdated.

Although job evaluation procedures are important in establishing true worth, they are more relevant to establishing relative job prices than absolute job prices. To help establish absolute job prices, organizations often use market surveys, particularly for those jobs that have identical or nearly identical counterparts in the marketplace. Conducting market surveys to directly price jobs that are not found in other organizations should be done with caution. It involves subjectivity; therefore, it is open to potential wage discrimination charges. Fair evaluations should be conducted to help reduce that likelihood.

In establishing wages, organizations can rely on job evaluations and market surveys and they can utilize inputs from the employees themselves. Evidence supports the fact that employees can responsibly set their own wages. In fact, in the few companies that have tried it, employees have set their own wages without management having to alter the procedures or change decisions. The method is most successful, however, in organizations where employees and management have a mutual trust, and employees are provided with information to help them understand the financial status of the company.

Establishing wages and determining which job evaluation method to use are only two components, although very important ones, of compensation. Other components include selecting the best performance-based pay plan and obtaining benefit from indirect compensation. These and others are discussed in detail in the next two chapters.

Discussion Questions

1. What is total compensation and what types of rewards are associated with it?
2. What are the major purposes of total compensation?
3. Explain why there is a critical link between job analysis and compensation.
4. A plethora of laws and Acts have been passed that influence organization policies. Discuss the ramifications of these laws and Acts on compensation policies.
5. What is the issue of comparable worth and how is it related to compensation?
6. What are the basic wage issues in determining compensation and how are these issues resolved?
7. What are the pros and cons of various job evaluation methods?
8. What factors contribute to whether employees will be satisfied with their pay?
9. How can an organization's total compensation package be assessed?
10. How can the true worth of jobs be determined?

CASE STUDY

The Pay Gap

"No way those guys on our shift will make more money than us," growled Mike Durrand during the bi-weekly supervisor's meeting. Mike was a first-line supervisor for Krugpot, a pulp and paper company. He had been a supervisor for more than 15 years. The reason for his discontent was that, for the first time in the company's history, subordinates were receiving higher pay than the supervisors.

"You are absolutely right," yelled Bud Sampson from another corner of the room. "Nowadays it's better to be a unionized worker in this company than a manager. At least as a worker you're paid for overtime, and can make a lot more money," he added angrily.

Van Nguyen, the director of personnel for the division, who was at the meeting, said, "Guys, you know that this company has always maintained a healthy, favourable, differential pay balance between management and the workers. This year, unfortunately, profit is down, and the company decided to limit pay raises for its exempt employees to 8% tops across the board. The collective agreement with the Federation of Pulp and Paper

Union, signed a year ago, provides for an automatic raise of COLA and a 10% additional raise for most jobs. It also is true that the contract with the union provides for a 1½ overtime pay rate. But this is only temporary, and I'm certain that the situation will be corrected in the future."

Added Inge Koblin, a recently promoted supervisor, "You know, my subordinates laugh at me constantly. They have good reason to suggest that there really are no incentives to become a supervisor in this company. We have more responsibility, we work more hours, and our final pay in dollars and cents is lower than most of theirs. I find it extremely demoralizing."

Van suggested, "Why don't you write a memo to me about this situation and mail a copy to Joe Rustiak, the vice-president, so that management will know how you feel about this situation. Maybe they'll realize the problems and do something about it."

Case Questions

1. What arguments can you present in favour of differential pay for the unionized employees and the first-line supervisors?
2. What would you do about the situation if you were Joe Rustiak?
3. If the corporation does not change its compensation policy, what should the personnel director do for this division?

Endnotes

1. E. E. Lawler III, *Pay and Organization Development* (Reading, MA: Addison-Wesley, 1981). R. E. Sibson, *Compensation*, rev. ed. (New York: AMACOM, 1981). G. T. Milkovich and J. M. Newman, *Compensation* (Plano, TX: Texas Business Publications, 1984).
2. The use of categories facilitates discussion of compensation. This is just one way to divide up the components of compensation. For an alternative way, see R. I. Henderson, "Designing a Reward System for Today's Employee," *Business*, July–Sept. 1982, pp. 2–12.
3. E. E. Lawler III, "The Strategic Design of Reward Systems," in R. S. Schuler and S. A. Youngblood (eds.), *Readings in Personnel and Human Resource Management*, 2nd ed. (St. Paul: West Publishing Co., 1984), pp. 253–259. R. Kanungo, "Reward Management: A New Look," in S. L. Dolan and R. S. Schuler (eds.), Canadian Readings in Personnel and Human Resource Management (St. Paul: West Publishing Co., 1987). R. M. Tomasko, "Focusing Company Reward Systems to Help Achieve Business Objectives," *Management Review*, Oct. 1982, pp. 8–12. B. R. Ellig, "Gearing Compensation to Market Cycles," *Management Review*, Nov.–Dec. 1982, pp. 17–21. *Elements of Sound Pay Administration* (Berea, OH: American Compensation Association and American Society for Personnel Administration, 1981).
4. "Employee Benefits: 1981," *Bulletin to Management*, December 9, 1982, pp. 3–4.
5. S. Lippman and J. McCall, "The Economics of Job Search: A Survey," *Economic Inquiry, 14*, 1976, pp. 155–190. D. P. Schwab, "Recruiting and Organizational Entry," in K. M. Rowland and G. R. Ferris (eds.), *Personnel Management* (Boston: Allyn & Bacon, 1982). F. S. Hills and T. Bergmann, "Professional Employees: Unionization Attitudes and Reward Preferences," *Personnel Administrator*, July 1982, pp. 50–54.
6. Tomasko, endnote 3, pp. 8–9. Lawler, endnote 3. R. J. Greene and R. G. Roberts, "Strategic Integration of Compensation and Benefits," *Personnel Administrator*, May 1983, pp. 79–86.
7. "Women, a force to be reckoned with in the Canadian economy," *The Globe and Mail*, July 15, 1985, p. B7.
8. "Population: Worked in 1980—Employment Income by Selected Characteristics," *Census of Canada 1981*, Catalogue 92–931.
9. Cited in W. F. Werther, Jr., K. Davis, H. Schwind, H. Das, and F. C. Miner, Jr., *Canadian Personnel Management and Human Resources*, 2nd ed. (Toronto: McGraw-Hill Ryerson Ltd.), p. 343.
10. "Beatrice Harwatiuk v. Pasqua Hospital," *Canadian Human Rights Report*, vol. 4, decision 73a, D/1177–1181, 1983.
11. D. J. Thomsen, "Compensation and Benefits," *Personnel Journal*, May 1981, pp. 348–354. *Elements of Sound Pay Administration*, p. 7. The use of the term *job evaluation* here represents a more restricted definition. Some people use the term to include the element of market pricing as well as internal job-content analyses.
12. Other methods of job evaluation similar to these include "slotting" and "scored questionnaires." For a discussion of the frequency of use of different job evaluation methods, see J. W. Steele, *Paying for Per-*

formance and Position (New York: American Management Association, 1982), pp. 18–19.
13. R. B. Pursell, "R & D Job Evaluation and Compensation," *Compensation Review*, 2nd quarter, 1972, pp. 21–31. T. Atchinson and W. French, "Pay Systems for Scientists and Engineers," *Industrial Relations*, 1967, pp. 44–56.
14. J. D. Dunn and F. M. Rachel, *Wage and Salary Administration: Total Compensation Systems*, p. 175. Copyright 1971 by the McGraw-Hill Book Company.
15. "An Approach to Bias-Free Job Evaluation Procedures," Office of the Deputy Premier, Ontario Women's Directorate (undated).
16. A. Nash and S. J. Carroll, Jr., *The Management of Compensation* (Belmont, CA: Wadsworth, 1975).
17. E. E. Lawler III, *Pay and Organizational Development* (Reading, MA: Addison-Wesley, 1981).
18. "An Approach to Bias-Free Job Evaluation Procedures," endnote 15, p. 2.
19. Ibid., p. 3.
20. Ibid., p. 4.
21. Ibid., addendum. Used with permission of the Ontario Women's Directorate.
22. Thorne, Stevenson & Kellogg Salary Surveys, 1984.
23. G. T. Milkovich and W. F. Glueik, *Personnel, Human Resource Management: A Diagnostic Approach* (Plano, TX: BPI, 1985), pp. 528–530. M. A. Conway, "Salary Surveys: Avoid the Pitfalls," *Personnel Journal*, June 1984, pp. 62–65.
24. For a discussion on the validity of job-evaluation systems see T. A. Mahoney, "Compensating for Work," in K. M. Rowland and G. R. Ferris (eds.), *Personnel Management* (Boston: Allyn & Bacon, 1982), pp. 257–258.
25. R. J. Greene, "Which Pay Delivery System is Best for Your Organization?" *Personnel*, May–June 1981, pp. 51–58. See also *Fair Employment Practices Guidelines #18, 9*, 1980, pp. 7–8.
26. L. Dyer, D. P. Schwab, and R. Theriault, "Managerial Perceptions Regarding Salary Increases Criteria," *Personnel Psychology*, vol. 29(2), 1976, pp. 232–242.
27. E. E. Lawler III, "Workers Can Set Their Own Wages-Responsibility," *Psychology Today*, February 1977, pp. 109–112.
28. Mary Zippo, "Roundup," *Personnel*, Sept.–Oct. 1980, pp. 43–45.
29. For further discussion of equity and its relationship to performance, see K. E. Weick, "The Concept of Equity in the Perception of Pay," *Administrative Science Quarterly, 11*, 1966, pp. 414–439. R. T. Mowday, "Equity Theory Predictions of Behavior in Organizations," in R. M. Steers and L. W. Porter (eds.), *Motivation and Work Behavior*, 3rd ed. (New York: McGraw-Hill, 1983), pp. 91–112. R. D. Daft and R. M. Steers, *Organizations: A Micro/Macro Approach* (Glenview, IL: Scott, Foresman & Co., 1986), pp. 99–101.
30. For the U.S.: "Executive Pay: The Top Earners," *Business Week*, May 7, 1984, pp. 88–108. For Canada, data is more sketchy. Information, however, is based on a small-scale executive compensation survey conducted by Heidi Markowitz, Business Psychology, Inc. (unpublished report, 1985.)
31. For further details on internal and external equity considerations see R. Theriault, "Key Issues in Designing Compensation Systems," in Dolan and Schuler (eds.), endnote 3.
32. J. C. Toedtman, "A Decade of Rapid Change: The Outlook for Human Resources Management in the '80s," *Personnel Journal*, Jan. 1980, pp. 29–33.

CHAPTER 10
Performance-Based Pay and Administration

PHRM in the News

Performance-Based Pay Systems
Purposes and Importance of Performance-Based Pay
Relationships of Performance-Based Pay
Legal Considerations in Performance-Based Pay

Merit Pay Plans
Merit Pay Guidelines
Merit Versus Cost-of-Living Adjustments

Incentive Pay Plans
Individual-Level Incentive Plans
Group-Level Incentive Plans
Organization-Level Incentive Plans

Administrative Issues in Performance-Based Pay
Obstacles to Performance-Based Pay Plan Effectiveness
Auditing the Merit Pay System
Participation in Performance-Based Pay Plans

Assessing Performance-Based Pay

Summary

Discussion Questions

Case Study

Endnotes

PHRM in the News

What Those Who "Have It Made" Make

David Culver
CEO, Alcan Aluminum Ltd.
Cash compensation: $566 453
Benefits: $9 155 plus $34 200 cash from stock options
1983 income: $609 808
1982 income: $437 901
1983 corporate sales: $6.5 billion
1983 corporate net income: $90 million

Jean de Grandpré
Chairman, CEO, Bell Canada Enterprises Inc.
Cash compensation: $658 000
Benefits: $70 000 in future retirement benefits
1983 income: $658 000
1982 income: $551 000
1983 corporate sales: $8.9 billion
1983 corporate net income: $830 million

Charles Baird
Chairman, CEO, Inco Ltd.
Cash compensation: US$329 000
Benefits: 22 officers receive varying portions of a US$78 000 noncash benefits package calculated at 3% of US$2.6 million
1983 income: US$329 000
1982 income: US$361 000
1983 corporate sales: US$1.2 billion
1983 corporate net loss: US$235 million

Maurice LeClair
CEO, Canadian National Railway Co.
Cash compensation: $232 950
Benefits: not reported
1983 income: $232 950
1982 income: $213 931
1983 corporate sales: $4.6 billion
1983 corporate net income: $212 million

Angus MacNaughton
Chairman, CEO, Genstar Corp.
Cash compensation: US$916 515, including US$400 000 cash bonus
Benefits: US$43 722
1983 income: US$960 237
1982 income: US$308 502
1983 corporate sales: $1.8 billion
1983 corporate net income: $103 million

Robert Welty
Chairman, CEO, Asamera Inc.
Cash compensation: $267 924
Benefits: $764 910 from stock options
1983 income: $1 032 834
1982 income: $216 189
1983 corporate sales: US$396.5 million
1983 corporate net loss: US $19 million

Donald McIvor
Chairman, CEO, Imperial Oil Ltd. *
Cash compensation: $516 150
Benefits: not reported
1983 income: $516 150
1982 income: $556 500
1983 corporate sales: $9 billion
1983 corporate net income: $290 million
*Moved to Exxon Corp. in April 1985

Phillip Urso
Chairman, CEO, McIntyre Mines Ltd.
Cash compensation: $570 000*
Benefits: company holds mortgage on home at 5% interest
1983 income: $570 000
1982 income: $292 159*
1983 corporate sales: $118.6 million
1983 corporate net loss: $7.5 million
*Includes $432 500 cash bonus paid partly in 1982 and partly in 1983

Howard Macdonald
Chairman, CEO, Dome Petroleum Ltd.
Cash compensation: $687 861
Benefits: $337 778 for loss of potential benefits on joining Dome, $100 000 relocation allowance; option to buy three million shares at $5.87 each
1983 income: $687 861
1982 income: not reported*
1983 corporate sales: $2.6 billion
1983 corporate net loss: $1.1 billion
*Joined Dome in June 1983

Cash compensation includes salaries, directors' fees, bonuses applicable for 1983 or earlier, plus any other cash. *Benefits* include securities; properties; the value of perks such as company cars and club memberships; insurance; other company-paid benefits; stock awards; interest-free loans; the value of stock options when converted to cash; long-term incentive programs contingent upon certain obligations; and retirement plans if they differ from the company plans.

Source: Wayne Lilley, "Pays and Perks, a Compensation Special," (excerpts), *Canadian Business,* April 1985, pp. 48–56. Used with permission of the author.

Pay for Performance

If you show up practically anywhere in the management hierarchy these days, something like this (although not likely on the same scale) could happen to you. The recession made companies lean but not totally mean: expendable people were chopped, but those who remain are being treated well. Says Bill Scott, Canadian operations manager of compensation consultants Hewitt Associates in Toronto: "Productivity has become the watchword, and that's been translated into pay for performance or merit pay."

That doesn't mean, however, that there's a simple relationship between a company's revenue and earnings and the amount on its pay stubs. As this special report points out, corporate Canada has become increasingly sophisticated in the way it rewards people. "Five or six years ago, the question that most companies had was, 'How much should we pay?'" says Terry Lynch, regional vice-president of Hay Associates Canada Ltd., another Toronto compensation specialist. "But when the phone rings now, the question is, 'How can we pay and how can we use compensation as an effective communicator and motivator to help us better achieve our business objectives?'"

Source: Wayne Lilley, "Pays and Perks, a Compensation Special," (excerpts), *Canadian Business*, April 1985, p. 50. Used with permission of the author.

Compensation Trends in 1986

TORONTO—Pay plans for 1986 look much like 1985, according to the Conference Board of Canada's annual survey on compensation trends. There is, however, considerable variation in projected salary increases reported by employers from various sectors, largely based on ability to pay, according to the director of the Board's Compensation Research Centre, Sally Luce. The survey findings were interpreted by Luce at the Board's 12th Annual Compensation and Human Resources conference earlier this month.

While the specter of pay cuts and concessions is dying out, an increasing number of organizations are adopting pay for performance schemes, according to Luce. In 1986 outstanding performers will receive average pay increases of 7.2% and satisfactory performers will receive an average of 4.6%. Benefits cost an average 23% of payroll costs in 1985 and although most employers forecast no change for 1986, some upward pressure exists, said Luce.

According to vice-president and chief economist for the Board, James G. Frank, as Canada's economic performance slows in 1986 after a strong performance in 1985, the unemployment rate should dip to 9.8%. He added that training and recruitment may surface as an issue in the latter part of the 1980s as fewer workers come on-stream and the market slowly begins to tighten.

On the industrial relations scene, 1986 will be a light bargaining year with little pressure expected from the union side. About 24% of respondents reported that they planned lower increases (3.8% on average) for union than for non-union employees. About 20% plan reduced start-rates for new employees, according to Luce. However, the national director of the Energy and Chemical Workers Union, Reginald Basken, said that unions will remain resistant to two-tier wage schemes as well as merit pay systems. He did agree that unions would display "more sanity" in wage demands and said the key feature in 1986 would be job security. Local issues will increasingly be removed from the bargaining table and dealt with on an individual basis as part of a growing trend toward "continuing dialogue."

Source: Human Resources Management in Canada, Report Bulletin No. 33, November 1985, p. 1. © 1986 Prentice-Hall Canada Inc. Used with permission.

These "PHRM in the News" articles illustrate the extent to which pay is linked with performance and the impact that this can have on productivity.

While Chapter 9 emphasized the multiple objectives of total compensation (attraction and retention of employees within a given legal framework), this chapter emphasizes the aspect of motivating employees to achieve high performance. This most often is achieved through use of **performance-based pay**. The two components of performance-based pay to be examined are *merit pay systems* and *incentive systems*. Note that while organizations may desire several types of behaviour from their employees, job performance is the behaviour of primary focus in this chapter. However, pay also is critical in motivating the other behaviours, particularly attendance and membership.

Performance-Based Pay Systems

Performance-based pay systems relate pay to performance. The extent of the relationship and the method of measuring performance are used to differentiate the two major types of performance-based pay systems or plans: incentive pay plans and merit pay plans. In incentive pay plans performance is often, but not always, measured by standards of productivity and direct indexes of the output of individuals, groups, or organizations. By contrast, merit pay plans generally use less direct measures of performance, such as rankings or ratings made by supervisors. The major portion of an individual's compensation, under this system, is from incentive pay. Since the level of compensation varies with performance, the level of an individual's compensation can vary greatly. Thus merit pay plans affect a relatively small percentage of an individual's total salary because merit pay generally is used only to move an individual's compensation within a rate range, and this adjustment is made only once a year. Traditionally, incentive pay plans have used only money as a reward. More recently, such non-monetary rewards as praise, participation, and feedback are also being tied to performance.[1]

Although many people are rewarded by performance-based pay, it is primarily under merit pay plans. Consequently, much of the compensation people receive is primarily not related to performance, but rather to the results of job evaluation and steps in rate ranges (discussed in Chapter 9). In either case, performance-based pay plans can motivate workers to perform at high levels. This is, in large part, the purpose and importance of performance-based pay systems.

Purposes and Importance of Performance-Based Pay

Money can be an extremely powerful motivator of performance. Says TPF/C's Mr. Crystal:

> People who question the motivational value of money tend to be mostly in academia or the news media. They have a much lower greed content than executives in industry and are motivated by other things. And that's good, because if they measured their success by the money they make, they'd probably kill themselves.[2]

Studies have shown that individual incentive plans can improve performance on an average of almost 30% in comparison to non-performance-based pay plans. Group incentive plans can increase performance 15 to 20%.[3] These figures are impressive given that other PHRM programs such as goal setting, participation plans, and job enrichment have less of an impact on productivity.[4]

If pay is going to influence employee performance, two sets of conditions must exist: One describes the employee's perspective and the other describes the organization's perspective. For the employee, the following are important:

- The employee must perceive a close relationship between performance and pay—pay must be perceived as contingent upon performance.
- Pay must be important or of high value to the employee.
- The employee must be able to perform (i.e., have the ability and know what is expected).
- The employee must not be placed in jeopardy or conflict by working for the extra pay. For example, he or she must not fear physical injuries, rate cutting, job insecurity, or ridicule from co-workers.
- Performance measurement must be fair. If performance evaluations are viewed as biased, many employees will not be motivated by pay.

In order that these conditions exist for the employee, the organization must do its part, which involves the following:

- There must be a high level of trust between the organization and the employees.
- The employee must understand how the pay program works.
- The employee must be able to control the performance on which the pay is based.
- The performance appraisal system must be free from potential bias.
- Managers must be trained in giving feedback.
- The amount of money set aside for merit or incentive pay must be sufficiently large to make extra effort worthwhile.

- The job evaluation must be valid, so that the overall salary relationships are equitable.

Different performance-based pay plans are appropriate under different conditions. Knowing which conditions currently exist in an organization is critical in successfully using performance-based pay plans. A list of plans to choose from is shown in Exhibit 10.1. Both the pay plans and the conditions under which they are more or less effective will be discussed in this chapter.

Relationships of Performance-Based Pay

The relationships between performance-based pay and other PHRM activities are discussed here.

Training and Development. Managers must be made aware of the effects of contingent (performance-based) rewards on performance. They must be trained to observe employee performance accurately and to provide employees feedback as quickly as possible after the desired behaviour, via pay, praise, and other rewards. In addition to management training, several other organization development programs can be used in conjunction with performance-based pay to improve productivity and the quality of work life (see, chapter 13).

Union-Management Relations. Since wages are a bargainable issue, whether or not an organization has a performance-based pay plan may depend on whether a union wants it. And because unions have traditionally opposed performance-based pay plans for several reasons, organizations must convince the union of the benefits of these pay plans. Once shown the benefits and even the necessities of such pay plans, some unions appear to be willing to co-operate and be instrumental in implementing performance-based pay plans.

Performance Appraisal. When pay is based on employee performance, how this performance is measured becomes of paramount importance.[5] The performance appraisal system must be accurate and reliable and appraise the behaviours and results needed most by the organization.

Performance-Based Pay Plans by Level — *Exhibit 10.1*

Individual	Group	Organization
• Piecework plan	• Production incentive	• Profit-sharing
• Standard hour plan	• Department head	• Scanlon plan*
• Measured day work	• Staff/professional	
• Sales incentive plan	• Senior officer	
• Managerial incentive plans		
• Suggestion systems		

*Discussed later in this chapter.

328 Compensating

Legal Considerations in Performance-Based Pay

As indicated in previous chapters, the various human rights Acts apply not only to staffing issues, but also to pay decisions. Of particular importance is the fact that a supervisor may be charged with unlawful discrimination by an employee who belongs to a protected group if the employee thinks a pay raise was denied on the basis of factors unrelated to performance. However, no cases of this type have been reported yet.

It is within this context of systemic relationships and legal considerations that merit pay and incentive pay plans operate. While incentive pay plans appear to have substantially more motivational value, merit pay plans are used much more frequently. The range of both types is shown in Exhibit 10.1.

Merit Pay Plans

The results of a recent U.S. Conference Board survey on merit pay plans indicate that this type of plan is widely used in non-union companies.[6] Of the companies surveyed, merit pay is granted to 96% of their non-exempt salaried employees, 99% of the exempt, and 98% of top management. In contrast, only 7% of the unionized hourly employees receive merit pay hikes, which usually are awarded in combination with a general increase. Non-union hourly workers are granted merit hikes by 39% of the companies, with 45% of the merit-paying firms also granting a general increase. Non-exempt salaried employees earned a median merit increase of 8% in 1977 and 1978—a figure that declined to 7.7% in 1979. Exempt salaried employees received median merit increases of 8% in each of the surveyed years, while the median merit hikes for top management were 8.1% in 1977, 8.2% in 1978, and 8% in 1979. Median merit hikes declined substantially in 1982 and 1983 to approximately 5.6%, due largely to the decline in the rate of inflation and slow economic activity.[7]

A survey conducted in 1983 by the Conference Board of Canada shows very similar trends. Approximately 75% of the companies surveyed said they linked pay with performance.[8] In 1986, for example, outstanding performers received an average pay increase of 7.2% and satisfactory performers received an average of 4.6%.[9]

Effective use of merit pay plans necessitates the determination of the size of merit pay raises, the times at which they are to be given, and the relationship between merit pay increments and position in the salary range. Particularly during times of high inflation, organizations must address the general relationship between merit pay and cost-of-living adjustments.

Merit Pay Guidelines

A typical example of a merit plan is shown in Exhibit 10.2. As illustrated, the pay increments depend not only on employee performance but also on employee position in the salary range.[10] Position is determined by expressing the employee's current salary as a percentage of the salary that is the midpoint of the range of salaries for that job. The lower the position in the range (the first quartile is the lowest), the larger the percentage of the merit raise.

It is important to monitor the number of people in each quartile. Although the percentage of merit increases is greater in the lower quartiles, the absolute size of increases is often larger in the higher quartiles. The more people in the higher quartiles, the larger the budget necessary for merit increases. Therefore, the compensation manager must monitor the line managers, who may attempt to push their employees to the top of the ranges in each job as a way to offer more rewards. The compensation manager ends up playing the role of police officer, particularly in a highly centralized operation. Unpleasant as it may be, this role is necessary for budget purposes and to ensure equity for all employees in the organization. Employees who perform equally well on the same job generally should not be paid different salaries and given different merit increases.[11]

Merit Versus Cost-of-Living Adjustments

Many large organizations grant **cost-of-living adjustments** (COLAs) or general (non-performance related) increases to their employees, particularly firms in which unions have written COLAs into their contracts. Neither COLAs nor general increases are based on performance, yet they can account for the lion's share of money available for compensation increases. And where unionized workers have COLA guarantees, the pressures are great to provide the same benefits to non-union, often white-collar, employees.

Sample Merit Pay Plan

Exhibit 10.2

Performance Rating	Current Position in Salary Range			
	First Quartile	*Second Quartile*	*Third Quartile*	*Fourth Quartile*
Truly outstanding	13–14% increase	11–12% increase	9–10% increase	6–8% increase
Above average	11–12% increase	9–10% increase	7–8% increase	6% increase or less
Good	9–10% increase	7–8% increase	6% increase or less	delay increase
Satisfactory	6–8% increase	6% increase or less	delay increase	no increase
Unsatisfactory	no increase	no increase	no increase	no increase

Many organizations would rather eliminate their COLAs in favour of merit pay plans, primarily because COLAs often are rather expensive and have no relationship to performance.[12] In addition, COLAs often take some salary control out of the hands of the organization and the compensation manager. Since most COLAs are tied to the Consumer Price Index, salaries increase arbitrarily as the Index goes up. The greater the COLA budget, the smaller the pot for merit increases. Some people argue that, because merit increases must be substantial to have any effect, the issue in times of high inflation becomes whether to use the entire salary budget for COLAs or for merit increases. The incentive value of merit raises tends to be modest in even the best economic circumstances. This is due to the relatively small size of the average merit increase, and to the relatively small differences (in absolute dollars) between getting the top increase and the lowest increase. Consequently, organizations look to incentive pay plans when they desire more motivational value from their compensation dollar.

Incentive Pay Plans

In Canada, most incentive plans are either piecework or standard hour plans.[13] In general, there is a great deal of variation in the type of incentive used, by type of industry and even by region. For example, a significant percentage of the employees in the textile, clothing, cigar, and steel industries are covered by incentive plans, while a much smaller percentage in the service industry and very few public employees are paid under incentive plans. Broadly speaking, it is more likely that incentive plans will be used if labour costs are high, the market is cost-competitive, technology is not advanced, and one employee's output is relatively independent of another employee's. These factors also may influence the specific type of plan used. The easiest way to discuss these plans is by the level at which they are applied—individual, group, or organization. Each type of plan is generally unique to a specific level.

Individual-Level Incentive Plans

Individual-level incentive plans include the following:
- Piecework plan
- Standard-hour plan
- Measured day-work plan
- Sales-incentive plan
- Managerial-incentive plan
- Suggestion systems
- Positive-reinforcement system

Piecework Plan. Piecework is the most common type of incentive pay plan. Under this plan, employees are guaranteed a standard pay rate for each unit of output. The pay rate per unit frequently is determined by the time-and-motion studies of standard output and the current base pay of the job. For example, if the base pay of a job is $30 per day and the employee normally can produce 30 units a day, the piece rate may be established at $1 per unit. The "normal" rate is usually more than the time-and-motion studies indicate, because it is supposed to represent 100% efficiency. The final rate will be adjusted to reflect the bargaining power of the employees, economic conditions of the organization and community, and what the competition is paying.

Standard-Hour Plan. The second-most-used incentive is the standard-hour plan. It essentially is a piecework plan, except that standards are denominated in time per unit of output rather than money per unit. Tasks are broken down by the amount of time it takes to complete them. This can be determined by historical records, time-and-motion studies, or a combination of both. The time to perform each task then becomes a "standard time."

Measured Day-Work Plan. Measured day-work plans play down the connection between rates and standards. Again, formal production standards are established, and employee performance is judged against these standards. But with measured day work, the typical standards are less precise. For example, standards may be determined by the results of a rating or ranking procedure rather than by an objective index, such as units produced.[14]

Sales-Incentive Plan. All of the incentive plans discussed previously share an important characteristic: they are usually applied to blue-collar employees and in some cases to office employees. Incentive plans for salespeople and managers are referred to as **commissions**. About two-thirds of all salespeople are paid a base salary plus commission.[15] In real estate sales however, almost 75% of the people are paid straight commissions. Only 22% of all other salespeople are paid straight commissions, and only 11% of all salespeople work without some guaranteed minimum pay.[16]

Managerial-Incentive Plan. Incentive plans for managers generally take the form of cash bonuses for good performance of the department, division, or organization as a whole. Other forms of compensation that can be used as managerial incentives are stock options and performance shares. A **stock option** is an opportunity for a manager to buy organization stocks at a later date but at a price established when the option is granted. The idea is that managers will work harder to increase their performance and the profitability of the company (thus increasing the price of the company's stock) if they can share in the profits over the long run. If the market price of the stock increases over time, managers can use their options to buy the stock at a lower price and to realize financial gain. Moreover, governments also recognize stock-option purchase as a boost to the economy. To encourage this trend, the province of Québec, for example, grants employees tax deductions for purchasing shares of the companies for which they work.

Performance shares provide a very close connection between individual performance (as reflected in company profitability) and rewards, because the manager or executive is rewarded only if established goals are met. The goals are usually stated in terms of earnings per share. If the goal is met, the manager receives shares of stock directly. Usually the manager receives cash (called "bonus units") as well as stock, in order to pay taxes on the stock. Receipt of just the shares, however, is usually a substantial reward on its own.[17]

The current trend in managerial incentive plans is toward long-term options. This strategy incorporates many advantages to both the company and the individual,[18] in that it

- provides executives with a means of accumulating capital at comparatively favourable tax rates;
- provides favourable tax treatment for the company, and in many cases for the employee;
- minimizes potential negative cash flow and dilution of earnings;
- motivates managers to maximize the future growth and profitability of the company; and
- retains outstanding executives and attracts others from the outside labour market.

Suggestion Systems. This form of incentive compensation, which rewards employees for money-saving or money-producing suggestions, is important because it is used so extensively. Approximately 80% of North America's 500 largest corporations have suggestion systems.[19] Suggestion systems are also important because they can result in substantial sums of money for the employees as well as significant savings for the company. Some organizations allow employees as much as 30% of the savings realized during the first year after implementation. Since the inception of Eastman Kodak's suggestion system, more than 1.8 million suggestions have been made by Kodak employees and approximately 30% have been accepted. As much as $2 million per year has been awarded to Kodak employees for their suggestions. IBM Canada Ltd. paid out $680 000 in awards for savings of $2.5 million, and the Treasury Board of Canada awarded $250 000 in 1983 for savings of almost $11.5 million.[20]

Nevertheless, suggestion systems generally do not have a very favourable reputation because individual awards often are not as large as those mentioned above. Also, employees sometimes never learn the results of their suggestions, and companies often grant smaller monetary rewards than the employees expect, based on company savings. In some cases, an individual's suggestion is at first ignored but is later put into operation by management—with no reward to the employee. This creates hostility, resentment, and distrust between management and employees. The suggestion box itself, in these cases, may become an object of ridicule and games.

Although most suggestion systems are designed to elicit and reward individuals' suggestions, some systems are designed for groups of employees. Such a system is part of the Scanlon plan, which is discussed in the section on organizational-level incentives. The suggestion system is a unique incentive system because it is designed to increase the number of good ideas rather than the output of products.

Positive-Reinforcement System. The **positive reinforcement system** lets employees know how well they are meeting specific goals, and rewards improvements with praise and recognition. In this respect it is also a unique incentive system:

> To establish a positive reinforcement program, the employer must define the behavioral requirements of the work to be done and evaluate how well it is being done. Job performance goals must be formulated in measurable terms, such as the meeting of deadlines, quality levels, and volume. Once these are established, employees must be provided with timely data on their goal performance.[21]

One of the basic premises of positive reinforcement is that behaviour can be understood and modified by its consequences. In fact, all incentive systems are based on this premise: performance is elicited because of the consequence of getting rewards. In many organizations, the consequences of behaving well are not monetary.

In order for a positive-reinforcement system to effectively elicit the repetition of desired behaviour/performance, several conditions must be met. The parameters of effective reinforcement in compensation include:

1. *Nature of the reinforcer:* Only praise that is valued by the employee is effective.
2. *Time of the reinforcer:* Only reinforcers that immediately follow the desired behaviour are effective. A response such as, "You did a good job, so I will recommend a pay raise in the next year's budget," is an example of an ineffective reinforcer.
3. *Magnitude of the reinforcer:* Only reinforcers that have sufficient magnitude and are tied strongly to the desired behaviour are effective.
4. *Specificity of the reinforcer:* Only reinforcers that are very specific and clearly understood by the employee are effective. Vague and non-specific feedback such as, "You did a good job," may not be an effective positive reinforcer.
5. *Routineness of the reinforcer:* Reinforcers that superiors use repetitively lose their effect over time. People get used to them and eventually take for granted the anticipated reward. An annual Christmas bonus is an example of a reinforcer that loses its effect over time.
6. *Schedule of the reinforcer:* Most rewards could be classified into one of two groups: continuous or partial reinforcement. Continuous reinforcement is administered every time a desired behaviour occurs. For example, a manager could praise (or pay) employees every time that they

perform properly. Partial reinforcement is administered at specific intervals, not every time that a desired performance is exhibited. Research has shown that partial reinforcement elicits slower learning but leads to stronger, more permanent retention. Exhibit 10.3 shows four types of reinforcement schedules and their effect on behaviour.

Individual-level incentive plans, whether based on monetary rewards or verbal praise, often have substantial motivational value. However, conditions under which they have this value do not always exist. Group-level incentive plans may be more effective in some situations.

Group-Level Incentive Plans

As organizations become more complex, a growing number of jobs become interdependent in either of two senses. Some jobs are part of a sequence of operations: the jobs that precede and follow them affect their performance. Other jobs are part of a joint effort that is necessary to achieve results.[22]

In either case, measurement of individual performance is difficult at best. Individual-level incentives are not appropriate under these conditions because they fail to reward co-operation, whereas group-level incentives can do this. Therefore, individual-level incentive plans may become less common if changing technologies make jobs increasingly interdependent.

Most group-level incentive plans are adaptations of individual plans. The standard-hour and performance-sharing plans are frequently used, but in

---

Exhibit 10.3   *Schedules of Reinforcement*

Schedule of Reinforcement	Nature of Reinforcement	Effects on Behaviour When Applied	Effects on Behaviour When Perceived	Example
Fixed interval	Reward on fixed-time basis	Leads to average and irregular performance	Quick extinction of behaviour	Weekly pay cheque
Fixed ratio	Reward consistently tied to output	Leads quickly to very high and stable performance	Quick extinction of behaviour	Piece-rate pay system
Variable interval	Reward given at variable intervals around some average time	Leads to moderately high and stable performance	Slow extinction of behaviour	Monthly performance appraisal and reward at random times each month
Variable ratio	Reward given at variable output levels around some average output	Leads to very high performance	Slow extinction of behaviour	Sales bonus tied to selling X accounts, but X constantly changes around some mean

Source: R. M. Steers, *Introduction to Organizational Behavior,* 2nd ed. (Glenview, IL: Scott, Foresman, 1984), p. 199. Copyright © 1981, 1984 by Scott, Foresman and Company. Reprinted by permission of the publisher.

group applications, base rates are paid for a group standard output, and group performance above this standard determines the premium for the individuals in the group.

For group-level incentive systems to motivate performance effectively, they must incorporate objective standards and measurable goals. The individuals in the group must believe that, as a whole, they can achieve these objectives through effective performance. Also, the system must be perceived as rewarding co-operation as well as individual performance. When these conditions exist, the results can be quite favourable. One well-publicized case comes from Nucor Corporation, a U.S. steel company.

The Nucor Example. In 1971, Nucor Corporation had sales of $64.8 million dollars and profits of $2.7 million dollars. In 1980, the corporation had sales of $482.4 million dollars and profits of $45.1 million dollars. This growth of more than 6090% in sales and 1500% in profits was generated entirely internally and was due to a number of factors such as modern technology, aggressive management style, and most importantly, substantial improvements in productivity.[23] The substantial improvement in productivity was due in large part to the various group-incentive plans. Since these plans can be adopted by other organizations, it is appropriate and useful to use Nucor as the basis for discussing group-level incentive plans here.

Nucor has four group-level incentive compensation plans. The plans are for production employees, department heads, secretaries, accounting clerks, accountants, engineers, and senior officers, and are set up as follows:

- *Production Incentive Program:* About 2500 employees within Nucor work under this program. Employee incentive groups are generally no larger than 25 or 30 people. For each of the steel mills there are nine bonus groups: three in melting and casting, where the bonus is based on good billet tons per hour; three in rolling, where the bonus is based on good shear tons produced; and three in straightening, where the bonus is based on good straightened tons produced. Measurements and totals are calculated on a weekly basis and bonuses are paid together with employees' regular pay the next week. To help ensure that these bonus plans work well, Nucor makes sure that the operation and output of each group are definable and measurable.

- *Department-Head Incentive Program:* At the department-head level the company has an incentive compensation program based on the *division's* contribution to overall profits or the profits of the division relative to its expenses.

- *Staff/Professional Incentive Program:* This third program covers employees who do not fit into the production or department-head groups. For example, included in this program may be groups composed of an accountant, an engineer, a secretary, and an accounting clerk. The bonus incentive for these groups is based on either the division return on assets or the company's return on assets.

- *Senior-Officer Incentive Program:* The senior officers at Nucor receive no profit sharing, no pension plans, nor many other executive "perks." Pay for these executives is roughly 70% of the salary that executives at similar levels in other companies receive. All other compensation is in the form of a bonus, half of which is paid in cash and half of which is deferred. The bonus derives from 10% of pre-tax earnings set aside for the senior officers according to their salary.

The Nucor example shows how an entire firm can operate under several different incentive plans, not just one for all employees. Sometimes, neither single nor multiple group-level incentive plans are appropriate for an organization. Organizational conditions may be more amenable to organization-level incentive plans.

Organization-Level Incentive Plans

Because many organizations need high levels of co-operation among their employees, they use some form of incentive on an organization-wide basis. Many Canadian firms use either plant-wide bonus plans or profit-sharing arrangements.[24]

Under these systems, employees receive as a bonus a percentage of their base wage if the organization reaches some goal. Employees receiving the same base wage or salary rate therefore receive the same incentive. Profit-sharing plans often are not considered a form of incentive compensation because individual employees have only partial and indirect control over organizational profits. However, since the extent of employee control over performance in a profit-sharing plan is a matter of degree rather than kind, profit-sharing plans are included here as an organizational-level incentive.

Profit-Sharing Plans. Many profit-sharing plans are registered with Revenue Canada to comply with current tax laws. There are two major types of profit-sharing plans that organizations can use. **Cash plans** provide for payment of profit shares at regular intervals, typically monthly or yearly. The percentage of profits distributed ranges from 8 to 75%. If profits are not realized by the company, no cash payments are made to employees. For this reason, many profit-sharing plans are also called "gain sharing." Gain sharing leads to enhanced productivity and subsequently creates additional profits in which all parties share.

Wage-dividend plans base the percentage of profits paid to employees on the amount of dividends paid to stockholders. These plans are assumed to increase understanding between employees and stockholders and are often perceived as more fair to employees than regular cash plans.

Profit sharing among Canadian corporations is growing fast. In the mid-1950s there were 2000 registered plans in Canada, by the mid-1970s there were 8000 plans, and by the mid-1980s, more than 25 000.[25] Companies such as IPSCO Steel of Regina, Dominion Envelope, Supreme Aluminum Industries, DOFASCO, Canadian Tire Corporation, and Simpsons department store are only a few examples of companies that use this system. However, while virtually all of the U.S. plans involve all employees, more than 95% of Canadian profit-sharing plans limit participation to senior executives. A study conducted in the U.S. demonstrated that, on all financial measures, the profit-sharing companies out-performed the non-profit-sharing companies by a substantial measure.[26]

Although these two types of plans are the most common, organizations continue to develop new plans that fit their unique circumstances. An example of such a plan is the one developed by steelmaker IPSCO of Regina. IPSCO asks profit-sharing participants to put from $200 to $500 of their own money into the plan through payroll deductions. The employees' money is then put together with the profit-sharing pool to buy IPSCO shares on the open market. The $200 contributor gets two-fifths of the shares allotted to a $500 contributor. Those who are eligible also can shield their share purchase in a group registered retirement savings plan so that they can benefit from immediate tax deductions. The IPSCO plan differs from conventional approaches in two major ways: all participants share *equally* in the profits, and the shares bought by the plan are vested immediately, although employees can sell their shares at any time.[27]

The Scanlon Plan. The Scanlon plan represents as much a philosophy of management-employee relations as it does a company-wide incentive system. It emphasizes employer-employee participation in the operations and profitability of the company. Scanlon plans are adaptable to different companies and changing needs, and are used in unionized as well as nonunion plants.[28]

The Scanlon plan reflects the fact that efficiency of operations depends on company-wide co-operation, and that bonus incentives encourage such co-operation. The bonus is determined on the basis of savings in labour costs, which are measured by comparing the payroll to the sales value of production on a monthly or bi-monthly basis. Previous months' ratios of payroll to sales value of production help to establish expected labour costs. Savings in labour costs are then shared by employees (75%) and the employer (25%). Because all employees share in the savings, one group does not gain at the expense of another. Each employee's bonus is determined by converting the bonus fund to a percentage of the total payroll and applying this percentage to the employee's pay for the month. In one Canadian company, The Canadian Valve and Hydrant Manufacturing Co., the ratio of payroll costs to net sales revenue was dramatically improved after a Scanlon-type plan was introduced.[29]

Although Scanlon plans can be successful, their real incentive value can be short-lived. This can occur if the employees feel that they no longer can work smarter or harder and, therefore, feel that they cannot improve on previous months' payroll-to-sales-value-of-production ratios. At this point, employee performance levels off and the Scanlon plan loses its incentive value. This problem, however, is greatly minimized where work methods and products are always changing. Under these conditions employees are more likely to feel that they can always find better ways to work.

Administrative Issues in Performance-Based Pay

Although performance-based pay plans are capable of substantially improving productivity, there often are many obstacles in design and implementation that limit their potential effectiveness.

Obstacles to Performance-Based Pay Plan Effectiveness

Obstacles in the design and implementation of performance-based pay plans can be grouped into three general categories: (1) difficulties in specifying and measuring job performance; (2) problems in identifying valued rewards (pay being just one of many rewards); and (3) difficulties in linking rewards to job performance.[30]

In order to reward job performance, one must first specify what job performance is, determine the relationships between levels of job performance and rewards, and accurately measure job performance. This is often difficult because of the changing nature of work, its multi-dimensional nature, technological developments, lack of supervisory training, and the manager's value system. The problems are presented in more detail in Exhibit 10.4, along with their implications for management.

A second set of obstacles applies to the selection of appropriate monetary as well as non-monetary rewards. Rewards other than pay may have more motivational value than pay, particularly for employees whose pay increments may be largely consumed by increased taxes. Consequently, it is important for the manager to learn which kind of rewards are valued by the employees and contingently administer those that are most reinforcing. This process is filled with potential problems, as shown in Exhibit 10.4.

The third set of obstacles relates to the difficulties in linking rewards to job performance. It can be difficult, for example, to create appropriate contingencies or accurate performance-appraisal measures. In addition, employee opposition is sometimes a major obstacle in successfully implementing performance-based pay, particularly incentive plans. This opposition is due to a large number of beliefs that employees may have about incentive plans, including

- that incentive plans result in work speedup;
- that rates are cut if earnings under the plan increase too much;
- that incentive plans encourage competition among workers and the discharge of slow workers;
- that incentive plans result in unemployment through "working yourself out of a job";
- that incentive plans break down crafts by reducing skill requirements through methods study;
- that workers do not get their share of increased productivity;

Obstacles to the Design of Effective Reward Systems and Their Implications for Management

Exhibit 10.4

Obstacles	Causes	Implications for Management
A. Difficulties in specifying and measuring performance	1. Changes in the nature of work • Increase in service-oriented jobs • Increase in white-collar, managerial, and professional jobs • Increases in the interdependencies and complexity of work 2. Multi-dimensional nature of work • Single-item measures of performance are often inadequate • In many jobs today, multiple criteria are necessary to assess performance 3. Technological developments • Technological developments often result in new and untested methods of work • Machine-paced jobs permit little variation in performance 4. Lack of supervisory training • Use of untrained, inexperienced supervisors in the evaluation process • Perceptual biases 5. The manager's value system • Lack of interest in or inability to differentiate among high and low performers • Failure to see long-range outcomes of differential rewarding	1. Develop techniques for specifying desirable behaviours and clarifying the objectives of the organization. 2. Utilize evaluation procedures that recognize the multi-dimensional nature of performance 3. Develop a reliable and valid performance appraisal system based on results and/or behavioural standards 4. Train supervisors to use the performance appraisal system appropriately and to understand potential sources of bias 5. Clearly define long-term consequences of performance-contingent and non-contingent reward practices
B. Problems in indentifying valued rewards	1. Choice of rewards • Choosing a reward that is not reinforcing 2. Utilizing rewards of insufficient size or magnitude • Lack of resources • Company policy 3. Poor timing of rewards • Size of organization: bureaucracy • Standardization/formalization of feedback mechanisms • Complexity of feedback system	1. Make managers aware of the effects of rewards on employee performance and satisfaction 2. Train managers to identify rewards for their subordinates 3. Administer rewards of sufficient magnitude 4. Administer rewards as quickly after desirable responses as possible

Continued on next page

Exhibit 10.4 Continued

Obstacles	Causes	Implications for Management
C. Difficulties in linking rewards to performance	1. Failure to create appropriate contingencies between rewards and performance • Lack of knowledge, skill, experience • Belief system • Difficulty of administration 2. Creating inappropriate contingencies • Rewarding behaviour that does not increase performance • Rewarding behaviour A, but hoping for B 3. Nullifying intended contingencies • Using improper performance appraisal instrument • Improper use of performance appraisal instrument • Failure to use information obtained • Inconsistently applied 4. Employee opposition • Individually: mistrust, lack of fairness, inequity • Socially: restrictions due to fear of loss of work • Outside intervention: union	1. Train manager to establish appropriate contingencies between rewards and performance 2. Use information obtained from appraisals of employee performance as basis for reward allocation decisions 3. Administer the reward system consistently across employees 4. Obtain employee participation in the design and administration of the pay plan

Source: P. M. Podsakoff, C. N. Greene, and J. M. McFillen, "Obstacles to the Effective Use of Reward Systems," *Readings in Personnel and Human Resource Management,* R. S. Schuler and S. A. Youngblood (eds.), 2nd ed. (St. Paul: West Publishing Co., 1984).

- that incentive plans are too complex;
- that standards are set unfairly;
- that industrial engineers are out to rob workers;
- that earnings fluctuate, making it difficult to budget household expenditures and even to obtain home mortgages;
- that incentive plans are used to avoid deserved pay increases;
- that incentive plans increase the strain on workers and may impair their health;
- that incentive plans increase the frequency of methods changes;
- that incentive plans ask workers to do more than a fair day's work; and
- that incentive plans imply a lack of trust in workers by management.[31]

All in all, many of these stereotypical beliefs emerge from lack of trust in management. This lack of trust has immediate implications for the establishment of rates and standards on which incentive systems are based. Workers may stage elaborate charades for the benefit of time-study engineers doing the work measurement described in Chapter 3. To further complicate matters, the engineers (who know that workers sometimes try to be misleading) may incorporate into their data estimates that take these charades into account. This combination of scientific observation and measurement and educated guessing can result in inaccurate or unfair rates, which reduce the incentive value of the system, the profitability of the company, or both.[32]

Auditing the Merit Pay System

Critical to the success of any merit pay system is that it be administered so as to maintain integrity—that it be administered accurately and fairly across employees and divisions/units in a company. It is important for all employees to know that their merit raise is being determined in the same way, regardless of the supervisor, and that the determination is based on an accurate measure of job performance. While ensuring accuracy of appraisals may be addressed effectively by a behavioural-based performance-appraisal method such as BARS or BOS (see Chapter 7), ensuring fair and consistent administration within the pay structure is done through the use of compra-ratios and performance ratios.

Compra-ratios and performance ratios used together can highlight pay and job performance relationships by individual employee, by salary grade, by level in the organization, or by department or division in the company. The **compra-ratio** is the measure of an individual's salary in relation to the mid-point of the range for a salary grade. This ratio is determined by dividing an individual's salary by the mid-point of the salary range and multiplying by 100. A ratio of 110, for example, means that the individual is being paid 10% over mid-point. Assuming a normal distribution of job performance and experience levels, the average compra-ratio in any department or division should be close to 100. Ratios higher than 100 may suggest leniency and therefore inaccuracy in a supervisor's appraisals, and ratios less than 100 may suggest the opposite. Differential ratios across departments or divisions may indicate inconsistent merit pay administration.

Similar conclusions can be drawn from the use of **performance ratios**, which indicate where the performance rating of any employee stands relative to the other employees. This is done by determining the mid-point of a performance range and dividing that into each employee's performance rating and multiplying that figure by 100. This process can be facilitated by using a performance appraisal method with points rather than relative rankings. Most performance appraisal methods discussed in Chapter 7, except the relative approach, can be used in determining performance ratios. Again, assuming normal performance distributions, the average performance ratio for a department or division should be close to 100. Variations from 100 may suggest unfair and inconsistent merit pay practices.

Participation in Performance-Based Pay Plans

Employee participation can take place at two critical points in performance-based pay plans: (1) in the design stage, and (2) in the administration stage.

Design Stage Participation. Many pay plans are designed by top management and installed in a fairly authoritative fashion. It appears, however, that employees can not only design pay plans, but design them more effectively. Also, the employees are more likely to understand and accept a plan that they helped to design. Participation in plan design also helps to reduce the resistance that accompanies almost any change in an organization. As a consequence of all of this, employees are more motivated to increase performance.

Administration Participation. As indicated in Chapter 9, employees can determine responsibly when and if other workers should receive pay increases. This also appears to be true for individuals determining their *own* pay increases. An example in a U.S. company, Friedman Jacobs, illustrates this point:

Friedman decided to allow his employees to set their own wages, based on their perception of their performance. This radical approach apparently has worked well. Instead of an all-out raid on the company coffers, the employees displayed responsible behaviour. They set their wages slightly higher than the scale of the union to which they belonged and apparently find their pay quite satisfactory. When one appliance serviceman who was receiving considerably less than his co-workers was asked why he did not insist on equal pay, he replied, "I don't want to work that hard." [33]

Assessing Performance-Based Pay

Regardless of organizational conditions, performance-based pay plans can be assessed on the basis of three criteria:[34] (1) the relationship between performance and pay—that is, the time between performance and the administration of the pay; (2) how well the plan minimizes the perceived negative consequences of good performance, such as social ostracism; and (3) whether it contributes to the perception that rewards other than pay (such as cooperation and recognition) also stem from good performance. The more it minimizes the perceived negative consequences and the more it contributes to the perception that other good rewards are also tied to performance, the more motivating the plan is likely to be. Exhibit 10.5 presents an evaluation of individual, group, and organizational plans based on these three criteria.

In Exhibit 10.5, three measures of job performance to be rewarded are sales or units made (productivity), cost effectiveness or savings below budget, and traditional supervision ratings. The more objective measures gen-

Effectiveness of Performance-Based Pay Plans

Exhibit 10.5

	Type of Plan	Performance Measure	Tie Pay to Performance	Minimize Negative Side-Effects	Tie Other Rewards to Performance
Merit	Individual plan	Productivity	+2	0	0
		Cost effectiveness	+1	0	0
		Superiors' rating	+1	0	+1
	Group	Productivity	+1	0	+1
		Cost effectiveness	+1	0	+1
		Superiors' rating	+1	0	+1
	Organization-wide	Productivity	+1	0	+1
		Cost effectiveness	+1	0	+1
		Profit	0	0	+1
Incentive	Individual plan	Productivity	+3	−2	0
		Cost effectiveness	+2	−1	0
		Superiors' rating	+2	−1	+1
	Group	Productivity	+2	0	+1
		Cost effectiveness	+2	0	+1
		Superiors' rating	+2	0	+1
	Organization-wide	Productivity	+2	0	+1
		Cost effectiveness	+2	0	+1
		Profit	+1	0	+1

Source: E. E. Lawler III, *Pay and Organizational Effectiveness*, p. 165. Copyright © 1971 by McGraw-Hill Book Company. Reprinted with permission.

erally have higher credibility, are more valid, and are more visible and verifiable than the traditional supervisor ratings. Consequently, the objective measures (productivity and cost effectiveness) are more likely to link pay to job performance than they are to minimize negative side-effects. This evaluation is based on the belief that people do what elicits rewards. More objective measures tend to make it very clear what is rewarded and what is not. This may produce more keen competition with other workers, result in more social ostracism, and lead workers to perceive that good job performance may reduce the work available to them.

The overall evaluation of plans suggests that, compared to individual-level incentive plans, group- and organization-wide incentive plans, although not high in relating individual performance with pay, result in fewer negative side-effects (the exception is with intergroup competition) and additional benefits besides pay, such as esteem, respect, and social acceptance from other employees.

No one of the three levels of incentive pay plans is superior on all criteria. Incentive plans have more incentive value than seniority increases, across-the-board raises, and merit pay plans. Thus, the situation for motivating job performance with pay is not hopeless. In fact, in a recent study of 54 companies with incentive programs, the average increase in productivity over their previous non-incentive programs was 22.8%. Furthermore, it appears that even larger gains are possible and likely to be maintained, when the conditions shown in Exhibit 10.6 exist.

Unfortunately, it is difficult for many organizations to meet all of these conditions. In addition, as the cost of indirect compensation continues to grow for most organizations, the amount of money left for performance-based pay decreases. Consequently, organizations look to their indirect compensation to provide some motivational value, as is discussed in the next chapter.

Summary

Performance-based pay plans are gaining popularity in Canada, attracting the attention of PHRM managers and even CEOs who search for means to motivate their employees. Yet the experience with merit pay is mixed: many managers have found that pay is not always a motivator of increased performance.

The success of many incentive plans depends on the circumstances under which they are implemented. For example, implementation of incentive pay plans requires an effective performance-appraisal program. The more objective the measures of job performance, the more value incentive plans

Exhibit 10.6   *Conditions Necessary for Performance-based Pay Plans*

- The employee must perceive a close relationship between performance and pay
- Pay must be important to the employee
- The employee must have the ability, be able to perform, know what's expected, and perceive minimal conflicts in performing the rewarded behaviours, both in the short and long run
- The employee must not be placed in jeopardy or conflict by working for the extra pay. For example, there must be no fear of physical injuries, rate cutting, job insecurity, or ridicule from co-workers
- Performance must be measurable and fair
- There must be a high level of trust between the organization and the employees
- The employee must know and understand how the pay program works
- The employee must be able to control the performance on which the pay is based
- The performance-appraisal system must be free from potential bias
- Managers must be trained in giving feedback
- The amount of money set aside for merit or incentive pay must be sufficiently large to make extra effort worthwhile
- The job evaluation must be valid so that the overall salary relationships are equitable

Source: R. S. Schuler and S. A. Youngblood, *Effective Personnel Management* (St. Paul: West Publishing Co., 1986), p. 342. Used with permission.

have. But many organizations do not have effective appraisal programs. As a result, pay is not based on job performance but rather on non-performance factors, such as the cost of living or seniority. To retain some appearance of rewarding job performance, some organizations may use merit pay plans. Consequently, most organizations are not able to provide the full incentive value of pay. Nevertheless, a few organizations are attempting to remove the obstacles to incentive plans by allowing a great deal of employee participation in implementation and administration, which provides employees with a clear understanding of the plan. This system allows employees to appeal pay decisions, and provides rewards as soon as possible after the job performance.

Yet, despite the potential motivational value of performance-based pay plans, the majority of organizations continue to choose essentially non-performance-based plans. Some organizations think that it is not possible to have performance-based pay plans because of the lack of appropriate conditions or because it is too costly. However, if the pay system is fair and effective, paying for performance increases performance, which should in turn increase profitability. This increased profitability should provide more than enough cash to enable the organizations to pay for the cost of the performance-based pay plan.

The choice of performance-based pay plans must be determined by several factors, such as the level at which job performance can be accurately measured (individual, group, or organization), the extent of co-operation needed between groups, and level of trust between management and non-management. Several plans can be used in the same company to reward different groups of employees for good job performance. However, there may be limits on a specific organization's use of performance-based pay—limits such as management's desire to have performance-based pay; management's commitment to take the time to design and implement one or several systems; the extent to which employees really influence the output; and the degree of trust that exists in the organization.

Discussion Questions

1. What are the parameters of effective reinforcement in compensation?
2. What is the difference between a merit pay plan and an incentive pay plan?
3. What conditions are necessary for effective performance-based pay systems?
4. How are cost-of-living adjustments related to merit pay?
5. What factors enhance the likelihood of using incentive pay plans?
6. Under what conditions are group-level incentive pay plans more appropriate than individual-level incentive pay plans?
7. What are organization-level incentive pay plans, and how do they work? Give examples.

8. Why do merit plans fail so often?
9. Employee opposition is often a major obstacle in effecting good performance-based pay systems. Discuss why this statement is true.
10. How can an organization determine whether merit pay is administered accurately across all employees or all units and divisions?

C A S E   S T U D Y

If the Hat Fits, Wear It

Ricky Hernandez has worked at the Halifax Hat Factory for more than one-third of his 34 years. Ricky first began work at Halifax Hat during the summers when he was a high-school student. Ricky's dad, Bob, had worked at Halifax Hat for 36 years, and had just retired the previous year. The only time that Ricky had not worked for Halifax Hat was during the two years after graduation from high school when he enlisted in the army and was stationed in Québec. After completing his army tour, Ricky decided to return to Halifax and settle near his family.

The hat business, while somewhat cyclical, provided about 120 steady jobs. Although the pay at Halifax Hat is somewhat below average for semi-skilled workers in the area, Ricky likes the incentive pay system that the company has used for the past five years. Under this system, workers are guaranteed a minimum wage per hour plus an incentive based on the number of finished hats completed above the standard. For the past two years, Ricky has been working the same job his father worked: utility man.

One of Ricky's favourite jobs as utility man is the finish job, which requires the worker to soften the brim of freshly pressed felt hats. According to the procedures taught to new employees, this job requires the use of both hands to knead the brim to remove the stiffness created when the hat is pressed. Needless to say, this requires considerable dexterity and stamina, and is one job on which it is difficult to produce over the standard.

Ricky, however, had learned from his father how to do the finish job effectively. In fact, about two years before his father retired, Bob shared with his son his secret invention—a labour-saving steel mandrel that he had devised more than 10 years previously to help him finish hats after arthritis began to make handwork difficult. Bob had showed his supervisor, Lynn Wilson, his invention and Lynn even got the owner and general manager of Halifax Hat, Mari Sperdakos, to evaluate it. But after several employees had used the mandrel rather unsuccessfully and damaged several expensive felt hats, the tool was banned from further use.

Bob was disappointed at the time, particularly because the company owner had never bothered to ask him to demonstrate the proper use of the mandrel. Bob believed that the trial use of the mandrel failed because the other employees had received inadequate training. From that point on, he hid the mandrel in his tool box. Lynn had sympathized with him, so he permitted the continued use of the tool but cautioned Bob to keep a keen eye out for management. Lynn knew that if Bob was ever caught violating the ban, they both could be severely disciplined and their jobs possibly jeopardized. But at the same time, Lynn knew that with this tool, Bob could produce at a rate approximately four times that of standard.

So Ricky inherited the secret mandrel and continued its covert use. Lynn Wilson knew that the tool, in experienced hands, could increase productivity to such an extent that the payroll department would catch on if Ricky were allowed to work the finish job for more than just a few hours each day. So Lynn was willing to let Ricky continue the illicit practice, but never for more than a few hours each day. Ricky came to look upon the tool as a way to earn slack time in case he needed time to relax a little on the job or as a means to earn a few extra dollars to spend on his family, particularly before holidays.

The cat-and-mouse game of using the secret tool bothered Ricky at first, but after a while, he could see no reason why he should try to convince management of their error in rejecting his father's invention. To ease his conscience, he would sometimes recall that management didn't exactly play fair and square with their large customers. For example, a common practice at Halifax Hat was to run extra hats on large contracts with retailers to produce private-label hats. The extra hats would then be restamped on the sweatband in such a way as to conceal the original label and add the Halifax Hat logo. These hats were then shipped to the company's own outlet stores and sold.

One day while Ricky was working on the finish job with the mandrel, he got careless and began to daydream about an upcoming fishing trip that he and his dad were planning. Before he knew it, Mari Sperdakos had rounded the corner like the wind on a nasty day, and saw Ricky manoeuvring a felt hat over the mandrel, totally oblivious to Sperdakos' approach.

Endnotes

1. P. M. Podsakoff, C. N. Greene, and J. M. McFillen, "Obstacles to the Effective Use of Reward Systems," in R. S. Schuler and S. Youngblood (eds.), *Readings in Personnel and Human Resource Management*, 2nd ed. (St. Paul: West Publishing, 1984).
2. *Industry Week*, May 4, 1981, p. 66.
3. K. W. Bennett, "Employee Incentives Plus New Technology Equals Productivity," *Iron Age*, Feb. 2, 1981, pp. 43–45. "Roundup," *Personnel*, Nov.–Dec. 1979, pp. 57–59. E. E. Lawler III, *Pay and Organization Development* (Reading, MA: Addison-Wesley, 1981). E. E. Lawler III, *Pay and Organizational Effectiveness: A Psychological View* (New York: McGraw-Hill, 1971).
4. Although goal-setting and job-enrichment programs are ways to increase productivity, incentive compensation appears to be able to produce larger increases in productivity.
5. P. J. Stonich, "The Performance Measurement and Reward System: Critical to Strategic Management," *Organizational Dynamics*, Winter 1984, pp. 45–57. R. N. Kanungo, "Reward Management: A New Look," in S. L. Dolan and R. S. Schuler (eds.), *Canadian Readings in Personnel and Human Resource Management* (St. Paul: West Publishing, 1987).
6. C. A. Peck, *Compensating Salaried Employees During Inflation: General vs. Merit Increases* (New York: The Conference Board, 1981), p. 14. D. J. Thomsen, "Salary Increases vs. Incentives," *Personnel Journal*, Dec. 1980, p. 974.
7. J. S. Lublin, "Small Pay Raises Expected Again as Slump Persists, Inflation Cools," *The Wall Street Journal*, Jan. 5, 1983, p. 23. J. Bettner, "Many Executives Forego Usual Big Pay Raises, Thanks to Recession and Lowered Inflation," *The Wall Street Journal*, Nov. 1, 1982, p. 56.
8. D. Alexander, "Pay for Performance," *Mercer Breakfast Seminar*, Toronto, January 19, 1984 (unpublished report).
9. *Annual Survey on Compensation Trends*, Conference Board of Canada, 1985.
10. Other factors influencing merit pay that can be legally defended when they are equally applied to all employees include: (1) position in salary range; (2) time since last increase; (3) size of increase; (4) pay relationships within the company or department; (5) pay levels of jobs in other companies; (6) salaries of newly hired employees; and (7) budgetary limits.
11. J. G. Goodale and M. M. Mouser, "Developing and Auditing a Merit Pay System," *Personnel Journal*, May 1981, pp. 391–397.
12. C. R. Deitsch and D. A. Dilts, "The COLA Clause: An Employer Bargaining Weapon?" *Personnel Journal*, March 1982, pp. 220–223. B. L. Metzger, *Profit Sharing in Perspective*, 2nd ed. (Evanston, IL: Profit Sharing Research Foundation, 1966), p. 45. H. Risher, "Inflation and Salary Administration," *Personnel Administrator*, May 1981, pp. 33–38, 68. J. D. Schwartz, "Maintaining Merit Compensation in a High Inflation Economy," *Personnel Journal*, Feb. 1982, pp. 147–152. Peck, endnote 6. D. J. Thomsen, "Compensation Trends in 1981," *Personnel Journal*, Jan. 1981, p. 22.
13. D. Nightingale, "Profit Sharing: New Nectar for the Worker Bees," *The Canadian Business Review*, Spring 1984, pp. 11–14.
14. J. D. Dunn and F. M. Rachel, *Wage and Salary Administration: Total Compensation Systems* (New York: McGraw-Hill, 1971), p. 236.
15. *Incentive Plans for Salesmen*, Studies in Personnel Policy 217 (New York: National Industrial Conference Board, 1970).
16. *Compensating Field Representatives*, Studies in Personnel Policy 202 (New York: National Industrial Conference Board, 1966).
17. R. J. Bronsteing, "The Equity Component of the Executive Compensation Package," *California Management Review*, Fall 1980, pp. 64–70. For an excel-

lent discussion of the entire area of executive (managerial) compensation see M. Bentson and J. Schuster, "Pay and Executive Compensation," in S. J. Carroll and R. S. Schuler (eds.), *Human Resource Management in the 1980s* (Washington, DC: The Bureau of National Affairs, 1983). A. Nash, *Managerial Compensation* (Scarsdale, NY: Work in America Institute, Inc., 1980). "After the Qualified Stock Option," *Business Week*, May 25, 1981, pp. 100–102. P. Meyer, "Executive Compensation Must Promote Long-Term Commitment," *Personnel Administrator*, May 1983, pp. 37–44. D. Rankin, "Warm Welcome for Incentive Options," *The New York Times*, June 13, 1982, p. F15.

18. W. F. Cascio, *Managing Human Resources: Productivity, Quality of Work, Life, Profits* (New York: McGraw-Hill Book Co., 1986), pp. 412–413.

19. M. A. Tather, "Turning Ideas into Gold," *Management Review*, March 1975, pp. 4–10. V. G. Reuter, "A New Look at Suggestion Systems," *Journal of Systems Management*, Jan. 1976, pp. 6–15.

20. For U.S. data, see A. W. Bergerson, "Employee Suggestion Plan Still Going Strong at Kodak," *Supervisory Magazine*, May 1977, pp. 32–33. For Canada, see W. Carr, "Communicating with ESP," "Current Matters/New Ideas" *Human Resources Management in Canada*, Prentice-Hall Inc., 1985, p. 5,342.

21. W. J. Kearney, "Pay for Performance? Not Always," *MSU Business Topics*, Spring 1979, p. 6. Division of Research, Graduate School of Business Administration, Michigan State University.

22. D. W. Belcher, *Compensation Management*, 3rd ed. (Englewood Cliffs, NJ: Prentice-Hall, 1974), pp. 323–324.

23. J. Savage, "Incentive Programs at Nucor Corporation Boost Productivity," *Personnel Administrator*, Aug. 1981, pp. 33–36, 49.

24. "The Compensation Special Report," *Canadian Business*, April 1985, pp. 48–57. Also, regarding about profit sharing in Canada see D. Nightingale, "Profit Sharing: New Nectar for the Worker Bees," *The Canadian Business Review*, vol. II, no. 1, 1984, pp. 11–14.

25. Ibid., Nightingale, p. 13.

26. B. L. Metzger, *Profit Sharing in Perspective*, 2nd ed. (Evanston, IL: Profit Sharing Research Foundation, 1966). More information on profit sharing in Canada can be obtained by writing to the Profit Sharing Council of Canada, 1262 Don Mills Rd., Don Mills, Ontario M3B 2W7. The following material has been published by the Council: *Profit Sharing—An Innovative Approach to Effective Management*, 1982; *The Profit Sharing Handbook*, 1983; *Profit Sharing and Employee Ownership*, 1980.

27. "A fairer share of the wealth: Steelmaker IPSCO shows its employees how the capitalist system works—for them," "A Compensation Special," *Canadian Business*, April 1985, p. 55.

28. B. E. Moore and T. L. Ross, *The Scanlon Way to Improved Productivity: A Practical Guide* (New York: John Wiley & Sons, 1978). A. J. Geare, "Productivity from Scanlon-Type Plans," *Academy of Management Review*, July 1976, pp. 99–108. R. J. Schulhof, "Five Years With a Scanlon Plan," *Personnel Administrator*, June 1979, pp. 55–63. L. S. Tyler and B. Fisher, "The Scanlon Concept: A Philosophy as a System," *Personnel Administrator*, July 1983, pp. 33–37.

29. W. B. Werther, Jr., et al., *Canadian Personnel and Human Resource Management*, 2nd ed. (Toronto: McGraw-Hill Ryerson, 1985), p. 350.

30. These have been identified and discussed by Podsakoff et al., endnote 1. See also R. I. Henderson, "Designing a Reward System for Today's Employee," *Business*, July–Sept. 1982, pp. 2–12.

31. S. Barkin, "Labor's Attitude Toward Wage Incentive Plans," *Industrial and Labor Relations Review*, July 1948, pp. 553–572. These issues are reviewed in more detail in E. Lawler III, *Pay and Organizational Development*, endnote 3; R. B. Goettinger, "Why Isn't Incentive Compensation Working?" *Personnel Journal*, June 1982, pp. 436–442.

32. J. D. McMillan and V. C. Williams, "The Elements of Effective Salary Administration Programs," *Personnel Journal*, Nov. 1982, pp. 832–838. T. A. Mahoney, "Compensating for Work," in K. N. Rowland and G. R. Ferris (eds.), *Personnel Management* (Boston: Allyn & Bacon, 1982), pp. 227–262.

33. E. E. Lawler III, *Pay and Organizational Development*, endnote 3, p. 110.

34. Ibid. R. B. Goettinger, "Compensation and Benefits," *Personnel Journal*, Nov. 1981, pp. 840–842.

CHAPTER 11

Benefits Pay and Administration

PHRM in the News

Benefits Pay
Purposes and Importance of Benefits Pay
Relationships of Benefits Pay
Legal Considerations in Benefits Pay

Private Protection Programs
Retirement Benefits
Early Retirement Benefits
Insurance Benefits
Supplemental Unemployment Benefits

Pay for Time Not Worked
Off the Job
On the Job

Employee Services and Perquisites
Golden Parachutes

Administrative Issues in Benefits-Pay Compensation
Determining the Benefits Package
Providing Benefit Flexibility
Communicating the Benefits Package

Assessing the Benefits of Indirect Compensation

Summary

Discussion Questions

Case Study

Endnotes

PHRM in the News

The Third Wave in Employee Benefits

A snapshot of the ideal benefits package envisaged by practitioners today would probably look like this:

Life Insurance:	4 times annual earnings
Sickness, Accident, Disability Benefits:	6 months' salary continuance; LTD benefits of 75% salary to age 65, fully indexed, WCB top-up if applicable continuation of pension accrual
External Health Care:	private hospital room plus full coverage in excess of government plans; 100% co-insurance; $25 deductible
Prescription Drugs:	pay-direct plan (35 cents deductible)
Dental Plan:	100% coverage of all services; $25 deductible; current year's schedule of fees;
Pension Plan:	2% final earnings; fully indexed to C.P.I. and integrated with C.P.P. or Q.P.P.

A practitioner assessing this snapshot (after an initial reaction of "Rich, very rich—must be government") should ask if it is "ideal but unfortunately too rich," or if it is just "too rich." After a long period of consistency in structure, [benefit] plan designs are now beginning to show the effects of many changing influences. With benefits running between 30% and 40% of payroll costs, justifying the expense is now raising many questions.

Today's benefit structures, with their higher value levels, merely seem to be richer versions of the structures of the 1940s. An analogy would be buying a car in 1985 with digital stereo, air conditioning, and computerized readouts added onto the engine and chassis of a 1940s gas-guzzler. Extremely expensive, but hardly ideal.

Source: J. Wallace and D. McPherson "Optimizing Benefits: The Third Wave in Employee Benefits," *Human Resources Management in Canada*, Dec. 1984, pp. 5,327–5,328. Prentice-Hall Canada Inc., Toronto, 1986. Used with permission.

Flexible Benefits Package Could Become New Standard

The much-talked-about practice of allowing employees to choose their own package of benefits remains just so much consultants' chitchat. From all accounts, only a handful of companies give workers any significant choice.

Employers, of course, are more concerned these days about maintaining or paring down their workforces. Company-paid benefits are definitely in second place.

However, the workforce is changing—there are more younger people, women and two-income couples—and these changes call for other changes in the approach to noncash compensation. The standard benefits package doesn't do the trick it used to.

One solution is to allow employees to mix and match their benefits—within some predetermined value.

Frank Livsey, a benefit consultant at Hewitt Associates, says "flexible" is loosely applied in some plans. For example, it may only mean a choice of life insurance coverage equal to one-, two- or three-times salary.

A truly flexible plan is much more wide-ranging, although there may be a core of mandatory benefits. Livsey gives the example of lower life coverage and less vacation and higher dental or medical coverage or additional contributions to a pension plan.

Hewitt Associates allows its Canadian employees to weigh individual benefits as they see fit. Employees are given an annual allocation of $100 for each year of service—up to a maximum of $1,000—which they can use to buy company benefits (after having worked for three years).

Their typical choices? Employees reimburse themselves for deductibles or co-insurance expenses in the medical plan, pay dental expenses (no company coverage), or contribute to the deferred profit-sharing plan.

By 1985, he forecasts about 10 companies here will have flexible compensation, growing to 100 during the 1990s.

Without making any predictions, John Trimble, benefits manager at T. Eaton Co., expects employees to have more say in how they receive employers' compensation. Among other choices, Eaton's plan allows employees more control of their vacation time, sick time and other time off. And, Trimble says, "our data tell us employees make intelligent choices—they know what they need. In cafeteria-style, you walk down the counter and pick up what you want until you run up a certain bill. Cafeteria-style would not apply to Canada whole hog but some degree of flexibility would apply in Canada."

Health-insurance coverage is a logical benefit choice since people may be already covered by their spouses' employers. Trimble says Eaton's will pay a single employee's health coverage, or the cash equivalent if the health coverage is not chosen. Family health coverage can be obtained by paying the extra cost.

Source: "Benefits and Pensions," *The Financial Post,* March 19, 1983, p. 29. Used with permission.

In the Boardroom

Employee benefits usually run the gamut of pension, medical and profit-sharing plans, with the occasional creative perk, such as paid tuition for employee children. IBM Canada Ltd. has added a new wrinkle. IBM pays *80% of the administrative cost of adopting a child*, to a maximum of $1,500 per family, for all regular and retired employees. It also provides financial assistance for each child for families with physically or mentally handicapped children.

Source: "In the Boardroom," *The Financial Post,* March 29, 1986, p. 20. Used with permission.

These "PHRM in the News" articles highlight several aspects of benefits pay and administration. One is the magnitude of benefits-pay costs. In some cases, these may equal to or even exceed those of direct compensation (see figures for CEOs in "PHRM in the News," Chapter 10). But, as the first article indicates, benefits costs tend to total 30 to 40% of the direct compensation.

The second article points to a new trend in benefits content and administration—the flexible package. The rising costs of benefits has led to a search for new ways to render them more effective, to meet the compensation objectives. The flexibility in fringe benefits packages offered at the T. Eaton Co. are aimed at achieving these goals.

The third article demonstrates the continued search for even more avant-garde benefits packages that reflect a company's social responsibility to society at large, as well as to selected employees. IBM Canada, for example, in an effort to boost its corporate image (thereby increasing the likelihood of attracting and retaining employees) has recently decided to pay 80% of the administrative cost of adopting a child. Other companies also are exploring some unique avenues in benefits-pay plans.

Many employees are vitally concerned about benefits. After all, this form of compensation is tax-free in many cases. From the organization perspective, as the cost of benefits in proportion to the total payroll cost grows, employers are becoming interested in choosing only benefits that are cost-effective—those that employees really value. Consequently, benefits-pay and administrative issues become a dynamic and vital personnel activity for both employees and employers.

Benefits Pay

Almost all organizations offer some form of benefits-pay program. For some of these organizations, as noted in the first "PHRM in the News" article, this indirect compensation may make up as much as 40% of the cost of total compensation (the terms "indirect compensation" or "fringe benefits" are occasionally used here to denote benefits-pay, because many organizations still refer to them as such). Furthermore, the percentage of total compensation devoted to benefits is expected to rise. Because the costs of benefits pay are becoming so significant, organizations question whether the benefits provided really are worthwhile. The answer depends on the purposes of benefits pay and what it really is.

Employee benefits can be defined as those rewards provided by the organization to employees for their membership and/or participation in the organization. Benefits pay can be divided into three categories: [1]

1. Protection Programs:
    –public
    –private

2. Pay for Time Not Worked:
    –on-the-job
    –off-the-job

3. Employee Services and Perquisites:
   –general
   –limited

Although some of these benefits are mandated by federal and provincial governments and therefore must be administered within the boundaries of laws and regulations, many others are provided voluntarily by organizations. Partly because such rewards are so diverse and employees' preferences are so varied, indirect compensation is not always valued or seen as a reward by all employees. When benefits are matched with employee preferences, however, many of the purposes of indirect compensation can be more readily attained.

Purposes and Importance of Benefits Pay

As was mentioned earlier, benefits-pay costs as a percent of direct compensation is growing substantially. As illustrated in Exhibit 11.1, the total benefits-pay cost for Canadian companies grew from approximately 24% in 1964 to 31% in 1984. Out of these, the legally required payments such as unemployment insurance, workers' compensation, etc., grew from approximately 1.5% in 1964 to 4.5% in 1984. Pension and other agreed-on payments grew from 9% (1964) to 13.5% (1984); paid rest periods did not change much, but payments for time not worked grew from about 8% in 1964 to 11% in 1984.[2] Note that 1980 represents a peak in benefits pay; a slight decline was marked for the early 1980s (a recessionary period). Also, note that profit-sharing payments and bonuses are excluded from this analysis.

Furthermore, it should be noted that benefits pay varies greatly across industries and by level of employee in the organization. A marked difference in benefits, for example, exists between the private sector versus the federal government. Whereas benefits received by federal employees used to be inferior to those received by private sector employees, the federal package is now estimated to be as good or even superior. However, regardless of salary level or sector of the economy, the cost of benefits to organizations is enormous.

For a proper appreciation of employees benefits, Exhibit 11.2 shows the breakdown of the benefits costs in relation to the total compensation cost. The average employer cost per employee for 1984 also is illustrated in Exhibit 11.2.

Through provisions of these benefits, organizations seek to

- attract good employees;
- increase employee morale;
- reduce turnover;
- increase job satisfaction;
- motivate employees;
- enhance the organization's image among employees; and
- make better use of compensation dollars.

Exhibit 11.1 Benefits and Other Non-wage and Salary Cost Comparisons for Canadian Companies from 1964 to 1984

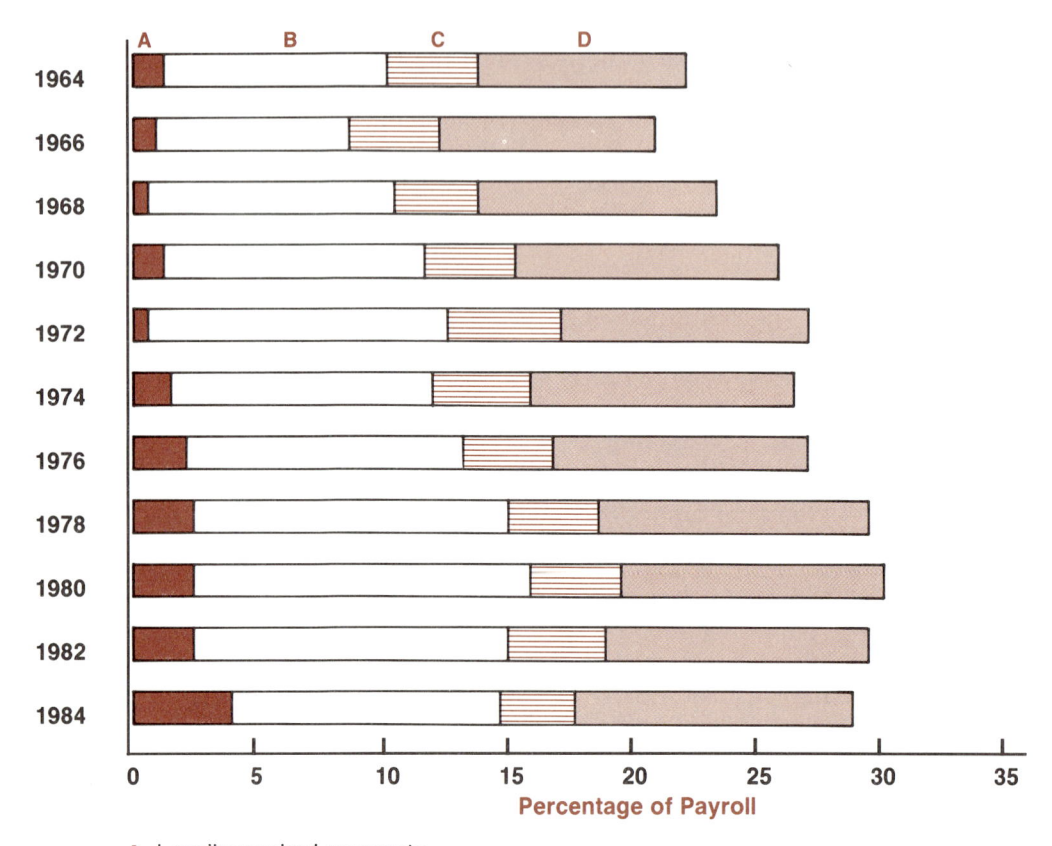

A: Legally required payments
B: Pension and other agreed-upon payments
C: Paid rest periods, lunch periods, etc.
D: Payments for time not worked

Source: "Employee Benefit Costs in Canada," *Annual Surveys from 1954–1984*, Thorne, Stevenson & Kellogg, Toronto. Used with permission.

Only rarely are all of these purposes actually achieved. "There is ample research to demonstrate that these purposes are not being attained, largely because of inadequate communication."[3] The argument can be made, however, that some of these purposes cannot be attained at all with indirect compensation, even in the absence of communication problems. For example, it is possible to motivate employees with incentives because the rewards are tied closely to performance, but the rewards of indirect compensation are tied only to organizational membership. Thus no direct reason exists why increased indirect compensation should motivate employees to perform better.

Benefits Pay and Administration

In addition, many employees regard compensation benefits not as rewards but as conditions or entitlements of employment.[4] They may think of indirect benefits as safeguards provided by the organization as part of its larger social responsibility:

> Workers have an expanding sense of what is due them as rights of employment. From pension, health care, long vacations to a high standard of living,

---

Average Cost and Percentage of Benefits Pay in Proportion to Total Compensation in Canada **Exhibit 11.2**

Compensation Components

ELEMENTS OF COMPENSATION	Average Cost per Employee* $/a
1. Straight-time pay for hours worked	19 526
2. Premium pay for overtime hours	599
3. Premium pay for shift differential	152
4. Premium pay for working on holidays	328
5. Incentive and production bonuses	1 155
6. Other direct wage and salary payments	1 177
(71.92%)**	22 937
7. Paid time-off for vacations	1 786
8. Paid time-off for holidays	1 031
9. Paid time-off for coffee breaks and rest periods	1 035
10. Paid time-off for bereavement, jury duty, and military service	39
11. Paid time-off for change time, call-in, and personal leave	216
(12.88%)	4 107
12. Legally required payment for unemployment insurance, workers' compensation, and Canada/Quebec pension plans	1 175
13. Organization pension plan	1 204
14. Welfare plans such as life insurance, survivor benefits, hospital, surgical, medical, dental plans, non-occupational sickness and accident, etc.	1 435
15. Cash benefits such as termination and severance pay, savings, bonus and profit-sharing plans	761
16. Other non-cash benefits such as free meals, cafeteria, free lodging, recreation facilities, parking and transportation, education subsidies	275
(15.20%)	4 850
TOTAL COMPENSATION	31 894

* Dollar figures derived from Thorne, Stevenson & Kellogg Survey: "Employee Benefit Costs in Canada, 1984."
** Percentage of total compensation.

Source: John T. Wallace and D. L. McPherson, "Employee Benefit Plans," *Human Resources Management in Canada*, Prentice-Hall Canada Inc., Toronto, 1986. Used with permission.

the perception by workers of what constitutes their rights is inexorably being enlarged. Concomitant with this spiraling sense of rights has been a declining sense of responsibility.[5]

Relationships of Benefits Pay

Although the relationships between total compensation and other PHRM activities described in Chapter 9 are applicable here, it is appropriate to highlight a few of those that apply to benefits pay. This is particularly important for staffing (both recruitment and selection) and health and safety functions.

Recruitment and Selection. As individuals demand more in terms of indirect compensation, an organization must offer more in order to attract a pool of potentially qualified job applicants. Without providing benefits comparable to those offered by others in the same industry or same area, an organization may lose qualified individuals to other employers.[6] Often, however, an individual may not learn of an employer's indirect compensation package until after being recruited. If this is the case, recruitment may not be as negatively affected as selection. A job applicant may go through the several, rather expensive, selection steps described in Chapter 5, only to reject a job offer because of an inadequate benefits compensation package.

Just as an organization's recruitment and selection activities can be adversely affected by a poor benefits-pay package, a sound indirect compensation plan can attract many potential job candidates. Organizations such as the federal government or the Toronto Transit Commission are attractive because of their benefits.

Health and Safety. As health and safety problems in organizations increase, the level of workers' compensation rates also often increases. This in turn increases the cost of indirect compensation to organizations. In addition, even if indirect compensation costs do not increase, it is possible that greater costs from damage suits against the employer could result and effectively increase total compensation costs. (This is further explored in the discussion of workers' compensation in Chapter 14.)

Legal Considerations in Benefits Pay

Benefits have been paid in Canada since World War I, starting with the establishment of the Workers' Compensation Board in Ontario, but only a small segment of the population could benefit from or rely on these programs. Not until 1927 was a federal/provincial constitutional conflict resolved, enabling the federal government to institute the Old Age Pension, which constitutes the basis for today's pension system. Unemployment policies emerged following the Depression and were translated into laws in the early 1940s. The post-war economic growth in the fifties and sixties led to the development of a web of social programs and benefits legislation. Much of the influence on Canadian benefits laws came from European and British laws, rather than from the U.S. Today, Canadian benefits (social and welfare legislation) are considered some of the most progressive in the western hemisphere. Currently, the government is trying to trim the enormous cost of these programs to reduce an increasing national deficit. In the following section, the entire web of legal benefit plans for Canadians will be presented.

Canada/Québec Pension Plans. The Canadian pension plan system is based on the existence of a three-tiered structure. Each tier is just as important as others in generating a source of income for retirement:

- Tier 1–Government income security plans
- Tier 2–Employer-sponsored retirement plans
- Tier 3–Personal retirement savings

The Canada Pension Plan (in effect since January 1, 1966) and the Québec Pension Plan are mandatory plans for all self-employed persons and all employees in Canada. Both plans are joint contributory: at the present time, the employer contributes 1.8% of a year's maximum pensionable earnings (YMPE), and the employee contributes 1.8%. To receive these pension benefits an employee must have resided in Canada for a minimum of 10 years, including the year prior to retirement. The retirement pension, approximately 25% of the contributory earnings up to the YMPE, is paid monthly for the contributor's lifetime.

In addition, a number of benefits are attached in case of disability, death (survivor's benefits), and moving to other countries. If the contributor becomes disabled, a monthly pension based on a fixed nominal amount plus an additional lump sum is payable to the employee. If the contributor dies, a maximum of 10% of the YMPE is paid in one lump sum to the contributor's estate. This is followed by a monthly pension to the surviving spouse. The amount varies depending on the age of the spouse at the time of death. Furthermore, a set amount is payable monthly to each dependent child. Canada has international agreements with several countries to protect the acquired social security rights of the eligible individual. Benefits are paid regardless of the country of residence after qualification to receive the pension payments.

Pension Benefits Standards Act. This Act regulates pension plans of firms under the jurisdiction of the federal government (such as Crown corporations, chartered banks, etc.). In addition, five provinces (Alberta, Saskatchewan, Québec, Nova Scotia, and Manitoba) have similar pension benefits Acts. The Act requires that pension funds be held in trust for members and that the funds not be completely controlled by either the employees or the employer. To accomplish this, a third party such as a life insurance agency, a trust company, or even the Government of Canada, is registered as custodian of the fund and administers it.

Old Age Security Act. All Canadians who meet the required age and residency requirements are entitled to payment of a minimum income under the Old Age Security Act.

Unemployment Insurance. All workers in insurable employment must pay a premium of 2.35%, which is deducted from their income. Employers must also contribute to this fund. Employers' premiums are calculated at 1.4 times the employee premium rate.

There are two types of unemployment insurance payments: regular and special. In order to receive the regular benefits, the applicant must have an interruption of earnings for at least seven days, and must have worked in insurable employment for a period of at least 10 weeks in the previous 52 weeks. Special benefits are paid to people who are sick, injured, pregnant, or in quarantine. The duration of regular unemployment benefits is determined by an entitlements formula. The weekly benefit rate is based on 60% of the claimant's average insured earnings for the previous 20 weeks in the qualified period.

Workers' Compensation Laws. Workers' compensation legislation gives employees protection for job-related accidents and industrial illnesses. Every province in Canada has its own Workers' Compensation Act. The administration of the Act is the responsibility of provincial Workers' Compensation Boards. Employers are classified into groups depending on the special industrial hazards that exist in each group. These groups of employers collectively pay the cost of compensation for any injured workers employed by the firms in that group. The annual contribution rate from each employer is determined on a pro-rata basis according to total annual payroll figures. It is possible for an employer to be charged a higher premium than this pro-rata basis due to a higher-than-average accident record compared with other organizations in this group. This provides a monetary incentive for enhancing the work environment.

Benefits provided under workers' compensation include: (1) medical care, (2) lump-sum death payment to a spouse and pension in case of death, (3) compensation in non-fatal cases, including wage loss for temporary disability, and (4) rehabilitation services.

Provincial Hospital and Medical Benefits. While Canada does not have a national health insurance plan as such, all Canadians are covered through a series of arrangements under the Canada Health Act (1984). Some provinces such as Manitoba and Québec provide a full health plan (even if Québec residents are travelling outside the province), while other provinces provide only minimum coverage. Manitoba and Québec, however, collect additional taxes of 1.5% and 3%, respectively, from all employers to cover the extended plan. Alberta, British Columbia, and Ontario charge premiums that are payable by the resident or an agent (usually the employer). In Alberta, for an employee group of 5 or more, and in Ontario, for a group of 15 or more, it is mandatory for all employers in this category to provide enrollment and collect premiums.

Private Protection Programs

Private protection programs are those offered by organizations, private and public, that are not required by law, although their administration may be regulated by law. The programs provide benefits for health care, income after retirement, and insurance against disability or loss of life. Almost all employers provide these programs for their employees.

Retirement Benefits

Approximately 40% of all Canadian employees are covered by private pension plans.[7] Most employers contribute to these plans. Pension coverage is most likely to exist for unionized employees in manufacturing firms. The average firm spends approximately 6.3% of its total payroll costs on pension plans.[8]

Employers can select from two types of pension plans: **contributory** and **non-contributory**. While regulations always require the employer to make minimal contributions, it may be necessary or desirable for employees also to contribute. The advantages of contributory plans include the following: (1) either a larger benefits fund or a lesser burden on the employer, (2) greater employee interest in and appreciation of the cost of a pension plan, and (3) tax-deductible contributions (up to $5500 annually at the present time). The non-contributory plans also have advantages, namely: (1) lower payroll and bookkeeping costs, (2) possibility of greater employee loyalty with less demand for wages and other benefits, and (3) more autonomy in making plans and investment decisions.[9]

Over the years, two significant problems have developed in the administration of pension plans in many industrial nations. First, some employers go out of business, leaving the pension plan unfunded or only partially funded. Second, the gap between yearly benefits paid and contributions keep widening, and the amount of unfunded liabilities keeps growing. The reason for this growing gap, according to two experts, is because "Many plans (in both the private and public sectors) have been installed over the years where the key decision makers had no understanding of the financial liabilities created by their pension plan." [10] Both of these problems have been buffered in Canada through the imposition of expert custodial administration under the Pension Benefits Standards Act.

Early Retirement Benefits

Thousands of Canadians have taken advantage of corporate offers of financially alluring early retirement programs. This trend began during the 1981–82 recession and continues today.[11] Employers—many of whom have not fully recovered from the recession—have devised strategies that encourage their older and usually their most highly paid employees to retire before they reach retirement age, as a way of reducing operating costs. Among the corporate leaders in the field are Vancouver-based forest products giant MacMillan Bloedel Ltd., with 12 000 employees; Metropolitan Life Insurance Co. of Ottawa with 2800 employees; Oshawa-based General Motors of Canada Ltd. with 45 000 workers; and Imperial Oil Ltd. of Toronto with a staff of 14 700. These companies have introduced plans that allow them to save as much as 30% of the cost of carrying their older employees through to age 65.

In order to make early retirement plans attractive, companies have to offer a wide variety of inducements. Most of the programs partially compensate older employees for the loss of that portion of the pension that they would have received if they had worked until they were 65. Some firms also provide a one-time cash settlement that can be converted, along with the pension, into tax-sheltered registered retirement savings plans (RRSPs), and they allow retirees to retain other benefits such as life insurance and medical plans.

Insurance Benefits

There are three major types of insurance programs: life, health, and disability. These insurance programs are provided by most organizations at a cost far below what would be charged to employees buying their own insurance. These programs have grown substantially, both in the dollar amount of benefits and the percentage of employees covered.

Life insurance programs cover almost all employees. A survey of 171 Canadian companies indicated that 98.8% provide life insurance programs for all of their employees.[12] The benefits are equal to about two years' income, but this tends to be more true for managerial employees than non-managerial employees.

Non-managerial, clerical, and blue-collar employees usually are covered for an amount that is less than one year's income. After retirement the benefits continue for most employees, but they may be reduced substantially. A majority of the life insurance programs offered by organizations are non-contributory—the employee does not pay into the program. There is, however, also a trend toward providing more coverage, particularly coverage of family members. Despite the cost, organizations are doing this to keep up with other organizations.

A similar philosophy supports the popularity of **supplementary health insurance plans**. All Canadian citizens are covered by provincial health care programs (for basic hospital care and medically required services); the supplemental health insurance plans provide coverage for those services that are excluded from the provincial plans. They include private or semi-private rooms in a hospital, ambulance services, extended rehabilitation services in case of lengthy recovery, and other supplementary services.

Dental insurance is the fastest growing addition to benefits pay.[13] A recent survey in Canada showed that 86% of the employers who participated in the survey offered dental plans.[14]

While health insurance programs generally cover short-term absences from work due to sickness, short-term absences due to disability are covered by *short-term disability insurance*. Longer-term absences are covered by *long-term sickness and disability insurance*. Both types of disability insurance generally supplement provincial disability programs, often referred to as *workers' compensation insurance*. However, short-term disability protection usually is offered by more organizations than is long-term disability protection. Virtually all of the organizations surveyed in 1984 offered short-term paid sick leave plans.[15]

Supplemental Unemployment Benefits

A small number of organizations offer employees protection against loss of income and loss of work before retirement, called **Supplemental unemployment benefits**. When such benefits are combined with unemployment compensation benefits, laid-off employees can receive as much as 95% of their average incomes.[16] The size of these benefits makes it easier for employees with many years of service to accept layoffs, thus allowing employees with less service, often younger, to continue working. These programs exist in a limited number of industries, and all are the product of labour-management contracts.

Supplemental unemployment benefit plans must be approved by Employment and Immigration Canada or payments will result in a reduction in unemployment insurance benefits. To avoid this, managers must design supplemental plans in line with Unemployment Insurance Canada regulations. These regulations outline acceptable supplemental plan provisions such as duration, funding, vesting, eligibility, and separation payment clauses.

Pay for Time Not Worked

Pay for time not worked is less complex to administer than benefits from protection programs, but it is almost as costly to the organization. Pay-for-time-not-worked plans continue to grow, in both amount and types. Recently, however, the effects of concessionary bargaining between union and management have meant fewer, not more, paid vacation days and holidays (see Chapter 17).

There are two major categories of pay for time not worked: off-the-job and on-the-job.

Off the Job

Payments for time not worked (referred to primarily as **off-the-job benefits**) constitute a major portion of the total cost of indirect compensation. The most commonly provided off-the-job benefits are vacations, sick leave, holidays, and personal days.

Specific policies concerning holidays and vacations vary from organization to organization. For example, paid vacation may vary from two weeks per year to four weeks or more. Paid holidays range from 6 to as many as

13. Some common holidays in Canada are New Year's Day, Good Friday, Victoria Day, Canada Day, Labour Day, Thanksgiving, Christmas, and Boxing Day.

On the Job

With increased awareness of the relationship between job stress and coronary heart disease and other physical and mental disabilities, organizations have become more concerned with finding ways to alleviate stress whenever possible.[17] People who are in good physical condition and who exercise regularly can often deal with stress better and suffer fewer negative symptoms. By providing athletic facilities on company premises, organizations are encouraging their employees to be physically fit and to engage in exercise. Paid time for physical fitness is clearly pay for time not worked on the job, but organizations often offer it because of its on-the-job benefits.

Employee Services and Perquisites

The final component of indirect compensation is employee services and perquisites, which may consist of the following:

- Food service costs
- Employee discounts
- Day-care centres
- Employer-sponsored scholarships or tuition assistance for employees and their dependants
- Employee counselling and advisory services (legal, tax, and personal problems)
- Low-cost loans
- Company-leased or -owned vehicles for business or personal use
- Child adoption subsidies

Perquisites primarily provided for top executives include:

- Annual company-paid physical examinations
- Company-paid memberships in country clubs, athletic and social clubs
- Use of company expense accounts to cover personal travel, meals, and entertainment
- Subsidized housing
- Business and personal use of corporate aircraft
- Sabbaticals
- Relocation costs

Although services and perks represent the smallest percentage of indirect compensation, they are highly rewarding to some employees and necessary to others. Some perks represent an important element in the status system of the organization. Others, such as the provision of day-care services, represent a means by which working is made possible.

Golden Parachutes

A recent development in executive compensation is the **golden parachute** arrangement. These arrangements generally provide financial protection for top corporate executives in the event of a change in control in the company. This protection is in the form of either guaranteed employment or severance pay on termination or resignation. The need for golden parachutes came about with the rapid flurry of mergers and acquisitions in the early 1980s. The parachutes were devised to soften top-management resistance to mergers or acquisitions that can financially help some companies and shareholders. Top managers who might be replaced as the result of a takeover would still be financially well off, in some cases, more so than previously. Because golden parachutes can be beneficial devices for the companies, executives, and shareholders involved, it is likely they will continue to be used.

Golden handcuffs are essentially the opposite of golden parachutes. When an organization wishes to retain (as opposed to lay off) a particular executive, they make it too costly for the executive to leave an organization. Types of compensation such as stock options and retirement packages are the most common golden handcuffs. By leaving, the executive forfeits these financially attractive benefits. Wise use of golden handcuffs can help in the retention of valued employees.

Administrative Issues in Benefits-Pay Compensation

Although organizations tend to view benefits pay as a reward, recipients do not see it this way. Benefits are often taken for granted; therefore, the organization gets little or no productivity return on its indirect compensation investment. As a result, there is much concern with the administration of indirect compensation.

Determining the Benefits Package

The benefits package should be selected on the basis of what is good for the employee as well as for the employer. Being aware of employee preferences often can help to determine which benefits package the employer should offer. Employees may indicate strong preferences for certain benefits over others: for instance, employees may indicate a strong preference for dental insurance, rather than life insurance, even though dental insurance is only one-fourth the cost of life insurance to the company.[18] The most desired benefit appears to be time off from work in large chunks. For older workers, there is a consistent increase in the desire for increased pension benefits. This is also the case for employees with rising incomes. These diverse preferences argue strongly for the provision of benefit flexibility.

Providing Benefit Flexibility

When employees can design their own benefits package, both they and the company benefit.[19] At least that's the experience at companies such as Eaton's, Cominco, and other Canadian companies. Seventy-five percent of Cominco's 1800 eligible employees have chosen to participate in a flexible benefits program. The company provides a core package of benefits to all employees, covering provincial medical plan payment; extended medical coverage with $500 deductible; life insurance offering one year's salary to the beneficiary; accident, death, and dismemberment coverage equal to three times the annual salary; short- and long-term disability insurance; vacations; a company pension; and a group-registered retirement savings plan. In addition, each employee can choose, cafeteria-style, from a variety of optional benefits. Some core benefits can be "sold" back to Cominco to add to the individual's cash account. For instance, if an employee's spouse is already covered by the provincial hospital plan, the employee can obtain a credit in flexible dollars for this hospital plan. And, depending on years of service with the company, a maximum of five holidays can be converted to flexible dollars to purchase other benefits. The options can include extended medical coverage with $25 deductible, three ranges of dental insurance, life insurance upgraded by six increments, and increased insurance for accidental death, dismemberment, and long-term disability.[20]

Communicating the Benefits Package

Providing benefit flexibility is good not only because it gives employees what they want, but also because it makes employees aware of the benefits that they are receiving and increases their morale.[21] Many employees are unaware of both the types and the costs of the benefits they are receiving.[22] If employees have no knowledge of their benefits, then there is little reason to believe that the organization's benefit program objectives will be attained. Many organizations indicate that they assign a high priority to telling employees about their benefits, although a majority spend only 1% of their payroll doing this.[23]

Many benefits program objectives are not currently attained, probably due to ineffective communication techniques. Almost all organizations use impersonal, passive booklets and brochures to convey benefits information; only a few use more personal, active media, such as slide presentations and regular employee meetings.[24] A technique that communicates the total compensation components every day, such as "benefits calendars," would be highly effective. Each month, the calendar shows a company employee receiving a compensation benefit. For example, one month may feature a photo of an employee building a new home made possible through the company's incentive program and savings plan. Another month may feature a benefit of the company's medical plan. By educating employees about the benefits package and providing employees with benefit flexibility, the positive impact of indirect compensation may be increased.

Assessing the Benefits of Indirect Compensation

Listed at the beginning of this chapter are several purposes of indirect compensation. The impact of the chosen indirect benefit program on these purposes is one-half of the equation for measuring the effectiveness of the benefits package. The other half involves determining the costs. Another way is to determine the effectiveness of the indirect benefits program, and then compare the costs and benefits.

An organization can determine the dollar value of the costs of indirect compensation in four ways:

1. Total cost of benefits annually for all employees
2. Cost per employee per year divided by the number of hours worked
3. Percentage of payroll divided by annual payroll
4. Cost per employee per hour divided by employee hours worked [25]

These costs then can be compared with the benefits, such as reduced turnover, less absenteeism, or an enhanced company image among employees. The dollar value of these benefits, although difficult to specify exactly, can be estimated, thus enabling the organization to compare directly the dollar costs of benefits against the dollar savings they afford.

After the company determines these cost/benefit ratios, it can further assess the benefits of its indirect compensation by

- examining the internal cost to the company of all benefits and services by payroll classification, by division or profit centre, and for each benefit. This information also helps to monitor benefit costs and helps to ensure some degree of uniformity across levels and divisions in the organization. Thus, this information serves a role similar to that served by compra-ratios and performance ratios, as discussed in Chapter 10;
- comparing the company's costs for benefits to external norms. For example, the company can compare its costs for the entire package or for each benefit to averages by industry, as reported in credible surveys. This data can help to ensure that a company is not spending more than it must to attract and retain individuals. It also can help to determine how much the company needs to spend if it wants to have a recruitment advantage over other companies;
- analyzing the costs of the program to employees. Determine what each employee is paying for benefits, overall and by benefit;
- comparing the data in the above step with externally published data; and
- analyzing how satisfied the employees are with the organization's current program—and as compared to competitors' programs.

The above methods focus on assessing the current benefits provided by an organization. Two other methods focus on assessing the alternatives available, by

- exploring the costs and benefits of alternative benefit possibilities such as flexible or cafeteria-style benefit plans. Costs in this case involve those associated with the benefits themselves as well as the administrative costs. The latter are particularly critical in cafeteria-style plans; and
- comparing the costs and benefits of alternative benefit possibilities with those of the current benefit program. Although the current program may be providing benefits at rather high costs, the costs of the benefits from alternative programs may be even greater and therefore less affordable.[26]

Summary

Chapters 9, 10, and 11 address the most frequently asked questions in organization orientation programs: "How much do I get paid?" and "How long is my vacation?" Although most organizations have been responding to both questions with, "More (or longer) than ever before," the growth in benefits-pay compensation has been double that of direct compensation. This doubling has occurred despite the lack of evidence that indirect compensation is really helping to attain the purposes of total compensation. Money, job challenge, and opportunities for advancement appear to serve the purposes of compensation as much as, if not more than, pension benefits, disability provisions, and services, particularly for employees aspiring to managerial careers.

This is not to say, however, that employees do not desire indirect benefits. Organizations are offering them at such a rapid rate in part because employees desire them. However, employees do not always value the specific indirect benefits offered by an organization, nor do all employees know what benefits are offered. The current evidence suggests that employees' lack of awareness of the contents and value of their benefit programs may partially explain why they are not perceived more favourably. As a result, some organizations solicit employee opinions about their preferences for compensation programs. Also, organizations are becoming more concerned about the communication of information about their benefits programs. Increased communication and more employee participation in the development of benefits packages may increase the likelihood that organizations will receive some gains from providing indirect compensation. However, these gains do not come without cost. In order to ensure that an organization is getting the most from its indirect compensation, thorough assessments must be made of what the organization is doing, what other organizations are doing, and what employees prefer to see the organization doing.

However, even if indirect as well as direct compensation programs are administered as effectively as possible, their potential effectiveness vis-à-vis increasing employee performance through enhanced motivation can be constrained by employee ability. Since enhancing performance depends on both motivation and ability, it is appropriate to examine ways to improve employee ability. This is discussed in the next chapter, where the emphasis is placed on the training and development functions of the PHRM manager.

Discussion Questions

1. Why is it necessary for organizations to be concerned with benefits pay?
2. What is indirect compensation and how can it be conceptualized?
3. What are the purposes of benefits pay?
4. How are the organization's recruitment and selection, direct compensation, and safety and health activities affected by indirect compensation?
5. What federal legislative Acts have influenced the rate and type of indirect compensation an organization must offer its employees?
6. How are unemployment benefits derived, and what is the status of unemployment compensation?
7. Identify and describe the major private protection programs that employers offer employees.
8. What are the major types of pay for time not worked, and what is their relative cost to organizations?
9. What considerations must be taken into account in determining the indirect compensation benefits package?
10. What are the pros and cons of flexible benefits programs?

C A S E   S T U D Y

To Be Sick with Pay: A Right or a Fringe Benefit?

On December 1, Metro Hospital had concluded a new sick-pay agreement with the union. The agreement stated, in part, that all employees with more than three years of service were entitled to 10 days of sick leave per year (without proof of medical certificate) and that, at no time, could more than 15 days be accumulated. Sick pay was full salary for the employee. The contract further stipulated that a doctor's certificate might be requested for sick leave that exceeded three consecutive days.

In the previous five years, the average absenteeism among the nurses due to sick leave was approximately 2.5 days. The work was of such nature that, when a nurse called in sick, someone else had to be found to perform his or her duties. Thus, under the old contract, no one drew sick pay for short-term illnesses because additional expenses were incurred in hiring replacements for sick employees.

When the new agreement had been in effect for six months, some alarming symptoms developed:

the average sick leave taken by the hospital's nurses jumped to 6 days, and in some units such as intensive care and the emergency room, it was even higher—an average of 7.5 days.

This worried Tom Watson, the director of personnel for Metro Hospital. Not only did it cause severe administrative disturbances, such as those entailed by trying to find replacements at the last minute, but also it significantly boosted the deficit in the personnel operating budget. He called his staff for a special meeting to discuss possible remedies to this situation.

Case Questions

1. What suggestions would you give Tom Watson?
2. How could the hospital ensure that the nurses not misuse sick leave?
3. Aside from compensation strategy, what other strategies could be considered?

Endnotes

1. J. F. Sullivan, "Indirect Compensation: The Years Ahead," *California Management Review*, Winter 1972, pp. 65–76. R. I. Henderson, "Designing a Reward System for Today's Employee," *Business*, July–Sept. 1982, pp. 2–12.
2. Thorne Stevenson and Kellogg, "Employee Benefit Costs in Canada," *Annual Surveys from 1964–1984*.
3. R. C. Huseman, J. D. Hatfield, and R. W. Driver, "Getting Your Benefit Programs Understood and Appreciated," *Personnel Journal*, Oct. 1978, p. 562. K. Yukich, "Benefits Communications: Beyond the Booklet," *Benefits Canada*, September 1985, pp. 33–38.
4. D. W. Belcher, *Compensation Administration* (Englewood Cliffs, NJ: Prentice-Hall, 1974), p. 376.
5. J. O'Toole, "The Irresponsible Society," in *Working in the 21st Century*, C. S. Sheppard and D. C. Carroll (eds.), (New York: John Wiley & Sons, 1980), p. 156.
6. For an excellent discussion of what attracts individuals to organizations, see D. P. Schwab, "Recruiting and Organizational Participation," in K. M. Rowland and G. R. Ferris (eds.), *Personnel Management* (Boston: Allyn & Bacon, 1982), pp. 103–128.
7. W. B. Werther et al., *Canadian Personnel Management and Human Resources*, 2nd ed. (Toronto: McGraw-Hill Ryerson, 1985), p. 361.
8. "Employee Benefit Costs in Canada," endnote 2, p. 20.
9. J. T. Wallace and D. L. McPherson, "Employment Benefit Plans," *Human Resources Management* in Canada, Prentice-Hall Canada Inc., Toronto, 1986, pp. 45,041–45,042.
10. Ibid., p. 45,041.
11. A. Finlayson, "The Lure of Early Retirement," *Maclean's*, February 1985, pp. 40–42.
12. *Benefits and Working Conditions*, vol. 1. Pay Research Bureau, Ottawa, Public Service Staff Relations Board, January 1980.
13. B. King, "Dental Plan Trend: Something to Smile About," *The Financial Post*, May 9, 1981, p. 42.
14. "Employee Benefit Costs in Canada," endnote 2, p. 13.
15. *Benefits and Working Conditions*, endnote 12, p. 76.
16. Wallace and McPherson, endnote 9, pp. 45, 70.
17. For more on the stress connection see S. L. Dolan and A. Arsenault, "The Organizational and Individual Consequences of Stress at Work: A New Frontier to Human Resource Administration," in V. V. Veysey and G. A. Hall, Jr. (eds.), *The New World of Managing Human Resources* (Pasadena, CA: California Institute of Technology, 1979), pp. 4.01–4.22. See also S. L. Dolan and D. Balkin, "A Contingency Model of Occupational Stress," *The International Journal of Management*, 1987 (in press).
18. See for example S. Nealy, "Pay and Benefit Preferences," *Industrial Relations*, Oct. 1963, pp. 17–28.
19. "Flexible Compensation Trends," *Bulletin to Management*, April 19, 1984. "Flexible Benefits," *Personnel Journal*, August 1981, p. 602. "Flexible Benefits Package Could Become New Standard," *The Financial Post*, March 19, 1983, p. 29. R. Yukich, "Flexible Health Care Benefits at Eaton's," *Human Resources Management in Canada*, 1983, Prentice-Hall Canada Inc., pp. 5,107–5,113.
20. "A Compensation Special," *Canadian Business*, April 1985, p. 57.
21. "Pay Off . . . ," *The Wall Street Journal*, July 8, 1982, p. 1. R. Foltz, "Communique," *Personnel Administrator*, May 1981, p. 8. Huseman, Hatfield, and Driver, endnote 3, pp. 560–566, 578. "How Do You Tell Employees About Benefits?" *Personnel Journal*, Oct. 1980, p. 798. R. M. McCaffery, "Employee Benefits Beyond the Fringe?" *Personnel Administrator*, May 1981, pp. 26–30, 66.
22. P. W. Cooke, "Telling Employees About Benefits," *Human Resources Management in Canada*, Prentice-Hall Canada Inc., 1985, pp. 5,337–5,340. K. Yukich, "Benefits Communications: Beyond the Booklet," *Benefits Canada*, 1985, pp. 33–38.
23. Cooke, endnote 22, p. 5,339.

24. Yukich, endnote 3, p. 35.
25. B. Ellig, "Determining the Competitiveness of Employee Benefits Systems," *Compensation Review*, 1st quarter, 1974 (New York: AMACOM, a division of American Management Association, 1974), p. 9. M. D. Demner, "Benefit Cost Control Mechanisms," *Human Resources Management in Canada*, Prentice-Hall Inc., 1983, pp. 5,122–5,125.
26. For suggestions on redesigning the benefits-pay compensation package for greater motivational value and enhanced productivity see S. C. Bushardt and A. R. Fowler, "Compensation and Benefits: Today's Dilemma in Motivation," *Personnel Administrator*, April 1982, pp. 23–26. D. L. Salisbury, "Benefit Trends in the '80s," *Personnel Journal*, Feb. 1982, pp. 104–108. J. Dunphy, "Redesign Time-Off Benefits," *Benefits Canada*, July–August 1980, pp. 13–15. J. Wallace and C. McPherson, "Managing Employee Benefits Through and After the Recession," *Human Resources Management in Canada*, Prentice-Hall Inc., 1983, pp. 5,117–5,121.

SECTION VI
Enhancing Human Potential

CHAPTER 12
Training and Development

CHAPTER 13
Quality of Work Life and Productivity

CHAPTER 12

Training and Development

PHRM in the News

Training and Development
Purposes and Importance of Training and Development
Relationships of Training and Development
Legal and Policy Issues in Training and Development

Determining Training Needs
Organizational Needs Analysis
Job Needs Analysis
Person Needs Analysis
Type of Training Needs

Implementing Training Programs
Training Considerations
Training Programs
Selecting a Program
Problems and Pitfalls in Training

Assessing Training Programs
Evaluation Designs

Developing Employees' Potential
Facilitating Employee Development
Formal Programs of Employee Development

Career Planning and Development
Individual-Centred Career Planning
Organization-Centred Career Planning

Summary

Discussion Questions

Case Study

Endnotes

PHRM in the News

Public Policy Strategy on Training in Canada

Employers are calling the biggest shake-up ever of Ottawa's multibillion-dollar employment programs everything from a major breakthrough on the training front to unrealistic in terms of how business works.

But whatever the final verdict on the streamlined six-program package, unveiled late last month by Employment Minister Flora MacDonald, one thing is clear: In carrying out the wholesale restructuring, the Mulroney government is placing its unwavering faith in business and the provinces on the line.

The big question: Will they deliver?

Despite skepticism in some business organizations and at least one province, just about everybody seems to agree it's too early to say. The regulations have yet to be published, and the new programs won't even be fully operational until sometime this fall.

Certainly the sweeping $2.1-billion-a-year Canadian Jobs Strategy portends large-scale changes. Gone will be an entire array of largely short-term make-work training schemes—everything from Canada Works, Lead & Career Access, to Critical Skills Training, General Industrial Training, Job Corps and others.

From now on the emphasis will be on what business can do for the unemployed over the longer term. The crucial test of private-sector involvement, for example, will be the success or failure of the $350-million Job Entry program (for youth and women having difficulty entering the labor market), and the $700-million Job Development program, aimed at the hard-core unemployed.

These two programs offer wage subsidies to employers to encourage them to take on and train local unemployed. But to qualify for this federal funding, the employer will have to offer a program of career-oriented employment, likely including some off-site educational training.

No menial jobs

In contrast with earlier practice, hiring unemployed people to do menial jobs, just to keep them busy, is a thing of the past, officials say. Employers, it is hoped, will participate in Local Advisory Councils being set up in Canada Employment Centre districts across the country to help establish training-and-work experience programs for local unemployed.

Says Geoffrey Hale, vice-president of the Canadian Organization of Small Business: "We salute the new emphasis on on-the-job training, as well as local involvement in designing training projects." But he admits, "There probably isn't a harder program to sell to employers than Job Development, where you are dealing with long-term unemployed who may have lost the habit of doing a day's work."

The new schemes do, indeed, represent a fundamental shift from a crazy-quilt of direct subsidies to a determined top-to-bottom upgrading of skills. Among the key implications of the recent ministerial announcement:

- A new and much-expanded role for locally based business in the design and delivery of training-and-work projects for the unemployed. Says one senior federal official: "There's a clear philosophical shift away from the old reliance on the public sector to provide work experience and educational training programmed from Ottawa."

- At the centre of the new theology is a drive to leave the subsidized unemployed with more than a new ticket to unemployment insurance after their brief period of work.

"We're not interested in funding six months of planting flowers or painting fences," says one senior aide to Employment Minister MacDonald. Instead, the Tory programs ambitiously aim to provide a mix of on-the-job and educational training that will leave recipients with identifiable work skills.

Source: G. Gherson, "Jobs Gauntlet Thrown Down" (excerpts), *The Financial Post*, July 13, 1985, pp. 1–2. Used with permission.

Computer-Assisted Training Program at Toronto Dominion Bank

Dave Fisher, Manager of Training Research and Development for the Toronto Dominion Bank, is going to be a very lonely man in 1984. A five-year veteran in his job at Canada's fifth largest bank, Fisher, an MBA graduate from Windsor, has convinced the brass at T-D to fund one of the most innovative training schemes in Canada. It will eventually provide upwards of 40% of all clerical training at the T-D as well as significant middle and senior management applications. If successful, it will give T-D a definite edge in an industry that has grown intensely competitive over the past few years. But if Fisher's ideas fail, he stands to become another target for the Orwellian social commentators hunting for Big Brother.

Fisher's past record in introducing innovative training packages is impressive. In the past three years, he has developed 19 new programs that are in the process of training T-D's 18,000 employees. "Sometimes you get so close to a new program," said Fisher, who acts as the brain trust for the bank's 85 training personnel, "that you lose track of what you have been doing." Keeping track of numbers, however, is not the only important job in Canadian banking, which has come a long way from the days of isolated street-corner branches.

"We have, for example, about 1,500 people involved just in our operations division—people who run the on-line computers system, and data processing," says Fisher. There is also a large number at head office—mortgage and investment personnel, controllers, a large international division, to name just a few. Most of us, however, are only familiar with any number of 950 branches, whether it is one with only 3 or 4 employees or the one with almost 700 people. From a training point of view, the logistics of delivering training packages for every employee—from a teller in rural Canada requiring customer service training to high-flying corporate lenders dealing only in oil patch companies—are not for the faint-hearted. Given the seven training centres the T-D bank has throughout the country, Fisher is still stuck with the fundamental problems of designing course materials and distributing them to all the training centres at the appropriate times.

Source: Barry Conway, "Computer-Assisted Training Program at the T-D Bank," *Human Resources Management in Canada*, December 1983, pp. 5,151–5,152. Reprinted with permission of Prentice-Hall Canada Inc., Toronto: 1986.

These "PHRM in the News" articles highlight important aspects of training and development. First, a considerable amount of money is spent on training the unemployed to help them become a viable part of the skilled Canadian workforce. Some Canadian companies are spending vast resources on training and developing their employees, although this is not a universal practice.

Although business and government together spend as much as $2 to $3 billion a year on training, Canada still ranks far behind Japan, the United States, and many European nations. Exact figures on training activity in Canada are scant, but one survey sponsored by the federal government found that, in 1983, the average large Canadian company provided about 4.5 days of formal training annually to about 20% of its employees.[1] This translates into an average of approximately one day per person employed. Although other studies came up with slightly higher figures, Canada is still far behind Japan, where a typical worker receives six to eight days of training, and a beginning manager as much as ten weeks in the first year of work.

In the future, however, companies will be forced to invest substantially more in training, given the fast obsolescence of knowledge and the accelerated introduction of new technologies in the workplace. Four out of every five employees polled by Gallup said that they would support the introduction of training systems that would allow them time off work to improve skills and keep pace with new technology.[2]

Because training and development are both important and costly, organizations want to conduct them effectively. This requires awareness and use of many training and development techniques and programs. In this chapter the purposes of training and development are discussed, along with training techniques and programs that organizations can provide. This chapter also will discuss the types of needs analysis that must be conducted in order to determine who should receive training, what skills are necessary, and at what level they should be taught. Implementing a successful training and development program involves creating proper conditions for learning.

The first part of the chapter will emphasize training issues, while the second part will focus on issues related primarily to employees' development.

Training and Development

Employee training and development activities refer to any attempt to improve current or future employee performance by increasing, through learning, an employee's ability to perform, usually by increasing his or her skills, knowledge, and/or attitudes. Given that employees' performance (P) could be determined by the following formula,

P = f (knowledge, skills, attitudes, situation)

training is the answer when performance deficiency could be attributed to gaps in the employee's skills, knowledge, and/or attitudes. Although performance also could be affected by situational factors (e.g., technology, quality of supervision), this simple formula could aid organizations in determining performance deficiencies on the basis of the questions:

- Skills: Is the employee *able* to do the job?
- Knowledge: Does the employee *know* how to do the job?
- Attitudes: Does the employee *want* (is motivated) to do the job?

All training programs are addressed to answer one or a combination of these questions.[3]

Although this is a rather simple formula, it may be difficult for an organization to determine exactly what level of performance is desired, particularly in the future, and what level of performance employees are currently exhibiting or are likely to exhibit in the future. Nevertheless, organizations that engage in training and development attempt to make these estimates in order to increase the potential effectiveness of their programs.

Purposes and Importance of Training and Development

A major purpose of training and development is to remove performance deficiencies, whether current or anticipated, that are the result of the employee's inability to perform at the desired level. Training for performance improvements is particularly important to organizations with stagnant or declining rates of productivity. Training also is important to organizations that are rapidly incorporating new technologies and consequently increasing the likelihood of employee obsolescence. For example, in 1983 IBM Canada spent $36 million in training and retraining its personnel, much of which was related to dealing with obsolescence and upgrading skills for dealing with clients.[4]

Another purpose of training and development that is particularly relevant to organizations that are rapidly incorporating new technologies, is that of making the current workforce more flexible and adaptable. If an organization can increase the adaptability of its workforce through training and development, it can increase the adaptability of the organization itself, thus increasing its potential for survival and profitability.

Training and development also can increase the level of commitment of employees to the organization and increase their perceptions that the organization is a good place to work. Increased commitment can result in less turnover and absenteeism, thus increasing an organization's productivity. Training and development also are important because it generally is recognized that society can benefit by enabling individuals to be productive and participative members of organizations.[5]

Relationships of Training and Development

As shown in Exhibit 12.1, training and development involve a large number of procedures and processes that are extensively related to many of the PHRM activities discussed so far.

376   *Enhancing Human Potential*

Exhibit 12.1   Training and Development Processes and Procedures

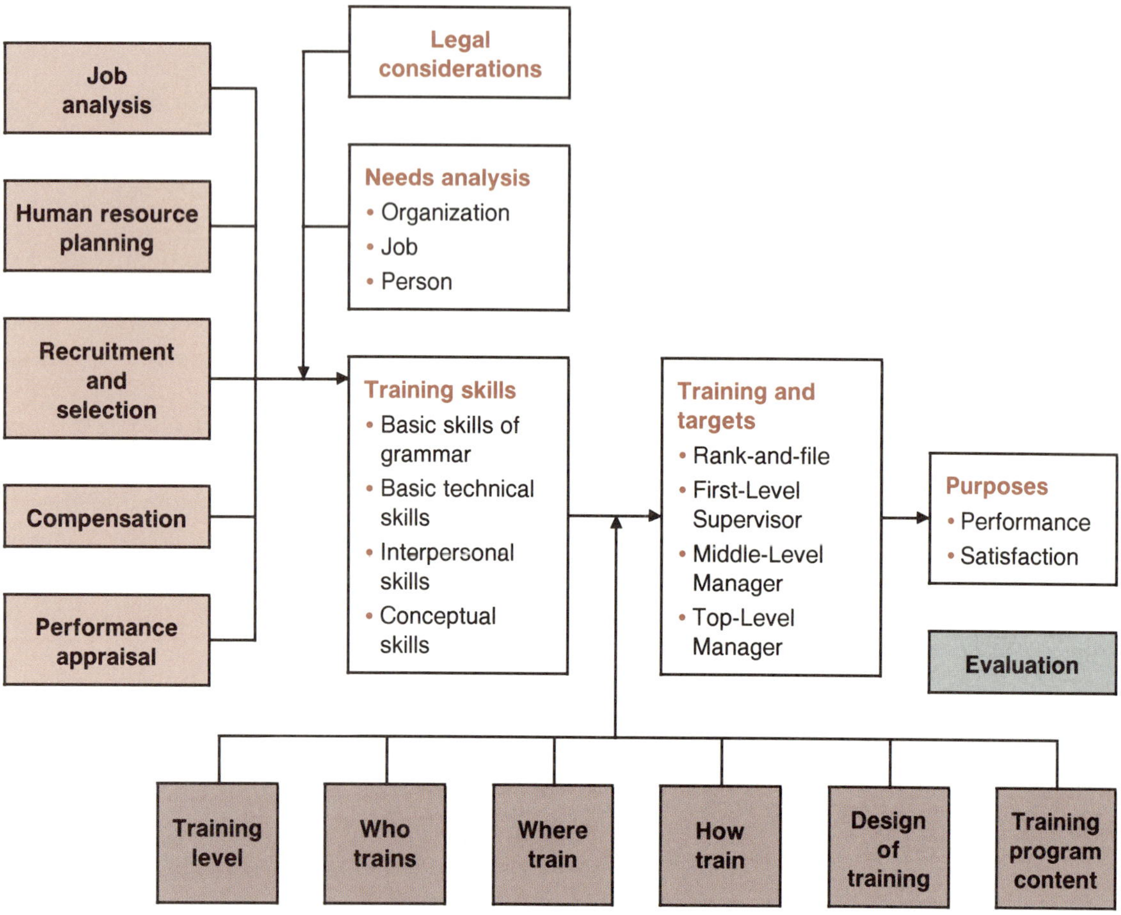

```
Job analysis ──┐
               │   ┌─────────────────┐
               ├──→│ Legal           │
Human resource │   │ considerations  │
planning ──────┤   └─────────────────┘
               │   ┌─────────────────┐
               ├──→│ Needs analysis  │
Recruitment    │   │ • Organization  │
and            │   │ • Job           │
selection ─────┤   │ • Person        │
               │   └─────────────────┘
Compensation ──┤   ┌──────────────────┐   ┌──────────────────┐   ┌──────────────┐
               │   │ Training skills  │   │ Training and     │   │ Purposes     │
Performance    │   │ • Basic skills of│   │ targets          │──→│ • Performance│
appraisal ─────┴──→│   grammar        │──→│ • Rank-and-file  │   │ • Satisfaction│
                   │ • Basic technical│   │ • First-Level    │   └──────────────┘
                   │   skills         │   │   Supervisor     │
                   │ • Interpersonal  │   │ • Middle-Level   │   ┌──────────────┐
                   │   skills         │   │   Manager        │   │ Evaluation   │
                   │ • Conceptual     │   │ • Top-Level      │   └──────────────┘
                   │   skills         │   │   Manager        │
                   └──────────────────┘   └──────────────────┘
```

| Training level | Who trains | Where train | How train | Design of training | Training program content |

Human Resource Planning. The determination of the organization's training and development needs often depends initially on its personnel and human resource planning requirements. These requirements, as discussed in Chapter 2, are derived from the organization's overall plans and objectives, its projected human resource needs (by skill, type, and number), and the anticipated supply of human resources to fill these needs. As a result of changing technology, organizations are finding it increasingly difficult to fill some of their human resource needs with already-trained employees. They are finding it increasingly necessary to do more of their own training and to develop talent from within the organization.[6] Human resource planning helps to formalize this necessity, and articulates management's concern for effectively utilizing its human resources now and in the future.

Job Analysis and Performance Appraisal. Whereas human resource planning helps to establish the general context within which training and development take place, job analysis and performance appraisal help to identify specific training and development needs (this process may be particularly well facilitated by behavioural-based performance appraisal methods such as BOS or BARS, described in Chapter 7). Performance appraisal results may reveal a performance deficiency and further analysis may indicate the cause. This information, used in conjunction with job analysis, can then determine the specific training needs required to remove the deficiency. The entire process, however, may indicate that the supervisor is unable to make valid performance appraisals and thus training and development programs need to be directed toward removing *that* deficiency.[7]

Recruitment and Selection. Even though an organization determines that it needs training and development programs, it may still choose to recruit trained individuals rather than train its current employees. This may save training and development costs, but when organizations do this for jobs above the entry level, they reduce promotional options that could be used as incentives for current employees. Consequently, many organizations have programs to enhance skills for both future jobs and current jobs.

Occasionally, organizations need a uniquely skilled individual and therefore choose to recruit externally, but even external recruitment does not guarantee that adequately trained job applicants will be found. As a result, organizations may choose to develop and implement pre-employment training programs. They can use the recruitment activity to identify potentially *qualifiable* as well as potentially *qualified* job applicants. Potentially qualifiable applicants then are provided with the opportunity for pre-employment training. After successfully completing this training they may be hired, or placed in a pool of potentially qualified applicants.

Compensation. It is important for rewards to be attached to any training and development activity, because an employee may not be interested in improving performance for its own sake. For instance, to encourage managers to train their employees, organizations often reward managers for performing this function well. The use of incentives is important not only for getting employees into training and development programs but also for maintaining the positive effects of these programs. Employees may revert to previous performance levels or behaviours if they are still rewarded, or not "punished." Therefore, the successful implementation and maintenance of training and development programs depend on establishing a compensation system that will motivate employees to perform.

Success begins with the proper determination of training and development needs. Before discussing training and development in further detail, it is important to examine the relevant legal and policy considerations.

Legal and Policy Issues in Training and Development

Legal and policy considerations are relevant to several aspects of training and development. One aspect is the determination of the training and development needs of job applicants.

In Chapters 5 and 6, various issues related to job discrimination were discussed. Discrimination in training and development practices are of similar concern. Although no human rights tribunal has yet ruled on the discriminatory impact of training and development programs, relevant legislation does cover this type of PHRM responsibility. Complainants from protected groups can file with human rights commissions if they are differentially prohibited from taking on or completing training programs, or even if they receive disparate treatment during training.[8]

Under the broad guidelines of affirmative action policy, the Canadian Employment and Immigration Commission has been steadily increasing the level of funding for industry-based training through expansion of the Canada Manpower Industry Training Program. Funding has grown in both absolute terms and in relation to expenditures on institutional-based training.[9]

In 1982, The National Training Act was established to provide occupational training for the labour force, to better meet the need for skills created by a changing economy and to increase the earning and employment potential of individual workers. The National Training Program includes courses ranging from basic skill development to language and apprenticeship training. Some of the special features of the Act promote not only training for trade skills and general industrial training, but also non-traditional training for women.[10]

Under the Adult Occupational Training Act of 1967, the federal government can support employer-centred training. Currently, employers may receive funding for up to three years. Within the context of these subsidy schemes, particular emphasis is placed by government on the training of certain disadvantaged groups: women, visible minorities, the handicapped, and native people.[11]

In its job strategy, unveiled during the summer of 1985, the federal government stated its intention to establish Community Industrial Training Councils across Canada, made up of employers, unions, and educational representatives. It also called for the establishment of employer-based trust funds that will enable employees to upgrade their skills in the face of technological change. In order to encourage the establishment of such funds, the federal government agreed to contribute 50% of the amount paid by the participants, up to $400 000 over a three-year period. These training funds also would allow individual employees to put money into tax-sheltered accounts designed to underwrite retraining expenses.[12]

Determining Training Needs

The three major phases of any training program are (1) the **assessment phase**, which determines the training and development needs of the organization, (2) the **implementation phase** (actual training and development), in which certain programs and learning methods are used to impart new attitudes, skills, and abilities, and (3) the **evaluation phase**. The relationships among these three phases are shown in Exhibit 12.2.

The next section focuses on the assessment phase, which consists of the analysis of the organization's needs, the job's needs, and the person's needs.[13]

Model for an Instructional System* Exhibit 12.2

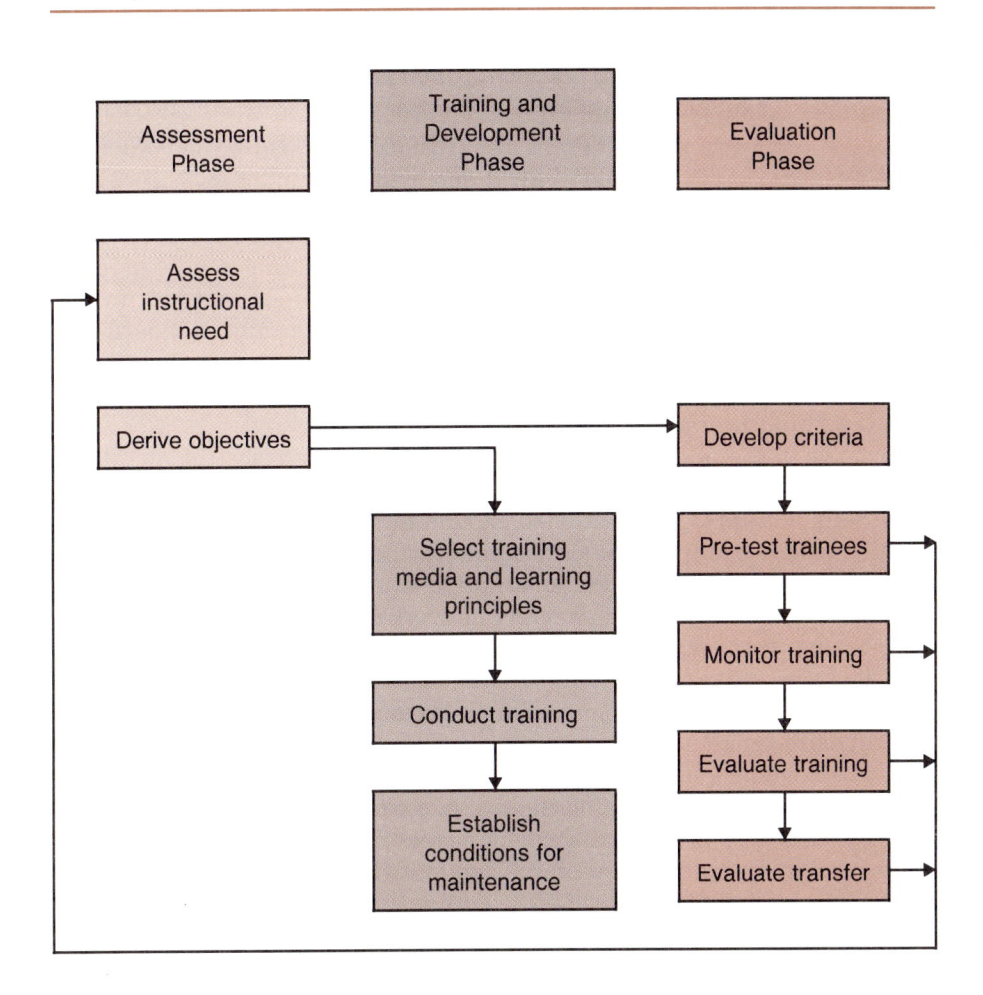

```
[Assessment Phase]    [Training and Development Phase]    [Evaluation Phase]

Assess instructional need
    ↓
Derive objectives ──────────────────→ Develop criteria
    │                                      ↓
    └──→ Select training media             Pre-test trainees
         and learning principles              ↓
              ↓                           Monitor training
         Conduct training                    ↓
              ↓                           Evaluate training
         Establish conditions                ↓
         for maintenance                 Evaluate transfer
```

*There are many other models for instructional systems in the military, in business, and in education. Some of the components of this model were suggested by these other systems.

Source: Adapted from I. I. Goldstein, *Training Program Development and Evaluation*, p. 8. Copyright © 1974 Wadsworth, Inc. Reprinted by permission of the publisher, Brooks/Cole Publishing Company, Monterey, CA.

Organizational Needs Analysis

Organizational needs analysis begins with an examination of the short-term and long-term objectives of the organization and the trends that are likely to affect these objectives. According to one expert "Organizational objectives should be the ultimate concern of any training and development effort."[14] In addition to examining the organization's objectives, the organizational needs analysis also consists of human resource analysis, analysis of efficiency indexes, and analysis of the organizational climate. Although analyses of the efficiency indexes and organizational climate help to identify training needs, they are useful primarily in the evaluation of training and development programs.

Human resource analysis translates the organization's objectives into the demand for human resources, skills required, and programs needed for supplying these skills and human resources. Training and development programs play a vital role in matching the supply of human resources and skills with the demands.

An analysis of efficiency indexes provides information on the current efficiency of work groups and the organization. Indexes that can be used include costs of labour, quantity of output, quality of output, waste, equipment use, and repairs. The organization can determine standards for these indexes and then analyze them to evaluate the general effectiveness of training programs and to locate training and development needs for groups within the organization.

Analysis of the organizational climate is used to describe the quality of the organization, how the employees feel about it, and how effective the employees are. Like the analysis of efficiency indexes, it can help to identify where training and development programs may be needed, and provide criteria against which to evaluate their effectiveness once implemented. Measures of the quality of the organizational climate include absenteeism, turnover, grievances, productivity, suggestions, attitude surveys, and accidents.

These three aspects of the organizational needs analysis present only a general definition of the organization's need for training and development. They are extremely important in isolating where the training and development programs should be focused and in providing some criteria against which to evaluate the effectiveness of the programs. Many organizations fail to conduct this analysis, preferring to jump in and train simply because everyone else is doing it.

Job Needs Analysis

Just as important and perhaps just as frequently overlooked, is the second phase of any needs analysis. Because the organizational needs analysis is too broad to identify detailed training needs for specific jobs, it is necessary to conduct a **job needs analysis**. Essentially, this analysis provides information concerning the tasks to be performed on each job (the basic information contained in job descriptions), the skills necessary to perform those tasks (from the job specifications or qualifications), and the minimum acceptable standards of performance. These three pieces of information may be gathered independently from current employees, the PHRM department, or current supervisors. They also may be gathered simultaneously by teams of individuals representing different areas of the organization. Exhibit 12.3 depicts the process of job needs analysis.

Person Needs Analysis

The **person needs analysis** can be accomplished in two different ways. Employee performance discrepancies may be identified either by comparing actual performance with the minimum acceptable standards of performance or by comparing an evaluation of employee proficiency on each required skill dimension with the proficiency level required for each skill. Notice that the first method is based on the actual, current job performance of an employee; therefore, it can be used to determine training and development needs for the current job. The second method, on the other hand, can be used to identify training and development needs for future jobs.

A relevant training question for the first method is: Will the employee be able to do the job assigned? For the second method, the relevant question is: Will this employee or new job applicant be able to do some job he or she has yet to do? Both of these questions have important implications for equal employment opportunity and affirmative action. To ensure employment equity and affirmative action, the basis for the above answers must be a validated set of measures that will enable the organization to determine current performance and potential performance, as described in Chapter 7.[15]

An increasingly popular technique used to gather information in person needs analysis is self-assessment. Self-assessment can elicit from the individual an appraisal of training needs for his or her present job or those necessary for desired future jobs.

Type of Training Needs

Based on the organizational, job, and person needs analyses, the appropriate type of training can be determined. Although many types of training exist, here they have been grouped into four categories for ease of discussion. These correspond to the skills and abilities that the training is intended to improve.

- *Basic skills of grammar, math, safety, reading, listening, and writing:* These skills often are missing in new employees, and sometimes in executives who have been around a long time.
- *Basic job-specific skills of a technical nature to do a specific job:* These skills might include how to type, file, or how to weld a pipe or fix a car. Budgeting and scheduling skills are included here. Other basic skills can be specific not only to a job, but to a particular company.

Exhibit 12.3 *The Process of Job Needs Analysis*

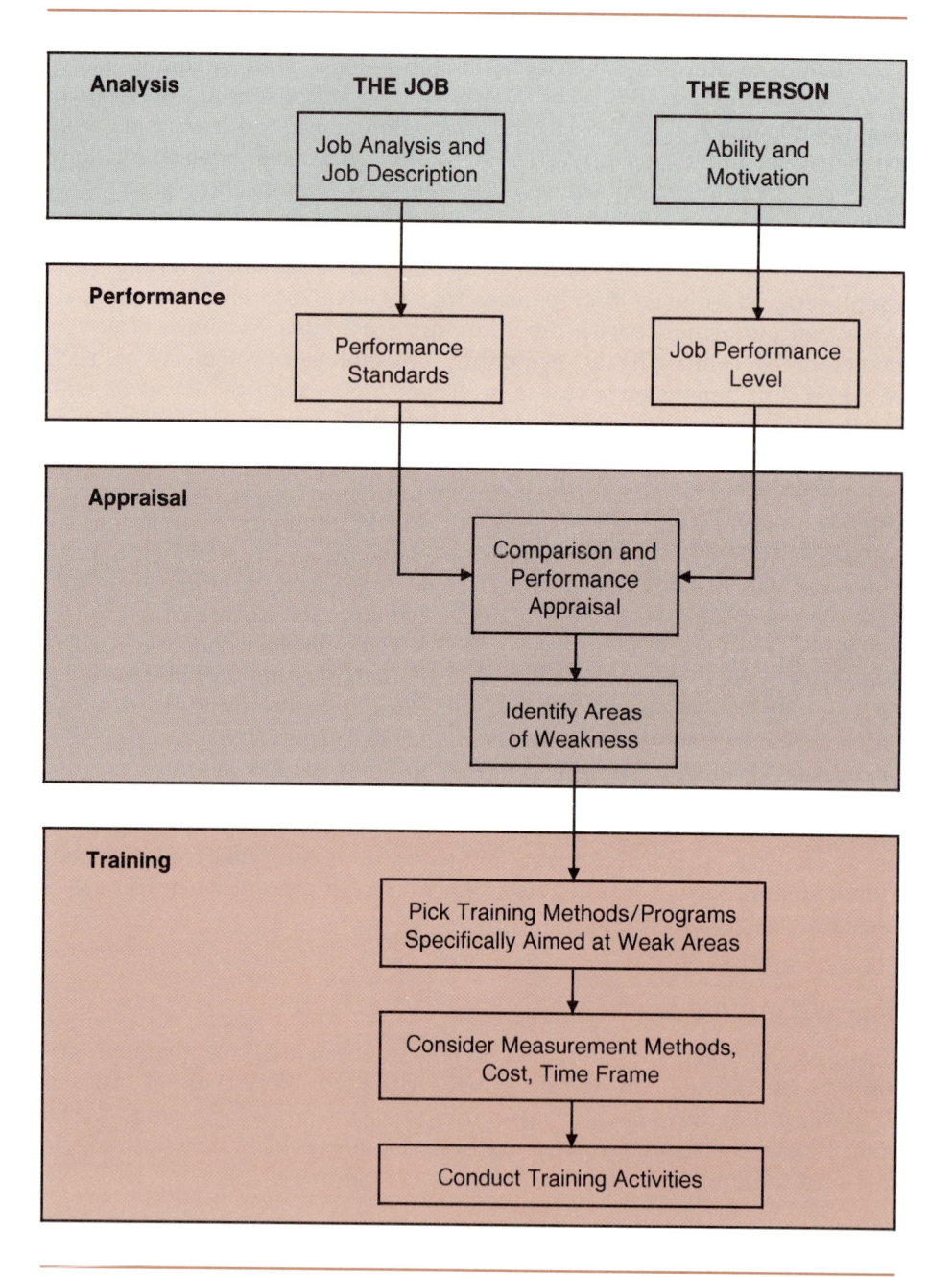

Analysis

- THE JOB: Job Analysis and Job Description
- THE PERSON: Ability and Motivation

Performance

- Performance Standards
- Job Performance Level

Appraisal

- Comparison and Performance Appraisal
- Identify Areas of Weakness

Training

- Pick Training Methods/Programs Specifically Aimed at Weak Areas
- Consider Measurement Methods, Cost, Time Frame
- Conduct Training Activities

Source: R. L. Mathis and J. H. Jackson, *Personnel: Human Resource Management,* 4th ed. (St. Paul: West Publishing Co., 1985), p. 292. Used with permission.

- *Interpersonal skills including communications, human relations, leadership and labour relations:* Also included here are skills related to legal considerations, and even organizational and time-use skills. Perhaps nowhere is the demand and need for these skills greater than for the first-time supervisor, although such skills are integral at all levels of management.
- *Broader-based conceptual integrative skills, such as strategic and operational planning, and organizational design and policy skills:* Also included here are decision-making skills and skills in adapting to complex and changing environments—often components of top- and middle-management responsibility.[16]

Implementing Training Programs

Successful implementation of training programs depends on selecting the right programs for the right people under the right conditions. Needs analysis helps identify the right people and the right programs, and several training considerations help identify the appropriate conditions.

Training Considerations

Several considerations are associated with implementing training programs. Each of these must be addressed appropriately in order to increase the likelihood that the program will be effective:

- Who participates in the program?
- Who teaches the program?
- What media are used to teach?
- What should be the level of learning?
- What learning principles are needed?
- Where will the program be conducted?

With these considerations in mind, the PHRM manager selects a training and development program from among the many that are available. Effective selection depends on an in-depth knowledge of the programs that are available.

Who Participates? Generally, training and development programs are designed specifically to teach particular skills because in most instances only one target audience is in attendance. However, there are times when training two or more target audiences simultaneously may be helpful. For example, rank-and-file employees and their supervisors may effectively learn about a new work process or machine together so that they will have a common understanding about the new process and their respective roles. Bringing several target audiences together also may facilitate group processes such as problem solving and decision making, and skills useful in quality circle projects and semi-autonomous work groups.

Who Teaches? Training and development programs may be taught by one of several people, including

- immediate supervisors;
- co-workers, as in buddy systems;
- members of the personnel staff;
- specialists from other parts of the company;
- outside consultants;
- industrial associations representatives; and
- faculty members from universities.

The selection of a teacher often depends on where the program is held and which skill is being taught. For example, programs teaching basic skills usually are conducted by members of the PHRM staff or specialists from other parts of the company, whereas interpersonal skills and conceptual, integrative skills for management are often taught at universities. However, large organizations such as McDonald's, IBM, Xerox, and Air Canada, which have large numbers of employees seeking management skills, provide their own management and advanced management skills programs.

What Media? There are several methods of delivering training information. In many colleges and universities, the basic methods used are lectures, lecture/discussion combinations, case discussions, and some self-programmed instructions. These are the methods also used in many training and development programs. Some additional training techniques include the following:

- Role playing
- Behaviour modelling
- Group participation exercises
- One-on-one counselling
- Demonstrations
- Videotape recording and playback
- Computer-assisted programs

Often combinations of these techniques are used. For example, some retail stores are training their department managers by using a videotape/behaviour modelling combination. First, the management trainees view a videotape of a manager (really an actor) behaving in an ideal way. Then the managers are given a chance to "model" the behaviour of the actor on the videotape. Some large transportation companies use similar methods in conducting safety training for their truck drivers, such as Montréal-based Provost Transport.

The rule of thumb in selecting training media is: The more active the trainee is within the selected media, the higher the retention rate. Various training media enable different degrees of a trainee's active participation. Lectures allow a minimum amount of participation, while videotape and behaviour modelling allow a great deal of participation. However, there is a direct trade-off in terms of cost: the simple media, such as lectures are low cost, and the more sophisticated media involve substantially higher costs.

What Level of Learning? There are three levels at which needed skills can be learned. At the lowest level, the employee or potential employee must develop **fundamental knowledge**, which means developing a basic understanding of the field and becoming acquainted with the language, concepts, and relationships involved in it. The goal of the next-highest level is **skill development**, or acquiring the ability to perform in a particular skill area. The highest level aims for increased **operational proficiency**, which means obtaining additional experience and improving skills that already have been developed.

Each of the four skill categories discussed can be learned at all three levels. How effectively they are learned depends on several learning principles.

What Are the Learning Principles? Training and development programs are much more likely to be effective when they incorporate several critical learning principles. These include

- employee motivation;
- recognition of individual differences;
- practise opportunities;
- reinforcement;
- knowledge of results (feedback);
- goal setting;
- transfer of learning; and
- follow-up.

If employees are **motivated to change** and to acquire different behaviours, training is likely to be easier and more successful. Sometimes the knowledge that a new job is available or that a raise is possible is enough to provide employees with sufficient motivation. In other instances, motivation could be significantly lowered due to the conditions under which the training is taking place and the capabilities of the trainer.

Recognition of individual differences also is required. Some individuals learn more rapidly than others, some have had more experience than others, and some may be more physically able to exhibit the behaviours resulting from the training. For these reasons, many professional trainers prefer to screen trainees according to their capacity to learn. It is often suggested that creating more homogeneous groups (in terms of learning patterns similarity) can enhance training effectiveness. This principle is used in many educational institutions.

Regardless of individual differences, whether a trainee is learning a new skill or acquiring knowledge of a given topic, the person should be given the

opportunity to practise what is being taught. Practise is also essential even after the individual has been successfully trained. It is almost impossible to find a successful professional tennis player or piano player who does not practise several hours every day.

According to the principles of **reinforcement**, people will do what is rewarded and avoid doing what is not rewarded or what is punished.[17] And although learning can be rewarding for its own sake, it is generally regarded as a difficult and distasteful process that must be rewarded extrinsically to ensure its effectiveness. Managers therefore should praise their employees for learning a new skill, and the organization could provide promotion opportunities for those who successfully complete a training and development program. These extrinsic or contingent rewards are said to reinforce an individual's behaviour (for example, learning a new skill) because they are given on the basis of that behaviour. Because the principles of reinforcement are so important in learning, the implementation and maintenance of effective training depend in part on the effective management of contingent rewards.

Although the evidence indicates that contingent rewards and punishments are effective if they are administered properly, managers occasionally claim that there are few rewards to give. Yet they often fail to provide what is probably the single most important reinforcement and incentive—**knowledge of results**.[18] People sometimes cannot judge whether they are learning a new behaviour correctly. Managers can play an important role at this point simply by telling employees how well they are doing. Adding rewards for properly performed behaviours and imposing punishments for improper behaviours accelerates learning considerably.

Goal setting also can accelerate learning, particularly when it is accompanied by knowledge of result. Individuals generally perform better and learn more quickly when they have goals, particularly if the goals are specific and appropriately challenging. Goals that are too easy or too difficult have little motivational value. It is only when people consider themselves capable of reaching the goal that they really become motivated.

The motivational value of goal setting also may increase when employees participate in the goal-setting process.[19] When the manager or trainer and the employee work together to set goals, the employee's unique strengths and weaknesses can be identified. Then aspects of the training and development program can be tailored to specific employees, which may increase the effectiveness of the training program.

While goal setting clearly affects the trainee's motivation, so also do the expectations of the trainer. Research has demonstrated that expectations are often self-fulfilling prophecies, so that the higher the expectations, the better the trainees perform. The self-fulfilling prophecy is also known as the **Pygmalion effect**. Legend has it that Pygmalion fell in love with a statue and, because of his prayers, it was given life. Pygmalion's fondest wish, his expectation, came true.

One serious mistake in designing training and development programs is the "failure to provide definite systems, policies and/or follow-up programs to ensure the learners' effective use of their newly acquired skills, knowledge, and attitudes *on the job*."[20] As a result, what an employee learns in a training program may never be tried in the actual job situation. Or if the newly learned behaviour *is* tried, it may quickly be extinguished due to lack of support. It therefore is important that provisions be made in training programs for the positive **transfer to the job of the behaviours learned** in training.

There are three ways to do this. One is to have conditions in the training program that are identical to those in the job situation. The second is to teach principles for applying the behaviours learned in the training program to the job situation, and the third is the contract plan, discussed below.

A final important design principle is **follow-up**. Once a participant leaves the training program, the PHRM manager should provide a means of follow-up to help to ensure that he or she will actually do what was taught. All too often, participants who do want to change their current behaviour get back to work and slip into the old patterns. This greatly decreases the effectiveness of the training program.

One approach to help prevent this from happening is the **contract plan**. Its simplicity is a key factor in its success. Near the end of a training program each participant drafts a statement indicating which aspects of the program he or she feels will have the most beneficial effect back on the job, then agrees to apply those aspects. Each participant also is asked to give another participant from the program a copy of the contract; this individual then agrees to check up on the participant's progress every few weeks.[21]

Although it is desirable to incorporate these principles of learning, many training programs do not have them or are designed without consideration of individual differences, motivation, reinforcement, feedback, and goal setting. However, application of these principles of learning can increase the chances of successfully implementing a training and development program.

Where Conducted? A final consideration in implementing a training program is the location: Where will training be conducted? There are three basic options:

- On the job
- On-site, but not on the job, for example in a training room in the company building
- Off the site, such as in a university or college classroom, a hotel, or a conference centre

Typically, the basic job skills are taught on the job and the basic grammar skills are taught on-site. Much of the interpersonal and conceptual integrative skill training is done off the site. In the following discussion, the term *on the job* encompasses both on the job and on-site locations, and *off the job* refers to off-the-site locations.

Training Programs

A multitude of training and development programs exist for both managers and non-managers. These programs most often are distinguished by who participates (for example, managers or non-managers); where the programs are conducted (on the job or off the job); and what employee ability is being improved (technical skills and knowledge, interpersonal skills and attitudes, or conceptual skills and knowledge). The abilities gained by the employee in any of these programs can be used to reduce current, or prohibit future, performance deficiencies.

On-the-Job Programs. As shown in Exhibit 12.4, several programs can be conducted on the job. These programs often are formally developed and implemented by the organization, but some training and development is informal. One such informal method is supervisory assistance, which can be provided for both non-managerial and managerial employees.

Generally, **on-the-job training programs** are used by organizations because they provide hands-on learning experience that facilitates learning transfer, and because they can fit into the organizations' flow of activities. Separate areas for training and development therefore are unnecessary, and employees can begin to make a contribution to the organization while still in training.

On-the-job training programs, however, are not without their disadvantages. For example, have you ever been waited on by a trainee in a restaurant? Or have you ever had to wait in line a particularly long time because the bank was "breaking in" several teller-trainees? On-the-job programs may result not only in customer dissatisfaction but also in damage to equipment, costly errors, and frustration for both the trainer (most likely a co-worker or supervisor) and the trainee.

The disadvantages of on-the-job training can be minimized by making the training program as systematic and comprehensive as possible. **Job in-**

Exhibit 12.4 *Major Training and Development Program Availability*

On-the-Job Training and Development
Job Instruction Training
Apprentice training*
Internships and assistantships
Position (job) rotation (the job itself)
Multiple management
Supervisory assistance—coaching, feedback, performance appraisal

Off-the-Job Training and Development
Formal courses—self (programmed or computer-assisted instruction; other (lecture/reading/correspondence course)
Simulation—vestibule, management games, assessment centres
Human relations, role playing
Human relations, sensitivity training

*These programs are actually composed of off-the-job as well as on-the-job components.

struction training** is such a technique, developed "to provide a guide for giving on-the-job skill training to white- and blue-collar employees as well as technicians."[22] Since job instruction training is a technique rather than a program, it can be adapted to training efforts for all employees in off-the-job as well as on-the-job programs.

Job instruction training consists of four steps: (1) careful selection and preparation of the trainer and the trainee for the learning experience to follow; (2) a full explanation and demonstration of the job by the trainer, to be repeated by the trainee; (3) a trial on-the-job performance by the trainee; and (4) a thorough feedback session between the trainer and trainee to discuss the trainee's performance and the job requirements.

Another method for minimizing the disadvantages of on-the-job training is combining it with off-the-job training. Apprenticeship training, internships, and assistantships are programs based on this combination. **Apprenticeship training** is mandatory for admission into many of the skilled trades, such as plumbing, electronics, and carpentry. To be effective, the on- and off-the-job components of the apprenticeship program must be well integrated and appropriately planned, must recognize individual differences in learning rates and abilities, and be flexible enough to meet the changing demands and technology of the trades.

Somewhat less formalized and extensive than apprenticeship training are the internship and assistantship programs. **Internships** often are part of an agreement between schools and colleges and local organizations. As with apprenticeship training, individuals in these programs earn while they learn, but at a rate that is less than that paid to full-time employees or master craftworkers. The internships, however, function not only as a source of training but also as a source of exposure to job and organizational conditions. Students on internship programs often are able to see the application of ideas taught in the classroom more readily than students without any work experience. **Assistantships** involve full-time employment and expose an individual to a wide range of jobs. However, since the individual only assists other workers, the learning experience is often vicarious. This disadvantage can be eliminated through the use of job or position rotation and multiple-management programs.

Both job-rotation and multiple-management programs are used to train and expose employees to a variety of jobs and decision-making situations. Although **job rotation** does provide employee exposure, the extent of training and long-run benefit it provides may be overstated. This is because the employees are not in a single job for a long enough period to learn very much and are not motivated to "dig in" because they know the situation is temporary.

In **multiple-management** programs, lower- and middle-level managers participate formally with top management in the planning and administration of corporate affairs. In essence, the top level of management makes decisions that take into consideration the advice of the middle and lower levels. Involving managers from all levels allows management to identify and select top-management candidates. In a sense, it becomes an on-the-job assessment process. Being part of a multiple-management program can be an important step in an individual's career. Because of the relatively limited number of positions in the multiple-management program and the valuable rewards associated with these positions, competition for them can be great.

The most informal program of training and development is **supervisory assistance**.[23] This method of training is a regular part of the supervisor's job. It includes day-to-day coaching and counselling of workers on how to do the job and how to get along in the organization. The effectiveness of coaching and counselling as a technique for training and development depends in part on whether the supervisor creates feelings of mutual confidence, provides opportunities for growth to employees, and effectively delegates tasks.

Off-the-Job Programs. Exhibit 12.4 listed four categories of off-the-job development programs. The first two—formal courses and simulation—are applicable to both non-managerial and managerial employees; the last two are primarily for managerial employees.

The **formal course method** of training and development can be accomplished either by self-training, which is facilitated by programmed or computer-assisted instruction, reading and correspondence courses, or by formal classroom lectures. Although many training programs use the lecture method because it efficiently conveys large amounts of information to large groups of people in one sitting, it does have several drawbacks:

- It perpetuates the authority structure of traditional organizations and hinders performance because the learning process is not self-controlled.
- Except in the area of cognitive knowledge and conceptual principles, there is probably limited transfer of useful material from the lecture to the actual skills and abilities required to do the job.
- The high verbal and symbolic requirements of the lecture method may be threatening to people with low verbal or symbolic experience or aptitude.
- The lecture method does not permit individualized training based on individual differences in ability, interests, and personality.

Because of these drawbacks, the lecture method is often complemented by self-training methods.

The two predominant auto-instructional methods are the linear programming method and the branch programming method, both of which are types of **programmed instruction**. In each, the learning material is broken down into "frames." Each frame represents a small component of the entire subject to be learned, and each frame must be learned successfully before going on to the next. To facilitate the learning process, feedback about the correctness of the response to a frame is provided immediately.

The successful use of programmed instruction requires that the skills and tasks to be learned be broken down into appropriate frames. Once this is done, the probability of an individual learning by this method is high, because it allows individuals to determine their own learning pace and to get immediate and impersonal feedback. However, many skills and tasks cannot be broken down into appropriate frames, so other methods, such as simulation, are used for off-the-job training.

Simulation presents participants with situations that are similar to actual job conditions. It is used for both managers and non-managers. A common technique for non-managers is the vestibule method, which simulates the environment of the individual's actual job. Since the environment is not real and generally is safer and less hectic than the actual environment, adjustment from the simulated training environment to the actual environment may be difficult. Because of this, some organizations prefer to do the training in the actual job environment. But the arguments for using the simulated environment are compelling: It reduces the possibility of customer dissatisfaction that can result from on-the-job training; it can reduce the frustration of the trainee; and it may save the organization a great deal of money, because fewer training accidents occur.

An increasingly popular simulation technique for managers is the **assessment centre method**, which is discussed in Chapter 5 as a device for selecting managers. However, certain aspects of the assessment centres, such as the management games and in-basket exercises, are excellent for training and need not be utilized only for selection purposes. Assessment centres are particularly useful for identifying potential training needs. Whether used for training or selection, assessment centres appear to be a valid way to make employment decisions.[24]

Regardless of where they are used, management or business games usually entail various degrees of competition between teams of trainees. In contrast, **in-basket exercises** are more solitary. The trainee sits at a desk and works through a pile of papers of the type that would be found in the in-basket of a typical manager, prioritizing, recommending solutions to problems, and taking any action necessary according to what is contained in the papers.[25]

Although the in-basket exercise tends to be an enjoyable and challenging exercise, the extent to which it improves a manager's ability depends in part on what takes place after the trainee has gone through the in-basket exercise. The debriefing and analysis of what happened, and what should have happened, should help the trainee to learn how to perform like a manager. Without the debriefing and analysis, however, the opportunity for improvement may be drastically reduced; the trainee has no expertise in deciding what to transfer to the job from the game or exercise.

Whereas the simulation exercises may be useful for developing conceptual and problem-solving skills, there are three types of human relations or process-oriented training that are used by organizations to develop in its managers "interpersonal insights—awareness of self and of others—for changing attitudes and for practice in human relations skills, such as leadership or the interview."[26] There are three basic types of human relations oriented programs.

Role playing focuses on emotional (human relation) issues rather than on factual ones. The essence of role playing is to create a realistic situation and then have the trainees assume various personalities in the situation. The usefulness of role playing depends heavily on the extent to which the trainees really "get into" the parts they are playing. If you have done any role playing, you know how difficult this can be and how much easier it is to just "read" the part. But when the trainee does get into the role, the result is a greater sensitivity on the part of the trainee to the feelings and insights that are presented by the role.

One method of interpersonal training that has been quite popular is **sensitivity training** or laboratory training. Individuals in an unstructured group exchange thoughts and feelings on the "here-and-now" rather than the "there-and-then." Although the experience of being in a sensitivity group often gives individuals insight into how and why they and others feel and act the way they do, critics claim that these results may not be beneficial because they are not transferable to the job.[27]

A summary of the advantages and disadvantages of all of the training programs reviewed is provided in Exhibit 12.5.

Selecting a Program

A knowledge of the principles of learning, the four categories of skills needed by individuals in organizations, and the methods of training avail-

Exhibit 12.5 — *A Summary of the Advantages and Disadvantages of the On-the-Job and Off-the-Job Training Programs*

Type of Program	Advantages	Disadvantages
Job Instruction Training	Facilitates transfer of learning Does not need separate facilities	Interferes with performance Damages equipment
Apprenticeship	Does not interfere with real job performance Provides extensive training	Takes a long time Expensive May not be related to job
Internship	Facilitates transfer of learning	Not really a full job
Assistantship	Gives exposure to real job	Learning is vicarious
Rotation	Exposure to many jobs Real learning	Does not involve full responsibility Too short a stay in a job
Multiple Management	Involves high-level responsibility Good experience	Not many positions available May be costly
Supervisory Assistance	Informal, integrated into job Inexpensive	Effectiveness rests with supervisor Not all supervisors may do it
Formal Course	Inexpensive for many Does not interfere with job	Requires verbal skills Inhibits transfer of learning
Simulation	Helps transfer of learning Creates life-like situations	Can't always duplicate real situations exactly
Role Playing	Good for interpersonal skills Gain insights into others	Can't create real situations exactly—still role playing
Sensitivity	Good for self-insight Promotes understanding of others	May not transfer to job May not relate to job

able and their advantages and disadvantages provide the necessary information to select the training programs that are most appropriate for specific organizations. Program selection is based on the answers to three questions:

- What skills do the employees need to learn?
- At what level do these skills need to be learned?
- What training and development programs are most appropriate for the required skills and level?

Skills Needed. The answers to the first two questions are determined by the results of the needs analyses. For example, if there are performance deficiencies among the supervisory and rank-and-file employees, most of the training should be aimed at increasing technical skills. On the other hand, interpersonal skills would be the primary need of middle-management employees, and top-level managers would most be in need of conceptual or managerial and administrative skills. These matches between type of employee and the predominant type of skill training needed are useful guides to training employees for current and future jobs. Knowledge of these matches can be used to facilitate employee career development and the organization's planning regarding training and development programs.

Level Needed. To use these matches for the benefit of the individual and the organization, it still is necessary to know the appropriate level of skill training: increased operational proficiency, skill development, or fundamental knowledge. The results of the job and person needs analyses determine the necessary level, particularly for current job training. The levels required for future job training depend on the organizational needs analysis as well as job and person needs analyses.

Program Needed. The final step is to determine which programs are most appropriate to teach the targeted skills at the level needed. A guide for this determination is shown in Exhibit 12.6. For example, apprenticeship training is appropriate for those who need to increase their operational proficiency in basic technical skills, whereas the case discussion method is appropriate for conceptual or managerial and administrative skill training at all three levels.

Unfortunately, selection of the appropriate program does not ensure the success of a training effort. Success also depends on the effective use of the principles of learning, the skills of the trainers, and the systematic and supportive organizational policies for training and development of employees.

Problems and Pitfalls in Training

This training and development stuff is all good, but it's my boss who really needs it.—Middle- and lower-level managers

Exhibit 12.6   Selecting a Training and Development Program

		Skills Required		
		Basic Skills	**Interpersonal Skills**	**Conceptual Integrative Skills**
Level of Skill Required	**Fundamental Knowledge**	job rotation multiple management apprenticeship training job instruction training	role playing sensitivity training formal courses	job rotation multiple management simulation case discussion
	Skill Development	job rotation multiple management simulation supervisory assistance	role playing sensitivity training job rotation multiple management simulation	job rotation multiple management simulation case discussion
	Operational Efficiency	job rotation multiple management apprenticeship training job instruction training simulation internship and assistanceship supervisory assistance	role playing job rotation multiple management apprenticeship training job instruction training simulation	job rotation multiple management simulation case discussion

Source: Adapted from T. J. Von der Embse, "Choosing a Management Development Program: A Decision Model," *Personnel Journal,* Oct. 1973, p. 911. Reprinted with permission of *Personnel Journal,* Costa Mesa, CA. All rights reserved.

If top management would only show active support of the program, it would be a certain success.—Staff training specialist

Management development? Active support? Why, I'm doing that all the time.—Top management [28]

As shown by these three quotations, misperceptions and the tendency to assign blame and responsibility to others are common in discussion about training in organizations. These techniques are partly responsible for the lack of success of some training efforts. But there are other reasons for failure as well, including: [29]

- Performing hasty and shallow needs analyses and thus failing to define what the real training needs are and who should receive the training
- Substituting training for selection and relying too heavily on the "magic" of training to increase the ability of individuals who lack the capability
- Limiting the training and development effort to only formal courses and ignoring all other methods
- Lumping together all training and development needs and thus failing to implement programs appropriate for different needs
- Failing to give consistent attention to the entire training and development effort
- Failing to provide for practical application and organizational support systems for the newly learned behaviours

Observers of the Canadian scene note that, in addition to these general problems, many Canadian training programs have other unique pitfalls, including

- the fact that management training is given a low priority; and
- the scarcity of skilled trainers (many executives in charge of training have very limited experience).[30]

Assessing Training Programs

Assessment of training programs is a necessary activity for PHRM departments: without assessment, evaluation is not feasible. As discussed in Chapter 1, PHRM departments must demonstrate their effectiveness and worth to the rest of the organization. Assessment involves determining what data and criteria are relevant for a valid evaluation, and then gathering and analyzing this. Methods by which to gather data, as discussed in previous chapters, include interviews, tests, performance appraisal results, and surveys of other companies. Once the relevant criteria are known, evaluation becomes possible. Effectiveness can be measured by comparing two or more sets of criteria.

Without evaluation, effectiveness cannot be known, yet many organizations fail to evaluate their training and development programs for a number of reasons. Frequently, firms are willing to accept programs at face value and are unaware of the importance of evaluation. Other times, managers are fearful of discovering that the programs really are not working. There also may be a lack of understanding of the evaluation methods and disagreements about the best criteria of effectiveness.[31]

To assess the effectiveness of any training program, the following questions should be answered:

- Did change occur?
- Is the change due to training?
- Is the change positively related to the achievement of organizational goals?
- Will similar changes occur with new participants in the same training program?[32]

In evaluating training programs, measures of change fall into four categories:

1. *Reaction:* How do participants feel about the training program? This is the most commonly used, but can be the most misleading (i.e., no evidence of change as a result of the program is apparent).
2. *Learning:* To what extent have trainees learned what was taught?
3. *Behaviour:* What on-the-job changes in behaviour occur because of attendance at the training program?
4. *Results:* To what extent have cost-related behavioural outcomes (e.g., turnover, productivity, or quality improvements) resulted from the training?

Evaluation Designs

In addition to determining the appropriate criteria to evaluate the program, the PHRM manager must select an **evaluation design**. Evaluation designs are important because they help the PHRM manager to determine if improvements have been made and if the training program caused the improvements. In addition to aiding in the evaluation of training programs, evaluation designs can (1) aid in evaluating any PHRM program aimed at improving productivity and the quality of work life; and (2) aid in evaluating the effectiveness of any PHRM activity.[33] Combining the data collection tools (i.e., organizational surveys), which are discussed in Chapter 13, with knowledge of evaluation designs can prove essential for demonstrating the effectiveness of PHRM programs and activities to the rest of the organization. Because the combination of data collection and evaluation design is vital for PHRM, evaluation design is discussed in more detail here.

There are three major classes of evaluation designs: pre-experimental, quasi-experimental, and experimental. Although it is preferable to use the experimental design, which is the most rigorous, a variety of organizational constraints make this impractical. Therefore, PHRM managers often utilize the moderately rigorous quasi-experimental design. Even when quasi-experimental designs are feasible, most evaluations that are done rely on the pre-experimental design. This design is used because it is easier and quicker. Unfortunately, this design is a very poor one for most purposes. An illustration of all three designs is shown in Exhibit 12.7, which also shows how programs can be evaluated using these designs and what is required.

The better designs in Exhibit 12.7 are those that make use of a control group. A control group consists of employees who are not trained but who are measured. Using such a design provides for comparisons. Panel A in Exhibit 12.7 shows the most common design used in organizations today. It also is the poorest in judging training effectiveness, because the base line in knowledge or skills for people who entered training is not known. Panel B is an improved design, taking into account some information about the initial skills, knowledge, and aptitudes of trainees prior to training. However, even if change results after training, it cannot be attributed to the training activities in this design. Panel C, which shows a post-measure-only design with control, may not require a pre-measure, but one has to be careful in comparing two very similar groups if conclusions about change and causality are to be made. Panel D is a full pre-post with control procedure. Evidence for training effectiveness can be inferred when pre-post changes are greater for the trained than the untrained personnel. This is, however, a rather costly procedure. Finally, Panels E and F provide for time series design without (E) and with a control group (F). These designs provide for collection of several initial measurements of critical skills, knowledge, and aptitudes, and involves monitoring of changes after training for a period of time. The trend that emerges provides important estimates of the stability of both pre-training and post-training. It helps to eliminate unnecessary training where experience alone improves skills, knowledge, and aptitudes over time (i.e., maturity curve). It also could provide estimates as to the retention rate of the newly acquired skills, knowledge, and aptitudes. For these and other reasons, many experts believe that multiple measures seem to be the best, because they minimize the so-called measurement and intervention interaction effects.[34]

Many of these design considerations also would apply to measurement of the effectiveness of employee development programs. However, although employee development commonly is associated with the concept of training, it is different in two areas, *focus* and *formality*. While training programs are set primarily to meet the organization's need, development focuses on the individual employee needs. It seeks to identify the continued needs that are exhibited by employees, in order to help them to be more effective and more content in their work. This individual focus represents an evolution in the role that many organizations assign to their PHRM officers. In fact, some organizations have even changed the title of their chief PHRM officer to emphasize this philosophy. For example, the title of the vice-president responsible for personnel at McDonald's restaurants recently was changed to "Vice-President of Individuality."

This focus on the individual means that the development process can be much less formal and structured than training programs. Because of the growing importance of employee development in organizations, the following section will elaborate on the formal and less formal PHRM activities undertaken in employee development and career planning.

Exhibit 12.7 **Major Classes of Evaluation Designs to Help Determine Program Effectiveness**

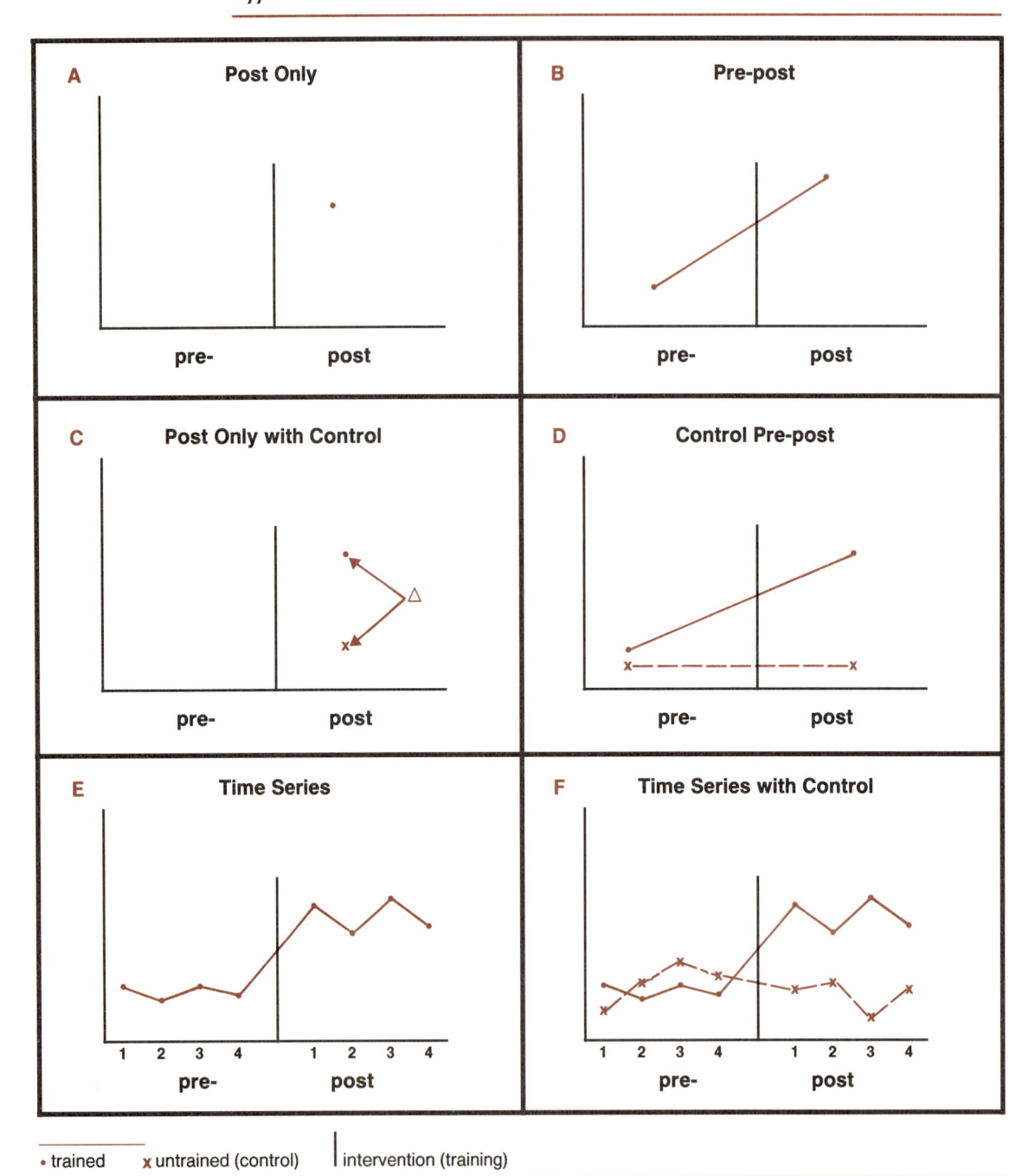

A Post Only

B Pre-post

C Post Only with Control

D Control Pre-post

E Time Series

F Time Series with Control

• trained   x untrained (control) | intervention (training)

Source: R. Haccoun, "Improving Training Effectiveness through the Use of Evaluation Research," in S. L. Dolan and R. S. Schuler (eds.), *Canadian Readings in Personnel and Human Resource Management* (St. Paul: West Publishing Co., 1987). Used with permission.

Developing Employees' Potential

The purposes of developing employees' potential are numerous. Although development usually is concerned with the improvement of intellectual or emotional abilities, other PHRM objectives could be met during the developmental process, such as to

- enhance employees' job satisfaction and quality of work life;
- help employees to discover new interests and potential that have been under-utilized;
- increase the job-performance effectiveness of the employee;
- prevent the employees' skills and knowledge from becoming obsolete; and
- sustain enthusiasm of employees, to avoid burn-out.

Employee development depends in many instances on the relationships and attitudes that the employee maintains with the immediate supervisor. By concentrating on the individual employee's goals and potential, a manager can significantly affect the employee's development. In this sense, almost all managers have an informally assigned responsibility to contribute to employees' development, a responsibility that recently has been labelled the **mentoring function**. Mentoring "is a relationship between a junior and senior colleague that is viewed by the junior as positively contributing to his or her development." [35]

Two types of functions contribute to the development of the junior person: first, a range of career advancement activities (i.e., sponsorship, coaching, exposure and visibility, protection, and challenging work assignments) and second, a range of personal support activities that help the junior member to develop a sense of personal identity (i.e., role modelling, counselling, acceptance and confirmation, and friendship).[36]

Facilitating Employee Development

Employee development is much broader than the acquisition of a specific skill. Therefore, a number of conditions are critical for employee development: an organizational philosophy that promotes development and is well supported by top management, and a real understanding of the interrelated nature of development.

Top-management back-up is a central condition in facilitating development; opportunities for development are in fact created by top management. Delegating decision-making responsibilities to lower-level positions to develop young employees, cultivating a climate that provides opportunities for frequent and open communication between people at different hierarchical levels, and the reward system for mentors are all desirable functions of top-management philosophy. If top management is not committed to employee development, it is not likely to result.

A relationship exists between the employee development efforts and other PHRM activities such as selection, placement, compensation, and appraisal. Neglect of any of these PHRM functions inhibits development efforts throughout the organization.[37] However, development is not a substitute for proper selection or placement. If a person is chosen to perform in a job that he or she is unable to do (lack of skills or knowledge), no amount of development will change that. Likewise, improper placement seldom can be rectified by development.

In addition to the on-going informal process of developing employee potential, many companies have attempted to devise more formal development plans. One study found that about 50% of surveyed companies had put such programs into effect for their first-line supervisors.[38] Many of these formal programs are administered by the organizations' PHRM departments.

Formal Programs of Employee Development

A variety of employee development methods is used in organizations. The basic goal of many formal programs is to develop people skills, job-specific skills, or planning and conceptual learning skills.[39] Exhibit 12.8 shows the extent to which each method is suited to each of the three goals.

Coaching is the continued process by which an immediate supervisor guides and monitors very closely a subordinate during the developmental program. **Committee assignments** allow a potentially promising employee to observe how decisions are made, by sitting on some important committees in the organization. This is considered to be beneficial for an employee who is being groomed for promotion in the company.

Job rotation involves the employee being assigned to different situations/jobs/departments (one at a time) for a limited period. The employee gains first-hand knowledge of the types of problems and processes commonly experienced in different jobs and sections of the firm, and theoretically becomes much more well-rounded in understanding organizational realities. Many banks in Canada use a 12-month job rotation process for their future managers.

Assistant-to methods are very similar in scope to coaching, although in this case the trainee works as an assistant to the assigned manager, usually in a staff capacity. Many development programs include **classroom courses**, in which employees attend a variety of general skill courses such as speed reading or word processing. Many companies encourage continuing education by paying employees to attend college courses, or even to study for advanced degrees at night school courses. Some of the Canadian companies who promote such individual development are Canadian Liquid Air, Sperry Canada, and Northern Telecom. The pace and direction of this phase of the developmental program is left to the choice of the individual employee.

Other organizations grant **project leaves of absence**, including sabbaticals. Sabbaticals have been very popular among university professors, enabling them to recycle their teaching skills and advance their research. Many firms have adapted similar approaches for their senior and professional employees. Given that a paid sabbatical can be an expensive proposition, many employers prefer to grant leaves of absence. In some

Matching Development Goals and Methods

Exhibit 12.8

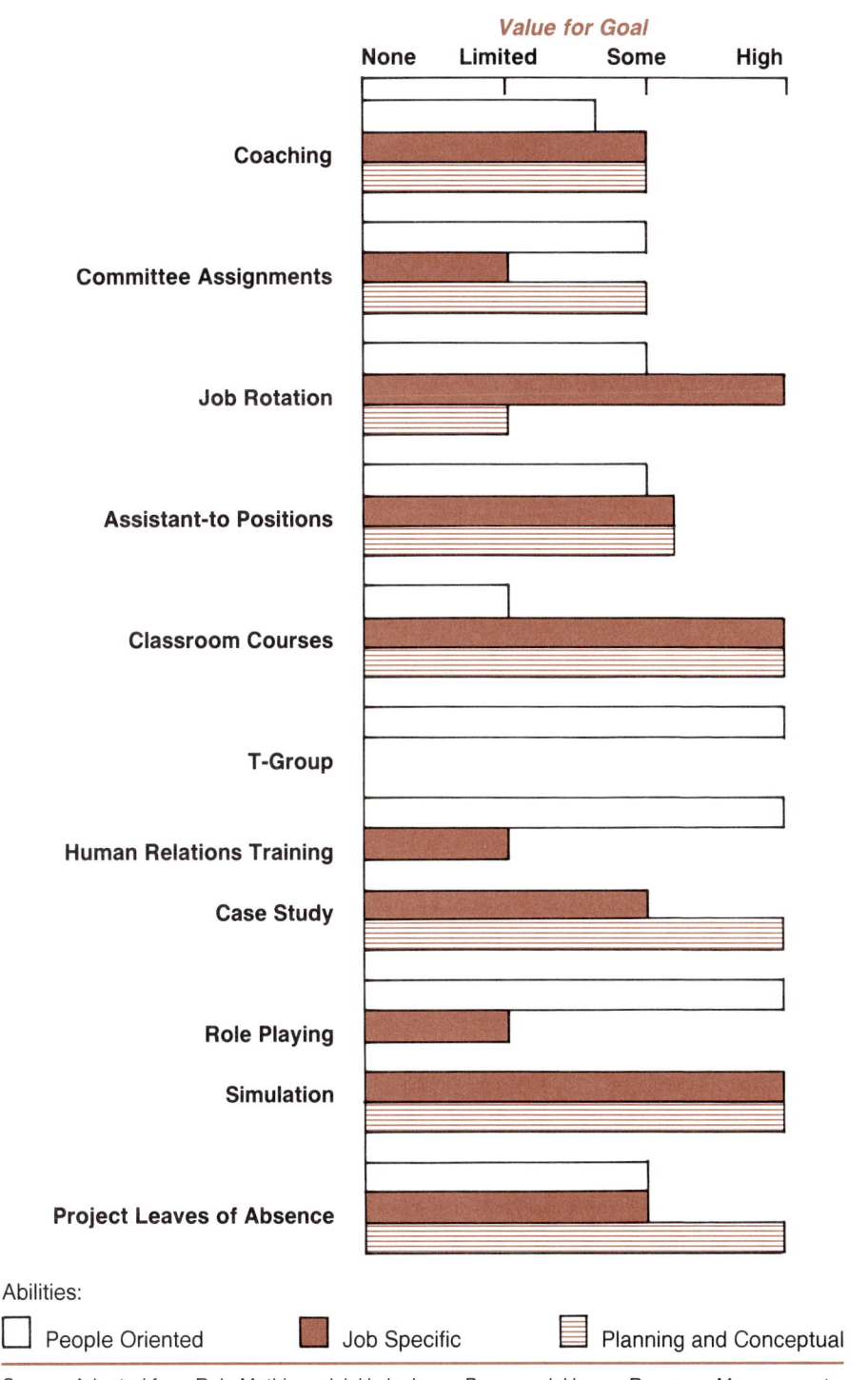

Value for Goal

Method	People Oriented	Job Specific	Planning and Conceptual
Coaching	Some	Some	Some
Committee Assignments	Some	Limited	Some
Job Rotation	Limited	High	Limited
Assistant-to Positions	Some	Some	Some
Classroom Courses	Limited	High	High
T-Group	High	None	None
Human Relations Training	High	Limited	None
Case Study	None	Some	High
Role Playing	High	Limited	None
Simulation	None	High	Some
Project Leaves of Absence	Some	Some	High

Abilities: □ People Oriented ▬ Job Specific ≡ Planning and Conceptual

Source: Adapted from R. L. Mathis and J. H. Jackson, *Personnel, Human Resource Management,* 4th ed. (St. Paul: West Publishing Co., 1985), p. 314 (used with permission).

organizations, rights for these leaves of absence also have been incorporated for non-exempt employees by virtue of collective agreements.

T-Groups and human relations training were very popular during the 1960s and the 1970s. Both are considered to be more related to individual development rather than to formal organizational development, except when carried out as integral parts of an organizational development program. **T-Group** training has also been called sensitivity training, or encounter group, marathon group, and laboratory training, and was introduced to Canadian industry by the U.S. National Training Laboratory. It is a technique that heavily emphasizes principles of group dynamics, and is geared toward developing skills for learning about oneself and others by observing and participating in a group situation. **Human relations** training is aimed at "humanizing" the employee to be more tuned to "people problems." This school of thought stemmed from the well-known Hawthorne studies.

Case studies, role playing, and **simulations** also are being used in developmental programs for employees. Most frequently, organizations use these methods with management trainees where the emphasis is on application and experience rather than memorization. Some organizations use these methods not only for developmental purposes but also for "conflict management," or both. For example, all 30 managerial employees of one of Krugers' pulp and paper plants meet every Friday, once a month, for a "confrontation meeting." Managers are encouraged to air their personal grievances and interpersonal conflicts with each other in the room. Conflicts are "managed" then, through use of role playing and simulations.

Career Planning and Development

In the past, career planning and development was confined to high-school or college students. Today, many organizations offer guidance and counselling to employees who want to develop a career. According to some experts, a number of forces have converged to stimulate the popularity of career activities in organizations,[40] including

- spillover effects of the affirmative action and equity laws that were extended from women and minorities to many other categories of employees;
- an increasing number of two-career couples, making career planning necessary to permit more balance between work and home;
- greater employee concern for quality of life, and the higher aspirations of a better-educated work force;
- growing need for career planning among the Baby-Boom generation in order to avoid career plateauing and obsolescence; and
- career management has become essential for organizations as a way to cope with an economy that swings between near-depression and very slow growth.[41]

All of these forces make it beneficial to both employees and employers to develop a strategy for long-term utilization and development of the employee's talent in the organization.

There are two different strategies of career planning available for organizational use: one centres on **individual planning needs** and the other on **organizational human resource planning needs**. Individual career planning focuses on people's plans for satisfying their personal needs for growth and development. Organizational career planning focuses on jobs and on constructing career paths that provide for logical progression of people from job to job. Exhibit 12.9 provides an example of career development activities.

Individual-Centred Career Planning

Studies often have indicated that career choices are influenced by four individual traits: *interests, self-identity, personality,* and *social background*.[42] Consequently, there are many manuals, textbooks, and videocassettes that can help individuals to diagnose their own career potential. Paper-and-pencil psychological tests, often provided by the organization, can help individuals to focus on their vocational interests and preferences. Personality and self-identity inventories are available for planning workshops and seminars, where employees learn how to better present themselves (prepare for an interview, prepare a résumé, etc.), how to be more forceful in communicating their career goals, and how to assess different career paths and make a choice. The content of such workshops varies from company to company.

Many companies do not apply their career programs across the board, but rather to individuals who wish to more systematically diagnose their self-image or personal needs for power, affiliation, or achievement. Such inventories can provide useful information if the results are properly interpreted. Interpretation requires understanding of the psychometric characteristics of the paper-and-pencil tests (particularly with regard to

Career Development Activities — Exhibit 12.9

Organization-Centred Career Planning		Mutual Focus Manager-Assisted Career Planning			Employee-Centred Career Planning	
Corporate succession planning	Corporate talent inventories	Development assessment centres (with feedback)	Manager-employee career discussions (includes separate training for managers)	Corporate seminars on organizational career	Company-run career planning workshops	Self-directed workbooks and tape cassettes

Note: This is a sample of program activities to illustrate different points on the continuum between individual-centred and organization-centred career planning. This is not a complete list of possible career development activities.

Source: Adapted from D. T. Hall and J. G. Goodale, *Human Resource Management* (Glenview, IL: Scott, Foresman and Company, 1986), p. 392.

validity and reliability, see Chapter 6) and should not be left to the novice. Therefore, many organizations provide career counselling by a human resource specialist, sometimes coupled with outside career specialists.

Organization-Centred Career Planning

The organizational career planning activity is similar to the individual appraisal activity. The major difference is that career planning by the organization is designed to meet its specific human resource planning goals. For this reason, many organizations devise programs ranging from job progression paths (clear policy that is communicated to the employees) to career accommodation in the form of retirement or early retirement.

Career progression paths represent "ladders" that each employee can climb to advance in certain organizational units. For example, the essence of Sears' job progression program is the identification of job demands. Sears uses the Hay plan to analyze jobs on three basic dimensions: know-how, problem solving, and accountability. Because these dimensions require different employee skills, a rational sequence of job assignments consists of jobs with different dimensions (e.g., sales, accounting, budget). Consequently, Sears can use its program to identify rational paths to target jobs (those that represent the end of employees' paths); to classify paths according to speed and level of development attained; and to justify and identify lateral and downward moves.[43]

Career paths are not always linear, nor do they always have to move up the organizational structure. In fact, many professional and technical employees, such as engineers and scientists, become part of what is called "*the dual-career ladder.*" Those who want to proceed in their technical-professional job are given the opportunity (although the career paths are very narrow), and those who wish to advance usually move into management. The dual career therefore provides opportunities for either the management ladder or the technical ladder.[44]

In order to enable organizations to better plan career pathing and career accommodation, many of them use computerized data banks containing information on the career histories, skills inventories, and career preferences of employees. Taking into consideration career opportunities, individuals may be identified for positions that are consistent with their career goals. The Canadian Armed Forces is using such a talent inventory at some of its divisions, and Canadian National has been experimenting with various talent inventories for the purpose of using them in their succession planning program. Succession planning was discussed in Chapter 2.

The core of succession planning however, is the review of key positions, the incumbents, and the development of a list of back-up candidates. One by-product of succession planning in recent years has been outplacement or other similar activities that *facilitate exit*. With promotion opportunities becoming scarcer as growth slows and layers of managerial positions are diluted, it is in the organization's best interest to help individuals to search for alternative careers outside of the organization. Although this involves the loss of important managers, blocking advancement and/or forcing managers to do the same things repeatedly might turn out to be more counter-productive in the long run.[45]

The Canadian government recognized this problem and in 1971 created a program entitled "Interchange Canada." With the dual objectives of enhancing employees' development and creating new opportunities for employee mobility, the program arranges for private sector managers to spend up to three years on temporary assignments with the federal government and vice versa. Between 1971 and 1985, more than 1100 managers benefited from this service.[46]

Summary

As employees enter and progress through various jobs within the organization, the need to acquire new skills and abilities is both a function of the employee changing jobs and of jobs changing with time. Effective personnel management requires that organizations accurately pinpoint where training and development needs exist and identify how to effectively address those needs.

Training and development activities are clearly linked to other personnel functions such as planning, performance appraisal, selection and recruitment, job analysis, job design, and compensation. Weak links between these functions obviously will limit the effectiveness of training and development programs. At a minimum, job analysis and performance appraisal are essential for each of the three phases of training and development: needs assessment, program implementation, and evaluation.

Evaluation of training program effectiveness requires a commitment by the company to engage in a rigorous, preferably experimental, design for program evaluation. Although similar to predictive validation designs, experimental designs are more costly to implement both in terms of time and money. Quasi-experimental designs and the use of existing performance appraisal information can enable the personnel manager to evaluate effectively the training and development decisions.

Developing employees' potential has a dual focus: to help individuals perform in jobs that are consistent with their interests and preferences, and to help organizations to match available jobs to the skills, knowledge, and aptitudes of their workforce. Facilitating employees' development utilizes both formal and informal activities, and the result is mutually beneficial to the organization and to the individual employee.

Because organizations are dynamic and present a variety of job transitions (staffing at entry levels with new recruits, promotions and transfers, layoffs, discharges, and retirement), career planning and development activities are relevant to all members of the organization. Career development is a continuous process.

From the organizational perspective, career development activities can contribute to other key personnel functions that enable the company to simultaneously attract and retain the best people. The employee, however, shares the responsibility of finding a job that fits his or her skills, knowledge, and aptitude, as well as interests and preferences. Individual-centred career planning can lead to proactive career decisions that enable the employee to manage numerous transitions during a career. Organization-centred career planning can lead to better utilization of human resources, and keep the employees content with the range of career opportunities that the organization may offer.

Discussion Questions

1. What steps are involved in the assessment phase of determining training needs?
2. Discuss the four basic categories of training and identify to what types of employees these categories of training generally are related.
3. List and briefly describe several training and development design principles.
4. What is job instruction training and how can it be used to minimize the disadvantages of on-the-job training programs?
5. What are the major drawbacks of using formal course methods (off the job) of training and development?
6. What are three critical questions to ask when selecting a training program?
7. What are some design principles that can enhance the learning that takes place in training programs?
8. Why do organizations often overlook or lack proper evaluation of employee training programs?
9. Why do organizations engage in employee development programs?
10. What is the role of top management in facilitating employee development programs? Why is it so critical?
11. Distinguish between "formal" and "informal" employee development programs.
12. Distinguish between individual-centred and organization-centred career planning programs.

CASE STUDY

A Training Misdiagnosis or Mistake?

Sue Catallo, training representative for the regional office of a large service organization, had been very excited about a new training program. The personnel department at head office had informed her six months previously that it had purchased a speed-reading training program from a reputable firm, and statistics showed that the program had proven to be very effective in other companies.

Sue knew that most individuals in the regional office were faced on a daily basis with a sizeable amount of incoming correspondence, including internal memoranda, announcements of new and revised policies and procedures, reports of federal legislation, and letters from customers. So a course in speed reading certainly should help most employees.

Head office had flown regional training representatives in for a special session on how to conduct the speed-reading program, so Sue had begun the program in her office with great confidence. She led five groups of 30 employees each through the program, which consisted of nine two-hour sessions. Sessions were conducted in the on-site training facilities. Altogether, 1200 employees in the organization participated in the training, at an approximate cost to the company of $110 per participant, including training materials and time away from work. The program was very well received by the participants, and speed tests administered before and after training showed that, on average, reading speed increased 250% with no loss of comprehension.

A couple of months after the last session, Sue informally asked a couple of employees who had gone through the training if they were applying the speed-reading principles in their work and maintaining their reading speed. They said they were not using it at work but did practise their new skill with their off-the-job reading. Sue checked with several other participants and heard the same story. Although they were applying what they had learned to their personal reading and for school courses, they were not using it on the job. When Sue asked them about all of the reading material that crossed their desks daily, the typical response was, "I never read those memos and policy announcements anyway!" Sue was concerned about this information but did not know what to do with it.

Case Questions

1. Did Sue waste valuable training funds?
2. Should Sue now start a program to get the employees to read the memos and policy announcements?
3. How could Sue have avoided the situation she now faces?
4. Should organizations provide training programs to help improve employee skills that can be used off the job?

Source: Adapted from R. S. Schuler, S. A. Youngblood, and L. K. Trevino, *Instructor's Manual, Effective Personnel Management*, 2nd ed. (St. Paul: West Publishing Co., 1986), p. 337. Used with permission.

Endnotes

1. R. Rajsic, "Organized Learning: Training That Pays," *Human Resources Management in Canada* (Prentice-Hall Canada Inc., 1985), p. 5,434.
2. "Feature Report: Trends in Training," *Human Resources Management in Canada* (Prentice-Hall Canada Inc., 1983), p. 5,143.
3. I. L. Goldstein, "Training in Work Organizations," *Annual Review in Psychology*, 1980, *31*, pp. 229–272. K. N. Wexley and G. P. Latham, *Developing and Training Human Resources in Organizations* (Glenview, IL: Scott, Foresman and Company, 1981). K. N. Wexley, "Training Human Resources in Organizations," *Annual Review in Psychology*, 1984, *35*, p. 519.
4. J. Lafrenière, "IBM, un chef de file qui se prèoccupe de ses produits et encore davantage de son personnel," *Formation et Emploi*, Feb.–Mar. 1985, *1(8)*, p. 10.
5. T. R. Horton, "Training: A Key to Productivity Growth," *Management Review*, September 1983, pp. 2–3.
6. R. Szawlowski, "Training and Development: Current and Future Trends in the High Technology Industry," in S. L. Dolan and R. S. Schuler (eds.), *Canadian Readings in Personnel and Human Resource Management* (St. Paul: West Publishing Co., 1987).
7. R. B. McAfee, "Using Performance Appraisals to Enhance Training Programs," *Personnel Administrator*, Nov. 1982, pp. 31–34. J. Carroll and C. E. Schneier, *Performance Appraisal and Review Systems* (Glenview, IL: Scott, Foresman and Company, 1982). H. J. Bernardin and M. R. Buckley, "A Consideration of Strategies in Rater Training," *Academy of Management Review*, 1981, *6*, pp. 205–212. H. J. Bernardin, "Effects of Rater Training on Leniency and Halo Errors in Student Ratings of Instructors," *Jour-*

nal of Applied Psychology, 1978, 63, pp. 301–308.
8. S. F. Cronshaw, "Future Directions for Personnel Psychology in Canada," paper submitted to a special issue of Canadian Psychology (pre-publication of draft, 1986), p. 18.
9. R. D. Phillips, "Affirmative Action as an Effective Labour Market Planning Tool of the 1980's," Technical Study No. 29, Supply and Services Canada, 1981, p. 59.
10. "Affirmative Action and Human Resource Planning for the 1980's," Affirmative Action Consulting Service, Ontario Region, Employment and Immigration, Canada, March, 1984.
11. R. Adams, "An Overview of Training and Development in Canada," in S. L. Dolan and R. S. Schuler (eds.), endnote 6.
12. This was recommended by the MacDonald Commission Report: Report of the Royal Commission on the Economic Union and Development Prospects for Canada (Ottawa: Supply and Services Canada, 1985).
13. I. L. Goldstein, Training: Program Development and Evaluation (Monterey, CA: Brooks/Cole, 1974). W. McGehee and P. W. Thayer, Training in Business and Industry (New York: Wiley, 1961). M. L. Moore and P. Dutton, "Training Needs Analysis: Review and Critique," The Academy of Management Review, July 1978, pp. 532–545. S. D. Truskie, "Getting the Most from Management Development Programs," Personnel Journal, Jan. 1982, pp. 66–68. J. Laurie, "Diagnosis Before Prescription: Data Collection, Part I," Personnel Journal, July 1982, pp. 494–498. J. Laurie, "Begin at the Beginning: Data Collection, Part II," Personnel Journal, Aug. 1982, pp. 568–569.
14. T. J. Von der Embse, "Choosing a Management Development Program: A Decision Model," Personnel Journal, Oct. 1973, p. 908. Reprinted with permission Personnel Journal, Costa Mesa, CA. Copyright October 1973.
15. For identification of both current and future performance potential, see Carroll and Schneier, endnote 7; G. P. Latham and K. N. Wexley, Increasing Productivity Through Performance Appraisal (Reading, MA: Addison-Wesley, 1981), on the use of behavioural measures such as BOS and BARS to validly measure performance, as discussed in Chapter 8.
16. "Supervisory Training: HR Issues and Intricacies," Bulletin to Management, April 26, 1984, 2, p. 7. B. J. Middlebrook and F. M. Rachel, "A Survey of Middle Management Training and Development Program," Personnel Administrator, Nov. 1983, pp. 27–31.
17. B. M. Bass and J. A. Vaughan, Training in Industry: The Management of Learning (Belmont, CA: Wadsworth, 1966), p. 62.
18. B. M. Bass and J. A. Vaughan, Training in Industry: The Management of Learning (Belmont, CA: Wadsworth, 1966), p. 66.
19. R. Likert, "Motivational Approach to Management Development," Harvard Business Review, 37, 1959, pp. 75–82. W. C. Hamner and E. P. Hamner, "Behavior Modification on the Bottom Line," Organizational Dynamics, 1976, 4, pp. 3–21.
20. Bass and Vaughan, endnote 18, p. 62.
21. S. R. Siegel, "Improving the Effectiveness of Management Development Programs," Personnel Journal, Oct. 1981, pp. 770–773.
22. Bass and Vaughan, endnote 18, p. 88.
23. T. DeLone, "What Do Middle Managers Really Want From First-Line Supervisors?" Supervisory Management, Sept. 1977, pp. 8–12. W. E. Sasser, Jr., and Frank S. Leonard, "Let First Level Supervisors Do Their Job," Harvard Business Review, March–April 1980, pp. 113–121. The Woodlands Group, "Management Development Roles: Coach, Sponsor, and Mentor," Personnel Journal, Nov. 1980, pp. 918–921.
24. V. R. Bohem, "Assessment Centers and Management Development," in K. M. Rowland and G. R. Ferris (eds.), Personnel Management (Boston: Allyn & Bacon, 1982), pp. 327–363. A. Tziner, "The Assessment Center Revisited: Practical and Theoretical Considerations," in S. L. Dolan and R. S. Schuler (eds.), Canadian Readings in Personnel and Human Resource Management (St. Paul: West Publishing Co., 1987).
25. S. Carey, "These Days More Managers Play Games, Some Made in Japan, as a Part of Training," The Wall Street Journal, Oct. 7, 1982, p. 35.
26. J. R. Hinrichs, "Personnel Training," in M. D. Dunnette (ed.), Handbook of Industrial and Organizational Psychology, 2nd ed. (New York: John Wiley & Sons, 1983), p. 855.
27. B. Mexoff, "Human Relations Training: The Tailored Approach," Personnel, March–April 1981, pp. 21–27. J. P. Campbell, M. D. Dunnette, E. E. Lawler III, and K. E. Weick, Jr., Managerial Behavior, Performance and Effectiveness (New York: McGraw-Hill, 1970).
28. R. J. House, "Experiential Learning: A Social Learning Theory Analysis," in R. D. Freedman, C. L. Cooper, and S. A. Stumpf (eds.), Management Education (London: John Wiley and Sons, Ltd., 1982), pp. 9–10.
29. J. W. Taylor, "Ten Serious Mistakes in Management Training Development," Personnel Journal, May 1974, pp. 357–362.
30. R. Rajsic, "Organized Learning: Training That Pays," Human Resources Management in Canada (Prentice-Hall Canada Inc.) October, 1985, p. 5,434.
31. S. Monat, "A Perspective on the Evaluation of Training and Development Programs," Personnel Administrator, July 1981, pp. 47–52. J. W. Newstrom, "Evaluating the Effectiveness of Training Methods," Personnel Administrator, Jan. 1980, pp. 55–60. R. D. Arvey and P. Shingledecker, "Research Methods in Personnel Management," in K. M. Rowland and G. R. Ferris (eds.), Personnel Management (Boston: Allyn & Bacon, 1982), pp. 24–50.

32. I. L. Goldstein, *Training: Program Development and Evaluation* (Monterey, CA: Brooks/Cole, 1974).
33. D. L. Kirkpatrick, "Evaluation Training Programs: Evidence vs. Proof," *Training and Development Journal*, 1977 (31), pp. 9–12. D. L. Kirkpatrick, "Four Steps to Measuring Training Effectiveness," *Personnel Administrator*, 1983 (28), *11*, pp. 19–25. R. Haccoun, "Improving Training Effectiveness through the Use of Evaluation Research," in Dolan and Schuler (eds.), endnote 6.
34. E. F. Huse and T. G. Cummings, *Organization Development and Change*, 3rd ed. (St. Paul: West Publishing Co., 1985), p. 383.
35. K. F. Kram, *Mentoring at Work* (Glenview, IL: Scott, Foresman, 1984).
36. K. F. Kram, "Phases of the Mentor Relationship," *Academy of Management Journal*, December 1983, *26*, pp. 605–625.
37. For more details, see R. W. Waters, "Developing Future Managers: Systems Approach," *Personnel Administrator*, August, 1980, p. 47.
38. H. Z. Levine, "Consensus," *Personnel*, November–December 1983, p. 4.
39. R. L. Mathis and J. H. Jackson, *Personnel, Human Resource Management*, 4th ed. (St. Paul: West Publishing Co., 1985), p. 313.
40. D. T. Hall and J. G. Goodale, *Human Resource Management* (Glenview, IL: Scott, Foresman, 1986), Chapter 14.
41. Ibid., pp. 390–391.
42. T. D. Hall, *Careers in Organizations* (Pacific Palisades, CA: Goodyear Publishing, 1976), pp. 11–13.
43. The Sears example is abbreviated from R. S. Schuler and S. A. Youngblood, *Effective Personnel Management*, 2nd ed. (St. Paul: West Publishing Co., 1986), p. 428 (used with permission).
44. For more information on dual-career paths for professionals and technical employees, see L. Bailyn, "Technical Careers," *Technology Review*, November–December 1982, p. 42; T. Danforth and A. Alden, "Dual Career Pathing: No Better Time, No Better Reason," *Employment Relations Today*, Summer 1983, pp. 189–201.
45. See for example, the rationale advanced by Exxon, "Succession Planning at Exxon," *Career Development Bulletin*, 1980, 2(1), p. 1.
46. N. Gallaiford, "Interchange Canada: Seeing How the Other Half Works," in "Feature Report: Employee Development," *Human Resources Management in Canada* (Prentice-Hall Canada Inc., 1985), p. 5,389.

CHAPTER

13

Quality of Work Life and Productivity

PHRM in the News

Productivity and the Quality of Work Life
Purposes and Importance of QWL and Productivity
Relationships of QWL and Productivity Programs
Policy Considerations in QWL and Productivity Programs

Programs for QWL Improvements
Communicating with Employees: Organizational Surveys
Semi-autonomous Work Groups
Quality Circles
Organizational Restyling

Programs for Productivity Improvements
Task Changes
Automation
Office Design
Productivity Improvements—The Total Management Approach

Assessing QWL and Productivity Programs
QWL Programs
Productivity Programs

Summary

Discussion Questions

Case Study

Endnotes

PHRM in the News

A "Souper" Company Plan

Campbell Soup Co. Ltd., the icon of the grocery trade whose familiar red-and-white cans can be found in most Canadian kitchens, tells its shareholders that it is in the "well-being" business. But two years ago, when the 55-year-old Toronto-based company hired the president of its major rival, Thomas J. Lipton Inc.'s David Clark, as its new chief executive officer, it was far from well. Clark was the ninth top manager to be brought in to save the company in 11 years. The firm had suffered declining sales for six of the previous seven years. And office politics were rife, according to Clark. That, he said, was due to a paternal and punitive "cover your ass" management which had acquired a "loser's image." With instability in the executive suite, Campbell's 2,000 "pent-up" employees had no "shared vision," said Clark, and the organization was "ripe for change."

Dynamic

Clark, a 46-year-old MBA from Hamilton, Ont., who is a self-admitted corporate zealot, immediately set about to make changes. His first mission was to reform marketing and management and galvanize the staff at the company's nine plants and three farms. To do that, he paid human resources consulting firm Achieve Enterprises Ltd., which opened shop in Edmonton in 1978 and has, since 1980, on average, doubled its earnings every year, $50,000 to transform Campbell from a staid company into a dynamic one. Clark increased the salaries of those whom he considered to be good workers, reduced the work week to 4½ days for salaried workers and staggered working hours.

In an attempt to involve middle managers in decision making, he divided the 90 Ontario managers into 15 "task forces" to tackle specific goals. In Campbell's nine plants in five provinces he grouped employees into "quality circles" to address and solve workplace problems. He also named a company ombudsman, invited seven employees to have 90-minute breakfasts with him every two weeks and established an annual award for an exemplary company employee. Last year the winner was 59-year-old Bill Clark, a maintenance manager in the Listowel, Ont., plant who was given a gold ring for designing pieces of machinery to overcome production problems.

Clark also began holding "information forums" for employees, a move that helped workers feel more secure in their own roles. The company also subsidized a fitness program and weight-training program, put new sofas and easy chairs in the women's washrooms, formed a 10-woman "women's advisory committee" and in May held an open house at the Toronto plant attended by more than 3,000 relatives of workers. One of the biggest hits with employees was the remodelled cafeteria in Toronto that, Clark said, "you wouldn't take your dog to before." And in an effort to get both managers and employees alike committed to the company, he encouraged employees to go out and meet retailers of Campbell's products (which include such brand names as Franco-American, Swanson's TV dinners, Pepperidge Farm desserts, Allen's apple juice, V–8, A–1 Sauce and Gattuso pastas).

The cost of instilling what Clark calls "a profound respect for people" at Campbell was about $200,000. The results, in financial terms, were dramatic. In 1984, the year after Clark installed what he called his "Serendipity" program, productivity went up by 8 per cent and net sales jumped by 4.6 per cent to $265 million. Sales are expected to rise another five per cent in 1985.

Sunny

Other changes were more subtle. Said Ethel Pokonzie, timekeeper at the 600-employee Campbell Toronto plant and an employee for 40 years: "Until a couple of years ago there was always a line drawn between the plant and office people. There isn't now. It's just a nice atmosphere. Now there's hardly a person who doesn't say 'Hi'." Added Ed Dzikowski, a 35-year-old supervisor of a soup production line at Campbell's Portage la Prairie, Man., plant: "It's a new mood, the difference between a cloudy day and a sunny one." Dzikowski is a member of one of his plant's "quality circles," one which last month changed a working procedure so that losses were reduced. Campbell vice-president for human resources Peter Barkla said that the nature of office politics has changed too: now that workers know more about what is going on, there are fewer rumors and less dissension.

Clark is now planning to produce a videotape on a strategy for excellence to be shown to the hourly rated production employees: "I believe we have shaken the limbs of the organization," he told *Maclean's*. "If we haven't shaken the trunk yet, I believe we will." Clark said that a management style "that has much to do with the tenets of religion made some of my colleagues feel a bit uncomfortable." But Clark, who is just two years into his five-year "corporate vision," is pressing on. Last week Campbell's middle managers awarded stickers to employees who excelled in their work that read, "Thanks for a souper job well done." Said Clark, "My feeling is that people will kill for them."

Source: Glen Allen, "A Souper Company Plan," *Maclean's*, July 15, 1985, p. 37. Used with permission.

QWL in the Atlantic Provinces

An experiment in the Atlantic provinces to develop QWL facilitators has given birth to several innovative changes in work methods among government, industry and educational groups.

The Work Improvement Training Program was begun in 1984 by Dalhousie University's Institute of Public Affairs. Funded by Labour Canada, the project aims at increasing the number of people familiar with QWL concepts and their application.

Eight organizations from Nova Scotia, New Brunswick and Prince Edward Island have been taking part in the program. The 25 participants representing industry, government and education had to comply with basic criteria for acceptance:

- strong support from their senior management;
- management representation by line managers able to effect change without prior approval within their own work groups;
- attendance by a union representative within these work groups;
- substitution of a worker representative where an organization did not have a bargaining unit.

An intense one-week course in the principle of socio-technical systems began the program. Subsequently, participants attended a two-day workshop each month and in between were expected to develop and implement a QWL change project in their work area. During the workshops, much time was spent by participants learning about the progress and difficulties of their individual QWL projects.

During the two-year period of the program several working examples of applied QWL have been developed. A municipality is revising its snow and ice clearing program in equal partnership with the union. In another case, members of a work group in a food distribution warehouse planned and carried out the move for an addition to the plant. Workers at a textile mill are designing new floor layouts for each of the units in the mill.

The initial concept for the program was developed to deal with geography and population problems in the Atlantic provinces. The land mass is larger than Britain yet its two million people are scattered in small pockets. Unfortunately, the resource base of QWL expertise in the area is small, which ruled out direct consulting at individual work sites. The solution was to bring representatives to one location on a regular basis and use education/classroom techniques. Core teaching and the consulting work has been done by five regular tutors, with other specialists flown in from other parts of Canada.

The Work Improvement Training Program has proved extremely cost effective for a large, thinly populated area, according to Jack Dougall, assistant director of the Institute of Public Affairs and director of the Advanced Management Centre at Dalhousie University.

The lessons learned in applying QWL, he says, have been outstanding.

"An interesting dimension of the program is that it was set up as an action research project, with the intent of evaluating productivity, job satisfaction and attitudes both before and after the program. It is intended to write up the outcomes of these findings in the form of case studies, both of the program as a whole and the individual projects."

Source: J. Dougall, "QWL in the Atlantic Provinces," *QWL Focus*, The News Journal of the Ontario Quality of Life Centre, Ministry of Labour, Province of Ontario, vol. 5(1), March 1986, p. 15. Used with permission.

Union Endorses Quality of Working Life

Quality of working life provides team-building and problem-solving tools and related attitudes at the workplace. The experience of the Union of National Defence Employees has been that the approach usually resolves situations that otherwise lead to formal grievances. Many grievances in the public service are ultimately resolved by employers to their sole and immediate advantage. This, of course, is a guarantee of poor long-term employee relations.

Source: N. D. Porter, "Union Endorses Quality of Working Life," *Canadian Business Review*, vol. II(4), Winter, 1984, p. 10. Used with permission of the Conference Board of Canada.

These three "PHRM in the News" articles highlight several aspects of quality of work life and productivity programs. Broader employee participation used in manufacturing firms such as Campbell Soup lifts morale, improves the sense of identity and commitment and, in general, contributes to higher productivity. As the second "PHRM in the News" article indicated, open communication, direct information, and participation not only improved the quality of work life for employees but also proved to be extremely cost effective for organizations in the thinly populated area of Atlantic Canada. The experience suggests that QWL programs can be taught and, if properly implemented, could gain union support, thereby contributing to the quality of labour-management relations. While not all unions favour QWL programs—more for ideological than practical reasons—the few who have co-operated in implementing QWL projects are committed to extend this experience.

Productivity and the Quality of Work Life

Declining Canadian productivity is a dilemma increasingly discussed in executive suites and by almost all personnel managers. Reversing the decline in productivity is a major goal for many organizations. Yet one of the most perplexing aspects of improving productivity is defining and measuring it. While almost no one challenges productivity's traditional definition, *output divided by input*, there is some debate about what is output and what is input. At first glance it appears impossible to measure the output or input of a nursing home, a bank, a big city orchestra, or many of the thousands of service and professional organizations. It appears equally impossible to measure the work that individual employees do in these types of organizations.

At a second glance, however, organizations are discovering that the task is not impossible, just difficult. Measures of productivity must be tailored to each organization, and to the goals of each organization. In general, **productivity** is defined as the output of an individual, group, or organization, divided by the input needed by the individual, group, or organization for the creation of output. Linking this definition to the discussion in Chapter 7, it can be assumed that increased employee performance and reduced employee absenteeism and turnover increase productivity no matter how an organization may define the term. Those measures can be used as well as organizational survival and competitiveness to evaluate productivity improvement.[1]

Quality of work life is as difficult to define and measure as productivity. Nevertheless, a QWL program is defined here as a process by which all members of the organization, through appropriate and open channels of communication set up for this purpose, have some say in decisions that affect their jobs in particular and the work environment in general, resulting in greater job involvement and satisfaction and reduced levels of stress. In essence, QWL represents an organizational culture or management style in which employees experience feelings of ownership, self-control, responsibility, and self-respect.[2] Exactly what organizations do to produce these feelings in their employees varies. Generally, however, in an organization characterized as having a high QWL, suggestions, questions, and criticism that might lead to improvement of any kind are encouraged and welcomed. In such a setting, creative discontent is viewed as a manifestation of constructive caring about the organization rather than destructive griping. Management encouragement of such feelings of involvement often leads to ideas and actions for upgrading operational effectiveness and efficiency as well as environmental enhancement. Increased productivity, measured in terms of work quality as well as quantity, is thus likely to result as a natural by-product.[3]

Purposes and Importance of QWL and Productivity

Although related, the importance and purposes of QWL and productivity serve different organizational objectives.

QWL. The attention now being paid to the quality of work life reflects the growing importance attached to it and a general concern for Match 2. It appears that a substantial number of workers are unhappy with their jobs and are demanding more meaningful work. Employees are beginning to demand changes in both economic and non-economic outcomes from their jobs. The importance of non-economic rewards is increasing relative to the importance of economic ones, particularly among white-collar and highly educated workers.[4] It appears that there is a need—and considerable room—for improvement in the quality of work life of many contemporary Canadian workers.

Some people attribute part of the present productivity slowdown and decline in the quality of products in Canada to deficiencies in the quality of work life and to changes in the interests and preferences of employees. People are demanding greater control and involvement in their jobs. They prefer not to be treated as a cog in a machine. When they are treated with respect, given a chance to voice their opinions, and given a greater degree of decision making, employees respond favourably:

> "I wasn't involved for over a year because of my suspicions. I am still suspicious, but my suspicions have changed since I have seen many improvements. Let's take a simple case of stockroom requisitions. Before, if you wanted a stupid pair of 75-cent gloves, you had to find a foreman to sign for them. Meanwhile, you're operating equipment worth thousands of dollars and you're the only one making decisions on it. Now we do our own requisitions, and work orders too."[5]

Productivity. An equal if not greater level of attention is being paid to productivity. Because companies and managers are evaluated by the level of profitability, ways to improve productivity are always of interest to them. This is particularly true now, however, as the rate of productivity growth in Canada has slowed to a point where it now is less than that in many other industrialized countries, and it should become more competitive in both national and international markets.

Increasing productivity also is seen as important because more Canadians realize that their standard of living is actually declining. Furthermore, if the current trend continues, the present generation will live less well than the previous generation, the first time this will ever have happened in Canada.

In summary, interest in the quality of work life and productivity usually focuses on techniques for changing the organization in order to improve employee satisfaction and productivity, increase job involvement and performance, and reduce stress, turnover, and absenteeism. It appears as if it is possible to achieve all of these benefits at once.[6]

Relationships of QWL and Productivity Programs

QWL and productivity programs have a significant impact on several other PHRM activities. Although the effects of these programs may reduce the necessity for other activities to improve productivity and the quality of work life (remember that all PHRM activities are assessed in part by their impact on productivity and QWL, as discussed in Chapter 1), the implementation of programs to improve QWL and productivity often requires changes in the other activities. Occasionally, a program to improve the QWL and productivity is based almost entirely on a specific PHRM activity, such as pay plan programs.

Recruitment and Selection. Recruitment and selection activities often are directly affected by QWL and productivity programs that reduce absenteeism and turnover. With high absenteeism and turnover, companies need to recruit and select more job applicants. In addition, the organization may be forced to hire applicants it would prefer not to hire, simply because so many positions need to be filled. These employees in turn may be more likely to be absent and quit, thus perpetuating a damaging cycle. A QWL or productivity program (such as career development) that reduces absenteeism and turnover will have a positive effect on the staffing function.

Job Analysis. When task-change programs are used to improve productivity or QWL, the purposes, duties, and characteristics of jobs often are changed. These changes generate a need for job analyses of the new jobs. Although new jobs are most readily created by job-enrichment programs, they also are created by workflow changes.

Training and Development and Human Resource Planning. QWL projects also influence personnel and human resource planning. Because turnover and absenteeism may be reduced by these projects, human resource needs may be reduced. Training needs, on the other hand, may increase, at least initially. This is true particularly for supervisors who must adjust to new supervisory roles as a consequence of QWL programs. QWL programs usually affect the jobs of first-level supervisors, whose co-operation therefore is most needed to ensure the success of the programs.

Health and Safety. As discussed in more detail in Chapter 14 many programs instituted to improve the QWL also effect an improvement in occupational health and safety conditions. Consider jobs where workers are likely to have accidents due to the boredom experienced on the job: QWL programs can reduce the boredom and, therefore, reduce the accidents as well. As one consequence of QWL programs such as job redesign or improved communications, workers become more involved and motivated.

Union-Management Relations. Unions can play a very important role in QWL and productivity programs.[7] Such programs often involve changing the conditions of employment and therefore are often subject to bargaining between union and management. But unions also can play a proactive role by pushing for programs that will save jobs or enhance the QWL for those who have jobs. Not all unions care to be a party to improvement programs, however, let alone play a proactive role. Some unions feel that such involvement blurs the distinction between the respective roles of management and labour in the workplace. Such involvement also can mean association with a program that is neither desired by the employees (the rank-and-file union membership) nor successful.

A summary of the relationships of other personnel activities to QWL and productivity appears in Exhibit 13.1.

Policy Considerations in QWL and Productivity Programs

QWL programs were formally introduced in Canada in 1978 through the initiative of the federal government and the creation of the QWL Unit of the Employment Relations Branch of Labour Canada. The QWL Unit was advised by E. Trist, an international scholar and pioneer in QWL, who accepted a position at York University in Toronto. The activities of this organization over the past few years have been quite diverse. Rather than immediately implementing QWL projects, the Unit held a series of workshops across Canada and invited interested academics, managers, trade unionists, and management consultants. The Unit also produced and distributed widely many publications on QWL, including a newsletter of QWL events, articles about different initiatives, and books of QWL readings. The process appeared to be an effective way to diffuse much information on QWL techniques, particularly about socio-technical concerns and quality circles. The Labour Canada QWL Unit provided a steady stream of activities and workshops, and also provided financial and technical assistance for QWL training and research projects. Finally, this branch developed a network of qualified QWL experts across the country.

Parallel activity has been undertaken by the Treasury Board of Canada since 1975. Experiments in the creation of semi-autonomous work groups were undertaken in 1975 in three federal departments, in collaboration with three different public sector unions, despite some hesitation on the part of the latter.[8] These first-generation experiments were soon followed by a second-generation series of experiments in two other departments in 1978. These experiments, although not always successful, were highly publicized and other organizations became interested.[9]

The Canadian Labour Market Productivity Centre was established in 1984. Although the Centre is well funded (about $7 million per year), its

Exhibit 13.1 Programs for Productivity and Quality of Work Life Improvements

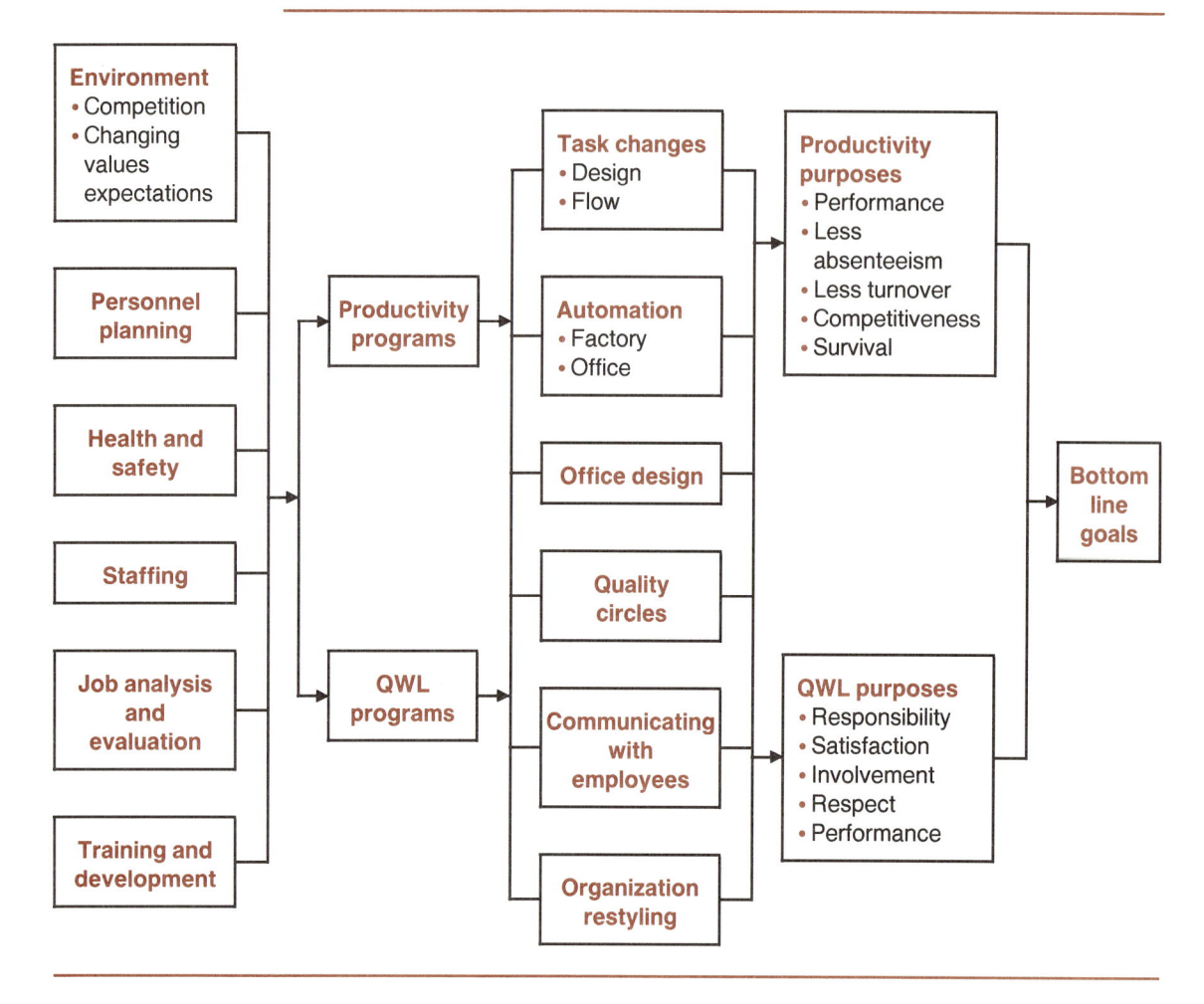

Environment
- Competition
- Changing values expectations

Personnel planning

Health and safety

Staffing

Job analysis and evaluation

Training and development

Productivity programs

QWL programs

Task changes
- Design
- Flow

Automation
- Factory
- Office

Office design

Quality circles

Communicating with employees

Organization restyling

Productivity purposes
- Performance
- Less absenteeism
- Less turnover
- Competitiveness
- Survival

QWL purposes
- Responsibility
- Satisfaction
- Involvement
- Respect
- Performance

Bottom line goals

---

mission is still not very clearly established.[10] It remains uncertain as to whether it will take an active role in promoting innovative work arrangements.

At the provincial level, most activities are less institutionalized. Different provinces set up different policies regarding QWL and productivity centres. In relative terms, however, Ontario is by far more committed to these innovations than the other provinces. In Ontario, the Department of Labour began to research innovative work arrangements in the late 1970s. At the end of 1978, the Ontario government created the Ontario Quality of Working Life Centre, which immediately became the best-funded and most professionally organized of the QWL organizations in Canada. The Centre's activities include consultation, information services, research and field activities, and educational programs. It also publishes one of the most professional journals on QWL topics, entitled *QWL Focus*.

Other provinces have let their respective universities and research centres take the lead in establishing QWL programs. For example, both McGill University and the University of Montréal in Québec have QWL centres; in Vancouver, a QWL forum was created under the umbrella of the British Columbia Research Council; in Atlantic Canada, the Institute of Public Affairs at Dalhousie University, founded in 1984, experimented with implementations of QWL projects in eight organizations (see the second "PHRM in the News" article). However, only a few provinces have established their own productivity centres and one, Québec's Institute for Productivity, has been discontinued after only a few years of operation.

Trade union support for QWL in Canada has been positive but not universal. It also has been subject to the politics of trade union organization. While commitments to QWL exist in the official platforms of many major Canadian industrial unions and some public sector unions, it still remains an anathema to some unions, particularly those whose relations with employers are poor or those who are strongly ideologically driven.[11]

Programs for QWL Improvements

Some programs for QWL improvements require limited changes to the organization, others more extensive changes. All of the programs share an orientation of concern and respect for the employee. Typically, the organization exhibits more openness and more willingness to invest in programs that benefit the individual as well as the organization. Such programs include the following:

- Communicating with employees: organizational surveys
- Semi-autonomous work groups and quality circles
- Organizational restyling

Communicating with Employees: Organizational Surveys

Second only to improving productivity, establishing ways to communicate with employees is considered by the top management of organizations to be one of PHRM's top priorities.[12] Improvement of communication is seen as an effective way to improve both productivity and the QWL. It facilitates the transmission of employee ideas into product improvements (as in quality circles) and organizational changes, and at the same time enhances employee job involvement, participation, and feelings of self-control. In addition, training programs can be established to improve supervisory communications and the PHRM department can conduct organizational surveys.

What Surveys Measure. As discussed in previous chapters, PHRM data frequently has been used either to measure job performance or as predictors of job performance. But the PHRM manager often has a need for other types of data. For example, in order to develop ways to improve employee job performance, the PHRM manager needs to measure employee perceptions of organizational characteristics, including the consequences of job performance, organizational policies, frequency of feedback, job-design qualities, task-interference characteristics, aspects of goal-setting, role conflict and awareness, and supervisor behaviours. It is equally necessary to gather data on the employee's reactions to the organizational conditions, the quality of work life, job involvement, and employee stress.

In addition to gathering data from employees on their perceptions of and reactions to organizational characteristics (subjective or reactive measures), it is useful to determine the actual or objective qualities (non-reactive measures) of organizational characteristics. For example, in order to make improvements in the design of jobs, it may be necessary to know what the actual characteristics of jobs are that the employees perceive as highly repetitive. This information, combined with information about the employees' reactions, can facilitate effective job-design changes.

It is important to gather objective measures of these reactions. Many of these reactions can be symptoms of employee stress, some of which can be measured physiologically (blood pressure and heart rate).[13] Since one of the criteria for the effectiveness of PHRM is employee health, these additional measures of employee reactions may become more common in organizational surveys. Other employee behaviours to be measured objectively include job performance, absenteeism, turnover, rates and types of accidents, and incidence of sickness.

Purposes of an Organizational Survey. An organizational survey serves several purposes. First, it helps to determine the effectiveness of PHRM functions and activities. Second, it measures the quality of the organization's internal environment and therefore helps to locate aspects that require improvement. Finally, the survey aids in the development of programs to make the necessary changes, and helps in evaluating their effectiveness.

Steps in an Organizational Survey. Several important steps and issues must be considered by the PHRM manager or an outside consultant when conducting an organizational survey, including careful planning, actual data collection, and ensuring employee participation.[14] These become necessary, however, only after top management has given its support for the survey. As the first step, the PHRM manager must consider the following:

- Specific employee perceptions and responses that should be measured
- Methods that will be used to collect the data, including observations, questionnaires, interviews, and personnel records
- Reliability and validity of the measures to be used
- People from whom the data will be collected—all employees, managerial employees only, a sample of employees, or only certain departments within the organization

- Timing of the survey, particularly if it is part of a longer-term effort
- Types of analyses that will be made with the data
- Specific purposes of the data—to determine reasons for the organization's turnover problem, for example

This last consideration is important because, by identifying the problem, the PHRM manager can determine which models or theories will be relevant to the survey. Knowing which model or theory to use tells the PHRM manager what data are needed and what statistical techniques will be necessary to analyze the data.

The next step is the actual collection of data. Three things are important here. It must be decided who will administer the questionnaire—the line manager, someone from the personnel department, or someone from outside the organization. It also must be decided where, when, and in what size of groups the data will be collected. Both of these considerations are influenced by the method used to gather the data. For example, if a questionnaire is used, larger groups are more feasible than if interviews are conducted. Finally, employee participation in the survey must be ensured. This can be done by gathering the data during company time and by providing feedback—for instance, by promising employees that the results of the survey will be made known to them.

The actual feedback process is the third step in the survey. As part of this process, the data are analyzed according to the purposes and problems for which they were collected. The results of the analysis then can be presented by the personnel department to the line managers, who in turn discuss the results with their employees. The feedback sessions can be used to develop solutions to any problems that are identified, and to evaluate the effectiveness of programs that may already have been implemented on the basis of results of an earlier survey.

The extent to which employees actually participate in the development of solutions during the feedback process depends on the philosophy of top management. Organizations that are willing to survey their employees to ask how things are going usually are willing to invite employee participation in developing plans for improvements. It is this willingness that allows organizational surveys to be used most effectively.

A Sample Questionnaire. "The paper-and-pencil questionnaire is the most common method of obtaining survey data."[15] Exhibit 13.2 is a questionnaire that asks employees to describe the degree to which they know what is expected of them (role ambiguity) and how much work they face in doing what is expected (job overload). Measures of role ambiguity and job overload have been used extensively in organizational surveys. If you are not working now, recall the last job (even a part-time one) that you held. Circle the appropriate numbers in the questionnaire before reading any further.

Once you have completed the questionnaire, add up the numbers you circled in items 1, 2, 3, and 4. This is your **role ambiguity** score. Now add up the remaining numbers you circled in the second part to determine your **job overload** score.

Exhibit 13.2 Role Ambiguity and Job Overload Questionnaire

These questions deal with different aspects of work. Please indicate how often these aspects appear in your job. *Circle one number per item.*

	Very Often	Fairly Often	Sometimes	Occasionally	Rarely
1. How often do you understand exactly what your job responsibilities are?	1	2	3	4	5
2. How often can you predict what others will expect of you on the job?	1	2	3	4	5
3. How often are your work objectives well defined?	1	2	3	4	5
4. How often are you clear about what others expect of you on the job?	1	2	3	4	5
5. How often does your job require you to work fast?	5	4	3	2	1
6. How often does your job require you to work very hard?	5	4	3	2	1
7. How often does your job leave you with little time to get things done?	5	4	3	2	1
8. How often is there a great deal to be done?	5	4	3	2	1

Next, circle the response in Exhibit 13.3 that measures your overall level of satisfaction in your job. How does your score on satisfaction compare with your scores on role ambiguity and job overload? Are you high on all three, low on all three, or do you have a mixed pattern?

What is the importance of these scores? In most organizational surveys, employees are asked for their perceptions of and attitudes toward many aspects of the organization. These surveys generally reveal very definite patterns. Satisfaction, for instance, tends to have a negative relationship with role ambiguity, but one that is consistent with job overload. Role ambiguity and job overload also are frequently related to stress and to employee performance. Therefore, role ambiguity and job overload scores reveal a great deal about an employee.

Semi-autonomous Work Groups

A human group is a collection of individuals (1) who have significantly interdependent relations with each other; (2) who perceive themselves as a group by distinguishing members from non-members; (3) whose group identity is recognized by non-members; (4) who have differentiated roles in

| Job Satisfaction Questionnaire | Exhibit 13.3 |

1. Knowing what you know now, if you had to decide all over again whether to take the type of job you now have, what would you decide?

    I would:

1	2	3
Decide without hesitation to take the same type of job	Have some second thoughts	Decide definitely not to take this type of job

2. If you were free right now to go into any type of job that you wanted, what would your choice be?

    I would:

1	2	3
Take the same type of job as I now have	Take a different type of job	Not want to work

3. If a friend of yours expressed an interest in working at a job like yours, what would your advice be?

    I would:

1	2	3
Strongly recommend it	Have doubts about recommending it	Advise against it

4. All in all, how satisfied would you say you are with your job?

1	2	3
Satisfied	Somewhat satisfied	Not satisfied

the group as a function of their own expectations and those of other members and non-members; and (5) who, as group members acting alone or in concert, have significantly interdependent relations with other groups.

This definition of a human group is generally descriptive of effective **semi-autonomous work groups**, the basic function of which is to work together to produce a final product. In addition, they make a number of employment decisions partially independent of the personnel department (hence the name, semi-autonomous work groups). For example, they make decisions on how to discipline their colleagues, what salary increases members should receive, and even who should be hired and who should be terminated.

The essence of semi-autonomous groups is illustrated in Exhibit 13.4. Panel A in this exhibit shows a group of people who, having accepted responsibility for a common goal, are in the process of learning how to use their own resources and abilities. Panel B, in contrast, shows the traditional bureaucratic form of work organization. The striking difference between

Exhibit 13.4 Traditional versus Semi-autonomous Structure

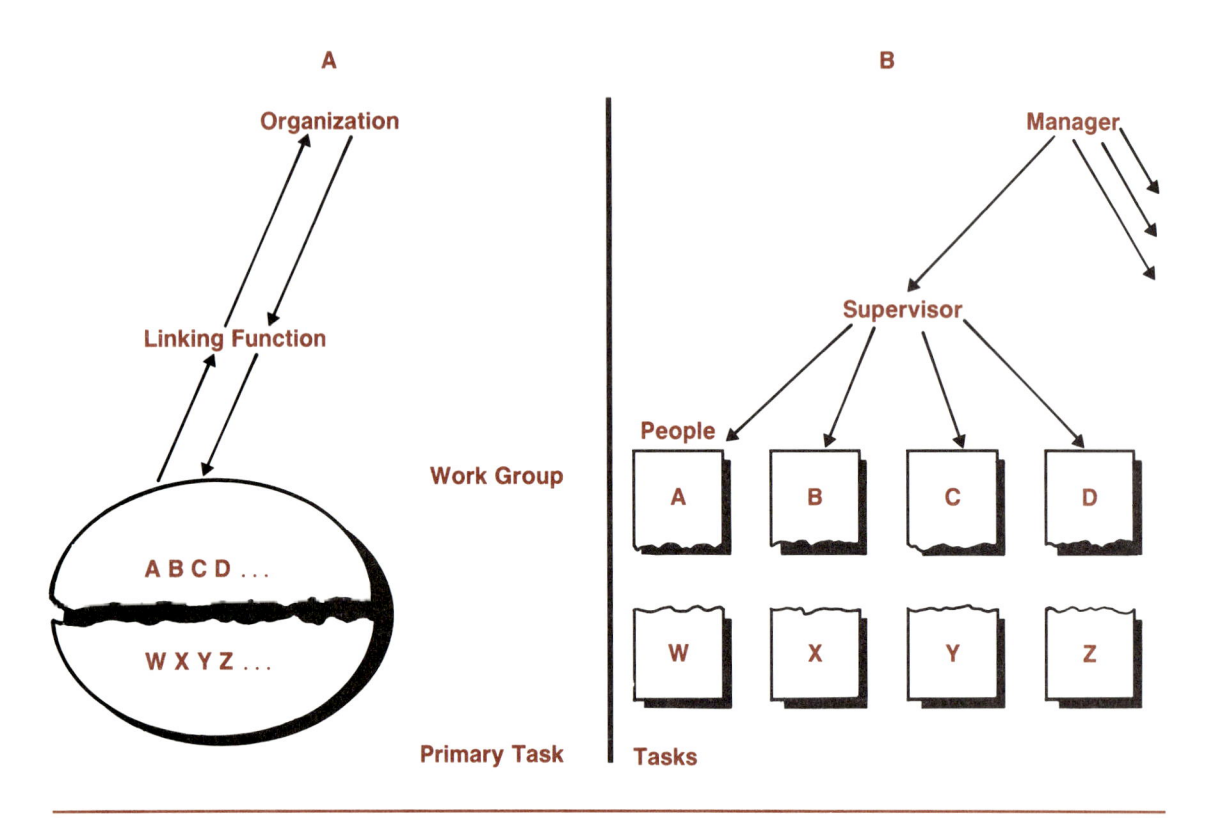

A

Organization ↕ Linking Function ↕ Work Group (ABCD... WXYZ...) — Primary Task

B

Manager → Supervisor → People (A, B, C, D) — Tasks (W, X, Y, Z)

Source: E. Emery, "Learning and the QWL," *QWL Focus*, News Journal of the Ontario Quality of Working Life Centre, Ministry of Labour, Province of Ontario, vol. 3(1), February 1983, p. 4. Used with permission.

these two forms points to the simple fact that when responsibility is given to a group of workers to achieve an agreed-on goal, they must learn to share and allocate all of the requirements for control and co-ordination of responsibilities, as well as learn the specific skills involved in each of the separate tasks. Given the above characteristics, one can roughly divide the skills required of semi-autonomous groups into six categories:

1. Direct job skills
2. Communication and decision-making skills
3. Perceptual skills in extracting information from the group's various environments
4. Work-design skills
5. Managerial skills
6. Skills to set and maintain a productive human atmosphere [16]

Volvo was a pioneer in the implementation of the semi-autonomous work group. In 1974, Volvo incorporated such a group into its QWL program at its Kalmar, Sweden, plant, attracting worldwide attention. Now, more than 10 years after start-up, the experience demonstrates consistent success in terms of production volume, productivity, quality of cars, and other measures.[17]

Whether this experiment is easily transportable to other countries and cultures remains uncertain. Canada has had its share of experiences, many of which were not successful. However, two Canadian cases are well remembered. The first involved the refund services branch of Air Canada's finance department in Winnipeg, where more than 50 000 refunds were being processed monthly. After altering its structure to self-management teams with greater autonomy in handling refunds for its region, an increase in job satisfaction and morale as well as a 30% increase in job performance was reported.[18]

In another case, Steinberg Ltd., a large supermarket chain that employs more than 25 000 people, created semi-autonomous production groups in its frozen-foods distribution centre in Montréal. The results of involving the employees and the unions in the implementation of the program were an increase in morale, a 3½-year absence of complaints from the stores receiving the deliveries, an absence rate of 5% as compared with 15% prior to the change, and a productivity rate 35% higher than the rate prior to the implementation of the program.[19]

Canadian unions, according to one report, are changing their attitude towards these particular experiments from a defensive one to an offensive one by participating in them and closely monitoring the consequences of these experiments, which relate to their survival.[20]

Quality Circles

Quality circles are an innovative management concept that have contributed to Japan's dynamic industrial growth. This technique considers a company's own workforce to be its most valuable resource because it often is the most qualified to identify and solve work-related problems.

Following 20 years of successful experiments in Japan as well as more recent successes in Europe and the U.S., hundreds of Canadian companies have implemented quality circles during the 1980s. Whether the quality circle is a fad or a permanent addition remains to be seen.

Quality Circle Teams. A **quality circle** consists of seven to ten people from the same work area who meet regularly to define, analyze, and solve quality and related problems in their area. Membership is strictly voluntary, and meetings are usually held once a week for an hour. During the group's initial meetings, members are trained in problem-solving techniques borrowed from group dynamics, industrial engineering, and quality control. These techniques include brainstorming, Pareto analysis, cause-and-effect analysis, histograms, control charts, stratification, and scatter diagrams.

Quality Circles and Unions. In general, unions have not opposed the introduction of quality circles. The fact that participation is voluntary forestalls possible union objections. If membership were mandatory, the union might decide to make the circles a bargaining issue, reasoning that workers were being ordered to do something that was leading to greater profits for the company.

The Supervisor as Team Leader. In many instances, the first-line supervisor runs the team meeting, acting as the facilitator. This is because this relationship is compatible with the existing organizational authority pattern, and also facilitates communications between the supervisor and employees. The team leader undergoes a basic training course in group dynamics, problem solving, and other techniques (often given by personnel staff), while members often receive preliminary training on establishing priorities and brainstorming.[21]

Results of Quality Circles. Do workers have the expertise to improve production and work life? There are a few spectacular examples where knowledge of day-to-day production intricacies benefited companies enormously. At the General Motors Packard Electric plant, creation of worker-management teams to advise on construction of four factories resulted in a $13.5 million overall cost reduction and a $4.5 million reduction in inventory costs. It also achieved the lowest injury, grievance, and absenteeism rates in the division. In another case, Bethlehem Steel reduced operating costs by $225 000 over a two-month period, after worker-management teams identified ways to exploit mill downtime for production. At the Westinghouse Defense and Electronic Systems Center, a purchasing department quality circle noticed waste in the way that vendors were sending supplies and saved the plant $636 000.[22]

Essentials for Quality Circles. Characteristics essential to quality circles include the following:

- The role of the facilitator is the most important aspect of a quality circle program. He or she must be able to work with people at all levels of the organization, be creative and flexible, and be aware of the political atmosphere of the organization.
- Management must support the quality circle program. If a union is involved, it also should support the program, and its views should be solicited.
- Participation should be voluntary for employees, but management should encourage the establishment of circles.
- Within established limits, circle members must feel free to work on problems of their choosing.
- Facilitators must keep management informed of what the circles are doing and on their progress.
- Quality, not quantity, should be the first consideration.
- A successful program adheres to the concepts and principles of effective quality circles. One of the facilitator's most crucial tasks is to see that circles follow correct procedures. If they do not, they become non-productive and eventually dissolve.[23]

Organizational Restyling

Popular ways to restructure or restyle an organization include (1) increased levels of participation and (2) Theory Z management.

Increased Participation. While quality circles represent one form of increased employee participation, other extensive efforts are being undertaken as well. One of the first attempts at industrial democracy on a broad scale occurred in West Germany under the title of co-determination. It enables workers' representatives to discuss and vote on key management decisions that affect them (see Chapter 18 for more details). Other models of participation in Europe include the Workers Council in Yugoslavia and the Israeli kibbutz system, a totally co-operative enterprise.

Canadian firms have had mixed results in experimenting with different models and degrees of participation schemes. Although in theory, these efforts should increase profits and workers' satisfaction, in reality this has not always been the case. In one particular example, that of Tricofil in St.-Jérôme, Québec, the workers bought the company, restyled it along the lines of a completely self-managed model, and went bankrupt a few years later. Analysis of this case suggested that a number of extraneous conditions need to exist in order for self-management to succeed, including proper market conditions, proper management skills, and clear vision of goals and responsibilities.[24] On the other hand, a co-operative structure formed at Harpel Printing Industries in Montréal yielded higher employee satisfaction as well as significant productivity gains.

These examples illustrate that there are limits to the extent to which participation in management of organizations can be increased. The effectiveness of participation in decision making (such as found in quality circle programs) depends on several factors: (1) the desire of the employees for participation in decision making; (2) the type and scope of decisions in which employees participate—whether employees decide only issues related to their jobs or to the total organization; (3) the amount of information that the organization is willing to share with employees; and (4) the willingness of supervisors and managers to allow their employees to participate. Exhibit 13.5 shows some of the activities that can be appropriate for employee participation and the limitations that might apply.

Theory Z Management. While participatory systems and quality circles definitely improve the quality of work life, these programs may represent limited changes to the organization itself. Some are QWL efforts that combine several programs and have far more extensive impact on the organization and the way it regards its people. Excellent examples of what amounts to a restyling of the corporation are Westinghouse and Honeywell, where quality circles are emphasized. In addition, both companies are adopting many of the organizational concepts involved in **Theory Z management**. This approach represents a modification of the more traditional North American management (Theory A) that incorporates some of the ideas from traditional Japanese management (Theory J).

Exhibit 13.5 *Activities Appropriate for Employee Participation and Potential Constraints on Their Use*

Activities	Potential Constraints
Performance appraisal	Limited change frequency
Compensation	Extensive rules and procedures
Job assignment/job design	Current leadership styles and beliefs
Safety	Top management preferences
Employment decisions—hiring, firing, etc. Work schedules	Willingness to change—management and employees
Stress management strategies	Personnel department climate and leadership
Change	Information access and availability

The characteristics of Theory Z, falling between Theory J and Theory A, include the following:

- Employment of a longer-term nature, informally stated
- Relatively slow promotion and evaluation period
- Career paths that "wander" through different functions in the organization
- Extensive planning data and accounting data used for purposes of information and collective decision making rather than for control
- Decisions made on the basis of sound data and on whether it fits the entire organization rather than just one sub-part
- Sharing of responsibility for making and implementing decisions, although decisions are often guided by one individual

As with Theory J and Theory A, in practice Theory Z takes many forms. It can be adapted not only to the North American culture but also to the unique styles and needs of each corporation. Modification of Theory J recognizes the fact that the cultures of Canada and Japan are quite different, so that it is impossible to do here exactly what is done in Japan. In fact, looking at the situational factors of Theory Z applications reveals a mixed picture:

- Canada has been characterized as a cultural mosaic, and the various ethnic groups tend to maintain their cultural identities, a force that would work against the uniformity of values in Type Z firms.
- Another potential factor that would inhibit a Type Z firm would be the relatively high degree of unionization in Canada. An adversarial union is a competing factor for employees' loyalty.[25]

Despite these factors, a study of the 100 top firms in Canada (published by *The Financial Post*, 1986) shows a number of companies that are considered exemplary of Type Z. Among them are Canadian Tire Corporation, Northern Telecom Canada, Four Seasons Hotel, Great-West Life Assurance, Syncrude Canada, Labatt's, and others.[26] The characteristics of such firms are very similar to those of the Type Z firm, including a strong organizational culture, employment stability, continuity of leadership, as well as promotion from within, and a generally high concern for employees.

Recently, however, Theory Z has been under attack. A recent article suggested that what actually motivates Japanese managers and makes the system work is Theory F—fear. The culture does not tolerate failure: the penalty for failure is termination. Fear is a powerful motivator.[27]

Programs for Productivity Improvements

As with QWL, productivity improvements can result from a wide range of programs. Programs clarifying performance expectations, job descriptions, and job duties not only reduce stress, but are instrumental in improving productivity.

Task Changes

The way that people do their work has a significant impact on their productivity. The impact is a result of (1) how the worker reacts to the job or task itself, and (2) the arrangement of the separate tasks distributed among the employees and departments in the organization in order to produce the final product. Whereas the first is effected through **task design**, the second is through the **work flow**.

Task Design. Although the various approaches to task design discussed in Chapter 3 can be used, job enrichment and socio-technical designs are most likely to improve the QWL and productivity.[28]

Job enrichment alters the levels of the following characteristics:

- Skill variety
- Job identity
- Job significance
- Autonomy
- Job feedback

The effect of job enrichment programs on productivity and bottom-line dollar savings can be substantial. Other conditions in the organization may need to be modified, however, to sustain any improvements.

Furthermore, the relationships among the five core job dimensions and the outcomes and the potential effectiveness may not apply equally to everyone. Not all employees have the same psychological needs or preferences, nor can job enrichment satisfy all of these needs. Job enrichment is limited in its impact because it can serve only some of the employees' psychological needs. The socio-technical approach to job design overcomes some of these limitations.

The **socio-technical approach** to job design arose in response to the views that (1) jobs, as organizational units, are not conceptually appropriate bases for the analysis and design of work systems, and (2) jobs are not an appropriate unit to use for making changes in organizations to improve the quality of work life. The socio-technical approach is based on the fact that jobs are people-made inventions designed to suit a number of technical and social systems' needs, and as such they are constantly changing. The objective of socio-technical design, such as the example at Volvo, is to bridge the two worlds—social and technical—so that the resources of the two are optimally used to co-produce an outcome that is desired by the employees of the organization. More often than not, the socio-technical approach is an important part of the semi-autonomous work groups discussed earlier.

The decision as to which job design program to implement is a complex one that includes the following steps:

1. Recognize a need for a change and gather pre-change data for evaluation
2. Determine that task design is the appropriate change
3. Diagnose the organization, workflow, group processes, and individual needs
4. Determine how, when, and where to design jobs
5. Provide for training and support if necessary
6. Make the job design changes
7. Evaluate the changes by comparing post-change data with pre-change data

One of Canada's celebrated QWL projects that utilizes the socio-technical design is that of the Shell chemical plant in Sarnia, Ontario. The success of this program is attributed not only to the initial socio-technical design, but also to a variety of other QWL concepts that have been integrated into the system, including the following:

- The team co-ordinator participates in employee recruitment processes
- A clear philosophy statement is prepared by management and communicated to all employees
- By design, a minimum number of rules and regulations prevail in the plant; norms emerge from the teams
- Self-management skills training is provided to all interested employees [29]

Workflow. Workflow changes result in improved productivity by utilizing the principles of industrial engineering (presented in Chapter 3) and organization design. These principles include the following:

- Breaking tasks into discrete, small duties
- Measuring how long the duties take
- Setting standards of performance for the duties
- Devising methods of meeting the standards and performing the duties
- Measuring how well the duties are performed and the standards are attained
- Feeding back the results to the employees and organization

- Monitoring the workflow
- Correcting the workflow as needed

These principles, as in the case of job enrichment, can be applied in the office as well as in the factory and to white-collar service work as well as to blue-collar manufacturing work.

Automation

After a decade of decline in the face of low-cost, high-quality imports, Canadian industry is beginning to automate at a pace that soon will change the face of Canadian factories and offices. Computer-controlled systems of robots are replacing many humans on plant floors and are responsible for unprecedented gains in productivity. Automated equipment also is moving into offices. Together these changes will affect millions of jobs during the next 20 years.[30]

Because automation is so significant and likely to be a major contributor to improving productivity, it is critical for PHRM departments to understand it and utilize it to improve productivity and the QWL. Automation is particularly critical to PHRM because it has the potential of changing the nature of so many jobs and creating many new jobs. These changes in turn will impact employee recruitment and selection, performance appraisal, and training.

Computer-integrated manufacturing, flexible manufacturing systems, and computer-aided design and manufacturing (CAD/CAM) are appearing increasingly in many Canadian factories. In relative terms, however, Canada is lagging behind Japan, Germany, and the U.S. in installing CAD/CAM equipment. Evans Research Corporation in Toronto reports that 90% of the $100 million that Japan spent for CAD/CAM equipment in 1983 was for equipment imported from North America, and that West Germany has absorbed 32% of European sales in installing this technology. The ironic fact is that Canada is successful in selling the most advanced technologies to its most virulent competitors. If Canadian productivity is to be increased, this trend must change in the years to come.

What is happening to the factory is also happening to the office. More and more offices across Canada are becoming automated. The biggest gains in office productivity are predicted to come from automating the jobs of professionals and managers.[31]

This surge of new technologies, if not carefully implemented, may result in employees' resistance out of fear and uncertainty, and be counterproductive. A number of studies concluded that the introduction of new technologies needs to be planned and executed carefully in order to minimize this resistance.[32] Therefore, the PHRM department should act as facilitator in introducing these new technologies. Ideally, the human resource department should be involved in the planning process before a computer system is introduced. The role of the PHRM officer is to foresee requirements in areas such as relocation, counselling, handling grievances, dealing with health and safety concerns, managing staff redundancies, and meeting new training needs. More often than not, however, the PHRM department ends up dealing with the aftermath of the decision to automat-mate. This is a *reactive response*; PHRM strategy should be proactive in order to ensure more positive outcomes.[33]

Office Design

Corning Glass Works of the U.S., a recognized leader in using behavioural science principles on the job, redesigned its engineering division by consolidating four physically separate departments into one well-designed building. It is estimated that productivity might increase by as much as 15%, since the new design allows for close, personal interaction and it is believed that engineers get more than 80% of their ideas through face-to-face contact with colleagues. The major design aspects of the building include the following:

- The building centres on a glass atrium that includes a cafeteria that most employees enter from the parking area. Thus many employees start their day by meeting casually with colleagues over coffee.
- A variety of stairways, escalators, ramps, and elevators encourages easy circulation from floor to floor.
- Twelve more coffee lounges are scattered throughout the building. They are equipped with beverage machines, high stools, and wall-sized washable writing boards. The aim is to encourage informal gatherings and casual brainstorming.
- Except for lab areas, all offices are enclosed only by 1.6m (62-inch) high partitions or floor-to-ceiling glass screens. Everyone has access to daylight and a view. Most labs have a view of the outside, and executive offices overlook the atrium.
- Ample strategic use of mirrored glass on balcony areas lets engineers glimpse activities on other floors and in other areas.[34]

Similar design considerations were used in the construction of the Scarborough Municipal Building in Ontario. Thousands of people work in a four-storey building that has no fixed-wall offices. Surprisingly enough, the work environment is very pleasant, not too noisy, and the municipality's employees seem to be very content. In fact, the building has become so well known that many tourists come to visit this "twentieth century industrial wonder."

While the engineers in the Corning and Scarborough buildings find easy access and interaction vital to productivity, many people who work in these offices find the increased interaction more hindrance than help. Consequently, office design should allow employees to have some privacy and some quiet.[35]

Individuals can and do implement quiet time on their own, but the greatest benefits occur when groups do it together. An entire office, department, division, or company can observe quiet time as a unit: everyone in the office makes a special effort to do their work quietly and not to bother their co-workers. External interruptions are minimized where possible. The fewer the number of interruptions allowed during this quiet period, the more work that will be successfully accomplished.[36]

Productivity Improvements—The Total Management Approach

Programs for productivity improvement rarely work well in isolation. They work best under the following conditions:

- Top management visibly supports the programs
- There is a philosophy of productivity improvement
- Employees are adequately trained
- Employees are fairly rewarded
- Employees are involved and receive feedback
- Appraisal systems are seen as fair and used in compensation decisions

In other words, productivity programs, like those to improve the QWL, work best when they are supported by management.

Assessing QWL and Productivity Programs

As shown in Exhibit 13.1, the programs aimed at improving the QWL and productivity have different purposes. However, because QWL programs also can achieve the intended purposes of productivity programs, they can be assessed by how well they attain all of these outcomes.

QWL Programs

As with other PHRM activities, assessing the benefits of QWL programs solely on the basis of dollars and cents is almost impossible. Consider the difficulties involved in assessing the dollar value of the benefits of raising the level of employee self-control or satisfaction by 10%, yet it is necessary to determine this. However, do all QWL programs have to be justified on the basis of dollars and cents? Or can they be justified solely on the basis of increased self-control, satisfaction, involvement, and self-respect—essentially all employee benefits?

Although corporations consider individual benefits to be important, many QWL programs are supported by corporations and employees because they also provide benefits to the organization. This diminishes the difficulty of evaluating QWL programs in terms of dollars and cents, although productivity gains resulting from a QWL program may not occur until several years after program implementation.

Productivity Programs

The process of assessing productivity programs is less complex than that for QWL programs because outcomes are much more measurable. For example, productivity can be assessed by individual job performance and reductions in absenteeism and turnover. Productivity programs at the organizational level can be evaluated in terms of profitability, competitiveness, and survival.[37]

Summary

Faced with increasing international competition and changing social and individual values, Canadian companies are confronted with a productivity crisis of major proportions. This crisis has led some Canadian companies to implement programs for productivity and QWL improvements, although not all companies are responding this way. Others have had productivity and QWL programs for many years.

This chapter reviews a few of the many programs being used by Canadian companies to improve their productivity and QWL. Increased productivity can be achieved in many ways, so it is important for each company to diagnose its situation to determine what is needed and what would have the greatest desired impact. Once this is done, an organization can choose from among several programs, many directly related to its PHRM activities. Wholesale adoption of programs because they are popular or "everyone else is doing it" is not likely to result in success. Regardless of the particular program, the evidence suggests that employee involvement in program design and/or implementation enhances the success of the program.

There also are many ways to improve the QWL. In addition, it is possible that, by improving the QWL, much of the productivity crisis also would be solved. In solving productivity and QWL problems, organizations may be able to benefit from Japanese or European ideas, with adaptations made to take into account cultural differences.

Wholesale adoption of the techniques of others is rarely likely to be successful. For example, Theory Z management is a modification of Japanese techniques for the Canadian environment: it represents a midpoint between traditional Japanese management and traditional North American management. While some large Canadian companies are shifting to Theory Z, it is too early to tell if this will be successful. Undoubtedly, new concepts and ideas will continue to emerge.

Discussion Questions

1. How are programs for productivity and QWL improvement related to each other?
2. To what PHRM activities and in what ways are productivity and QWL programs related?
3. Evidence suggests that the quality of the work experience affects behaviours and attitudes off the job. Can you think of an example to

illustrate this? What implications does this phenomenon have for PHRM?
4. What types of information related to productivity and QWL can be obtained through the use of survey measures?
5. What are the purposes of an organizational survey?
6. What are the important factors to consider in assessing the effectiveness or utility of increased participation in decision making?
7. Identify some of the characteristics of Theory Z management.
8. What are the essential characteristics of any quality circle effort?
9. Considering the total management approach, discuss how programs for productivity improvement work best.
10. Why are the benefits of QWL programs more difficult to ascertain than the benefits associated with productivity programs?
11. Some people claim that QWL is a fad, others believe that it is here to stay. Think of arguments for and against these two polarized views.

CASE STUDY

Quality of Work or Leisure?

Morag Kavanagh of Management Decisions Systems, Inc., a highly respected management consulting firm, had been asked by one of her clients to conduct a feasibility study for the implementation of a quality of work life intervention. Her client, Teletalk, is a large public utility that provides telecommunication services.

The idea for QWL intervention originated with Morgan Roth, Teletalk's vice-president of industrial relations, who learned of the concept at a conference sponsored by the Ontario Quality of Life Centre that he had attended. Morgan believed that a QWL program might be the answer to the alarming increase in absenteeism at Teletalk over the past five years.

Teletalk had been contending with the problems related to technological innovations of the telecommunications industry, which had resulted in two major reorganizations and a threatened strike over automation by the union, the Communication Workers of America, that represents nearly all of Teletalk's non-exempt employees.

Morag, after meeting with Morgan and his staff, arranged to interview some of the Teletalk employees, including workers from four different departments, their supervisors, a member of the support staff, the medical director, and the union. While Morag wanted to gain an understanding of the worker reactions to a QWL program, she was equally interested in finding out the workers' explanation for the singular increase in absenteeism at Teletalk.

The first group with which Morag met comprised three young women who had recently undergone training for craft positions (installers, line repair, switch equipment technicians) and had completed six months in their new jobs. The positions, which have been predominantly male-occupied, pay considerably more than the jobs of operator or service representative that women have traditionally held with Teletalk. When questioned about the absenteeism rates, particularly the significantly higher rates observed for female Teletalk employees, all three women agreed that the problem was that women were victims of occupational segregation by Teletalk. The skilled, better-paying, and more challenging jobs had not been available to the women until very recently. Furthermore, in response to Morag's question about a possible QWL program, Jacqueline Gauthier, the most articulate of the three, said, "Frankly, we don't need a QWL program, we don't want it, and moreover, if personnel sends us one more survey to fill out, we're going to throw up! We're sick of it!"

The next group was made up of four supervisors drawn from the largest departments, who gave Morag an entirely different perspective on the problem of absenteeism. According to the supervisors, absenteeism was not their problem and they had the data to support their argument. For reporting purposes, Teletalk divided absenteeism into two categories: incidental and medical. Incidental absences were any episodes of seven days' duration or less. Medical absences, by definition, were any episodes of greater than seven days' duration, and therefore required a clearance from the medical department before the absent employee could return to work. The supervisors then showed Morag graphs of a five-year trend of incidental and medical absences. For each of their departments, the trend was unmistakably consistent: incidental absence exhibited a gradual decline while medical absence was showing a marked increase. The supervisors agreed that Morag should forget the QWL program because the problem was the medical department's fault.

Morag's next stop was to see Dr. Virgil Gangstead, the medical director of Teletalk. While Virgil was sympathetic to the supervisors' viewpoint, he felt that they were misguided. In fact, Virgil challenged Schuler Associates, Inc. to do a job-attitude study of the correlates of incidental and medical absenteeism and, he predicted, they would discover that incidental and medical absences shared the same work-related causes. Virgil also felt that the medical department was the victim of poor assessment and gamesmanship by the organization. He explained, "This QWL project is no different than the other programs management has tried in the past—it will roll in like a large wave and then retreat to the ocean to be swallowed up, just like all of the other programs!"

According to Virgil, the real problem was management's belief in the infallibility of the absenteeism recording system. Supervisors were rewarded for holding down incidental absence, which amounted to an insignificant amount of the total lost time. Moreover, each department interpreted differently the absenteeism coding scheme, created by the accounting department for payroll purposes.

"The problem is so bad that the craft departments won't even consider transfer applications from the service departments because they simply don't trust their absenteeism records. And I must admit that in some departments, we have cultivated an absence 'culture' for years," Virgil said.

Finally Virgil suggested that if Morag really wanted to identify the problem, she should talk to the union representatives who had negotiated the last contract. Not a bad idea, decided Morag, and scheduled the union president, John Mobley, for an interview that afternoon.

Morag had been warned that John could be feisty but, to the contrary, she found him to be quite gracious and informative. When asked about the contract provision that permitted any worker with five or more years of seniority to be paid for the second through the seventh day of absenteeism, John explained without any hint of defensiveness or apology, "Our workers are not stupid. They know that under this arrangement it pays, to a limit, to take more rather than less time off the job if you choose to be absent. For some of our workers, this compensates for below-standard wages. For others, it simply legitimizes the worker's right to be absent for whatever reason without undergoing an interrogation. This organization has its faults, but after all, we don't live in Russia!

"Besides, I think management has learned from its previous attempts at absenteeism control that the workers can always invent an antidote to the poison of a new absence-control program."

As for the QWL program idea, John just laughed. "Listen, Morag, management better wake up. Absenteeism is not the exclusive domain of the non-exempt employees. We all have a need for leisure, including management. The QWL program idea is fine, but you won't find us supporting it. Our members want more paid time off to pursue their leisure activities."

Morag concluded the interview with John and drove to her office to dictate some notes for her QWL feasibility report to Morgan Roth. She certainly had obtained more data than she had expected.

Endnotes

1. "The Revival of Productivity," *Business Week*, February 13, 1984, pp. 92–100. J. L. Graham, "White Collar Productivity: Misunderstandings and Some Progress," *Personnel Administrator*, August 1981,

pp. 27–32. J. M. Rosow (ed.), *Productivity Prospects for Growth* (New York: Van Nostrand, 1981). E. W. Glaser, "Productivity Gains Through Worklife Improvements," *Personnel*, January–February 1980, p. 72. J. Savoie, "Productivity: A Challenge for the Eighties," *Quality of Working Life: The Canadian Scene*, 1981, vol. 4(1), pp. 24–26.

2. L. E. Davis and A. B. Cherns (eds.), *The Quality of Working Life* (volumes I and II) (New York: The Free Press, 1975). B. A. Macy, "A Public Sector Experiment to Improve Organizational Effectiveness and Employees' Quality of Work Life: The TVA Case," paper presented at the Forty-first Annual Meeting of the Academy of Management, Aug. 2–5, 1981, San Diego, CA. D. A. Nadler and E. E. Lawler III, "Quality of Work Life: Perspectives and Directing," *Organizational Dynamics*, Winter 1983, pp. 20–30. J. R. Hackman and J. L. Suttle, *Improving Life at Work* (Santa Monica, CA: Goodyear, 1977). Jim Rosow, "Quality of Work Life Issues for the 1980's," *Training and Development Journal*, March 1981, pp. 33–37. R. P. Quinn and G. L. Staines, *The Quality of Employment Survey* (Ann Arbor, MI: Survey Research Center, Institute for Social Research, The University of Michigan, 1979).

3. E. W. Glaser, "Productivity Gains Through Worklife Improvements," *Personnel*, Jan.–Feb. 1980, p. 72. "Corporate Culture Determines Productivity," *Industry Week*, May 4, 1981, pp. 82–86. J. Mansel and T. Rankin, "Changing Organizations: The Quality of Working Life Process," *Issues in the QWL*, no. 4, September 1983, Toronto QWL Centre, Ontario Ministry of Labour.

4. D. Lacey, "What Will Workers Want in Post-Recession America?" *Personnel Administrator*, May 1983, pp. 71–78.

5. Interview with K. Ashton, union representative at Eldorado Resources, *QWL Focus*, vol. 4(1), Spring 1984, p. 8.

6. For an elaboration on these dual goals, see Hans Van Beinum, "Playing Hide and Seek with QWL," in *QWL Focus—The Emergence of QWL Domains*, vol. 5(1), March 1986, pp. 7–9.

7. See the entire issue of *QWL Focus*, "A Labour Perspective on QWL," vol. 4(1), Spring 1984.

8. J. Mears and L. Brunet, "Overview: QWL Activities in Canada," in N.Q. Herrick (ed.), *Improving Government: Experiments with QWL Systems* (New York: Praeger, 1983), pp. 5–11.

9. M. Cameron, "A Crown Corporation: Process Versus Outcome," in N.Q. Herrick (ed.), ibid., C. Jones, "Major Obstacles to QWL's Development in the Canadian Federal Public Service," in Herrick (ed.), ibid., pp. 21–29.

10. H. Kolodny, "Canadian Experience in Innovative Approaches to High Commitment Work Systems," in S. L. Dolan and R. S. Schuler (eds.), *Canadian Readings in Personnel and Human Resource Management* (St. Paul: West Publishing Co., 1987).

11. Ibid.

12. ASPA survey results reported in *Personnel Administrator*, Sept. 1982; R. G. Foltz, "Productivity and Communications," *Personnel Administrator*, July 1981, p. 12. For more recent, see E. F. McDonough III, "How Much Power Does HR Have, and What Can It Do to Win More?" *Personnel*, January 1986, pp. 18–25.

13. For more information on the importance of both subjective and objective data for proper diagnosis of job stress, see S. L. Dolan and A. Arsenault, *Stress, Santé et Rendement au Travail*, Monograph No. 5, School of Industrial Relations, University of Montréal, 1980. S. L. Dolan, "Job Stress Among College Administrators: An Empirical Study," *International Journal of Management*, 1987 (in press). S. L. Dolan and D. Balkin, "A Contingency Model of Occupational Stress," *International Journal of Management*, September 1987. R. S. Schuler and S. E. Jackson, "Managing Stress Through PHRM Practices: An Uncertainty Interpretation," in D. M. Rowland and G. R. Ferris (eds.), *Research in Personnel and Human Resource Management*, vol. 4 (Boston: JAI Press, 1986).

14. R. B. Dunham and F. J. Smith, *Organizational Surveys* (Glenview, IL: Scott, Foresman, 1979), Chapter 5, pp. 91–97.

15. Ibid., p. 13.

16. "Learning and the Quality of Working Life," *QWL Focus*, vol. 3(1), February 1983, p. 4.

17. T. Rankin, "Volvo Kalmar: Ten Years Later," *QWL Focus*, vol. 5(1), March 1986, p. 20.

18. P. Roddick, "Work Improvement Plan at Air Canada," *Quality of Working Life: The Canadian Scene*, vol. (1), Autumn 1978, p. 2.

19. P. Pelletier, "Semiautonomous and Autonomous Production Groups," *Quality of Working Life: The Canadian Scene*, vol. (3), 1980 (1), pp. 22–25.

20. M. Brossard, "North American Unions and Semiautonomous Production Groups," *Quality of Working Life: The Canadian Scene*, vol. 4(1), 1981, pp. 1–5.

21. "Quality Circle Boom Part of Growing American Trend," *Supervision*, September 1981, pp. 8–11.

22. D. Hage, "Goal Is Improving Work Place," *Minneapolis Star*, November 19, 1981.

23. Extracted from: "Quality Circles on the Rise," *Performance*, May 1981, p. 2 (U.S. Office of Personnel Management); and A. Lemeliln, "Quality of Working Life or Quality Circles?" *Human Resources Management in Canada* (Prentice-Hall Canada Inc., 1983), pp. 5,097–5,102.

24. For more information on the Tricofil experience, see M. Simard, "L'Autogestion a Tricofil," *Reprint No. 33*, School of Industrial Relations, University of Montréal, 1979.

25. A. M. Jaeger, "The Applicability of Theory Z in Canada: Implications for the Human Resource Func-

tion," in Dolan and Schuler (eds.), endnote 10.

26. For complete details of these firms, see E. Innes, R. L. Perry, and J. Lyon, *100 Best Companies to Work for in Canada*, (Toronto: Collins, 1986).

27. J. Kotkin and Y. Kishimota, "Theory F," *INC. Magazine*, April 1986, pp. 53–60.

28. R. Griffin, *Task Design—An Integrative Approach*, (Glenview, IL: Scott, Foresman, 1982). J. R. Hackman and G. R. Oldham, *Work Redesign* (Reading, MA: Addison-Wesley, 1980).

29. N. Halpern, "Sustaining Change in the Shell Sarnia Chemical Plant," *QWL Focus*, vol. 2(1), May 1982, pp. 5–11.

30. D. E. Close, "Productivity and Technology: Top Management and the Challenge," ("Current Matters—New Ideas"), *Human Resources Management in Canada* (Prentice-Hall Canada Inc., June 1984), pp. 5,214–5,216.

31. M. Mass, "In Offices of the Future: The Productivity Value of Environment," *Management Review*, March 1983, pp. 16–20.

32. For example, see S. Zuboff, "New Worlds of Computer-mediated Work," *Harvard Business Review*, vol. 60(5), 1982, pp. 142–152. S. Dolan and D. Roy, "Implementing New Technologies in the Office: A Comparative Threat," paper presented at the International Research Symposium on New Techniques and Ergonomics, Valenciennes, France, May 31–June 2, 1983.

33. For more information on proactive strategy in dealing with automation in Canadian firms within the QWL context, see the entire issue of *QWL Focus*, vol. 1(3), August 1981.

34. "Corning Builds for Productivity," *Behavioral Sciences Newsletter*, Oct. 12, 1981. Used by permission.

35. "Work Environment: Its Design and Implications," *Personnel Journal*, Jan. 1981, pp. 27–31. H. E. McCurdy, "Crowding and Behavior in the White House," *Psychology Today*, April 1981, pp. 21–25. J. T. Yenckel, "Offices: Designs for Efficiency," *The Washington Post*, Feb. 26, 1981, p. D5.

36. M. E. Douglass and D. N. Douglass, "Quiet Time Increases Productivity," *Personnel Administrator*, Sept. 1981, p. 22.

37. C. R. Day, Jr., "Solving the Mystery of Productivity Measurement," *Industry Week*, Jan. 26, 1981, pp. 61–66. J. W. Forrester, "More Productivity Will Not Solve Our Problems," *Business and Society Review*, Spring 1981, pp. 10–19.

SECTION VII
Maintaining Effective Industrial Relations

CHAPTER 14
Occupational Health and Safety

CHAPTER 15
Employee Rights

CHAPTER 16
Unionization

CHAPTER 17
Collective Bargaining

CHAPTER 14

Occupational Health and Safety

PHRM in the News

Occupational Health and Safety in Organizations
Purposes and Importance of Improving Health and Safety
Relationships of Occupational Health and Safety

Legal Considerations of Occupational Health and Safety
The Canadian Jurisdictional Framework
Federal Health and Safety Legislation
Provincial Health and Safety Legislation
The Right to Know
The Right to Refuse Work
Joint Health and Safety Committees
Accident Reporting and Inquiries

Work Hazards
Factors Affecting Occupational Accidents
Factors Affecting Occupational Diseases
Factors Affecting Low Quality of Work Life
Sources of Organizational Stress

Occupational Health and Safety Strategies for Improvement
Strategies for Health and Safety Improvement in the Physical Work Environment
Strategies for Health and Safety Improvement in the Socio-psychological Work Environment

Assessing Occupational Health and Safety Activities
Physical Work Environment Strategies
Socio-psychological Work Environment Strategies

Summary

Discussion Questions

Case Study

Endnotes

PHRM in the News

Sick-Time Claims Soar Under Québec Law, GM Says

QUÉBEC (CP)—Workers at the General Motors of Canada Ltd. plant near Montréal claim three times as much paid leave for job illness and accidents as Ontario autoworkers because of Québec's lax health and safety program, GM officials say.

In a report, officials from the plant at Ste. Thérèse say GM's costs for the program, financed by employers' contributions, have jumped 290 per cent since it was introduced in 1977.

The 16-page report obtained by the *Canadian Press* includes graphs illustrating what officials call "the very sudden and drastic increase in claims for compensation" after adoption of the program, hailed in 1977 as the most advanced in North America.

The report says the law is "extremely attractive and virtually devoid of any control mechanisms to check for abuse" and allows "an interpretation of the term 'work accident' to include almost any situation that occurs in the work place."

GM officials say they have begun to control the problem by insisting that workers take medical examinations after filing claims for compensation, taking photos and testimony of witnesses after a work accident and improving company presentations at the health and safety commission's appeal board.

Claims for time lost due to work-related illness or accidents rose by 127 per cent one year after enactment of the legislation, the GM officials wrote.

In 1980, 32 per cent of the approximately 3,900 Ste. Thérèse workers submitted such claims, compared with 9 per cent of workers at GM's foundry and plant at St. Catharines and Oshawa, Ont., respectively.

Last year, 33 per cent of Ste. Thérèse workers submitted claims, compared with 11 per cent for Ontario workers.

The Québec health and safety program calls for automatic payment of benefits during the first five days that an employee is absent as a result of an occupational injury or illness.

"There is no doubt these increases are the direct result of the automatic five-day advance scheme and the increase in the benefit rate from 75 per cent (of gross earnings) to 90 per cent (of net earnings) adopted in 1979," says the GM report.

The authors note that GM's cost for health and safety premiums was $2 for $100 of gross earnings, or $835,000 in 1977, before the plan was enacted. The figure shot up to $3.3 million or $5.81 per $100 by 1982. It has fallen steadily since and is projected at $4.58 per $100 of gross earnings for 1985 because of management controls.

Claude Petelle, who worked at the plant for eight years and represented injured workers for the United Auto Workers union, reacted angrily to the report. "You can use statistics to prove anything," Petelle said. "In fact, our studies show that lost-time claims at Ste. Thérèse are well below the average for plants in Canada and the U.S." Petelle charged that GM complained to the government about absenteeism at the plant, and the government told the health and safety commission to reject more claims. He said international officials of the United Auto Workers encouraged GM to avoid recognizing the workers' health and safety committee as the law requires, and the commission has never forced the company to do so.

Source: The Gazette, Montréal, Saturday, June 15, 1985, p. D3. Reprinted by permission of *The Canadian Press.*

Union Granted Approval to Sue Asbestos Firms

EDMONTON (CP)—The Workers' Compensation Board has given a union permission to sue American manufacturers of asbestos products. Bill Spring, business agent for Local 110, International Association of the Heat, Frost Insulators and Asbestos Workers Union, said the union local needed permission before launching court action. The lawsuits will seek unspecified damages for pain, suffering and shortened lifespans of 30 Alberta insulators.

All 30 have had or have advanced cases of respiratory disease or asbestos-related cancer of the lungs or stomach, he said. Two have died. The workers handled U.S. insulation products in the 1950s and 1960s.

The compensation board first approved the lawsuits last summer, but withdrew that approval after lawyers from the United States said their fees could go as high as 40 per cent of the settlement. The board changed its mind after the union argued the insulators wouldn't get any money if court action wasn't allowed.

Source: The Gazette, Montréal, April 17, 1986, p. B11. Reprinted by permission of *The Canadian Press.*

New Directions in Occupational Health and Safety, Worker Participation and Job Design

The last decade and a half has been an era of growing concern for health and safety in the workplace. Since the late '60s, the labour movement in most countries has made occupational health and safety a top priority. Most industrial nations revised their health and safety legislation in the '70s. Tremendous union, management and societal resources have been allocated to making the workplace a safe and healthful environment.

Over the same period, there has been growing interest in the redesign of the workplace to increase union and employee participation and to eliminate repetitive, unchallenging, over-supervised dead-end jobs. These innovations, normally subsumed under the quality of working life or QWL label, have been promoted by management as a means to greater organizational effectiveness, by unions as a move toward industrial democracy and more human dignity in the workplace, and by governments as central to developing and maintaining more mature labour-management relations.

Rarely has any substantial connection been made in North America between quality of working life issues and workplace health and safety. At best, health and safety (viewed primarily in terms of hazard control and accident prevention) has been seen as a key component in the quality of worklife. At worst, the concerns of quality of working life proponents have been viewed as irrelevant or frivolous by companies, unions, and governments grappling with a myriad of highly visible occupational health and safety problems.

There is growing evidence, however, that health and safety and quality of working life issues are closely related to each other. The reason goes beyond the undeniable fact that traditional health and safety issues should be dealt with in conjunction with issues of employee participation and job design. There are now powerful arguments being put forth that many occupational health and safety issues cannot be effectively addressed unless the content of jobs and the nature and extent of employee participation are also addressed.

Source: J. Mansell, "New Directions in Occupational Health and Safety, Worker Participation and Job Design," *QWL Focus*, vol. 5(1), March 1986, p. 10. Reprinted by permission of *QWL Focus*, News Journal of the Ontario Quality of Working Life Centre, Ministry of Labour, Province of Ontario.

These "PHRM in the News" articles illustrate important aspects of health and safety in the workplace. The issue is a complex one, and many groups have become involved: the federal and provincial governments, the unions, management, and employees. While the work environment can have severely negative effects on workers, it is difficult to assign responsibility for these hazards. The first article suggests that progressive health and safety legislation could cost companies significant amounts of money, particularly when workers can abuse the law. The second article points to the increased role of unions in health and safety matters. The third article suggests an integrative framework that could be undertaken by industry to improve the management of health and safety, based on concepts borrowed from QWL philosophy (see also Chapter 13).

Occupational Health and Safety in Organizations

With a mandate to be more cost effective and to play a more significant role in the management of human resources, personnel and human resource managers can prove their value by concerning themselves with occupational health and safety in organizations. Indeed, many PHRM functions and activities are related to occupational health and safety, and neglect can result in substantial costs to the organization. Therefore, the personnel and human resource manager should develop an awareness of occupational health and safety matters, and devise strategies for improving these in the organization.[1]

Occupational health and safety refers to the physiological/physical and socio-psychological conditions of an organization's workforce, resulting from the work environment. If an organization takes effective health and safety measures, fewer of its employees suffer physiological, physical, or socio-psychological harm.

Common occupation-caused physiological and physical maladies include cardiovascular diseases, various forms of cancer, emphysema, and actual loss of life or limb. Other occupation-caused maladies include leukemia, white-lung disease, brown-lung disease, black-lung disease, sterility, central nervous system damage, and chronic bronchitis.

Common harmful socio-psychological conditions, the major causes of a low quality of work life, include stress, dissatisfaction, apathy, withdrawal, projection, tunnel vision, forgetfulness, inner confusion about roles or duties, mistrust of others, vacillation in decision making, inattentiveness, irritability, procrastination, and a tendency to become distraught about insignificant matters.

Purposes and Importance of Improving Occupational Health and Safety

The enormous costs that result from inadequate health and safety conditions—both in monetary and human terms—are enough to justify workplace improvement programs. The purposes of improving health and safety conditions are primarily to protect employees, thereby reducing these costs.

Costs. Between 1975 and 1985, an average of 1000 Canadian workers have died annually as a result of workplace accidents. In 1982, direct costs of compensation payments to injured workers totalled $2 billion, and it is estimated that indirect costs increase that figure to an alarming $10 billion dollars.[2] Furthermore, the number of industrial accidents does not seem to be decreasing. Every six seconds of the working day, an injury occurs at a Canadian organization.[3] Not only has the number of injuries increased over the years but also, in a number of provinces, workplace injury severity, as measured by work days lost per claim, has been greatly increased. Exhibit 14.1 shows the average number of days of temporary total disability per disabling injury claim for selected provinces. A large increase in the average days lost per claim occurred from 1979 to 1983.

In addition, enormous costs to organizations are associated with *organizational stress* and a *low quality of work life*. For example, alcoholism, often the result of an attempt to cope with job stress and a low quality of work life, is estimated to cost organizations and Canadian society more than $21 million per day.[4] Perhaps more difficult to quantify, but just as symptomatic of stress and poor quality of work life, are the workers'

Exhibit 14.1   *Average Days of Temporary Total Disability Per Disabling Injury Claim*

Year	Ontario	Manitoba	Alberta	Nova Scotia
1979	24	13.4	24.5	23.3
1980	23	13.4	23.1	20.3
1981	26	13.8	23.1	29.8
1982	30	19.5	26.5	33.6
1983	37	19.9	33.7	31.6

Note: Each province has its own method of accounting, thus rendering the interprovincial comparisons imprecise.

Source: P. Lewycky, "Are Workplace Injuries Becoming More Severe?" *At the Centre* (the official newsletter of the Canadian Centre for Occupational Health and Safety), vol. VIII, no. 2, July 1985, p. 11. Used with permission.

feelings of lack of meaning and involvement in their work and loss of importance as individuals.

To reduce these two sets of harmful conditions in the organization, one must attack their sources. The two general environments that may prove hazardous are the *physical work environment* and the *socio-psychological work environment.* Harm caused by aspects of either environment will result in a lack of organizational effectiveness in terms of lower productivity and increased absenteeism, turnover, worker compensation claims, and medical costs. It must be kept in mind that these environments will not affect all workers in the same way. What is harmful for one may not be for another. Together, the harmful physiological/physical and socio-psychological conditions, their sources and their outcomes, constitute a model of occupational health and safety in organizations. This model is discussed later in this chapter.

Benefits. If organizations reduce their rates and severity of occupational accidents, diseases, and stress, and improve the quality of work life for their employees, the following benefits can occur: (1) more productivity due to fewer lost work days; (2) more employee efficiency due to increased involvement with their jobs; (3) reduced medical and insurance costs; (4) lower worker compensation rates and direct payments due to fewer claims; (5) greater flexibility and adaptability in the workforce as a result of increased participation and feeling of ownership; (6) better selection ratios because of the increased attractiveness of the organization as a place to work; and (7) fewer deaths.

Because the costs of inadequate occupational health and safety are so enormous, and the benefits of safe conditions are so extensive, it is not surprising that organizations are concerned with improving their work environments.

Relationships of Occupational Health and Safety

Health and safety activities have extensive relationships with other PHRM activities. A summary of the many relationships is shown in Exhibit 14.2.

Recruitment and Selection. To the extent that an organization can provide a safe, healthy, and comfortable work environment, it may increase its success in attracting and retaining a qualified, productive workforce. If organizations develop reputations for being unsafe places to work, they will find it more difficult to recruit more qualified employees.

PHRM Programs for Improving QWL. Since a low QWL is associated with several costly socio-psychological conditions, programs for improving QWL are directly associated with occupational safety and health. Because QWL often depends on the employees' perceptions of organizational policies and structures, many Canadian companies have commissioned organizational surveys to measure these perceptions. More informal mechanisms to en-

Exhibit 14.2 Relationships of Health and Safety and other PHRM Activities

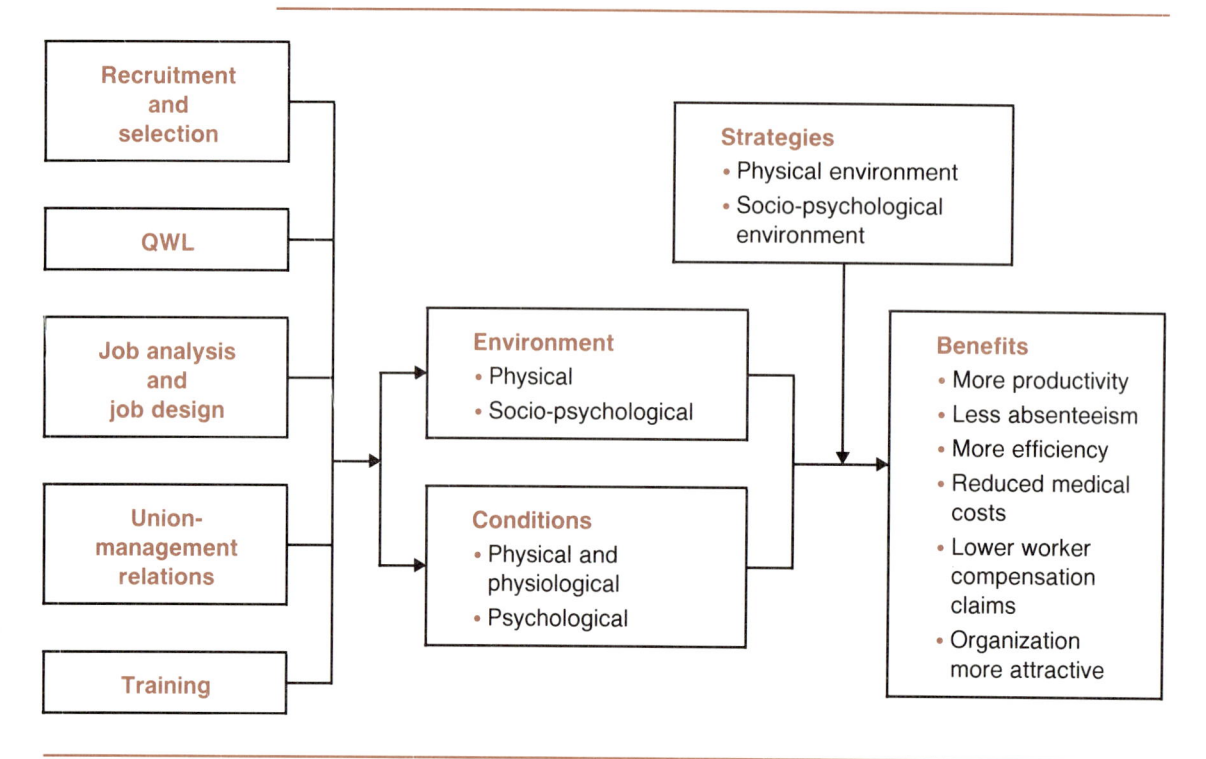

```
┌──────────────┐
│ Recruitment  │
│     and      │──┐
│  selection   │  │
└──────────────┘  │
                  │
┌──────────────┐  │                                    ┌──────────────────┐
│              │  │                                    │ Strategies       │
│     QWL      │──┤                                    │ • Physical       │
│              │  │                                    │   environment    │
└──────────────┘  │                                    │ • Socio-         │
                  │                                    │   psychological  │
┌──────────────┐  │                                    │   environment    │
│ Job analysis │  │        ┌──────────────────┐        └────────┬─────────┘
│     and      │  │        │ Environment      │                 │
│  job design  │──┼───────▶│ • Physical       │                 │         ┌─────────────────────┐
│              │  │        │ • Socio-         │                 │         │ Benefits            │
└──────────────┘  │        │   psychological  │                 │         │ • More productivity │
                  │        └──────────────────┘                 ▼         │ • Less absenteeism  │
┌──────────────┐  │                                                       │ • More efficiency   │
│   Union-     │  │                                        ───────────────▶│ • Reduced medical   │
│ management   │──┤        ┌──────────────────┐                            │   costs             │
│  relations   │  │        │ Conditions       │                            │ • Lower worker      │
└──────────────┘  │───────▶│ • Physical and   │                            │   compensation      │
                  │        │   physiological  │                            │   claims            │
┌──────────────┐  │        │ • Psychological  │                            │ • Organization      │
│   Training   │──┘        └──────────────────┘                            │   more attractive   │
└──────────────┘                                                           └─────────────────────┘
```

hance communications also are being implemented. In addition, safety committees and quality circles often are instrumental in developing strategies to improve the work environment.

Union-Management Relations. Occupational health and safety is one of the major concerns of unions. Many union contracts have some type of safety provision that complements the basic Canadian laws regarding health and safety, with particular emphasis on the right to refuse unsafe work. Other clauses include a union/employer pledge of co-operation in the development and operation of safety and health programs, the right to protest unsafe work, the right to discipline employees for violating safety rules, regulation of crew size, posting rules of safety, and right of inspection by a joint or union safety committee.

Job Analysis and Job Design. As described in Chapter 3, the ways in which jobs are physically designed has an important impact on people's performances. Ergonomic problems, stemming from a failure to properly match people and machines, account for many workplace accidents. Matching the physical abilities of the employee with those required by the job may mean redesigning the job.

Training. Occupational health and safety training are becoming an integral function of PHRM departments. Because of the complicated web of health and safety laws, companies conduct training sessions for their employees in order to increase compliance with the laws. Many companies also conduct safety drills and training with the aim of increasing awareness of safety features. Other companies hold stress workshops to help their employees to better cope with the socio-psychological work environment.

Legal Considerations of Occupational Health and Safety

According to the President and CEO of the Canadian Centre for Occupational Health and Safety: "Occupational health and safety in Canada represents a complex mix of jurisdictions, roles, responsibilities and duties which not only overlap, but at times conflict." [5]

Occupational health and safety legislation lies in the federal, provincial, and territorial jurisdictions. Of Canada's employed workforce, less than 10% are covered by the federal jurisdiction, and slightly more than half of this group are the federal government's own employees. What differentiates Canadian occupational health and safety legislation from that of most other countries is the emphasis that it gives to the rights of workers. This legislation allows workers to refuse dangerous work, to be informed about hazardous materials or dangerous conditions in the workplace, and to participate in worksite occupational health and safety committees. These often are referred to as the three basic rights of occupational health and safety, and they are of special interest to PHRM departments.[6]

The Canadian Jurisdictional Framework

Canada differs from the United States in the extent of existing federal jurisdiction for health and safety. In Canada, there is no national equivalent of the U.S. Federal Occupational Safety and Health Act. In Canada there is not one government approach but thirteen—those of the ten provinces, two territories, and the federal government. The Canadian Constitution determines the parameters of federal and provincial jurisdiction over workplace health and safety. Under that Act, the federal government's power to legislate is limited to federal government employees and to industries coming under federal jurisdiction. Federally regulated industries include interprovincial railways, communications, pipelines, canals, ferries, shipping, air transport, banks, grain elevators, uranium mines, certain Crown corporations, and atomic energy. Generally, the federal government's power to regulate is related to areas of a national, international, or interprovincial nature. Each province, on the other hand, has wide regulatory powers over matters within its boundaries relating to the working environment and the employer/employee relationship in the workplace. Thus, each province has its own health and safety legislation with its own unique features, although there are common themes and trends.

Federal Health and Safety Legislation

There are three federal acts of particular significance to occupational health and safety—The Hazardous Products Act, The Transportation of Dangerous Goods Act, and the Act that underlying the establishment of Canadian Centre for Occupational Health and Safety.

The Hazardous Products Act, passed in 1969, has wide application to industry across Canada. Primarily it is directed toward the protection of the consumer, which affects industry in two ways:

1. It prohibits the sale or import of certain specific products, for example, children's furniture painted with material containing more than the acceptable level of lead.
2. It establishes hazard-identification and -labelling requirements applying to the sale or import of specified products. Thus products sold for consumer use must be labelled to indicate the hazards of the chemicals they contain, plus information about necessary precautions and emergency treatment.

Although the Act is directed primarily at consumer safety, it also protects the many small companies that purchase these products from retail outlets for use in the workplace.

The Transportation of Dangerous Goods Act, passed in 1981, establishes a single legislative authority (Transport Canada) to deal with the handling and movement of hazardous materials by all federally regulated modes of transport in Canada. The aim of the Act is to ensure that dangerous goods are identified, known to the carrier, and classified according to a coding system.

The Canadian Centre for Occupational Health and Safety Act, passed in 1978, created a national body concerned with the study and co-operative advancement of occupational health and safety in Canada. The Canadian Centre, which the Act established, has no regulatory authority; rather its purpose is to provide a forum for the collection of health and safety information across Canada. The objectives of the Centre are to

- promote the concept of a safe working environment;
- co-ordinate research and advisory services; and
- promote information sharing.

The Centre, which is located in Hamilton, Ontario, is an autonomous body that does not come under the administration of a government department. It is governed by a board composed of representatives from federal and provincial governments, industry, and trade unions.

To date, the main contribution of the Centre has been advisory services in the area of occupational health hazards—particularly chemicals. It has set up an elaborate computer information system, and is a useful source of information for all those concerned with occupational health and safety. More than 250 organizations, including governments, now have access to this information system through local terminals, and access is publicly available.

Provincial Health and Safety Legislation

As mentioned before, each province in Canada has its own health and safety legislation. Although each province's regulation varies in content and administration, during the last decade most of the regulations were reshaped to include the following common characteristics:

- Consolidation of various previous pieces of legislation into one comprehensive Act
- Changes in the administrative structure, e.g., consolidation under one ministry or the establishment of a separate commission
- Greater attention paid to occupational health concerns
- Emphasis on employee involvement through statutory rights

Exhibit 14.3 lists the various provincial health and safety laws, along with their administrative bodies. The major ways in which the various provincial governments control health and safety in the workplace is through the implementation of the laws through the following control mechanisms:

- Incorporating general duty clauses into the legislation. A general duty clause places the overall responsibility for compliance on a specified party.
- Issuing regulations under the authority of the Acts. In general, a wide range of regulations on health and safety matters is specified. Regulations are issued at any time. In some provinces these require only the signature of the lieutenant-governor to become effective, and in other provinces certain regulations are subject to public hearings before they can be instituted.
- Setting out statutory rights such as the right to refuse to work, involvement in joint health and safety committees, and receiving health and safety information.
- Enforcing and inspecting the health and safety procedures: appointed inspectors have the right to enter the workplace and issue orders for remedial corrections where compliance with the Act is lacking. These inspectors also can prosecute those responsible for violations of the Act.
- Referencing standards and codes so that compliance becomes mandatory.

Major changes have taken place in most of the provinces in recent years in the administrative structures applying to health and safety legislation. Two trends are (1) the consolidation of standard-setting and enforcement functions under one government body, and (2) the establishment of tripartite, consultative or policy-setting forums.

Essentially three functions are involved in government occupational health and safety administration: legal standard-setting and enforcement,

Exhibit 14.3 Provincial Health and Safety Laws

Province	Main Agency
Alberta Occupational Health and Safety Act, 1976, amended 1983	Alberta Workers' Health, Safety and Compensation Ministry—Occupational Health and Safety Division
British Columbia Workers' Compensation Act, 1979, amended 1980 Industrial Health and Safety Regulations, amended 1979, Factory Act, 1979 Occupational Environment Regulations; Mines Act, 1980 (for health and safety provisions)	Workers' Compensation Board
Manitoba Workplace Safety and Health Act, 1976, amended 1983	Department of Environment and Workplace Safety and Health
New Brunswick Occupational Health and Safety Act, 1983	Occupational Health and Safety Commission, which consists of 7 members—3 from labour, 3 employers, and an independent full-time chairman appointed by government—and is responsible to the Ministry of Labour and Manpower
Newfoundland Occupational Health and Safety Act, 1978, amended 1980; The Workers' Compensation Act, 1970, amended 1980	Department of Labour and Manpower, Occupational Health and Safety Division
Nova Scotia Industrial Safety Act, 1967, amended 1981; Health Act, 1967 Occupational Health Regulations, amended 1977	Ministry of Labour, Occupational Safety (Industrial Safety) Division
Prince Edward Island Workers' Compensation Act, 1974, amended 1980 Industrial Safety Regulations, 1974	Workers' Compensation Board
Ontario Occupational Health and Safety Act, 1978	Ministry of Labour, Occupational Health and Safety Division

Continued

Exhibit 14.3

Province	Main Agency
Québec An Act Respecting Occupational Health and Safety, 1979; Environment Quality Act, 1977; Quality of the Work Environment, 1981; Workers' Compensation Act, 1964	Health and Safety Commission of the Department for Social Development, which consists of 15 members—7 from labour, 7 employers, and a full-time chairman appointed by the government
Saskatchewan Occupational Health and Safety Act, 1977; Occupational Health and Safety Regulations, amended 1981	Department of Labour, Occupational Health and Safety Division

Source: Dilys Robertson, "Occupational Health and Safety," *Human Resources Management in Canada*, Prentice-Hall Canada Inc., Toronto: 1986, p. 60,042. Used with permission.

workers' compensation, and accident-prevention education. These functions are not all integrated under one government agency in all of the provinces, although in British Columbia, for example, they are in fact integrated under the Workers' Compensation Board. In Alberta they all come under the Workers' Health, Safety and Compensation Ministry. In other provinces (e.g., Québec and New Brunswick), all of these functions come under the general policy direction of a commission.

Some highlights of the provincial administration of health and safety legislation are summarized in the following:

- In Newfoundland, Nova Scotia, Ontario, and Saskatchewan, the major administering body for occupational health and safety legislation is the provincial Ministry of Labour.
- In British Columbia and Prince Edward Island, the major administering body is the provincial Workers' Compensation Board.
- Québec and New Brunswick have established commissions that include labour and management representation, and these commissions effectively provide policy direction for the setting, administration, and enforcement of the health and safety laws, as well as compensation and accident prevention.
- Manitoba, Saskatchewan, Alberta, Ontario, and Prince Edward Island have advisory councils established through legislation that include management and labour representatives. The councils provide their respective provincial Ministry of Labour with advice on health and safety matters.
- In the Northwest Territories and the Yukon, territorial jurisdiction is exercised through a commissioner and a territorial government that has power to issue ordinances over a wide range of local matters, including health and safety. Some such ordinances—for example, Mining Safety and Workers' Compensation—deal specifically with occupational health

and safety. Others deal with health and safety generally, fire prevention, for example. In some cases, administration of these ordinances is handled by the appropriate federal government department.

- In most of the provinces, accident prevention information and advice and education is provided through either the Ministry of Labour, the Workers' Compensation Board or a commission. In Ontario, accident prevention associations were established early in the century and their funding was ensured through statutory provision in the Workers' Compensation Act.
- Québec's Act allows for industrial sector-based associations to be set up through joint agreements between employers' associations and unions. Once established, the object of each sector-based association is to provide training and assistance to the workplaces in the sector. They are funded through a commission.[7]

The Right to Know

Many provinces are preparing right-to-know legislation, which is patterned on a federal provincial task force that Labour Canada initiated in 1982, and is entitled "Workplace Hazardous Materials Information System." Under provincial legislation, suppliers are responsible for evaluating and classifying their chemicals for toxicity and such other hazards as flammability. Under the legislation the information delivery system should have three complementary components: labels, data sheets, and workers' education programming.[8]

The first legal test of these guidelines occurred recently in Ontario, where Justice D. Steele of the Ontario Supreme Court awarded $350 000 to a worker who was blinded on a construction site. The worker was E. Meilleur, and he was sprayed in the face and eyes with a chemical, Uni-Crete XL, which is used with concrete to seal the interior of rock excavations. Although Meilleur received Workers' Compensation payments, the Compensation Board allowed him to sue the manufacturer and distributor of the product. The case focused on the quality of warning provided by the manufacturer, Uni-Crete Canada and Diamond Shamrock and on the danger of the chemical with which Meilleur was working. Justice Steele found that although the worker was 75% responsible for the accident because he failed to wear safety goggles, Uni-Crete Canada was 20% responsible, and Diamond Shamrock 5%.[9]

The Right to Refuse Work

A distinctive feature of the reforms that have taken place in most Canadian health and safety legislation is the emphasis placed on a worker's right to refuse unsafe work. Even prior to such reforms, any worker had a right, under common law, to refuse work that would place him or her in imminent danger. In addition, most existing legislation laid a duty on workers not to do unsafe work. However, pursuing such rights under common law is usually expensive, difficult, and time-consuming, and it therefore was never a practical option for most workers.

When the right was first introduced into legislation in various provinces, many employers expressed concern that the right would be abused—particularly by the trade unions—and that this legal right would prove to be disruptive to industry. With a few exceptions, these fears have so far proved to be unfounded. In practice, work refusals should not occur in an organization that has sound communications policies and good safety programs. Those concerned with human resources management must ensure that company procedures exist to minimize the need for work refusals, and also to deal legally, fairly, and efficiently with any refusals that may occur.

Generally, the right to refuse work is not dependent on the worker's ability to prove that a hazard exists. In most cases, all that is required is "reason to believe" that the work is unsafe. However, in most jurisdictions, this right does not apply to certain types of work. In Ontario, for example, certain workers are specifically excluded—policemen, firemen, workers in correctional institutions, workers in hospitals, for example, where the safety of other people would be placed in jeopardy by their refusal. In Québec, on the other hand, all workers covered by the Act are not permitted the right of refusal where exercise of the right would jeopardize the safety of others or where danger is a normal part of the job.

Joint Health and Safety Committees

The federal government and all of the provinces except Nova Scotia and Prince Edward Island have legal regulations that require the establishment of joint health and safety committees for specific types of workplaces. The overall intent of this regulation is to place emphasis on the necessary role of workers in establishing health and safety programs and to encourage employers to resolve health and safety problems through their own internal responsibility systems. Government support for joint committees in occupational health and safety can be seen in two ways:

1. The statutory provisions with regard to committees and their rights and responsibilities
2. The way in which joint committees are drawn into the government inspection and enforcement process

The legal role of joint committees varies among the provinces. In general, Québec's and Saskatchewan's legislation gives joint committees more authority than do those of the other provinces.

Although joint labour-management committees have been in place in Canada for only a short time, the evidence from preliminary studies indicates that, where co-operation is high, this instrument is effective in reducing occupational injuries and diseases.[10] However, many of the committees across industry in Canada have not yet matured. More information will be available when committees in all industries have had more experience.

Accident Reporting and Inquiries

In all of the Canadian jurisdictions, employers are required to report accidents that cause injury or occupational diseases to the Workers' Compensation Board, for the purpose of administering compensation and rehabilitation programs. However, most of the jurisdictions also require separate reporting of specified accidents and illnesses to the ministry that administers and enforces occupational health and safety legislation. These reporting requirements generally are for the purpose of administration and law enforcement.

Provisions relating to the reporting of accidents differ among the various jurisdictions. Most require immediate notification of accidents that cause fatalities or critical injuries, and explosions that might have caused serious injury or death. Notification when an employee has contracted an occupational disease or illness usually is required also. In general, it is required that the employer not disturb evidence unless necessary to prevent further injury. Some jurisdictions also require the employer to investigate accidents and submit written reports.

Work Hazards

As shown in Exhibit 14.4, both the physical and the socio-psychological aspects of the work environment influence occupational safety and health. Each aspect has its own hazards to health and safety. On the physical side, it is diseases and accidents; on the socio-psychological side, it is low QWL and stress. Traditionally, only the physical environment has received the attention of most companies and health and safety laws. Increasingly, however, companies are admitting to the impact of socio-psychological hazards on health and safety.[11]

Consequently, efforts to improve occupational health and safety must include strategies to remove hazards from both work environments. Developing effective strategies begins with understanding the factors affecting health and safety in organizations.

Factors Affecting Occupational Accidents

Certain organizations, and even certain departments within the same organization, have higher accident rates than others. There are several factors that explain this difference.

Organizational Qualities. Accident rates vary substantially by industry. For example, firms in the construction and manufacturing industries have higher accident rates than firms in service businesses, finance, insurance, and real estate. Small and large organizations (those with fewer than 100 employees and more than 1000, respectively) have lower rates than medium-sized organizations. This may be because supervisors in small organizations are better able to detect safety hazards and prevent accidents than those in medium-sized organizations. Also, larger organizations have more resources than medium-sized organizations to hire staff specialists who can devote all of their efforts to safety and accident prevention.

Model of Occupational Health and Safety in Organizations   Exhibit 14.4

Environmental Hazards

Physical
- Occupational accidents
- Occupational diseases

Socio-psychological
- Low QWL
- Organizational stress

Conditions

Physical-physiological
- Loss of limb
- Cancer
- Leukemia

Psychological
- Dissatisfaction
- Apathy
- Confusion

Outcomes

High turnover/absenteeism

Dissatisfaction

Medical claims

Low productivity

Low efficiency

High workers' compensation costs

Low job involvement

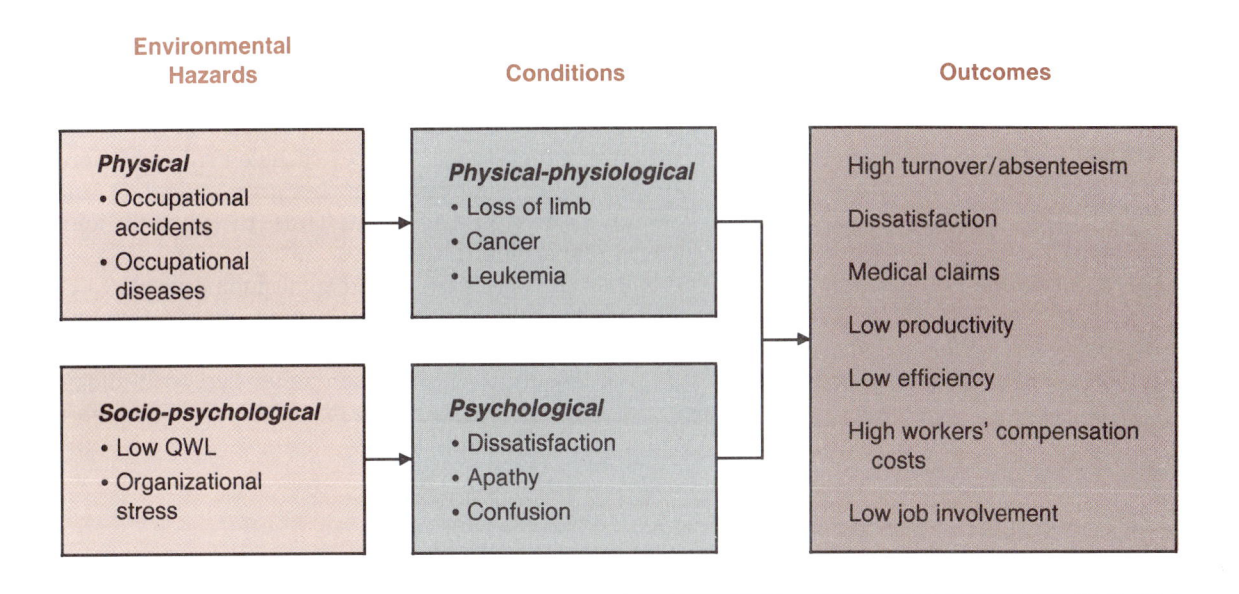

Safety Programs. Organizations differ in the extent to which they develop techniques, programs, and activities to promote safety and prevent accidents. The effectiveness of these techniques and programs varies by the type of industry and size of organization. For example, in large chemical firms, greater expenditures for off-the-job safety, medical facilities and staff, safety training, and additional supervision are associated with decreased work-injury costs.[12] On the other hand, work-injury costs can actually increase due to ineffectively applied expenditures for correction of unsafe physical conditions, for safety staff, for employee orientation, and for safety records. As a result, some organizations in the same industry may have higher injury costs per employee than others. And, of course, those organizations that have no safety programs generally have higher injury costs than similar companies that have implemented such programs.

The Unsafe Employee. Although organizational factors play an important role in occupational safety, many experts point to the employee as the cause of accidents. Accidents depend on the behaviour of the person, the degree of hazard in the work environment, and pure chance. The degree to which the person contributes to the accident is often regarded as an indicator of proneness to accidents.

Accident proneness cannot be considered a stable set of traits that always contribute to accidents. Nevertheless, there are certain psychological and physical characteristics that make some people more susceptible than others to accidents. For example, employees who are emotionally low have more accidents than those who are emotionally high, and employees who have had fewer accidents have been found to be more optimistic, trusting, and concerned for others than those who have had more accidents.

Employees under greater stress are likely to have more accidents than those under less stress, and those with better vision have fewer accidents than those with poorer vision. Older workers are less likely to be hurt than younger workers. People who are quicker in recognizing differences in visual patterns than at making muscular manipulations are less likely to have accidents than those who are the opposite. Many psychological conditions that may be related to accident proneness—for instance, hostility and emotional immaturity—may be temporary states. Thus, they are difficult to detect until after at least one accident.

Because none of these characteristics is related to accidents in all work environments, and since none is always present in employees, selecting and screening job applicants on the basis of accident proneness is difficult. Even if it were possible, aspects of the organization, such as its size, technology, management attitudes, safety programs, and quality of supervision, could still be important contributors to accidents.

Factors Affecting Occupational Diseases

The potential sources of work-related diseases are as distressingly varied as are the ways that they affect the human organism:

> Typical health hazards include toxic and carcinogenic chemicals and dust, often in combination with noise, heat, and other forms of stress. Other health hazards include physical and biological agents. The interaction of health hazards and the human organism can occur either through the senses, by absorption through the skin, by intake into the digestive tract via the mouth, or by inhalation into the lungs.[13]

The fastest-growing category of occupational diseases includes illnesses of the respiratory system (see second article in "PHRM in the News"). Cancer, however, tends to receive the most attention since it is a leading cause of death in Canada, second after heart disease. Many of the known causes of cancer are physical and chemical agents in the environment. And because physical and chemical agents theoretically are more controllable than human behaviour, an effort is made to eliminate them from the workplace.

Legislation is concerned with many other categories of occupational diseases and illnesses in addition to cancer, including occupation-related skin diseases and disorders; dust diseases of the lungs; respiratory conditions due to toxic agents; poisoning (systemic effects of toxic materials); disorders due to physical agents; and disorders associated with repeated trauma.

Occupational Groups at Risk. Miners, construction and transportation workers, and blue-collar and lower-level supervisory personnel in manufacturing industries experience the majority of both occupational diseases and injuries. The least safe occupations are firefighting, mining, and law enforcement. In addition, large numbers of petrochemical and oil refinery workers, dye users, textile workers, plastic-industry workers, painters, and industrial chemical workers are particularly susceptible to some of the most dangerous health hazards.

Of course, occupational diseases are not exclusive to the blue-collar workers and manufacturing industries. The "cushy" office job has evolved into a veritable nightmare of physical and psychological ills for white-collar workers in the increasingly growing service industries. Among the common ailments are varicose veins, low-back pain, deteriorating eyesight, migraine headaches, hypertension, coronary heart disorders, respiratory problems, and digestive problems. Situational factors causing these disorders include (1) too much noise; (2) interior air pollutants such as cigarette smoke and chemical fumes, for example, from photocopy machines; (3) uncomfortable chairs; (4) poor office design (see Chapter 13); (5) chemically treated paper; and (6) new office technology such as video display terminals. In addition, dentists routinely are exposed to radiation, mercury, and anaesthetics, and cosmetologists suffer from high rates of cancer and respiratory and cardiac diseases connected with their frequent use of chemicals.

Individuals at Risk. Scientists estimate that approximately 1600 diseases are caused by genetic defects. Some individuals are more susceptible to a variety of illnesses due to their vulnerable genetic makeup.[14] This assertion, which is difficult to validate, has sparked a new controversy regarding the future role of PHRM departments in conducting genetic screening and genetic monitoring.

Theoretically, genetic screening would be used to evaluate the genetic makeup of a given job applicant. This evaluation, along with a knowledge of chemicals used, could indicate what chemicals could cause diseases, such as cancer. By identifying the individual's propensity to contact a given chemical-caused disease, companies could (a) reject the applicant, (b) place the applicant in a work environment away from the hazard, or (c) institute policies (e.g., require protective clothing) to lessen the probability of later disease. At present, there are no laws at either the federal or provincial level specifically governing the use of genetic tests in the workplace.

Although not extensively used at present, many large corporations are considering turning to genetic tests in the future. Yet, in no case has the research reported a clear relationship between either possession of a trait or deficiency (which can be measured reliably) and the eventual development of disease. Many who possess a trait or deficiency do not encounter health problems at a later date. Although it may be useful to test the applicants for susceptability, it would not seem reasonable, advisable, or fair to reject candidates without better estimates of potential risk.

Genetic monitoring may be a better course of action than genetic screening. In monitoring, the focus is on providing ongoing testing of employees exposed to potentially harmful substances, to detect changes in genetic material that could lead to health risks later on. Monitoring, if used to identify potential toxins, may lead to transfer of those seemingly vulnerable and, where possible, rid the workplace of the suspected chemical or agent. This could be extremely beneficial to the worker and the company alike.[15]

Factors Affecting Low Quality of Work Life

For many workers a **low quality of work life** is associated with conditions in the organization that fail to satisfy important preferences and interests, such as a need for responsibility, challenge, meaningfulness, self-control, recognition, achievement, fairness or justice, security, and certainty.[16] Common organizational conditions causing these preferences and interests to remain unsatisfied include (1) jobs with low significance, variety, identity, autonomy, feedback, and qualitative underload (see Chapters 3 and 13 for a discussion of these); (2) high levels of one-way communication and minimal involvement of employees in decision making; (3) pay systems not based on performance or based on performance that is not objectively measured or under employee control; (4) supervisors, job descriptions, and organizational policies that fail to convey to the employee what is expected and what is rewarded; (5) personnel and human resource policies and practices that are discriminatory and of low validity; and (6) employment situations where employees can be dismissed arbitrarily.

Many conditions in organizations also are associated with organizational stress. Remember, however, that a condition contributing to stress or low QWL for one individual may not have the same effect on another, because of differing preferences and interests.

Sources of Organizational Stress

Prevalent causes of **organizational stress** include the four Ss: (1) supervisor; (2) salary; (3) security; (4) safety.[17]

Major stressors that employees associate with the supervisor are petty work rules and relentless pressure for more production. Both deny workers their fulfilment of the needs to control the work situation and to be recognized and accepted.

Salary is a stressor when it is perceived as being given unfairly. Many blue-collar workers feel that they are underpaid relative to their white-collar counterparts in the office. Teachers think they are underpaid relative to people with similar education who work in private industry.

Employees experience stress when they are unsure whether they will have their jobs next week, next month, or even the next day. For many employees, lack of job security is even more stressful than jobs that are unsafe generally. At least the employees *know* that the jobs are unsafe, whereas with a lack of job security, the employees are always in a state of uncertainty.

Organizational Change. Changes made by organizations are often stressful, because usually they involve something important and are accompanied by uncertainty. Many changes are made without advance warning. Although rumours often circulate that a change is coming, the exact nature of the change is left to speculation. People become concerned about whether the change will affect them, perhaps by displacing them or by causing them to be transferred. The uncertainty surrounding an impending change causes many employees to suffer stress symptoms.

Work Pace. Work pace, particularly who or what controls the pace of the work, is an important potential stressor in organizations. Machine pacing gives control over the speed of the operation and the work output to something other than the individual. Employee pacing gives the individual control of the operations. The effects of machine pacing are severe, since the individual is unable to satisfy a crucial need for control of the situation. It has been reported that workers on machine-paced jobs feel exhausted at the end of their shifts and are unable to relax for some time after work because of increased adrenaline secretion on the job. In one study of 23 white- and blue-collar occupations, assembly workers reported the highest level of severe stress symptoms.

Work Overload. While some employees complain about not having enough to do, others have far too much. In fact, some have so much to do, it exceeds their abilities and capacities. The result of this situation, if prolonged, can be fatal.

Physical Environment. Although office automation can improve productivity, it does have its stress-related drawbacks. Video display terminals, for example, have specific stress-related drawbacks, although the findings on just how serious an effect these screens have on workers are not yet complete. Other aspects of the work environment associated with stress are crowding, lack of privacy, and lack of ability to change aspects of the environment, e.g., to move the desk or chairs or even to hang pictures in a work area in an effort to personalize it.[18]

Occupational Health and Safety Strategies for Improvement

To improve the occupational health of an organization's workforce, the sources of the harmful conditions first must be identified, then strategies for improving these can be developed. The success of the strategies can be determined by comparing occupational health and safety ratings before and after the strategy is implemented. Only by doing this can organizations determine whether what they are doing is effective. A summary of these strategies as well as the occupational health and safety maladies is shown in Exhibit 14.5.

Strategies for Health and Safety Improvement in the Physical Work Environment

Common to improving both accidents and diseases in the physical work environment is the use of records. These records can be used to assess where

Exhibit 14.5 *Summary of Maladies and Strategies for Occupational Health and Safety*

Physical Work Environment

Occupational accidents	Redesigning the work environment
	Setting goals and objectives
	Establishing safety committees
Occupational diseases	Measuring the work environment
	Setting goals and objectives

Socio-psychological Work Environment

Quality of work life	Redesigning jobs
	Increasing participation in decision making
Organizational stress	Establishing organizational stress programs
	Establishing individual stress strategies

the organization is in terms of current incidences of accidents and diseases, in essence forming a baseline against which to compare and evaluate other specific strategies for workplace improvements. Because the process of gathering such data creates an awareness of health and safety problems, it could be regarded as a strategy for workplace improvements as well as a process that helps to determine the effectiveness of other strategies.[19]

Health and Safety Rates. Health and safety rates are described in terms of their frequency, severity, and incidence. Organizations are required to maintain records of the incidence of accidents and illnesses for comparison purposes; many organizations also maintain frequency and severity records of accidents and illnesses. Since the PHRM department generally is responsible for health and safety, it is important for PHRM personnel to know how to compute health and safety rates.[20]

The **incidence rate** is most explicit in combining both illnesses and injuries, as shown by this formula:

$$\text{Incidence rate} = \frac{\text{Number of recordable injuries and illnesses} \times 1 \text{ million}}{\text{Number of employee exposure-hours}}$$

Suppose an organization has 10 recorded injuries and illnesses and 500 employees. To compute the number of employee exposure-hours, it would multiply the number of employees by 40 hours and by 50 work weeks or 500 × 40 × 50 = 1 million. In this case, the incidence rate would be 10.

The **severity rate** reflects the hours actually lost due to injury or illness, recognizing that not all injuries and illnesses are equal. Four categories of injuries and illnesses have been established: deaths, permanent total disabilities, permanent partial disabilities, and temporary total disabilities. The severity rate is calculated by this formula:

$$\text{Severity rate} = \frac{\text{Total hours charged} \times 1\text{ million}}{\text{Number of employee hours worked}}$$

Obviously, an organization with the same number of injuries and illnesses as another but with more deaths would have a higher severity rate.

The **frequency rate** is similar to the incidence rate except that it reflects the number of injuries and illnesses per million hours worked rather than per year:

$$\text{Frequency rate} = \frac{\text{Number of disabling injuries} \times 1\text{ million}}{\text{Number of employee hours worked}}$$

Occupational Accidents. This aspect of the physical work environment concerns immediate physical injury to workers, ranging from minor cuts and bruises to loss of limb or even life. Designing the work environment to minimize the likelihood of accidents is perhaps the best way to prevent accidents and improve safety. Among the safety features that can be designed into the physical environment are guard devices on machines, handrails in stairways, safety goggles and helmets, warning lights, self-correcting mechanisms, and automatic shut-offs. The extent to which these features actually will reduce accidents depends on employee acceptance and use. For example, eye injuries will be reduced by safety goggles only if employees wear the goggles correctly. The effectiveness of any safety regulation depends on how the regulation is implemented and whether it is obeyed. If employees are involved in the decision to make some physical change to improve safety, they are more likely to accept the change.

Another way to alter the work environment and to improve safety is to make the job itself more comfortable and less fatiguing. This approach is generally referred to as **ergonomics**. Ergonomics considers changes in the job environment in conjunction with the physical and physiological capabilities and limitations of the employees. As a result, employees are less likely to make mistakes due to fatigue and tiredness.

Whereas ergonomics focuses on the physical and physiological, another approach focuses on the psychological. Job redesign also can help prevent accidents, by increasing employee motivation and reducing boredom. The result may be increased alertness and fewer accidents.

The personnel department can be instrumental in accident prevention by assisting the supervisors in their training efforts and by implementing safety motivation programs. Many organizations, for example, display signs indicating the number of days or hours worked without an accident. Many organizations display posters saying "Safety First." In safety contests, prizes or awards are given to individuals or departments with the best safety record. These programs seem to work best when employees are already safety conscious and when physical conditions of the work environment provide no extreme safety hazards.[21]

Many organizations have set up management by objectives programs to deal with occupational health. The five basic steps of these programs are

1. identifying existing hazards based on personnel records;
2. evaluating the severity and risk of these hazards;
3. implementing appropriate programs to control, prevent, or reduce accidents (setting objectives);
4. establishing a system for objectively assessing improvements and giving positive feedback for correct safety procedures; and
5. monitoring the progress of programs against stated objectives and making revisions as needed.[22]

Occupational Diseases. More harmful and costly to organizations and employees than occupational accidents are occupational diseases. In addition, the physical environment has a more subtle impact on occupational diseases than on occupational accidents. Therefore, it generally is more difficult to develop strategies to reduce the incidence of occupational diseases. Nevertheless, four strategies can be suggested:

1. Record keeping
2. Setting objectives
3. Recognition
4. Educational programs

The records must include the date, number of samples taken, length of time over which the sampling was done, procedure used, analytical method, the employees' names, social insurance numbers, and job classifications, where the employees work in the organization, and the protective equipment used. Often a physician is involved in the process of gathering this information, but the responsibility for gathering and processing the information lies with the organization. The organization should keep this information for as long a period as is associated with the incubation period of the specific disease—it could be as long as 40 years. These records contribute to the knowledge of such fields as epidemiology, and are useful when making decisions about how to improve future work environments.

The second strategy is setting objectives, implementing programs, and maintaining records of diseases. This strategy uses the information collected in the first strategy and follows the same steps as management by objectives programs for reducing occupational accidents. A third strategy is for organizations to recognize the importance of previously neglected ailments and make a committed effort to help workers with those ailments. For example, since long exposure to asbestos could generate serious ailments, several asbestos companies in Québec have undertaken jointly a program with the School of Medicine at Mount Sinai Hospital to assist and monitor employees who have worked for the companies for more than a few years. Even former employees were invited to participate in the program.

A final strategy is worker education and physical fitness programs.[23] Educational programs on arthritis, for example, are now being conducted at General Motors. A part of worker awareness is informing them of clinics across the nation to which workers can go if they suspect they are ill due to workplace exposures. Physical fitness programs are discussed later in the chapter.

Strategies for Health and Safety Improvement in the Socio-Psychological Work Environment

Many techniques can be used to improve the socio-psychological work environment. Techniques to improve the QWL include career management, job redesign, quality circles, and organizational restyling. Since these were described in Chapters 12 and 13, emphasis here is given to techniques to manage stress.

Organizational Stress Management Programs. Specific programs can be designed to improve aspects of the organization such as the supervisor's role, work overload, the physical environment, the salary structure, and job security, and while it is unlikely that an organization would use all of these programs, many are using at least a few of them.

The Children's Aid Society of Metropolitan Toronto developed an interesting program to reduce stress hazards among entering frontline social workers in child welfare. The program, which radically differs from other approaches, includes several steps:

1. Hiring frontline workers in batches
2. Keeping these newly hired workers in small groups of five or six for their first six months on the job
3. Gradually increasing their caseload so that it eventually reaches 60% of the normal caseload by the end of the six months
4. An enhanced supervisor's role emphasizing education, accompanied by a reduction of other supervisory duties
5. An improved training program: one or two days of training every two weeks
6. Increased social support for the group [24]

Other organizations use alternative organizational stress management strategies such as "team building," issuing new or clear policies regarding work when it is ambiguous, and providing counselling to distressed employees.[25]

Individual Stress Management Strategies. Time management can be an effective individual strategy for dealing with organizational stress. Other individual strategies that should be included in individual stress management include (1) good diets; (2) regular exercise; (3) monitoring of physical health; and (4) the building of good social support groups.[26] Many Canadian organizations will pay for their employees (usually professional and managerial) to join fitness clubs. A few organizations have built first-rate gym facilities on their premises, complete with qualified staff. Research conducted within two large Canadian insurance companies located in Toronto demonstrated that high levels of workers' satisfaction and QWL and higher levels of productivity are associated with use of fitness programs. Absenteeism also was reduced by 22% among the employees who participated in the program.[27]

There are many activities or programs that organizations can offer in order to improve physical and socio-psychological work conditions in organizations. Selecting the most appropriate activity depends on a thorough diagnosis of the causes. An assessment of past activities and those used by others also can be useful in this selection process.[28]

Assessing Occupational Health and Safety Activities

The effectiveness of health and safety activities run by organizations can be assessed by using the outcome data associated with health and safety shown previously in Exhibit 14.4. However, assessing strategies improvement targeted at the physical work environment differs from the evaluation of the strategies targeted at the socio-psychological work environment.

Physical Work Environment Strategies

The effectiveness of these strategies often is measured by the effects of a specific strategy on employee absenteeism and turnover, medical claims and worker compensation rates and costs, productivity (quantity and quality), and efficiency. The effects of these strategies also can be seen in a change in the rates of accidents or the incidences of specific diseases. The relative effectiveness of these strategies can be measured by determining the cost of the program and the relative benefits. For example, it is suggested that workplace safety can be increased substantially by correcting person-machine mismatching through ergonomics. Since ergonomic changes are relatively quick and inexpensive, ergonomics may be the most effective strategy to use for physical work environment changes.

Socio-psychological Work Environment Strategies

The effectiveness of this class of strategies is determined by assessments of the psychological indicators of health and safety levels and employee dissatisfaction and job involvement. In addition, effectiveness can be measured by using the same assessments as those used for determining the effectiveness of physical work environment strategies. Indeed, it is very appropriate to measure the effectiveness of stress management strategies against the physical and physiological indicators.

Even so, it is often very difficult to establish a cause-and-effect assessment between stress strategies and most physical and physiological indicators. To do so requires using measures that are relatively sensitive to stress reduction such as heart rate or blood pressure. Often, indirect measures of performance, such as absence records, could be used as a substitute.[29]

Summary

The health and safety of employees in organizations will become increasingly important in the years ahead. Employers are becoming more aware of the cost of ill health and the benefits of having a healthy workforce. The federal and provincial governments, through a complex web of laws, make it more necessary for employers to be concerned with employee health and safety. The current concern is primarily with occupational accidents and diseases caused by the physical environment, but organizations can choose to guard employee health by improving the workers' socio-psychological environment as well. Although many of the latter efforts are voluntary, the government may prescribe, in the near future, regulations for socio-psychological conditions. Therefore, it would pay organizations to be concerned with both aspects of the work environment now. Effective programs for both environments can significantly improve both employee health and the effectiveness of the organization.

When adoption of programs for improvement is being considered, it is important to involve the employees. As with many quality of work life programs being implemented in organizations, employee involvement in improving health and safety is not only a good idea but one likely to be preferred by the employees.

The physical and the socio-psychological environments are each quite different, and each has its unique components. While some improvement strategies may work well for one part of the work environment, they will not work in other parts. A careful diagnosis is required before programs are selected and implemented.

The bottom line from a PHRM perspective is that these programs can reduce costs in the form of insurance premiums and claims, workers' compensation, litigation, and productivity loss due to disability, accidents, absenteeism, turnover, and even deaths.

Discussion Questions

1. What is occupational health and safety? Give examples to support your definition.

2. What is the strategic importance of improving occupational health and safety?
3. How are programs for improving QWL related to improvements in occupational health and safety?
4. What are the legal requirements of health and safety legislation in Canada?
5. What factors affect occupational accidents and occupational diseases?
6. Identify and describe the four Ss of organizational stress.
7. What are the steps necessary to develop a strategy for improving an organization's health and safety?
8. In what ways can an organization prevent occupational accidents?
9. Discuss the importance of occupational diseases to organizations.
10. How can physical work environment strategies and socio-psychological work environment strategies be assessed?

C A S E   S T U D Y

Stress Management at Metropolitan Hospital

A stress-management program was carried out over a one-year period at Metropolitan Hospital. The initial impetus for the project was widespread complaints from the nurses about feeling stressed, overworked, lonely, and subject to unexpected changes in hospital policies and procedures. The hospital administrators sought help in dealing with these problems from a local management consulting firm that had conducted a similar program at another hospital.

The initial stage of the project consisted of diagnosing the causes and consequences of stress experienced at the hospital. Understanding the sources of stress was seen as a necessary prelude to developing an appropriate plan for managing stress.

The consultants developed a questionnaire to collect data from a sample of 300 nurses representing different wards of the hospital. The questionnaire included items about various organizational stressors, including both ongoing, recurrent stressors and those associated with recent changes. It also included questions about the nurses' use of stress-management techniques, such as exercise, nutritional planning, and the available support systems.

The questionnaire ended with items about experienced strain symptoms (for example, irritability, sleeping difficulties, and changes in eating and drinking patterns) and longer-term effects (for example, health problems, dissatisfaction, and decreased work effectiveness). In addition, the consultants requested access to the personnel files of the nurses who participated in the study, including absenteeism records for the previous 12 months and performance appraisal data.

Analysis of the diagnostic data showed that many of the organizational changes and ongoing working conditions were significantly related to nurses' levels of strain and longer-term stress effects. Among the most stressful organizational-change events were major and frequent changes in instructions, policies, and procedures; numerous unexpected crises and deadlines; and sudden increases in the activity level or pace of work. The ongoing working conditions contributing most to negative effects of stress included quantitative work overload, feedback only when performance was unsatisfactory, lack of confidence in administration, and role conflict and ambiguity.

The nurses reported little if any use of stress-management techniques to help them to cope with these stressors. Only 20% engaged in regular physical exercise and, surprisingly, 60% had marginally or poorly balanced diets. Among the most commonly reported health problems were tension headaches, diarrhea or constipation, common colds, backaches, and depression.

Based on the diagnostic data, the hospital administrators and the consultants implemented several organizational improvements. In order to reduce work overload and role ambiguity, positions were analyzed in terms of work distribution, job requirements, and performance standards. This resulted in more balanced workloads across the jobs and in clearer job descriptions. The hospital administrators also began working with wards to define job expectations and to provide ongoing performance feedback. The nurses were given training in how to better organize their workload and time and in how to more effectively seek social support on a continuing basis.

In order to reduce stress caused by organizational changes, hospital administrators spent more time informing and educating the nurses about any forthcoming changes. Top management also held information meetings with senior nurses on a quarterly basis in order to clear up misunderstandings, misinterpretations, and rumours.

While the above changes were aimed at reducing organizational stressors, additional measures were taken to help the individual nurses to identify and cope with stress more effectively. The hospital instituted yearly physical examinations to detect stress-related problems. It also trained nurses to identify stress symptoms and problems both in themselves and their peers. The hospital developed an exercise club and various sports activities and offered weekly yoga classes. It also created a training program combining nutritional awareness with techniques for coping with tension headaches and backaches. Fresh fruit was made available as an alternative to doughnuts at all meetings and training sessions.

Initial reactions to the stress management program were positive, and the hospital currently is assessing the longer-term effects of the intervention. The total cost for the one-year trial period was estimated at $150 000.

Source: Based on a case described in E. F. Huse and T. G. Cummings, *Organizational Development and Change*, 3rd ed. (St. Paul: West Publishing Co., 1985, p. 332. Adapted with permission.

Endnotes

1. R. S. Schuler, "Occupational Health in Organizations: Strategies for Personnel Effectiveness," *Personnel Administrator*, Jan. 1982, pp. 47–56. R. S. Schuler, "Occupational Health in Organizations: A Measure of Personnel Effectiveness," in R. S. Schuler, J. M. McFillen, and D. R. Dalton, (eds.), *Applied Readings in Personnel and Human Resource Management* (St. Paul: West Publishing Company, 1981), pp. 39–53.
2. *At the Centre*, vol. VIII, no. 1, March 1985, p. 7. Canadian Centre for Occupational Health and Safety, Hamilton, Ontario.
3. From a speech by federal labour minister Bill McKnight, February 6, 1985.
4. "Special Report on Alcohol Statistics," Minister of National Health and Welfare Canada and the Minister of Supply and Services Canada, 1981.
5. G. Atherley, "Occupational Health and Safety: Acts, Actors, and Actions," in S. L. Dolan and R. S. Schuler (eds.), Canadian Readings in Personnel and Human Resource Management (St. Paul: West Publishing Co., 1987).
6. Ibid. (cited with permission).
7. Summary is based on D. Robertson, "The Scope of Occupational Health and Safety in Canada," in *Human Resources Management in Canada*, Prentice-Hall Canada Inc., 1984, revised February 1985, pp. 60,038–60,039.
8. For more information on these three components, see G. Atherley, "The Right to Know: Challenge and Opportunity," ("Current Matter—New Ideas"), *Human Resources Management in Canada*, February 1986, pp. 5,470–5,476.
9. *At the Centre* (the official newsletter of the Canadian Centre for Occupational Health and Safety), vol. VIII, no. 2, July 1985, p. 13.
10. G. K. Bryce and P. Manga, "The Effectiveness of Health and Safety Committees," *Relations Industrielles/Industrial Relations*, vol. 40(2), 1985, pp. 257–283.
11. B. Rice, "Can Companies Kill?" *NIOSH*, and other reports and articles from *NIOSH*, such as B. Wilkes and L. Stammerjohn, "Job Demands and Worker Health in Machine-Paced Poultry Inspection," all published by the U.S. Department of Health and Human Services, Cincinnati, OH, May 1981. M. J. Colligan and L. R. Murphy, "Mass Psychogenic Illness in Organizations: An Overview," *Journal of Occupational Psychology*, 52, 1979, pp. 77–90. M. J. Colligan and M. J. Smith, "A Methodological Ap-

proach for Evaluating Outbreaks of Mass Psychogenic Illness in Industry," *Journal of Occupational Medicine, 20,* 1978, pp. 401–402.
12. F. C. Rineford, "A New Look at Occupational Safety," *Personnel Administrator,* Nov. 1977, pp. 29–36.
13. N. A. Ashford, "The Nature and Dimension of Occupational Health and Safety Problems," p. 45. Reprinted with permission from the Aug. 1977 issue of *Personnel Administrator.* Copyright © 1977, The American Society for Personnel Administration, 30 Park Drive, Berea, OH 44017.
14. W. Matthewman, "Title VII and Genetic Testing: Can Your Genes Screen You Out of a Job? *Harvard Law Review, 27,* 1984, pp. 1185–1220.
15. For more information on genetic testing, see J. Olian and T. Snyder, "The Implications of Genetic Testing," *Personnel Administrator, 29,* 1984, pp. 19–27; T. Murray, "Genetic Testing at Work: How Should It Be Used? *Personnel Administrator,* September 1985, pp. 91–102; S. Dolan and B. Bannister, "Emerging Issues in Employment Testing," paper presented at the 4th International Congress in Work Psychology of the French Language, Montreal, May 5, 1986.
16. For a set of references identifying and discussing many of the preferences and interests listed here, see R. S. Schuler "Definition and Conceptualization of Stress in Organizations," *Organizational Behavior and Human Performance, 23,* 1980, pp. 184–215. R. S. Schuler, "An Integrative Transactional Process Model of Stress in Organizations," *Journal of Occupational Behavior, 3,* 1982, pp. 3–19. R. S. Schuler, "Organizational and Occupational Stress and Coping: A Model and Overview," in R. S. Schuler and S. A. Youngblood (eds.), *Readings in Personnel and Human Resource Management,* 2nd ed. (St. Paul: West Publishing, 1984). S. Dolan and D. Balkin, "A Contingency Model of Occupational Stress," *The International Journal of Management,* September 1987.
17. A. B. Shostak, *Blue Collar Stress* (Reading, MA: Addison-Wesley, 1980).
18. For extensive discussion of office space and physical design issues, see R. S. Schuler, L. R. Ritzman, and V. Davis, "Merging Prescriptive and Behavioral Approaches for Office Layout," *Production and Inventory Management Journal, 3,* 1981, pp. 131–142. E. Sundstrom, "Interpersonal Behavior and the Physical Environment," in L. Wrightsman (ed.), *Social Psychology,* 2nd ed. (Monterey, CA: Brooks/Cole, 1977). F. I. Steele, *Physical Settings and Organization Development* (Reading, MA: Addison-Wesley, 1973). D.D. Umstot, C. H. Bell, and T. R. Mitchell, "The Effects of Job Enrichment and Task Goals on Satisfaction and Productivity: Implications for Job Design," *Journal of Applied Psychology, 61,* 1976, pp. 379–394.
19. H. M. Taylor, "Occupational Health Management-by-Objectives," *Personnel,* Jan.–Feb. 1980, pp. 58–64. H. J. Hilaski, "Understanding Statistics on Occupational Illnesses," *Monthly Labor Review,* March 1981, pp. 25–29. B. Hopkins, B. Conard, and D. Duellman, *Behavior Management for Occupational Safety and Health* (U.S. Department of Health, Education and Welfare, 1979).
20. For more information about these measures, see "Injury Frequency and Severity Rates: A Primer," *At the Centre* (the official newsletter of the Canadian Centre for Occupational Health and Safety), vol. VIII, no. 2, July 1985, pp. 10–11.
21. A. Czernek and G. Clark, "Incentives for Safety," *Job Safety and Health,* Oct. 1973, pp. 7–11. D. Hampton, "Contests Have Side Effects, Too," *California Management Review, 12,* 1970, pp. 86–94.
22. H. M. Taylor, "Occupational Health Management-by-Objectives," *Personnel,* Jan.–Feb. 1980, pp. 58–64. For a discussion of counselling on an individual basis, see M. D. Glicken, "Managing a Crisis Intervention Program," *Personnel Journal,* April 1982, pp. 292–296.
23. "Editor to Reader," *Personnel Journal,* July 1981, pp. 514–520.
24. N. E. Falconer and J. P. Hornick, *Attack on Burnout: The Importance of Early Training,* Children's Aid Society of Metropolitan Toronto, 1983.
25. For more information on alternative stress remedies available for PHRM officers, see S. L. Dolan and A. Arsenault, "The Organizational and Individual Consequences of Stress at Work: A New Frontier to Human Resource Administration," in V. V. Veysey and G. A. Hall (eds.), *The New World of Managing Human Resources* (Pasadena, CA: Institute of Technology, 1979), pp. 4.01–4.22.
26. M. T. Matteson and J. M. Ivancevich, "The How, What and Why of Stress Management Training," *Personnel Journal,* Oct. 1982, pp. 768–774. S. E. Jackson and R. S. Schuler, "Preventing Employee Burnout," *Personnel,* March–April 1983, pp. 58–68. R. W. Driver and R. A. Ratliff, "Employers' Perceptions of Benefits Accrued from Physical Fitness Programs," *Personnel Administrator,* Aug. 1982, pp. 21–26. R. Burke, "Stress and Burnout in Organizations: Implications for Personnel and Human Resource Management," in S. L. Dolan and R. S. Schuler (eds.), endnote 5.
27. R. J. Shepard, M. Cox, and P. Corey, "Fitness Program Participation: Its Effect on Worker Performances," *Journal of Occupational Medicine,* 1981, *23,* pp. 359–363. M. Cox, R. J. Shepard, and P. Corey, "Influence of an Employee Fitness Program upon Fitness, Productivity, and Absenteeism," *Ergonomics,* 1981, *24,* pp. 795–806.

28. For more information about two particular individual stress management techniques, see M. Shain, H. Suurvali, and M. Boutilier, *Healthier Workers: Health Promotion and Employee Assistance Programs* (Lexington, MA, and Toronto, Canada: D.C. Heath and Co., 1986).

29. A. Arsenault and S. L. Dolan, "The Role of Personality, Occupation and Organization in Understanding the Relationship between Job Stress, Performance and Absenteeism," *Journal of Occupational Psychology*, 1983, vol. 56(2), pp. 227–240.

CHAPTER 15
Employee Rights

PHRM in the News

Employee Rights
Purposes and Importance of Employee Rights
Relationships of Employee Rights

Legal Considerations in Employee Rights
Employee Rights to Job Security
Employee Rights on the Job

Strategies for Employee Rights
Employer Strategies for Employee Job Security Rights
Employer Strategies for Employee Rights on the Job

Assessing Employee Rights Activities

Summary

Discussion Questions

Case Study

Endnotes

PHRM in the News

Challenge to Laws Requiring Workers to Pay Union Dues

Labor laws that require employees to pay union dues and to join unions against their will are oppressive and unfair, the result of "direct state interference and dictatorship," says a new group sponsored by the right-wing National Citizens Coalition.

The group, called Freedom of Choice, held a news conference yesterday to take on big unions and big government and to announce plans for a court challenge to the labor laws. It has hired lawyer Morris Manning.

The group was formed to attack government laws and is not anti-union, Mr. Manning said before introducing members of the group.

Mr. Manning said he will argue before the Supreme Court of Ontario that forced union membership and forced payment of dues and the use of dues for political purposes infringe on rights guaranteed by the Charter of Rights and Freedoms.

He said the group is challenging what he called compulsory unionism and the breaking of direct dialogue between an individual employee and management, which occurs when a union is certified to represent all employees.

Included in Mr. Manning's argument will be a challenge brought last year by Dolly Foran, the owner of a crane rental company in Hamilton, that any individual has the right to refuse to join a union and pay dues.

(Last year, the Ontario Labour Relations board suggested in a tentative opinion that the Charter does not appear to give an individual a right to reject union membership and payment of union dues. An exemption from paying dues can be granted on religious grounds, but only if the equivalent of the union dues is paid to a charity.)

"We want all the compulsory section (of the Ontario Labour Relations Act) struck down, as long as they recognize that each and every individual has to have the respect and dignity to make up his own mind. The rest of it they can keep," said Mrs. Foran, a member of Freedom of Choice.

Mrs. Foran said she represents about 2,000 owners of small businesses, but her membership list must remain confidential because many employers fear their buildings and machinery might be blown up by militant union people.

She said the group was confident it could raise the more than $500,000 it will cost to fight the labour laws through the courts. "There's no way I could have hired the country's top constitutional lawyer" without substantial support, she said.

Hugh Peacock, the legislative representative for the Ontario Federation of Labour, said in a telephone interview yesterday that Freedom of Choice is engaging in union-busting. "What they're really after is a totally unregulated business environment," he said. "These people are throwbacks to the era of social Darwinism and rugged individualism. What they want is the law of master and servant," he said.

Source: B. Marotte, "Employee Rights," excerpts from *The Globe and Mail*, July 4, 1985, p. 19. Used with permission.

The Right Not to Be Harassed

SASKATOON—A transport company which failed to take action after an employee complained of being sexually harassed by her supervisor has agreed to pay $5,000 in compensation following a settlement conciliated by the Canadian

Human Rights Commission. The employee complained to the president of Kindersley Transport Ltd. that her supervisor had grabbed her breasts while she was working in the computer room. She alleged that no action was taken after she complained and that following her complaint she was awarded a lower annual salary increase than usual. She subsequently resigned. Under the terms of the settlement the company also agreed to implement a written anti-harassment policy and have supervisors and managers attend a half-day CHRC workshop.

Source: Report Bulletin No. 36, *Human Resources Management in Canada,* February 1986, p. 4. © 1986 Prentice-Hall Canada Inc. Used with permission.

No Desk, No Work for Union Official

QUÉBEC—A Québec Justice Department computer analyst charged yesterday that he is being humiliated and harassed because he is an union official.

Jean-Marc Lafrenière, an analyst with the department since 1979, said he was stripped last year of his office, telephone, computer, and work assignments as a result of a dispute over his union activities.

Lafrenière earns about $35,000 a year to do nothing at a desk set up in a Justice Department lunchroom. He is one of about 100 so-called "tablettés"—civil servants with job security who have fallen victim to their superiors' wrath. "I've been put on stand-by," Lafrenière told reporters.

He said having to sit in a lunchroom all day with nothing to do is humiliating and "it's damaging me." He said union activities also are impossible because he cannot be reached by telephone and because employees don't want to discuss problems with him in the open.

The charges came a week after a labor arbitrator ruled Lafrenière's superiors had abused his rights. Labor arbitrator Marcel Morin ruled last Thursday the department violated Lafrenière's rights three times in 1984 by refusing to allow him to attend union functions. Lafrenière is an officer of the union of government professionals, the Syndicat des professionelles et professionels du government du Québec, and administers union business on behalf of 550 members in his section.

Source: J. Robinson, "No Desk, No Work for Union Official," *The Gazette*, Montréal April 15, 1986, p. A5. Used with permission.

These three "PHRM in the News" articles illustrate what is becoming a very prominent issue in PHRM: employee rights. As viewed by some managers, employee rights are seen as a mechanism by which employees can second-guess management's decision. Some managers believe that the currently increasing employee rights are ushering in an age of employee control of the organization. As viewed by unions and many employees, however, employee rights help to ensure that management decisions are made on a sound, justifiable basis and that employees are protected from arbitrary and vindictive actions by management.

Obviously, these views are in sharp contrast. It is unlikely that the differences will be resolved in the near future, and PHRM staff should understand both positions, keep up to date with current legal considerations, and develop strategies for organizations to use in addressing employee rights.

These scenarios also describe three specific employee rights. One is the right to not join a union, the second is the right to work in an environment free of sexual harassment, and the third is the right to pursue union-related activities without being harassed by management.

This chapter follows the conventional method of distinction found in research and practice and discusses employee rights in terms of two major headings: job security and rights on the job. A definition of employee rights and their increasing importance in PHRM is followed by a review of major legislation, court rulings, and some arbitration decisions that have created the present legal climate.

The major issue in job security is the erosion of the traditional doctrine of an arbitrary termination. Significant on-the-job issues involve privacy rights and access to employee records, co-operative acceptance, particularly in regard to various forms of harassment, and notification and assistance concerning a plant or office closing. Employer success in ensuring employee rights in both areas depends on establishing effective organizational communication as well as setting out clear policies for grievances, progressive discipline, privacy, and safe work environment.

Employee Rights

Although much of the current discussion of employee rights addresses the right of employers to "terminate arbitrarily," employee rights cover much more, including the employee's right to a job under almost any conditions, and also the employee's right to fair, just, and respectful treatment while on the job.

Within these two broad areas of employee rights are several more specific issues, including freedom from sexual harassment; the right of plant closing notification; due process treatment in discharge cases; freedom from discriminatory treatment based on gender, marital status, race, religion, or national origin; and the right to have personal records remain confidential. While some of these rights are protected by law or collective bargaining agreements, others are not. This leaves the majority of the non-unionized work force unprotected.

Employee rights are defined here as those rights desired by employees regarding the security of their jobs and the treatment administered by their employer while they are on the job, irrespective of whether or not those rights are currently protected by law or collective bargaining agreements. As these employee rights become recognized by employers, the extent of management rights, the prerogatives that management has in dealing with its workforce, diminishes. Thus, employee rights have significant impact on PHRM activities. Concern for employee rights demands a careful balance between management rights and employee rights.

Purposes and Importance of Employee Rights

The discussion of recruitment and selection in Chapters 4, 5, and 6 focused on the methods of attracting and placing job applicants into organizations; attention now is directed toward the considerations involved in establishing and maintaining relationships with the job applicants who are hired. The previous chapters have stressed the importance of making sure that employees, new and old, are informed about what is expected of them and what opportunities are available in the organization. This chapter stresses issues of fairness in relation to employee-employer relationships. This, after all, is the thrust of employee rights.

Treating employees fairly and with respect is important to organizations. Where there is legal protection of employee rights (e.g., the right to not be discriminated against in employment decisions), violations can result in penalties and fines (see Chapters 4 and 5).

The violation of employee rights that do not have explicit statutory protection is also becoming costly to organizations. That is, rights for which no Acts or collective agreements have been put in place. Such is the case of the protection given by the courts and arbitrators against wrongful dismissal. For example, a complainant's dismissal was ruled unjust when she was dismissed on the grounds of unsatisfactory job performance. The adjudicator decided that the complainant's 12 years of service with the employer should be recognized and that the company should pay her severance in recognition of her long service—eight months' pay rather than the seven weeks' pay she had received.[1]

In another example, the Supreme Court of Ontario ruled that a car dealership must pay a former employee $93,940 plus 15% interest from the time of the dismissal, for his "callous summary dismissal." Robert Eyers took a holiday from his position as general sales manager for City Buick Pontiac Cadillac Limited after suffering a heart attack in June 1982. Incorrectly assuming that he was permanently disabled, the company stopped paying Eyers' salary in August while he was still away and without informing him.

On his return, Eyers was pronounced fully recovered and fit for work by his doctors. Shortly after contacting his employer in mid-September, Eyers received what looked like a termination letter. It stated that "due to the economic climate, the position of general sales manager ... no longer exists and will not be created until such time as the economy brightens up."

During the trial, the company professed concern about Eyers's health and his fitness to cope with a more stressful position. Supreme Court Justice Joseph Potts deemed the health concern a "smokescreen." Potts asked, "What is the difference between telling a person 'you're fired' ... a senior man in the company ... and telling him 'the job you had before is no longer there'?"

Eyers was an eight-year employee earning $40 000 per year plus fringe benefits and bonus. He was offered a position as Cadillac sales manager at a salary of $14 000, which the judge ruled he should not have been required to accept to mitigate his damages. "He would likely have been fired from his new position," said Potts.

Under normal circumstances, appropriate notice for an eight-year employee is one year, said Potts, but because of the lack of courtesy with which Eyers was treated and the fact that he was not even informed when he was taken off the payroll, Potts ruled that the period of notice for which Eyers should be compensated was 17 months, effective August 1, 1982.[2]

Relationships of Employee Rights

As shown in Exhibit 15.1, employee rights are related extensively to other PHRM activities, such as recruitment and selection. The relationships shown in Exhibit 15.1 are some of the most important.

Union-Management Relations. Where unions exist, employee job security rights generally are protected by the union-management contract. However, because only about one-third of the labour force is unionized, many employees are left without this protection. If job security becomes a major issue, it may stimulate union organizing activity, as is suggested in Chapter 16.

Relationships and Aspects of Employee Rights — *Exhibit 15.1*

```
Union-management         Legal
relations                considerations

Training and
development
                         Employee rights to
                         job security:
                         • Justifiable dismissals      Purposes
Staffing                 • Unjustifiable              • Reduced legal
• Recruitment              dismissals                   costs
• Selection                                           • Retain
                                                        employees
                         Employee rights on          • Attract
Appraising               the job                       employees
performance              • Privacy
                         • Cooperative
                           acceptance
                         • Closing notification
```

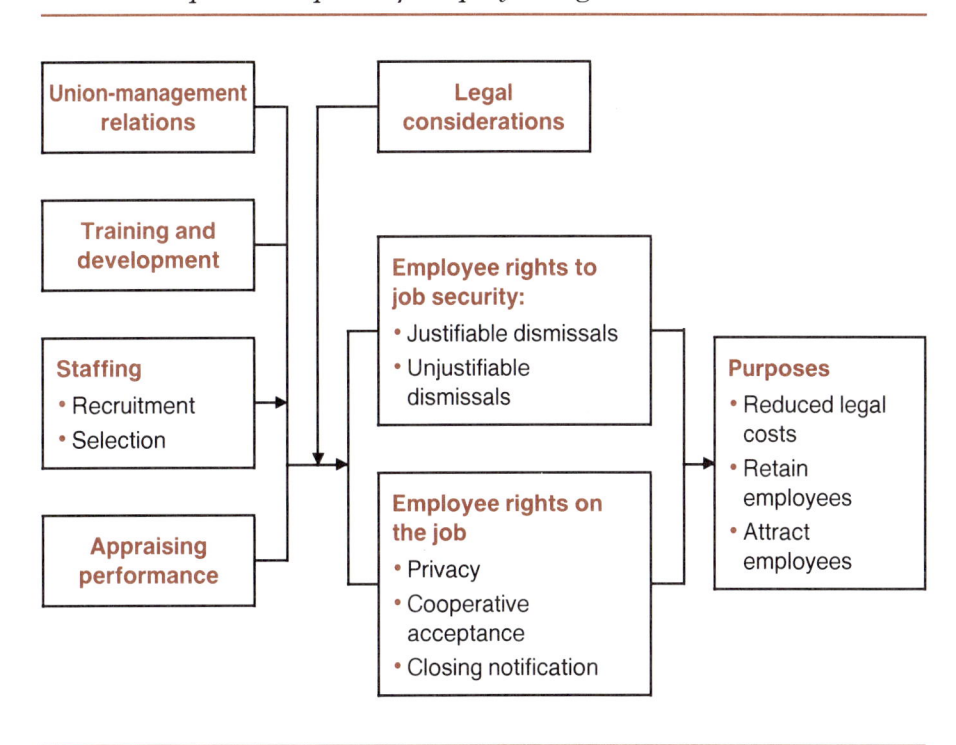

Training and Development. Supervisors are more likely to dismiss employees unjustifiably and commit sexual harassment offences if they have not received effective training on these issues. Consequently, a frequently suggested approach to the issue of sexual harassment is to develop an organizational policy and an educational program for all supervisors and managers to help them to avoid comitting such offences.[3]

Appraising Performance. Supervisors often use poor employee performance as grounds for dismissal. When asked by the court to show evidence in these cases, however, supervisors and PHRM managers often are unable to produce it. Often, records of employee performance are either not accurately maintained or are inaccurately used. Sometimes employees are not informed when they are performing inadequately, nor are they given a chance to respond to charges of poor performance or given an opportunity to improve (lack of due process). Because employees are winning "unjustifiable dismissal" suits, organizations probably will intensify efforts to train supervisors and managers to conduct valid appraisals, to maintain accurate PHRM records, and to establish grievance procedures that ensure due process.

In discussing these relationships and in describing the purposes and importance of employee rights, legal considerations must be included.

Legal Considerations in Employee Rights

Employee rights entail a web of legal considerations, so this section is much larger than in previous chapters. After discussing the legal issues surrounding employee rights, PHRM strategies that can facilitate employer recognition of these rights are discussed.

Employee Rights to Job Security

If neither collective agreement nor a specific statute governs an employee dismissal, the common law rules of the master and servant relationship apply. Such is the case in the majority of dismissals in Canada,[4] but each termination is judged according to the common law of each province.

In Canada, the definition of "cause for dismissal" has changed significantly over time. In the past, terminating employees for reasons such as misconduct, negligence, and disobedience was done almost automatically, but now the employee's behaviour must constitute a serious breach of contractual obligations to merit such action. The Canadian employment situation, through common law precedents, has tended to become a "lifetime" contract. Most employees are hired under an implied contract; others, generally those in management, have written contracts. Implied contracts usually have no established time frames. In many cases of wrongful dismissal, the employee has claimed that employment under this "implied contract" was terminated without "just cause." Since employment is considered a contract; termination without cause is considered a breach of that contract. A small mistake in the performance of the job, for instance, does not justify summary dismissal, since the courts consider employees fallible human beings. The fault or misconduct must amount to a repudiation of the employment contract.[5]

In addition, Canadian jurisdictions prohibit dismissal on certain specific grounds. For example, dismissal for union activity is unlawful in all of the provinces as well as in the federal government. Dismissal for reasons such as pregnancy and wage garnishment have been the object of a statutory ban in several provinces. According to one expert, however, these legislative interventions do not provide a higher degree of job security to non-unionized workers, because of their limited scope.[6]

Just Cause for Dismissal. Cause for dismissal under common Law includes any act by the employee that could have serious negative effects on the operation, reputation, or management of the firm. This could include, for example, fraud, drunkenness, dishonesty, forgery, insubordination, continual absenteeism, or refusal to obey reasonable orders. The onus for proving the existence of just cause is on the employer.

In any case, the protection offered to employees under Canadian common law remains very limited for a number of reasons, including (1) provided that lawful notice is given of the intent, an employer can dismiss an employee without cause; the majority of the Canadian workforce receives only the statutory period of notice (one or two months); and (2) the remedies for dismissed workers under common law are very limited. For instance, the dismissed person can obtain damages that amount to only the wages that would have been earned during the notice period. Reinstatement is not provided under common law, except in very special cases.[7] Also, traditionally, the employer does not have to respect the requirements of "fair dismissal", and is not obliged to communicate to the employee the reasons for discharge nor to provide the employee with an opportunity to explain his or her actions.[8]

Statutory Protection Against Wrongful Dismissal. To date, three Canadian jurisdictions have enacted general statutes to protect employees against wrongful dismissal: Nova Scotia, Québec, and the federal government.

Nova Scotia was the first to draft legislation that provides all employees with protection against unjust dismissal. Under such legislation, an employee can appeal to the Director of Labour Standards, who attempts first to conciliate. If agreement is not reached, the Director has the authority to issue a decision that is binding, unless either side appeals to the Labour Standards Tribunal. The Director may require the reinstatement of the employee. Protection under this Act, however, is available only for employees with at least 10 years of service with the same employer.

Section 61.5 of the Canadian Labour Code covers federal employees who are not part of any collective agreement, and who have completed 12 months of continuous employment. When an employee files a complaint for unjust dismissal with Labour Canada, an inspector will attempt to settle the problem. The Minister of Labour may appoint an adjudicator, who will determine whether the complainant was wrongfully dismissed. Extensive remedial powers are given to the adjudicator, including the authority to reinstate the complainant in the former job.

In 1979 Québec enacted *The Act Respecting Labour Standards*. Similar to the previously mentioned provisions, it enables employees with five years of uninterrupted service with the same employer to engage an arbitrator appointed by the Commission of Labour Standards. This arbitrator also has extensive remedial powers.

Constructive Dismissal and Reasonable Notice. Once an employee is hired, neither party can unilaterally change the terms of the hiring contract, unless both willingly agree. If, as a result of a change in employment status, the employee resigns, this may be considered constructive dismissal. Examples of changes in employment status that could lead to constructive dismissal include

- a change in job function;
- a reduction in salary or benefits;
- a change in reporting relationships;
- a demotion; and
- reassignment to a new job or location.

If there is no cause, an employee can be terminated as long as the employer gives reasonable notice. Apart from the statutory minimum notice periods, no time frames for reasonable notice have been established by law. Over the years, reasonable notice has been decided by judges on the basis of individual cases. It would appear, however, that the courts take the following factors into consideration:

- Length of service
- Age of employee
- Availability of similar employment
- Experience and training
- Level of responsibility
- Degree of specialization
- Method of recruitment [9]

Damages. When an employer terminates an individual's employment, it is understood that either reasonable notice will be given or an amount equal to the employee's salary for the notice period will be paid. Should the employee sue for more compensation and win, this amount is considered damages. However, to be entitled to damages, the employee must have suffered a loss (of income, for example). In awarding damages, the courts apparently are also considering such things as benefits and commissions, but only those to which the employee would have been entitled during the notice period. Bonuses might also be considered if the employee's bonus formed part of the total compensation. Other awards for damages have included moving expenses incurred in accepting a new job in a new location, reasonable telephone charges, and professional dues.

Since the late seventies, judges have been awarding damages for "mental distress or suffering" in many cases. Mental distress can result from factors that range anywhere from the manner in which the termination was handled, the suddenness of the termination, loss of reputation, seniority, or status. A classic example of this is the case of Pilon v. Peugeot of Canada.

Pilon, after 17 years with Peugeot, was summarily dismissed. He obtained another position within days, but he became physically ill. He sued his former company. The judge, in assessing the merits of the case, found that Peugeot did not live up to the implied contract. Pilon was awarded $7 500 for mental distress brought on by the nature and suddenness of termination.

Job Security Under Collective Agreement. The greatest achievement of many collective bargaining agreements in Canada regarding job security has been the removal of management authority to terminate any employee without cause and/or due notice. Moreover, job security is enhanced under the collective agreement by regulation of the two specific situations under which employees could be terminated: job redundancy and employee failure to meet obligations. Under the management-rights provisions of most collective agreements, an employer may reduce the workforce due to automation and/or other causes of job redundancies, but must respect criteria set by the collective agreement as to which employees are laid off.

In addition, although the employer can dismiss an unsatisfactory employee, nearly all collective agreements state that the employer can do it only with just cause. Disputes arising from the application of collective agreements usually are referred to grievance arbitration for adjudication. The expression "just cause" is left purposely vague and provides the arbitrator high flexibility in his or her judgements. Despite this flexibility, the general trend that emerges points to the fair treatment of employees at all times.

Employee Rights on the Job

Employee rights on the job include privacy of and access to employment records, co-operative acceptance, freedom from sexual harassment, the right to a safe environment, and special plant-closing arrangements.

Rights to Privacy of and Access to Government Records. Since the early 1980s 1980s when Bill C–43 was introduced, Canadians have had the right of public access to government records and are protected by privacy clauses that represent a refinement of Part IV of the Canadian Human Rights Act, which enables the court to examine any government record to determine whether to order that it be produced in litigation proceedings.

The Access of Information Act contained in Bill C–43 adopts the main structural features of the American Freedom of Information Act. The central principle of the act is that the public is entitled to obtain government records, unless they are specified as exempt. Further, the bill provides for judicial review of governmental decisions to deny access to particular records.[10] The major departure from the philosophy of disclosure that is central to the Freedom of Information Act is the exemption relating to personal information. Section 19 of Bill C–43 prohibits disclosure of "any record" that "contains personal information" unless the individual in question has consented to the disclosure or unless the information is "publicly available."

Rights to Co-operative Acceptance. Co-operative acceptance refers to the right of employees to be treated fairly and with respect regardless of race, gender, national origin, physical disability, age, or religion, while on the job, as well as in obtaining a job and maintaining job security. Not only does this mean that employees have the right to not be discriminated against in employment practices and decisions, but also it means that employees have the right to be free of any type of harassment, including sexual.

All provincial legislatures and the federal government prohibit discrimination in employment on the basis of gender. Yet sexual harassment has become a serious and growing problem in the workplace. Several Human Rights Commissions report a continuing increase in the number of complaints in the sexual harassment area. In Ontario, for example, the number of complaints rose from 35 to 122 between 1978 and 1983.[11] In British Columbia and Saskatchewan, about one-quarter of all employment discrimination complaints in 1983 and 1984 pertained to sexual harassment.[12]

Recent amendments to the Canada Labour Code (effective from March 1, 1985), have made it mandatory for employers under federal jurisdiction to develop and issue sexual harassment policies, and to provide a redress mechanism for the victims of sexual harassment.

Employer responsibility in the case of sexual harassment has been illustrated clearly by the results of several court cases. For example, in Kotyk v. Employment and Immigration Canada (1983), the tribunal found that the manager of a Canada Employment Centre had made unwanted sexual advances toward two complainants who were his subordinates. In addition to finding the manager liable for sexual harassment, the tribunal also found his employer liable because of a lack of a policy regarding sexual harassment and lack of clear instructions to their supervisory personnel regarding such matters.

A recent case in Saskatchewan echoes on a provincial level this concept of employer responsibility. Chief commissioner of the Saskatchewan Human Rights Commission, Ron Kzuzewiski, commented that "It is the employer's responsibility to ensure a non-discriminatory environment," and warned that those "who try to ignore sexual harassment in the workplace will be responsible for the discriminatory results."[13]

Rights to a Safe and Healthy Environment. As discussed in Chapter 14, health and safety issues at work are becoming a growing concern in

Canada. The various federal and provincial laws require explicit labelling of hazardous materials and warning signs in areas where these are used or stored. Some provinces have invoked legislation that enables workers to refuse dangerous work.

A marked emphasis on the right to a pollution-free environment also is spreading among Canadian firms. Some companies have taken proactive measures against substances in the work environment that until recently were not considered to be critical. For example, Boeing Canada has imposed a ban on smoking on the job. Other organizations also are attempting to reduce the stress induced by unhealthy socio-psychological conditions in the work environment.

Plant-Closing Arrangements. The federal and some provincial governments have shown their concern for terminated employees by passing legislation that requires employers to establish committees to assist those employees affected by staff reduction. The committees consist of employee and management representatives and an independent chairman. Their role is to assist employees affected by large-scale terminations to find other employment. In addition, the various governments have special branches designed specifically to assist employers and employees affected by a group reduction.

On the federal level, there is the Industrial Adjustment Service, which is a branch of the Employment and Immigration Canada Commission. It acts as a catalyst to bring employers and workers together to discuss changes in the workplace, to formulate adjustment measures to alleviate the problems that change can bring, and to monitor and evaluate the implementation of plans developed.

The Service offers technical advice, guidance, and financial incentives wherever there is a technological or economic problem affecting workers. Several reasons for layoffs may be identified, and the efforts and recommendations of the service are tailored to the specific situation. Causes of layoffs include plant expansion, contraction, closure, relocation, technological change, industrial slowdown, manpower planning, or labour instability.

Employment and Immigration Canada, through the Industrial Adjustment Service, may provide financial incentives to assist in the implementation of the negotiated agreements. The federal contribution is usually 50% of the cost, the balance being the responsibility of the company.

A committee is formed, made up of members from the company, the union (or a representative of the employees), and an impartial chairman, supported by a representative of the provincial Ministry of Labour and an Industrial Adjustment Service consultant.

While there may be industrial relations implications in the consultant process (for example, the recognition of seniority and transfer provisions in the collective agreement), the Industrial Adjustment Service is not intended to carry out any industrial relations functions that may interfere with the normal collective bargaining process. The Service will terminate all discussions with management and labour when a dispute is in progress or when bargaining is taking place.[14]

The Ontario government established its Plant Closure Review and Employment Adjustment Branch in 1980 to support the government's initiative on layoffs and plant closures. This branch's mandate is

- to become aware of any announced or impending plant closures or major reduction of operations as early as possible;
- to make contact with companies considering closure and also with the employee representatives or unions, as required;
- to obtain information about the closures and advise the government on the possibility of maintaining the operation;
- where the closure is unavoidable, to attempt to resolve any disagreements concerning termination rights and benefits and recommend the mediation services of the Ministry of Labour, as required; and
- to co-ordinate the involvement of the ministries of Colleges and Universities, Intergovernmental Affairs, Industry and Trade, and Community and Social Services, on a particular closure situation. This ensures that available Ontario government programs are focused effectively on the needs of those affected by the closure.

The provincial branch works closely with the Industrial Adjustments Service. The Ministry of Labour is a financial contributor to manpower adjustment committees in layoff situations.

A program involving both group and individual employee counselling sessions is available in large closure situations, involving 50 or more employees. The program is funded by the Ontario Ministry of Labour, offered at local community colleges, and co-ordinated through the provincial Ministry of Colleges and Universities.

Strategies for Employee Rights

Because of several legal and humane considerations, it is important that organizations develop and implement strategies for recognizing employee rights. Effectively implementing other PHRM activities discussed in this book is one general way to help to ensure that many of the legally sanctioned employee rights are recognized. In addition, organizations can implement specific programs, including employee privacy policies, employee assistance programs, outplacement activities, and sexual harassment prevention training.

Employer Strategies for Employee Job Security Rights

In addition to adhering to the applicable job security laws, employers should ensure fair and legal termination by communicating expectations and prohibitions, establishing grievance procedures and due process, and following progressive discipline procedures.

Communicate Expectations and Prohibitions. Although ignorance of rules is generally no excuse in society at large, it does apply in employment settings. Generally, employees may be disciplined only for conduct that is not in accordance with what they know or reasonably understand is prohibited or required. Employers must ensure that performance expectations are conveyed to employees, along with information about what is prohibited. Employers can do this by issuing written policy statements, job descriptions, and performance criteria. Written standards also should exist for promotions.

Treat Employees Equally. If the employer discharges one employee for five unexcused absences, then other employees who have had five unexcused absences also must be discharged. Periodic training for supervisors can help to ensure that such policies are communicated and administered consistently by all supervisors.

Grievance Procedures and Due Process. Not only should grievance procedures be established to ensure due process for employees, they should also be administered consistently and fairly.[15] For example, evidence should be available to employee and employer, and both parties should have the right to call witnesses and refuse to testify against themselves. Furthermore, these grievance procedures should be set out clearly as company policy and communicated as such to employees. The contents of a typical grievance policy are shown in Exhibit 15.2.

Establish Progressive Disciplinary Procedures. A formal grievance policy should be accompanied by a progressive disciplinary policy. For most violations of company rules, firing should be the last step in a carefully regulated system of escalating discipline, often called **progressive discipline**. Maintaining accurate records during all phases of this process is crucial for building a valid justifiable cause for disciplinary discharge. As discussed in Chapter 8, the steps possible in progressive disciplinary procedures include the following:

- *Warning* may be oral at first, but should be written, signed by the employee, and a copy kept in the personnel files. Valid personnel files, along with a progressive discipline policy for discharge can be the best defence according to several court cases that dealt with discharge for excessive absenteeism (see, for example, Henry v. Unique Envelope Inc., 1985, Ontario).
- *Reprimand* is official, in writing, and placed in the employee's file.
- *Suspension* can be for as short a time as part of a day, or for as long as several months without pay, depending on the seriousness of the employee's offence and the circumstances.
- *Disciplinary transfer* may take the pressure off a situation that might explode into violence, or one in which personality conflict is a part of the disciplinary problem.
- *Demotion* can be a reasonable answer to problems of incompetence, or an alternative to layoff for economic reasons.

484   *Maintaining Effective Industrial Relations*

Exhibit 15.2   A Typical Grievance Procedure

With good working relations it is to be expected that supervisory personnel and department heads will recognize and work to resolve employee problems and dissatisfactions at their first appearance and, therefore, that this appeal procedure should have limited usage.

Step 1: Discuss the problem or dissatisfaction with your supervisor who will attempt to resolve it in accordance with established personnel policies within *two working days,* unless there are extenuating circumstances.

Step 2: Should the problem remain unresolved, your supervisor will endeavor to make an appointment for you to discuss the matter with your department head within the next *three working days.*

Step 3: Should the problem continue to remain unresolved, the employee should present the problem or dissatisfaction in writing (see attached form) and forward it to the director, employee relations, who will either schedule a meeting with all interested parties, or will present a recommendation within *five working days* for a resolution of the problem based upon personnel policies and practices.

Most matters of employee concern should be resolved at the conclusion of Step 3. However, for that unusual problem which may not have been resolved to the employee's satisfaction, the employee may request that the matter be brought to the attention of administration for consideration and decision. An administrative decision will be rendered and communicated in writing to all interested parties within *ten working days.* This decision will be final and binding.

Source: Reprinted by permission of the publisher, from "Consensus: Grievance Procedures for Nonunionized Employees," by Thomasine Rendero, *Personnel,* January–February 1980, p. 7. © 1980 American Management Association, New York. All rights reserved.

- *Discharge* is the last resort, used only when all else has failed, although it might be a reasonable immediate response to violence, theft, or falsification of records. But firing can be exceedingly painful, even if it is justified and well planned. Therefore, some organizations carefully diagnose performance deficiencies prior to termination and occasionally reassign employees to different parts of the organization or trade top-level managers to other organizations.[16]

An optional additional step in progressive discipline is the "last chance agreement." Before resorting to firing, an employer may be willing to grant an employee one more chance, but with several stipulations. For example, instead of suspending or terminating an employee for excessive absenteeism, the employer may grant the employee one final fixed time period in which to improve.

Taking all of these steps does not ensure that the problem will be solved—termination may still be necessary. The following advice may help in performing this difficult task:

- The termination interview should be brief. Normally, a 10–15 minute meeting is sufficient. A longer meeting increases the opportunity for the company representative to make a mistake. Some mistakes can be costly.

- It is best to conduct the termination meeting in that person's office or in some office other than your own. If conducted in your office, you may be trapped into a lengthy harangue by a disgruntled individual who is using you to vent ... hostility, anger, and frustration.
- Many individuals hear very little after they understand they have lost their job. This is understandable. They often begin to think of their future [or] the anxiety and stress of having no job, and there is a strong concern about their family, especially if the individual is the chief wage earner in the family.
- Hence, have a written description of benefits and/or salary continuation, if applicable. Also include how the individual is to be paid.
- It is a good idea to role play with someone before you actually do the termination. It is better yet if you can videotape the role play(s). Practice can help iron out the bugs and the discomfort and make it easier and less cumbersome in the actual termination meeting.[17]

Employer Strategies for Employee Rights on the Job

In order to protect employee rights on the job, employers must develop effective policies, procedures, and programs in regard to privacy of access to records; co-operative acceptance, particularly in regard to sexual harassment; and plant or office closings.

Employee Privacy Rights and Record Access. Concern for the privacy of personnel records and employee access to personnel files has been emphasized only since the early 1980s. As discussed previously, privacy legislation generally does not cover private employer-employee relationships. Nevertheless, many organizations are moving ahead on their own to establish policies and rules governing employee privacy and access rights. Early efforts in this area produced only definitions of employee privacy. Today, however, a significant number of companies have written policies regarding the privacy of personnel records, and provide employees access to records containing information about themselves.

Employer concerns about employee privacy rights also are influencing pre-employment screening and the use of polygraph tests. Pre-hire practices are being examined to ensure that only job-related information is collected, because collecting non-job information now is considered an invalid intrusion into the private lives of job applicants. Similar opinions are becoming widespread on the use of polygraph test results (discussed in Chapter 5) in selection and placement decisions.[18]

Employee Rights to Co-operative Acceptance. While many issues are associated with employee rights to co-operative acceptance, sexual harassment has recently become a prominent concern for many employees and employers. Although this aspect is being focused on here, race, age, disability, national origin, and religion also should be considered because these are significant aspects.

What was once regarded as good-natured fun between supervisors or managers and employees may today constitute sexual harassment according to various human rights guidelines. Because employers ultimately are responsible, they need to be particularly concerned with the development of strategies to prevent sexual harassment by their employees. One such strategy includes the following steps: [19]

- Raise affirmatively the issue of harassment, and the fact that it exists, to the rest of the organization. The PHRM manager should persuade top management to make it a rule that all discharges must be reviewed by a senior corporate officer or review board.
- Set up grievance procedures for those who have been harassed. Because the employer is liable for sexual harassment except where it can be shown the organization took immediate and appropriate corrective action, it pays to have an established policy and system in place.
- Establish procedures for corroborating a sexual harassment charge. That is, the PHRM manager should make sure that the person charged with sexual harassment has the right to respond immediately after charges are made by the alleged victim. Due process must be provided to the alleged perpetrator as well as to the alleged victim.
- Specify a set of steps in a framework of progressive discipline for perpetuators of sexual harassment. These could be the same steps used by the organization in treating any violation of organizational policies (see the progressive discipline procedures discussed earlier).
- Finally, make all employees aware of the company's position on sexual harassment. Provide support, such as training programs for managers and supervisors.

Although implementing these steps does not guarantee elimination of sexual harassment, it establishes a clear-cut policy in this important human resources management area.

Employee Rights in Plant/Office Closings. Basically, employers are not legally obligated to notify employees if a facility is to be closed down or relocated. As in cases of discharge without cause, employers resist making this notification immediately because it limits their flexibility. In addition, some employees argue that it really is better for them also if management holds backs such information because this could contribute to the survival of the company.

These arguments, however, are beyond the immediate interest of the employees involved in a potential or actual plant closing. And despite their resistance, employers are recognizing the employees' humane right to assistance when facilities are closed. Therefore, some notify employees well in advance of the actual closing. While recognition of this right has been initiated primarily by the pressure of unions on management, many nonunion companies now are providing help, usually in the form of outplacement assistance.

Outplacement assistance usually is offered to individuals who are discharged or displaced, but it can have more dramatic value for entire work forces displaced because of plant or office closings. Outplacement assistance programs typically offer a number of benefits to employees, including

- severance pay;
- enhanced benefits;
- four-week termination notification period;
- training and development programs to help employees to develop new skills and find other jobs;
- double pay for overtime work needed to get the facility ready to close down; and
- retention bonuses to encourage employees to stay until the time of actual closing.

Assessing Employee Rights Activities

When organizations recognize employee rights and establish programs to ensure that these are observed, they can achieve a match between employee and employer rights and obligations. In achieving this match, both the organizations and the employees benefit. Organizations benefit from reduced legal costs, since not observing certain employee rights is illegal. In addition, an organization's image is enhanced by its readiness to recognize employee rights, making it easier for the organization to recruit good, potentially qualified applicants. And although it is suggested that expanded employee rights, particularly those relating to job security, may reduce needed management flexibility, it may be an impetus for better planning, resulting in increased profitability.

Increased profitability also may result from the benefits that employees receive when their rights are observed: they feel that they are being treated fairly and with respect, and they experience increased self-esteem and a heightened sense of job security. Employees who perceive job security may be more productive and committed to the organization than those who do not, and the organization may benefit through reduced wage increase demands and greater flexibility in job assignments. This is happening in many of the traditionally unionized manufacturing industries where the protection of employee rights, particularly job security, is considered as much a matter of survival as profitability. As discussed in Chapters 16 and 17, it is also a matter of concern for a new era of union-management relations.

An organization's employee rights activities can be assessed in many ways, some of which are more appropriate than others. For example, evaluating employee rights activities by the size of legal costs certainly is appropriate in the areas of co-operative acceptance and unjustifiable dismissal. Where employee rights are not legally protected, using legal costs to assess these activities may be less appropriate. However, if organizations fail to observe those humane rights not now legally protected they soon may find themselves having to use legal costs to evaluate all of their employee rights activities. Many organizations recognize this and are moving to observe humane rights as well as legal rights. This seems particularly true for employee rights to privacy of and access to records, and facility-closing arrangements.

Summary

The area of employee rights is gaining considerable attention in the 1980s. Although employees have won many legal rights over the years, the most controversial rights are those not yet legally protected or those that are left to employers' discretion. Thus, tribunals have a potentially significant role in the future of employee rights. Whether the courts and the legislative and executive bodies move to increase the number of legally protected rights of employees depends to some extent on how employers behave in the area of unprotected employee rights. If they take a proactive position, the courts and the legislative bodies may be less inclined to legislate both job security and on-the-job employee rights. At this time, a great deal of momentum has already gathered to provide some type of legal protection for job security rights. PHRM managers and employers still can have an impact in shaping the form of such legal protection.

Although many employers claim that many of their rights have been taken away, they still retain the right to terminate workers for poor performance, excessive absenteeism, unsafe conduct, and generally poor organizational citizenship. It is critical, however, for employers to maintain accurate records of these employee actions, and to inform the employees where they stand. To be safe, it is also advisable for employers to provide a grievance process for employees, to ensure that due process is respected.

Today it is more important than ever to keep objective and complete personnel files, as evidence that employers have treated their employees fairly and with respect and have not violated any laws. Without these, organizations may get caught on the short end of a law suit. Many employers are taking the initiative by giving their employees the right to access their personnel files and prohibiting disclosure of the file information to others without consent. In addition, employers are omitting from their personnel files any non-job-related information and avoiding hiring practices that solicit that type of information.

Although employers have the right to close down a facility without any notification, many employers are notifying their employees in advance of such closings, even in non-union companies. In addition to giving notification, some employers are implementing outplacement assistance programs that offer employees retraining for new jobs, counselling and aid in finding new jobs or in getting transfers, provisions for severance pay, and even retention bonuses for those who stay until closing time. Closing a facility with notification and with outplacement assistance seems to produce positive results for the organization and minimize the negative effects for the employees.

Finally, in the area of employee rights to co-operative acceptance, it is particularly important for employers to prevent sexual harassment. This can be done with top-management support, grievance procedures, verification procedures, training for all employees, and performance appraisal and compensation policies that reward those who practice anti-harassment behaviour and punish those who do not. Where appropriate, it also is useful to develop such policies in co-operation with the union. Union co-operation should be sought on many issues, as is discussed in the next two chapters.

Discussion Questions

1. What is the strategic importance to the organization of protecting employee rights?
2. Discuss some legal protections now offered employees, resulting from federal Acts and court/tribunal decisions.
3. On what grounds can employees be legally discharged?
4. Identify and discuss the laws that have an impact on employee rights to privacy of and access to employee records.
5. What is the bottom line in protection offered to employees concerning plant closings or relocation?
6. What strategies exist for employers to ensure employee job security rights?
7. Outline and discuss what is meant by a progressive disciplinary procedure.
8. Under what conditions can an employer be held legally responsible for sexual harassment of its employees?

CASE STUDY

What's Wrong with What's Right?

Stuart Campbell, 35, moved slowly down the steps of the courthouse and squinted into the last rays of sunlight that pierced through downtown Winnipeg. It had been a long day for Stuart, who had been forced to relive two tortuous years of his past in front of the Manitoba Superior Court.

Stuart had spent the day recalling for the court the details of his former employment as a regional sales representative for Nako Electronics, a major marketer of audiotapes in Canada. Nako Electronics had and still has a considerable stake in Stuart Campbell. Today, both sides had made concluding arguments before the court in a trial initiated by Nako Electronics to overturn a private arbitrator's rule that Nako had wrongfully terminated Stuart. The arbitrator's decision and the award to Stuart of $500 000 plus interest of $82 083.50 was a bitter pill for Nako to swallow.

Stuart hesitated for a moment at the foot of the steps and came back to the present; he had agreed to meet his attorney at a nearby restaurant. His spirits began to pick up as he manoeuvred through the city traffic, but he couldn't help thinking how, in just a year, his good job had gone bad.

Five years previously, Stuart Campbell had been riding high as the regional representative for Nako for all of western Canada. Stuart, a hard worker, had boosted the sluggish sales of Nako audiotapes from less than $200 000 to $1 million in only 14 months. In fact, business was going so well that Stuart had bought himself a Mercedes-Benz 450 SEL. That's when Mike Hammond, Nako's vice-president of marketing, took notice of Stuart.

On one of his visits to Stuart's territory, Mike commented to Stuart that he really liked the Mercedes but he'd settle for a Buick when he visited Vancouver in the near future.

Stuart testified, "He said he didn't want anything as fancy as I had, that a new Buick would be adequate and I could pay for it!"

Mike unfortunately couldn't be in court to defend himself—he had died unexpectedly the previous year of a heart attack. However, during the trial, Nako Electronics had to answer to a number of allegations made against Mike Hammond. It seemed that some of Stuart's fellow workers had suffered similar fates.

In addition to turning down the car proposition, Stuart had refused to invest in a phonograph cartridge business started by Mike, believing it to be (forgive the pun) phoney. In fact, Mike had approached all of the Nako sales representatives to invest in the cartridge company at $1250 a share, while Mike and two other associates had paid only $1 a share for 80% of the company's stock. Stuart's attorney, Anne Blasco, had made sure that two of Stuart's former fellow sales representatives testified at the court proceedings that they were mysteriously fired after refusing to invest in Mike's company.

In the year following Stuart's successful boosting of sales of Nako audiotapes and Mike's thwarted shakedown attempts, Nako increased Stuart's sales quota by more than 75% and, Stuart alleged, Nako sabotaged a substantial proportion of his sales by refusing to give his major customers promotional assistance. In the fall of that year, Nako fired Stuart without explanation.

Nako argued in court that the company didn't need a reason to fire Stuart, and besides, he wasn't meeting his increased sales quota. Moreover, the company argued, Mike could not very well defend himself against the charges of Stuart and the others.

Stuart rehashed these details many times with his attorney both during the private arbitration hearing and during numerous rehearsals for the trial. He hoped he finally would be able to put these memories behind him.

At the restuarant, Anne summarized the day's court proceedings and expressed cautious optimism about the final outcome. "But you know, Stuart," mused Anne, "if you had kicked in the 10 or 15K that Mike demanded for the shares, you'd have a business worth more than $4 million in sales today, and you wouldn't have had to go through all this agony."

Endnotes

1. Clarke Transport Canada Inc. and L. L. Desrosiers (secretary), cited in *Arbitration Service Reporter*, March 1986, vol. 10(3), pp. 2–3.
2. "Report on the Law," *Report Bulletin No. 24*, February 1985, p. 3. Prentice Hall Canada Inc., 1985.
3. See, for example, H. C. Jain, "Sexual Harassment: Issues and Policies," *Research Working Paper No. 239*, July 1985. Faculty of Business, McMaster University, Hamilton, Ontario.
4. G. Trudeau, "Employee Rights vs. Management Rights: Some Reflections Regarding Dismissal," in S. L. Dolan and R. S. Schuler (eds.), Canadian Readings in Personnel and Human Resource Management (St. Paul: West Publishing Co., 1987). Used with permission.
5. G. England, "Recent Developments in Wrongful Dismissal Laws and Some Pointers for Reform," *Alberta Law Review*, 1978 (16), pp. 470–520.
6. Trudeau, endnote 4.
7. D. Harris, *Wrongful Dismissal* (Toronto: Richard DeBoo Publishers, 1984).
8. These three reasons are elaborated on in Trudeau, endnote 4.
9. K. Bullock, "Termination of Employment," in *Human Resources Management in Canada*, Prentice-Hall Canada Inc., revised, August 1985, pp. 75,023–75,024.
10. J. D. McCamus, "Bill C–43: The Federal Canadian Proposals of the 1980s, in J. D. McCamus (ed.), *Freedom of Information: Canadian Perspectives* (Toronto:

Butterworths, 1981), pp. 266–305.
11. H. Jain, "Sexual Harassment: Issues and Policies," *Research and Working Paper Series No. 239*, July 1985. Faculty of Business, McMaster University.
12. Ibid., p. 1.
13. "Report Bulletin No. 37," *Human Resources Management in Canada*, March 1986, p. 4. Prentice-Hall Canada Inc.
14. For more information on plant closures and comparison with the U.S. system, see W. L. Batt, Jr., "Canada's Good Example with Displaced Workers," *Harvard Business Review*, July–August, 1983, pp. 6–22.
15. T. Rendero, "Grievance Procedures for Nonunionized Employees," *Personnel*, January–February 1980, pp. 4–10.
16. For cases involving wrongful dismissal decisions based on badly documented performance records, see Anderson v. Pirelli (1984), Ontario; Birman v. Four Twenty Seven Investments, Ltd. (1985), Ontario.
17. L. D. Foxman and W. L. Polsky, "Ground Rules for Terminating Workers," *Personnel Journal*, July 1984, p. 32. See also, Bullock, endnote 9.
18. S. L. Dolan and B. Bannister, "Emerging Issues in Employment Testing," paper presented at the 4th Congrès International de Psychologie du Travail de Langue Française (proceedings in press), Montréal, May 5–7, 1986.
19. G. E. Biles, "A Program Guide for Preventing Sexual Harassment in the Workplace," *Personnel Administration*, June 1981, pp. 49–56. Jain, endnote 11, pp. 13–14.

CHAPTER 16
Unionization

PHRM in the News

Unionization of Employees
Purposes and Importance of Unionization
Relationships of PHRM and Unionization

Legal Considerations in the Unionization of Employees
The Early Days
Labour Relations Legislation Today

The Attraction of Unionization
The Decision to Join a Union
The Decision Not to Join a Union

The Development and State of Unionization
The Early Days
Today
Structure and Function of Unions in Canada

The Organizing Campaign
The Campaign to Solicit Employee Support
Determination of the Bargaining Unit

Assessing the Unionization of Employees

Summary

Discussion Questions

Case Study

Endnotes

PHRM in the News

Decline of Organized Labor

Public opinion polls in Canada show declining support for organized labor, despite the fact that almost 40 per cent of Canadian workers belong to a union. The most recent Gallup poll, published in December, found that 35 per cent of Canadians were hostile to the union movement. And the *Maclean's*/Decima Poll, published in January, showed that only 10 per cent of those surveyed thought that unions safeguarded their economic interests. Said Harvard University labor law specialist Paul Weiler, a former professor at Toronto's York University: "The unions have fallen into disfavor because of strikes in the public sector and because some people believe they have too much influence on public policy during elections."

Dispute

Increasingly, the public has made its dislike of strikes evident—especially when they cause inconvenience. Contract talks have broken down between the 23,000-member Canadian Union of Postal Workers and Canada Post Corp. after eight months of negotiations, much of which involved job-security demands. CUPW's 1981 strike interrupted Canadian mail service for six weeks. Roughly 3,500 Ontario brewery workers were threatening to strike Molson Ontario Breweries Ltd., Labatt's Ontario Breweries Ltd., and Carling O'Keefe Breweries Canada Ltd. in a dispute over the companies' introduction of aluminum cans. The Brewery Malt and Soft Drink Workers union contends that the cans will ultimately lead to fewer jobs.

At least one strike in progress has profound significance for the Canadian labor movement's future. National attention has focused on a three-month-old strike by 1,500 recently organized members of the Retail, Wholesale and Department Store Union (RWDSU), employed by six southern Ontario outlets of the privately owned T. Eaton Co. The strikers are demanding a first contract from the huge retailer, which has 35,000 employees across the country. According to some labor specialists, the Eaton's strike is a litmus test of organized labor's prospects for signing up white-collar workers in Canada's service sector, including banks, the booming computer industry and even fast-food operations. Instead, the service industries in the private sector, where most new jobs are expected to emerge, are labor's last frontier in the march to expand union membership. Said textile union director Clark: "If this Eaton's strike is ever busted, it will be a long and frosty year before another group of retail people will ever sign a union contract."

Aware of the implications, the labor movement has rallied to support the strikers. The 800,000-member Ontario Federation of Labour has begun an advertising campaign directed at the general public urging a shoppers' boycott and setting out labor's side of the dispute. The stores have continued to do business as usual and show no sign of giving in to the unionized workers' demands. But Robert McKay, the union's chief negotiator, said the public is sympathetic to the strikers, and added, "We have letters by the thousands from consumers." According to Charles Ireton, business agent for Local 204 of 65,000-strong Service Employees International Union, which represents hospital, nursing home and cemetery workers, "The Eaton strike is a fight we fought in the 1930s and 1940s—a fight for basic rights."

Power

At least some analysts said that business has become increasingly intransigent toward organized labor, partly because of leaner operations arising from the 1981–82 recession and partly because the seemingly intractable unemployment crisis has made individuals more concerned with personal job security than with collective rights. According to Harry Glasbeek, a labor law professor at York University, unions are losing their struggle with business for economic power. Said Glasbeek: "Business is telling labor, 'Unless you give us the conditions we want, we will invest our money in Taiwan.' Business is using its economic power for political ends in a way that labor cannot do."

Source: Excerpts from R. Miller, "Big Labor's Weakening Grip," *Maclean's* Magazine, March 4, 1985, pp. 38–40. Reprinted with permission.

Canadian UAW: Leadership, Crisis, and Critical Decisions

The setting was more suitable to black tie than blue collar, and the hotel menus tended toward haute cuisine rather than the meat and potatoes supposedly preferred by organized labor. But the luxurious Sheraton Bal Harbour resort near North Miami, Fla., where a two-room suite costs as much as $410 (U.S.) a night, played host last week to the high priests of North America's troubled unions. The executive council of the American Federation of Labor–Congress of Industrial Organizations (AFL–CIO)—each of the council's 35 members is a powerful union boss in his own right—gathered in an opulent conclave to ponder labor's uncertain future in a job-short, high-technology world. Among the painful subjects on the AFL–CIO agenda were problems increasingly familiar to Canadian union leaders: organized labor's declining political influence and its failure to make a major breakthrough in recruiting white-collar workers outside the public sector.

Divorce

For AFL–CIO council member Owen Bieber, president of the 1.3-million-member United Auto Workers union, the Florida meetings were doubly difficult. No easy solutions emerged during the private sessions. And Canadian UAW director Robert White, 49, was in Bal Harbour to begin the delicate negotiations expected to lead to an autonomous union for Canadian UAW workers by next fall. White, Bieber and two other American UAW executives—secretary-treasurer Raymond Majerus and board member Joseph Tomasi—spent five hours Wednesday discussing a property settlement in the impending White-inspired divorce of roughly 120,000 Canadian UAW members from their American colleagues. Among assets to be divided: the UAW strike fund, which totals almost $800 million (Cdn.), and such union-owned real estate as its modern two-storey national headquarters building in suburban Toronto.

White proposed the controversial divorce, after nearly 50 years of marriage, on Dec. 10, 1984, and the union's international leadership accepted it in principle on the very same day. Last week's preliminary negotiations were officially described as amicable and a further meeting of the four-man committee was scheduled for March 11 in Detroit. Said White: "There wasn't a lot of animosity but we didn't accomplish anything. It really was an exploratory first meeting."

Leaders of other unions on both sides of the border were keeping a close watch on the UAW developments. Of the 2.6 million Canadians who belong to private sector unions, no fewer than 1.5 million are in so-called international organizations, most of which are dominated by their American members. At least some Canadian labor executives expressed support for the concept of all-Canadian unions. Said Vancouver's Cathy Walker, staff representative of the Canadian Association of Industrial, Mechanical and Allied Workers: "True international solidarity is built between strong national independent unions. Canada is the only country in the world whose unions have been controlled from another country." But Charles Clark, co-director of the Toronto-based Amalgamated Clothing and Textile Workers Union, disagreed. Clark said that he believed the UAW "will be all right." But he added: "It is not the path for all international unions. We have autonomy, yet it is the strength of the Americans and the number of the American-owned companies in this country that make our union as effective as it is."

Oppose

White cited the differences "in political climate" between the United States and Canada as one reason for his willingness to lead his UAW followers out of the American-dominated fold. But, more important, his decision stemmed from a fundamental disagreement between the U.S. and Canadian UAW leadership on bargaining tactics. Canadian UAW executives, including White, emphatically oppose an increasing willingness by the U.S. union to forgo annual wage increases and accept lump-sum increases, a share of future profits and job security guarantees from the automakers instead. White, who left school at the age of 15 and later became a UAW member when he found employment at a Woodstock, Ont., woodworking plant, was unwilling to accept the car makers' argument that they needed wage concessions in order to survive.

Source: Excerpts from R. Miller, "Big Labor's Weakening Grip," *Maclean's* Magazine, March 4, 1985, pp. 38–40. Reprinted by permission.

These two "PHRM in the News" articles highlight important aspects of the unionization of employees. One is the rapid decline of the power of organized labour. Unions, as well as management, are having to fight for the survival of the very industries they organized many years ago. And now, instead of achieving wage gains in those industries, they are having to take wage cuts. In fact, many unions are engaging in active organizing campaigns as membership in traditional industries, such as steel and automobile, decline or, at best, do not grow.

Another issue within the Canadian labour movement is the tension between some international unions and their Canadian components. The most dramatic event was the withdrawal of the Canadian Section of the United Auto Workers Union to form an independent Canadian union in 1985–86. One of the major issues that brought about this split was the unwillingness of the Canadian section to follow the American parent union in giving concessions to employers during the depths of the recession in the early 1980s. An articulate and dynamic Canadian leader, Robert White, also was a contributing factor to that decision. More breakaway movements are anticipated in the future.[1]

This chapter discusses the importance of unionization from the perspective of both employees and employers. It presents the historical context of the union movement in Canada, including the major legislation, court decisions, and other rulings that have influenced the unionization process in both the public and private sectors. Specifically, the conditions that make unions attractive to employees are examined and the steps in a union organizing campaign are outlined. Chapter 17 will describe the collective bargaining process, which involves negotiating an agreement, resolving conflicts, and administering the union contract.

Unionization of Employees

Unionizing or **unionization** is the effort by employees and outside agencies (unions or associations) to band together and act as a single unit when dealing with management over issues related to their work. The most common form into which employees organize is the **union**, an organization with the legal authority to negotiate with the employer on behalf of the employees—over wages, hours, and other conditions of employment—and to administrate the ensuing agreement.

Purposes and Importance of Unionization

To employers, the existence of a union—or even the possibility of one—can exert a significant influence on the ability of the employer to manage its vital human resources. To employees, unions often can help them to get what they want (e.g., higher wages and job security) from the employers.

Importance to Employers. Understanding the unionizing or organizing process, its causes, and its consequences is an important part of personnel and human resource management. Unionization often results in management having less flexibility in hiring, job assignments, and the introduction of new work methods such as automation and inflexible job structures. And, as indicated in Chapter 15, unions obtain for their members rights that employees without unions legally do not have. This, of course, forces organizations with unions to consider their employees' reactions to many more decisions than would be the case otherwise.

In some cases, however, employers who are non-union and want to remain that way give more consideration and provide more benefits to their employees. Consequently, the claim that it is more expensive for a company to operate with unionized rather than non-unionized employees is not always true. Unions also assist employers through wage concessions or co-operation and assistance in workplace joint efforts, such as quality circles, Scanlon plans or safety committees, allowing employers to survive particularly difficult times and, in fact, remain profitable and competitive.

Importance to Employees. Although it has been suggested that unions are attractive because they directly satisfy people's social or affiliation preferences, this function does not appear to be as important as the union's influence in changing the work setting. A survey of workers by the University of Michigan Survey Research Center indicates that workers perceive the union's goals to be related primarily to job context factors. Of all the goals listed, 80.5% were related to wages, benefits, working conditions, or job security; 1.3% were concerned with job content; 6.5% had to do with union power, and 11.7% had negative associations, such as hurting employees, business, or the country. The same survey showed that 89% of the workers felt unions have power to improve wages and working conditions; 87% felt that they had power to improve job security, and 80% felt that they could protect workers.[2]

Surveys continue to show that the four most commonly expressed goals of employees (irrespective of whether or not they are unionized) are the following:

- Earning a living wage
- Working in a safe environment
- Having decent hours of work
- Having comfortable physical surroundings [3]

These goals are particularly interesting in light of the recent emphasis on other QWL programs such as employee participation, quality circles, and job enrichment. Such survey results suggest that for many workers having a good quality of work life means first having a decent income and working conditions. Once these are provided, other dimensions of the quality of work life may take on greater importance. By the same token, attempts at QWL improvements via more participation or quality circles are less appropriate during times when some employees are asked to make wage concessions and others are being laid off.

Relationships of PHRM and Unionization

As shown in Exhibit 16.1, the unionization of employees is related to many other PHRM functions and operates in a complex legal context. Because this legal context influences organizing as well as other collective bargaining activities, an entire section in this chapter is devoted to the discussion of the legal considerations for unionization and collective bargaining.

Recruitment and Selection. Unionization may have a direct impact on who is hired and the conditions under which applicants are hired. Also, employers are bound by jurisdictions regarding replacement of workers during a strike. In all Canadian jurisdictions except Québec (as per Bill 45, 1977), employers are permitted to hire workers to replace striking employees.

Unions also can play an important role in deciding who is to be promoted, given a new job assignment, put into training programs, terminated, or laid off. This role is facilitated by established seniority provisions in union-management contracts. It is strengthened further by courts and Human Rights Commission decisions that recognize seniority provisions as part of a bona fide seniority system.[4] The "last hired, first fired" principle is still common practice for unionized employees.

Employee Rights. When employers treat individuals with fairness and respect, employees are more inclined to exhibit loyalty toward their employ-

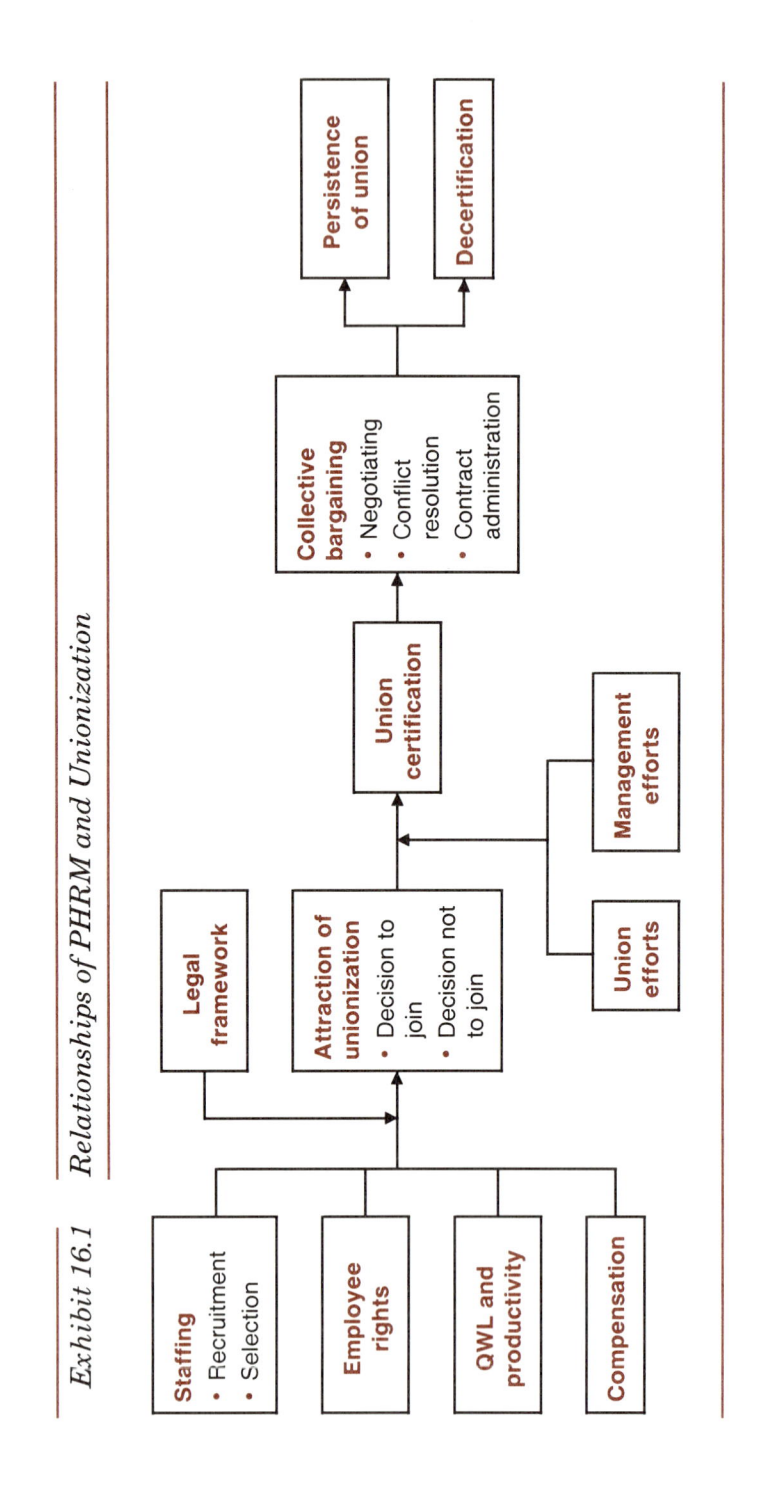

498 *Maintaining Effective Industrial Relations*

Exhibit 16.1 Relationships of PHRM and Unionization

```
Staffing                                                                          Persistence
• Recruitment                                                                      of union
• Selection                                                                            ↑
                     Legal                                                      Collective
Employee            framework                                                   bargaining
rights                 │                      Union          →                 • Negotiating
                       ↓                      certification                    • Conflict
QWL and         Attraction of                    ↑                              resolution
productivity    unionization      →              │                             • Contract
                • Decision to                    │                              administration
Compensation      join                           │                                     ↓
                • Decision not                   │                              Decertification
                  to join                        │
                       ↑
                       │
              ┌────────┴────────┐
         Union              Management
         efforts            efforts
```

ers. The more rights that the employers recognize and observe, the better employees feel, and the less likely employees are to form a union. Once unionized, however, the union will help to ensure that both legal and humane employee rights are observed.

Quality of Work Life and Productivity. As described in Chapter 13, many PHRM programs for QWL and productivity improvement are undertaken jointly by union and management. Although not all unions support the QWL programs, many unions do offer active support and the involvement (generally voluntary) of their members.

Compensation. One of the most important goals of employees is acceptable wages and adequate benefits. Because it is perceived that unions can force employers to provide these, employees are more likely to find unionization attractive. The threat of possible unionization, however, is often enough to cause employers to provide better than satisfactory wages and benefits.

Because unionization has such an extensive set of systemic relationships with other PHRM activities and because it serves so many purposes and is so important, employers must give it serious consideration.

Legal Considerations in the Unionization of Employees

Three basic beliefs underlie the legal framework for labour relations in Canada:

1. Employees should be free to organize
2. Representatives of employees should be able to engage employers in bargaining
3. Employees and employers should be free to invoke meaning and sanctions in support of their positions, employees should be free to withdraw services, and employers should be free to close their doors.

The Early Days

Historically, labour relations legislation in Canada comprised a multiplicity of legislation at both the federal and provincial levels. Separate Acts, or special clauses in the general legislation, exist for different sectors, industries, and workers. According to one expert, the Canadian constitutional division of powers led to the most decentralized industrial relations system in the world.[5] The federal government has jurisdiction over a number of industries such as inter-provincial transportation and communications, but manufacturing, mining, and other industries fall under provincial jurisdiction, even though companies may operate plants on a national basis. During times of national emergency, the federal government may invoke the War Measures Act of 1918 to legislate in the labour relations field for industries considered to be essential to the emergency. This occurred during World War II.

After this war, labour relations legislation reverted again to provincial jurisdiction, with the provinces obtaining jurisdiction over 90% of the labour force. For a number of years following World War II, many of the provinces passed legislation modelled after the federal Industrial Relations Disputes and Investigation Act (IRDI Act), 1948. It specified the rights for workers to join unions; made provisions for certification of unions as bargaining agents by a labour relations board; required unions and management to negotiate in good faith; and specified a number of unfair labour practices by both unions and management and a two-stage compulsory conciliation process that had to be complied with before strikes or lockouts became legal.

In the 1950s, several of the provinces began to move away from the IRDI Act model, introducing features into their own labour relations legislation to meet the special needs of their jurisdiction. It was at this time that labour legislation in Canada began to evolve into eleven different policies—one federal and ten provincial. The most radical departure from the IRDI Act model was the retreat from the two-stage compulsory conciliation procedure to alternatives that included greater flexibility, a greater degree of voluntarism, and allowed more options to governments in the method of settling disputes.

Labour Relations Legislations Today

It would be beyond the scope of this chapter to attempt to describe the contents of the labour relations legislation in each jurisdiction. Instead, the following section provides a cursory review of legislation that characterizes Canadian labour laws, with special emphasis on common features as well as distinct legislation.

Certification of Bargaining Units. Under Canadian legislation, an employer may voluntarily recognize a union and negotiate a collective agreement, except in Québec, where there is no legal status for voluntary recognition. However, if an employer refuses to voluntarily recognize the union, the union may apply to the Labor Relations Board for certification.

Since the 1950s, Canadian legislation has required that unions have a majority of employees in a bargaining unit as members before they could apply for certification. In recent years, however, some jurisdictions have made the requirement less than 50%, in the sense that they require 50% of *those voting* rather than 50% of all members of the bargaining unit (this is 40% in Ontario). Those who fail to cast ballots are no longer considered as voting against the certification of the union.

Except for British Columbia, the certification process in Canada is different from that in the U.S. in that the majority of unions are certified without a vote if an officer of the appropriate labour relations board finds, on the basis of signed membership cards, that the union truly does not have the support of the majority. In the U.S., and in British Columbia as the result of a change in 1984, it requires a vote in every case of union certification.

Labour Relations Boards. Labour relations boards exist in all jurisdictions except for the province of Québec, where these functions are carried out by a group of some 20 commissioners. The boards were set up to administer the labour relations Acts. Usually they are tripartite, composed of union representatives, management representatives, and a neutral chair (usually a government representative). Labour relations boards have much flexibility in their procedures, particularly those for solving conflicts.

Determination of the unit appropriate for collective bargaining is one of the more important functions of the board. A board may accept the unit described in the union's application or it may alter it, usually by adding or dropping employees in order to ensure homogeneity, viability, and representation of the characteristics of the employing organization. Units may include all plant workers of one employer, plant workers of several employers in the same area, workers in more than one plant of the same employer, parts of a plant, or particular occupations or crafts. Most of the Acts provide some guidelines as to what constitutes an "appropriate" unit. For example, they may suggest that professional employees would constitute a single unit or that particular crafts or occupations such as carpenters, watchmen, supervisors, etc., may each have their own bargaining units.

Most Acts also specify certain categories of workers that are not covered by the legislation. Generally these include management and employees working in a confidential capacity, as well as doctors, dentists, and lawyers. This means that these employees do not have the protection of the legislation should they wish to establish unions to represent them in negotiations with their employers.

In establishing the appropriate unit, boards generally pay close attention to the wishes of the employees, the history of bargaining in similar units, types of union organization (industrial or craft), and the employees involved (plant, office, technical, professional, and craft). Most determinations involve a single plant, and this is a principal reason why collective bargaining operates on a local plant basis.

Considerable time may elapse between an application for certification and the determination by the labour relations board of the need for a vote. During this period, employees could be swayed against the certification or lose interest for one reason or another—for example, because of inaction due to a delay.

Since these delays usually have little to do with the applicant union, several of the Acts provide for pre-hearing votes. Under such a provision, the labour relations board will conduct a vote on receipt of the application. In Ontario, Québec, and the federal government, for example, a pre-hearing vote will be held at the request of the union, if the board is satisfied that at least 35% of the employees in the voting constituency are members of the trade union. A pre-hearing vote usually covers the unit specified in the application, although it may be modified by the board on the basis of an examination of its records. The resulting ballots are sealed until the certification proceedings have been completed. Depending on the outcome of these proceedings, the ballots then will be counted to determine whether the union is to be certified.

Decertification. All Acts provide orderly procedures for decertifying unions. Generally application for decertification can be made if the certified union fails to bargain, if after a certain period either another union claims majority support of the employees, or the majority of employees indicate that they do not want to be represented by a union. Where an agreement has been signed, application for decertification can be made only at specified periods, generally within two months before the agreement's termination.

Applications for decertification may be made by the employees in the unit or by the employer if the union fails to bargain. Some provincial laws—for example those in Ontario and Manitoba—allow for application to the labour relations board to terminate bargaining rights of a union that originally acquired those rights through the voluntary action of the employer—no formal certification exists in these situations. The federal statute does not provide procedures for termination of bargaining rights in these instances of voluntary recognition.

Accreditation. A recent provision in labour relations legislation concerns certification rights for employer associations. The term used to describe the process of granting these rights is *accreditation*. Accreditation is particularly important in the construction industry, where much of the bargaining takes place between unions and employer groups. The purposes of accreditation are to ensure the unification of employers in bargaining, to force unions to recognize majority employer associations for bargaining purposes, and to ensure the adherence of all employers to the agreement negotiated between the accredited association and the union. Procedures for acquiring accreditation are similar to those for acquiring certification.

Unfair Labour Practices. Certain practices involving either the company or the unions are considered unfair, and rules regarding them are subject to enforcement by the labour relations boards or the courts. The following are examples of unfair practices on the part of employers:

- Interference with the rights of employees to select the union of their choice for collective bargaining purposes, or discrimination against employees for union activity. By law, employers cannot dismiss, discipline, or threaten employees for exercising their right to unionize. Employers cannot make promises that will influence an employee's choice of a union—for example, promising better benefits should the employee select one union rather than another or vote for no union. This legislation, however, does not prevent employers from presenting their case in support of one union or another, or for no union. What the employer can say under these circumstances, the manner in which it can be said, and the

type of forum that can be used are matters that are open for review by the relevant labour relations board.
- Employer participation in the formation, selection, or support—financial or otherwise—of unions representing the employees.
- Unilaterally changing the terms of collective agreements or changing the wages and working conditions during certification proceedings or during collective bargaining, if the purpose is to undermine the union. By law, employers are compelled, as are unions, to bargain in good faith—that is, to demonstrate serious intentions to bargain fairly.

Some unfair labour practices on the part of unions include the following:

- Interference with or participation in the formation or administration of an employers' organization.
- Interference with the bargaining rights of a certified union.
- Discrimination against union members or employees in the bargaining unit.
- Intimidation or coercion of employees to become or remain members of the union.
- Forcing employers to discriminate against, dismiss or discipline union members.
- Failure to provide fair representation for all employees in the bargaining unit, whether in collective bargaining or in grievance procedure cases.[6]

Conciliation and Mediation. In their legislation, all jurisdictions provide for conciliation and mediation services, yet legislation varies in scope and extent of government intervention. Québec, for example, has abolished its conciliation boards, and allows employees to strike 90 days after a union request for the appointment of a conciliation officer. Most other jurisdictions still enforce the compulsory two-stage conciliation approach.

Typically, legislation specifies that no strike action is permitted before a conciliation effort has been made and has failed. Conciliators and mediators are appointed by the federal or provincial labour ministers at the request of either one or both of the parties involved or at the discretion of the ministers. If the dispute still is not settled, a conciliation board may be appointed, comprising appointees of the parties and a neutral chairman. The board will try to effect a settlement; failing that, it will report to the government its recommendations for a settlement. Again, the term of the board is set down in the legislation and may be extended by the parties. Most of legislations require a 7- to 14-day waiting period following the delivery of the board's report before the parties have the right to strike or to lock out.

Conciliation boards seldom are used now since they have been sharply criticized for the time lapse in their decision-making process and their lack of success. Conciliation and mediation will be elaborated on in Chapter 17.

Arbitration. All jurisdictions, with the exception of Saskatchewan, require that collective bargaining agreements include a provision for final settlement by arbitration (i.e., of issues relating to interpretation of the collective agreement), without stoppage of work. This means that, as long as a collective agreement is in force, any strike or lockout is illegal. The arbitrators' decision is final and cannot be changed or revised, except in cases of error, proven corruption, fraud, breach of natural justice, or if the arbitrator exceeds the recognized limits of authority.

The Attraction of Unionization

To understand the union movement today, it is necessary to consider the reasons for which employees decide either to join or not to join unions. A great deal of research has been conducted in an attempt to analyze why workers unionize. Although no single reason exists, three separate conditions appear to be strong influences on an employee's decision to join a union: dissatisfaction, lack of power, and union instrumentality.

The Decision to Join a Union

Dissatisfaction. When an individual takes a job, certain conditions of employment (wages, hours, type of work) are specified in the **employment contract**. A **psychological contract** also exists between employer and employee, which consists of the unspecified expectations of the employee about reasonable working conditions, requirements of the work itself, the level of effort that should be expended on the job, and the amount and nature of the authority that the employer has in directing the employee's work.[7] These expectations are related to the employee's desire to satisfy certain personal preferences in the workplace. The degree to which the organization fulfils these preferences determines the employee's level of satisfaction.

Dissatisfaction with either the employment contract or the psychological contract will lead the employee to attempt to improve the work situation, often through unionization. A major study found a very strong relationship between level of satisfaction and the proportion of workers voting for a union. Almost all workers who were highly dissatisfied voted for a union, but almost all workers who were satisfied voted against the union.[8]

Therefore, if management wants to make unionization less attractive to employees, it may consider making work conditions more satisfying. Management and the PHRM department often contribute to the level of work dissatisfaction by doing the following:

- Giving unrealistic job previews, creating expectations that cannot be fulfilled
- Designing jobs that fail to use the skills, knowledge, and abilities of employees and are not compatible with their personalities, interests, and preferences

- Practising such day-to-day management and supervisory behaviours as poor supervision, unfair treatment, and lack of upward communication
- Failing to tell employees that the company would prefer to operate without unions and that management is committed to treating employees with respect.[9]

Lack of Power. Unionization is seldom the first recourse of employees who are dissatisfied with some aspect of their jobs. The first attempt to improve the work situation is usually made by an individual acting alone. Someone who has enough power or influence can effect the necessary changes without collaborating with others. The features of a job that determine the amount of power the job holder has in the organization are **essentiality**, or how important or critical the job is to the overall success of the organization, an **exclusivity**, or how difficult it would be to replace the person. An employee with an essential task who is difficult to replace may be able to force the employer to make changes. If, however, the individual task is not critical and the employee can easily be replaced, employees are likely to consider other means, including collective action, to increase their power to influence the organization.[10] Labour economists refer to this phenomenon of employees debating whether to fight for improvement of working conditions or to quit the organization as the "exit-voice debate."

In considering whether or not collective action is appropriate, employees also are likely to consider the likelihood that a union would be able to obtain the desired aspects of the work environment, and weigh those benefits against the costs of unionization. In other words, the employees would determine union instrumentality.[11]

Union Instrumentality. Employees who are dissatisfied with many aspects of a work environment, such as pay, promotion opportunity, treatment by supervisor, the job itself, and work rules, often perceive a union as being instrumental in removing such negative aspects. The more that employees believe that a union is likely to obtain positive work aspects, the more instrumental the union is for the employees.

The employees then determine the value of these benefits and the costs of unionization, such as the bad feelings of supervisors and managers, a lengthy organizing campaign, and the resentment of other employees who may not want a union. When the benefits exceed the costs, employees will be more willing to support a union.

Exhibit 16.2 summarizes the reasons that employees might have for deciding to join a union. In general, the expectation that work will satisfy personal preferences may induce satisfaction or dissatisfaction with work. As the level of dissatisfaction increases, individual workers seek to change their work situation. If they fail, and if the positive consequences of unionization seem to outweigh the negative consequences, individuals will be inclined to join the union. This, however, will not always be the case. Employees may choose not to join a union.

The Decision Not to Join a Union

The question of whether or not to join a union involves an assessment of the negative consequences of unionization. Employees may have misgivings about how effectively a union can improve unsatisfactory work conditions. Collective bargaining is not always successful; if the union is not strong, it will be unable to convince an employer to meet its demands. Even if an employer does respond to union demands, the workers may be affected adversely. The employer may not be able to survive when the demands of the union are met, and thus the company may close down, costing employees their jobs. The organization may force the union to strike, inflicting economic hardship on employees who may not be able to afford being out of work, or it may in some cases attempt reprisals against pro-union employees, although this is illegal.[12]

Beyond perceptions of unions as ineffective in the pursuit of personal gains, employees also may resist unionization because of general negative attitudes toward unions. Employees may identify strongly with the company and have a high level of commitment to it. They therefore would tend to

Exhibit 16.2 *Processes in the Decision to Join a Union*

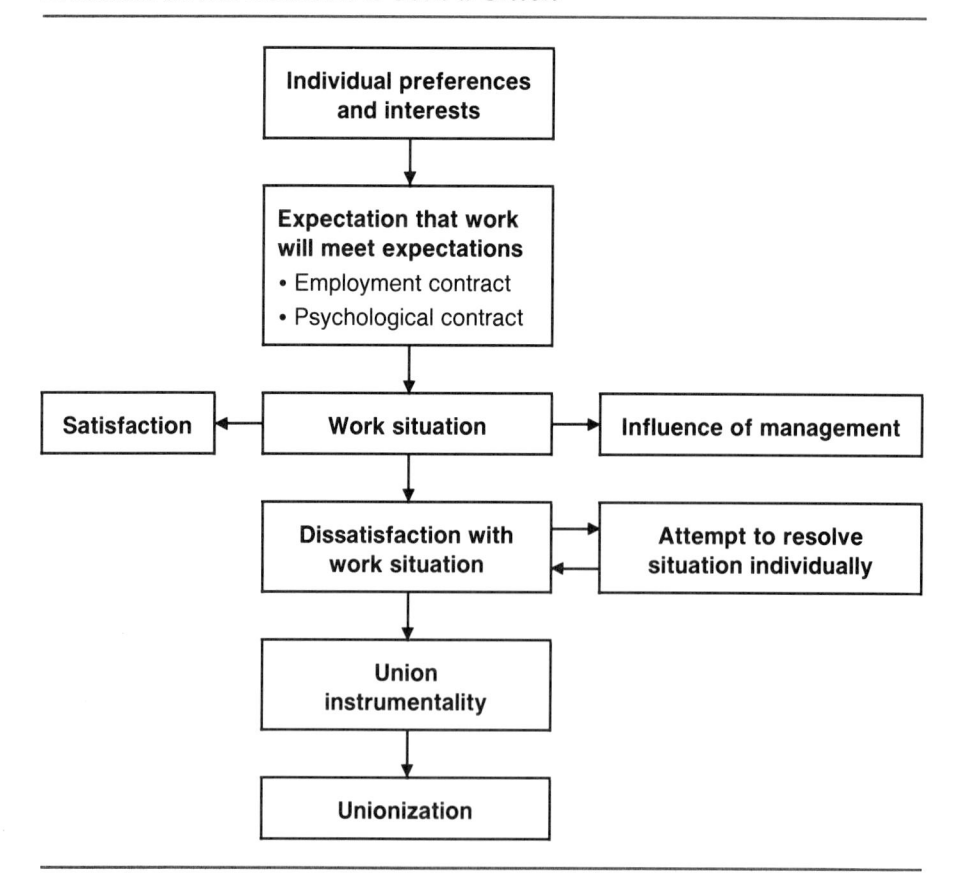

```
          Individual preferences
               and interests
                    │
                    ▼
          Expectation that work
          will meet expectations
          • Employment contract
          • Psychological contract
                    │
                    ▼
  Satisfaction ◄── Work situation ──► Influence of management
                    │
                    ▼
          Dissatisfaction with ──► Attempt to resolve
            work situation    ◄──  situation individually
                    │
                    ▼
                  Union
              instrumentality
                    │
                    ▼
               Unionization
```

view the union as an adversary and would be receptive to company arguments against unions. Employees also may perceive the goals of the union to be objectionable, intending to harm the company and the free enterprise system in general (see the first "PHRM in the News" article). They may object to the concept of seniority or even to the political activities of the unions. Moreover, certain employees—for example, engineers or university professors—view themselves as professionals and find collective action to be contrary to such professional ideals as independence and self-control.[13]

The decision not to unionize can be influenced by management as well. Employers may influence the employees' decision not to join a union by establishing good management practices: fostering employee participation in planning and decision making, opening channels of communication, setting up processes for handling employee problems and grievances, developing employee trust, and offering competitive wages—all characteristics of PHRM discussed throughout this book.[14]

The Development and State of Unionization

The study of labour unions is enhanced a great deal by an appreciation of their historical context. A better understanding of the attitudes and behaviours of both unions and management also can be gained through a knowledge of past labour-management relations. It is useful to compare the evolution of legislation discussed earlier with this historical presentation.

The Early Days

In the last century, Canada's economy was largely agricultural, with a few large concentrations of population and industry. However, a few labour unions existed in the early 1800s. There are, for example, records of several craft unions in the maritime provinces that existed before the end of the War of 1812. There is evidence, too, of the existence of a printers' union in Québec City as early as 1827, and a few shoemakers' unions in Montréal in the 1830s. According to one labour historian, printers were organized in Toronto also at about this time, and in Hamilton in 1833.[15] However, little organization of workers beyond individual local units was evident until the latter half of the last century.

The development and growth of unions in Canada have been influenced primarily by events and developments in the United States. In the decade preceding Confederation, unions that had been operating south of the border began to form locals in Upper Canada. This was the beginning of international unionism as we know it in Canada today. The first international unions were British, the most important of which were the Amalgamated Society of Carpenters and Joiners and the Amalgamated Society of Engineers. Iron moulders and printers were the first of the U.S. unions to establish branches in Canada.[16]

In subsequent decades a number of attempts were made to establish a central labour federation. All of these failed except the Trades and Labour Congress of Canada (TLC), which was established in 1886. A close link developed between the American AFL and the Canadian TLC. Many of the international unions that became members of the AFL also had Canadian districts that helped to form the TLC. The TLC also included strictly Canadian unions at that time. In 1902, the TLC acceded to the wishes of the AFL and barred dual unionism.

The fastest growth in the Canadian labour movement occurred between 1913 and 1920. In 1919, union membership was more than 778 000.[17] Some of the major reasons for this growth included favourable economic conditions and population growth, and economic and industrial expansion in the aftermath of World War I.

The TLC experienced an uneven pattern of growth during the 1930s and the 1940s. While the Depression period led to a decline in membership, an increase was realized following the passage of the U.S. Wagner Act of 1935. This gave unions the right to organize and required employers to bargain in good faith. With the passage of the Act, new industry-wide unions spread into Canada and contributed to further growth of the labour movement.

Initial growth was achieved in affiliation with the TLC, but these new industrial unions generated tension and were finally expelled from the TLC. Later they were welcomed into the more nationalistic Confederation of Canadian Labour (CCL). The merger of the two congresses (CCL and TLC) occurred in 1956, and together they formed the Canadian Labour Congress (CLC).

The evolution of the labour movement was different in French Canada. The growing militancy of the CCCL resulted in the discarding of religious ties in 1960 to become an independent militant federation, the Confederation of National Trade Unions (CNTU). In 1972, a third federation, the Confederation of Democratic Unions broke off from the CNTU. However, this federation remains small.

In sum, since 1956 most unions in Canada have been affiliated with the CLC or the CNTU. In 1981, however, the CLC suspended 14 international building trade unions with more than 229 700 members for non-payment of affiliation fees. In 1982, the expelled unions founded the Canadian Federation of Labour (CFL).

Today

While traditionally Canadian unions have had adversarial relationships with management, most unions now seem to be moving toward a more cooperative relationship.[18] Another trend in the Canadian labour movement today is a breaking away from international unions and an establishment of independence. These current trends are influenced by a number of factors, such as a decline in membership and the distribution of membership.

Decline in Membership. Although union membership in Canada is close to 39% in comparison with only 18% in the U.S., growth has been stopped in the last few years, and in many unions, membership is declining. Union membership grew to a peak of 39% in 1978 and has levelled off since then.[19] In 1985, 3 662 000 non-agricultural workers were unionized. Recent reports from Labour Canada suggest that in 1984–85, most unions were able to maintain the same number of members.[20] In Québec, which was considered to be the fortress of unionism, membership in unions reached its lowest point for many years, declining from 34.2% in 1974 to 27% in 1984.[21] Exhibit 16.3 shows the trends for union membership in Canada and in Québec between 1969 and 1985.

Factors that contribute to this decline include the increase in white-collar jobs, creation of small- and medium-sized enterprises, a decline in employment in industries that are highly unionized, high levels of unemployment, decline in the influence of union leadership (see the second article in "PHRM in the News"), public anti-union feelings, and a more effective non-union policy being undertaken by management. In addition to these factors, in some provinces such as British Columbia and Newfoundland, recent legislation contributed to the thinning of the ranks of the provincial trade union movement. Certification of union bargaining units fell dramatically in 1984 as a result of the passage of an Act that requires the endorsement of a minimum of 55% of employees in a secret ballot. De-certification also has been on the rise in British Columbia as a result of the difficulties created by the new labour code.[22]

Statistics on Union Membership in Canada: 1969–1985 — *Exhibit 16.3*

Year	Canada Non-Agricultural Workforce	Canada Civilian Labour Force	Québec
1969	32.5	26.3	32.6
1970	33.6	27.2	32.9
1971	33.6	26.5	33.8
1972	34.6	27.6	33.6
1973	36.1	29.2	32.5
1974	35.8	29.4	34.2
1975	36.9	29.8	31.7
1976	37.3	30.6	31.2
1977	38.2	31.0	30.5
1978	39.0	31.3	28.9
1979	N/A	N/A	29.5
1980	37.6	30.5	29.6
1981	37.4	30.6	30.4
1982	39.0	31.4	28.7
1983	40.0	30.6	28.6
1984	39.6	30.6	27.0
1985	39.0	30.2	N/A

Source: *Labour Canada,* "Labour Organizations in Canada 1985"; *La Presse,* July 27, 1985, p. A13.

Distribution of Membership. While membership in unions in general remains relatively high, the distribution across different industries is uneven. For example, in 1982 the highest proportion of Canadian unionization was within the public sector (68.7%), followed by 61.8% in construction, and 44.3% in manufacturing.[23] Historically, membership has been concentrated in a small number of large unions. In 1985, the largest and most important federation within the Canadian labour movement was the Canadian Labour Congress, which accounts for almost 58% of all unionized employees. Exhibit 16.4 lists the 17 largest unions and their affiliation and membership numbers in 1982, 1984, and 1985.

Structure and Function of Unions in Canada

Central federations such as the CLC exist in most industrial countries. These federations have much input into public policy decisions. However, since jurisdiction over labour relations policy in Canada is primarily at the provincial level, national federations have organizational entities at that level that attempt to influence the formulation of provincial policies. At a lower level are local labour councils and the local unions.

The most prominent and numerically dominant central federation in Canada is the CLC. Like the American AFL–CIO, the Canadian Labour Congress is a loose and very weak federation. The power in the Canadian labour movement rests with the sovereign national and international unions and in varying degrees at the local union level. The primary function of the CLC is to look after labour's interest at the national level. Research has suggested that, in the past, the CLC could block negative legislation, but it did not have the power to compel legislation over the opposition of other influencial groups.[24]

In addition to its political role, a central federation such as the CLC attempts to resolve conflicts among its constituent components and to ensure that they follow the policies adopted by the periodic national conventions. To this end they have a number of sub-bodies that meet between conventions to assess the extent to which policies are being followed, and to guide the senior executive officers in the ongoing conduct of federation affairs.

The major umbrella organization for national and individual unions in Canada, as mentioned earlier, is the CLC. The CLC is something like a "union of unions" since it brings together a number of national unions, Canadian branches of international unions, and directly-chartered local unions. Exhibit 16.5 presents the structure of the CLC and the relationship of some of its components to the AFL–CIO in the U.S.

The supreme governing body of the CLC meets at biennial conventions to develop policy and amend its constitution. The CLC attempts to achieve its objectives at the national level in a number of ways. Each winter it has traditionally presented its annual memorandum to the government of Canada. In this memorandum the CLC president outlines to the prime minister and the cabinet the objectives that the CLC thinks the government should pursue. Often the recommendation implies criticism of federal policy. In 1976, for example, the CLC discontinued this annual presentation of an all-inclusive memorandum to the cabinet as part of its protest against wage and

Unions With Largest Membership in Canada
(50 000 members or more)

Exhibit 16.4

		Membership	
	1982	1984	1985
1. Canadian Union of Public Employees (CLC)	274 742	293 700	296 700
2. National Union of Provincial Government Employees (CLC)	230 000	242 300	245 000
3. United Steelworkers of America (AFL–CIO/CLC)	197 000	148 000	148 000
4. Public Service Alliance of Canada (CLC)	157 633	181 200	181 500
5. United Food and Commercial Workers (AFL–CIO/CLC)	135 000	140 000	146 000
6. International Union, United Automobile, Aerospace and Agricultural Implement Workers of America (CLC)	121 829	110 000	135 800
7. International Brotherhood of Teamsters, Chauffeurs, Warehousemen and Helpers of America (Ind.)	93 000	91 500	91 500
8. United Brotherhood of Carpenters and Joiners of America (AFL–CIO)	89 010	78 000	73 000
9. Social Affairs Federation (CNTU)	84 000	93 000	93 000
10. Québec Teaching Congress (Ind.)	82 122	86 200	90 000
11. International Brotherhood of Electrical Workers (AFL–CIO/CFL)	70 993	72 900	68 000
12. Canadian Paperworkers Union (CLC)	66 210	63 200	63 000
13. Service Employees International Union (AFL–CIO/CLC)	65 000	65 000	70 000
14. International Association of Machinist and Aerospace Workers (AFL–CIO/CLC)	64 384	66 600	58 600
15. International Woodworkers of America (AFL–CIO/CLC)	63 000	55 800	51 200
16. Labourers' International Union of North America (AFL–CIO)	55 447	59 300	51 400
17. Québec Government Employees Union (Ind.)	N/A	55 200	55 200

Source: *Directory of Labour Organizations in Canada: 1982 and 1985,* Labour Data Branch, Labour Canada (Ottawa: Supply and Services Canada, 1982 and 1985), pp. 16–17. Reproduced by permission of the Minister of Supply and Services Canada.

price controls.[25] In order to back its demands, the CLC developed an action plan—a one-day national work stoppage. This demonstrated to the government that the CLC could mobilize a demonstration of considerable proportion.[26]

Less formal tactics utilized quite often by the CLC include, for example, meetings with senior government officials. In addition, when Statistics

512   *Maintaining Effective Industrial Relations*

Exhibit 16.5 *The Structure of the CLC-Affiliated Segment of the Canadian Labour Movement*

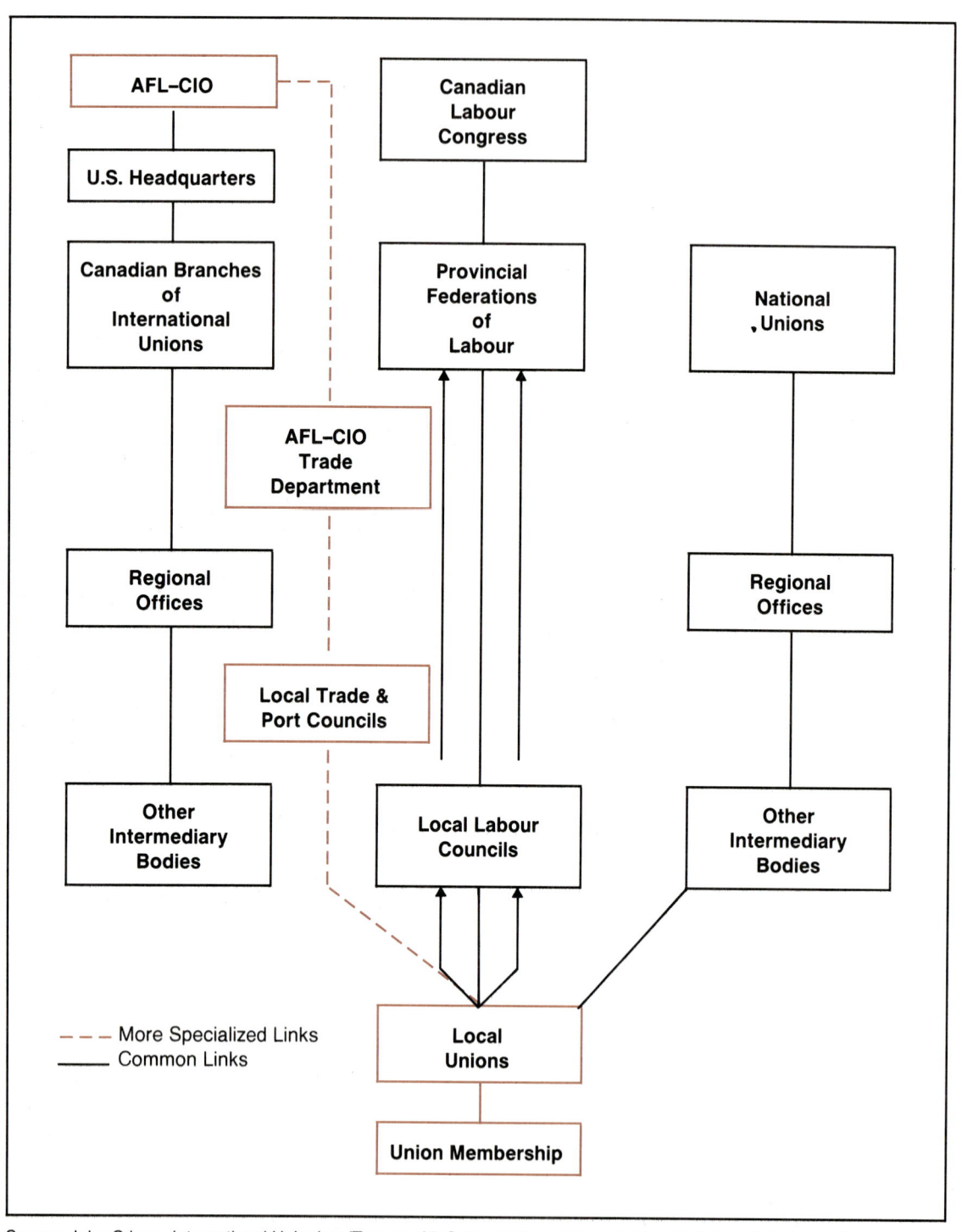

Source: John Crispo, *International Unionism* (Toronto: McGraw-Hill Co. of Canada Ltd., 1967), p. 167. Used with permission of the author.

Canada releases its monthly figures on the cost of living and unemployment rate, the CLC frequently prepares press releases to ensure that "Canadians become aware that we are not hostile as a labour movement and that we have done some great things for this country." The CLC also monitors the courts for anti-union challenges under the Charter of Rights and Freedoms, and makes clear to the government of Canada its stand against free trade with the U.S.[27]

The CLC attempts to influence the formulation and administration of public policy at the national level and maintain peace with the Canadian Labour Congress by resolving jurisdictional issues. It also suggests policies that it thinks the government should pursue in light of the changes in prices, the rate of unemployment, and other economic indicators.

Another important function of the CLC is that of defining, organizing, and ironing out problems of conflicting jurisdiction of its affiliates. For example, these problems arose when the Auto Workers Union and the Machinists Union tried to organize aerospace workers in the same plants.

Tactics of operation and agenda for action have been influenced significantly by the various CLC leaders throughout the years. For example, while the former president (until 1986) tended to act like a one-man band, eventually alienating many people with his speeches salted with profanities, the newly elected leader has a different style. Shirley Carr, who is referred to as "the coal miner's daughter," presented to the press the following items as the pressing agenda for the CLC future:

- Emphasis on consolidation both inside and outside the CLC
- Development of a new and aggressive strategy to tackle and organize workers in the finance sectors of the economy, mainly financial institutions.

As indicated earlier, the CLC consists of slightly more than 50 Canadian branches of international unions and more than 20 national unions. Each national union usually is given a mandate to organize within a particular jurisdictional area as defined in its constitution. Not only does the national or international branch serve its local unions, but also it helps to organize campaigns. Also, during contract negotiations, the representatives of the national union may assist the local negotiating committee in the formulation and negotiation of its demands and even in the actual negotiations. The national unions also assist the local unions in processing grievances.

The **local union** is the basic unit of labour organization, formed in a particular plant or locality.

> The members [of the local] participate directly in the affairs of their local including the election of officers, financial and other business matters.[28]

A worker's first contact with unionism is usually with a local union. It represents the basic building block of the labour movement structure. There are an estimated 13 000 locals in Canada, the number of which per union varies. Some unions have fewer than 10 locals, while others have more than 100. Local unions are of varying sizes, ranging from a few members to many thousands.

Activities of union locals revolve around collective bargaining and handling grievances. In addition, locals hold general meetings, publish newsletters, and otherwise keep their members informed. Typically, however, the members are apathetic about union involvement. Unless a serious problem exists, attendance at meetings is usually very low, and often elections of officers draw votes from less than one-fourth of the membership.

The Organizing Campaign

One of the major functions of the labour relations boards is to conduct the selection of unions to represent employees. This is accomplished through a certification election to determine if the majority of employees want the union. Under Canadian labour laws, the union that is certified to represent a group of employees has the exclusive right to bargain for that group.

Because unions may acquire significant power through certification, employers may be anxious to prevent this. In addition to this potential union-management conflict, there may be more than one union attempting to win certification as representative of a group of employees, creating competition and conflict between unions.

Several steps in the regular certification process can be identified. These are presented in Exhibit 16.6. A union also may organize a majority of the employees and obtain voluntary approval by the employer, in which case, it would not need to follow to the steps shown in Exhibit 16.6.

Different jurisdictions have different provisions for the percentage of support needed to apply for certification or in situations where boards are mandated to certify without a vote. Also, the percentages required to certify a union are different in the bargaining unit than those based on individuals voting. Exhibit 16.7 provides a summary of these provisions across jurisdictions.

Exhibit 16.6   *Certification Process*

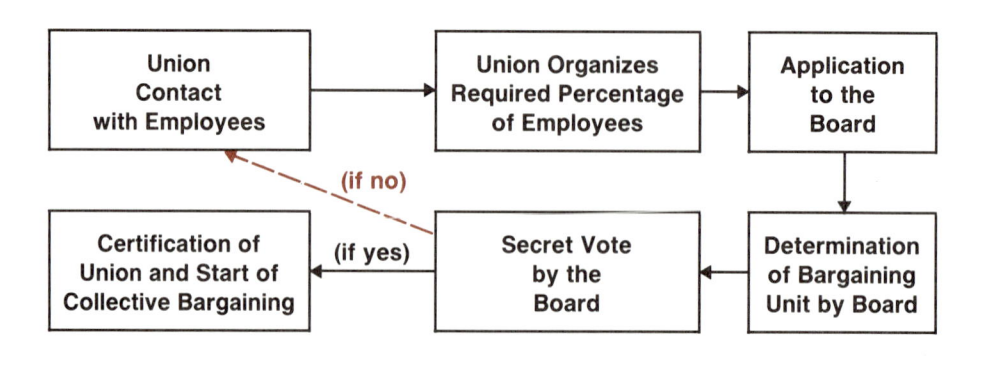

```
Union Contact          Union Organizes         Application
with Employees    →    Required Percentage  →  to the
                       of Employees            Board
      ↑                                          ↓
      ⋯(if no)⋯                                  
Certification of       Secret Vote            Determination
Union and Start of ← (if yes) Board       ←   of Bargaining
Collective Bargaining                         Unit by Board
```

A Comparison of Provisions Dealing with Union Certification

Exhibit 16.7

Jurisdiction	Percent support needed to apply for certification	Percent support where boards are mandated to certify without a vote	Percent support needed to apply for a pre-hearing vote [a][b]	Percent support necessary for a union to be certified when a vote is taken — 50% of those in the bargaining unit	50% of those voting
Federal	35	50 or more	35%		X (If over 35% vote)
Newfoundland [c]	50		N/R	X	
Prince Edward Island	50		not specified		X
Nova Scotia	40	50 or more	N/R		X
New Brunswick	40–60	60 or more	40	X	
Québec	35	50 or more	N/R	X	
Ontario	45–55	55 or more	35		X
Manitoba	50		N/R		X
Saskatchewan	25				X (If over 50% vote)
Alberta	50	50 or more	N/R		X
British Columbia	45–55	55 or more	45		X (If over 50% vote)

[a] In most jurisdictions, the boards usually have the power to certify the union or bargaining agent without a vote if there is concrete evidence that over 50% of the members want the union.
[b] Includes those statutes that make specific reference to a pre-hearing vote.
[c] In Newfoundland, the Board may direct its chief executive officer to conduct an investigation where an application has been made and if not less than 40% and not more than 50% of members are in good standing in the union, the chief executive officer *shall* cause a representation vote to be taken.
N/R No reference to a pre-hearing vote in the statute.

Source: A. W. J. Craig, *The System of Industrial Relations in Canada,* 2nd ed. (Scarborough, Ontario: Prentice-Hall Canada Inc., 1986), p. 129. Used with permission of Prentice-Hall Canada Inc.

The Campaign to Solicit Employee Support

In the campaign to solicit employee support, unions generally attempt to contact the employees and obtain sufficient support in order to be certified. Many major unions employ field organizers. These are people who spend most of their time going from company to company attempting to organize workers. The life of a typical organizer was well depicted in the movie *Norma Rae*. Most organizers possess fine organizational and verbal skills, and have complete knowledge of the relevant laws. Their techniques may vary as a function of the composition of the workforce and the problems at hand.

Some organizers cater to specific populations. The United Steelworkers Union in Canada, for example, employed a Canadian-Italian person who specialized in organizing workers of Italian origin.[29] Others specialize in organizing blacks, women, or white-collar professionals.

Establishing Contact. Contact between the union and employees can be initiated by either party. National or international unions may contact employees in industries or occupations in which they traditionally have been involved. Most union organizing drives start with a few disgruntled workers who are dissatisfied with their salaries and/or working conditions, and they call or visit the local office of a union. On initial contact, the union official will assess the situation and if it looks reasonably promising, the official will set up a plan of action. From then on, the organizer works as a strategist, educator, counsellor, and companion to members of the workforce in an effort to enlist support to secure certification.

In communities where one or two well-known non-union companies operate amid a preponderance of unionized firms, the initiative often comes from the national or international union. Such was the case when labour managed to organize the employees of the T. Eaton Company store in Brampton, Ontario. The concentration on this store snowballed into an historic organizing drive that eventually affected three of Canada's largest department store chains—Eaton's, Sears, and Simpson's.[30]

In all campaigns, a list of all employees in the bargaining unit is needed. To obtain such a list without the employer's knowledge is difficult, so organizers resort to many devices. Some organizers obtain this by referencing the members' vehicle licence plates through the provincial Ministry of Transportation, which is legal in Canada. Once the list is compiled, demographic and socio-economic analyses are conducted. These analyses play an important role during the campaign.

Sign-ups. Once contact has been made, the union begins to pressure employees to sign membership cards as soon as possible. Through the work of a nucleus of committed employees, many unions employ tactics such as house visits. Such a strategy may help to persuade undecided workers to go along with the unions. Different organizers aim for different percentages of sign-ups, although all aim beyond the minimum required by the certification law. During the sign-up campaign many organizers try to give the impression that the union is there to stay.

Employer Resistance. The employer usually resists the union's campaign. One of the best tactics for preventing unionization is to keep the employees content. This is difficult; no matter how good the working conditions, some workers always are dissatisfied. Some employers call in consultants, who resort to one or more of the following tactics:

- Use of doctored statistics, such as selective wage surveys, to make employees believe that company conditions already are superior to most

- Making threats or promises contingent on victory or defeat of the union. For example: "We may eventually close the plant and move to another province"
- Secretly promoting the formation of an employees' association and encouraging the association itself to apply for certification.[31]

However, in most jurisdictions, employers are legally constrained from interfering with an employee's freedom of choice. The following actions by an employer are illegal:

- Promising improvement in wages or working conditions contingent on defeat of the union
- Granting of wage increases or making other PHRM changes that cannot be proven to be "normal"
- Taking any action that the labour relations board believes could deceive employees as to the degree that they are able to vote freely on vital issues.

During the union campaign and election process, therefore, it is important that the PHRM manager caution the company against engaging in unfair labour practices, which, when identified, generally cause the election to be set aside. Severe violations by the employer can result in certification of the union as the bargaining representative, even if it has lost the election.

Determination of the Bargaining Unit

A bargaining unit is usually defined as a unit of employees who are considered "appropriate" for collective bargaining. Usually, statutes are set out in broad terms and it is up to the labour relations boards to determine who should or should not be included in the units. A typical unit may consist exclusively of craft employees, technical employees, or workers with various skills. It is necessary to have at least two employees to form a bargaining unit.

The statute governing the definition of "appropriate unit" is rather broad in most jurisdictions in Canada. For example, in Alberta, Nova Scotia, and Prince Edward Island, excluded from bargaining units are members of the medical, dental, legal, architectural, and engineering professions. Ontario excludes the same professions except engineers, and adds to the list land surveyors and people employed in agriculture, hunting, trapping, and horticulture, as well as domestic employees. All jurisdictions in Canada exclude employees who are considered to act in a confidential capacity in matters relating to industrial relations or who perform managerial functions.

Assessing the Unionization of Employees

Although there may be occasions when management wants to have its employees unionized, this generally is not the case. Consequently, the personnel manager's roles are to monitor employee attitudes and take steps as necessary to reduce dissatisfaction. In other words, the effectiveness of the personnel and human resource manager in this area can be measured by how satisfied and involved the employees are with the company. Their mood can be assessed by means of organizational surveys, as discussed in Chapter 13.

Because union-management activities are enmeshed in a web of federal and provincial laws, another measure of effectiveness is how well the personnel manager avoids violating these laws while maintaining relationships with the workforce. Moreover, PHRM corporate officers who are responsible for developing labour relations policies across provincial lines (in the case of multi-plant or multi-provincial locations) have the duty of monitoring closely the different labour relations statutes and complying with them. By the same token, effectiveness can be judged by how well the personnel manager negotiates and administers contracts if the employees are unionized.

Summary

Union membership in proportion to the labour force is in decline, more so in some provinces and/or sectors of the economy than in others, and the overall influence of organized labour also is diminishing. Unions historically have adapted to change in order to survive in Canada. Strategically, unions have had to adjust to the decline in employment in traditional industries such as steel, automobile, and mining. In addition, the labour force has shifted to services and from blue- to pink- and white-collar occupations. Unions have yet to capture new labour force entrants, particularly women. Although the fastest growing unions in the past have been in the public sector, this growth has slowed down in relation to population growth. Organized labour is concerned about its image and is making renewed efforts to move with geographical, industrial, occupational, and demographic shifts in the labour force.

The effective PHRM manager, particularly in non-union companies, should understand the history of union-management relations and the basic legal framework that guides collective bargaining in Canada. A knowledge of the role that labour relations boards play is critical if organizations are to avoid unfair labour practices.

An understanding of why unions appeal to workers also has implications for the design of effective PHRM functions. Research has demonstrated that workers join unions because of dissatisfaction, notably over wages and working conditions. In addition, unions appeal to workers because of union power to bargain and obtain concessions from management. Where unions are perceived as instrumental in providing workers with a voice and preventing arbitrary treatment by management, union representatives are more likely to be able to organize workers. Learning what unions do has important implications for both unionized and non-unionized organizations. The next chapter examines the collective bargaining process in detail.

Discussion Questions

1. Why have unions appealed to workers historically? Are the reasons today different than those in the past?
2. What is a labour relations board? How do these boards help to promote the policy of free collective bargaining in Canada?
3. Explain the structure and purposes of the Canadian labour movement, with emphasis on the role and functions of the CLC.
4. Why are unions losing power?
5. Identify and explain the major steps in the certification process.
6. What are the major ingredients for a successful campaign to solicit employees' support?
7. What legal strategies could be undertaken by employers to devise a campaign against unionization?

CASE STUDY

A Blow to Unionization!

Following a flurry of union activity at 16 of Eaton's, Simpsons, and Sears Canada outlets, efforts to organize Canada's more than 800 major and junior department stores have slowed down considerably. Due to recent developments, the very existence of the union is threatened.

While union officials may insist otherwise, many observers contend that the recent move by workers at four Toronto-area Eaton's stores to decertify their union will strike a major blow to labour's continuing effort to organize Canada's largely union-free department store sector.

The demise of unionization would be, according to industry officials, a significant boost to the recovering department store industry. The threat of nationwide unionization, which began in 1984, came just as department stores, emerging from the recession, endured their greatest losses. A renewed push to organize, according to the same sources, would again place a heavy pressure on the industry's slim profit margins. Labour costs already represent 20% of sales for companies operating with 3% profit margins. Therefore, an increase in labour costs of even 1% would have a significant impact on the bottom line. In addition, industry sources indicate that, during 1985, department stores have worked hard to realize higher profits; they don't want to see the unions come in and negate their efforts.

Retailers say that unions threaten management autonomy. "We don't want somebody else running our business," Richard Sharpe, Sears' chairman and CEO said during an interview.

Workers at three Eaton's stores last week filed to decertify their union with the Ontario Labour Relations Board. A fourth store in Ontario is still gathering petition signatures in an attempt to decertify the recently certified Retail, Wholesale, and Department Store Union. Since 1984, union efforts to organize department store employees resulted in about 10% success. Observers argue that sweeping changes in the department store industry may prevent unions from future successes.

PHRM specialists feel that the trend to more part-time workers, more commissioned salespeople, and more licensing of store space to outsiders for royalties or percentages of sales fees means that the interests of these people will be divergent from the interests of the collective, so that the cohesion and coherence of workers that unions need is not the same as it was in the past. In addition, retailers say that they will respond to the union threat by developing better labour relations and attempting to meet more of the needs of employees, thereby lessening the role unions might play.

At the same time, many employees are realizing that unions cannot guarantee job security. For example, in 1985 Eaton's moved to lay off half of its workers at a unionized store in Brandon, Manitoba, in response to the provincial government-imposed agreement guaranteeing substantial wage increases under first-contract legislation. This experience has led some observers to conclude that the unions really have not accomplished half or even a third of what they promised, because what they promised was unaffordable. In addition, these observers concluded that it is a different reality these days, with employees concerned about keeping their jobs and therefore accepting not wage increases, but wage rollbacks.

Case Questions

1. What makes unionization of department stores in Canada different from unionization of other sectors?
2. Why, would you speculate, are some employees attempting to decertify the RWDSU?
3. What are the factors operating in favour of the industry and against the RWDSU? Should this be the case? What information is missing from the observations quoted in the case study?
4. If you were an organizer for RWDSU, what would be your strategy? What rationale for unionization would you advance?

Endnotes

1. A. W. J. Craig, "The Canadian Industrial Relations System," in S. L. Dolan and R. S. Schuler, (eds.) Canadian Readings in Personnel and Human Resource Management (St. Paul: West Publishing Co., 1987).
2. R. P. Quinn and G. C. Stains, *The 1977 Quality of Employment Survey* (Ann Arbor, MI: Institute for Social Research, Survey Research Center, University of Michigan, 1979).
3. P. Farish, "PAIR Potpourri," *Personnel Administrator*, Sept. 1981, pp. 23–24.
4. G. Trudeau, in Dolan and Schuler (eds.), endnote 1, 1987. W. S. Tarnopolsky, *Discrimination and the Law in Canada* (Toronto: R. DeBoo Ltd., 1982).
5. A. W. J. Craig, "The Canadian Industrial Relations System," S. L. Dolan and R. S. Schuler, (eds.) endnote 1.
6. This summary was based primarily on G. Saunders, "Union Management Relations: An Overview," *Human Resources Management in Canada* (Prentice-Hall Canada Inc., 1983), pp. 55,035–55,036.
7. E. H. Schein, *Organizational Psychology* (Englewood Cliffs, NJ: Prentice-Hall, 1965).
8. J. G. Getman, S. B. Goldberg, and J. B. Herman, *Union Representation Elections: Law and Reality* (New York: Russell Sage Foundation, 1976).
9. J. F. Rand, "Preventive Maintenance Techniques for Staying Union Free," *Personnel Journal*, June 1980, p. 498.
10. J. M. Brett, "Behavioral Research on Unions," in B. M. Staw and L. L. Cummings (eds.), *Research in Organizational Behavior*, vol. 2 (Greenwich, CT: JAI Press, 1980). J. M. Brett, "Why Employees Want Unions," *Organizational Dynamics*, Spring 1980, pp. 47–59. W. C. Hamner and F. J. Smith, "Work Attitudes as Predictors of Unionization Activity," *Journal of Applied Psychology*, Aug. 1978, pp. 415–421.
11. J. Fossum, *Labor Relations: Development, Structure, Process*, 2nd ed. (Dallas, TX: Business Publications, Inc., 1982). S. A. Youngblood, A. D. Denis, J. Molleston, and W. H. Mobley, "The Impact of Work Attachment, Instrumentality, Beliefs, Perceived Labor Union Image, and Subjective Norms on Union Voting Intentions and Union Membership," *Academy of Management Journal*, 27, 1984, pp. 576–590.
12. Getman, Goldberg and Herman, endnote 8.
13. F. Bairstow, "Professionalism and Unionism: Are They Compatible?" *Industrial Engineering*, April 1974, pp. 40–42. P. Felville and J. Blandin, "Faculty Job Satisfaction and Bargaining Sentiments," *Academy of Management Journal*, Dec. 1974, pp. 678–692. B. Husaini and J. Geschwender, "Some Correlates of Attitudes Toward and Membership in White Collar Unions," *Southwestern Social Science Quarterly*, March 1967, pp. 595–601. L. Imundo, "Attitudes of Non-Union White Collar Federal Government Employees Toward Unions," *Public Personnel Management*, Jan.–Feb. 1974, pp. 87–92. A. Kleingartner, "Professionalism and Engineering Unionism," *Harvard Business Review*, March–April 1971, pp. 48–54.
14. J. H. Hopkins and R. D. Binderup, "Employer Relations and Union Organizing Campaigns," *Personnel Administrator*, March 1980, pp. 57–61.
15. F. J. McKendy, "History and Structure of the La-

bour Movement in Canada," in S. M. A. Hameed (ed.), *Canadian Industrial Relations* (Toronto: Butterworth and Co., 1975), p. 109.
16. S. Jamieson, *Industrial Relations in Canada* (Toronto: Macmillan of Canada, 1973), p. 13.
17. A. W. J. Craig, *The System of Industrial Relations In Canada* (Scarborough: Prentice-Hall Canada Inc., 1983), p. 65.
18. R. J. Adams, "Industrial Relations and the Economic Crisis: Canada Moves Towards Europe," in M. Juris, M. Thompson, and W. Daniels (eds.), *Industrial Relations in a Decade of Economic Change* (Industrial Relations Research Association, 1985), pp. 115–149.
19. Ibid, p. 125.
20. *La Presse*, July 5, 1985, p. B6.
21. *La Presse*, July 27, 1985, p. A13.
22. J. Danylchuk, "B.C. Laws Hit Unionization," *The Globe and Mail*, July 15, 1985, p. B3.
23. A. Allentuck, "Union Demands: Tinkering with Tradition," *The Financial Post*, March 1, 1985, p. 10.
24. D. Kwavnick, "Labour's Lobby in Ottawa: How the CLC Influences Government Policy," *Labour Gazette*, July 1973, pp. 441–443.
25. R. Lang, "Labour's Manifesto for Canada: A New Independence?" Proceedings of the 29th Annual Meeting of the Industrial Relations Research Association, Madison, WI, IRRA, 1977, pp. 91–99.
26. R. J. Adams, endnote 18, p. 178.
27. P. Maser, "The Coal Miner's Daughter and the CLC," *The Gazette*, April 12, 1986, p. B5.
28. *Directory of Labour Organizations in Canada*, Labour Data Branch, Labour Canada, 1982, p. 281.
29. D. A. Peach and D. Kuechle, *The Practice of Industrial Relations* (Toronto: McGraw-Hill Ryerson Ltd., 1975), p. 81.
30. T. Brodie, "Department Stores Gain Upper Hand," *Financial Times of Canada*, March 24, 1986, p. 4.
31. Peach and Kuechle, endnote 29, p. 87.

CHAPTER 17

Collective Bargaining

PHRM in the News

Collective Bargaining

The Collective Bargaining Process
Union-Management Relationships
Processes of Bargaining
Management Strategies
Union Strategies
Joint Union-Management Strategies

Negotiating the Agreement
Negotiating Committees
The Negotiating Structure
Issues for Negotiation

Conflict Resolution
Strikes and Lockouts
Mediation
Arbitration

Contract Administration
Grievance Procedures
Grievance Issues
Management Procedures
Union Procedures

Assessing the Collective Bargaining Process
Effectiveness of Negotiations
Effectiveness of Grievance Procedures

Summary

Discussion Questions

Case Study

Endnotes

PHRM in the News

GM Demands Concessions—or Else

The president of General Motors of Canada warned yesterday that workers at its Ste. Thérèse assembly plant will have to shape up and change their attitude if they want to hang onto their jobs.

George Peapples came to Montréal yesterday to meet Québec Premier Robert Bourassa amid rising fears the province will lose its only automotive assembly plant and its 4,000 jobs.

Bourassa requested the meeting, but got no assurances GM will keep the Ste. Thérèse assembly plant open beyond the summer of 1987.

At a news conference following the meeting, Peapples restated GM's position that it has too many assembly lines and Ste. Thérèse has one of the lowest quality levels of GM's North American operations.

Peapples said bad labor relations at the plant have contributed to the low quality.

"Until very recently there was a very adversarial relationship between union and management," he said. He acknowledged both labor and management were to blame.

Efforts by the workers and management in recent months have brought some improvements, he said. "We are encouraged by what we're seeing, but we definitely have to see significantly more progress."

The facility now produces rear-wheel-drive cars, but that production is scheduled to end by 1987.

GM has several U.S. plants also producing conventional-drive models, and has said the quality of the plants will be a major factor in determining which will get new investment.

Despite the hard line taken by GM, Bourassa said he does not believe it is too late to save the plant.

The struggle to keep the plant will be a test of how well Québec can perform in the increasingly competitive North American marketplace, Bourassa said.

After listening to Peapples's assessment of the Ste. Thérèse situation, Bourassa said: "I'm moderately optimistic. I'll have to see what happens in the next few months."

Bourassa said the government is willing to work with the United Auto Workers Canada (UAW) to persuade the automaker to keep the plant open, and will also press Ottawa to make similar arguments.

Before meeting with Peapples, Bourassa met UAW president Bob White, Québec UAW leaders and Louis Laberge, president of the Québec Federation of Labour.

White said GM has an obligation to remain in Québec where residents buy 35 per cent of the GM cars sold in Canada.

White said the union is worried about the plant, but hasn't given up on it. "We're going to try whatever means we can and meet with whomever we have to trying to get them (GM) to understand that it is important to make an investment here."

Source: S. McGovern, "No Concessions for Premier on GM Plant," *The Gazette*, Montréal, April 8, 1986, p. A–4. Used with permission.

Battle Over Right to Strike Splits Public-Service Union

By the end of the convention the T-shirts were a hot item. Bold red lettering on a white background boasted: "I survived the 1985 PSAC convention."

For a week PSAC—the Public Service Alliance of Canada, the country's third largest union—had seen its convention floor turned into a battlefield.

The armies were the militant and conservative factions within the union.

The principal skirmish centered on the right to strike.

In April, PSAC's chief negotiator, Daryl Bean, signed an agreement with Robert de Cotret, president of the Treasury Board—the federal government department that plays the role of employer.

PSAC would be allowed to negotiate a master contract covering non-monetary issues for 160,000 of its 180,000 members.

PSAC now holds separate negotiations for 39 different bargaining units. It wastes time as negotiators run from one bargaining table to another.

A master agreement, particularly one including common expiry dates for all bargaining units, has been the union's goal for a decade. It would not only be easier to work with, it would give them strength in numbers.

But the agreement Bean brought back did not have common expiry dates, it dealt only with non-monetary issues and the price he paid infuriated the militants: the right to strike over non-monetary issues.

"Some union leaders died in fighting to put on the map union principles like the right to strike," said Denis Gagnon, head of PSAC's postal communications employees section, who led the militant opposition.

More than 200 Montréal members walked out on the first day of the convention because, as observers, they were not permitted to speak.

"The grassroots wanted to deliver a simple message that we don't want to give up the right to strike," said André Senechal.

By the end of the convention, delegates had given leaders a clear mandate to go back to the government and try to obtain a master agreement covering monetary and non-monetary issues without surrendering the right to strike.

The battle is important to more than the union. Sometimes called the "sleeping giant," PSAC has the ingredients needed to be a powerful union. It has the members, the money and the capacity to shut down services essential to a large number of Canadians—such as the issuing of federal cheques.

"We'd only have to be 50-per-cent as militant as the postal workers to get as much as they did (in their contracts) because we've got so many members," said Joane Hurens, PSAC's Québec director.

Québec, with 55,000 members, has long been part of the militant faction within the union, Hurens said.

Unions have played a role in Québec's history for generations. Federal civil servants have witnessed the common fronts and epic battles of their provincial counterparts. And, Hurens said, PSAC's Québec division has established strong communications links among its members—unlike western Canadian regions whose members are isolated and scattered over geographic areas as large as the Northwest Territories.

Traditionally, Québecers have received little support for their militancy.

"The public service tends to lord its white-collar mentality," said Bill Doherty, a former PSAC vice-president who is writing a history of federal government unions.

Many members come from areas where unions are disdained, they feel far more secure in their jobs and they view PSAC more as a staff association than a union, he said.

Though it is Canada's third largest union, PSAC "hasn't really been rubbing noses with organized labor," Doherty said.

But Québec was not alone this time. "We had allies all over the country," Hurens said, "British Columbia, Toronto, some of the Maritimes."

With a new Conservative government talking about reducing 15,000 civil-service jobs and new technology threatening to wipe out others, "the golden years are gone," she said.

People in Saskatoon are going to realize they need a union, she said, and "I don't think they'll care what their neighbors think."

For several months unions representing Québec's provincial civil servants unsuccessfully battled provincial legislation that will limit their right to strike.

Pointing to a study that showed Québec civil servants had "maximum union rights combined with a system that ensures the maximum impact of pressure tactics" and arguing public sympathy was on its side, the provincial government adopted its legislation this month.

Hospital workers will, effectively, have no right to strike. Other civil servants will be allowed to strike over money issues once every three years.

Many of their non-monetary issues—those pertaining to working conditions—will be negotiated in local schools, hospitals and government offices without the right to strike.

Though union leaders decried the law, arguing it would eliminate their right to negotiate, they knew they were up against an apathetic membership and an unsympathetic public.

PSAC's Bean also knows which way the political winds are blowing.

During the convention Bean was elected president of PSAC, polling 226 votes to Gagnon's 137.

Bean told reporters he would immediately seek a meeting with de Cotret to try to obtain a master agreement covering all monetary and non-monetary issues with the right to strike, but he would not predict the outcome.

"We know what Tory governments have normally meant to us," Bean told reporters. "Tory governments have been traditionally anti-labor."

That's why Doherty, who described himself as a militant, believes many of PSAC's leaders should be described as pragmatic rather than conservative.

PSAC is governed by the Public Service Staff Relations Act, "a rather Draconian piece of legislation," Doherty said. "We're up against the biggest and toughest employer in the country." It's an employer that can change the rules of the game any time play is not going its way.

Source: S. McGovern, "Battle Over Right to Strike Splits Public-Service Union," *The Gazette*, Montréal, June 29, 1985, p. B-4. Used with permission.

Labor Strike Overrated

Union leaders have always lamented the inordinate attention that goes to the tiny minority of wage negotiations that result in a strike. In most years, more than 90% of all union contracts are renewed without employees resorting to job action.

Labour Canada reports 1985 was no exception. By the end of October, nearly 700,000 employees in major bargaining units had reached agreement on new contracts—and only 8.4% of them had been involved in a shutdown. At the same time, however, only 35% renewed wage pacts without the assistance of third parties. Sixteen percent of the new agreements required arbitration, and another 38% saw the use of a government-appointed conciliator or arbitrator.

By year-end 1985, the situation had improved—about 1.1 million union members were involved in direct wage talks with their employers and only 0.3% were on strike.

Source: The Financial Post, April 12, 1986, p. 10. Used with permission.

These "PHRM in the News" articles highlight important issues in the union-management collective bargaining relationships. At one time, a major trend toward concessionary bargaining characterized many American unions while Canadian unions were less concessionary. The new demands from GM in Québec, although they do not explicitly call for concessionary bargaining, show a trend toward stiffer management demands for improved labour-management relationships as well as higher commitment to productivity improvements. Similarly, an historical battle regarding the right to strike has plagued public-service unions. Militant unions' members (particularly from Québec) view the recent concessions on the right to strike as not worthy of consideration.

The third article sheds light on an important phenomenon: most collective contracts are concluded with peaceful negotiations that do not lead to the parties engaging in either strikes or lockouts. Relationships between union and management could be highly adversarial on the one hand, or highly co-operative on the other. It also appears that unions' concessions will continue to be an issue in the 1990s, if companies are to compete successfully in a global economy.

This chapter discusses the traditional adversarial union-management relationship and more recent co-operative efforts. Also, bargaining processes and strategies will be examined, as well as the many parts that make up the collective bargaining process, including negotiating the contract, conflict resolution, and contract administration.

Collective Bargaining

The core of union-management relations is **collective bargaining**. It generally includes two types of interaction. The first is the negotiation of work conditions that, when written up as the collective agreement (the contract), become the basis for employee-employer relationships on the job. The second is the activity related to interpreting and enforcing the collective agreement (contract administration) and the resolution of any conflicts arising out of it.[1]

When addressing contemporary issues in collective bargaining, one should ask the following questions:

- What is the role of unions in helping to attain higher productivity?
- Should public employees have the right to strike?
- How can union-management co-operation be facilitated?
- Are union-management relationships in Canada shifting from traditional adversarial to contemporary co-operative? And if yes, what are the implications for the collective bargaining process?

This chapter discusses all of these questions. First, however, the quality of the union-management relationship is discussed, since this has such a powerful influence on the negotiating process, the settlement of grievances, and the rest of the collective bargaining process.

The Collective Bargaining Process

Collective bargaining is a complex process in which union and management negotiators both manoeuvre to win the most advantageous contract. How the variety of issues involved are settled depends on the following:

- The quality of the union-management relationship
- The processes of bargaining used by labour and management
- Management's strategies in the collective bargaining process
- Union's strategies in the collective bargaining process
- Joint union-management strategies

Union-Management Relationships

An understanding of union-management relationships is facilitated by seeing them set in a **labour relations system**. Using a simplified explanation of open systems theory, it is possible to define the labor relations system as comprising "a complex of private and public activities, operating in a specified environment, which is concerned with the allocation of rewards to employees for their services and the conditions under which these services are rendered." [2]

Exhibit 17.1 summarizes the forces and actors operating within the labour relations system. Based on the pioneering work of John Dunlop, Exhibit 17.1 identifies the major components and sub-units of the LRC.[3] It shows that LRC is influenced by a number of environmental sub-systems such as the economic, political, legal, and social sub-systems, as well as the goals, values, and power of the main actors in the labour relations system: labour, management, and the government.

Labour may be non-exempt employees or union members; management are the exempt employees (they may also be the owners); and governments and public agencies such as labor relations boards or public sector employees comprise the third party.[4] These three components were labeled by John Dunlop as "actors," denoting both individuals and groups. The actors, therefore, include managers as individuals or management teams, and employees or their organizations (associations or unions) formed to represent their collective concerns.

Each of the groups identified in the labour relations model traditionally has had different goals. Workers are interested in improved working conditions, due process, wages, and opportunities; unions are interested in their own survival, growth, and acquisition of power, which depend on their ability to maintain the support of the employees by providing for their needs. Management's goals are concerned with profits, certainty, market share, and growth, and the organization also seeks to preserve managerial prerogatives to direct the workforce, to receive promotions, and to achieve personal goals. Government is interested in a stable and healthy economy, protection of individual rights, due process, and safety and fairness in the workplace.

528   *Maintaining Effective Industrial Relations*

Exhibit 17.1 A Framework for Analyzing Labour Relations Systems

Environmental Sub-systems
(External Inputs)

Ecological Sub-system
- Physical surroundings
- Natural resources
- Climate

Economic Sub-system[a]
- Product market
- Labour market
- Money market
- Technology

Political Sub-system
- Legislative action
- Executive action

Legal Sub-system
- Statutory law
- Common law
- Administrative law

Social Sub-system
- Goals and values as influence on actors in labour relations system
- Social structures
- Public opinion pressure

Labour Relations System
(Internal Inputs)

Actors
- Labour
- Government and Private Agencies
- Management

Goals | Values | Power

Mechanisms for Converting Inputs into Outputs
- Day-to-day interpersonal relations to satisfy social and psychological needs
- The negotiation process
- Conciliation officer and board
- Mediator
- Fact-finding
- Arbitration of interest and rights disputes
- Creative bargaining, continuous committees
- Special inquiry commissions
- Strikes and lockouts[b]

Organizational Outputs
- Management rights
- Union recognition
- Union security
- Dues check-off

Worker-Oriented Outputs
- The wage and effort bargain
- Job rights and due process
- Contingency benefits

Feedback Loop (flow of effects into labour relations system and environmental sub-systems)

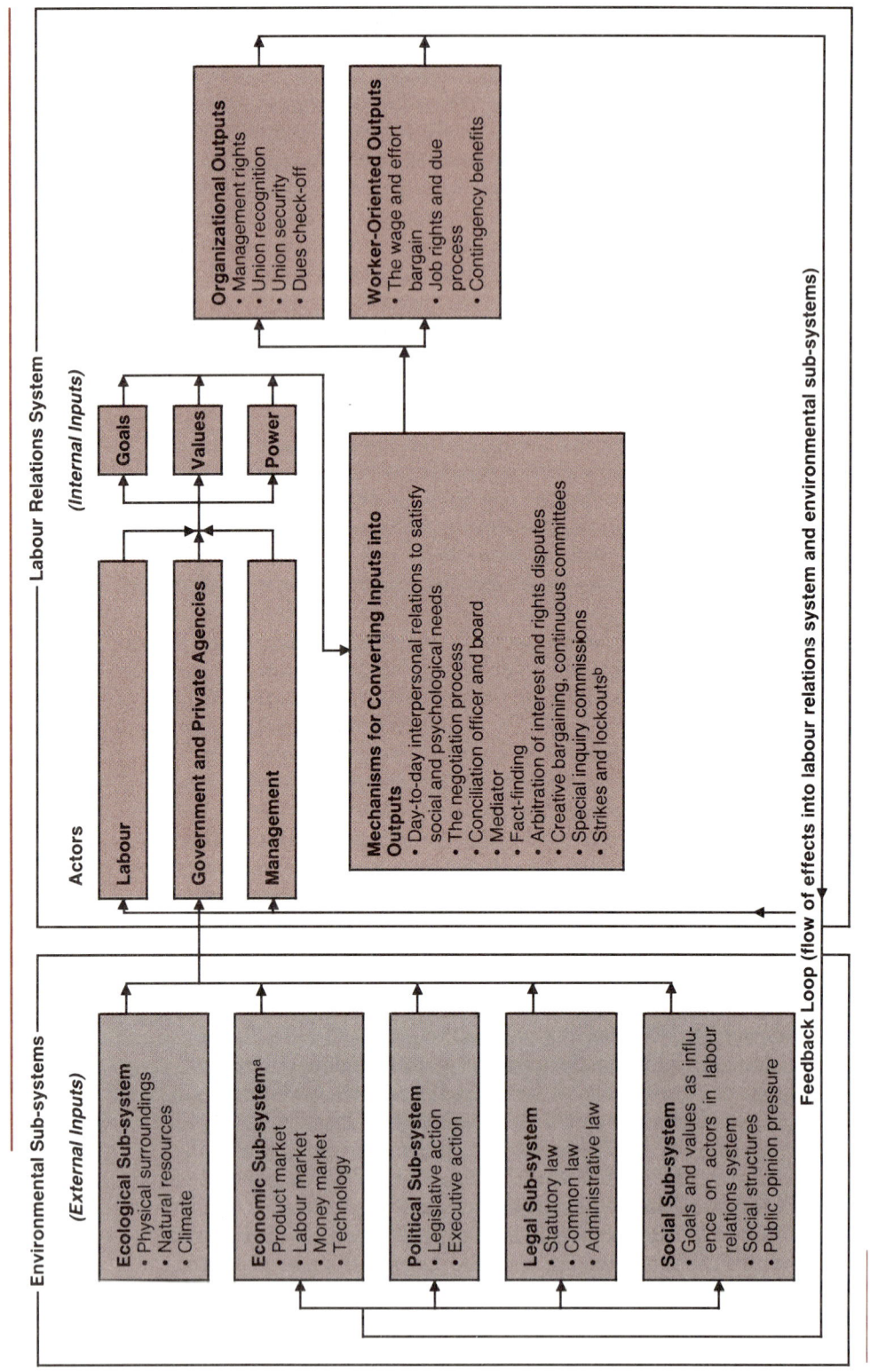

[a] This model presupposes but does not explicitly show the interrelationship between the various societal sub-systems.
[b] A work stoppage also may be considered an outcome or output of the labour relations system.

Source: A. W. J. Craig, *The System of Industrial Relations in Canada*, 2nd ed. (Scarborough: Prentice-Hall Canada Inc., 1986), p. 3. Used with permission.

These sets of goals, particularly those of unions and those of management, are important because they influence the nature of the relationship between union and management. For example, if the goals of union and management are seen as incompatible, an adversarial relationship may exist between the two parties. If the goals are seen to be complementary, then a more co-operative relationship may exist. It also is possible, however, to view these relationships somewhat differently. For example, if it is presumed that the union-management relationship is adversarial, the goals of union and those of management may be seen as incompatible. Understanding the compatibility of goals is important to understanding the union-management relationship. Therefore, the nature of the possible relationships between union and management are discussed here in detail.

The Adversarial Relationship. In this relationship the goals of union and management generally are seen as incompatible. When seen this way, an **adversarial system** emerges, in which labour and management both attempt to get a bigger cut of the pie while government attempts to protect its interests.

> In an adversarial system of union-management relations, the union's role is to gain concessions from management during collective bargaining and to preserve those concessions through the grievance procedure. The union is an outsider and critic.[5]

Historically, unions have adopted an adversarial role in their interactions with management. Their focus has been on wages and working conditions, and they have attempted continually to get "more and better," respectively. This approach works well in economic boom times but becomes difficult when the economy is not healthy. In fact, high unemployment and the threat of continued job losses recently have induced unions, as well as management, to revise their relationship. Many unions have begun to enter into new, collaborative efforts with employers.[6]

A Co-operative Relationship. In a **co-operative system**, the union's role is that of a partner, not a critic, and the union becomes jointly responsible with management for reaching a co-operative solution. Thus, a co-operative system requires that union and management engage in problem solving, information sharing, and integration of outcomes. Co-operative systems have been a major component of the labour relations system in countries such as Sweden, Yugoslavia, and West Germany. There, they have built a co-operative mechanism (co-determination is discussed in Chapter 18) into the labour system. There have been occasions, however, when Canadian management and labour have worked together to solve a problem. Most job-redesign projects undertaken by management require acceptance by the union to be successful. Active co-operation with the union is one of the best ways to gain this acceptance.

Successful projects like the Shell Sarnia plant (discussed in Chapter 13) involve the union in a co-operative effort to solve problems of concern to both parties. Another dramatic example of the emerging co-operative union attitudes in 1986 is provided by the country's steel industry. During May of

1986, top executives met with the United Steelworkers union in Sault Ste. Marie, Ontario, in an attempt to thrash out common strategies for dealing with the industry's weak points. This marked the second year in a row that the groups have met.

In 1985, the two groups formalized their relationship by creating the Canadian Steel Trade Conference, a combination of think tank and lobby organization. Because the steel firms and the United Steelworkers have agreed to set aside collective bargaining sore points, issues like technological change and adjustment to free trade were addressed with less than the usual acrimony. In fact, the steel group's experiment attracted attention elsewhere in the country. Among the unions said to be interested in pursuing similar arrangements are the Energy and Chemical Workers and the International Woodworkers of America.

Another co-operative approach is the use of an in-house fact-finder, appointed by mutual agreement of management and union, to develop and suggest alternative solutions to problems associated with labour relations. The fact-finder is a neutral party who has the trust and confidence of both labour and management and whose primary concern is employee participation in decision making. The fact-finder often is able to alter an adversarial relationship between union and management.

A Macro-Perspective of Labour Relations Systems in Canada. Although traditionally the labour relations system in Canada was very adversarial, the economic shocks of the late 1960s have resulted in a state of co-operation by all parties involved. Labour, management, and the government now focus more on achieving a consensus and on the expansion of workers' participation by right.[7]

Until the early 1960s, the major Canadian labour federation, the Canadian Labour Congress, sought to protect and enhance the terms and conditions of employment of their members via negotiations with employers. Bread and butter today rather than pie in the sky tomorrow was the primary union strategy. The labour movement had little direct influence on government policy.

Canadian employers were fragmented in their approach to organized labour. Although many employers' associations existed, some on a provincial and some on a national level, no common strategy for dealing with unions was undertaken by them. Because of the general unwillingness of employers to bargain collectively unless forced to do so, relations between labour and management were, in general, strained and distant.

During this period of adversarial relations, the government considered its primary role to be that of protecting the public from the disruptions that could result from industrial conflict.[8] Yet, as an employer, during the early 1960s government had avoided "Wagner Act-style" bargaining with its own employees. Namely, consultation began to take place with various employees' associations, with impasses resolved unilaterally by the employer. At that time, public sector unionism grew rapidly, and government employees who were discontent with consultation were demanding the same rights as private sector workers, and legislation towards that end was introduced in many jurisdictions.[9]

The labour relations system was changed during the period between the 1960s and the 1980s. The economic recession and high inflation led to an increase in union militancy. For example, during the 1970s, Canada had the second-highest level of time lost due to strikes in the western world.[10] Several approaches were tried by the Canadian government to control or influence the outcomes of collective bargaining during that period. Policies ranged from wage-price guidelines (1969–70) to mandatory wage-price controls (1975–78), and to complete public sector compensation control in the federal and several provincial jurisdictions.

The unilateral imposition of controls on wages and prices triggered strong opposition from both labour and management. Government was then led to search for alternative means to foster consensus in the labour relations system. Experiments with various procedures, such as fact-finding, first contact arbitration, grievance mediation, and bargaining by objectives followed. At the same time, a great deal of new legislation was passed in order to improve substantive conditions, not only for unionized workers but also for non-union employees, in the area of health and safety and human rights.[11]

During the early 1980s, the Canadian labour relations system was influenced again by the deep recession. Employers adopted a tougher stance at the bargaining table. At the same time, Canadian unions resisted demands for concessions more effectively than their U.S. counterparts. Whereas in the U.S. as many as three or four agreements at that period contained concessions, in Canada the rate was no more than one in ten. Nevertheless, wage and price increases slowed down significantly during 1983–84.

Although on the surface it looked as if the Canadian labour relations system remained adversarial, in fact, from the early 1960s until the 1980s, a slow but systematic shift toward a more co-operative relationship between the partners took place. One expert labelled this shift "tripartism," which refers to formal or quasi-formal decision-making structures in which representatives of labour, business, and government attempt to reach consensus on policy issues of mutual concern.[12] The major features of this co-operative tripartism included the following developments:

- The increased influence of the Canadian Labour Congress on government policies.
- The emergence of a loose national employers' organization, the Business Council on National Issues, which became the most influential business actor at the national level.
- The creation by the federal government of task forces composed of both labour and industry, to study the problems and prospects of 23 Canadian industries. Similarly, a Major Projects Task Force was created to develop a strategy for implementing major construction projects. The equal composition of labour and business representatives gave rise to the issuance of a consensus report in 1981.
- The creation of a National Labour Market and Productivity Centre composed of representatives of labour and business.

All in all, on a national level the Canadian labour relations system seems to be characterized by tripartism. Yet, this does not necessarily mean that the same level of co-operation is characteristic of the plant level.

Regardless of whether union and management share an adversarial relationship or a co-operative one, they still engage in processes of bargaining to arrive at a union-management contract. These processes often are influenced by the type of relationship union and management have at the local level. For example, an adversarial relationship is more likely to accommodate a process of distributive bargaining, while a co-operative relationship is more likely to accommodate a process of integrative bargaining.

Processes of Bargaining

The most widely used description of the bargaining processes incorporates four types of bargaining in contract negotiations: distributive bargaining, integrative bargaining, attitudinal structuring, and intra-organizational bargaining.

Distributive Bargaining. **Distributive bargaining** takes place when the parties are in conflict over an issue and the outcome represents a gain for one party and a loss for the other. Each party tries to negotiate for the best possible outcome. Some experts refer to this process as a "zero-sum" game.

Exhibit 17.2 outlines the distributive bargaining process. On any particular issue, union and management negotiators each have three identifiable positions. The union has an **initial demand point**, which is generally more than they expect to get; a **target point**, which is their realistic assessment of what they may be able to get; and a **resistance point**, which is the lowest acceptable level for that issue.

Management has three similar points: an **initial offer**, which is usually lower than the expected settlement; a **target point**, which is the point at which it would prefer to reach agreement; and a **resistance point**, which is its upper acceptable limit. If, as shown in Exhibit 17.2, management's resistance point is greater than the union's resistance point, there is a **positive settlement range** where negotiation can take place. The exact agreement within this range depends on the bargaining behaviour of the negotiators. If, however, management's resistance point is below the union's, there is no common ground for negotiation. In such a situation, there is a **negative settlement range**, and a bargaining impasse exists.[13]

For example, in regard to wages, the union may have a resistance point of $5.40 per hour, a target of $5.60, and an initial demand of $5.75. Management may offer $5.20 but have a target of $5.45 and a resistance point of $5.55. The positive settlement range is between $5.40 and $5.55, and it is very likely that this is where the settlement will be. Note, however, that only the initial wage demand and offer are actually made public at the beginning of negotiations.

Because many issues are involved in a bargaining session, the process becomes much more complicated. Although each issue may be described by the above model, in actual negotiations there is an interaction among issues. Union concessions on one issue may be traded for management concessions on another. Thus the total process is dynamic.

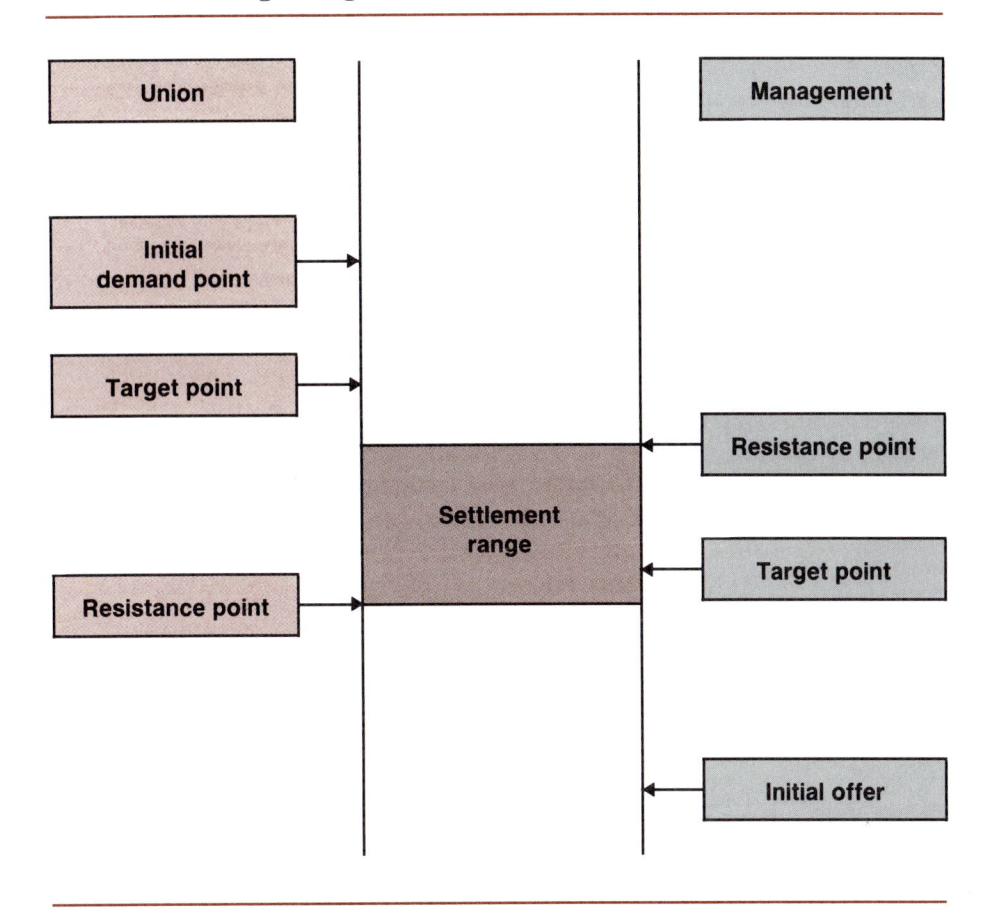

Distributive Bargaining Process *Exhibit 17.2*

```
Union                                    Management

Initial
demand point      →

Target point      →
                              ← Resistance point
                  Settlement
                    range     ← Target point

Resistance point  →


                              ← Initial offer
```

Source: U.S. Department of Labor Bureau of Labor Statistics, *Occupational Safety and Health Statistics Concepts and Methods,* BLS Report 438, (Washington, D.C.: Bureau of Labor Statistics, 1975), p. 2.

The ritual of the distributive bargaining process is well established, and deviations often are met with suspicion. The following story illustrates this point:

> A labour lawyer tells the story of a young executive who had just taken over the helm of a company. Imbued with idealism, he wanted to end the bickering he had seen take place during past negotiations with labor. To do this, he was ready to give the workers as much as his company could afford. Consequently he asked some members of his staff to study his firm's own wage structure and decide how it compared with other companies, as well as a host of other related matters. He approached the collective bargaining table with a halo of goodness surrounding him. Asking for the floor, he proceeded to describe what he had done and with a big smile on his face made the offer.
>
> Throughout his entire presentation, the union officials stared at him in amazement. He had offered more than they had expected to secure. But no

matter, as soon as he finished, they proceeded to lambaste him, denouncing him for trying to destroy collective bargaining and for attempting to buy off labor. They announced that they would not stand for any such unethical maneuvering, and immediately asked for 5 cents more than the idealistic had offered.[14]

Integrative Bargaining. **Integrative bargaining** is the situation in which management and the union work to solve a problem to the benefit of both. For instance, issues of work-crew size may be addressed, or union concerns for job security. Most quality-of-work-life changes involve integrative bargaining. The new work setting will benefit employees as well as the employer. Given the adversarial nature of labour-management relations, integrative bargaining is not common, although the recent interest in co-operative relations is changing, particularly in the field of health and safety (see Chapter 14).

The federal government, through its Department of Labour, developed a wide-ranging reform in order to foster more integrative bargaining and co-operation, but it had limited success.[15] The initiatives included steps to remove irritants that could give rise to conflicts, such as the outlawing of professional strikebreakers in a few jurisdictions (Ontario, Québec, and British Columbia); the removal from collective bargaining of the requirement for employers to deduct union dues directly from pay cheques and remit them to the union (the Rand Formula) was removed from collective bargaining; and the introduction of binding arbitration of first contracts in case of impasse by several Canadian jurisdictions. These initiatives were all intended to foster a climate of integrative bargaining.

Finally, Labour Canada QWL initiatives aimed at improving employee satisfaction and enhancing productivity are another example of government tripartism on the plant level designed to foster a more co-operative labour relation system and bargaining climate. Not all bargaining processes, however, determine who gets how much or result in the solving of problems. In some bargaining processes, the union or management tries to influence the attitudes of the other. This is referred to as "attitudinal structuring."

Attitudinal Structuring. The relationship between labour and management results in **attitudinal structuring**, or the shaping of attitudes toward one another. Four dimensions of this relationship have been identified: (1) motivational orientation, or tendencies that indicate whether the interaction will be competitive and adversarial or co-operative; (2) beliefs about the legitimacy of the other, or how much a party believes the other has a right to bargain; (3) level of trust in conducting affairs, or belief in the integrity and honesty of the other party; and (4) degree of friendliness, or the likelihood that interactions will be friendly or hostile. As the bargaining process proceeds, these attitudes may be altered. The attitudes emerging from the negotiations will have a serious impact on the administration of the contract and future negotiations.

Intra-organizational Bargaining. During negotiations, the bargaining teams from both sides may have to engage in **intra-organizational bar-**

gaining, or confer with their constituents about changes in bargaining positions. Management negotiators may have to convince management to change its position on an issue—for instance, to agree to a higher wage settlement. Union negotiators eventually must convince their members to accept the negotiated contract, so they must not only be sensitive to the demands of the membership but realistic as well. When members vote on the proposed package, they will be influenced strongly by the opinions of the union negotiators.

Within the range of these bargaining processes, unions and management can engage in a wide variety of actual bargaining behaviour. The process chosen and the specific behaviours enacted often are a product of strategies they choose to pursue, either separately or jointly.

Management Strategies

Prior to the bargaining session, management negotiators develop the strategies and proposals they will use. Four major areas of preparation have been identified:

1. Preparation of specific proposals for changes in contract language
2. Determination of the general size of the economic package that the company anticipates offering during the negotiations
3. Preparation of statistical displays and supportive data that the company will use during negotiations
4. Preparation of a bargaining book for use by company negotiators. Typically this contains a compilation of information on issues that will be discussed, giving an analysis of the effect of each clause, its use in other companies, and other facts.[16]

An important part of this preparation is calculation of the cost of various bargaining issues or demands. The relative cost of pension contributions, pay increases, health benefits, and other provisions should be determined prior to negotiations. Other costs also should be considered.[17] For instance, what is the cost to management, in terms of its ability to do its job, of union demands for changes in grievance and discipline procedures or transfer and promotion provisions? The goal is to be as well prepared as possible by considering the implications and ramifications of the issues that will be discussed and by being able to present a strong argument for the position that management takes.[18]

Union Strategies

Like management, unions need to prepare for negotiations by collecting information. The more thorough the investigation, the more convincing the union will be during the negotiations. Since collective bargaining is the major means by which a union can convince its members that it is effective and valuable, this is a critical activity. Unions should collect information in at least three areas:

1. The financial situation of the company and its ability to pay

2. The attitude of management toward various issues, as reflected in past negotiations or inferred from negotiations in similar companies
3. The attitudes and desires of the employees

The first two areas give the union an idea of what demands management is likely to accept. The third area is important but sometimes is overlooked. The union should be aware of the preferences of the membership.[19] For instance, is a pension increase preferred over increased vacation or holiday benefits? The preferences will vary with the characteristics of the workers. Younger workers are more likely to prefer more holidays, shorter work weeks, and limited overtime, whereas older workers are more interested in pension plans, benefits, and overtime pay. The union can determine these preferences by using a questionnaire to survey its members, as discussed in Chapter 13.

Joint Union-Management Strategies

Consistent with co-operative union-management relationships and integrative bargaining are joint union-management strategies. There are three major types of such strategies: productivity bargaining, concessionary bargaining, and continuous bargaining.

Productivity Bargaining. A relatively recent method of negotiating is **productivity bargaining**. This is a special form of integrative bargaining. Labour agrees to scrap old work habits and work rules for new and more effective ones desired by management, and in exchange, management returns some of the gains of modernization and increased efficiency to labour in the form of new and better work incentives.

Some unions have been hesitant to agree to this approach, because they fear that their members will lose jobs, that the company will require excessive work, or that technological change eventually will eliminate more jobs. Despite this hesitancy, productivity bargaining has been used successfully. One notable result is that the bargaining process changes from distributive to integrative. Labour and management work together, not only to create the agreement itself, but to create an atmosphere of ongoing co-operation. Another notable result is that significant cost savings are realized, enabling the company to survive and providing continued jobs for union members.

Concessionary Bargaining. As mentioned earlier, **concessionary bargaining** is prompted by severe economic and near-bankruptcy conditions of employers. Seeking to survive and prosper, employers seek concessions from the unions, giving in return promises of job security. Concessions sought by management from the unions may include wage freezes, wage reductions, work rule change or elimination, fringe benefit reductions, delay or elimination of COLAs, and more hours of work for the same pay. Although some rank-and-file union members may not be pleased with the concessions and therefore reject tentative contracts that have concessions, their alternatives seem to be limited. Either concessions must be made or plants will be closed or moved or the company may have to declare bankruptcy.

Another alternative that a few organizations have tried is having the employees buy the company or parts of it. Such purchases can be facilitated through employee stock ownership plans, described in Chapters 10 and 11.

Continuous Bargaining. Like affirmative action, health and safety requirements and other government regulations continue to complicate the situation for both unions and employers. As the rate of change in the work environment continues to accelerate, some labour and management negotiators are turning to **continuous bargaining**. Under this approach, a joint committee meets on a regular basis to explore issues and to analyze and solve problems of common interest. Several characteristics of continuous bargaining have been identified:

- Frequent meetings during the life of the contract
- Focus on external events and problem areas rather than on internal problems
- Use of outside experts in decision making
- Use of problem-solving (integrative) approach [20]

The intention is to develop a union-management structure that is able to adapt to sudden changes in the environment in a positive and productive manner. This continuous bargaining approach is different from, but an extension of, the emergency negotiations that unions have insisted on when inflation or other factors have substantially changed the acceptability of the existing agreement. Continuous bargaining is a permanent arrangement intended to help avoid the crises that often occur under traditional collective bargaining systems.

Negotiating the Agreement

Once a union is certified as the representative of a bargaining unit, it becomes the only party that can negotiate an agreement with the employer for all members of that unit. This is, therefore, an important and potent position. The union is responsible for negotiating for what its members want and it has the duty to represent all employees fairly. The union is a critical link between employees and employer. The quality of its bargaining is an important measure of union effectiveness.

Negotiating Committees

The employer and the union select their own representatives for the **negotiating committee**. Neither party is required to consider the wishes of the other. Management negotiators, for example, cannot refuse to bargain with representatives of the union because they dislike them or do not think they were an appropriate choice.

Union negotiating teams typically include representatives of the union local, often the president and other executive staff members. In addition, the national union may send a negotiating specialist, who is likely to be a labour lawyer, to work with the team. The negotiators selected by the union do not have to be members of the union or employees of the company. The general goal is to balance bargaining skill and experience with knowledge and information about the specific situation.

At the local level, when a single bargaining unit is negotiating a contract, the company usually is represented by the manager and members of the labour relations or personnel staff. Finance and production managers also may be involved. When the negotiations are critical, either because the size of the bargaining unit is large or because the effect on the company is great, such specialists as labour lawyers may be included on the team.

In national organizations, top industrial relations or personnel executives frequently head a team made up of specialists from corporate headquarters and perhaps managers from critical divisions or plants within the company. Again, the goal is to have expertise along with specific knowledge about critical situations.

The Negotiating Structure

Most contracts are negotiated by a single union and a single employer. In some situations, however, different arrangements can be made, with mutual agreement. When a single union negotiates with several similar companies—for instance, the construction industry or supermarkets—the employers may bargain as a group with the union. At the local level this is called **multi-employer bargaining**, but at the national level it is referred to as **industry-wide bargaining**. Industry-wide bargaining occurs in both the public and the private sector. National negotiations result in contracts that settle major issues, such as compensation, whereas issues relating to working conditions are settled locally. This split bargaining style is common in the United Kingdom and Israel.

When several unions bargain jointly with a single employer, they engage in **co-ordinated bargaining**. Although not so common as the others, co-ordinated bargaining appears to be increasing, particularly in public sector bargaining.[21] One consequence of co-ordinated and industry-wide bargaining is often **pattern settlements**, where similar wage rates are imposed on the companies whose employees are represented by the same union within a given industry. Pattern settlements can be detrimental because they ignore differences in the employers' economic condition and ability to pay. The result of this can be settlements that are tolerable for some companies but cause severe economic trouble for others. As a partial consequence of this, pattern settlements resulting from co-ordinated and industry-wide bargaining now do not occur very often. Nevertheless, the incentive to use these bargaining structures usually is related to efficiency and the relative strength of union and management.

In multi-employer bargaining, the companies negotiate very similar contracts to eliminate the time and cost of individual negotiations. Since this also saves the union's time and money, the union may be willing to accept this type of bargaining if its own bargaining position is not weakened. Where local conditions vary substantially, there may be a need for splitting the bargaining between the national and local levels—settling the major issues at the national level and leaving specific issues for the local level, where they can be adjusted to meet local needs.

Given the fact that in Canada there is a high degree of provincial jurisdiction over the private sector, it is very difficult for employers and unions to negotiate on a national basis. However, some incidents of multi-provincial negotiations have taken place in a number of industries. For example, while the main negotiations for the Steel Company of Canada occur at its Hamilton-Ontario headquarters, negotiators from other locations in Canada assist the process. Only when the terms of the settlement in Hamilton are acceptable to negotiators from Montréal and other locations is agreement reached.

In some provinces, such as British Columbia, multi-employer bargaining takes place frequently. In British Columbia, this is due to the legislation that enables employers' associations in any industry to be accredited and to bargain on behalf of all of their members. Accreditation in the other provinces is confined mainly to the construction industry.[22]

Issues for Negotiation

There is no typical format for negotiations. Issues may range from wages and working conditions to agreements regarding benefits, grievance handling, and other items that determine working conditions. Today's list of issues for negotiation is voluminous. A recent analysis by Labour Canada summarizes the most important items typically found in agreements—a total of 164 items, classified under 26 main headings. Some of the most prevalent items will be briefly summarized in the next paragraphs.

Although there are no formal or legal rules governing the issues that are subject to bargaining, there are a few exceptions in public sector negotiation, in which the law limits the issues that can be negotiated and included in an agreement. The Public Service Staff Relations Act, which was introduced in 1967 and governs collective bargaining rules for federal public employees, enables all issues to be negotiated except matters that would require a change in statute. A fairly large number of issues may be handled by a conciliation board. Arbitration, the alternative to the conciliation/strike route, is severely restricted in the items that may be addressed by an arbitration board. Parties who fail to reach an agreement and choose to submit the matter to arbitration may submit only the following issues: rates of pay, hours of work, leave entitlements, standards of discipline, and other terms and conditions of employment directly related to those items.

Wages. Probably no issues under collective bargaining continue to give rise to more difficult problems than do wages and wage-related subjects. Wage conflicts are the leading cause of strikes. Difficulties here are understandable: a wage increase is a direct cost to the employer as is a wage decrease to the employee.

The wages that an employee is paid are primarily determined by the basic pay rate for a certain job. This pay then may be increased by several other factors, all of which are subject to collective bargaining. Although management would prefer that basic pay be related only to productivity, this is seldom the case. Three additional standards are frequently used: (1) comparative norm, where rate of pay is influenced by the rates provided for similar jobs in other companies within an industry or even by comparative rates between industries; (2) ability to pay, where the pay rate is influenced by the financial capability of the company and particularly its profit figures; and (3) standard of living, where changes in the cost of living influence the rate of pay.

Recently, due to the productivity crisis and increased international competition, firms are having profitability problems. In turn, they are asking unions to forego wage increases and in some cases to take a wage reduction. As described in the section on concessionary bargaining, however, when employers ask for wage concessions, unions ask for job security in return. In turn, to facilitate being able to provide job security, employers provide early retirement incentives for all of their employees.

Wages, however, comprise only one general category of payment to employees. The other is economic supplements, or indirect (fringe) benefits. Collective bargaining deliberations may include discussion of how an increase in compensation will be split between these two types of payments. This is an important question, because the cost to the company of wages and fringe benefits may differ.

Economic Supplements. An increasingly important part of the pay package is the section covering **economic supplements**, fringe benefits such as vacations, holidays, pensions, and insurance. These benefits can run as high as 40% of the cost of wages, and are now a major factor in collective bargaining.

Provisions written into the bargaining agreement are very difficult to remove. If the union wins a new medical plan, for example, management will not be able to negotiate for its removal at the next bargaining session. Since management has less control over fringe benefits than over wages, it tends to be cautious about agreeing to costly benefits.

Occasionally, economic circumstances are so extreme that the union will agree to reductions in fringe benefits. The general rule, however, is that once something becomes part of the agreement, it remains. Common economic supplements include the following:

- *Pensions:* Once management has decided to provide a pension plan, the conditions of the plan must be determined (when the benefits will be available, how much will be paid, and whether they become available according to age or years of service). Finally, the organization must decide how long employees must work for the company in order to receive minimum benefits (vesting) and whether the organization will pay the whole cost or whether employees or the union will be asked to help.

- *Paid vacations:* Most agreements provide for paid vacations. The length of vacation is usually determined by length of service, up to some maximum. The conditions that qualify an individual for a vacation in a given year also are specified. Agreements occasionally specify how the timing of vacations will be determined. Also, employees may be given their choice of vacation time according to seniority. For example, a survey conducted by Labour Canada found the following paid vacation clauses in collective agreements covering 700 or more employees:
    - 62% of agreements provide two-week paid vacations and require a minimum of one year of service
    - 20% of agreements grant three-week paid vacations after one year of service
    - 20.6% of agreements grant five-week paid vacations for employees with more than 20 years of service [23]
- *Paid holidays:* A substantial proportion of collective agreements stipulate that employees will be paid for statutory holidays on which they do not work. In order to be eligible for this payment, however, employees must meet certain conditions in relation to days worked before and/or after the statutory holidays. For example, about 50% of collective agreements (covering about 35% of employees) stipulate that employees must work the working days preceding and following the holiday in order to be paid for it.[24]
- *Sick leave:* Unpaid sick leave allows the employee to take time off for sickness without compensation. Paid sick leave usually is accumulated while working. Typically, one-half to one-and-a-half days of paid sick leave are credited for each month of work.
- *Life insurance:* The employer may be required to pay some or all of the costs of life insurance plans.
- *Dismissal or severance pay:* Occasionally employers agree to pay any employee who is dismissed or laid off due to technological changes or business difficulties.

Institutional Issues. Some issues are not related directly to jobs but nevertheless are important to both employees and management. **Institutional issues** that affect the security and success of both parties include the following:

- *Union security:* Union security clauses define the relationship between the union and its members. There are four types of union security clauses in Canada. Under the **closed shop** agreement, the company agrees to hire and retain union members only. Closed shops very frequently are found in construction and are often associated with "hiring halls." Closed shops are not a very popular form of union security since only 4% of agreements discuss them. A **union shop** agreement requires all employees to become union members; 25.3% of collective agreements in Canada stipulate this provision. A **modified union shop** exempts from compulsory membership all employees who are not union members at the time of the agreement, but requires workers hired in the future to join the union; 21.1% of agreements in Canada contain this provision.[25] The final union security clause is the **Rand Formula**, which requires all employees within the bargaining unit (including non-union employees) to pay the equivalent of union dues as a condition of retaining employment.

- *Checkoff:* Unions have attempted to arrange for payment of dues through deduction from employees' pay cheques. Some provinces, such as Québec, have legislated to make the checkoff compulsory. Yet checkoff clauses in other provinces may contain provisions regarding the type of checkoffs: compulsory for all employees; compulsory for union members only; voluntary revocable. About 86% of union contracts contain this provision.
- *Managerial prerogatives:* More than 80% of the agreements today stipulate that certain activities are the right of management. In addition, management in most companies argues that it has "residual rights"—that all rights not specifically limited by the agreement belong to management.[26]

Administrative Issues. The last category of issues is concerned with the treatment of employees at work. **Administrative issues** include the following:

- *Breaks and cleanup time:* Some contracts specify the time and length of coffee breaks and meal breaks for employees. Also, jobs requiring cleanup may have a portion of the work period set aside for this procedure.
- *Job security:* This is perhaps the issue of most concern to employees and unions. Employers are concerned with restriction of their ability to lay off employees. Changes in technology or attempts to sub-contract work are issues that influence job security. One agreement illustrating this point was reached by the Canadian Brotherhood of Railway, Transport and General Workers in 1985 and VIA Rail. The agreement stipulated that employees with four years or more of continuous service would be protected from layoffs caused by technological, operational, or organizational changes. In return for this clause, the VIA union agreed to overhaul the pay structure for train service employees so that workers would have to work for all money that they are paid.[27]
- *Seniority:* Length of service is used as a criterion for many personnel decisions in most collective agreements. Layoffs are usually determined by seniority. "Last hired, first fired" is a common situation. Provisions for layoff on the basis of strike seniority are contained in 16% of agreements, covering 17% of employees, and 34% of agreements covering an additional 33% of employees include provisions for seniority with other factors such as ability, skill, knowledge, and physical fitness.[28] Seniority also is important in transfer and promotion decisions.
- *Discharge and discipline:* This is a touchy issue, and even when an agreement addresses these problems, many grievances are filed concerning the way employees are disciplined or discharged.
- *Health and safety:* Although various occupational health and safety Acts specifically deal with this issue, some contracts have provisions specifying that the company will provide additional safety equipment, first aid,

physical examinations, accident investigations, and safety committees. Hazardous work is covered by special provisions and pay rates. Often the agreement will state generally that the employer is responsible for the safety of the workers, so that the union can use the grievance process when any safety issues arise.
- *Production standards:* The level of productivity or performance of employees is a concern of both management and the union. Management is concerned with efficiency, but the union is concerned with the fairness and reasonableness of management's demands.
- *Grievance procedures:* This is a significant part of collective bargaining, and is discussed in more detail later in the chapter.
- *Training:* The design and administration of training and development programs and the procedure for selecting employees also may be bargaining issues.
- *Duration of the agreement:* Agreements can last for one year or longer, with the most common period being three years.

Conflict Resolution

Although the desired outcome of collective bargaining is agreement on the conditions of employment, negotiators often are unable to reach such an agreement at the bargaining table. In these situations several alternatives are used to resolve the impasse. The most visible response is the strike or lockout, but third-party interventions such as mediation and arbitration also are used.

Strikes and Lockouts

When the union is unable to get management to agree to a demand that it feels is critical, it may resort to a strike. A **strike** is the refusal by employees to work for their employer. Management may refuse to allow employees to work, which is called a **lockout**, but this is not a frequent occurrence. Exhibit 17.3 presents the industrial conflict picture in Canada for the years 1963 to 1983. The percentage of working time lost to strikes is influenced by the number of collective agreements negotiated each year. The second series in Exhibit 17.3 represents the percentage of large unit settlements involving a work stoppage. The two series, however, present a clear picture: except for 1977 and 1978 (years of mandatory wage and price controls), strikes in Canada were frequent between 1966 and 1982. During the 1970s, Canada had the second-highest level of time lost due to strikes in the western world (following Italy), and double that of the U.S. during this period.[29]

In recent years, the number of days lost due to strikes and lockouts is decreasing significantly (see the third "PHRM in the News" article), although public sector compensation is controlled by law in the federal and

Exhibit 17.3 Strikes and Lockouts in Canada: 1963–1983

	Strikes and Lockouts as Percent of Estimated Working Time[a]	Percent of Large Unit Settlements Involving a Work Stoppage[b]
1963–65	0.12	10.4
1966–70	0.35	12.2
1971	0.16	14.4
1972	0.43	13.0
1973	0.30	18.3
1974	0.46	15.6
1975	0.53	12.7
1976	0.55	13.5
1977	0.15	5.5
1978	0.34	6.3
1979	0.34	11.2
1980	0.38	12.3
1981	0.37	13.9
1982	0.25	6.1
1983	0.19	7.1

[a]1963–1980: Labour Canada, *Strikes and Lockouts in Canada* (Ottawa: annual); 1981–1983: Labour Canada, *Work Stoppages December 1983* (Ottawa: 1984).
[b]1963–1980: Labour Canada, *Collective Bargaining Review* (Ottawa: annual); 1981–1983: Labour Canada, *Work Stoppages December 1983* (Ottawa: 1984). Large unit settlements refer to bargaining units with 500 or more employees.

several provincial jurisdictions. The frequency of strikes is affected by a variety of circumstances, including the general health of the economy, union-management relations, and internal union affairs.[30]

In order to strike, the union must hold a strike vote to get its members' approval for a strike if the negotiations are not successful. Strong membership support for a strike strengthens the union negotiators' position. If the strike takes place, union members picket the employer, informing the public about the existence of a labour dispute in the hope that the public will boycott this company during the strike. A common practice is the refusal of union members to cross the picket line of another striking union. This gives added support to the striking union.

Employers usually attempt to continue operations while the strike is in effect. They either run the company with supervisory personnel and people not in the bargaining unit or hire replacements for the striking employees. However, many jurisdictions have passed "anti-scab" laws, which do not permit the employer to hire replacements, as in Québec, for example.

The success of a strike depends on its ability to cause economic hardship to the employer. Severe hardship usually causes the employer to concede to the union's demands. Thus it is paramount, from the union's point of view, that the company not be able to operate successfully during the strike, and that the cost of this lack of production be high. In addition, the timing of the strike is often critical. The union attempts to hold negotiations just prior to the period when the employer has a peak demand for its product or services, when a strike will have maximum economic impact.

Although strikes are common, they are costly to both the employer, who loses revenue, and employees, who face loss of income. If the strike is prolonged, it is likely that the cost to employees will never fully be replaced by the benefits gained.[31] In addition, the public interest generally is not served by strikes. They are often an inconvenience to the public and can have serious consequences to the economy as a whole.

The right to strike in the public sector is even more debatable—the public services employee withholds services from the general public in an attempt to gain concessions from the public employer. The public, therefore, is held hostage to the public sector union's strike. For these reasons, all jurisdictions in Canada that grant the right to strike to the public sector also use a designation process to deal with essential services. Some jurisdictions such as British Columbia and Québec have statutes that specify which services are essential and must be maintained either wholly or in part. In 1982 Québec established the Essential Services Council, which is empowered to designate the level of service to be maintained if the parties cannot agree on the number of employees required, or if the union does not designate a sufficient number of employees.

Conflict resolution interventions such as arbitration, mediation, and other measures often are required.

Mediation

Mediation is a procedure in which "a neutral third party assists the union and management negotiators in reaching voluntary agreement."[32] The mediator has no power to impose a solution, but attempts to facilitate the negotiations between union and management. The mediator may make suggestions and recommendations, perhaps bringing objectivity to the often emotional negotiations. To have any success at all, the mediator must have the trust and respect of both parties and have sufficient expertise and neutrality to convince the union and employer that he or she will be fair and equitable.

As indicated in Chapter 16, conciliation is compulsory in all jurisdictions in Canada except Saskatchewan. Conciliation as prescribed by legislation in some jurisdictions provides for the appointment of a mediator. In the late 1970s and early 1980s, data published by Labour Canada indicated that at least 55% of all settlements were achieved through some form of third-party interventions, and of this it was estimated that a mediator was involved in about 20% of the settlements. The same data also indicates that there has been an increasing use of mediation in recent years in the private sector in Canada.[33]

Arbitration

Arbitration is a procedure in which a neutral third party studies the bargaining situation, listening to both parties and gathering information, and then makes recommendations that are binding on the parties. The arbitrator, in effect, determines the conditions of the agreement.[34]

Three types of arbitration have developed. The first is an **extension of bargaining**: the arbitrator attempts to reach a rational and equitable decision acceptable to both parties. The second type is called **final-offer arbitration**, which involves the arbitrator choosing between the final offer of the union and the final offer of the employer. The arbitrator cannot alter these offers but must choose one as it stands. Since the arbitrator chooses the offer that appears most fair and since losing the arbitration decision means settling for the other's offer, pressure exists for both parties to make as good an offer as possible. The intention of final-offer arbitration is to encourage the parties to make their best offer and to reach an agreement before arbitration becomes necessary. This also is true in relation to the use of **closed-offer arbitration**, in which the arbitrator receives information on only the parties' original positions without any information on the bargaining progress up to that point.

Once the impasse is resolved, union and management have a binding contract. Adhering to this contract is the essence of contract administration. However, there are times during contract administration when arbitration is again necessary, as in the case of a grievance being filed. This type of arbitration is referred to as **grievance arbitration**.

In contrast to grievance arbitration, the arbitration process described above that deals with the contract terms and conditions is called **interest arbitration**. While interest arbitration is relatively infrequent in the private sector, it is more common in the public sector. In the public sector, most jurisdictions in Canada force arbitration. Most of the statutes set out fairly broad criteria for arbitrators to follow, yet some provinces request that the arbitrator keeps the interests of the public to the fore. Ontario and Alberta require that arbitrators or arbitration boards consider the government's fiscal policies when rendering their interest arbitration awards. Consequently, the use of arbitration in Canada has increased significantly since the 1960s.

Therefore, grievance arbitration in the private sector receives the most attention and concern. The role of grievance arbitration and the arbitrator is considered in step 4 of the grievance procedures in the following discussion of contract administration.

Contract Administration

Once signed, the collective agreement becomes "the basic legislation governing the lives of the workers."[35] That is, the daily operation and activities in the organization are subject to the conditions of the agreement. Since it is impossible to write an unambiguous agreement that will anticipate all of the situations that will occur over its life, there inevitably will be disputes about interpretation and application of the agreement. The most common method of resolving these disputes is a **grievance procedure**.

Virtually all agreements negotiated today provide for a grievance process to handle employee complaints.

Grievance Procedures

Basically, a grievance is a "charge that the union-management contract has been violated."[36] A grievance may be filed by the union for employees or by employers, although management rarely does so. The grievance process is designed to investigate the charges and to resolve the problem. Five sources of grievances have been identified:

1. Outright violation of the agreement
2. Disagreement over facts
3. Dispute over the meaning of the agreement
4. Dispute over the method of applying the agreement
5. Argument over the fairness or reasonableness of action [37]

In resolving these sources of conflict, the grievance procedure should serve four separate groups: the *employers* and *unions*, by interpreting and adjusting the agreement as conditions require; the *employees*, by protecting their contractual rights and providing a channel of appeal; and *society* at large, by keeping industrial peace and reducing the number of industrial disputes in the courts.[38]

Grievance procedures typically involve several stages. The collective bargaining agreement specifies the maximum length of time that each step may take. For example, it may require the grievance to be filed within five days of the incident that is the subject of dispute. The most common grievance procedure, shown in Exhibit 17.4 involves four steps, with the final step being arbitration.

- *Step 1:* An employee who feels that the labour contract has been violated usually contacts the union steward, and together they discuss the problem with the supervisor involved. If the problem is simple and straightforward, it is often resolved at this level. Many contracts require the grievance to be in written form at this first stage. However, there may be cases that are resolved by informal discussion between the supervisor and the employee and therefore do not officially enter the grievance process.
- *Step 2:* If agreement cannot be reached at the supervisor level, or if the employee is not satisfied, the complaint can enter the second step of the grievance procedure. Typically, an industrial-relations representative of the company now seeks to resolve the grievance.
- *Step 3:* If the grievance is sufficiently important or difficult to resolve, it may be taken to the third step. Although contract provisions vary, top-level management and union executives usually are involved at this step. These people have the authority to make the major decisions that may be required to resolve the grievance.
- *Step 4:* If a grievance cannot be resolved at the third step, most agreements require the use of an arbitrator to consider the case and reach a decision. The arbitrator or panel of arbitrators must be neutral and

Exhibit 17.4 Typical Grievance Procedure

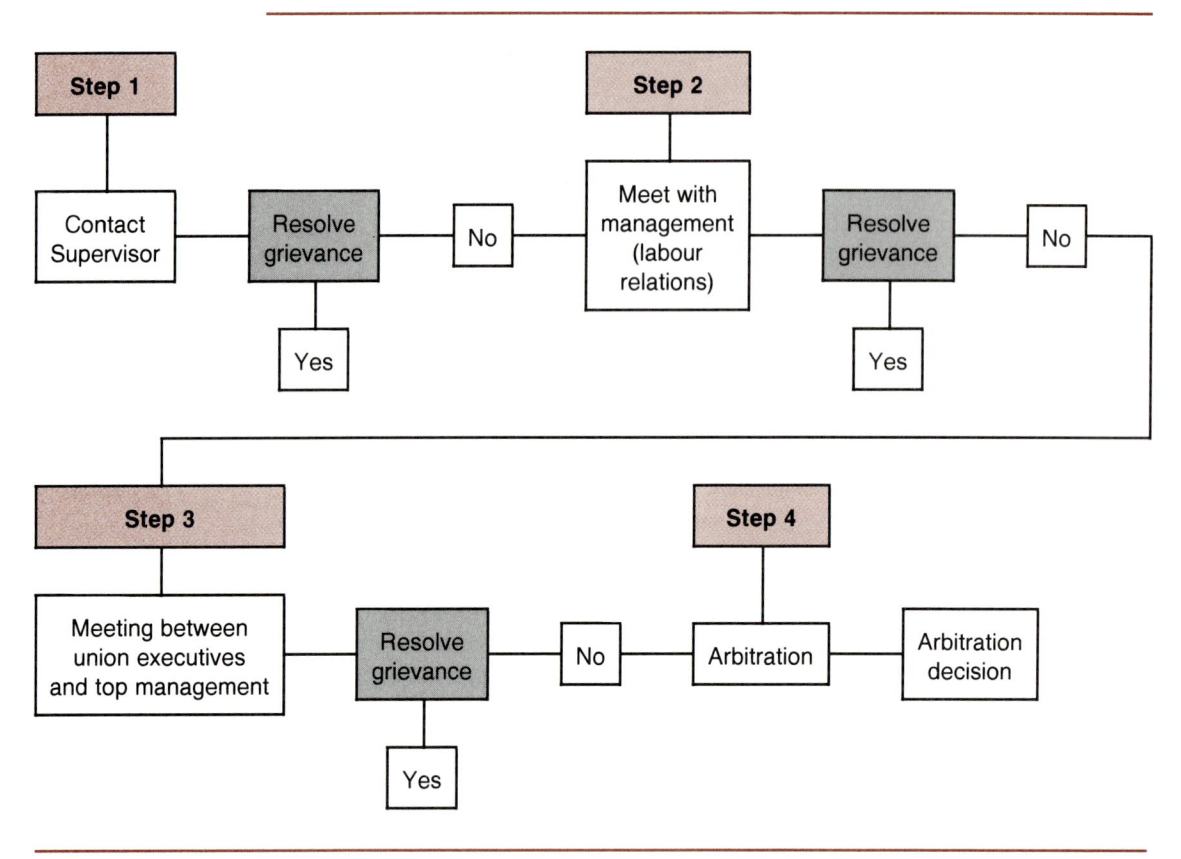

Step 1: Contact Supervisor → Resolve grievance? Yes / No
Step 2: Meet with management (labour relations) → Resolve grievance? Yes / No
Step 3: Meeting between union executives and top management → Resolve grievance? Yes / No
Step 4: Arbitration → Arbitration decision

Source: R. S. Schuler, *Personnel and Human Resource Management,* 2nd ed. (St. Paul: West Publishing Co., 1984), p. 573.

mutually acceptable. However, if the parties are unable or unwilling to select the arbitrator(s) then in practically all jurisdictions in Canada, the labour ministers have the right to make the nomination. Also, some provinces supply the parties with a list of arbitrators and when both parties have selected the same name, that person becomes the arbitrator. The arbitrator holds a hearing, reviews the evidence, then rules on the grievance. The decision of the arbitrators is usually binding.

Since the cost of arbitration is shared by the union and the employer, there is some incentive to settle the grievance before it goes to arbitration. Moreover, given that the arbitrators' fees in Canada range from $300 to $1000 per day, along with other fees, the parties have incentive to resort to less expensive methods of resolving the conflict. A newly suggested method is the **grievance mediation**, which is, according to some experts, cheaper, quicker, and remains confidential, hence mediated settlements are not published.[39] Air Canada, for one, uses this new approach.

Occasionally, the union will call a strike over a grievance in order to resolve it. This may happen when the issue at hand is so important that the union feels it cannot wait for the slower arbitration process, which takes a long time. This "employee rights" strike may be legal, but if the contract specifically forbids strikes during the tenure of the agreement, it is not legal and is called a **wildcat strike**. Wildcat strikes are not common, however, since most grievances are settled through arbitration.

Grievance Issues

Grievances can be filed over any issue relating to the workplace that is subject to the collective agreement, or they can be filed over interpretation and implementation of the agreement itself. The most common type of grievance that reaches the arbitration stage is concerned with discipline and discharge, although many grievances are filed over other issues. It is generally conceded that management has the right to discipline employees. The grievance issue usually relates to just cause for the discipline and the fairness and consistency of the action taken. Because disputes can arise over the definition of "just cause," discipline and discharge actions are prone to grievances.

Although it is accepted that absenteeism, for example, can constitute grounds for discharge, the critical issue is the determination that the absenteeism in question is excessive. Insubordination usually is either failure to do what the supervisor requests or the more serious problem of outright refusal to do it. If the supervisor's orders are clear and explicit and if the employee is warned of the consequences, discipline for refusal to respond is usually acceptable. The exception is when the employee feels that the work endangers health.

Since seniority usually is used to determine who is laid off, bumped from a job to make way for someone else, or rehired, its calculation is of great concern to employees. Promotions and transfers also use seniority as one of the criteria to determine eligibility, so management must be careful in this area, to avoid complaints and grievances.

Compensation for time away from work, vacations, holidays, or sick leave is also a common source of grievances. Holidays cause problems because there often are special pay arrangements for people working on those days.

Wage and work schedules also may lead to grievances. Disagreements often arise over interpretation or application of the agreement relating to such issues as overtime pay, pay for reporting, and scheduling.

Grievances have been filed over the exercise of management rights—management's right to introduce technological change, use subcontractors, or change jobs in other ways. This type of behaviour also may be the source of charges of unfair labour practices, since these activities may require collective bargaining.

Occasionally other activities prompt grievances. Wildcat strikes or behaviour that is considered to be a strike (mass absences from work, for example) may result in a management grievance. The major focus of grievances, however, is in the administration of the conditions of the agreement.

Management Procedures

Management can affect significantly the grievance rate by adopting proper procedures when taking action against an employee. One of the areas most in need of such procedures is that of discipline and discharge. The issue of just cause and fairness is central to most discipline grievances. Employers must ensure that the employee is adequately warned of the consequences of poor performance or role violations, that the rule involved is related to operation of the company, that a thorough investigation is undertaken, and that the penalty is reasonable. The following activities have been identified as being useful in meeting these conditions:

- Explanation of rules to employees
- Consideration of the accusations and facts
- Regular warning procedures, including written records
- Involvement of the union in the case
- Examination of the employee's motives and reasons
- Consideration of the employee's past record
- Familiarization of all management personnel, particularly supervisors, with disciplinary procedures and company rules [40]

In areas outside of discipline and discharge, management can avoid some grievance problems by educating supervisors and managers about labour relations and about the conditions of the collective agreement. It has been found that the presence of supervisors with labour knowledge can significantly reduce the number of grievances.

Union Procedures

The union has an obligation to its members to provide them with fair and adequate representation and to speedily process and investigate grievances brought by its members. Thus, the union should have a grievance-handling procedure that will aid in effectively processing grievances without being guilty of unfair representation.

Unions may have an additional interest in grievances as a tool in collective negotiation. They may attempt to increase grievance rates to influence management as the time for collective bargaining approaches. Grievances also may be a way to introduce or show concern for an issue in negotiations. In some cases, grievances may be withdrawn by unions in exchange for some management concessions. This may be dangerous, however, since it may be an unfair representation of the employee.

An important influence on the grievance process is the union steward. Since the union steward generally is the first person to hear about an employee's grievance, the steward has substantial influence on the grievance process. A steward can encourage an employee to file a grievance, can suggest that the problem is really not a grievance, or can resolve informally the problem outside the grievance procedure. The steward, being in such a key position, can have a profound effect on the situation. Personality characteristics of stewards may, in fact, influence the number of grievances filed.[41] Because stewards are selected from the ranks of employees and may have little knowledge of labour relations, the union should provide training to improve their effectiveness. The company should support such training as well.

Assessing the Collective Bargaining Process

The effectiveness of the entire collective bargaining process and the union-management relationship can be measured by the extent to which each party attains its goals, but there are some difficulties associated with this approach. Because goals are incompatible in many cases and therefore can lead to conflicting estimates of effectiveness, a more useful measure of effectiveness may be the quality of the system used to resolve conflict. Conflict is more apparent in the collective bargaining process, where failure to resolve the issues typically leads to strikes. Another measure of effectiveness is the success of the grievance process, or the ability to resolve issues developing out of the bargaining agreement.

Effectiveness of Negotiations

Because the purpose of negotiations is to achieve an agreement, this becomes an overall measure of bargaining effectiveness. A healthy and effective bargaining process encourages the discussion of issues and problems and their subsequent resolution at the bargaining table. In addition, the effort required to reach agreement is a measure of how well the process is working. Some indications of this effort are the duration of strikes, the use of mediation and arbitration, the need for government intervention, and the resulting quality of union-management relations (whether conflict or co-operation exists). Certainly joint programs for productivity and QWL improvements could be regarded as successes resulting from the quality of union-management relations.

Effectiveness of Grievance Procedures

How successful a grievance procedure is may be assessed from different perspectives. Management may view the number of grievances filed and the number settled in management's favour as measures of effectiveness. Unions may also consider the number of grievances, but from their point of view, a larger number rather than a smaller number may be considered more successful.

Although the views of management and the union may differ, an overall set of measures to gauge grievance procedure effectiveness may be related to the disagreements between managers and employees. Measures that might be included are frequency of grievances; the level in the grievance procedure at which grievances are usually settled; the frequency of strikes or slowdowns during the term of the labour agreements; the rates of absenteeism, turnover, and sabotage; and the necessity for government intervention.

The success of arbitration often is judged by the acceptability of the decisions, the satisfaction of the parties, innovation, and the absence of biases in either direction. The effectiveness of any third-party intervention rests in part on its ability to reduce or avoid strikes.

Summary

Collective bargaining is a complex process in which union and management negotiators manoeuvre to win the most advantageous contract. This has been the process in the traditional union-management relationship. The traditional relationship has been changing, however, particularly with the development of the productivity crisis in Canada. In addition, government intervention of the labour relations system at all levels is becoming much more apparent. The aim of all parties concerned is to safeguard the basic rights to collective bargaining, yet at the same time move the parties from an adversarial relationship to a more co-operative one. Canada certainly seems to be shifting in this direction at both the national and local levels.

Although many obstacles exist to union-management co-operation, present economic conditions are prompting many firms to act in co-operation with unions for their mutual benefit. The need for more co-operation has been recognized by some union leaders, who recommend more involvement with management.

The positive efforts of both union and management are required to make the labour relations system work. Would you argue that someone *has to* stay married to someone who becomes a drunk, runs around, and abuses the rest of the family? Would you argue that someone *should* stay married to that someone? Would you argue that public employees *have to* keep working even if their employers fail to provide pay increases to at least keep up with increases in the cost of living? *Should* employees continue to work under even the most adverse conditions, where management disregards the rights and welfare of the employees?

Historically, the threat of a strike is necessary to bring concessions by management. Without the threat, these concessions become less likely, although some managements may grant them even without the threat. The strike threat is an integral part of union-management relations in the private sector. Is the public sector really different from the private sector? Arguments go both ways of course. It is hard to tell the difference, however, between an irresponsible management in the private sector and one in the public sector, regardless of how essential the services are to the community.

The quality of the union-management relationship can have a strong influence on contract negotiations. Labour and management each select a bargaining committee to negotiate the new agreement. The negotiations may be between a single union and a single company or multiple companies or between multiple unions and a single company. Bargaining issues vary in scope and content, thus issues could be grouped into wage issues, economic supplements issues, institutional issues, and administrative issues. Mandatory issues must be discussed, permissive issues can be discussed if both parties agree, and prohibited issues cannot be discussed.

Almost all labour contracts outline grievance procedures for handling employee complaints. The most common grievance is related to discipline and discharge, although wages, promotions, seniority, vacations, holidays, and management and union rights also are sources of complaints. Management can influence the results of grievances by developing a procedure that ensures that their actions are just and fair. Written records of actions taken are useful for potential arbitration. Unions have a legal responsibility to represent the employee fairly in grievances; therefore, they also need a grievance-handling procedure.

Discussion Questions

1. What is the current trend in union-management relations and what impact does this trend have on unions, management, and employees?
2. What is the labour relations system, how is it governed, and what interests are at stake?
3. Compare and contrast adversarial and co-operative union-management relations.
4. Discuss the strategies that managements and unions use to prepare for collective bargaining.
5. Identify and discuss the three major types of joint union-management strategies.
6. Economic supplements are a major factor in collective bargaining. What are economic supplements and to what is their importance attributed?
7. What alternatives are there for management and labour to resolve an impasse in collective bargaining?
8. What is the purpose of a grievance procedure, what are legitimate grievances, and what is the process by which grievances are resolved?
9. What steps can management take to limit the number and severity of grievances?

CASE STUDY

Negotiations in the Hi-Tech Plastics Company

In union-management relations, collective bargaining is essentially a power relationship. It is through the implied and actual use of power that parties are compelled to resolve their conflicts. This was the situation when the management of Hi-Tech Plastics Company sat down with the Amalgamated Plastics Workers to negotiate a new contract.

Allen Springer, the 40-year-old president and owner of Hi-Tech, was surprised at the list of demands presented by the APW business agent, Tony Mattson. But Springer was completely taken aback by the union's tenacity. Throughout the six-hour session, the union team refused to budge from its initial positions. It was not the first time that the APW had caught Springer off guard: the organizing drive that brought the union into Hi-Tech had also come unexpectedly.

Allen Springer took the reins of this Oshawa company following the untimely death of his father, the founder of the company. At that time, Oshawa automakers needed plastic body parts, trim pieces, and fasteners to meet government-mandated high-mileage standards. Allen took full advantage of this demand and shifted his company's output from consumer to industrial lines. As a result of this strategy, sales volume almost tripled and the employee roster doubled to its present size of 105 employees. Measured against the industry leaders, however, Hi-Tech is still a small firm.

In the third year of Springer's presidency, a recession caused major setbacks in the auto industry; Hi-Tech's revenues declined and unsold inventory stacked up. In the midst of this bad spell, Allen Springer was hit with another blow—his workers were signing cards and pressing for union certification.

Following the successful drive, the union represented 65 Hi-Tech employees. The first contract was easily drafted, and included a 6% wage hike in a one-year pact, but the renewal negotiations were more militant. Battle lines formed on three union demands:

1. A three-year agreement, with a 30% wage boost the first year of the contract and 13% for each of the following years.

    Because contract negotiations were time-consuming and expensive, Springer wanted the contract to run longer than the one-year term of the first contract, but not at the proposed wage increases. He offered what he believed was a generous 8% wage hike.

    But Tony Mattson claimed that stingy wage hikes over the preceding five years had cut severely into the union members' standard of living. A 30% increase, he stated, was just bridging the gap between past wage increases and the inflation rate, as measured by the Consumer Price Index.

2. A dental health plan. On this point the talks became heated. Mattson pounded on the table, jumped to his feet, and shouted, "How can management claim to care about their workers while ignoring their health?"

3. Reinstate service pins. From the time Hi-Tech opened its doors, the elder Springer had acknowledged employee loyalty with 24-carat gold service pins for 5, 10, 15, and 20 years of uninterrupted employment. But in the face of declining income and with gold prices at almost $400 per ounce, Allen Springer had halted the practice. The union was quick to respond with a grievance calling for the pins to be brought back. At contract negotiation time the issue was still unresolved, but the APW members were adamant—give us our pins, they said, or submit the entire issue to binding arbitration.

Aside from the specific demands, what troubled Springer the most was the apparent willingness of the members to strike if their demands were not met. Throughout the session the threat of a strike was implied. Several times Mattson hinted that the rank-and-file members already had voted for a strike if their demands were not met to the letter.

During a break in the negotiations, Mattson confided to Springer that, although he was personally against a strike, the members were prepared. His manner was in sharp contrast to the shouting and table-pounding during the bargaining. Now he was speaking in low, even tones. "The local has already rented office space across the street from the plant for strike headquarters," he said. "The central labour union is giving advice and the other labour unions have pledged their support. I'm afraid they mean business."

This information disturbed Springer. If the union employees went on a picket line, he would be left with only clerical personnel, a sales staff, and six production supervisors.

As Springer reflected on the demands and the strike threat, he was grateful that at least this was only the first bargaining session with two more to go, and that the present contract had 15 more days before it expired. He had three days to prepare for the next bargaining meeting.

Case Questions

1. What information does Springer need to prepare for the next session? How would the information be useful?
2. What past poor labour relations practices can you identify?
3. What strategy or strategies would you suggest Springer use? Should he take a strike or try to avert it? Why?
4. What could be done to develop more effective labour relations on a long-term basis?

Source: Adapted with permission from R. L. Mathis and J. H. Jackson, *Personnel: Human Resource Management*, 4th ed. (St. Paul: West Publishing Co., 1985), pp. 608–609.

Endnotes

1. For an informative view and in-depth discussion of collective bargaining, see A. R. Weber (ed.), *The Structure of Collective Bargaining* (New York: Free Press of Glencoe, 1961); A. Sloane and F. Whitney, *Labor Relations* (Englewood Cliffs, NJ: Prentice-Hall, 1972); R. C. Richardson, *Collective Bargaining by Objectives* (Englewood Cliffs, NJ: Prentice-Hall, 1977); L. Balliet, *Survey of Labor Relations* (Washington, DC: The Bureau of National Affairs, 1981); J. A. Fossum, "Union Management Relations," in K. M. Rowland and G. R. Ferris (eds.), *Personnel Management* (Boston, MA: Allyn & Bacon, Inc., 1982), pp. 420–460; J. A. Fossum, "Labor Relations," in S. J. Carroll and R. S. Schuler (eds.), *Human Resource Management in the 1980s* (Washington, DC: The Bureau of National Affairs, 1983); B. F. Beal, E. D. Wickersham, and P. Kienast, *The Practice of Collective Bargaining* (Homewood, IL: Irwin, 1976); A. M. Glassman and T. G. Cummings, *Industrial Relations: A Multidimensional View* (Glenview, IL: Scott, Foresman and Company, 1985).
2. A. W. J. Craig, *The System of Industrial Relations in Canada*, 2nd ed. (Scarborough, Ont.: Prentice-Hall Canada Inc., 1986), p. 1.
3. J. T. Dunlop, *Industrial Relations Systems* (New York: Henry Holt and Co. Inc., 1958). Details regarding development and Canadian applications of this model can be found in H. Jain (ed.), *Canadian Labour and Industrial Relations: Private and Public Sectors* (Toronto: McGraw-Hill Ryerson Ltd., 1975), pp. 2–12.
4. For more details on Canadian labour relations systems, see A. W. J. Craig, *The System of Industrial Relations in Canada*, 2nd ed. (Scarborough: Prentice-Hall Canada Inc., 1986).
5. J. M. Brett, "Behavioral Research on Unions," in B. M. Straw and L. L. Cummings (eds.), *Research in Organizational Behavior*, vol. 2 (Greenwich, CT: JAI Press, 1980), p. 200.
6. For more details on this shift, see S. L. Dolan, "The Shift in Labor-Management Relations as a Function of Changes in Social and Economic Conditions," working paper, School of Industrial Relations, University of Montreal.
7. R. J. Adams, "Industrial Relations and the Economic Crisis: Canada Moves Towards Europe," in H. Juris, M. Thompson, and W. Daniels, *Industrial Relations in a Decade of Economic Change* (Madison, WI: IRRA, 1985), p. 115.
8. H. D. Wood, *Labor Policy in Canada*, 2nd ed. (Toronto: MacMillan, 1973).
9. A. M. Ponack, "Public-Sector Collective Bargaining," in J. Anderson and M. Gunderson (eds.), *Union-Management Relations in Canada* (Don Mills, Ontario: Addison-Wesley, 1982).
10. Adams, endnote 7, p. 122.
11. I. Christie, *Employment Law in Canada*, (Toronto: B. U. Herworths, 1980).
12. Adams, endnote 7, p. 126.
13. J. A. Fossum, *Labor Relations: Development Structure Process*, 3rd ed. (Dallas, TX: Business Publications Inc., 1985), p. 10.
14. Excerpt from A. A. Blum "Collective Bargaining: Ritual or Reality?" *Harvard Business Review*, Nov.–Dec. 1961. Copyright © 1961 by the President and Fellows of Harvard College. All rights reserved.
15. K. G. Waldie, "The Evolution of Government Consultation on Economics Policy." Paper presented to a Conference on Labor-Management Cooperation in Canada, sponsored by the Royal Commission on the Economic Union and Development Prospects for Canada, Ottawa, June 22, 1984.
16. A. Sloane and F. Whitney, *Labor Relations*, 5th ed. (Englewood Cliffs, NJ: Prentice-Hall, 1985), pp. 191–201.
17. For a good example on how to cost out collective bargaining agreements, see C. Hajdu, "Using a Computer to Cost Out Collective Agreements," in "Current

Matter/New Ideas," *Human Resources Management in Canada*, Prentice-Hall Canada Inc., 1984, pp. 5,245–5,249.

18. For an interesting description of GM Canada's preparation for negotiations with the Canadian UAW during the critical period of 1982–83, see B. Conway, "Negotiating a Master Agreement," in "Current Matter/New Ideas," *Human Resources Management in Canada*, Prentice-Hall Canada Inc., May 1983, pp. 5,041–5,044.

19. To get a sense of union strategy, see the UAW preparation for the negotiation with GM, in B. Conway, "Leading the United Auto Workers," in "Current Matter/New Ideas," *Human Resources Management in Canada*, Prentice-Hall Canada Inc., 1983, pp. 5,045–5,049.

20. See J. A. Fossum, "Labor Relations," in S. J. Carroll and R. S. Schuler (eds.), *Human Resource Management in the 1980s* (Washington, DC: Bureau of National Affairs, 1983), pp. 395–396.

21. A classical example of multi-employer bargaining in Québec occurred during the late 1970s and the early 1980s through the creation of a national bargaining committee for several unions referred to as "The Common Front." This strategy seemed to be quite successful during the 1970s, but frictions and divergent interests among the coalition members, as well as unilateral government actions, led to the dismantling of The Common Front.

22. A. J. Craig, "The Canadian Industrial Relations System," in S. L. Dolan and R. S. Schuler (eds.), *Canadian Readings in Personnel and Human Resource Management* (St. Paul: West Publishing Co., 1987).

23. *Provisions in Collective Agreements in Canada Covering 200 and More Employees: All Industries (Excluding Construction)*, Agreement Analysis Section, Labour Data-Labour Canada (Ottawa: Supply and Services Canada, March 1981), pp. 31–34.

24. Ibid., p. 30.

25. Ibid., p. 1.

26. Ibid., p. 50.

27. "VIA Rail Employees Get Job Security in New Contract," *The Gazette*, Montréal, July 16, 1985, p. D–7.

28. *Provisions in Collective Agreements in Canada Covering 200 and More Employees*, endnote 23.

29. W. D. Wood and P. Kumar, *The Current Industrial Relations Scene in Canada* (Kingston, Ont.: Queen's University Industrial Relations Centre, 1983), p. 398.

30. See, for example; S. L. Dolan, "Determinants of Officers' Militancy," *Industrial Relations* (Canada), vol. 34, 1979, pp. 287–311; S. Cameron, "Historical Variations in the Impact of Union Density on Strike Frequency," *Industrial Relations* (Canada), vol. 40(2), 1985, pp. 367–370; R. Dubin, "Attachment to Work and Union Militancy," *Industrial Relations, 12*, 1973, pp. 51–64; R. K. Schutt, "Models of Militancy: Support for Strikes and Work Actions Among Public Employees," *Industrial and Labor Relations Review, 35*, 1982, pp. 406–422; A. Shirom, "Union Militancy: Structural and Personal Determinants," *Industrial Relations, 16*, 1977, pp. 152–162.

31. D. J. Mitchell, "A Note on Strike Propensities and Wage Developments," *Industrial Relations, 20*, 1981, pp. 123–127. T. A. Kochan and R. N. Block, "An Inter-Industry Analysis of Bargaining Outcomes: Preliminary Evidence from Two-Digit Industries," *Quarterly Journal of Economics, 91*, 1977. J. Kennan, "Pareto Optimality and the Economics of Strike Duration," *Journal of Labor Research*, 1980, *1*, pp. 77–94.

32. T. A. Kochan, "Collective Bargaining in Organizational Research," in B. M. Staw and L. L. Cummings (eds.), *Research in Organizational Behavior*, vol. 2 (Greenwich, CT: JAI Press, Inc., 1980). T. A. Kochan and T. A. Jick, "A Theory of the Public Sector Mediation Process," *Journal of Conflict Resolution, 23*, 1978, pp. 209–240. H. A. Landsberger, "The Behavior and Personality of the Labor Mediator: The Parties' Perception of Mediator Behavior," *Personnel Psychology, 13*, 1970, pp. 329–347.

33. Data for the period 1965–69 and 1981 is published in *Collective Bargaining Review*, Labour Canada, Ottawa; data for 1970–80 is published in *Wage Developments Resulting from Major Collective Bargaining Settlements*, Labour Canada, Ottawa, 1981.

34. "Judgment Day for Arbitrators," *Business Week*, April 19, 1982, p. 66. R. Johnson, "Interest Arbitration Examined," *Personnel Administrator*, Jan. 1983, pp. 53–59, 73. "More Support for Arbitration," *Business Week*, Oct. 5, 1981, p. 132. J. N. Draznin, "Labor Relations," *Personnel Journal*, April 1981, p. 256. D. King, "Three Cheers for Conflict!" *Personnel*, Jan.–Feb. 1981, pp. 13–22. J. F. Rand, "Creative Problem-Solving Applied to Grievance Arbitration Procedures," *Personnel Administrator*, March 1980, pp. 50–52. D. Sheane, "When and How to Intervene in Conflict," *Personnel Journal*, June 1980, pp. 515–518. "Arbitration Case Increase," *Personnel Journal*, Nov. 1981, p. 832. S. C. Walker, "The Dynamics of Clear Contract Language," *Personnel Journal*, Jan. 1981, pp. 39–41.

35. A. Cox, "Rights Under A Labor Agreement," *Harvard Business Review, 69*, pp. 601–657.

36. S. H. Slichter, J. J. Healy, and E. R. Livernash, *The Impact of Collective Bargaining and Management* (Washington, DC: The Brookings Institute, 1960), p. 694.

37. Ibid., pp. 694–696.

38. J. N. Draznin, "Labor Relations," *Personnel Journal*, July 1981, p. 528. J. N. Draznin, "Labor Relations," *Personnel Journal*, August 1980, p. 625. G. A. Jacobs, "Don't Take 'No' for an Answer," *Industry Week*,

Jan. 26, 1981, pp. 38–43. I. Paster, "Collective Bargaining: Warnings for the Novice Negotiator," *Personnel Journal*, March 1981, pp. 203–206.
39. F. Bairstow, "Grievance Mediation: A Better Way," in "Current Matter/New Ideas," *Human Resources Management in Canada*, Prentice-Hall Canada Inc., August 1985, pp. 5,410–5,413.
40. Bureau of National Affairs, *Grievance Guide*, 4th ed. (Washington, DC: Bureau of National Affairs, 1972), pp. 8–9.
41. D. R. Dalton and W. D. Todor, "Manifest Needs of Stewards: Propensity to File a Grievance," *Journal of Applied Psychology*, December 1979, pp. 654–659.

SECTION VIII
Contemporary Trends

CHAPTER 18
PHRM Agenda for the Future

CHAPTER 18
PHRM Agenda for the Future

PHRM in the News

Trends and Challenges in PHRM
Power of PHRM in the Organization
The Need for Professionalism in PHRM
PHRM and the Use of New Technology
Contemporary and Future Challenges

International PHRM
PHRM in Japan
PHRM in West Germany

Assessing PHRM in the 1990s
Qualitative Approaches
Quantitative Approaches

Summary

Discussion Questions

Endnotes

PHRM in the News

Facts and Fantasies about PHRM in the 1980s

A highly qualified, innovative human resources (HR) function is more important to companies today than ever before. Why? Because of such factors as the need to step up productivity in the face of foreign competition, the need to comply with an increasing number of regulations and laws, and the increasing need to compete with other companies for highly skilled employees. HR can play an important role in redesigning a company's structure, control systems, or reward systems. Moreover, it has the potential to make a significant contribution to a company's health, vitality, and survival.

Nevertheless, indications are that many senior managers—both HR managers and line managers—are dissatisfied with the role HR departments often play. They feel that HR too often simply responds to line managers' requests instead of acting strategically. As the number and effects of changes in the environment continue to escalate, it's likely that such dissatisfaction will grow, as will pressure on companies and HR executives to expand the HR department's role by making it a more proactive and strategic one.

But how can HR's potential be translated into real action? How do we transform a function traditionally regarded as a service arm into a full-fledged member of the senior management team? The answer lies in increasing its power and influence. Top managers must make a conscious and concerted effort to create a new order within the organization.

Source: Reprinted by permission of the publisher, from "How Much Power Does HR Have, and What Can It Do to Win More? by E. F. McDonough III, *Personnel*, January 1986, p. 18, © 1986 American Management Association, New York. All rights reserved.

Japan's Corporate System a Prison

Back in 1972, as Japan was well along in its drive to dominate the world's economy, Masanori Fujimoto left the green fields of his native Hokkaido to seek his fortune. With a degree in international economics earned at a local university, Fujimoto secured himself a job in Tokyo with Mitsubishi Corp., part of one of Japan's most venerable and powerful industrial groups. Hardworking and intelligent, Fujimoto did well at Mitsubishi, and in 1979 earned his M.B.A. from Stanford University under a company-sponsored scholarship. Now fully fluent in English and acquainted with the latest in American business practices, the lean, handsome executive returned to Japan with all the accoutrements necessary for a highly successful career in the elite ranks of Japanese business.

Yet today, Fujimoto, like a growing number of other highly qualified Japanese managers, finds the path to success so clogged as to be virtually impassable. With corporate growth slowing appreciably and a mounting oversupply of qualified executives, giant corporations such as Mitsubishi no longer generate enough executive positions to satisfy ambitious young *sarariman*.

"We don't have a very good dream anymore," Fujimoto said over lunch in the small apartment he shares with his wife and two children in a quiet Tokyo residential district. "We know that there will probably not be the promotions, the rise in position we expected. It's a gloomy reality."

Fujimoto's pessimism is surprising in a country that has enjoyed so much growth and prosperity. And it is in startling contrast to all the mythology about the Japanese miracle, especially the unique loyalty that is said to flow between the Japanese corporation and its employees.

"It's not really a question of loyalty," explains Fujimoto, who works an average of 60 to 70 hours each week selling large-scale power and electrical systems to North American customers. "The reason you don't go is there is nowhere to go."

"Nowhere," because switching firms or even starting your own company is not a realistic alternative. In the business culture of Japan, bigness denotes status, and changing jobs suggests personal failure. "Here you learn to live the frustration because everything else is too risky," Fujimoto complains. "You are a prisoner of society and the rules that govern your life."

Source: J. Kotkin and Y. Kishimoto, "Theory F." Reprinted with permission, *INC.* magazine, April 1986, p. 53. Copyright © 1986 by INC. Publishing Company, 38 Commercial Wharf, Boston, MA 02110.

These "PHRM in the News" articles highlight several significant aspects of present and future challenges to personnel and human resource management. One is that it is vital for organizations to grant PHRM more power and visibility in order to enable the department to be more proactive and strategic. This shift in focus will transform the PHRM department, traditionally regarded as a service arm of the organization, into a full-fledged part of senior management. With an increased dependence of companies and nations on events happening in the global market, it is becoming more important than ever to have some awareness of how other countries utilize their human resources. The second "PHRM in the News" article draws attention to recent phenomenon transforming the managerial cultures and PHRM practices in Japan.

Trends and Challenges in PHRM

The same forces described in Chapter 1 that have increased the importance of PHRM are also creating new trends and provoking comparisons with other nations.[1] However, these forces are changing. For example, while until 1985 productivity was declining (see Chapters 1 and 2), future projections indicate growth rather than decline or stagnation. Predicted growth rates to the middle of the 1990s are near the high end of Canadian historic averages. Yet, while during the 1980s many companies enjoyed productivity at the expense of high unemployment, this trend is expected to change during the 1990s in the country as a whole. Various predictions made in Canada (by the McDonald Commission, the Economic Council of Canada, and others) indicate that the anticipated productivity growth in the 1990s will not result in high unemployment. Furthermore, employment will remain a single-digit figure, and inflation will stabilize in the 5% to 6% range.[2]

The pace and complexity of technological change also will increase in the 1990s. There is some controversy regarding the impacts of this trend: some believe that it will cause future unemployment, while others claim that, historically, technological innovations create more jobs. Those espousing the latter assertion predict that new jobs created by technology will alter the composition of the workforce: future employees will be more educated, more skilful, and more inspired to interact with the new technologies. In the five major chartered banks in Canada, for example, one employee in fourteen is working in data-processing related occupations.[3] Continued upgrading of the training and management of this new breed of employees will present a major challenge to PHRM.

The international competition, the continued enactment of deregulation policies, and the current proposals to establish free trade between Canada and the U.S., will be strong and significant factors influencing the overall effectiveness of operations in Canadian companies. Many more companies will export their products and services around the globe, and an increase in multi-national structures is likely to occur. Multi-nationals such as Bell Canada, Northern Telecom, Alcan, and others will be forced to pursue PHRM policies relating to the local cultural, geopolitical, and economic realities of the countries in which they will operate. Consequently, a thorough understanding of international PHRM will become vital.

Although some trends in the workplace, such as reduced rates of absenteeism, may suggest some productivity improvement, it appears that many employees are continuing to feel alienated, bored, and dissatisfied with their jobs and are increasing their demands for a greater say in workplace decisions that affect them. This demand for a greater say in decision making is part of a larger desire on the part of employees to have more rights in the workplace. This trend, and hence the importance of the match between employee rights and management rights, is also likely to intensify in the 1990s. It is likely, therefore, that PHRM will have to recognize further legal considerations in utilizing human resources. If employees do not strive to increase their rights, the growth in the number of new legal considerations may not materialize, but the frequency of litigation, particularly relating to employment equity, sexual harassment, wage and salary discrimination, and health and safety, can be expected to increase.

Organizations are expected to remain concerned about productivity, quality of work life, and legal compliance, which also contributes to the growth in the strategic importance of PHRM. These organizational concerns can be expected to support and intensify the multiple roles PHRM can play and the pervasiveness of PHRM at all levels in the organization—operational, managerial, and strategic. These concerns are likely to enhance several contemporary themes of PHRM, including openness, proactiveness, and effectiveness. It also is expected that these concerns will continue to stimulate the interest that organizations have in learning about how other companies and nations utilize their human resources.

This chapter concentrates, therefore, on some of the challenges PHRM will face in the 1990s. First, the role and power of PHRM in the organization will be discussed, followed by a call for more professionalism among PHRM practitioners, and a birds-eye view of some specific challenges within each functional area of PHRM. Then, in order to have a general appreciation for international PHRM, a summary review of PHRM in Japan and Germany will be presented. The U.S. experience is omitted from the discussion primarily because of its similarity to PHRM practices in Canada and because of the wealth of literature on the U.S. that already is available. Finally, the purpose of the last chapter is to demonstrate various methods and procedures that could be used to assess the overall effectiveness of PHRM activities.

Power of PHRM in the Organization

As suggested in the first "PHRM in the News" article, in order for PHRM to be effective, its role and importance in the organization must be recognized. A recent study concerning the power of PHRM today concludes that although PHRM is gaining more influence, there is still room for improvement in most organizations. The study noted, however, a shift in PHRM focus from the early 1980s to the present. While staffing and compensation have been and continue to be priorities of the PHRM function, a shift in priorities from employment equity and collective bargaining to employee communication, human resources planning, and overall business planning has occurred.[4] Similar trends have been observed on the Canadian scene, with the exception perhaps of issues of employment equity, which will continue to dominate PHRM. Furthermore, the same survey indicates that PHRM senior executives view the following priorities for the 1990s in a descending order of importance:

- Developing human resources strategies
- Human resources planning
- Business planning
- Staffing
- Employee communication

Indirectly, surveys such as this suggest that PHRM is abandoning some more traditional priorities and replacing them with more activities related to strategic business plans. This shift implies an increase in the influence of PHRM compared to the past. While PHRM will continue to be involved in traditional functions, it will expand its scope of general activities into business decisions and planning, serving more frequently as a consultant to the business, and performing more regularly as an equal member of the management team.

As CEOs of many firms come to recognize the contribution of PHRM to the overall economic well-being of the organization, the trend toward "PHRM power" will probably be reinforced. In helping the PHRM department to expand its functions and influence, top management must first recognize PHRM as a field of expertise and must make sure that the department is staffed and trained accordingly.

The Need for Professionalism in PHRM

One of the major obstacles to progress and expansion of PHRM power and influence is the fact that many departments still consist of PHRM officers who lack proper training and education. While in Chapter 1 it was noted that this situation is improving in Canada (one in five PHRM practitioners possess university degrees), it is still a long way from the desired state. Many PHRM practitioners are not yet convinced that professionalism and a code of ethics are a must if they wish to be taken seriously. Ironically, PHRM itself often provokes the perception that professionalism is unnecessary. A senior executive in a large company summarized his view by admitting that his company had the habit of converting ineffective manufacturing personnel into PHRM staff members. This type of practice has diminished PHRM credibility and capacity.

In order to gain credibility, PHRM staff members need to be viewed as professionals. With proper compensation and delegation of authority, professionals could be attracted to the field. Reporting relationships in the organization are also in need of change. In organizations that undervalue their PHRM staff, the senior PHRM officer usually reports to the vice-president of administration, operations, finance, or marketing. This consequently puts PHRM in a position of relatively low status. On the other hand, organizations that value their PHRM assign the senior PHRM officer the title of vice-president, reporting directly to the executive vice-president or to the president of the company. Further, these organizations give their senior PHRM officers greater visibility and greater access to important information and committees.

Increasing the PHRM budget lets the department exercise more discretion over the hiring of professional staff and the initiation of new projects and activities. With an increased budget, PHRM departments can interact with many individuals and/or sections of the organization, providing guidance, support, and counselling in various matters. This may change the image of PHRM from being a policeman in charge of discipline and grievances or a record keeper handling employees' pay cheques and employees' personal information, into a business partner in charge of employees' career planning, training and development, and other essential services.

Professionals are defined by the body of knowledge that they possess in the occupation, and their adherence to a disciplined code of ethics that usually is reinforced and supervised by peers, via professional associations. Although the laws in Canada currently do not require licensing of PHRM professionals, some sort of certification probably will be required in the future. While many occupations, such as engineering, medicine, law, and psychology, require certain basic qualifications as well as membership in the respective professional association as a prerequisite to practise, none is required for today's practising PHRM professional. This is paradoxical in the sense that the public is not protected when critical decisions about employment hiring, discharges, promotions, and other issues are made by unqualified individuals. A decision by a non-professional PHRM officer actually could lead to an employee developing a severe mental and/or physical health problem. How would you like to be fired by someone who does not understand the situation, lacks the legal knowledge about the case, and does not abide by any ethical standards?

Although the recent developments in employee rights (as discussed in Chapter 15), unions pressures, and other conditions, limit today's arbitrary decisions, there are still many employees in Canadian organizations whose future is subjected to the whim of personnel laypersons. Consequently, it is hoped that governments, professional personnel associations (see the list of these in Appendix B), and concerned management will co-operate in setting guidelines and imposing codes of conduct on PHRM practitioners. Universities also should contribute to this effort by adding ethics and business conduct courses to their personnel curriculum.

PHRM and the Use of New Technology

In the future, not only will PHRM departments be confronted with challenges resulting from the introduction of technology and automation throughout organizations but also they will be utilizing more micro-electronic technology to improve their own effectiveness. PHRM departments have been low on the list for computerization, but new computer applications involving PHRM departments in overall corporate strategy are resulting in more companies allocating microcomputers to their PHRM departments. The Bank of Montreal, for example, installed more than 20 IBM PCs in its human resource division in 1984 and many more have been introduced since. Some of the many uses of microcomputers in the Bank of Montreal include organizational charting, succession planning, management of absenteeism, applicant tracking and staffing inventory.[5]

Human resource information systems are being introduced to many medium-sized and larger organizations at an ever-accelerating rate, to meet increased demands for efficiency: employees need fast responses to their enquiries, and government regulations force companies to monitor constantly such aspects as health and safety, equity, and other PHRM functions. The significant reduction of the cost of purchasing and maintaining microcomputers and mainframes is another factor.[6] More specifically, human resource information systems can be used in many of the PHRM functions discussed in this book. Brief suggestions for each of these applications follow.

Human Resource Planning. Effective planning, as discussed in Chapter 2, requires readily accessible information on the current state of affairs. The computer can be instrumental in establishing a checklist of goals and activities that minimize costs and maximize employee development and legal compliance. For example, absenteeism results in high costs, including the cost of total hours lost according to occupational group, the total cost of additional employee benefits, the total cost of additional supervisory hours, and other related costs unique to each organization. The computer helps to calculate total costs of absenteeism by processing and analyzing this wealth of data.

Job Design and Job Analysis. A vast amount of personnel information on job analysis and job design also can become part of a human resource information system. For example, changing organizational requirements for particular blends of skills, knowledge, and abilities, as well as interests and preferences can result in job descriptions and job specifications that do not accurately reflect current organizational needs. Computer technology can be instrumental in avoiding mismatches. Job-description and job-specification information relevant to job analysis components can be stored on a computer system and then used to match people with jobs. Survey results could be stored as well, and be used to determine if and how jobs should be redesigned.

Staffing. Human resource information systems could be instrumental in affirmative action plans that require a utilization analysis by particular job categories. This type of system also can improve recruitment effectiveness by tracking down the historical trends of recruiting sources in a variety of ways. For example, PHRM staff can determine the best source of candidates for one position or department as well as the percentage of candidates hired from a particular source.

Human resource information systems also could be used to decide which predictors or tests are relevant for a particular case; administering a multitude of predictors makes personnel work challenging. For example, PHRM staff could do a validation study quickly by correlating current job performance data with any of several predictors. Available data on validity also can increase a company's ability to comply with the law, thereby avoiding legal battles and/or costs due to discrimination charges. Finally, simulation capabilities may be used to forecast the effects of alternative selection procedures, thus avoiding the potentially exorbitant costs of full-scale implementation trials.

Performance Appraisal. In particular, computer technology can facilitate the link between performance appraisal and training and selection. By establishing a menu of skills, knowledge, and abilities needed for each position, the results of an employee review can be used as a basis for determining whether a performance deficiency necessitates training, transfer, or even dismissal. In addition, with performance appraisal information stored in a human resources information system, employees can obtain instant feedback. This feedback can prompt those who were assessed as being poor to improve their performance, and it will reinforce a continued drive for excellence on the part of those who achieved high appraisal results.

Compensation. Computer technology can be instrumental in managing total compensation and ensuring equity. Total compensation can be computed for each employee and the average for each position can be calculated. In conjunction with job evaluation, the PHRM department can determine whether compensable factors are being assigned monetary values systematically or randomly. This can help to minimize inequitable compensation.

Furthermore, computer technology can accommodate performance-based pay planning and administration in various forms. First, administration may be conducted by establishing a merit plan grid on a computer system. The computer can be programmed to post the appropriate percentage increase. Also, budget planning is facilitated by manipulating the percentage values on the grid, automatically changing each individual's pay. This is the essence of the many spreadsheet software programs available on the market (e.g., Lotus 1–2–3; Multiplan; DBase; RBase 5000, and others).

In addition, computer technology facilitates management manipulation of data that can be used to formulate projections concerning salary structure proposals, compra-ratio, total cost of selected configurations of benefits package, and the cost of compensation in the future under different rates of inflation. Finally, with such an information system, an organization can more easily implement and administer a flexible or cafeteria-style benefit package.[7]

Training, Development, and QWL. As with staffing, establishing a directory of employee's skills, knowledge, abilities, interests, and preferences as an integral part of the information data base aids personnel in identifying individuals for training opportunities. Individuals also may be identified for open positions that are consistent with their career goals. Career pathing could be planned with computer-assisted technology.

As part of QWL efforts, human resource information systems could be used to collect data on surveys of different natures, such as ones involving morale, climate, and stress. Analysis of such survey data aggregated by occupation, department, or division of an organization can provide useful clues to aid in the selection of more effective remedial programs. Current information in an information system also can be helpful in attempts to improve productivity. Data on performance, absenteeism, and turnover can be part of the system and can be used to measure levels of productivity in different areas of the organization.

Health and Safety. Use of human resource information systems to conduct epidemiological studies could be very effective, particularly for organizations that produce or handle hazardous material. The information system could be used to monitor employees' health, and risk factors due to exposure could be detected early enough to remedy the situation. Furthermore, with high levels of accidents, remedial costs stored in the system could be tallied and summarized across departments or the organization, and costs systematically coded by the nature of their cause could help the PHRM department to identify patterns of problems in the company.

Employee Rights, Unionism, and Labour Relations. With a human resources information system in place, the computer can monitor complaints involving violations of employees' rights. The PHRM department can generate confidential personal information in a variety of formats in a short time. Computer technology and an information system can facilitate decision making in union management relations by maintaining a data base of information about other union settlements in the same or different industries. Management could also simulate its offers to the union more quickly and easily, thus enhancing its bargaining strategies.[8]

Contemporary and Future Challenges

While computer technology is one of the factors affecting PHRM practices, many other forces are challenging future PHRM activities, including changes in the composition of the labour force and increased employees' expectations (see Chapter 1), changes in the life styles of working adults, and changes that will occur in the social and legal system. Following is a brief summary of anticipated changes in various PHRM activities resulting from all of these forces.

Human Resource Planning. Many organizations have engaged in various forms of planning for a long time. In most, however, human resource plans were built around decisions that already had been made.[9] This may have been feasible when human resources were abundant and organizations had a great degree of freedom to hire and fire, but it is no longer possible. Now human resource plans and decisions must be integrated with the strategic plans of the entire organization. Human resources should not be addressed to solve short-term problems but rather must be that PHRM undertaken on a long-term planning basis.

Such efforts may not be easy nor always successful, but PHRM departments cannot avoid the long-term planning task. These tasks could involve developing and implementing programs to facilitate expansion or even retrenchment or reduction of operations. Rapid technological changes also will increase the likelihood of employee obsolescence. Consequently, the PHRM department will need to anticipate the provision of more programs in training and development.

Finally, there will be a growing desire for personal flexibility, a greater need for personal privacy and civil liberties, a continued demand by women and other minorities for equal participation at all levels of the workforce, more dual-career couples, and a growing desire by individuals to have more leisure time. Consequently, careful planning will have to be executed in order to cater to new future demands.

Job Design and Job Analysis. As organizations attempt to meet employment-equity and affirmative-action requirements, there will be an increased need to justify staffing procedures and performance appraisal results. A critical basis for this justification is job analysis, which provides adequate details of both the duties that a job entails and the skills needed to perform those duties. Thus organizations without job analysis programs probably will institute them, and those that already have such programs will review their analyses to ensure that they are current and effective.

In addition to the conventional job descriptions, more job analyses will include a description of the results expected and even the rewards that are part of the job. Such a description might include design characteristics and context of the job. Consistent with the PHRM theme of openness, it is likely that more job descriptions and job specifications will be prepared with input from the supervisor and the job incumbent.

In the area of job design, a number of trends probably will emerge. First, to meet public pressures PHRM departments likely will design jobs to accommodate all types of employees, particularly the handicapped. Second, there will be a greater focus on altering jobs by implementing ergonomic principles, to enhance worker motivation, productivity, and safety.

Staffing. A number of interesting trends appear to be developing. The increased use of a work-sample approach will lead to a resurgence in testing for selection purposes. Growing emphasis will be placed on using structured interviews, and all interviewers will undergo effective training on both the legal and the normative problems associated with the process of interviewing. New selection instruments will be devised to match not only the employee's skills, knowledge, and aptitudes with the job requirements, but emphasis will be placed on matching interests and preferences. For example, tolerance to stress and preference for working as part of a team might be factors taken into consideration by the new selection processes. In addition, PHRM staff would be very sensitive to problems resulting from recruiting over-qualified individuals as well as under-qualified employees.

New future legal issues also will influence the staffing function. New regulations will be passed, for example, to either outlaw or control the usage of controversial tests being currently introduced, such as drug tests, polygraphs, and honesty tests. A recent survey regarding these new tests concluded that, by default, these tests are geared specifically to minimize error in selection rather than to maximize good decisions,[10] which is contrary to the spirit of many Canadian human rights legislations.

Performance Appraisal. Performance appraisal has been poorly conducted in most organizations. As the cost associated with poor appraisal systems increases, more companies will invest in developing reasonable and sound systems. Costs are rising for two major reasons: 1) arbitration; human rights commissions tend to rule in favour of individuals who have been subjected to discrimination in companies that did not have appropriate performance appraisal systems in place; and 2) the costs associated with lack of recognition of excellence and potential.

The training of personnel managers to provide appraisals based on job behaviour rather than on personality traits will continue to be a major concern. With retirement at the age of 65 no longer being a set policy, employers must develop legally defensible performance appraisal to be used in decisions related to older employees. Also, with the refinement of legislations concerning employee rights, a sound appraisal system must be in place to justify employees' dismissal. Finally, more effective ways of tying performance appraisals to pay systems probably will be developed, if organizations want to operate on performance-based pay systems.[11]

Compensation. Compensation administration is becoming increasingly complex. Rapid increases in benefit costs and a pressure for more individualized compensation flexibility will add even more complexity. Revisions of tax laws will force constant changes in the offers and administration of the compensation components to enable employees to optimize their benefits and to provide employers with the means to achieve their compensation goals of attraction, retention, motivation, and control of costs.

A particular challenge to existing compensation practices is the issue of pay equity between men and women doing similar jobs. More attention in the future will be devoted to reducing this inequity, possibly through the use of innovative, bias-free, job-evaluation systems.

Training, Development, and QWL. Although training and development have grown significantly in importance, so have their costs. In the future, more emphasis will be placed on assessing training and development effectiveness to ensure that the organization receives its money's worth. With the rapid obsolescence of knowledge, continual retraining of employees will become a necessity. In addition, with the massive introduction of new technologies, PHRM departments will have to design training to upgrade the skills and knowledge of their employees in these fields. To respond to and to manage these trends, PHRM departments not only will have to design and implement new training programs, but also will have to overcome the employees' resistance to the changes that are associated with the introduction of new technologies.[12]

Workers will continue to emphasize their desire for more participation and control over the workplace. As a result, the biggest challenge to PHRM departments will be to manage a workforce with a different value system. Again, attention will be focused on a variety of QWL experiments designed to instill and cultivate a new set of values shared by all workplace participants—employees, unions, and management.[13]

Health and Safety. Largely because of various federal and provincial health and safety requirements but also because of management awareness of its social responsibilities, personnel health and safety will continue to grow in importance.[14] Many health and safety experts will be added to the PHRM staff. In fact, some observers believe that in several provinces, such as Ontario, Manitoba, and Québec, occupational health and safety is becoming the fastest growing career track for individuals pursuing PHRM careers.

Occupational health and safety legislation will continue to evolve as a result of the many criticisms levelled at existing ones. One area that definitely will get more attention is the psycho-social work environment and its impact on employees' mental and physical health. Consequently, in addition to more traditional safety measures and health programs, companies also will design programs to monitor stress and implement a variety of stress management programs.[15]

Employee Rights, Unionism, and Labour Relations. A clear pattern that is emerging in relation to employee rights is a tendency of our society to place less responsibility on the individual and a greater responsibility on society at large not only to respect employee rights but also to provide a minimum standard of living.

The interface with labour organizations will continue to be a priority in many organizations. Others will increase their efforts toward improving the existing relationships with their employees in order to avoid unionization. Increased use of consultants and other sophisticated methods by nonunion employers probably will result, as they attempt to fend off unions.

Both union and management will be forced to utilize more integrative types of bargaining in order to remain competitive in their respective markets. Many PHRM officers who previously saw unions as villains will be forced to come to grips with the reality that unions are here to stay. PHRM departments would be wise to view unions as partners in the workplace rather than as adversaries.

Unions also will come to realize that they are becoming less attractive to many of their members. Although some union growth is still expected in the public and white-collar sectors, other unions will have to devise new strategies to maintain their current level of membership. Some unions are doing this by expanding their traditional concerns for bread-and-butter issues (extrinsic rewards) to more work content-related issues. It would not be surprising to find unions in the future negotiating such issues as career planning and advancement paths, and level of interest, challenge, and responsibility as defined in job analyses. Some public sector unions already emphasize similar issues in their official agenda.[16]

International PHRM

As the world becomes more interdependent and as international mobility characterizes many business organizations, management recognizes the need to be aware of PHRM practices in other cultures and nations. During the 1970s and the early 1980s when recession cut deep into the economy and businesses suffered as a result, companies looked to other countries in search of magic solutions to their problems.

This was a period when many new management tools and techniques imported from Japan, for example, were mentioned often in management circles. Quality circles and management by consensus also were two hot topics. Buzz words, such as "co-determination" from West Germany, were used frequently in Canada to denote a necessity for worker participation and QWL programs. Yet, when one examines closely many of these "new" concepts, it becomes evident that they are not so innovative: many of these ideas have been known to Canadian business for a long time.

Perhaps the most important discovery was that these ideas could be implemented successfully throughout the organization or even across the nation. However, a missing link is identified on closer examination of the reasons for the relative prosperity of Japanese or German firms during the periods when the rest of the world suffered from high inflation and high unemployment. This missing link is the realization that the reason for this situation was not the technologies of management, but rather certain cultural variables. Since the entire culture of one country cannot be imported to another, a more realistic view of the importable cultural ingredients should be examined.

The following section takes a critical look at PHRM practices in two countries, Japan and West Germany, presenting highlights of their systems and comparisons with Canada. Needless to say, it is not intended to provide a comprehensive summary of PHRM in these nations, but rather to stress some unique features of their PHRM practices.

PHRM in Japan

The commitment to lifetime employment is one of the most distinguishing features of the Japanese labour market. Referred to as *Shushin Koyo*, the practice is almost a guarantee that anyone hired by a company will stay with it until retirement age. Although not required by the law nor formalized by written contract, lifetime employment is encouraged and endorsed by the Ministry of Labor and *Nikkeiren*, the Japan Federation of Employers' Association, and is practised by all major employers. In contrast to North American norms, therefore, inter-organizational mobility in Japan is discouraged (see the second "PHRM in the News" article).

With lifetime employment, human resource planning is less flexible, yet it must be tied closely to broader corporate objectives. Moreover, lifetime employment in Japan generally has not been applied to female workers, who for the most part are expected to drop out of the labour market once they get married. This norm may explain the low level of unemployment in Japan. Imagine trying to solve unemployment problems in Canada by phasing out all married women from the labour market!

Because of the lifetime employment policy, recruitment is rather different in Japan than in Canada, where it might be said that the hiring emphasis is on skill or job qualifications. In Japan, emphasis is placed on the general attributes of the person being hired, including potential loyalty to the employer. All regular employees of the corporation are normally hired at one time of the year, usually in April, immediately following the end of the academic year. Initiation ceremonies then take place, in which the first and critical phase of moulding the individual into the organizational culture begins.[17]

All of those who are not hired at this time are considered to be non-regular. They are offered temporary and part-time employment, and a lifetime commitment is not made to them. They can be temporarily laid off or discharged as necessary. In fact, the non-regulars represent anywhere from 50 to 70% of the total national workforce, which helps to explain why this policy of lifetime commitment endures even during periods of economic fluctuations.

Although job descriptions and job assignments are carried out in Japan, employees are expected to possess multiple skills and perform many jobs, as the need arises. However, Japanese managers are encouraged to seek consensus before reassigning employees or imposing new rules and regulations. The Japanese are fond of saying there are three sacred treasures of the Imperial House: the first is lifetime employment; the second is the traditional seniority system that determines not only wages but the timing of promotions; and the third is the enterprise (or company) union, which will be discussed later in this section.

Under the seniority system, it is rare to find any employee working under someone with less seniority in terms of service length, assuming that both have similar educational backgrounds. This system has its roots in the traditional *Oyabum-Kobun*, or parent-child relationship, which attaches great respect to the older or senior member of the family.

During the past few years, however, much consideration has been given to the argument that if wages are paid on the basis of seniority only, then those who have more ability may not always work hard. Therefore, today, the predominant method for determining wage increases is one that incorporates both seniority and merit. Wage increments determined using this combined approach may also vary according to job responsibility and work requirements. Nevertheless, even if an employee's job responsibilities remain unchanged until the mandatory retirement age (raised recently to 60), earnings will increase annually based on seniority.

In a comparison of basic hourly wages, Japanese wages are found to be among the highest in the world. Starting in about 1965, Japanese trade unions initiated a concerted industry-wide campaign known as the "spring offensive," during which time many trade unions take simultaneous, instead of independent, actions in demanding wage hikes. Today, approximately 80% of the organized workers negotiate wage hikes in the spring. As a result of this trend, wage decisions in the major industries, such as steel, influence the outcome of other industries. This has resulted in relatively standardized wage-increase rates throughout Japanese industry.

One distinguishing feature of the Japanese wage system is the provision of a semi-annual bonus or wage allowance. This is separate from the annual incremental rate. Usually paid without exception, the bonus amount is determined through collective bargaining and is closely related to both the general economy and the profitability of the company. Generally the equivalent of five to six months' salary is paid in bonuses at midsummer and at the end of the year.

Given the very paternalistic nature of the Japanese system, workers customarily receive indirect compensation in various forms in addition to salary. This may include housing or a housing allowance; daily living support, including transportation, meals, and uniforms; cultural and recreational benefits; discount stores selling food and clothing; and medical and health care. This "invisible remuneration" varies according to the size and the profitability of the company.

In most large companies all job training is carried out within the company itself. The in-company form of training is looked on as a key to each company's productivity and managerial control. Regular employees are hired as either high-school or college graduates; they generally have academic training but few, if any, vocational skills. The company looks on training as a means of orienting employees to its needs. It is not unusual, for example, for a new employee to have anywhere from one to six months of training before actually starting work. Supplemental training usually continues throughout the first three years of an employee's career, with additional training provided as necessary throughout employment.

Descriptions of training programs generally reveal a greater emphasis on the company as a whole—its role in society, its relationship to the competition, its marketing goals and objectives, what it must do to meet these objectives, its disadvantages in comparison to the competition, and what can be done to remedy these weaknesses. In short, emphasis is placed on creating well-rounded workers rather than on training employees in narrow issues, as is characteristic of many training programs in Canada. Yet, in addition to this general training, Japanese job training also offers special emphasis on application of skills.

In order to decrease boredom and job fatigue, multi-skill training permits employees to rotate jobs, rotate shifts, and generally meet fluctuations in production requirements. All blue-collar workers are expected to be multi-skilled within four to five years after joining the company. Among white-collar workers, a new employee is rotated to a new assignment at three- to six-month intervals. This process, coupled with formal training, continues for the first three to four years of an employee's career. Following that period, individualized training is made available for those who desire development in a specific area. Employees are tested or selected for specialized training, which may be provided through a company's own education centre or through university study.

The consequence of these PHRM practices is a very committed and loyal workforce that produces high-quality products. Similar results are reported in North American plants managed by the Japanese.[18]

The third sacred treasure of the Imperial House is what is known as the enterprise union. Unlike the North American and the European experience where unions are organized horizontally and industry-wide, almost all trade unions in Japan are formed on a company-by-company, or enterprise, basis. In the late 1970s, almost 71 000 labour unions could be found in Japan, one existing in almost every organization. There also are four principal industry-wide federations of workers that serve as co-ordinators, formulators of unified and reliable standards, and sources of information.

As a result of the enterprise union's central role, problems in management-labour relations are dealt with more directly, without necessarily involving an outside body. The "mixed" union representation of all blue-collar workers and some white-collar workers proves to be valuable in determining more representative concerns. The greater union participation by employees has resulted in almost 16% of Japan's current top management having once been active labour union leaders.

Another unique feature of the enterprise union takes into account the employees' loyalty to the company. Workers do not look on the union solely as a negotiating body, but use its structure to deal with such questions as industry and technical reforms, new plant and equipment investments, and matters of personnel and productivity development.

A summary of Japanese PHRM in comparison with Canada's is provided in Exhibit 18.1. The Japanese PHRM practices look to long-term accomplishments. The corporation is regarded as a mechanism for attaining certain social objectives in addition to individual objectives, including full employment, prestige and loyalty, a lifetime job, and various other social benefits.

Yet, as the second "PHRM in the News" article indicates, some contemporary challenges to the traditional Japanese paternalistic system will arise in the 1990s. Already some employees perceive the current system to be a "prison." Moreover, the system worked well in a growth situation, but it may run into trouble in a declining economy. In addition, given that the Japanese tend to be less opportunistic than the Canadians, for example, they will miss out on fast-breaking opportunities. The strong pressures for conformity that have worked to their advantage until now will be threatened by the success resulting from creativity and innovation that characterizes the valued concept of individuality of the western culture.

PHRM in West Germany

Germans are perceived as paying particular attention to rules and regulations and to power and status symbols. This results in more formal management and operations styles than exist in Canada. Broadly speaking, many of the PHRM guidelines are translated into a network of rules and regulations, with which German workers and employers appear to feel more se-

Differences Between Canadian and Japanese PHRM Systems — Exhibit 18.1

PHRM Program Characteristics	Canadian	Japanese
Employment Relationship	Short-term	Lifelong
Promotion Criteria	Primary Merit	Primary Seniority
Pay-Increase Criteria	Primary Merit	Primary Seniority
Selection	Formalized and Statistical	Informal and Intensive
Training	Formal	Informal and Intensive
Labour-Management Relations	Adversarial	Co-operative
Motivational Emphasis	Individual	Group
Career Paths	Specialized	Non-specialized
Behaviour Control Methods	Feedback/Monitoring of Conformity to Standards	Feedforward/Indoctrination
Decision-Making Modes	Individual	Collective

Source: Modified with permission from S. J. Carroll and R. S. Schuler, "Professional HRM: Changing Functions and Problems," in R. S. Schuler and S. A. Youngblood (eds.), *Readings in Personnel and Human Resource Management* (St. Paul: West Publishing Co., 1984), p. 577.

cure. However, this does not prevent innovative PHRM ideas being implemented in West German firms.

Many West German workers perform in "work islands," where they can avoid boredom by rotating jobs, socializing, and working in cycles of up to 20 minutes rather then a few seconds. West Germany appears to be well ahead of other countries in modifying the conventional assembly line. This enlightened position in alternative job-design utilization is a product of the work humanization movement in West Germany, initially founded by the federal government in 1974 and maintained by the co-operative relationship between labour and management. Many companies also furnish their own funds for work-design innovation projects.

An interesting work arrangement not discussed in Chapter 4 is the experimental *flexiyear schedule* in West Germany, under which employees base their work schedule on a full year rather than a day or a week. Actual implementation of such schedules vary across organizations, but typically, employees indicate how many hours they want to work each month for the following year. Then the employer and the employee together reach agreement on the exact days and hours per day to be worked. As with many alternative work plans in Canada, a critical advantage of flexiyear schedules is the choice it provides the employees. The results thus far are extremely favourable: reduced absenteeism, reduced conflict between work and family commitments for many employees, and increased accommodation of employees' desires for more leisure time.[19]

A relatively unique feature of training and development in West German firms is the extensive and successful apprenticeship system. This system receives financial and organizational support from both labour and management. Apprenticeship training for many West German young people begins at age 15, when compulsory schooling ends. Youths then select one of several programs that last between two and three years. Currently, 451 jobs in West Germany require apprenticeship. In total, almost half of the West German youths between 15 to 18 are enrolled in almost half a million apprenticeships. The results of this system include well-trained workers and an unemployment rate among youths that is far less than that in Canada.

The belief that worker interests are best served if employees have a direct say in the management of the company is called *Mitbestimmung*, co-determination. The concept of co-determination originated in West Germany and it now is spreading into many other European countries. Co-determination means, for example, that unions are given seats on the boards of directors of corporations. In addition, managers are encouraged to consult with unions before making major organizational changes, whether these be mergers, investments, or plant closings or relocations. If management disagrees with the union position, management prevails. However, unions may veto subcontracts by the company, and they have access to all company records.

Under the political leadership of the Social-Democrat government in West Germany, a consensus was reached during the early 1980s to promote international competitiveness through technological superiority and to overcome barriers to innovations by integrating the trade unions into the process of change. The West German system of labour relations, with its key features of centralization, juridification, and participation seems to be functioning well, even in the face of changed socio-economic conditions. The efficiency and legitimacy of collective bargaining also seem to hold, given the co-determination practice and similar system flexibility. Low levels of conflict plus commitment to co-operation characterize the labour relations system in West Germany.[20]

Since its defeat at the hands of fascism in the 1930s, the West German labour movement has consisted of unions with unitary structures that are a synthesis of traditional elements of the socialist and the Catholic labour movement. Although labour is dominated by social democracy, the Catholic influence on the development of such concepts as co-determination, social partnership, or capital formation for employees has become an integral part of the West German trade unions' ideology. Also, trade unions in West Germany are organized on an industrial basis.

The dominant labour organizations are 17 trade unions affiliated with the DGB (Confederation of Trade Unions), which sets the pattern in negotiating for the majority of the workers. The other trade union federations (the DBB, Association of Civil Servants; the DAG, White-Collar Association; and the CGB, Christian Trade Unions) lack significant bargaining power, hence public service employees are not allowed to strike.

In the 1980s, unionized employees who were members of DGB affiliates made up a third of the labour force. However, their power and influence stretches significantly beyond their numbers. For example, employee support for unions far exceeds their readiness for unionization. In fact, during the election of workplace representatives, about 80% of all employees vote regularly for candidates who have been nominated by DGB unions. Another feature of the West German unions is their centralized authority: most internal decision making takes place in the upper echelons of union bureaucracy.

West German employers also are organized and centralized. There are employers' associations in several industries, often dominated by large companies. The largest employers' umbrella organization is the BDA (Federation of German Employers' Association). The BDA co-ordinates various kinds of legally binding agreements for its members. For example, in 1978 it published a "taboo catalogue" containing rules and provisions of the association designed to strengthen its bargaining power and limit the amount of management compromise required in bargaining. Among its instructions was that Saturday, usually not a working day, should be a working day in order to maximize the use of labour and machinery. Although this instruction was reversed in 1984, it illustrates the strategy of the employers' association to establish common policies.

A summary of the differences between Canadian and West German PHRM systems is presented in Exhibit 18.2. The notable efficiency of the West German PHRM practices could be explained by the strong connection of the major partners to the labour relations system and the adherence of West German employees to discipline, rules, and regulations.

Exhibit 18.2 *Differences Between Canadian and West German PHRM Systems*

PHRM Program Characteristics	Canadian	West German
Job Design Emphasis	Production-oriented	Employee-oriented
Training	Formal: Multiple	Formal: Emphasis on Apprenticeship
Motivational Emphasis	Individual: Informal	Collective: Formal
Behaviour-control Methods	Flexible	Rigid
Managerial Power Base	Charisma/Expertise	Legal/Structural
Collective Bargaining	Decentralized	Centralized
Labour-management Relations	Adversarial	Partnership

Assessing PHRM in the 1990s

Many organizations do not appreciate the magnitude of their investment in their PHRM activities unless they adopt a systematic framework for assessing these activities. At present, only large organizations in Canada engage in formal PHRM assessment. Many managers consider the PHRM contribution "intangible" and thus see little need to conduct a formal evaluation. By failing to develop a rigorous and systematic assessment, many organizations do not recognize the real input of the personnel department to the organizations overall productivity.

Senior managers are quick to proclaim that the major strength of their organization is their employees, but when asked to justify the PHRM budget, or even to explain PHRM budget cuts at times of economic difficulties, they are unable to provide a rational and empirically supported reason for these statements.[21]

Many PHRM managers themselves face a similar dilemma when they are asked to justify the economic rationale for the introduction of a new program or service. How would they present the anticipated tangible outcomes of an attitude survey or a new stress management program? Most business people understand and respect PHRM activities when their costs and benefits are translated into dollars and cents, so the need exists to develop a systematic framework for estimating, monitoring, and assessing PHRM activities in coherent logic. Without such a framework, a PHRM manager not only encounters difficulty in justifying the department's activities for others, but he or she does not have criteria against which to assess the effectiveness of the programs for the department's own purposes.

Assessment of PHRM activities therefore serves a number of purposes. It helps to

- evaluate the state of health of the PHRM system and to identify problem areas;

- evaluate and monitor the various PHRM activities in terms of tangible criteria (bottom-line contribution to the organization); and
- anticipate future problems and to initiate interventions.

At present there is a growing interest among organizations to learn how to conduct a systematic PHRM assessment. With the significant rise in labour costs and the increased importance attached to human assets, the search for evaluation methodologies intensifies. One area that has been found most instrumental in enhancing assessment is the use of human resource information systems, as discussed earlier. Other approaches, which are not necessarily mutually exclusive with each other or with information systems, are presented here.

Qualitative Approaches

Personnel Audit Approach. The most simple and straightforward approach for assessing PHRM effectiveness is the personnel audit. In its pure form, a **personnel audit** is simply a review of the many available personnel records to determine if key personnel policies and procedures are in place and are being followed. Similar to financial audits, personnel audits rely on existing records such as personnel budgets and allocations, grievances reports, types and number of training and development programs, and performance evaluation records. The personnel audit approach usually is implemented by developing a checklist of the required policies and procedures, as illustrated in Exhibit 18.3. The items usually are grouped by human resource activity, such as staffing, compensation, and labour relations.

A checklist is a very simple and elementary approach to assessment, but its interpretation is quite difficult.[22] In order to overcome some of the difficulties in interpretation, audits often are conducted by a team. Multiple audits designed for sections or units of the organization usually involve a team of PHRM specialists and line managers representing the section or unit. Some organizations conduct this type of audit on an annual or biannual basis. In order to facilitate interpretation, the unit's audit results could be compared with results from other units in the organization or from similar units in other organizations in the same industry. The comparison provides good insights into such PHRM activities as health and safety, compensation and benefits, and labour relations. Norms for indirect performance such as turnover and absenteeism also could be set by this comparative approach.

Often, the checklist approach to personnel auditing is complemented by data generated through interviews and/or surveys. The premise for this approach is that the effectiveness of the PHRM department is determined by its reputation with its constituents or clients.[23] If constituent satisfaction is used exclusively in the audit process it could lead to erroneous assessment. The attitudes of the various users should be used in conjunction with the checklist approach so that the audit can produce useful information pertaining to effectiveness.

Exhibit 18.3 An Illustration of a Personnel Audit (an interview with the operating manager)

1. What would you say are the objectives of your plant?
2. As you see it, what are the major responsibilities of managers?
3. Have there been any important changes in these over the last few years in the plant?
4. Are there any personnel responsibilities on which you think many managers need to do a better job?
5. What are some of the *good* things about employee relations in this plant?
6. Do you feel there are any important problems or difficulties in the plant? Causes? How widespread? Corrective measures?
7. Do you have any personnel goals for the year?
8. Overall, how well do you feel the personnel department does its job? Changes the department should make?

Community Relations
9. What are managers expected to do about community relations? Is there plant pressure? Reaction to pressures?
10. What have you done about community relations? Do you encourage subordinates to participate in them? What are your personal activities?

Safety and Medical
11. Who is responsible for safety in your area? Role of group leaders and lead men?
12. What things do you do about safety? Regular actions? Results achieved?
13. Do you have any important safety problems in your operation? Causes? Cures? How widespread?
14. What does the safety specialist do? How helpful are those activities? Other things could be done?
15. Are there any other comments or suggestions about safety you would like to make?
16. Have you any comments about the dispensary? Employee time involved? Types of service offered? Courtesy?

Communication
17. How do you keep your people informed? What are your regular communication activities? Particular problems?
18. How do you go about finding out information from employees? Channels and methods? How regularly are such channels used? How much information is passed on to employee superiors? How much interest do supervisors show? Does personnel provide information?
19. Has the personnel department helped improve communication in the plant? What assistance is needed? Nature of assistance provided?
20. Has the personnel department helped you with your own communication activities?

Communication Channels Available
21. What improvement is needed in these?
22. Are there any other comments about communication you'd like to make? Any changes or improvements you'd especially like to see?

Continued

Exhibit 18.3

Manpower Planning

23. What kind of plans do you have for meeting the future manpower needs of your own component? Indicate plans for hourly, nonexempt. How far do plans extend into the future?
24. What does your manager do about planning for future manpower needs? How is this planning related to your own planning?
25. What part does the personnel department play in planning for the future manpower needs of your component? Of the plant as a whole?

Personnel Development

26. How is the on-the-job training of employees handled in your group? Who does it? Procedures followed?
27. What changes or improvements do you think should be made in the on-the-job training of employees? Why?
28. What changes or improvements do you feel are needed in the amount or kind of classroom training given here? Why?
29. Have you worked with your subordinates on improving their current job performance? Inside or outside regular appraisal? Procedure? Employee reaction? Results? Improvements needed?
30. Have you worked with subordinates on plans for preparing for future job responsibilities? Inside or outside regular appraisal? Procedure? Employee reaction? Results? Improvements needed?
31. What does personnel do to help you with your training and development problems?
32. Do you have any other comments on personnel development or training?

Personnel Practices

33. How are employees added to your work group? New employees, for example. (*Probe*: Specify exempt, nonexempt, hourly. Procedure followed? How are decisions made? Contribution of personnel? Changes needed and reasons? Transfers?)
34. How is bumping or downgrading handled? (*Probe*: Specify nonexempt or hourly. Procedure followed? How are decisions made? Contribution of personnel? Changes needed and reasons?)
35. How are promotions into or out of your group handled? (*Probe*: Specify exempt, nonexempt, hourly. Procedure followed? How are decisions made? Contribution of personnel? Changes needed and reasons?)
36. Do you have any problems with layoffs? (*Probe*: Nature of problems? Possible solutions? Contribution of personnel?)
37. How do you handle "probationary" periods? (*Probe*: Specify hourly, nonexempt, exempt. Length of period? Union attitude? How handled?)
38. How are inefficient people handled? (*Probe*: Specify hourly, nonexempt, exempt. How do you handle? How do other supervisors handle? Frequency?)

Salary Administration—Exempt

39. What is your responsibility for exempt salary administration? (*Probe*: Position evaluation? Determining increases? Degree of authority?)

Continued on next page

Exhibit 18.3	Continued
	40. How do you go about deciding on salary increases? (*Probe*: Procedure? Weight given to merit? Informing employees? Timing?)
	41. What are your major problems in salary administration? (*Probe*: Employee-centered? Self-centered? Plan-centered?)
	42. Has the personnel department assisted you with your salary administration problems? How? (*Probe*: Administrator's role? Nature of assistance? Additional assistance needed and reasons?)
	Salary Administration—Nonexempt
	43. What is your responsibility for nonexempt salary administration? (*Probe*: Nature of plan? Position evaluation? Changes needed and reasons?)
	44. How has the personnel department helped in nonexempt salary administration? (*Probe*: Specify personnel or other salary administrators. Nature of assistance? Additional assistance needed and reasons?)

Source: Reprinted by permission from Walter R. Mahler, "Auditing PAIR," in D. Yoder and H. Heneman (eds.), *ASPA Handbook of Personnel and Industrial Relations*, p. 2–103. Copyright © 1979 by The Bureau of National Affairs, Inc., Washington, D.C. 20037.

The personnel audit approach tends to rely heavily on impressions. The quantitative approaches are based on statistical and mathematical models as well as on results obtained.

Quantitative Approaches

PHRM Indexes. Many organizations develop in-house PHRM indexes to be used in assessing the efficiency of the PHRM unit; these indexes are used frequently.[24] These PHRM indexes and ratios usually are grouped to correspond to the major activities of the PHRM department. They also can be grouped according to PHRM strategic concerns such as accidents, turnover, absenteeism, productivity, etc. Examples of typical PHRM indexes are provided in Exhibit 18.4.

Most organizations compare these indexes to the unit's own past data or to some desired objectives. Data also could be compared to the industry average. The results of these comparisons can indicate whether the unit is stable, improving, or declining. Analysis of the trend can provide valuable insights into the relationship between PHRM activities and unit performance.[25]

Cost/Benefit and Human Resource Accounting Approaches. Since the early 1950s, attempts have been made to develop cost/benefit analysis models for PHRM activities.[26] What makes this approach different from others is the quantification in financial terms of a set of common behavioural and performance outcomes. Although there are no generally accepted accounting procedures for employee valuation, attempts have been made to apply standard accounting principles to employee behaviour. Behaviours that are

Sample of PHRM Indexes — Exhibit 18.4

Planning
- Number of unpredicted new job openings
- Deviation between forecasted and actual needs

Staffing
- Average age of workforce
- Ratio of exempt and non-exempt employees
- Average amount of time it takes to recruit employees by skill types
- Advertising cost per hire/per referral
- Turnover and absenteeism rates
- Ratio of various selection devices (application blanks, tests, etc.,) to performance indexes

Compensation
- Number of employees above or below the standard wage rates
- Ratio of promotion by merit v. promotion by seniority
- Mean wage differential between departments, divisions, and/or critical categories of employees
- Number and types of employees participating in profit sharing
- Number and types of employees using services provided by the company (insurance plans, recreation facilities, etc.)

Training and Development
- Proportion of eligible employees who received skills training in the past year; new supervisors who received supervisory training
- Proportion of employees fully qualified for their jobs
- Product and service quality before and after training
- Training costs per employee and employee salary level

Health and Safety
- Frequency of accident rates
- Number of days/hours lost due to accidents
- Accidents by type
- Accidents/professional diseases by department/division or category of employee

Labour Relations
- Proportion of grievances won in the last year
- Average cost of grievance per employee
- Number of grievances and complaints filed
- Grievances by subject

---

measured using this approach are those associated with the PHRM functions of attracting, selecting, retaining, developing, and utilizing employees.

The definition of the cost of all PHRM functions includes two major parameters: **controllable** v. **uncontrollable**, and **direct** v. **indirect**. Therefore, it is necessary to recognize the impact of situational factors in developing costing formulas. For instance, consider employee absenteeism behaviour. The extent to which people are absent due to real illness or the sickness of children at home, or even the weather, represents an uncontrollable cost. However, employee use of their bank of sick-leave days because they are discontent with their salary or as a stress-reduction strategy *can* be controlled by the organization.

Direct measures refer to actual costs, such as the accumulated, direct cost of replacing an absent employee. The indirect measures usually are expressed in terms of time, quality, or quantity. In many cases, indirect costs exceed direct costs in terms of dollars and cents, although rarely are they taken into serious consideration by many organizations. For example, the indirect cost associated with replacing an absent employee may include the following:

- The administrative cost of searching for a replacement
- The cost in productive time of the supervisor responsible for orienting the replacement
- The short-term cost of training and orienting the replacement
- The cost associated with low morale on the part of other employees

Thus, indirect measures are valuable in that they supply part of the data needed to develop a direct measure. Estimating dollar values associated with outcomes can be very instrumental in calculating the benefits associated with programs intended to reduce these costs. The programs may include training, changing control systems in the organization, or changing the compensation policies. The real payoff to be gained from determining the cost of employee behaviours lies in being able to demonstrate a financial gain from an intelligent application of PHRM methods.

Human resource accounting attempts to treat human resources as assets rather than expenses. Under this approach the accounting conventions applied to capital assets also are applied to the workforce. Consequently, the asset value of human resources may be estimated by replacement costs and/or acquisition costs, and depreciation is possible. A number of recent applications of human resource accounting have been reported.[27]

A special application of human resource accounting is the **utility analysis**. In this approach, PHRM costs are measured by obtaining managers' estimates of the dollar values of the results expected from PHRM activities. For example, in one study managers were asked to estimate the dollar value of different performance levels of computer programmers. By pointing out the improvement in performance attributed to a new selection program, PHRM officers were able to estimate the dollar value of its results.[28] A few employers such as General Motors and IBM are beginning to experiment with utility analysis.[29]

Work Analysis and Budgeting Approaches. Both of these methods involve quantitative evaluation. Work analysis is based on work-sampling techniques that randomly examine PHRM staff activities with the purpose of drawing inferences about the total activities of the department. For example, using this technique one study concluded that the PHRM department spent more than 50% of its time on staffing and benefits, which was consistent with the department strategy.[30]

Budgeting can provide yet another clue with which to assess PHRM effectiveness: PHRM activities can be evaluated in terms of the percentage-budget allocated to each major activity. The amount of money allocated reflects the strategic importance of the activity. Changes in directions and magnitude of PHRM policies can be assessed over time, as well as compared with other PHRM activities.

Summary

Some of the future trends as well as current problems facing PHRM have been presented in this chapter. It has been shown that PHRM activities are in an accelerating state of evolution, and that the future holds even more difficult and complex tasks for PHRM practitioners, but these are matched by even more challenges and rewards. PHRM departments will be more visible in the organization—partners in obtaining the strategic goals of the enterprise. The emerging challenges will demand a more capable, better-educated, and thoroughly professional staff. More specifically, in addition to the traditional body of knowledge and adherence to a professional code of ethics, PHRM executives will need more scientific and technical skills in the areas of computers and robotics.

The overview of PHRM practices in other countries promotes appreciation of the similarities and the differences between practices in Canada and elsewhere. While it would be naïve to suggest that foreign PHRM practices can be transported easily to Canada, an understanding of them facilitates a rethinking of the assumptions that underlie Canadian PHRM practices.

Finally, a review of contemporary as well as emerging methods used to assess PHRM activities are discussed. Both qualitative and quantitative techniques can be used to conduct a systematic evaluation. The objective of the PHRM assessment is to further the development and application of improved means of human resource management in organizations.

Discussion Questions

1. Why is the PHRM department gaining power in organizations today? What are the roadblocks to this gain?
2. Should PHRM professionals be licensed? What is a PHRM professional?
3. What are the emerging uses of new technologies in PHRM work?
4. What important trends in HRP, job design, and staffing should be recognized by PHRM staff?

5. What important trends in appraisal and compensation should be recognized by PHRM staff?
6. What future challenges can be expected in the labour relations field?
7. Discuss the strengths and weaknesses of Japan's PHRM activities.
8. What are the most salient features of West Germany's PHRM activities?
9. Why should PHRM activities overall be assessed?
10. What is the difference between direct and indirect costs? Provide examples of each.
11. What is the value of conducting a qualitative PHRM assessment?
12. Discuss the pros and cons of two selected quantitative techniques of PHRM assessment.

Endnotes

1. For issues and trends projected for PHRM in the 1980s, see S. J. Carroll and R. S. Schuler (eds.), "Human Resource Management in the 1980s," in R. S. Schuler and S. A. Youngblood (eds.), *Readings in Personnel and Human Resource Management* (St. Paul: West Publishing Co., 1984). For discussion of issues and trends projected for the 1990s, see R. Adams, "Into the 1990's: The Human Resources Adjustment Agenda," in *Human Resources Management in Canada*, Prentice-Hall Canada Inc., April 1986, pp. 15,511–15,517.
2. This trend represents the authors view, based on various writings in the area. See also the main feature article of *Financial Times*, June 9, 1986.
3. Adams, endnote 1, p. 15,514.
4. E. F. McDonough III, "How Much Power Does HR Have, and What Can It Do to Win More?" *Personnel*, January, 1986, pp. 18–25.
5. P. Donohue, "Computers and Human Resources Management," in *Human Resources Management in Canada*, Prentice-Hall Canada Inc., 1984, p. 5,211.
6. For more information on human resource information systems in Canada, see D. Dimick, "On Line: HRIS and the Human Resources Function," in *Human Resources Management in Canada*, Prentice-Hall Canada Inc., 1985, pp. 5,441–5,447. E. Harvey and J. H. Blackely, "Maximizing Use of Human Resource Information Systems (HRIS)," in S. L. Dolan and R. S. Schuler (eds.), *Canadian Readings in Personnel and Human Resource Management* (St. Paul: West Publishing Co., 1987).
7. R. D. Huff, "The Impact of Cafeteria Benefits on the Human Resource Information System," *Personnel Journal*, April 1983, pp. 282–283.
8. Computer-assisted technology has been used successfully in the B.C. forest products industry and by other companies in the pulp and paper industry. For details, see C. Hajdu, "Using a Computer to Cost Collective Bargaining," in *Human Resources Management in Canada*, Prentice-Hall Canada Inc., 1984, pp. 5,245–5,249.
9. M. R. Schiavoni, "Employee Relations: Where Will IT Be in 1985?" *Personnel Administrator*, March 1978, p. 28.
10. S. L. Dolan and B. Bannister, "Emerging Issues in Employment Testing," paper presented at the Fourth Congress international de psychologie du travail de langue française, Montréal, May 5, 1986.
11. D. B. Gehrman, "Beyond Today's Compensation and Performance Appraisal Systems," *Personnel Administrator*, March 1984, pp. 21–33.
12. For more on the issues of resistance to change, see S. L. Dolan, "Implementing New Technologies in the Office: A Comparative Study of Perceived Threat," *Working Paper no. 85–03*, School of Industrial Relations, University of Montréal, July 1985.
13. H. Kolodney, "Canadian Experiences in Innovative Approaches to High Commitment Work Systems," in S. L. Dolan and R. S. Schuler (eds.), endnote 6. A. Jaeger, "The Application of Theory Z in Canada: Implications of the Human Resource Function," in S. L. Dolan and R. S. Schuler (eds.), endnote 6.
14. G. H. Atherley, "Occupational Health and Safety: Act, Actors and Actions," in S. L. Dolan and R. S. Schuler, endnote 6.
15. S. L. Dolan and André Arsenault, "The Organizational and Individual Consequences of Stress at Work: A New Frontier to Human Resource Adminis-

tration," in V. V. Veysey and G. A. Hall, Jr. (eds.), *The New World of Managing Human Resources* (Pasadena, CA: California Institute of Technology, 1979), pp. 4.01–4.22. R. Burke, "Stress and Burnout in Organizations: Implications of PHRM," in S. L. Dolan and R. S. Schuler (eds.), endnote 6. R. S. Schuler, "Managing Stress Through Personnel/HRM Practices: An Uncertainty Interpretation," paper presented at the P/HR program of the Academy of Management Meeting, Chicago, August 14, 1986.

16. For example, as this book is being written, the Police Brotherhood Association of Montréal is negotiating issues such as police patrolling concerns and career programs for its members.

17. An interesting depiction of Japanese hiring methods and the initiation ceremony can be seen in a film made recently by the National Film Board of Canada, Japan Inc.: *Some Lessons to North America*, 1983.

18. J. Main, "The Trouble with Managing Japanese Style" *Fortune*, April 2, 1984, pp. 50–56. "The Japanese Manager Meets the American Worker," *Business Week*, August 20, 1984, pp. 128–129. R. Novotny, "Working for the Japanese," *Personnel Administrator*, February 1984, pp. 15–19.

19. B. Teriet, "Flexiyear Schedules in Germany," *Personnel Journal*, June 1982, pp. 428–429.

20. Based on descriptions provided in O. Jacobi, "World Economic Changes and Industrial Relations in the Federal Republic of Germany," in H. Juris and M. Thompson (eds.), *Industrial Relations in a Decade of Economic Change* (Madison, WI: IRRA), pp. 211–246.

21. See the entire special report feature "Best Companies Conference," *The Financial Post*, June 7, 1986, pp. 17–20.

22. P. Sheibar, "Personnel Practices Review: A Personnel Audit Activity," *Personnel Journal*, March 1974, pp. 211–217

23. T. Connelly, E. J. Conlon, and S. J. Deutsch, "A Multiple Constituency Approach of Organizational Effectiveness," *Academy of Management Review*, 5(2), 1980, pp. 211–218. M. Hitt, R.D. Ireland, B. W. Keats, and A. Vianna, "Measuring Subunit Effectiveness," *Decision Sciences*, January 1983, pp. 87–102. A. S. Tsui, "A Tri-partite Approach to Research on Personnel Department Effectiveness," *Industrial Relations*, Spring 1984.

24. J. R. Lapointe, "Human Resource Performance Indexes," *Personnel Journal*, July 1983, pp. 545–600.

25. For details on indexes that include estimated costs associated with the behaviour related to them, see B. A. Macy and P. H. Mirvis, "A Methodology for Assessing the Quality of Work Life and Organizational Effectiveness in Behavioural and Economic Terms," *Administrative Science Quarterly*, June 1976, pp. 212–326.

26. For an example, see H. E. Brogdan and E. Taylor, "The Dollar Criterion: Applying the Cost Accounting Concept to Criterion Construction," *Personnel Psychology*, 1950 (3), pp. 133–154.

27. E. G. Flamholtz, *Human Resource Accounting*, 2nd ed. (San Francisco: Jossey-Bass Inc., 1985). W. F. Cascio, *Costing Human Resources: The Financial Impact of Behavior In Organizations* (Boston, MA: Kent Publishing Co., 1982).

28. J. E. Hunter, F. L. Schmidt, R. C. McKenzie, and T. W. Muldraw, "Impact of Valid Selection Procedures on Work Force Productivity," *Journal of Applied Psychology*, 64(1), 1979, pp. 107–118.

29. G. T. Milkovich and W. F. Glueck, *Personnel: A Diagnostic Approach*, 4th ed. (Plano, TX: BPI Inc., 1985), p. 631.

30. S. J. Carroll, Jr., "Measuring the Work of a Personnel Department," *Personnel*, July–August, 1960, pp. 49–56.

Appendixes

APPENDIX A

List of Employment-Standards Legislation in
Canada
(updated as of January 1986)

APPENDIX B

Selected Journals and Associations in Personnel
and Human Resource Management

APPENDIX A

List of Employment-Standards Legislation in Canada
(updated as of January 1986)

A
List of Employment-Standards Legislation in Canada
(updated as of January 1986)

Alberta

The Employment Standards Act, R.S.A.1980, c. E–10.1, as amended
  Exemption Regulation, A.Reg. 83/81
  Scheme of Employment Regulation, A.Reg. 101/81
  Minimum Wage Regulation, A.Reg. 145/81
  Adolescents and Young Persons Employment Regulation, A.Reg. 82/81
  Ambulance drivers and attendants, A.Reg. 77/81
  Construction industry and brush clearing, A.Reg. 81/81
  Field services, A.Reg. 73/81
  Highway and rail construction; brush clearing, A.Reg. 79/81
  Irrigation districts, A.Reg. 75/81
  Nursery industry, A.Reg. 76/81
  Oil well servicing, A.Reg. 74/81
  Taxi industry, A.Reg. 80/81
  Trucking industry, A.Reg. 78/81
The Child Welfare Act, R.S.A.1980, c. C–8
Coal Mines Safety Act, S.A.1974, c. 18
Individual's Rights Protection Act, R.S.A.1980, c. 1–2, as amended
Industrial Wages Security Act, R.S.A.1980, c. 1–3

British Columbia

Employment Standards Act, S.B.C.1980, c. 10, as amended by S.B.C.1983, c. 16 and S.B.C.1983, c. 10, s. 21
  Employment Standards Regulation, B.C. Reg. 37/81 as amended by B.C. Regs. 222/81; 451/81; 226/82; 457/82; 308/83; 340/83; 410/83; 115/84; 170/84 and 303/84
Human Rights Act, S.B.C.1984, c. 22
Public Construction Fair Wages Act, S.B.C.1976, c. 43

Manitoba

Employment Standards Act, C.C.S.M., c. E110
  Employment Standards Regulation E110–R1 as amended by M.R. 116/72, 129/73, 110/74, 143/75, 138/76, 89/81, 90/82 and 238/84
  Layoffs, M.R. 261/82
  Domestic workers, M.R. 222/82
  Crown employees exemptions: general, M.R. 251/76; Manitoba Telephone System, M.R. 138/77; summer students, M.R. 255/77
Construction Industry Wages Act, R.S.M.1970, c. C190, as amended by S.M.1974, c. 59; S.M.1981, c. 38; and S.M.1984, c. 28
  Heavy construction wage schedule, M.R. 99/85
  Greater Winnipeg and major building construction wage schedule, M.R. 180/85
  Construction outside Greater Winnipeg and not on major building projects wage schedule, M.R. 100/85
Payment of Wages Act, C.C.S.M., c. P15
Remembrance Day Act, R.S.M.1970, c. R80 as amended by S.M.1971, c. 41
Vacations with Pay Act, R.S.M.1970, c. V20 as amended by S.M.1972, c. 49; S.M.1976, c. 34; S.M.1977, c. 37; S.M.1978, c. 49; S.M.1982, c. 32; S.M.1982–83–84, c. 93 and Bill 75, in force 11 July 1985
Wages Recovery Act, R.S.M.1970, c. W10
Recent Changes: Three bills, proclaimed in force 11 July 1985, make the following changes:
  Bill 74 adds rights of paternity and adoption leave to the Employment Standards Act;
  Bill 75 changes and strengthens the procedures for the recovery of unpaid wages under the Payment of Wages Act; Bill 77 extends the periods of notice required for group terminations and allows the minister to appoint joint planning committees in such circumstances.

New Brunswick

Days of Rest Act, SNB 1985, c. D–4.2
  Exemption Regulation, N.B. Reg. 85–149
Employment Standards Act, SNB 1982, c. E–7.2 as amended by SNB 1983, cc. 8, 10, 30 and O–0.2; SNB 1984, c. 42
Minimum Employment Standards Act, R.S.N.B.1973, c. M–12 as amended by S.N.B.1974, c. 28 (Supp.); S.N.B.1975, c. 36; S.N.B.1976, c. 37; S.N.B.1981, c. 43; S.N.B.1983, c. 10

Exemptions Regulation, N.B. Reg. 84–83

Minimum Wage Act, R.S.N.B.1973, c. M–13, as amended by S.N.B.1974, c. 29 (Supp.); S.N.B.1976, c. 38; S.N.B.1981, c. 44

   Minimum Wage Order, N.B. Reg. 82–143, as amended by N.B. Reg. 83–84

Vacation Pay Act, R.S.N.B.1973, c. V–1 as amended by S.N.B.1976, c. 58, S.N.B.1981, c. 78, S.N.B.1982, c. 65.

Recent Changes: Sections 45 to 60 and 85 of the Employment Standards Act were proclaimed in force 16 May 1985. These created new administrative bodies to administer the rest of the new Act when it comes into force. The Days of Rest Act came into effect 1 September 1985, followed by an Exemption Regulation on 20 September 1985. The Act prohibits employment on Sundays or specified holidays unless the employment falls under one of the many exemptions in the Act or regulations.

Newfoundland

Child Welfare Act, S.N.1972, c. 37 as amended

Labour Standards Act, S.N.1977, c. 52, as amended by S.N.1979, c. 35; S.N.1983, c. 20; S.N.1984, c. 29; S.N.1984, c. 40; S.N.1985, c. 11

   Labour Standards Regulations, 1985, N. Reg. 271/84

Newfoundland Human Rights Code, R.S.N.1970, c. 262 as amended

Nova Scotia

Labour Standards Code, S.N.S.1972, c. 10 as amended

   General Regulations, O.C. No. 76–1203, as amended by N.S. Reg. 17/83

   General Minimum Wage Order, N.S. Reg. 125/84

   Minimum Wage Order—Beauty Parlour

   Minimum Wage Order—Logging and Forestry

   Minimum Wage Order—Road Building and Heavy Construction

Ontario

Employment Standards Act, R.S.O.1980, c. 137 as amended by S.O.1981, c. 22; S.O.1983, c. 55; S.O.1984, c. 31

   General Regulations, R.R.O.1980, Reg. 285 as amended by O.Reg. 802/83 and O. Reg. 189/84

   Benefit Plans, R.R.O.1980, Reg. 282

   Termination of Employment, R.R.O.1980, Reg. 286 as amended by O.Reg. 531/83; O.Reg. 301/84 and O.Reg. 120/85

   Ambulance Services, R.R.O.1980, Reg. 281 as amended by O.Reg. 803/83

   Domestics and Nannies, R.R.O.1980, Reg. 283 as amended by O.Reg. 75/84

   Fruit, Vegetable and Tobacco Harvesters, R.R.O.1980, Reg. 284 as amended by O.Reg. 241/81 and O.Reg. 342/84

   Residential Care Workers, Reg. 440/82

One Day's Rest in Seven Act, R.S.O., c. 326

Industrial Standards Act, R.S.O.1980, c. 216

P.E.I.

Labour Act, R.S.P.E.I.1974, c. L–1 as amended by S.P.E.I.1975, c. 17; S.P.E.I.1982, c. 15; S.P.E.I.1983, c. 25 and S.P.E.I.1984, c. 1

   Notice of termination exemption regulations, EC522/71

   Minimum Wage Order 1/82, EC44/82

Minimum Age of Employment Act, R.S.P.E.I.1974, c. M–11 as amended by S.P.E.I.1984, c. 1

Québec

An Act representing labour standards, R.S.Q. c. N–11, as amended

   Regulation respecting labour standards, O.C. 873–81

   Register regulation, O.C. 1915–80

   Exemption regulation, O.C. 2566–83

   Exclusion of health and social services regulation, O.C. 756–80

   Ordinance No. 14, Retail Food Trade, O.C. 783–73, as amended

Charter of Human Rights and Freedoms, R.S.Q. c. C–12

Civil Code, Arts. 1165a–1668

Manpower Vocational Training and Qualification Act, R.S.Q. c. F–5

National Holiday Act, R.S.Q. c. F–1.1

Saskatchewan

Labour Standards Act, R.S.S.1978, c. L–1 as amended by S.S.1979, c. 69; S.S.1979–80, c.

84; S.S.1979–80, c. 92; S.S.1981, c. 63; S.S.1983, c. 11; S.S.1983, c. 66; S.S.1983, c. 16
Labour Standards Regulations, S.Reg. 317/77 as amended by S.Reg. 374/77, S.Reg. 126/81 and S.Reg. 34/84
Minimum Wage Board Orders: No. 1 (1981) S.Reg. 201/80; No. 2 (1981) S.Reg. 203/80; No. 3 (1981) S.Reg. 204/80; No. 1962 "A"
Minimum Wage Board Regulation No. 1
Wages Recovery Act, R.S.S.1978, c. W–1 as amended by S.S.1979, c. 92

Northwest Territories

Fair Practices Ordinance, R.O.N.W.T.1974, c. F–2, as amended
Labour Standards Ordinance, R.O.N.W.T.1974, c. L–1, as amended
   Annual Vacations—Reg. 88
   Labour Standards Wages—Reg. 89
   Employment of Young Persons—Reg. 90
   Educational Work Experience—Reg. 91
   Labour Standards Meal—Reg. R–085–82
Mining Safety Ordinance, c. 12 (3rd) 1982
Wages Recovery Ordinance, R.O.N.W.T.1974, c. W–1, as amended

Yukon

Employment Standards Act, S.Y.T.1984, c. 5
   General Exemption Regulation, O.I.C. 1984/344
   Minimum Wage Order No. 84/1, O.I.C., 1984/340
   Fair Wage Schedule Order No. 85/1, O.I.C. 1985/61, as amended by Order 85/2, O.I.C. 1985/165
   General Exemption Regulation, O.I.C. 1984/344
   Minimum Wage Order No. 84/1, O.I.C. 1984/340

Recent Changes: The Fair Wages Schedule for public works contracts was approved 29 March 1985 and amended 29 July 1985. An exemption from the hours of work and overtime provisions was created by O.I.C. 1985/91, dated April 19, 1985.

Federal Regulation

Canada Labour Code, R.S.C.1970, c. L–1, as amended
   Canada Labour Standards Regulations SOR/72–7, as amended
   Minimum Hourly Wage Order 1980, SOR/80–659
Canadian Human Rights Act, S.C.1976–77, c. 33, as amended
   Equal Wages Guidelines, S1/78–155
Fair Wages and Hours of Labour Act, R.S.C.1970, c. L–3
   Fair Wages and Hours of Labour Regulations, SOR/67–95 as amended
Holidays Act, R.S.C.1970, c. H–7

Recent Changes: An Act to Amend the Canada Labour Code and the Financial Administration Act (Bill C–34) received royal assent 29 June 1984. Part III, Labour Standards, was proclaimed 1 March 1985. Substantial changes were made to the leave provisions of the Code and sexual harassment provisions were added. Other changes were made to holiday pay entitlements, penalties, minimum wage exemptions, and unjust dismissal procedures.

APPENDIX B

Selected Journals and Associations in Personnel and Human Resource Management

B
Selected Journals and Associations in Personnel and Human Resource Management

I Research and Academic Journals

Academy of Management Journal, published quarterly by the Academy of Management (U.S.).

Canadian Journal of Administrative Sciences, published quarterly by the Administrative Sciences Association of Canada, Faculty of Administrative Studies, York University, Toronto, Ontario.

Canadian Journal of Behavioral Sciences, the Canadian Psychological Association publishes articles about applied psychology, including organizational behaviour and development, psychometrics, and social psychology.

Ergonomics, Taylor and Francis, Ltd., Red Lion Court, Fleet Street, London, England. Emphasizes human engineering; combines approaches of human biology, anatomy, physiology, and psychology with mechanical engineering.

Gestion (French), published by H.E.C. University of Montréal, Montréal, Québec. Various articles about management functions are covered, including PHRM topics. Similar in style and form to the *Harvard Business Review*.

Harvard Business Review, Graduate School of Business Administration, Harvard University, Soldier's Field, Boston, MA. A review of the general field of business, with frequent articles on industrial relations.

Human Organizations, Society for Applied Anthropology, New York State School of Industrial and Labor Relations, Cornell University, Ithaca, NY. Intercultural approach to problems of human relations, including industrial relations.

Human Resource Management, published by the Graduate School of Business, University of Michigan, Ann Arbor, MI 48109.

Human Resource Planning, published by the Human Resources Planning Society, P.O. Box 2553, Grand Central Station, New York, NY 10017.

Industrial and Labor Relations Review, New York State School of Labor and Industrial Relations, Cornell University, Ithaca, NY. Opinions and reports of studies on labour legislation, collective bargaining, and related subjects.

Industrial Medicine and Surgery, Industrial Medicine Publishing Company, 605 North Michigan Avenue, Chicago, IL. Emphasizes health programs in industry, with reports on health hazards, occupational diseases, handicapped workers, medical services, and related subjects.

Industrial Relations, Institute of Industrial Relations, University of California, Berkeley and Los Angeles, CA. Ideas and opinions as well as reports on research in the field.

Industrial Relations/Relations industrielles, Department of Industrial Relations, Laval University, Ste. Foy, Québec. Reports on labour legislation, collective bargaining, and related PHRM topics.

Journal of Applied Psychology, American Psychological Associations, 1313 Sixteenth Street N.W., Washington DC. All phases of applied psychology, with numerous reports on personnel research.

Journal of Occupational Behaviour, published by John Wiley & Sons Ltd., Baffins Lane, Chichester, Sussex P.O. 19100, England. Has published various issues related to occupational behaviour.

Journal of Occupational Psychology, a journal of the British Psychological Society, St-Andrews House, 48 Princess Rd. E., Leicester LE1 7DR, England.

Journal of Personnel Administration and Industrial Relations, Personnel Research Publishers, Washington DC. Reports original studies and theoretical analyses on all phases of industrial relations.

Labour/Le travailleur, published by the Department of History, Memorial University of Newfoundland, St. John's, Newfoundland AIC 5S7.

Labour Law Journal, Commerce Clearing House, Inc., 214 N. Michigan Avenue, Chicago, IL. Usually presents non-legalistic discussions about legal phases of industrial relations.

Personnel Psychology, P.O. Box 6965, College Station, Durham, NC. Emphasizes reports on research on psychological aspects of personnel and industrial relations.

II Practitioner and Trade Journals

The Employment Law Report, published monthly by Concord Publishing Ltd., 70 Yorkville Ave., Toronto, Ontario M5R 1B9.

Formation et Emploi (French), published in Québec.

Human Resources Management in Canada, a two-volume information service with monthly report bulletins and updates. Published by Prentice-Hall Canada Inc., 1870 Birchmount Rd., Scarborough, Ontario M1P 2J7.

Management Record, The Conference Board, 247 Park Avenue, New York, NY. Numerous reports on both experience and research, surveys conducted by the NICB staff, and digests of symposia.

Management Review, American Management Association, 330 West 42nd Street, New York, NY. General coverage of all phases of management.

Monthly Labor Review, Bureau of Labor Statistics, U.S. Department of Labor, Washington DC. Summaries of staff studies on industrial relations; statistical sections include continuing series on industrial disputes, employment, payrolls, and cost of living.

Personnel, American Management Association, 330 West 42nd Street, New York, NY. Broad coverage of the field of industrial relations, with numerous reports on surveys, studies, and experience.

Personnel Journal, published at 866 West Eighteenth Street, Costa Mesa, CA. Covers a broad spectrum of topics in personnel and labour relations.

Personnel Management, formerly the *Journal of the Institute of Personnel Management*. Institute of Personnel Management, Management House, 80 Fetter Lane, London, England. Theory and practice in both personnel management and labour relations.

Personnel Management Abstracts, Bureau of Industrial Relations, University of Michigan, Ann Arbor, MI. Abstracts of books and articles in both personnel management and labour relations.

Public Personnel Quarterly, published by the International Personnel Management Association, 1859 K Street N.W., Washington DC.

Personnel Administrator, published by the American Society for Personnel Administration, 606 Washington Street, Alexandria, VA 20221. Information on taking the ASPA examinations to become a certified personnel administrator can be obtained by writing to the ASPA.

QWL Focus, published by the Ontario Quality of Working Life Centre, Ontario Ministry of Labour, Toronto.

III Associations

Association of Human Resource Professionals of the Province of Québec, 1253 McGill College Ave., Suite 192, Montréal, P.Q. H3B 2Y5.

Calgary Personnel Association, P.O. Box 1737, Calgary, Alberta T2P 2L2.

Canadian Council on Working Life, P.O. Box 567, Station B, Ottawa, Ontario K1P 5P7.

The Canadian Industrial Relations Association, Department of Industrial Relations, Laval University, Ste. Foy, Québec G1K 7P4.

Canadian Public Personnel Association, 220 Laurier Avenue W., Suite 720, Ottawa, Ontario K1P 5Z9.

Canadian Pension Conference, 121 Bloor St. E., Suite 3000, Toronto, Ontario M4W 3M5.

Canadian Public Personnel Management Association, 270 Laurier Ave. W., Suite 720, Ottawa, Ontario K1P 5Z9.

Halifax and District Personnel Association, P.O. Box 592, Halifax, Nova Scotia B3J 3C8.

The Industrial Accident Prevention Association, 2 Bloor St. W., 31st Floor, Toronto, Ontario M4W 3N8.

Industrial Relations Management Association of British Columbia, 501–540 Bussard St., Vancouver, B.C. V6C 2K1.

The New Brunswick Occupational Health and Safety Commission, P.O. Box 600, Fredericton, N.B. E3B 5H1.

Ontario Municipal Personnel Association, 110 University Ave., Suite 902, Toronto, Ontario M5J 1V6.

The Ontario Society for Training and Development, 111 Caveen St. E., Suite 355, Toronto, Ontario M5C 1S2.

Personnel Association of Edmonton, Box 1392, Main Post Office, Edmonton, Alberta T5J 2N2.

Personnel Association of Ontario, 2 Bloor St. W., Suite 601, Toronto, Ontario M4W 3E2.

Personnel Association of Winnipeg, 155 Carlton St., Suite 700, Winnipeg, Manitoba R3C 0H6.

Profit Sharing Council of Canada, 1262 Don Mills Rd., Suite 91, Don Mills, Ontario M3B 2W7.

Regina Personnel Association, 199 North Leonard St., Regina, Saskatchewan S4N 5X5.

Glossary

Absentee employee who is scheduled to be at work but is not present.

Absolute Standards an approach that allows superiors to evaluate each subordinate's performance independent of the other subordinates and often on several dimensions of performance.

Accreditation/Certification the process by which the standards and credentials for members of a profession are established. Also, the process used to certify an organization of employees as the bargaining agent for a unit of employers/employees.

Achievement Tests measures of an individual's performance on the basis of quality and/or quantity. These may be actual work samples of the job or paper-and-pencil tests.

Administrative Issues issues concerning the treatment of employees, such as breaks and clean-up time.

Adversarial System a view of labour and management that depicts each of the two parties in conflict over achieving incompatible goals.

Adverse Impact a significantly higher percentage of a protected group is rejected for employment, placement, or promotion.

Affirmative Action Programs programs that are designed to ensure proportional representation of employees and to undo the result of past discrimination on grounds of race, creed, gender, or national origin.

Alternative Ranking a comparative approach in which the superior alternates between ranking the best and the worst until all subordinates are ranked.

Alternative Work Arrangements schedules that make available hours of work and days of work that differ from the more traditional 9–5, Monday-to-Friday schedule.

Application Blank a form that requires information about the job applicant's background and present conditions and is used to make hiring decisions.

Apprenticeship Training a training format based on learning a job while doing it for a long time before being recognized as competent, full-fledged employee.

Aptitude Tests measures of an individual's potential to perform. Intelligence tests are aptitude tests.

Arbitration a procedure in which a central third party studies the bargaining situation, listens to both parties, gathers information, and then reaches a decision that usually is binding for the parties.

Assessment the process of measuring and comparing costs and benefits to determine effectiveness or value, particularly as these relate to each personnel activity and the entire personnel department of a company.

Assessment Centre Method used to determine managerial potential of employees. Evaluates individuals as they take part in a large number of activities conducted in a relatively isolated environment. It also is useful for identifying potential training needs.

Assistantships a type of on-the-job training that involves full-time employment and exposes the individual to a wide range of jobs as they assist other workers.

Association a formal group of individuals that represents a much larger group. In many ways similar to a union except that an association often is involved in fewer functions than a union.

Attitude Survey systematic method of soliciting employees' opinions about different aspects of their employment.

Attitudinal Structuring the relationships between labour and management during collective bargaining that result in the shaping of attitudes toward one another.

Attrition decrease in the number of employees that results when employees leave the organization and are not replaced.

Audit an in-depth, critical analysis of the activities of a unit, with the aim of determining the unit's effectiveness.

Authorization Cards cards signed by employees if they want to be represented by a labour organization.

Autonomous Work Groups a variety of arrangements that enable employees to decide how they will meet their job requirements.

Autonomy the degree to which the job provides substantial freedom, independence, and discretion to the worker in performing the job.

Award in labour-management arbitration, the final decision of an arbitrator, binding on both parties in the dispute.

Band Width the maximum span of work day from which an employee can choose the hours he or she will work.

Bargaining Unit the heart of the labour-management relationship. A group of employees certified by a labour relations board to be part of a union.

Base Rate the ratio of applicants who would succeed on the job relative to the total number of applicants, when the test is not used for selection.

Behaviourally Anchored Rating Scale (BARS) a quantitative absolute form that expands on the conventional rating form by specifying more extensively the anchors on behavioural dimensions used to evaluate a subordinate.

Behavioural Observation Scale (BOS) similar to BARS except in development of the dimensions, scale format, and scoring.

Benchmark Jobs jobs against which the worth of other jobs are determined by an analysis of the compensable factors and their dollar values and by comparison to other jobs.

Biographical Information Blank a form on which an applicant may indicate information about past accomplishments, interests, and preferences that can be used to supplement an application blank.

Bona Fide Occupational Qualification is a defence against adverse impact. For example, hiring only males to play male roles in theatrical productions.

Bona Fide Seniority System a formal system of seniority that has been and is maintained with the intent to not discriminate, in compliance with various human rights Acts.

Business Games a type of work sample test used in managerial selection. Business games may be similar to in-basket exercises or simulation tests, however, they are called games because there generally are rules for play, and a winner.

Business Necessity used as a basis for defending adverse impact. Business necessity suggests that the essence of the business operation would be undermined by hiring members of the protected group.

Cafeteria Benefit Plan plan that allows an employee to select the mix of benefits and services that he or she prefers.

Canada Employment Centres centres administered by the Canada Employment of Immigration Commission that matches job seekers with employers who have job opening.

Canada Labour Code the main Act regulating labour relations for federal jurisdiction.

Canada Labour Relations Board a board whose powers and duties include the determination of appropriate bargaining units, the certification and decertification of unions, and decisions as to unfair labour practice.

Canada Pension Plan a mandatory, contributing pension plan applicable to all self-employed individuals and employees in Canada, except those who work for the federal government.

Canadian Classification and Dictionary of Occupations a publication of the federal government providing detailed definitions for all jobs in Canada.

Canadian Labour Congress (CLC) a central labour congress in Canada formed in 1956 that represents more than half of organized labour in Canada.

Canadian Human Rights Act a federal law, enacted in 1977, prohibiting discrimination on the basis of race, national or ethnic origin, colour, religion, age, gender, marital status, or physical handicap.

Career Development Programs organizational programs designed to match employees' needs, abilities, and goals with current or future opportunities and challenges within the organization.

Career Management Programs concerted efforts in career planning and development aimed at satisfying a dual match between employee ability and job demands and employee needs and job rewards.

Career Pathing two major activities designed to identify employee abilities, values, goals, strengths, and weaknesses (career planning) and provide a set of job experiences that aid the employee in satisfying those attributes (job progression).

Career Planning Activities offered by the organization to help individuals identify strengths, weaknesses, and specific goals and jobs they would like to attain.

Carpal Tunnel Syndrome an illness characterized by numbness, tingling, soreness, and weakness in the hands and wrists, often resulting from the job.

Cash Plans a type of profit-sharing plan that provides for payment of profit shares at regular intervals.

Centralization a term applied to organizations where essential decision making and policy formulation is done at one location (e.g., headquarters).

Certification Election an election conducted to determine if a majority of the employees in a bargaining unit want the union to represent them all.

Closed-Offer Arbitration a type of arbitration in which the arbitrator receives information on only the parties' original positions without any information on the bargaining process up to the time that the arbitrator is selected.

Co-determination a system of governing an organization in which the employees and management help to run the company through union representation on the board of directors.

Cognitive Job Elements represent the specific parts of a job such as communicating, decision making, analyzing, and information processing.

Collective Bargaining bargaining or joint discussion over wages, hours, and conditions of employment between representatives of management and the employees.

Commissions individual incentive pay plans for sales people.

Company Union an employee organization, usually of a single company, that is dominated or strongly influenced by management.

Compa Ratio is the measure of the average salary for a given pay grade relative to the midpoint of that pay grade.

Comparable Worth proponents of this compensation issue contend that while the true worth of jobs may be similar, some (often held by women) are paid at a lower rate than others (often held by men). Resulting differences in pay that are disproportionate to the differences in the true worth of jobs amount to wage discrimination.

Comparative Standards or Comparative Approach in this approach to performance evaluation, subordinates are all compared against each other to determine their relative performance.

Compensable Factors yardsticks of factors against which jobs are compared or measured to determine their relative worth.

Compensatory Approach in a hiring process, an applicant's weak point can be made up for (compensated) by a strong point.

Compressed Work Weeks work weeks of fewer than the traditional five days yet equal in time to those of five days.

Concessionary Bargaining bargaining by unions where they give up or concede issues to management.

Conciliation a process in which a third party (usually the government) attempts to bring disputing parties to a resolution.

Concurrent Validation measures the relationship between a predictor (test) and a job criterion score (job performance), whereby the predictor and criterion are collected at the same time.

Confirmation Approach when a manager "loads the deck" to favour a particular candidate by selecting several candidates for final decision who are less qualified than the favoured candidate.

Construct Validity a measure of how well a test measures the constructs or dimensions that are judged to be critical for job performance.

Contaminated the degree to which a measure of performance measures more dimensions of performance than those that are related to the actual performance of an individual.

Confederation of Canadian Unions federation of unions dedicated to independence from international unions.

Confederation of National Trade Unions (CNTU) a Québec-based central labour body.

Content Validity an estimate of how well the test reflects elements of the job domain.

Contingent Rewards extrinsic rewards given to reinforce a particular behaviour. Reinforcement is an essential component of the training process.

Continuous Bargaining when unions and management representatives meet on a regularly scheduled basis to review contract issues of common interest.

Contract Plan an informal agreement written by each participant in training, specifying one aspect of the training that will be most beneficial and agreeing to effect that aspect once back on the job. An important dimension of the contract is selecting a "buddy" to follow-up or check on the trainee's success in implementing that aspect of the training.

Contrast Effect a good person looks even better when placed next to a bad person, and a good person looks not as good when placed next to a great person.

Contributory Programs a type of retirement plan in which both the employee and the organization contribute for benefits to be obtained at retirement.

Conventional Rating a quantitative absolute form in which a superior evaluates subordinates by checking how well they are doing on a form with several dimensions (traits) and numbers.

Co-operative Acceptance ensures that employees have a work environment free of sexual harassment.

Co-operative System a view of labour and management that depicts each of the two parties engaging in reciprocal problem solving, information sharing, and integration of goals.

Co-ordinated Bargaining when several unions bargain jointly with a single employer.

Core Time the time in which everyone must work; there is no choice about this work time.

Corporate Culture the values, norms, and statements about what is important to a company and how its employees should be treated.

Correlation Coefficient a measure of the degree of relationship between two variables (a test and job performance).

Cost-of-Living Adjustments (COLAs) salary or compensation variation that is related to economic conditions (cost of living changes) rather than performance.

Criteria the measures used (e.g., performance appraisal results) to indicate how well an employee is doing on the job; indications of job success.

Criterion-Related or Empirical Validity a validity strategy whereby a test or predictor is correlated with job performance or a criterion.

Critical Incidents an absolute form in which the superior records the critical or important events exhibited by a subordinate on a pre-determined list of critical incidents.

Critical Incident Technique method of job analysis whereby behavioural descriptions that have a critical or essential impact on the performance of a job (good, average, or bad) are recorded.

Cut-Off Scores scores on a test or predictor below which one decision is made (not to hire) and above which another decision is made (to hire).

Decentralization a term applied to organizations where essential decision making and policy formulation is done at several locations (i.e., in the divisions or departments of the organization).

Decertification removal of a union from representation if the employees currently represented by the union vote to do so.

Deficient the degree to which a measure of performance fails to measure all the essential elements of the actual performance of an individual.

Delphi Technique a number of experts take turns at presenting a forecast statement. As the process continues, the forecast is subject to other members' revisions until a viable forecast emerges.

Depth Interview an interview where the interviewer has only a general set of questions to ask and where the interviewee is asked to go into detail in answering.

Dictionary of Occupational Titles (DOT) source for obtaining the job descriptions of almost 30 000 different jobs in the U.S.

Differential Validity a comparison of validity coefficients or prediction models for two or more sub-groups of individuals.

Direct Compensation basic wages and performance-based pay, including merit and incentive pay.

Direct Index this assessment approach tends to be more objective because such things as actual units sold, scrap rate, absenteeism, and units produced are used to evaluate performance.

Discrimination in the workplace, unequal treatment of persons, whether in hiring, promoting, or discharging, on the basis of gender, age, marital status, race, creed, and other traits not related to direct job performance.

Distributive Bargaining a type of collective bargaining where both labour and management try to attain goals that would result in a gain for one party but a loss for the other.

Duties the specific activities that comprise a job are called duties.

Earned Time a positive behavioural control strategy to reduce absenteeism through a no-fault approach, which provides employees with days off as needed.

Economic Supplements a type of compensation for employees that includes things such as pensions, vacations, paid holidays, sick leave, health and insurance plans, and supplemental unemployment benefits.

Effective Feedback information given to employees in a performance appraisal context that enables them to use the information effectively to improve performance and facilitates acceptance of evaluation.

Effectiveness an indication of contribution or value to the organization such as personnel's contribution by improving the organization's productivity, quality of work life, and legal compliance.

Effective Personnel Management the recognition of the importance of an organization's workforce and the efficient and fair use of several functions and activities to ensure that the individual, the organization, and society benefit from them.

Effective Personnel Planning the first step in an effective personnel program. It predicts or estimates future human resource needs and establishes personnel activities to enable the organization to meet these future needs.

Empirical Validity *See* **Criterion-Related Validity**

Employee Assistance Programs (EAPs) programs specifically designed to assist employees with chronic personal problems (for example, marital dysfunctions, alcohol abuse) that hinder their job performance, attendance, and corporate citizenship.

Employee Contract a formal, and frequently a written, agreement between employer and employee, specifying the wages, hours, and type of work conditions.

Employee Pacing condition in which the pace or rate at which the employee works is determined by the employee and not by the machine. *See* MACHINE PACING

Employee Referral Programs essentially word-of-mouth advertising, involving current employees informally recruiting potentially qualified job applicants.

Employee Rights rights desired by employees regarding the security of their jobs and the treatment administered by their employers.

Employee Service and Perquisites a form of indirect compensation that varies depending on employee type and organization, to offset the problems associated with working (e.g., day care) or used to symbolize a status differential (e.g., company-paid memberships to country, athletic, and social clubs).

Employee Training and Development any attempt to improve current or future employee performance by increasing, through learning, an employee's ability to perform, particularly by changing an employee's attitudes and increasing his or her skills and knowledge.

Employment Contract an agreement between the employee and the employer regarding certain conditions of employment (e.g., wages, hours, and the type of work).

Ergonomics an approach to job design concerned with designing and shaping jobs and working conditions to fit the physical abilities and characteristics of individual workers.

Error of Central Tendency type of halo error where all dimensions are rated average or all individuals are given a more lenient rating.

Error of Strictness type of halo error where all dimensions are given an unfavourable rating or all individuals receive a tougher rating.

Essay Method a performance evaluation method in which the superior describes in writing (essay form) the performance of the subordinates.

Essentiality the amount of power a job holder (any employee) has, which is determined by how critical the job is to the organization and how difficult the job holder would be to replace.

Evaluation Designs methods by which training programs can be evaluated to determine how effective the training programs are (i.e., how much change is made).

Exclusivity the difficulty in replacing a job holder. Also, in a labour relations context, the right acquired by an employee organization to be the sole representative of the bargaining unit.

Exempt Employees for example, job incumbents who are not paid overtime for working overtime; they are exempt from the wage hour laws requiring overtime pay.

Exit Interviews conversations with departing employees to learn the reasons for their departure.

Extended Critical Incident Technique is the application of the critical incident technique to a variety of job domains identified by job incumbents.

Extension of Bargaining a situation in which the arbitrator attempts to reach a rational and equitable decision acceptable to both parties in arbitration.

External Equity determining the wage rates for different jobs on the basis of what other companies are paying for those jobs.

Face Validity a subjective assessment of how well a test will predict job success by examining the test items.

Fact-Finding a formal/informal dispute-resolution procedure for investigating and reporting on the facts of a situation.

Factor-Comparison Method similar to point rating in that it has compensable factors, but in factor comparison the factors have dollar not point values.

Fair Employment Practices the practice of employers (or unions) of offering workers equal employment opportunities.

False Negatives incorrect predictions that applicants will not perform well when, in fact, applicants will perform successfully.

False Positives incorrect predictions that applicants will perform well when in fact applicants will perform poorly.

Feasibility Assessment estimating the value of using a predictor by examining its costs and benefits and by comparing it against alternative ways.

Final-Offer Arbitration an arbitrator chooses between the final offer of either union or management.

Flexible Compensation an approach to compensation that gives individuals a chance to choose which types of compensation they prefer, as opposed to the organization just handing them a fixed compensation package.

Flexible Spending Plans plans that provide some form and level of pay to employees that is non-taxable to some extent.

Flexible Time the time a worker can choose to work within the band width, yet outside the core time.

Flexiyear Schedules a work system in which employees schedule work time over the span of a year rather than a day or week as in the case of flexitime schedules.

Flexitime a work schedule that gives employees daily choice in the timing of work and non-work activities.

Follow-Up once a person leaves a training program, it is important (in order to evaluate effectiveness of the training program) to find out how well the person is doing once back on the job.

Forced-Choice Form an absolute form on which the superior evaluates the subordinate by choosing which item in a pair of items better describes the subordinate.

Forced-Distribution Method a comparative approach in which the superiors are forced to place subordinates in ranks that represent groups or percentage clusters.

Formal Course Method an off-the-job training program that includes self-training and formal classroom courses and lectures.

Frequency Rate a formula to determine the frequency of accidents and diseases. Similar to the incidence rate except that it is calculated using the number of hours worked rather than on a per annum basis.

Functional Job Analysis (FJA) a description of the nature of jobs, job summaries, job descriptions, and employee specification.

Genetic Screening a process of selecting people or not selecting them on the basis of gene tests.

Goals a basis against which to evaluate how well employees are performing, particularly managers.

Goal Setting people learn quickly and perform better when specific, hard, and clear objectives are set.

Golden Handcuffs extremely favourable monetary arrangements that build up over time, making it more and more costly for an employee to leave an organization.

Golden Parachutes extremely large sums of money made available to executives if they lose their jobs due to mergers and acquisitions.

Grievance Arbitration arbitration that takes place during the life of a contract over a grievance filed by either party.

Grievance Procedure the most common method of resolving disputes between union and management over application and interpretation of the agreement or contract.

Guidelines-Oriented Job Analysis (GOJA) a person-focused job analytic technique based on the *Uniform Guidelines*. The process involves six steps that produce information helpful for the development of performance appraisal, training, and selection procedures.

Halo Error the tendency (erroneous) to rate an individual on several dimensions by how well they do on just one dimension.

Handicap an impairment that substantially limits one or more of a person's major life activities.

Hay Plan a structured procedure for analyzing jobs that is systematically tied into a job-evaluation and compensation system. The Hay plan includes information about the nature and scope of a position as well as how to reward the position.

Health Insurance Plans health and medical insurance provided to Canadian citizens by the various provincial governments and by private agencies.

Historical Records organizations often use information on how well employees have done in the past to establish what is average and also excellent performance.

Horizontal Loading the adding of duties to a job that are similar to those already part of the job and that require the same skills, knowledge, and aptitudes.

Human Resource Information System a method that allows more rapid and frequent data collection to back up a forecast of personnel needs.

Human Rights Legislation laws enacted by the federal and provincial governments against discrimination.

In-Basket Exercise a simulation training technique in which the solitary trainee sits at a desk and works through a pile of papers found in the in-basket of a typical manager, prioritizing, recommending solutions to problems, and taking any necessary action.

Incentive Pay Plan method of monetary and non-monetary compensation related to direct indexes of performance for the individual, group or organization. It generally represents a substantial proportion of an individual's direct compensation.

Incentive Stock Option individual incentive plan that awards stock, such as in stock-option plans for junior stocks.

Incidence Rate an explicit formula for determining the incidence of accidents and diseases per year by the number of employee-exposure levels.

Indirect Compensation rewards or benefits provided by the organization to employees for their organizational participation. Also known as fringe benefits or supplemental compensation.

Individual Contemporary a major classification of approaches to job design that focus on the individual worker/job-design interface or relationships.

Industry-Wide Bargaining a situation in which employers bargain as a group with the union at the national level.

Initial Demand Point a demand by the union for a wage settlement that is higher than what is expected to be granted.

Initial Offer made by management to represent what wages and conditions it will grant to the union.

Injunction a court order restraining one or more persons, corporations, or unions from performing certain acts that the court thinks will result in injury to property or other rights.

Institutional Issues issues not directly related to the job that affect the security and success of union and management, such as strikes and methods of dues collection.

Integrative Bargaining a type of collective bargaining where labour and management work to solve contractual problems to the benefit of both.

Interest Bargaining arbitration that deals with the terms and conditions of the contract.

Interest Tests a type of test intended to reveal an individual's interests and preferences. These tests are not necessarily predictive of job performance, but they can predict which job will be more in line with a person's interests.

Internal Equity determining the wage rates for different jobs within one organization on the basis of the relative worth of those jobs to the organization.

Internal Reliability the extent or degree of relatedness or similarity among items, dimensions, or statements that are supposed to measure or refer to the same thing, such as a 10-item test of mechanical aptitude or a 10-item supervisory measure of job success.

Internships training programs (often part of an agreement between schools, colleges, and universities with organizations) where an individual may work full-time but only for a short time.

Interpersonal Competence Tests measures of social intelligence. These include aspects of intelligence related to awareness of non-verbal and social information.

Intra-Organizational Bargaining the process of negotiating teams influencing their constituents over changes in bargaining positions.

Job Analysis the process of describing or recording the purposes, tasks characteristics, and duties of a job in a given organization setting, to determine a match for individual skills, experience, knowledge, and needs.

Job Banks places where computerized listings of jobs and their characteristics are maintained. These banks are generally associated with public employment agencies such as Canada Manpower Centres.

Job Burnout a specific set of symptoms brought on by severe or chronic stress directly related to the job rather than to personal difficulties. Related symptoms are chronic fatigue, low energy, irritability, and negative attitude toward job and self.

Job Classes used interchangeably with JOB FAMILIES.

Job Classification Method similar to ranking except that classes or grades are established and then the jobs are placed into these classes.

Job Description a detailed statement of the duties, purposes, and conditions under which a job is to be performed. *See* JOB ANALYSIS

Job Design results in a set of purposes, tasks characteristics, and task duties in a given organizational setting, based on a set of unique organizational and personnel qualities.

Job Enlargement an approach to job design that loads a job horizontally, adding more of the same types of duties that require the same skills.

Job Enrichment an approach to job design that loads a job vertically, increasing the number of skills needed and the sense of significance.

Job Evaluation comparison of jobs by the use of formal and systematic procedures to determine their relative worth within the organization.

Job Fairs events where many employers gather to talk with potential job applicants, often students, about job opportunities.

Job Families grouping together all jobs of nearly the same value to the organization for the purpose of establishing a wage structure that reflects internal equity.

Job Feedback the degree to which the job itself provides the worker with information about how well the job is being performed.

Job Identity the degree to which a job requires completion of a complete and identifiable piece of work.

Job Instruction Training a systematic technique for on-the-job training consisting of four steps: (1) careful selection and preparation of trainer and trainee for the learning experience to follow; (2) full explanation and demonstration by the trainer; (3) a trial on-the-job performance by the trainee; and (4) a thorough feed-back session highlighting job performance and job requirements.

Job Matching an essential function in effective recruiting that entails fitting the needs of people to the requirements of the job.

Job Needs Analysis an examination of the organization that provides information on the tasks to be performed on each job, the skills necessary to perform those tasks, and the minimum acceptable standards of performance.

Job Posting a procedure of posting within the organization a list of jobs that are available.

Job Profiles a major component of a job-matching system, which contains the descriptions of jobs that are available.

Job Progression Program a systematic effort by companies to tie individual career needs to the practical needs of the organization by identifying what individuals want and what organizations need and can offer.

Job-Relatedness refers to selection tests and qualifications being related to an employee's being successful on the job. If a test or qualification is shown to be job-related, an adverse impact charge can be defended.

Job Rotation an approach to job design that does not change the design of a job, but rather rotates the worker from job to job.

Job Sex-typing classifying a job as being suitable only for a male or a female (e.g., male: foreman; female: seamstress), generally reflecting a traditional sex-role bias.

Job Sharing arrangements for two people or more to share (split) the hours of one job (e.g., two people take one job and each works four hours daily).

Job Significance the degree to which the job has a substantial impact on the lives of other people.

Job Specification a detailed statement of the skills, knowledge, and abilities required of a person doing a given job. *See* JOB ANALYSIS

Judgemental Forecast a personnel planning forecasting technique that relies on the personal judgements of selected experts.

Junior Stock Plan an individual incentive plan involving the awarding of a special non-voting common stock at bargain prices.

Knowledge of Results the knowledge of how well a task was done. An important employee reinforcement technique.

Labour Relations Board a board set up in the federal and all provincial jurisdictions to administer labour relations legislation.

Labour Relations System a conceptual paradigm used to help elucidate the inter-relationships among management, union, and employees.

Leaderless Group Discussion a type of work-sample test in managerial selection in which applicants sit around and discuss a topic for a given period of time.

Learning Principles guidelines to the ways in which people learn most effectively.

Lie Detector Test polygraph tests are becoming an increasingly common part of selection procedures. Used to predict employees who are likely to lie or steal.

Local Union the basic unit of union organization formed in a particular plant or locality.

Lockout a refusal of management to allow workers to work.

Low Quality of Work Life a sociopsychological work environment component characterized by one-way communications, lack of respect for employee rights, poor personnel functions, and policies that produce unfavourable psychological conditions and outcomes.

Machine Pacing a condition under which the machine determines how fast the work must be done by the employee.

Management by Objectives (MBO) this approach evaluates the performance of managers (typically) on the basis of how well they have attained their pre-determined goals or objectives.

Management Position Description Questionnaires (MPDQ) a method of job analysis that relies on the checklist method to analyze jobs, particularly management jobs.

Management Rights as used in industrial relations, the term encompasses those aspects of the employer's operation that do not require discussion with or concurrence of the union.

Manager the person who directs and is responsible for other employees who are either supervisors or managers.

Managerial Estimate estimates of staffing needs made by either the top-down version or the bottom-up version.

Match 1 a match or fit between worker skills, knowledge, and aptitudes and organizational/job demands.

Match 2 a match or fit between worker preferences and interests and organizational characteristics.

Measurable Indicators ways to help measure the effectiveness of PHRM using measures of QWL, productivity, and legal compliance as general indicators and many others as specific indicators.

Measured Day Work an incentive pay plan where production standards are established, although not as precisely as in piecework plans, and employees are paid according to those standards.

Mediation a procedure in which a central third party assists union and management negotiators in reaching a voluntary agreement.

Mentor someone who offers informal career guidance and support to an employee on a regular basis.

Merit Pay Plans methods of monetary compensation (generally related to subjectively evaluated performance) that represents only a small percentage increment in an employee's direct compensation.

Method Analysis the use of individual activity units to describe the way a job is to be performed and evaluated. Also known as motion study. Best application is to nonmanagerial jobs.

Minimum Wage the rate of pay established by statute or by minimum wage orders as the lowest wage that can be paid to an employee.

Mixed Interview a performance appraisal interview in which the rater combines the tell-and-sell with the problem-solving type of interview.

Multi-employer Bargaining where employers bargain as a group with the union at the local level.

Multi-lateral Bargaining a type of collective negotiating wherein more than two parties are involved in the negotiating and there is no clear union-management dichotomy.

Multiple Cut-off Model a hiring process in which an applicant must exceed fixed levels of proficiency (do well on all tests) but in no particular sequence.

Multiple Hurdle Model a hiring process in which an applicant must do well on several tests or predictors and must do well in sequence.

Multiple Linear Regression an extension of simple linear regression where several independent variables (Xs) are used to more accurately predict or forecast future events. For example: productivity is predicted by an equation relating absenteeism (X_1), turnover (X_2), and waste (X_3) to the dependent variable productivity (Y).

Multiple Management Programs training programs for managers where lower- and middle-level managers get an opportunity to work with top-level managers.

Multiple Predictor Approach combining several pieces of information or predictors to make a selection decision.

Narrative Essay a written, open-ended statement of evaluation or appraisal of an employee. *See* ESSAY METHOD

National Union a basic unit of labour unions that organizes, charters, and controls member union locals and develops the general policies and procedures by which locals operate.

Negative Settlement Range when there is no overlap between union demands and management's concessions, thus resulting in no ground for settlement.

Negotiating Committee representatives from the union and management who meet to negotiate a contract.

Network a collection of friends, acquaintances, and colleagues, both inside and outside one's workplace, that can be summoned to provide some type of help or support.

Nominal Grouping Technique a structured group process in which several individuals list and identify their ideas. All ideas are considered by all members and action is decided on after a structured evaluation is completed.

Non-compensatory Approaches hiring processes where weak points cannot be made up for by a strong points.

Non-contributory Programs a type of retirement plan in which the employee is the sole contributor for benefits obtained at retirement.

Non-exempt Employees for example, jobs in which the incumbents are paid overtime for working overtime; they are not exempt from wage/hour laws not requiring overtime pay.

Non-verbal Cues clues to behaviour that do not involve words or speech. Examples include body movements, gestures, handshakes, eye contact, and physical appearance.

Objective Forms appraisals where the evaluation is done against specifically defined behaviours or outcomes, such as levels of output, level of specific goal attainment, or number of days absent.

Occupational Accidents accidents such as loss of limb, loss of hearing, or even loss of life as a consequence of the physical environment of the workplace.

Occupational Diseases diseases or illnesses such as cancer and leukemia that result from aspects of the physical work environment.

Occupational Safety and Health physical/physiological and socio-psychological conditions of an organization's workforce.

Off-the-Job Training Programs training programs that are taught outside the organization facility.

On-the-Job Training Programs a set of training programs that are conducted on the job or where the people are working.

Open Shop a shop in which union membership is not required as a condition of retaining employment.

Order Effects where the order or arrangement of information on job applicants influences the evaluation they receive.

Organizational Needs Analysis an examination of short- and long-term objectives of the organization, human resource needs, efficiency indexes, and organizational climate, as these relate to the training and development needs of the organization.

Organization Stress a socio-psychological work environment component characterized by organizational changes, work overload, poor supervision, unfair salaries, job insecurity, and physical insecurity, all producing uncertainty.

Organizational Surveys gathering data from individuals in a company to determine how things are going and how they feel.

Paired Comparison Method a comparative approach in which the superior compares each subordinate with every other subordinate in order to evaluate the subordinate's performance.

Panel Interview an interview where there are several interviewers for just the one interviewee.

Paper-and-Pencil Achievement Tests measures of job-related knowledge rather than work samples of the job itself.

Partial Reinforcement providing immediate reward or follow-up to individuals on an intermittent rather than a continuous basis.

Patterned or Structured Interview an interview that involves a specific set of questions in a fixed order.

Pattern Settlements a settlement between a union and management that is based on and similar to an agreement made by another company with the union.

Pay Fairness ensuring that what employees are paid is in relationship to what they and others give to the organization.

Pay for Time not Worked a form of indirect compensation received by an employee for time not spent working. There are two categories: *off-the-job*, vacations, sick leave, holidays, personal days, comprising the major portion of costs of indirect benefits, and *on-the-job*, lunch and rest periods, use of physical fitness facilities.

Pay Grades a range of pay for a particular job family or class. Grade structure is based on job evaluation points associated with a point-factor evaluation.

Pay Level the absolute pay or wage that employees receive.

Pay Secrecy the issue of whether employees should or should not have access to the organization's compensation schedule.

Perfectly Negative Validity where the degree of relationship between two variables is one-to-one and negative.

Perfectly Positive Validity where the degree of relationship between two variables is one-to-one and positive.

Performance Appraisal a system of measuring, evaluating, and influencing an employee's job-related attributes, behaviours and outcomes, and level of absenteeism, to discover at what levels the employee presently is performing on the job.

Performance Appraisal System the entire system, which incorporates the following: method used to gather the appraisal data; job analysis; establishment of validity and reliability of the method; characteristics of the rater and ratee that influence the process; use of the information for development and evaluation; evaluation of performance appraisal in relation to its stated objectives.

Performance-Based Pay Systems pay systems that relate pay to performance, including incentive pay plans and merit pay plans.

Performance Contracts an employment agreement with clearly specified objectives for a given period of time and the appropriate rewards or disciplinary action for meeting or failing to meet these goals.

Performance Criteria dimensions or factors used to judge an individual in performing a particular job.

Performance Ratios these ratios indicate where the performance rating of any employee stands relative to that of other employees.

Performance Shares under this managerial incentive plan, managers receive shares or stocks in a company as a performance reward, based on how well the company is doing.

Performance Standards indicators or levels attached to the performance criteria to enable a judgement to be made about how well an individual is performing.

Performance Part-Time fixed arrangements for regular employees to work fewer than five days per week or forty hours per week.

Permissive Issue those issues over which it is not mandatory to bargain but that are not specifically illegal.

Person-Needs Analysis an examination of the deficiencies between an employee's actual performance and the desired performance, or between an employee's proficiency on critical job dimensions and the desired proficiency required by the job dimensions.

Personal Appraisal identifying your own abilities, values, and goals across several life dimensions that are important to you. Strengths and weaknesses also are taken into account.

Personal Competence Test a test designed to measure whether individuals know how to make appropriate and timely decisions for themselves and whether they put forth the effort to do so.

Personality Inventories tests that measure individual traits or characteristics, for example, the California Psychological Inventory, the Minnesota Multiphasic Personality Inventory.

Personnel Generalist personnel staff with moderate experience of the language, needs, and requirements of the line workers. Generally found in organizations characterized by centralization.

Personnel Manager the person who heads up the personnel department.

Personnel Practices refers to all of the ways, techniques, and philosophies utilized in handling the organization's human resources. Included are all of the personnel functions and activities discussed in this text.

Personnel Roles the parts that can be played by a personnel department, including the roles of policy formulator, provider and delegator, auditor, and innovator.

Personnel Specialist a personnel department member with specific skills related to a particular area or department of the organization. Generally found in organizations characterized by decentralization.

Physical Abilities Analysis a person-focused method of job analysis that uses nine abilities to analyze the physical requirements of tasks.

Physical Job Elements these represent the specific physical properties of a job such as lifting, lighting, colouring, sound, speed, and positioning.

Physical Work Environment composed of the building, furniture, equipment, machines, lights, noise, heat, chemicals, toxins, and so on, that can be the cause of occupational accidents and diseases.

Physiological/Physical Conditions the conditions of the work environment that if not appropriate, can lead to occupational diseases and accidents.

Piecework Plan the most common type of incentive pay plan. Under this plan, employees get a standard pay rate for each unit of output.

Placement an activity concerned with ensuring that job demands are filled and that individual needs and preferences are met.

Point Rating or Point-Factor Method a job evaluation strategy that assigns point values to previously determined compensable factors and adds them to arrive at a total score used to determine wage levels.

Polygraph Test *See* **Lie Detector Test**

Position Analysis Questionnaire (PAQ) a structured procedure used in job analysis that describes jobs in terms of worker activities. PAQ is based on a person-oriented trait system that allows it to be applied across a number of jobs and organizations without modification. A salient disadvantage is its length.

Positive Reinforcement System an incentive system based on the assumption that behaviour can be understood and modified by its consequences. The system lets employees know how well they are meeting specific goals and rewards improvements with praise and recognition. No money is involved.

Positive Settlement Range overlap area between management's resistance point and the union's resistance point. Facilitates an acceptable settlement.

Predictive Validation similar to concurrent validation except that the predictor variable is measured some time before the performance variable.

Predictor Rate the proportion of correct decisions (true positive plus true negative) relative to the total number of decisions when a test is used for selection.

Predictors the tests or pieces of information used by personnel departments to predict how well an applicant is likely to do if hired.

Preference Tests a type of selection test that is used to match employee preferences with job and organizational characteristics.

Pre-retirement Counselling counselling given to employees before retirement in order to facilitate their transition from work to nonwork. This may result in early retirement decisions, but it need not always.

Primacy Effect an order effect where first information is given greater weight—the concept of a first impression.

Private Employment Agencies an external recruiting source that caters primarily to two types of job applicants: professional and managerial workers and unskilled workers. These agencies charge a fee for setting up connections between applicants and employers.

Problem-Solving Interview a participative performance appraisal interview in which the ratee and rater try to understand and solve performance problems.

Productivity the outputs of an individual, group, or organization divided by the inputs needed by the individual, group, or organization for the creation of outputs.

Productivity Bargaining a special form of integrative bargaining where labour agrees to scrap old work habits for new and more effective ones desired by management. Offers labour the gain of modernization and increased labour efficiency in the form of work incentives.

Profit-Sharing Plans an organizational incentive plan involving the awarding of money to employees if some level of company profit is attained.

Programmed Instruction a systematic and stepwise presentation of skills and tasks broken down into "frames," where each frame must be successfully completed before going into the next. Feedback concerning the correctness of response for each frame is provided immediately and allows individuals to pace themselves.

Progressive Discipline a system whereby employees are increasingly more severely disciplined or punished with the repetition of offences.

Prohibited Issues issues about which it is illegal for unions and employers to bargain.

Promotion from Within a practice and policy of promoting current employees to fill vacant positions and not hiring people from the outside.

Protection Programs indirect compensation designed to protect the employee and family if and when the employee's income (direct compensation) is terminated, and to protect the employee and family against the burden of health-care expenses in the event of disability.

Psychological Contract an informal and unwritten understanding between employees and employer about what is reasonable to expect from an employee in exchange for what is contained in the employment contract.

Psychomotor Tests aptitude tests that combine mental and physical aspects of individual ability; for example, the MacQuarrie Test for Mechanical Ability, the Tweeser Dexterity Tests.

Purposes the reason for the creation and existence of a job.

Pygmalion Effect the self-fulfulling prophesy of telling someone they will succeed and then observing that person succeed.

Quality Circles an innovative management concept that helps contribute to an organization's growth and well-being based on the philosophy that a company's workforce participation is its most valuable resource because employees are often the most qualified to identify and solve work-related problems.

Quality of Work Life (QWL) a process by which all members of the organization, through appropriate channels of communication set up for this purpose, have some say about the design of their jobs in particular and the work environment in general to satisfy their needs.

Quotas specific numbers of percentage goals established by an organization for minority hiring, to correct under-utilization or past discrimination in employment.

Rand Formula a union security plan developed by Judge Rand in an arbitration decision handed down in 1946, which requires the employer to deduct union dues from the pay of all employees.

Ranking Method a hierarchy or ladder of jobs constructed from the job analysis to reflect the relative value of the jobs to the organization.

Ratee the person being appraised in an appraisal. *See* SUBORDINATE

Rater the person doing the appraising in an appraisal. *See* SUPERIOR

Realistic Job Preview a recruitment technique by which the potential applicant is made aware of the positive and negative aspects of the organization. An applicant is encouraged to approach current employees and the line manager to ask questions about the appropriate fit between his or her needs and the organization's needs.

Reality Shock the career disappointment from having higher expectations of jobs than the jobs can fulfil.

Recency Effect an order effect where the last or most recent information is given greater weight.

Recency-of-Events Error *See* **Recency Effect**

Recognition Tests examples of past behaviour or performance that indicate the quality of an individual's work; for example, portfolios.

Recruitment the set of activities and processes used to obtain legally a sufficient number of the right people at the right place and time so that the people and the organization can make selections based on their own best short-run and long-run interests.

Redundancy Planning developing alternative strategies for obsolete employees to acquire skills necessary for other types of work. Planning includes counselling, training, and part-time employment.

Reference Verification a method for validating information provided by the applicant; for example, checking school records and transcripts, calling previous employers.

Reinforcement essentially means giving people immediate follow-up on their performance based on the premise that people will do what is rewarded and avoid doing what is punished.

Reliability the consistency of a test or test item on repeated measurement. *See* TEST-RETEST RELIABILITY

Relocation Program a company sponsored fringe benefit that assist employees who must move in connection with either transfer or discharge.

Replacement Planning replacement charts to help plan for whom will be able to replace whom in the event of a position becoming vacant.

Resistance Point the lowest acceptable level that the union can accept on behalf of its members or the highest acceptable level for management.

Responsibility Centres a method to appraise managers by measuring how well they do in relationship to costs, profits, or revenues for a given unit or division.

Right to Plant/Office-Closing or Relocation Notification the right to be informed before a company closes a plant or office or before it decides to move it.

Role Awareness the degree to which an individual knows what is expected and what authority he or she has.

Role Conflict the extent of conflict or incompatibility between doing what is expected and what it is possible to do.

Role Playing off-the-job training where a realistic situation is created and individuals learn by playing roles in the situation.

Safety Committee a committee that involves employees in safety-policy formulation and implementation.

Salary Compression a decrease in the range of pay between various positions (levels) in the organization.

Sales Incentive Plans administered for individuals engaged in selling; usually called commissions plans.

Scanlon Plan a type of company-wide incentive program emphasizing management-employee relations, particularly employee participation, and underscoring the principle of efficient operations through co-operation. In effect, employees share in organization profits as a result of contributing and co-operating to attain higher productivity.

Scattergram a plotting or visual display of the relationship between two variables for several individuals.

Scientific Approach an approach to designing jobs that minimizes the skills needed by the worker to perform the job. The result often is a job that is simple and repetitive.

Selection the process of gathering information for the purpose of evaluating and deciding who should be hired, under legal guidelines, for the short- and long-term interests of the individual and the organization.

Selection Ratio the proportion of individuals actually hired in relation to those who applied.

Sensitivity Training a method of training and development conducted in a group setting, intended to give individuals insight into how and why they and others feel and act the way they do.

Severance Pay a lump-sum payment by an employer to a worker whose employment has been terminated.

Severity Rate reflects the hours actually lost due to injury or illness by differentially weighting categories of injuries and illnesses.

Sex-Role Stereotyping the definition of a role as being or having a sex type; e.g., traditionally the role of the housekeeper was defined as being female and the job of the bread-winner as being male.

Sexual Harassment physical violation or verbal abuse of employees, particularly by managers and supervisors.

Simple Linear Regression a quantitative formula used to relate an independent variable (X) to a dependent variable (Y). For example, a forecast of future events such as sales (Y) is predicted by demand (X).

Simulation an off-the-job training program that presents individuals with situations that are similar to actual job conditions.

Simulation Tests a type of achievement test used in the selection process. The applicant is given a task to perform, although the situation in which the task is performed is not necessarily recreated.

Single Predictor Approach the use of one test or piece of information to choose an applicant for the job.

Skill-Based Evaluation a job evaluation strategy by which the organization compensates the employee by paying the person for skills and experience relative to the organization's mission.

Skill Variety the degree to which a job requires a number of different skills to perform it correctly.

Social Insurance a public-protection program devised by governments, that provides wage earners and their dependants with a minimum income during periods of disability or unemployment.

Socialization a process of bringing an individual into an organization and transmitting norms, values, and skills to that individual.

Social Support Groups individuals who provide unconditional support for the individuals in the group.

Socio-psychological Conditions conditions in the workplace that can lead to perceived stress and low quality of work life.

Socio-psychological Work Environment the non-physical parts of the work environment including such things as relationships with supervisors, company policies, structure of the organizations, organizational changes, uncertainty, conflicts, and relationships with co-workers.

Socio-technical Approach a productivity program under the heading of task redesign that is based on the concept that jobs are man-made inventions, related to a number of technical and social systems that are themselves constantly changing. The concept reflects a sensitivity to bridging technical and social systems in such a way as to be optimally productive.

Standard Hour Plan this second most widely used incentive pay plan pays on the basis of time per unit of output rather than the quantity of output.

Standard Résumé an organized chronological documentation of work and educational experience relating to one's career and qualifications. Generally prepared by an applicant for a position.

Statistical Projection a forecasting technique used in personnel planning that, for example, uses simple linear regression to predict employment growth as a function of sales growth.

Steel-Collar Workers refers to machines, particularly robots, that can be used to do the work instead of people.

Steward an employee elected by the work unit to act as the union representative on the work site and to respond to company actions against employees that violate the labour agreement.

Stock Option a managerial incentive plan where the manager is given an opportunity to buy stocks of the company at a later date but at a price established at the time the option is given.

Straight Ranking a comparative approach in which the superior lists the subordinates from best to worst, usually on the basis of overall performance.

Stress Interview an interview in which an applicant may be intentionally annoyed or embarassed by the interviewer to see how the applicant reacts.

Strike a refusal of employees to work for a company.

Strike Benefits union payments, usually a small proportion of regular income, to workers during a strike.

Structured Job Analysis the use of a standard format for job descriptions so that all organizations can use the same job categories.

Subjective Forms appraisal forms on which the raters evaluate an employee on the basis of subjective attributes such as leadership, attitude toward people, or loyalty.

Subordinate the term used to denote the person whose performance is being appraised by a person at a higher job level.

Succession Planning similar to replacement planning but tends to be longer term, more developmental, and offer more flexibility.

Suggestion Systems a form of incentive compensation paid to employees who are responsible for money-saving or money-producing ideas for the organization.

Superior the term used to denote the person at a higher job level who does the appraising of another's performance.

Supervisor the person who directs and is responsible for other employees who are non-supervisors and non-managers.

Supervisory Assistance an informal method of training, often involving discussions between a supervisor and his or her employee.

Supplemental Unemployment Benefits benefits received by employees who are on layoff from their company until returning to work or until the benefits expire.

Target Point a realistic assessment of what wages and conditions of employment the union is likely to get from management.

Team Contemporary a major classification of approaches to job design that focus on the group/job design interface or relationships.

Technological System refers to the machines, methods, and materials that are used to produce the organization's output.

Tell-and-Listen Interview a performance appraisal interview in which the rater informs the ratee of the evaluation and then listens to the ratee's opinion of the evaluation.

Tell-and-Sell Interview a performance appraisal interview in which the rater informs the ratee of the evaluation and sells the ratee on the evaluation.

Terminate for Good Cause to fire an employee for good reason.

Test-Retest Reliability demonstrating the relationship between the results of the same test given at two different times.

Tests any paper-and-pencil test, performance measure, or other information used as a basis for making an employment decision.

Theory Z Management a current management philosophy modifying some of the more traditional U.S. management concerns (Theory A) and integrating some of the ideas from conventional Japanese management (Theory J).

Time Study *See* **Work Measurement**

Timetables these identify specific dates when affirmative action goals and quotas are to be met.

Total Compensation the activity by which organizations evaluate the contributions of employees in order to distribute fairly the direct and indirect monetary and non-monetary rewards, within the organization's ability to pay and within legal regulations.

Training and Development any attempt to improve current or future employee performance by increasing an employee's ability to perform through learning. It can be accomplished by changing the employee's attitude or increasing his or her skills or knowledge.

True Negatives correct predictions that applicants will perform poorly who in fact do perform poorly.

True Positives correct predictions that applicants will perform well who in fact do perform successfully.

Uncertainty a lack of predictability or an inability to tell what things are or will be like.

Unfair Labour Practice a practice on the part of either union or management that violates provisions of federal or provincial labour laws.

Unfair Representation breach of the duty of a union to fairly represent all employees covered by the union-management contract.

Union an organization with the legal authority to negotiate with the employer on behalf of the employees and to administer the ensuing agreement.

Union Local the grass-roots unit of the labour organization that represents the employees who are in the same union unit at a given workplace.

Union Shop an organization that requires employees to join the union within a set number of days after initial employment.

Unionization or Unionizing the banding together of employees and outside agencies (unions and associations) to act as a single unit when dealing with management over issues related to their work.

Utilization Analysis process of determining the number of women and minorities in different jobs within an organization.

Valid Predictor any test used for staffing that predicts or correlates with actual job performance.

Validity the degree to which a predictor or criterion measures what it purports to measure, or demonstrates the job-relatedness of a test by showing how well an applicant will perform, based on the test predictions.

Validity Generalization demonstrates that the job-relatedness or validity of one test in one situation applies equally in other situations.

Vertical Loading the adding of duties to a job that are different from those already involved in the job and that require different skills, knowledge, or aptitudes.

Vested pertains to qualifications required to become eligible for an organization's pension benefits.

Wage-Dividend Plans a special type of cash plan where the percentage of profits paid to employees is determined by the amount of dividends paid to stockholders.

Wage Surveys published reports of what several different companies are paying for certain types of jobs.

Weighted Application Blank an application blank in which some information is given more importance or weight as a predictor of future success.

Weighted Checklist identical to a critical incidents format but with various points that differentiate the varying importance of different incidents.

Wellness Tests health assessments of employees that include measures of blood pressure, blood cholesterol, high density cholesterol, skin-fold evaluation of diet, life-change events, smoking, drinking, and family history of chronic diseases.

Whipsaw the process wherein unions use one contract settlement as a precedent for the next and force the employer to settle all contracts before work is resumed.

Wide-Area and Multi-Craft Bargaining a negotiating structure that exists in the construction industry, for example, where several separate construction unions may settle at the same time with one contractor.

Wildcat Strike a strike that is not legal because the contract forbids it, but the union strikes anyway.

Work Measurement the determination of standard times for all units of work activity in any task. Includes the assessment of "actual effort" exerted and the "real effort" required to accomplish a task. *See* METHODS ANALYSIS

Work Pacing refers to the rate or flow of work and who controls the rate or flow. *See* MACHINE PACING

Work Sample Test a test that consists of an actual simulation of the job or critical tasks associated with the job; for example, a keyboarding test used to select a secretary.

Work Sampling the process of taking instantaneous samples of work activities of individuals or groups of individuals. Activities then are timed and classified according to predetermined categories. The result is a description of the activities by classification of job and the percentage of time for each activity. *See* METHODS ANALYSIS

Work Sharing a plan by which available work is distributed as evenly as possible among all workers when production slackens, to reduce layoffs.

Work Standards Approach a type of goal-oriented evaluation, similar to MOB except that the pre-determined goals are dictated by management and often established by work measurement.

Workers' Compensation a program offered to cover worker sickness and disability.

Yellow-Dog Contracts contracts signed by employees when hired, promising that they will not join a union.

Index

A

AAI (ASPA Accreditation Institute), 30
Abella Commission, 159–160
Absolute standards, 243–251
Access Information Act, 479–480
Accidents
  Factors affecting, 454–456
  Reporting and inquiries, 453–454
Accreditation
  of employer associations, 502
  of PHRM, 30–31
Achievement tests, 180–182
Act Respecting Labour Standards (Québec), 478
Adult Occupational Training Act (AOTA), 378
Adverse impact, 163–164
Adversarial system, 529
Affirmative Action
  Atomic Energy of Canada, 120
  Canadian Human Rights, 125–126
  Canadian National (CN), 126
  Royal Bank of Canada, 126–128
Affirmative Action Programs and Recruiting, 125–128
Age discrimination, 153
Air Canada, 71, 153, 203, 425, 548
Alcan, 230–231, 562
All salaried workforce, 316–317
Almedia v. *Chubb Fire Security*, 236–238
Alternative work arrangements, 141–145
Application blanks
  Biographical Information Blank (BIB), 172
  Definition, 171
  Legal requirements, 171–172
  Research on, 172–173
  Weighted, 172
Appraisal by subordinates, 259
Appraisal by superiors, 258–259
Apprenticeship training, 389
Aptitude tests, 179–180
Arbitration, 503–504, 545–546
ASPA (American Society of Personnel Administration), 30
Assessment centre, 181–182, 254–255, 391
Assistantship, 389
Atomic Energy of Canada, 120
Attitudinal structuring, 534
Auditor, 17–18
Automation, 63–64, 431–432

B

Bank of Montréal, 565
Bargaining Unit
  Certification, 500–502
  Decertification, 502
  Determination, 517
Base rate, 211
Beatrice Harwatiuk v. *Pasqua Hospital*, 300
Behaviourally Anchored Rating Scale (BARS), 248–251
Behavioural Observation Scale (BOS), 248–251
Bell Canada, 151, 562
Benefit criteria (for PHRM), 21
Benefit pay and administration
  Administrative issues, 363–365
  Assessment, 365–366
  Definition, 352–353
  Employee services and perquisites, 362–363
  Legal considerations, 356–361
  Purposes and importance, 353–356
  Pay for time not worked, 361–362
Bias, 196
Bill C–34, 299
Bill C–43, 479–480
Bill C–62, 48–49, 157–158
Biographical Information Blank (BIB), 172
BNA (Bureau of National Affairs), 18, 137
Boeing Canada, 481
Bona Fide Occupational Requirement (BOFR), 162, 164, 203
  Air Canada, 153, 203
Bone v. *CFL*, 162
Bottom line, 10, 164
Brotherhood of Railway and Airline Clerks, 74
Business games, 181
Business necessity, 162

C

Cafeteria approach to compensation, 315
California Psychological Inventory, 182
Campbell Soup, 411–412
Camco Inc., 3
Canada Employment and Immigration Centre (CEC), 133–134
Canada Health Act, 358
Canada Labour Code, 296–299
Canada Manpower Industry Program (CMITP), 378
Canada Occupational Forecasting Program (COFP), 60
Canada Pension Plan, 357

Canadian Air Line Employees' Association (CALEA), 74
Canadian Broadcasting Corporation, 126, 194
Canadian Centre for Occupational Health and Safety, 448–449
Canadian Classification and Dictionary of Occupations (CCDO), 97–98
Canadian Human Rights Act, 125–126, 159–160, 479
  Historical developments, 159–161
Canadian Labour Congress (CLC), 510–514
Canadian Manufacturing Association, 13, 15
Canadian Mental Health Association, 280
Canadian National (CN), 126
Canadian Pacific Air (CP), 144
Canadian Tire Corporation, 336, 428
Candidate profile, 139
Careers
  in PHRM, 28–29
  Paths, 404
Career opportunities, 140
Career planning and development, *see* employee's development
Case study, 402
Centralization (of PHRM), 25–26
Central tendency, 257
Certification
  of bargaining units, 500–501
  of PHRM, 30–31
Charter of Rights and Freedoms, 159
Child care assistance, 141
Children's Aid Society (CAS), 463
Closed shop, 541
Closed offer arbitration, 546
CNR v. *Bhinder*, 162
Coaching, 400
Codetermination, 576
Cognitive job elements, 81
Colfer v. *Ottawa Board of Commissioners of Police*, 161
Collective bargaining
  Assessment, 551–552
  Contract administration, 546–551
  Conflict resolution, 543–546

Definition, 526
Negotiating agreement, 537–543
Process, 527–537
Combined approach to multiple predictors, 198–199
Cominco, 364
Community Industrial Training Council, 378
Comparable worth, 300
Compensable factors, 302–303
Compensation, *see* total compensation
Compensatory approach to multiple predictors, 198
Compra-ratio, 341
Compressed work week, 143–144
Computer-aided design (CAD), 431
Computer-assisted training program, 373
Computer-integrated manufacturing (CIM), 431
Concessionary bargaining, 536–537
Conciliation, 503
Confirmation approach, 202
Construct validity, 163
Constructive dismissal, 478
Continuous bargaining, 537
Contrast effect, 176–177
Control systems, 91
Conventional rating, 245–248
Cooperative acceptance, 480, 485
Cooperative system, 529–530
Cost criteria (for PHRM), 21–22
Cost-of-living adjustment (COLA), 329–330
Conventional statistical projection, 50
Counseling, 280–281
Craton v. *Manitoba Public Schools*, 203
Crises (in PHRM), 11–14
Criterion (criteria)
  Actual, 195
  Contamination, 196, 240
  Definition, 166–167
  Deficiency, 196, 240
  Ultimate criteria, 195
  Benefit, 21
  Cost, 21–23
  Evaluating PHRM, 20–23
  Job success, 195–196
Critical incident technique (CIT), 103, 244
  Extended, 103–105

Cronbach alpha, 204
Cut-off score, 212

D

Dangers (in dismissal), 478–479
Decentralization (of PHRM), 25–26
Decertification, 502
Delegator, 17
Delphi technique, 50
Dictionary of Occupational Titles (DOT), 97
Direct index approach, 253
Discrimination
  Adverse impact, 163–164
  Age, 153, 203
  Definition, 160–161
  Issues, 4
  Job description, 75
  Marital status, 4
  Retirement, 4
  Systemic, 160–164
Dismissal
  Cause for, 477
  Constructive, 478
  Statutory protection, 477–478
Distributive bargaining, 532
DOFASCO, 336
Dominion Envelope, 336
Dritnell v. *Michel Brent Personnel Place*, 161
Dual-career ladder, 404

E

Earned time, 276–277
Edwards personal preference schedule, 182
Eldorado Resources, Ltd., 280
Employee assistance programs (EAPs), 279–280
Employee benefits, *see* benefits pay and administration
Employee development
  Programs, 400–405
  Purposes and importance, 399
Employee referral programs (ERPs), 131
Employee rights
  Assessment, 487–488
  Definition, 473
  Legal considerations, 476–482
  Purposes and importance, 474–475
  Strategies for improvement, 482–487

Employment Agencies, 132–135
Enhancing human potential, 8–9
Ergonomics, 86–87, 461
Error (in selection), 196
Evaluation designs, 396–398
Exempt employee, 299
Eyers v. *City Buick Pontiac Cadillac Ltd.*, 474–475

F

Fact finder, 530
Factor comparison method, 308
Final offer arbitration, 546
Financial Administration Act (Bill C–34), 299
Flex time, 142–143
Flexiyear schedule, 576
Forced choice form, 245
Forced distribution method, 241–243
Ford Occupational Imbalance Listing (FOIL), 60
Forecasting
  Human resource demands, 49–51
  Human resource supplies, 51–53
  Techniques, 52
Formal course method, 390
Formulator, 17
Foster v. *Forest Products Ltd.*, 161, 162
Four Seasons Hotel, 194, 428
Frequency rate, 461
Functional job analysis (FJA), 97–98

G

General Motors of Canada, 360, 441, 523
Genetic screening, 185
Germany (PHRM), *see* PHRM in Germany
Goal programming, 53
Goal setting, 386
Golden handcuffs, 363
Golden parachutes, 363
Gordon personal profile, 182
Grade structure, 311–313
Great-West Life Assurance, 428
Grievance
  Arbitration, 546
  Issues, 549
  Mediation, 548
  Procedures, 547–551

Griggs v. *Duke Power Co.*, 161
Grote v. *Sechet Building Supplies Ltd.*, 161
Growth Need Strength Questionnaire, 88
Guidelines oriented job analysis (GOJA), 105–106
Guilford-Zimmerman Temperament Survey, 182

H

Halo effect, 176, 256
Harpel Printing, 427
Hay plan, 99–100, 307
Hazardous Products Act, 448
Health and Safety Joint Committees, *see* Occupational Health and Safety
Health and safety rates, 460–461
Help Wanted Index (HWI), 132
Honesty tests, 186–187
Hot stove principles, 278
Human relations, 402
Human relations training, 402
Human resource accounting, 584
Human resource management costs, 12–13
Human resource demand forecast, 49–51
Human resource supply forecast, 51–53
Human resource information system (HRIS)
  Definition, 46
  PHRM applications, 46–49
Human resource objectives and policies, 53–55
Human resource planning (HRP)
  Assessment, 65–66
  Changes in the 1990's, 60–65
  Control and evaluation, 58–59
  Definition, 41
  Phases of, 45–59
  Purposes and importance, 41–49
  Roadblocks, 59
Human resource programming, 55–58

I

IBM Canada, 332, 351, 352, 375
Imperial Oil, 72, 368

In-Basket, 181, 391
Incentive pay plans
  Managerial, 331–332
  Measured day work, 331
  Piecework, 330–331
  Positive reinforcement, 333–334
  Sales, 331
  Standard hour, 331
  Suggestions, 332–333
Incidence rate, 460
Individual contemporary (job design), 85–86
Industrial Relations Disputes and Investigation Act (IRDI), 500
Innovator (personnel role), 18
Insurance benefits, 360
Integrative bargaining, 534
Interchange Canada, 405
International PHRM, *see* PHRM in Japan; in Germany
Internships, 389
Interpersonal competence tests, 180
Interest arbitration, 546
Interest tests, 183
Intraorganizational bargaining, 534–535
Ipsco Steel, 336, 337

J

Japan, *see* PHRM in Japan
Job activity reference questionnaire (JAPQ), 88–90
Job analysis
  Assessment, 106–108
  Definition, 75–76
  Information, 92–93
  Legal considerations, 80
  Purposes, 76–78
  Techniques, 94–106
Job assignments, 220
Job autonomy, 81
Job classification method, 304–306
Job classes, 310–313
Job description, 92–94
  Example, 95–96
Job design
  Approaches, 85–87
  Assessment, 88–91
  Definition, 76
  Legal considerations, 80
  Qualities, 81–84
  Purposes, 76–78

Job enlargement, 86
Job enrichment, 86, 429
Job evaluation
  Definition, 301–302
  Discriminatory aspects, 308–310
  Methods, 302–308
Job feedback, 81
Job focused techniques (of job analysis), 96–101
Job identity, 81
Job instruction training (JIT), 388–389
Job matching, 139
Job needs analysis, 380–381
Job overload, 81, 421, 422
Job posting, 130–131
Job preferences, 61–62
Job profile, 139
Job rotation, 85–86, 389, 400
Job sharing, 144–145
Job search techniques, 132–136
Job significance, 81
Job specification, 76–78
Job stereotyping, 140
Job success, *see* criterion
Judgemental forecasts, 50
Just Cause (for dismissal), 477

K

Kotyk v. *Canada Immigration*, 480
Knowledge of results, 386
Kruger Inc., 58, 402
Kuder preference records, 183
Kuder-Richardson, 204

L

Labatt Brewing Co., 428
Labour Force
  Demographics, 60–61
  Job preferences, 61–62
  Survey, 132
Labour Relations Boards, 501–502
Labour Relations System (LRS)
  in general, 527–529
  in Canada, 530–532
Leaderless group discussion (LGD), 181
Learning principles, 385
Legal compliance, 15–16, 21
Leniency error, 256
Lie detector tests, 185–186
Lifetime employment, 572

Loading
  Horizontal, 86
  Vertical, 86
Local union, 513–514
Lockout, 543–544
Low QWL, 458

M

MacBean v. *Village of Plaster Rock*, 161
MacMillan Bloedel Ltd., 360
MacQuarrie test for mechanical ability, 179
Management by objectives (MBO), 251–252
Management Position Description Questionnaire (MPDQ), 98–99
Managerial estimate, 50
Managerial incentive plans, 331–332
Match 1, 57, 138, 169
Match 2, 57, 138, 170
Markov analysis, 53
Means et al. v. *Ontario Hydro*, 236
Measured day work, 331
Mediation, 503, 545
Medical examinations, 184–185
Mentoring, 399
Merit pay, 328–330
Methods analysis, 100–101
Metropolitan Life Insurance Co., 360
Minnesota Multiphasic Personality Inventory, 182
Multiple cutoff, 197
Multiple hurdle approach, 197–198
  Common pitfalls, 198
Multiple linear regression analysis, 51
Multiple management program, 389–390
Multiple predictor approach, 197–199

N

Narrative essay, 243–244
National Training Act, 378
National Training Program, 378
Negotiating committee, 537–538
Negotiating structure, 538–539
Nominal grouping technique, 50

Non-compensatory approach to multiple predictors, 197–198
Northern Telecom, 181, 428, 582

O

Occupational accidents, 461
Occupational diseases, 456–457, 462–463
Occupational Health and Safety
  Assessment, 464–465
  Costs, 444–445
  Definition, 443–444
  Joint committees, 453
  Legal considerations, 447–454
  Purposes and importance, 444–445
  Strategies for improvement, 459–464
O'Conner Finger and Tweezer Dexterity Test, 179–180
Off the job (training programs), 390–392
Office design, 432–433
Old Age Security Act, 358
Ontario Hydro, 181, 236
Ontario Quality of Life Centre, 418
On the job (training programs), 388–390
Order effect, 176–177
Organization
  of PHRM, 23–25
Organizational change, 458–459
Organizational needs analysis, 380
Organizational surveys, 419–422
Organizational restyling, 427
Orientation programs, 218–220

P

Paired comparison method, 241
Paper-and-pencil achievement tests, 180
Pay
  Administration practices, 316
  Equity, 316
  Level, 316
  Secrecy, 315
Peer appraisal, 259
Pension Benefits Standards Act, 357
Performance
  Gaps, 274–275
  Interviews, 271–273

Shares, 332
Strategies for improvement, 275–281
Performance appraisal
   Approaches, 241–253
   Assessment, 253–254, 281–284
   Conflicts in, 267–269
   Criteria, 240–241
   Definition, 231–232
   Design of, 269–271
   Interview, 271–273
   Legal considerations, 235–238
   Purposes, 232–233
   Standards, 240–241
Performance based pay
   Administrative issues, 338–341
   Assessment, 341, 342–344
   Definition, 325–326
   Incentive pay plans, 330–337
   Legal considerations, 328
   Merit pay plans, 328–330
   Purposes and importance, 326–327
Permanent part time, 144–145
Person needs analysis, 381
Personal competence test, 180
Personal Insurance Co. of Canada, 74
Personality inventory, 182
Personnel audit, 579–582
Personnel and human resource management roles, 16–18
   Auditor, 17–18
   Innovator, 18
   Policy formulator, 17
   Provider and delegator, 17
PHRM
   Assessment in the 1990's, 578–585
   Budgets, 27
   Careers, 28–29
   Contemporary challenges, 568–571
   Definition, 5–6, 34 (endnote 2)
   Earnings, 29
   Generalist, 28, 30–31
   in Germany, 575–577
   in Japan, 572–575
   Manager (qualities), 27–28
   New technology, 565–567
   Power in the organization, 563
   Professionalism, 563–565
   Roles, 16–18
   Scope of activities, 18–20
   Special interest, 18–20
   Specialist, 28, 30–31

Physical abilities analysis (PAA), 102–103
Physical abilities tests, 183–185
Physical job elements, 81
Piecework plan, 330–331
Pilon v. *Peugeot of Canada*, 479
Plant closing, 481–482, 486–487
Point rating method, 306–307
Polygraph test, 185–186
Position Analysis Questionnaire (PAQ), 101–102
Position description, 83–84
Positive reinforcement system, 333–334
Predictor, 166
Predictor rate, 211–212
Preference tests, 183
Preretirement counseling, 58
Primacy effect, 177
Productivity, 15, 21
   Assessment, 433–434
   Bargaining, 536
   Canada, 13
   Crisis, 13
   Definition, 414
   Programs for improvements, 433
   Purposes and importance, 415–416
   Ratios, 51, 52
Professional certification/ accreditation, 30–31
Professionalism in PHRM, 29–30
Profit sharing, 336–337
Programmed Instruction (PI), 390–391
Progressive discipline, 483–485
Promotion(s), 128–129, 200–204
Provider, 17
Provigo Inc., 119
Provost Transport, 384
Psychological contract, 504
Psychomotor tests, 179–180
Public Service Alliance of Canada, 524–525
Public Service Staff Relations Act (PSSRA), 539
Pygmalion effect, 386

Q

Quality of work life (QWL)
   Assessment, 433–434
   Definition, 15, 21, 414–415
   Policy considerations in Canada, 417–419

Programs for improvements, 419–429
   Purpose and importance, 415
Quality circles, 425–426
Québéc Pension Plan, 357

R

Rand formula, 534, 542
Ranking methods (in compensation), 303–304
Realistic job preview, 218
Reasonable notice, 478
Recency effect, 177
Recognition test, 180
Recruitment
   Assessment (of activity), 145–146
   Assessment (of methods), 137
   Definition, 121
   External sources, 131–136
   Internal sources, 128–131
   Legal considerations, 125–128
   Purposes and importance, 121–122
Redundancy planning, 57–58
Reference checks, 173–174
Regression analysis, 52
   Simple linear, 50
   Multiple linear, 51
Reliability
   Definition, 204
   Internal consistency, 204
   Split half, 204
   Test-retest, 204
Relocation assistance, 140–141
Renewal analysis, 53
Replacement planning, 53–54
Responsibility centre approach, 251, 252
Retirement benefits, 359–360
Right to know, 452
Right to refuse work, 452–453
Role ambiguity, 421
Role overload, 81
Role playing, 391–392, 402
Role underload, 81
Royal Bank of Canada
   Access program, 280
   Affirmative action, 126–128, 157
Ryan v. *Chief of Police, Town of North Sydney*, 161

S

Safety programs, 455

Salary survey, *see* wage and salary surveys
Sales incentive plans, 331
Scanlon plan, 337
Scattergram, 207
Scientific job design, 85
Scarborough county building, 432
Segrave v. *Zellers*, 174
Selection
  Criteria, 166–167
  Definition, 154
  Interview, 174–178
  Legal considerations, 157–164
  Predictors, 166–167
  Purposes and importance, 154–155
  Ratio, 212
  Tests, 178–187
Sexual harassment, 4
Self appraisal, 759
Semi-autonomous work groups, 422–425
Sensitivity training, 392, 402
Severity rate, 460–461
Shell Sarnia, 430
Simpsons Canada, 145, 336
Simulation tests, 180
Singh v. *Security and Investigation Services Ltd.*, 161
Single predictor approach, 196–197
Skill based evaluation, 308
Skill variety, 81
Socialization of new employees
  Definition, 216
  Methods, 217–220
  Purposes, 216–217
Sociotechnical approach, 429–430
Sorel v. *Tomerson*, 236
Split-half reliability, 204
Standard hour plan, 331
Standard work schedules, 142
Steinberg, 181, 425
Stochastic analysis, 51, 52
Stress
  Sources, 458–459
  Techniques to manage, 463–464
Strike, 543–545
Strong vocational interest test, 183
Succession planning, 53
Supervisory assistance, 390
Supplemental unemployment benefits, 361

Supreme Aluminum Industries, 336
Suggestion systems, 332–333
Surveys, *see* organizational surveys
Syncrude, 428

T

Task redesign, 429–430
Team contemporary (job design), 86
Temporary help agencies, 134–135
Test, 166
Test-retest reliability, *see* reliability
T-Group, *see* sensitivity training
Theory Z, 427–429
Time series analysis, 51, 52
Time study, 100–101
Toronto Dominion Bank, 373
Total compensation
  Assessment, 317–318
  Contemporary issues, 314–317
  Definition, 292
  Job evaluation, 301–310
  Legal considerations, 296–300
  Pay structure, 310–313
  Purposes and importance, 292–294
Training and Development
  Assessment of, 395–398, 405–406
  Definition, 374
  Determining training needs, 378–383
  Implementing training programs, 383–393
  Legal and policy issues, 377–378
  Problems and pitfalls, 393–395
  Purposes and importance, 375
Transfers
  of personnel, 129, 200–204
  of training, 387
Transportation of Dangerous Goods Act of 1981, 448
Treasury Board of Canada, 332
Trends (in PHRM), 11–14
Tricofil, 427
Tripartism, 531–532

U

Unemployment Insurance Laws, 358

Unfair labour practices, 502–503
Unionization
  Assessment, 517–518
  Definition, 496
  Determination of bargaining unit, 517
  History of, 507–510
  Legal considerations, 499–504
  Organizing campaigns, 514–517
  Purposes and importance, 496–497
  Structure and function of unions, 510–514
  Unfair labour practices, 502–503
Union instrumentality, 505
Union shop, 541
Unit demand forecasting, 51
United Steelworkers Union, 516, 530
Unsafe employee, 455–456
Utility analysis, 584

V

Validity
  Coefficient, 206
  Concurrent, 205
  Content, 80, 207–208
  Construct, 163, 208
  Criterion related, 205–207
  Definition, 205
  Differential, 209–211
  Face, 208
  Generalization, 211
  Predictive, 206–207
Values
  Toward mobility, 64
  Toward retirement, 65
  Toward work, 64
Vestibule training, 391
Volvo, 424–425, 430

W

Wage and salary surveys, 310–311
Wage dividends plan, 336
Warner-Lambert Canada, Ltd., 280
Wechsler Intelligence Scale, 179
Weighted application blanks (WAB), 172
Work flow, 430
Work measurement, *see* time study

Work overload, 459
Work pace, 459
Work preference questionnaire, 89–90
Work sampling, 101
Work sample tests, 181
Work standard approach, 252–253
Worker alienation, 14
Workforce composition, 13–14
Wrongful dismissal, 477–478

Y

Year's maximum pensionable earnings (YMPE), 357